THE
OPEN
LEARNING
FOUNDATION

An Active Learning Approach

People in Organisations

THE
OPEN
LEARNING
FOUNDATION

An Active Learning Approach

PEOPLE IN ORGANISATIONS

Kevin Gallagher,
Ed Rose, Bob McClelland,
John Reynolds, Steve Tombs

BLACKWELL
Business

Copyright © Open Learning Foundation Enterprises Ltd 1997

First published 1997

Reprinted 1997, 1998, 1999, 2002

Blackwell Publishers Ltd
108 Cowley Road
Oxford OX4 1JF, UK

Blackwell Publishers Inc
350 Main Street
Malden, Massachusetts 02148, USA

British Library Cataloguing in Publication Data
A CIP catalogue record for this book is available from the British Library

Library of Congress Cataloging in Publication Data
People in Organisations: an active learning approach / Steve Tombs ...
[et al.].
p.   cm. — (BABS)
At head of title: Open Learning Foundation
Includes bibliographical references (p.   ).
ISBN 0–631–20181–5 (alk. paper)
1. Organizational learning. 2. Industrial management. I. Tombs,
Steve. II. Series.
HD58.82.P463   1997   96–52855
658—dc21   CIP

Typeset in 10 on 12pt Times New Roman
Printed and bound in Great Britain by TJ International Ltd, Padstow, Cornwall

This book is printed on acid-free paper.

Copyright acknowledgments

Contents

Unit 2 Technology and Flexibility

Unit 4   The Nature of Organisations   221

Unit 6 Psychological Perspectives on Work and Organisations 373

Unit 7   Motivating the Workforce   435

Resources   639

GUIDE FOR STUDENTS

Course Introduction

Welcome to *People in Organisations*. The objectives of this guide are:

- to give you an outline of the subject of people in organisations;
- to explain why it is necessary for you to study people in organisations as part of your degree;
- to describe the nature of the material on which this workbook is based;
- to outline the programme which you will be following;
- to offer some practical hints and advice on how to study people in organisations using the open learning approach; and
- to point out some of the advantages to you of studying people in organisations by the method used in this book.

People in Organisations – what is covered?

Why do people in organisations feel and act in the way they do? What are the factors which influence the behaviour of people in organisations and hence what factors affect the operation of the organisation as a whole? How can organisations be designed and managed in order to influence people's behaviour and therefore to ensure more successful organisations?

People and organisations is a relatively new field of study which addresses crucial questions of this sort. It draws together a number of disciplines, (e.g. sociology, industrial psychology, management theory) each of which is concerned with how people's behaviour is influenced by the organisational setting in which they work. Such factors can include amongst others:

- the way people are managed;
- the work they are expected to carry out;
- the way in which the organisations reward them;
- the interpersonal relationships that they have with the organisation's members.

People and organisations is, similarly, concerned with the way in which people's behaviour influences the results and outcomes achieved by the organisation. For example:

- the flexibility and responsiveness achieved by the organisation;
- financial success;
- the standards of service provided to the organisation's customers.

From this very brief description it can be seen that people and organisations operate on a number of different levels of analysis. For instance it is interested in:

- people as individuals;
- people in interaction with others;
- the nature of organisations within which people work.

The early units of this module develop one further level of analysis, namely:

- the historical and social context of organisations.

By examining key sociological theories, the module explores such issues as the processes of social change, the development of industrialisation and capitalist forms of production and the changing ways in which managerial control is exercised. The functioning of organisations can best be understood in relation to their social and historical context. The module employs this insight in order to consider contemporary trends, such as the changing form and structure of organisations and the impact of new technology.

Clearly there are many types of organisations in contemporary society. But whether we think of manufacturers, retailers, prisons, universities, charitable organisations, or health care organisations, they can all be considered as *work organisations* and it is this aspect which is the dominant focus of this module. People in organisations is concerned with explaining organisations, both the general and the particular. For instance it is interested in developing general theories of decision-making or leadership or communications which might apply broadly to all organisations. Beyond this it is concerned with particularly the exploration of organisations by developing models which account for *differences* between organisations and which therefore can provide a more detailed framework for helping managers, and others, to influence organisational outcomes. You will come across a wide range of theories and ideas which provide general and particular accounts of organisations.

Why study people in organisations?

As part of the study of business a thorough understanding of organisations, and the people who work in and for them, is crucial. The majority of the working population is employed by organisations and we deal with organisations when buying and selling goods and services. The quality of our health and welfare services, our educational systems and even our political democracy, are largely the result of people in organisations, the decisions which they make and the effectiveness with which they function. The first reason for studying people in organisations therefore is simply that they are so crucial in delivering valued good and services and so important in influencing the overall quality of life.

The second reason for studying people in organisations is entirely practical. Management is frequently defined as 'achieving results through other people' and anyone who seeks to influence organisations, (whether or not they are called managers) requires an understanding of human behaviour, organisational processes and the interaction of the two. So, for instance, we need to understand these issues in order to achieve practical outcomes such as:

- introducing change into organisations;
- adopting a suitable style for communicating with others in the organisation;
- empowering employees to make full use of their skills and talents.

Some managers may achieve this level of understanding instinctively or by trial and error, but increasingly business is seeking to apply the insights of the disciplines that make up people in organisations. It is commonplace to read in company reports that 'our people are our greatest asset'. Increasingly it is apparent that long term business success will be achieved by those companies that develop effective strategies for developing and utilising the skills of their human resources.

A third reason for studying people in organisations is what might be termed personal insight and personal development. Through understanding the behaviour of others we may develop a better understanding of ourselves and therefore enhance the possibility of our own personal development. A manager with no insight into his or her own behaviour or the impact it has on others is likely to be less effective as a manager as a consequence. When reading the text and completing the activities it is therefore important that you consider how it connects with your own experience and how far the ideas help you understand the behaviour of people in organisations – yourself included!

What is in this workbook?

The core of the workbook is eleven study units. These have been written specifically for undergraduate business students by authors with considerable experience of teaching on BA (Hons) courses.

The units are particularly useful to students, like you, who may be following a course where an 'open learning' approach is being adopted. The features which make it particularly suitable for open learning include:

- very careful sequencing of the material so that there is a clear and logical progression;
- a step by step approach so that you will be able to understand each new point thoroughly before proceeding to the next one;
- a very clear layout with relatively short headed sections and paragraphs;
- numerous short case studies and examples which help illustrate the ideas and provide opportunities for analysis and developing understanding;

- lots of opportunities for you to check that you understand what you have just read;

- several 'review activities' in each unit which enable you to extend and apply your knowledge, for example, by relating it to case studies or extracts from journal articles;

- plenty of opportunities for you to test your progress through end-of-unit exercises to which solutions are provided.

Resources

At the back of the book there is a resources section, a collection of journal articles and extracts from texts. Particular features of this section are:

- a number of journal articles and extracts from texts, each dealing with a significant issue in people in organisations;

- up-to-date material, some of which deals with topical issues;

- fairly short articles and extracts written in clear, non-technical language;

- articles and extracts which are clearly linked to the review activities in the text.

Although the workbook is designed to be complete in itself, your understanding of the subject will be improved by wider reading. Each unit has a list of recommended reading to guide you towards some of the more important and useful literature.

Using the workbook

You should work through the units in the order which best fits in with your course. You should begin by noting the points which the unit outlines identify as the crucial aspects of the material. This will put the contents of the units into context and guide you through them.

Each unit is interspersed with a number of 'activities' and 'review activities'. All of these are intended to be attempted by you as they arise and completed before you move on. The suggested answers to each activity are given immediately following the relevant activity. The solutions to the review activities are given at the end of the relevant unit.

The activities are intended to be a combination of a check that you are following the unit and understanding it, on the one hand, and a way of making your learning a more active experience for you, on the other. By working through the activities, you can effectively divide your study time between that necessary to taking on new ideas and that which is necessary to reinforce those ideas. The review activities allow you to consider larger sections of the material, testing and extending your understanding by applying them to case examples or to articles in the resources section.

Typically, the activities will only take you a few minutes to deal with. By contrast, the review articles may take considerably longer. It is important that you discipline yourself to complete each activity, self-assessment question or exercise before you refer to the answer provided. You should read the items in the resources section when recommended.

Avoid rote learning

You should avoid any attempt at rote learning the material in this workbook. By working through the activities you should aim to understand the underlying 'logic' in the ideas being presented. Simply trying to 'learn the theories' is inappropriate and insufficient. Rather, you should endeavour to appreciate how different theoretical ideas and models lead to their own particular conclusions and insights and therefore point to particular types of solution to behavioural/organisational problems. You should also try to associate the names of authors with their key ideas. This will help you separate out the different theories and ideas and will help when you begin to read around the subject more widely.

Given the complexity of the subject matter, it is rarely, if ever, possible to present single solutions to behavioural organisational problems. Human behaviour cannot be predicted with complete accuracy and there is no single best way to explain behaviour. At various points in the workbook you will come across competing explanations and alternative schools of thought. This can be quite frustrating if you feel there should be right and wrong answers to questions but it is inherent in the subject. However, you should attempt to use the ideas creatively to form your own views on how behaviour can best be explained and on the most appropriate solutions to organisational problems.

Set aside time for your studies

Clearly, at the start of the study period you will not know how long it will take to do the necessary work. It is sensible therefore, to make a start on the work at an early stage in the study period. Try to discipline yourself to set aside particular times in the week to study, though not necessarily the same times each week. Experiment with different ways of studying the material to find the one which best suits you. Try skimming each unit to get a broad grasp of the material before you go through it in detail. Alternatively, try reading all the unit objectives and summaries before you ready the material in depth. Try to find the most suitable time to study when your concentration is at its highest and interruptions are at a minimum. And do set aside sufficient time to complete all the activities – they are a crucial part of the learning process.

People in Organisations

Introduction

People in Organisations is concerned with the functions of organisations and within them, why people behave and act in a particular way.

In studying the 10 units that make up this module you will be introduced to the range of functions and interactions that exist with people and with organisations in our society.

The module is written for students who are newcomers to these areas. The theories and concepts introduced are reinforced through activities and case studies to support theory through practice and directed observation.

Many of the units examine contextual issues on people in organisations, initially from historical and evolutionary perspectives to provide a basis for understanding their current impact. The module is introduced by an examination of administration and control and its development through classical management theories such as Fayol and Taylor.

The contextual issues are extended into a consideration of technology and flexibility, where in unit two particular consideration is made of Fordism (debating deskilling and alienation) and post Fordism (debating flexibility). These concepts are extended into unit three which examines continuity and change with emphasis on human action through authors such as Silverman, Goldthorpe and Lockwood and in consideration of the issues of managerial cycles of control.

The contextual issues are concluded with two units which are concerned, respectively with examinations of the nature of organisations and the nature of work. Organisations are examined as social networks, their classification and the nature and consequences of their structure and their activities are explored through a series of interactive student activities and case studies. The nature of work is examined through historical development through to current work culture and development (including gender issues). The unit examines work design issues and the changing nature and patterns of work both inside and outside the workplace.

Those units beyond unit five are concerned with content issues where the major focus is attached to psychological perspectives concerned with people. Unit six introduces a range of psychological perspectives on work and organisations such as personality theories, perception, the development of selection procedures through to an examination of the use of psychometric testing. This unit is further developed in unit seven where content process and control theories are examined with respect to motivating the workforce. Observations are made on motivation versus influence.

The content issues which are psychological in focus, conclude with two units concerned with group and group effectiveness and leadership. Unit eight examines the types and purpose of groups leading on to the effectiveness and development of groups in organisations. Unit nine examines Leaders leading and the led, which presents perspectives on the process of leadership, the relationship of leadership and management, the universal personality traits and contingency approaches to leadership and the distinction between transactional and transformational approaches to leadership.

The module concludes with unit ten where there is an examination of organisational communication as an overridingly important process to the successful operation and function within organisations. There are four main sections to the unit; communications theories and models, barriers to communication, formal and informal communication and communicating culture. The latter section revisits some earlier observations in psychology, such as personality and selection and expands these areas in the context of communication.

Each of the units is self contained and there are no pre-requisites attached to any one unit, however it is intended that the ordering of units is pedagogic in terms of contextual and content issues.

Due to the flexibility of materials lecturers and students can decide the units and their sequence to form the basis of an undergraduate module or a one year course on people in organisations.

We have identified suitable bibliographic and reference sources for each of the units and all units contain activities, case studies and are supported by a resource section containing relevant articles, where necessary. These inputs, along with the text, provide both a broad and deep approach to the subject, from which it is hoped both lecturers and students can benefit

Bob McClelland
Liverpool Business School, 1996

UNIT 1

ADMINISTRATION AND CONTROL

Introduction

What do you think of when someone says the word 'management'? Perhaps you think of a factory with employees toiling away on the 'shop floor' watched over and directed by the 'management' in their white coats or pinstripe suits from their offices 'upstairs'; or a design department with managers acting as a focus of co-ordination for specialised design activities carried out by 'colleagues'?

Many people have these sorts of images. Whether our experience of management is good or bad, we tend to assume that work has always been like it is today. We take for granted that organisations have people who report to others in an ordered hierarchical structure; that in the workplace there are laid down policies and procedures; that an attempt is made to define and solve problems systematically; that people are hired and promoted on merit and that attempts are made to motivate the organisation's employees. In short, we tend to regard management as a well established discipline which has been in its present form for many years.

In fact, the art of management as we know it today is vastly different from that of 100 years ago. Although we can say that management of some form must have existed to enable the planning, organising, leading and control of the work situation, we can also say that our general understanding of management has been lacking and ad hoc in the past. It is only relatively recently that concerted attempts have been made to analyse management as a separate function and to attempt systematically to improve output in the workplace by attention to it. Not until the latter half of the nineteenth century and the early part of the twentieth century were theories developed of how production processes and business organisation might be systematically managed. In this unit, we consider and review some of the earliest of these theories, and their impacts, past and present.

Essentially, we look at philosophies and mechanisms which were advocated as the means by which managers could improve the effectiveness and efficiency of the production (or service provision) process.

- **Effectiveness** we may define as 'doing the right jobs' in order to achieve the organisation's aims and objectives.
- **Efficiency** is sometimes defined as 'doing the job right' and is a measure of how well a person or machine is performing at a given task.

For example, with modern production methods we could produce a Model 'T' Ford, as manufactured in the 1920s, with great efficiency but few would wish to buy it. So, although the work effort might be efficient it would not be particularly effective.

We look at these philosophies and mechanisms from several angles: what prompted their introduction; the circumstances in which they were introduced; their effect upon management's goals of efficiency and effectiveness; and linked inextricably with the previous factor, the effect of these changes on the performance and attitudes of the workers. This is the linchpin for successful management in almost all cases. All of these considerations have, as their basis, the concept of management control.

We consider three main areas of early management theory:

- **scientific management** as developed by Taylor and others
- **Fayol's principles of administration**
- **human relations** as developed by Mayo.

You will find that each of these early theories approaches control in different ways:

- scientific management is concerned with an operational approach: the 'best way' of doing a particular job
- Fayol's principles of administration are concerned with organisational policies and guidelines to be adopted in the structure and operation of an organisation
- human relations concentrates on appreciation of people: their needs as individuals and groups; the way in which they interact socially; and how these activities impinge on their work activity.

We begin the unit by looking at the meaning of control and administration and then look in detail at these three main areas.

Objectives

Our main aim in this unit is to introduce the concepts of management, or administration, and control and the development of theories related to them.

By the end of this unit, you will be able to:

- distinguish between the concepts of management, administration, and control.
- use a present-day model to analyse what was meant by control in the time of the early management theorists.
- describe factors in the work and environmental context which affected management style and control during this period.
- list Frederick Taylor's major principles of scientific management and describe how they may be used in a particular situation.
- describe the contributions to scientific management of the Gilbreths and Gantt.
- highlight scientific management principles and techniques in a modern-day example and comment on their appropriateness for managerial control.
- explain Henri Fayol's 14 principles of management.
- explain Fayol's 'managerial activities'.
- analyse modern-day examples with reference to Fayol's managerial activities and principles of management and address Fayol's relevance today.

- describe the main findings from Mayo's relay assembly room experiment and the later experiments at the Hawthorne Plant.

- outline the impact of the Hawthorne Studies in the 1930s and 1940s on organisational studies, in particular, in the field of human relations.

- highlight human relations principles and techniques in modern-day examples and comment on their appropriateness, particularly in relation to managerial control.

SECTION 1

Control and the Art of Management

Introduction

In this section, we begin with a discussion of some different meanings of 'control' in a business context. We explain what the early management theorists meant by control and what they saw as its relationship with their ideas on administration and management. We use a present-day model of control to illustrate these points.

However, as the context in which control is administered is very significant, we consider socio-economic factors in the USA, between 1865 and 1940, which influenced the development of early management and control theory.

1.1 The background

In the unit introduction, we noted that:

- management theory is about philosophies and mechanisms which have been put forward as means by which managers could improve the effectiveness and efficiency of the production (or service provision) process

- the theories we look at in this unit develop control within organisations in one form or another

- together they represent some of the early developments over a range of aspects of business management: operations, organisations and human resources.

Before looking at the theories in detail, however, we need to:

● examine what the terms 'control' and 'administration mean in the context of these early theories

● review one central context where it was felt necessary to develop management control theory so we can appreciate how approaches and theories are influenced by particular contextual needs and circumstances.

For a number of reasons, the appropriate context for us to look at is that of the USA between the 1860s and 1940. Firstly, both scientific management and human relations theory were originally developed and widely practised in the USA, so it gives us an idea about the environment in which Taylor and Mayo and others were carrying out their experiments and research.

Secondly, Fayolism, though originating in France, was also influential in many of the huge American companies which tried out many of these management theories.

Finally, we consider Fordism, which was also developed and practised in the US context, in Unit 2.

1.2 Control and administration

ACTIVITY 1

What types of activity would you include when you use the word 'control' in a business context?

You may have thought of a number of possible meanings for 'control' – the control mechanisms for a process, checks on how a service is carried out, disciplinary control of a workforce, a company's control of its resources and so on.

John Child analysing control in a modern context in his book *Organisations* talks of two levels of control:

● **strategic**

● **operational.**

The first strategic level is defined by Child as 'control over the means and methods on which the whole conduct of an organization depends' (Child, 1984). It involves, for instance, the ability of a company to establish a new factory in terms of control of capital, its relationship with local authorities and its hold over the supply of a willing workforce from the community. This 'hold' includes not only the ability to hire and fire but the provision of benefits which tie the employee to the organisation, for example, company pension schemes, medical schemes, and subsidised mortgages.

The second operational level considers control over the production process and concerns the means and processes by which management attempts to keep a tight rein on all of those activities in the company related to its production or services. Power may be overtly used to ensure that employees comply with management's directives; this may be coercive or through a reward system and also through influence on the values and beliefs of individuals.

We concentrate on this second type of control because it was this type of activity or aspiration that the early theorists referred to. Although Mayo used an example of strategic control in the benevolent but nevertheless restricting paternalism of the Western Electric Company, 'control' in its original context referred very much to operational matters, by which management attempted to keep a tight rein over production and related activities. We see that this is what Fayol meant by control and that the concerns of the other early theorists reflected the same conceptions of what control involved.

Subsequent studies have suggested, as John Child (1984) tells us, that management control and the use of power involve complex variables and that the two levels of control do not exist independently. As Child puts it: 'The ability to exercise control within an organisation at this second [operational] level is largely dependent on, and certainly facilitated by, control at the first strategic level.'

MANAGEMENT CONTROL

A modern framework for management control as given by Child (Figure 1) is therefore shaped by both strategic and operational requirements and involves:

- **defining goals**
- **establishing standards** to measure against
- **controlling** the operating behaviour of subordinates
- **measuring output** against planned output
- **evaluating and rewarding performance.**

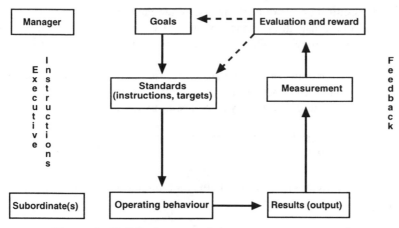

Figure 1: Child's framework for management control
Source: Child, 1984, Figure 6.1, p. 141

This type of model of control with its logical sequence of the process requirements needed to achieve specified goals may seem obvious to us now. However, it was not always so. At the time when the early theorists began their work, there was little recognition of the need for such defined and systematic control – not even for operational processes. In particular:

● Managers were given little guidance on how to plan the work operation. The field of work study did not exist. Even organisation charts which we take for granted today were not used. Managers may have had 'goals' but they were founded upon shaky ground and subject to their own idiosyncrasies rather than proven management principles.

● Subordinates used to set their own standards for the job and used their own forms of measurement of output.

We see that the early theorists provided the basis upon which modern models of management control, such as that of Child, were developed.

ACTIVITY 2

The title of this unit is 'Administration and Control'. What do you see as the relationship between these two?

You may have suggested that a company's administration or management is the means whereby control is effected. For company-wide control to be effective, appropriate policies and guidelines must be in place in organisations and adherence to them must be monitored. For Fayol, the early theorist of the principles of administration, administration meant the whole running of a business organisation and included control as one of its elements. When Fayol wrote of 'administration', now we might talk instead of 'management' but whichever word we use, there is a close relationship between administration and management and control.

Two of our areas for study in this unit are scientific management and principles of administration. Their titles signify links to the type of control, we have just been discussing. Your third topic for study is the development of human relations theory.

ACTIVITY 3

Do you see a possible relationship between human relations and the topic of administration and control?

Control involves measurement, standards, monitoring, etc. As a result, both now and in earlier times, managers have tended to think of control in terms of managerial and operational control systems so control could be regarded purely as a technical matter. Child saw it as 'a neutral phenomenon'.

However, production and service processes are carried out through people, and the term 'control' must therefore also concern the extent to which management can issue orders and have them willingly carried out by its workers.

To think purely in terms of control systems is to be completely unaware of the reality of the situation. After all, we talk of having control of 'the hearts and minds' of those we wish to lead. Child says: 'managers . . . need to secure motivation and feedback from those at whom control is directed'. In other words, management and control also involve influencing and motivating human beings; they require the management of human relations as well as of administrative and operational factors.

All of the aspects of early theory we have looked at in this unit are therefore related – both to control and business administration in general and to each other. They introduce you to pioneering work on the fundamental concepts and concerns still vital to effective business management.

1.3 Importance of context for management and control

ACTIVITY 4

Let us consider a modern-day example. A Japanese car manufacturer has established a production plant in Britain. In Japan, workers start the day by getting together as groups and performing a series of invigorating exercises. They then sing the company song.

What do you think would be the likely reaction of workers if these daily team- and culture-building activities were introduced in a British plant?

The question of exercise is debatable. Twenty years ago, exercise was considered to be for fanatics only. Perhaps today there would be more acceptance, although it is still doubtful that the majority of workers would do it willingly.

With regard to the company song, most British workers would, feel embarrassed to have to demonstrate their loyalty in this way. The team comes first in Japan; in Britain it is definitely of secondary importance to the individual.

Our example makes the important point that control and administration (or management) are tied very much to factors present in the actual situation. What works in one country or context may not work in another.

Similarly, it suggests that any critical understanding of the development of control and management theory needs to take into account the historical, cultural and socio-economic climate in which the theory or theories grew up.

Let us return now to our consideration of the three main areas: scientific management; principles of administration; and human relations. We then ask the question: Why did 'management' feel the need to develop these schools of thought?

To understand why and how these theories were developed you need to understand the extensive changes happening in industry in the latter half of the last and early part of this century, in other words, the context of their introduction. Central to this are developments in the USA.

1.4 The USA

We concentrate on these developments in the USA as:

- Both scientific management and human relations were originally developed within the USA. (Fayolism was developed in France.)
- The huge American companies of the time tried out these theories.

However, when we come to consider the relevance of these theories today we will broaden the scope and will use British examples as well. We now look at the USA between the 1860s and the 1930s. This will give you an appreciation of the environment in which Taylor, Mayo and others were carrying out their experiments and research. In Unit 2, you also consider Fordism as practised in the USA.

THEORETICAL DEVELOPMENTS AND THE AMERICAN CONTEXT

Two of the three theories we are considering originated in the USA and huge American companies were leaders in readily trying out all the early management theories. The American context is therefore of great importance for us to understand why and how the theories developed. Before looking at the individual theories, we review a range of the most important contextual factors and socio-economic changes occurring in the US between the 1860s and 1940. We look at:

- why management found the need to develop these theories
- how the theories themselves were influenced and shaped by the context of experiment and research.

RAPID GROWTH AND CHANGE IN INDUSTRIAL CONTEXT

It is hard to appreciate that only 150 years ago the USA was essentially an agricultural economy. It was not until after the end of the Civil War in 1865 that industry began its relentless and very rapid growth so that by around 1880 the USA could boast of an industrial economy. This is commonly defined as one in which less than 50% of society is concerned with 'primary' production.

Comparing this with the British economy of the time it is interesting to note the statistics given in Table 1.

	Population (Million)	National Income (Billion $)
Britain	5.1	5.2
USA	50.2	7.2

Table 1: The comparative population and national income of
Britain and the US in 1880
Source: Littler, 1983

However, by 1900, as Littler states, 'the American population and national income were almost double that of Britain's'.

A series of mergers of companies took place in two successive waves between 1898-1902 and 1926-30. As Littler says, the effect of this was that 'between 1896 and 1905 the 100 largest USA companies quadrupled in size controlling 40% of industry by 1905'. Clearly, if such rapid expansion in industry and company size was to be handled effectively, there was a need for improved management and control.

IMMIGRANT WORKFORCE

Another factor peculiar to the American situation was the influx of immigrants. The 14 million immigrants, Poles, Italians, Jews, Germans, in the period from 1860 to 1900 meant that in many industries well over half of the workforce were 'new' Americans. For these people, the source of support and the people they identified with were not work colleagues but family and religious groups. As immigrants, they were disadvantaged by:

- language barriers
- racial stereotypes relating to such things as intelligence, work motivation, aptitudes and skills
- lack of relevant industrial skills.

Such workforce factors influenced early management theorists by directing the attention to particular problems and concerns. Thus we see that Taylor in the 1890s, talks of Schmidt, a Dutchman who he used for testing out his theories of scientific management. (Schmidt had to do exactly as Taylor directed – he was being paid to 'do', not to think.) Later in the 1920s, we see Mayo conducting experiments with groups of people, many of them non-native or first generation Americans.

WAGES

Generally speaking workers in the USA enjoyed better wages than their British counterparts. This was due to a high wage, low cost philosophy as outlined in Schoenhof's *The Economy of High Wages* (1892). The basis for this philosophy was that high wages did not have to mean high costs for the employer. In fact, the reverse was true, by increasing the efficiency of the workers and gaining increases in output per worker, management could afford to pay higher wages and still reduce unit costs. This model assumes either fewer workers to produce the same quantity of goods (demand is limited) or that the same workers produce more goods which are then sold (demand is greater than supply). When you look at Fordism in Unit 3, you see that the supply of low price cars, for example, could not keep up with the demand for them by the public. These early theorists assumed that workers would be quite happy to go along with the efficiency development because they would benefit through higher wages.

LABOUR TURNOVER

The number of workers entering and leaving jobs within companies, labour turnover, was extremely high. In 1914, the average turnover of staff was in the region of 100% per year. This was due in large part to low skilled immigrants working their way up the job ladder as they became more skilled. This factor encouraged the tendency of management to treat their workers as a commodity, just like any other resource.

Another tendency was for management to break the job down into tasks requiring a much narrower range of skills so that semi- and unskilled workers could be quickly trained to do them. By the same token, workers were more likely to adopt an approach which concentrated on their pay and working conditions and which was complementary to the objectives of their (capitalist) employers. They believed in the American dream of mobility upwards.

THE GREAT DEPRESSION

The great depression of 1929-1933 was to have a serious impact upon manufacturing output in the USA. Industrial production fell by a half and a quarter of the workforce, 15 million people, lost their jobs. The later experiments of Mayo were conducted in this period.

UNIONS

Unions never became really popular in the USA in the way in which they did in Britain. Early unions emerged and grew as craft unions after the Civil War; but these for skilled workers only. The American Federation of Labour (AFL), formed in the 1880s, was concerned only with craft unions and was opposed to unskilled workers joining unions.

In general, employers did all they could to discourage unions, For example, they had 'yellow-dog' contracts, signed by employees at the time of employment, which stated that they would not join a union. Disputes and strikes did occur within certain industries, for example, the railroad strikes of 1877. But the sheer growth of industry soon overshadowed these. Note that unions were essentially non-political; they did not associate themselves with a 'Labour' party, seeing their prime role as one of securing better pay and conditions for their members.

UN-SKILLED WORKERS

So what happened to the immigrant workers and other non-skilled workers? How did they cope without a union to help them? The government was no help; it did nothing to counter anti-union employers.

Only after the great depression, when the power imbalance between employer and worker became so great that it could no longer be ignored, did the government bring in the 1935 Wagner Act which provided the legislation to ensure that unions could organise themselves. The Congress of Industrial Organizations (CIO) was formed for the masses of unskilled workers. The giant companies of the day – US Steel, Ford and General Motors – were to oppose unions violently at first but eventually they had to concede to the reality that unions were there to stay (Conlin & Renshaw, 1978).

ACTIVITY 5

What management concerns might these factors have raised in the American context? What influence might they have had on the approaches and practice of early management theorists?

There are many points you could have noted. Management might be concerned with:

● how new workers with low skills, possible language problems and a tendency to move on could be trained quickly to be as efficient as possible

● how they could best be enabled and encouraged to produce more efficiently and effectively

● what working conditions would be most conducive to this

● how processes could be broken down into the most simple and efficient methods requiring little initiative

● how standards could be set and performance measured

● what should be done if workers did not meet the standards, and so on.

As we look at the work of the theorists, particularly those involved in the development of scientific management, you can see these kinds of concern reflected in their focus and approach.

Their somewhat mechanistic approach to improving efficiency and control was perhaps influenced also by:

● the idea that greater efficiency would benefit workers too by producing high wages

● the relative lack of popularity of unions amongst workers

● the power imbalance which this and events, such as the Depression contributed to.

The human problems of the depression were also probably an influence on the work of the early human relations theorists with their attempts to develop a more humane, paternalistic approach to management and control, and their realisation of the importance of psychological as well as economic and physical factors in work motivation and performance.

REVIEW ACTIVITY 1

1 What did the early management theorists mean when they talked about control? Identify factors from the list below in your discussion. What level of control, strategic or operational, do these factors belong to. Which of the factors listed relate to our present understanding of management control?

(a) Ability of an organisation to hire and fire

(b) Company pension and medical schemes

(c) Measurement against standards

(d) A company's relationship with local authorities

(e) Monitoring output

(f) Evaluation of results

(g) Motivation of personnel

2. Complete Child's framework for control in Figure 2.

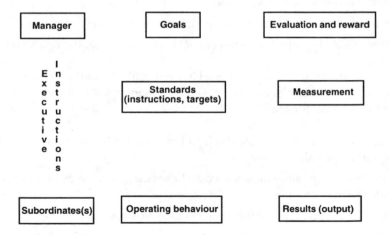

Figure 2: Child's framework for control, incomplete

3 Identify the three ideologies we looked at in depth in this section and explain briefly how each is linked to control.

(a) Management by objectives

(b) Scientific management

(c) Appraisals

(d) Human relations

(e) Total quality management

(f) Principles of administration

4 We have reviewed important factors in the US socio-economic setting during the period in which the early management theories were developed. Which of the following statements indicate why we need to understand the US context?

(a) It is only applicable to the USA

(b) Much of the theory was developed and adopted there

(c) All of the other major nations (such as Britain) already had their own well-developed theories of management

(d) The specific nature of theories is influenced by the context in which they originate, are practised and develop.

Summary

In this section, we have explained what we mean by administration and control and introduced you to early theories concerning different aspects of these. You have also looked at the context for some of these theories and highlighted the important role of context in management and control.

More specifically, in this section, you have:

- defined 'control'
- compared your ideas with Child's two levels of control and his model of management control
- considered the relationship between 'administration' and 'control'
- discovered that the early theorists considered 'control' as an element of 'administration' – a term often synonymous with what we now call 'management'
- examined the importance of context of control in a modern factory
- observed that control is linked to human relations as well as management systems
- looked at the American context in which the early theories were applied and examined the implications of rapid industrial expansion, immigrant influx and other relevant factors.

SECTION 2

Scientific Management

Introduction

In this section, we consider the growth of a new way of managing, known as 'scientific management', that was introduced in the latter part of the nineteenth century. We follow the work of Frederick Taylor and other major contributors to the movement from this time until the 1920s.

Following this, we examine the far-reaching consequences of scientific management to productivity and control of the work situation and the subsequent resistance to such control. Finally, we review the applicability of scientific management to modern organisations.

2.1 Frederick Taylor (1856-1915)

Originally trained as a machinist in the early 1870s, Taylor was to become one of the most important figures in management theory during the latter part of the nineteenth century and the early part of the twentieth century. Much of his work is associated with what became known as 'scientific management'. His first writings were published as *Principles of Scientific Management* in 1911.

Taylor was concerned with the efficiency with which machinists and other workers performed their jobs. Much of his work was with the Midvale and Bethlehem Steel Companies in the USA.

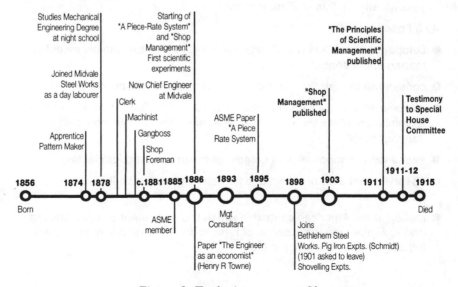

Figure 3: Taylor's career profile

ACTIVITY 6

Imagine you are a worker in 1875, employed as a general labourer at a large steel works in the USA; this was the sort of place in which Taylor worked. The production of steel involves, amongst other processes, the haulage and unloading of iron ore and coal from rail truck to the blast furnaces. From what you have learned of the general US industrial context and from your own knowledge, answer the following questions:

1   What sort of working environment do you think exists?

2   On what basis do you think you would be paid?

3   How secure do you think your job is?

4   How well educated are you likely to be?

5   What, in broad terms, would be your likely view of management and its attempts to get you to be more productive?

You will be in the open, performing heavy, manual tasks.

1   Work is likely to be characterised by:

   ● dusty, dirty and possibly very noisy atmosphere

   ● exposure to the heat and cold of the day

   ● never-ending toil of stooping and heavy lifting

   ● monotony of the job only broken by conversing with other workers.

2   You will probably be paid on a piece work rate, that is, by your output each day.

3   Your job is only as secure as your health and the whim of your employer. Although unions are now becoming much stronger they are for craftsmen, not general labourers!

4   You are unlikely to be well educated. You might be an immigrant with the added problems of a new language and culture to contend with.

5   You would probably have a definite 'them and us' attitude – managers are well educated you are not! You would not be highly receptive to change unless you saw very tangible benefits for yourself.

As you can see from his career profile in Figure 3, Taylor, who might have entered Harvard had his eyesight been adequate at the time, rose through the ranks of the Midvale Steel Company from labourer to chief engineer.

By his own account, and as you might have expected from Activity 6, Taylor had a fairly rough time of it at first. He refused to go along with the output being produced by the team he was in charge, knowing that it could easily produce more.

In fact, cajoling, threatening and laying off workers he managed to achieve the appropriate increases after about three years. But why did he have to do this?, he wondered .Why couldn't he simply demonstrate the amount of work which should be produced in a day by a skilled, competent, willing worker (a 'first-class worker' as opposed to a 'second-' or 'third-class worker') and then there would be no dispute? And so he began his study of work operations and how much a 'first-class worker' could be expected to produce on a regular basis.

2.2 Planning and doing – a new approach

What Taylor was advocating was revolutionary. Up until that time, the job of work and its planning had been largely left to the workers themselves. Managers were satisfied to leave the intricacies of the operations to the workers and paid them according to what they thought was appropriate. Some used an 'initiative and incentive' scheme in which they offered bonuses or other rewards, such as promotion, as incentives. They relied upon the initiative of the workers to enable them to meet whatever the nominal targets were. Workers used 'rules of thumb' to assist them, for example, they would assume that a man would take twice as long to shovel a load of material which was twice the density of another. (See Taylor's experiments on shovelling which follow.)

Taylor would argue that even when they had the intelligence, they did not have the time to carry out a detailed systematic study of how to improve their own efficiency.

ACTIVITY 7

Do you see any possible disadvantages in the earlier methods of managing?

Taylor was convinced that under this old system a good deal of 'soldiering' went on. We would call this 'laziness' and 'skiving'. He argued that there was:

● 'natural soldiering' – the natural inclination of a man (note he invariably used this term as most of his work was with men, although one of his studies involved women whose job it was to pick out defective bicycle ball bearings) to slow down to an easy pace

● 'systematic soldiering' – this was more of a deliberate attempt to slow down the rate of work to make it last longer (he cites the case of golf caddies who are paid by the hour)

However, if managers did not know what a fair day's work was, how could they stop, or even recognise, these practices? And how could they decide what was a 'fair day's work'? How could managers answer these questions?

ANALYSING THE JOB; SETTING THE STANDARD

Taylor recognised that answering these questions required managers to:

- carefully study the job, breaking it down into individual parts.

- identify what a good worker could do in a 'fair day's work'.

- the analysis of the job had to be the manager's responsibility in his view and no longer that of the workmen. The work was to be, in Taylor's view, a 50:50 split with managers planning and workers doing.

In his search to establish the standard for a fair day's work, Taylor categorised workers as first-, second- and third-class. The first-class worker was diligent, skilful and produced the greatest output. His original *First Class Shovellers,* for instance, were so concerned about producing at maximum rate that they preferred to purchase their own individual shovels and not the ones issued by the company.

TAYLOR'S PRINCIPLES OF SCIENTIFIC MANAGEMENT

Taylor's 'principles of scientific management' are:

1 'Develop a science for each element of a man's work which replaces the old rule of thumb method.'
   [This would identify the one best way for a job to be done and help ascertain what should be produced in a day by a skilled, competent worker.]

2 'Scientifically select and then train, teach, and develop the workman, whereas in the past he chose his own work and trained himself as best he could.'

3 'Heartily co-operate with the men so as to insure all of the work being done in accordance with the principles of the science which has been developed.'

4 'There is an almost equal division of the work and the responsibility between the management and the workmen. The management take over all work for which they are better fitted than the workmen, while in the past almost all of the work and the greater part of the responsibility were thrown upon the men.' (Taylor, 1947, p. 36)
   [Study and analysis of work methods and planning of the work were to be the manager's job.]

TAYLOR AND INCENTIVES

Taylor advocated the use of incentives, such as a differential piecework system that increased the daily or piecework rate of pay, for first-class workers. In one experiment, for instance, he offered Schmidt a rate of $1.85 which effectively increased his wages by 60% above that of other workers. His premise was that both worker and manager would benefit from scientific management, the worker from increased pay and management from increased output.

Indeed his 'bottom line' reason for scientific management was:

- higher wages for workers
- lower labour costs (per unit output) for management.

He did not believe that the increased rate of pay should be negotiated, as such, but determined by experiment. For example, he employed men at different rates and found the rate at which they would prefer to work under his direction, rather than revert to their old (self-determined) direction. However, he insisted that scientific management was not purely about incentives. It was to do with a whole mental revolution. Pay was just one of the factors.

ACTIVITY 8

As we have seen, the working day for some of the labourers where Taylor worked consisted of constant shovelling of large quantities of coal and iron ore – manually transferring material from stockpiles to supply the steel furnaces with their raw inputs. In general terms, how do you think Taylor might have applied his principles and his ideas on incentives to the situation? Who would he see as benefiting from their application?

Taylor might have:

- analysed how the shovelling was presently carried out and how it might be most efficiently done, perhaps looking at aspects like tools used, economy of position, physical action, etc
- measured how much ore could be moved by the most efficient methods and workers
- introduced bonus schemes to encourage people to adopt the most efficient methods
- introduced careful selection of the job personnel and training in the best methods.

Taylor would see both workers, through higher wages, and management, lower unit costs, as benefiting from the application of his principles.

2.3 Taylor's methods

Why did people listen to Taylor? People listened because quite simply Taylor proved by personal example that his methods could work. The results reported were dramatic, as the well-known examples which follow demonstrate.

Example 1: The science of shovelling

At the Bethlehem Steel Company, Taylor analysed two 'first-class shovellers' whose job it was to shovel ore. At first, the men used their own personal shovel irrespective of the job. The average shovel load was 38 lb and each man shovelled 25 tons per day. Taylor gave the men smaller shovels (he systematically cut off bits of the shovel) and the daily tonnage rose to 30 tons per day. Eventually he found that the optimum size of shovel was one which allowed a load of 21 lb. Different size shovels were introduced for different types of material, ore, coal, etc. Those men who could match the rates of the 'first-class shovellers' had their pay increased by 60%. Those who could not were given training in the 'science of shovelling'. After 3 years, the work of 400-600 men was being done by 140 men.

Example 2: The pig iron experiment and Mr Schmidt

In 1899, the Bethlehem Steel Company had to manually load 80,000 tons of iron onto freight trucks. This iron was in the form of 92 lb 'pigs'. The average worker was used to loading 12.5 tons per day. Taylor thought that it was possible to load 47 tons per day. People were shocked and incredulous at his claims.

However, to prove that scientific management principles could work Taylor chose a man called Schmidt who, after training, never failed to load at least 47 tons per day for three years. Other workers were picked and similarly trained. He found that, only one in eight men was physically capable of this: these would be his 'first-class' persons. The qualities for the job were to be physically very strong ('as an ox') but intelligence was not required, only the willingness to follow the directions and planning of the supervisor. Indeed, Taylor might argue that an intelligent man might be more suited to a more cerebral task.

ACTIVITY 9

Put yourself in the position of Schmidt at the beginning of the pig iron experiment. What would be your feelings about the experiment ? What about those of your colleagues (factors of age, skill, strength, motivation, etc)

● You are young and fit so the thought of loading additional tonnage under Taylor's direction might seem inconsequential.

● To those colleagues not in the same 'super league' as yourself the thought of you setting new standards could be a very real threat to them whatever their motivation. You may also be aware (or be made aware !) of this.

- Of course, you may feel that the additional pay was not worth the extra work and you may resent being told how to do your job.

- Perhaps you like to set your own pace and leave time to chat to your work colleagues. Perhaps you alter your work pattern now and again 'just for a change' to relieve the monotony.

- Perhaps you think it is a management trick and the new rate will become the norm.

TAYLOR'S ASSUMPTIONS

As you have probably already noted, Taylor made several sweeping and often questionable assumptions to support his theory:

- The worker was paid to produce. He would go along with new, more efficient methods .

- A differential piecework system, for example, £0.20 per standard piece and £0.25 per higher rate piece, would be welcomed by management.

- There was no reason why management and worker could not work together towards common goals.

- Management generally could study work as rigorously as he did – with the same time and expertise.

Although often regarded as the father of scientific management, Taylor was not its sole contributor, and others followed his work.

2.4 Other contributors to scientific management: the Gilbreths and Gantt

A society of purists was established in 1914, later re-named the Taylor Society in his memory, which issued bulletins about six times a year between 1914 and 1934 on scientific management.

Frank and Lillian Gilbreth and Henry Gantt were influential theorists whom we now consider briefly.

THE GILBRETHS

Frank Gilbreth was a successful building contractor who considered himself first and foremost as a skilled brickwork professional. He was to conduct studies which looked at the 'science' of bricklaying. As Taylor pointed out to the Special Committee of Representatives in 1912, when he was defending scientific management and citing the work of Gilbreth, the art of bricklaying had remained essentially the same for 4000 years, even the bricks themselves were similar. The inference was that no real progress had been made despite successive generations of bricklayers coming and going. Gilbreth, by his adoption of scientific management, was to change all of this (Gilbreth, 1908).

ACTIVITY 10

Can you suggest briefly how Taylor's first principle of scientific management might be applied to bricklaying?

Taylor's first principle is 'develop a science for each element of a man's work'. Gilbreth's studies were to make use of 'time and motion'. He was particularly interested in where the bricklayer stood when laying bricks, how far he had to stretch down to pick up a brick from a pile of bricks and how many movements the laying of one brick entailed. He carefully recorded all of this, using photographs as part of his analysis. It took him one and a half years to cut out the first movement by the bricklayer stepping to the right, and a further year and a half to cut out the constant stooping for a brick. He introduced a movable table so that the bricks were always at the right height. He even suggested that the consistency of the mortar was such that a brick could be placed by hand in one movement rather than needing to be tapped down with the bricklayer's trowel. The result was, on average, that the number of motions for laying a brick was reduced from 18 to 5 and the rate of bricklaying increased dramatically from 120 per man per hour to 350 per man per hour. He was to reward men who followed his system by paying them $6.50 per day as opposed to the normal $5 per day. If they would not (or could not) attain the required outputs he would lay them off.

Looking at a modern building site today it is possible to see principles in action still. Great attention is paid to the correct positioning of packs of bricks. There is a 'right way up' for many bricks (so rainwater flows off and is not trapped); thus, bricks are stacked as level with the bricklayer's grasp as possible, facing the correct way up. A person acting as hod carrier and another as mortar mixer keep the bricklayer constantly supplied with materials to hand; scaffold is constantly adjusted by other labourers as the brick work proceeds. However, possibly the consistency of the mortar is a problem or the practice hasn't spread to Britain for the tapping of bricks still goes on!

The Gilbreths also devised flow process charting to depict whole operations diagrammatically; this system is still used today.

ACTIVITY 11

Think of a modern-day example of time and motion study.

Of course, there are numerous examples. For instance, any repetitive operation which occurs many times is likely to have been studied in this way. Examples range from manufacturing, for example, car plant assembly, to catering, for example, a fast food hamburger.

LILLIAN GILBRETH

Lillian Gilbreth was a trained psychologist and, as Huczynski and Buchanan (1991) note, was influential in extending her husband Frank's work to include firstly studies into fatigue (Gilbreth & Gilbreth, 1916) and then investigations into ways of reducing fatigue. This was to lead to experiments to:

- reduce daily hours
- introduce restbreaks
- reduce actions which were fatiguing.

In fact, the studies went beyond this to include some of the psychological effects upon the worker of providing an atmosphere more conducive to work, for example:

- provision of canteens and rest rooms
- provision of entertainment and music into the factory.

As Huczynski and Buchanan point out (1991), this was 'the first realisation that workers may have a variety of different needs'.

In a paper to the Taylor Society in 1922, the Gilbreths introduced the idea of 'superstandards' (Gilbreth & Gilbreth, 1922). Essentially this was a refinement of Taylor's standards into even narrower areas. The establishment of the standard itself had to be subject to detailed examination. More than Taylor's 'carefully thought out method', the standard had to be of proven accuracy. Once these 'superstandards' had been defined the way was then open to make common the units, methods and devices of research.

Measuring as it did 'all those things that have to do directly to fatigue', the Gilbreths even mention posture as an element which their superstandards would address. This is a factor which is still a contentious issue with the recent development of personal computers work stations, along with the contentious 'repetitive strain injuries' (RSI). Superstandards also looked not only at the 'one best way' to do work but the 'one best learning process' by which to teach it.

Like Taylor, they believed that workers would be happy to go along with the establishment of high work standards (their superstandards) but not necessarily financial incentives. They believed that work achievement was important to the personal satisfaction of individuals. 'It is true that there is nothing more monotonous than working under standards that one knows are inferior, and that one can easily improve upon . . . Such conditions are ruinous to ambition, to the development of personal and individual expression, and to the creative instinct and joy in work.'

ACTIVITY 12

Summarise significant or valuable points in the work of the Gilbreths.

Your answer should have included the following points:

- time and motion studies; reduction of number of movements in a work operation; timing of work operations
- superstandards; the quest for standardisation of standards
- studies of fatigue; rest breaks and entertainment
- realisation that workers have needs other than purely financial

HENRY LAURENCE GANTT (1861-1919)

Gantt worked with Taylor at the Bethlehem Steel Works. He agreed basically with Taylor's approach to work but he felt that some managers were using the system to exploit the workers.

When he became a consultant in his own right, Gantt moved away from the differential piecework system, that is, the rate being dependent on first-class workers achieving targeted rates, to one in which the worker received a standard payment even if he did not achieve all of the tasks outlined on his card (Gantt, 1919). Those who did achieve more than on their card received a substantial bonus.

He also later extended his bonus system so that the foreman received a bonus for every one of his workers who exceeded the standard. His reasoning was that once someone had done this the other workers would quickly follow.

Taylor acknowledged the use of a worker bonus as beneficial and as a means of changing worker behaviour during the change-over from the 'slow pace of ordinary work to the high speed which is the leading characteristic of good management'. He was to defend his differential rate as good for an established operation while conceding that perhaps Gantt's bonus was good for use in short term, rapidly changing activities in which the worker could not hope to attain the (high) differential rate.

Gantt's approach differed from Taylor's in other respects too:

- He was not so rigid in his definition of 'one best way' to do a job but, as Cole states, talked instead of a 'way which seems to be best at the moment' (Cole, 1990).
- He seemed less biased towards the 'soldiering' view in which workers were assumed to be naturally lazy but, as Huczynski and Buchanan tell us (1991), he advocated that 'the policy of the future will be to teach and to lead'.

However, nowadays Gantt is best remembered for his charts. Gantt charts were first established to show each worker's progress publicly in the form of a horizontal bar whose length represented the quantity of work to be done. Black bars were shown on days when the worker met the standard, red bars when he hadn't.

Gantt was later to extend this idea to represent not just each worker's progress but the progress, against a barred 'plan', of all of the operations on the site. This system is extremely widely used today, especially in project planning and control, when the duration of activities is in days and weeks rather than hours. It not only shows how long individual activities will take but also how they can be most effectively 'fitted together'.

ACTIVITY 13

How might an individual react to this public display of red and black bars of their daily output?

An individual might react in either of two, very different, ways:

- A **motivator:** If a worker is achieving the black bar (and the bonus) he or she may feel elevated amongst their peers. It may also act as a motivator to other workers who were unsure if the standard was possible and as a visible signpost for those close to attaining it.

- A **de-motivator:** If a worker fears that he or she cannot achieve the standard, perhaps through factors which he or she can do nothing about – age, infirmity, disability, then to see this display and be constantly reminded of it by colleagues will be disheartening. It may reinforce antagonism to working at a 'management rate' and determination to stick to the 'old standard' a worker is used to.

2.5 Applicability of scientific management outside the work shop

Although the majority of literature concentrates on Taylor's work on the shop floor, it is crucial to note that, amongst members of the Taylor Society the application of scientific management was not bounded by location or type of corporate enterprise.

As Oliver Sheldon says in the *Bulletin of the Taylor Society,* 1924, when talking of 'Taylor the creative leader', 'Scientific management has come to be recognized as a philosophy which is applicable, not only to shop management, but also to every activity of a business, from accountancy to selling, and, further, to every corporate enterprise, whether it be a manufacturing concern, a professional society, or a municipal organization.'

In 'A Critical Analysis of Scientific Management', another paper delivered to the Taylor Society in 1919, Farquhar devotes a section to 'Application to broader fields'. In this analysis, Farquhar states that: ' . . . the managements of general offices in manufacturing plants, and banks, etc., particularly as regards layout and office procedure, are being reorganized in several instances in accordance with the principles found so effective in the factory'.

ACTIVITY 14

Consider a typing pool within the administration office of a modern manufacturing company. Tasks include:

- typing customer letters to confirm orders
- typing customer contracts
- typing internal reports and memos.

How could scientific management principles be applied in this situation?

This is clearly a very diverse management situation to one found on the shopfloor. However, the principles of scientific management may be applied along the following lines:

Science for the job
Each of the above jobs requires a different approach, even though the physical output is still typed words on a page.

At the most basic level, there are accepted ways in which letters, contracts, reports and memos should be typed. These are not inherent but must be learned by the typist. Positioning of address, heading, date and letter terminology, for example, when to use 'yours sincerely', are already established. These common standards are a form of the Gilbreth's 'superstandards'.

At a deeper level, the company could have standardised their own formats for letters to different types of customer and contracts, for example, one type of contract for use in the UK, another for use overseas. These would have been very carefully scrutinised by the company's own sales team and legal department to achieve the best possible standards for maximum coverage of the company's business.

Management may have decided to allocate typing of one particular sort to specific individuals, for example, giving one type of contract to one individual with specialist knowledge.

There are other points to note:

Selection
Have the typists been carefully selected? Do they have a typing qualification? Can they use a word processor? Have they worked in an office or legal environment before?

Training
Office environments vary. Training will need to be given to all new recruits so that they become accustomed to the organisation's methods.

Co-operation
The manager needs to work with those in the typing pool. He or she needs to take an interest in the output of the pool. Any changes in working practice, for example, work allocations, should ideally be agreed before implementation.

Division of work and responsibility
It isn't the manager's job to correct grammar and it isn't the typist's job to draft the terms of a contract. These responsibilities need to be clearly defined.

2.6 Resistance to scientific management

The resistance to scientific management, or **Taylorism** as it was to be called, was perhaps inevitable, given its huge shift in emphasis towards managerial control over the worker.

- Resistance had been felt right from the very start – from the time of Taylor's own attempts to impose his ideas over his team when he had been a gangboss at the Midvale Steel Works, still formulating his ideas on scientific management.

- Opposition to the system in its mature form was to come from both management and workers when Taylor was acting as an industrial consultant at the Bethlehem Steel Works where he was hired from 1898. Apparently his methods were so successful that they were having a dual 'knock-on' effect; the workforce was being reduced as Taylor's methods improved worker efficiency. This led to adverse industrial relations at the factory; tied to this was the fact that the management rented out houses to the workers as well as owning shops. This reduction in workforce was leading to a loss in their revenue. Having ignored requests by management to be more sensitive in his approaches, Taylor was dismissed from the company in 1901.

- Scientific management was criticised in England by the Iron and Steel Institute in 1905, and there were 'violent conflict and strikes' in 1912 when Renault introduced the system in France at Billancourt (Huczynski & Buchanan, 1991).

- In the USA, there was considerable opposition, which reached a peak in the first world war. From 1911 to 1915, there was a series of violent strikes in the Illinois Central and the Union Pacific Railroads. The most famous one at the Watertown Arsenal led to Taylor being called to account for his 'scientific management' before a House of Representatives Committee in 1912. The minutes of this hearing are included in Taylor's book, *Scientific Management,* 1947 and they make intriguing reading as Taylor explains his philosophy in some depth .

Though Taylor was grudgingly exonerated by the committee who accepted his methods had merit, it severely questioned the high level of control which managers enjoyed under scientific management. It was clear that the workers at the Watertown Arsenal were still extremely unhappy and opposed to Taylor's ideas, and ultimately the Senate was to decree that scientific management was not to be used in defence-related factories (Mullins, 1993).

However, the situation changed in the USA after the first world war and the resistance to scientific management lessened. Morris L Cooke led a group of more liberal-minded Taylorists which struck up a dialogue with the American Federation of Labor (the skilled craft unions). The AFL, led by Samuel Gon.pers from the 1880s till 1924, was to adopt a pragmatic approach. It wanted to develop a 'constructive' image with employers whilst still fighting fiercely for the pay and working conditions of its members.

R E Cole quoted in Littler (1983) describes the situation as follows: 'The emergent unions had two basic options. They could struggle to increase the amount of worker discretion on the job, thereby 'enlarging' the job, or even insist on a worker voice in job design. Alternatively the unions could accept the given framework of power and struggle to make quantitative improvements in worker rewards. The first one was clearly a radical one which the unions eventually rejected in the face of management and government power and lack of worker support.'

Resistance to the heavily directive controls of scientific management therefore became less important to the unions than recognition and reward improvements, and there was little ability or incentive in the rest of the labour force to resist its development.

Most workers were not in the AFL or any union. The CIO, which catered for un-skilled workers, was only formed in 1935. As we previously discussed, the workforce had been subjected to waves of immigration and as a result had a profusion of un-skilled and semi-skilled workers , many of whom had come from agricultural backgrounds. This, coupled with the generally better pay and conditions of the USA, compared to, say, European industrial nations, meant that there was limited resistance to the control aspects of scientific management – especially in the newer factories in Detroit and the Mid West.

ACTIVITY 15

Why was scientific management accepted by workers in the USA after the first world war?

In essence the reasons are two-fold:

● Firstly, many of the workers were low skilled immigrants who did not have the means of collective resistance (they did not belong to a union) and, in any case, they were apt to be resigned to what they saw as the status quo.

● Secondly, the skilled workers (whose union was the American Federation of Labor) took a pragmatic approach which was based on terms and conditions but which accepted management's right to manage in the way it thought fit.

2.7 Scientific management today

The lasting impact of scientific management appears to be a bone of contention for modern-day writers. There are those such as Rose (1988) and Fox (1985) who tend to look at the application of an ent',e management system of control and to view it as a power ideology rather than a contribution still valuable for modern management. Recalling that trust is the essential element in employee and employer working together in scientific management, they see an essential naiveté in Taylor's expectation of a high trust atmosphere between 'low discretion' employees with little power to make important decisions and a powerful management. They challenge the assumption that employees want 'more' and suggest that what drives them is parity of reward in a much broader sense. They summarise by questioning how such a system could ever be practical and conclude that scientific management is effectively 'dead'.

The other school of thought, whilst recognising that scientific management is rarely carried out in its entirety, asserts that it has survived. In fact, it has done much more than survive – the basic idea of 'best way to do a job' and its measurement, specialisation, selection of staff and training have in fact become the norm in many industries today.

Thus, Littler (1983) who is scathing in his attack on the critics, says: 'The popular notion that Taylorism has been 'superseded' by later schools of industrial psychology, or 'human relations', that it 'failed' – because of Taylor's naive views of human motivation or because it brought about a storm of labour opposition or because Taylor and various successors antagonized workers and sometimes management as well – or that it is 'outmoded' because certain Taylorian specifics like functional foremanship or his incentive-pay schemes have been discarded for more sophisticated methods: all these represent a woeful misreading of the actual dynamics of the development of management.'

Littler suggests that the reason for such radically differing views is that Taylorism is not just a power ideology, as it is viewed by Rose and Fox. It has structural implications as well – particularly for work design and the way in which work tasks are allocated to staff. These are significant and enduring.

Thus, modern management makes much more use of the 'scientific approach' – in which decisions are based on proven fact, rather than the rule-of-thumb measures or opinion – than is sometimes acknowledged. Key ideas deriving from it that are still in use today include:

- time and motion study, as used in modern operations management
- standardised tools and procedures
- specific goals assigned to individuals based on time and motion study.
- scientific selection of 'best workers', for example, psychological profiling
- training.

These observations lead Schermerhorn, Hunt and Osborn (1991) to conclude: 'Considering that it has been over 65 years since Taylor's death and that a knowledge explosion has taken place during these years, Taylor's track record is remarkable. The point is not, as is often claimed, that he was 'right in the context of his time' but that most of his insights are still valid today. The present authors agree with those who consider Taylor a genius.'

ACTIVITY 16

(i) Do you see any particular weakness or potential problem in the scientific management approach? (ii) Do you consider that any of the principles or practices are still relevant and valuable for management today?

(i)   Taylor's basic assumptions are flawed; managers and workers might not always work in harmony! Managers might try to increase targets once previous ones have been achieved. Managers might not want to pay the higher wage rates. Workers might attempt to conceal their true capabilities. Managers might not have the sort of analytical and planning skills which Taylor was prescribing they should use.

You might like to do your own planning as a worker. As a skilled worker, you might resent this even more as you observe unskilled workers doing the task element of your job and managers doing the planning of it. The possible monotony and boredom associated with increasingly specialised tasks is also a consideration.

(ii) The effects of scientific management are so pervasive that they are felt in many aspects of modern work. Times have changed and employers are more likely to consult their workers. However, many organisations use principles such as:

● work study, time and motion

● standardised tools and procedures

● scientific selection of 'best workers'.

REVIEW ACTIVITY 2

Suggested time: 25-30 minutes.

Read the case study below and then answer the questions at the end of it.

The Roving Area Representative

Jane Cassidy is the recently appointed sales director in a national company which packages and distributes various grades of motor oil to haulage contractors, travel operators and agricultural users. The company structure also includes a marketing department (with director in charge), a finance department (also with director) and an operations director in charge of two departments – packaging and haulage. Packaging has a foreman and a workforce of labourers, whilst haulage has a foreman and a workforce of drivers. All directors report directly to the managing director.

Jane is the product of a university education in which she studied marketing and commerce and has worked her way up the ranks in sales since getting her first job eight years ago. Jane's 'inherited' sales team consists of area representatives whose job it is to visit both existing and prospective clients. The majority of these managers have risen to their current positions by 'being in the right place at the right time', for example, taking over someone else's job after that person has left the company. They tend to have varying amounts of experience and have attended the occasional short sales course although few have any professional or academic qualifications. Even now it appears that there are some managers who are undoubtedly good at their job but, by the same token, there are some who Jane would rather get rid of.

Sales contracts are normally negotiated for a yearly period. The market is highly competitive and so area representatives have traditionally been given certain discretion, within boundaries prescribed by the sales director, to set contracts with their clients according to the variables of volume, price and delivery. They can receive up to 25% bonus depending upon the volume of business they generate and how this relates to agreed individual targets. Up until now the area representatives have operated on a written call card basis; these are cards which are kept for each client and which record details such as company name and address, key contact person(s), last date visited, type of contract, expiry date of contract, price, delivery terms, and other comments.

Information from these cards is summarised and has, in the past, been sent to the sales director so that he could co-ordinate on a national basis.

Area representatives like to feel that they lead exciting working lives, though, in reality, their job can be rather lonely so they constantly chat to one another over the car telephone during the long hours of motorway driving. Little 'cliques' exist which share local sales information and gossip. These have previously excluded the sales director

Jane feels that the reporting mechanism is far too slow for her purposes as oil prices fluctuate dramatically. Additionally, she feels that she is not always receiving the 'full picture' and that some of the area representatives are somewhat cavalier in their deals, to say the least. For example, she suspects it may emerge that they are offering unrealistic delivery times, giving 'freebies' such as oil storage tanks, etc. In a bid to obtain up-to-date, accurate and full information, Jane is thinking of giving area representatives portable laptop computers and a whole new system of working. The idea is that the area representatives would take the laptops on their travels and enter the information into them each night either at home or in their hotel room. They would have to 'report in' at least once a week or at pre-set times by downloading their laptop information via a modem to a central head office computer. Jane is also thinking of using the system in reverse, and sending messages to each area representative via her computer to their home computer terminal which they will be told to access upon their return. In the past, communication has proved problematic due to the roving nature of the area representatives also she is slightly suspicious that managers sometimes choose not to receive messages!

Jane also has doubts about whether or not all of her representatives can be relied upon to use this new technology. She intends to provide training specifically for this but has started to think that perhaps she should introduce a programme of careful recruitment of younger, more 'professional' staff, both from outside the organisation and through careful management development of promising 'high flyers' within the organisation.

Jane is also thinking of holding monthly meetings in her office at which all of the area representatives must be present. Each manager will be asked to give a report on progress within his or her area. The format of these reports will be standardised and will include details such as the number of clients visited, the number, type and value of successful contracts serviced and those obtained, as well as any contracts lost. Previously managers were more or less left to their own devices and there was little monitoring of their progress. She intends to initially use the reports as the basis for determining good performance, as given by these indicators. Given that the good performers are likely to be the sort of manager she is seeking to develop she intends to involve one or two of them in future development of specific sales methods and procedures. She will ask these good performers to assist in training and selection, using their existing knowledge of the industry.

She also would wish to go further than this by then applying her own ideas with regard to efficiencies to be gained through computer routing of calls (so as to minimise 'dead' time on the road between calls) and of drawing up schedules to visit existing clients (rather than waiting until their contract is almost expired). She has promised them that any useful suggestions will be looked at seriously. She also thinks that this would be a good time for area representatives to socialise with more than their immediate 'neighbour' and Jane intends meetings to be complete by 1pm so that a relaxed business lunch may be arranged. Jane is well aware of the coolness of relations between the area representatives and previous sales director and intends to adopt a more constructive approach in these situations. She intends also to arrange a company paid annual weekend break for managers and their partners at a 4-star hotel. Key customers will also be invited. An internal company magazine is a further idea which will be pursued and notable events covered.

And, of course there is the issue of bonuses. This has long been a thorny problem; it is true that large bonuses have been awarded in the past but the gripe has always been from those who were not awarded them that they did not reflect issues such as the number of contracts involved or the degree of competition. For example, one area representative received a large bonus whenever one particular very lucrative contract was renewed, allegedly because he was 'well in' with his opposite number and so required very little sales effort. The size of the market – the potential number of clients and how geographically spread they were – is also an issue. Some managers complained that in some areas a 'monkey could do the work and get a bonus' whereas in other areas it was 'well nigh on impossible' to hit the targets. Jane is aware of this unfairness and feels that it undermines the motivation of managers in poor areas and over rewards managers in 'good' areas.

Of course, if the managers follow the proposed new systems Jane is confident that they will soon be hitting targets they never thought possible and she has plans to make this a key note in her initial meetings with them. However, she proposes to devise a points system which would weight the bonus according to the degree of difficulty of achieving targets. In theory, the bonus maximum would remain at 25% but privately she is wondering if this is the right level. Certainly she intends to monitor the degree of difficulty allowed by her points system against the actual securing of individual contracts within her best managers' portfolios. She suspects that difficult targets which do not allow sufficient 'difficulty weighting' will restrict success because the payoff for additional work is seen not to be worthwhile. By systematically analysing targets, their difficulty weighting and actual performance achieved over the next 6 months, Jane will set the next set of targets.

List all of the elements of scientific management you can find in the case study with regard to Jane's proposal. Use the summary of Taylor's approach in sub-section 2.2 as a framework. Add brief notes, as you think appropriate.

Summary

In this section, you have explored scientific management, specifically you have:

- considered the work of Frederick Taylor
- looked at other contributors – the Gilbreths with their 'time and motion' studies, and Henry Gantt with his bonuses and Gantt Charts
- noted its applicability outside of the shopfloor
- discussed resistance to it
- reviewed its relevance today and its use as a control mechanism.

SECTION 3
Principles of Administration

Introduction

In this section, we explain the rationale behind the management theories of Henri Fayol and investigate the context in which these theories were introduced.

After working through you will be able to explain Fayol's '14 principles of management' and his 'managerial activities', and identify some differences between the approaches of Fayol and that of Taylor. You look at modern-day examples with reference to specific managerial activities and principles of management and address Fayol's relevance today.

3.1 Henri Fayol (1841-1925)

Henri Fayol was a French engineer who rose to prominence within the fields of coal mining engineering, mining geology and finally, management practice. His contribution to the theories of management (translated from the French 'administration') was to become very influential.

In order to appreciate the context in which Fayol introduced his ideas and the respect with which they were subsequently held, we look briefly at his success as an industrialist and as a management writer.

FAYOL: THE SUCCESSFUL INDUSTRIALIST

In 1860, although only 19, Fayol had already taken up the post of mining engineer with the Commentary group pits of the Commentary-Fourchambault Company. By 1866, he was the Manager of the Commentary pits, by 1872, he was the General Manager of the Commentary, Montvicq and Berry group of mines and, by 1888, the Managing Director of Commentary-Fourchambault. He led the company through difficult times and under his directorship it expanded to become an invaluable national asset which supplied France with vital coal reserves and steel during the 1914-18 war.

MANAGEMENT WRITINGS

Although Fayol had little time for writing, he published two papers (in 1900 and in 1908) in which he began to discuss management. Then, in 1916 he published 'Administration, industrielle et generale', a *Bulletin of the Societe de l'Industrie Minerale*. This was to become the most famous of his management writings. The first edition in English was published in 1929. His writings on administration and management extended to include the management of state institutions, for instance, the Posts and Telegraphs (1921). Fayol died before he could complete a projected book which would embody these and other ideas but the first two sections ('Necessity and possibility of management teaching' and 'Principles and elements of management') were published and appeared in English as *General and Industrial Management* in 1949 (Fayol, 1949).

FAYOL'S DEFINITION OF MANAGEMENT

Fayol (1949) identified six **industrial undertakings** which occurred in the workplace:

- **Technical activities** – production, manufacture, adaptation
- **Commercial activities** – buying, selling, exchange
- **Financial activities** – search for and optimum use of capital
- **Security activities** – protection of property and persons
- **Accounting activities** – stocktaking, balance sheet, costs, statistics
- **Managerial activities** – planning, organization, command, co-ordination, control

Fayol concerned himself principally with the last of these, managerial activities. He also espoused a set of guidelines which he said, that whilst not definitive, had worked in his experience. These he called **principles of management**.

FAYOLISM AND TAYLORISM – A DIFFERENT APPROACH

ACTIVITY 17

Can you already see any fundamental differences between Fayol and Taylor in the development of management theory and practice?

You will probably have noted immediately that whereas Taylor's theories approached management from a 'bottom-up' perspective, Fayol's was a 'top-down' approach. Taylor looked firstly at jobs and the 'one best way' of carrying them out, basing his research on the worker, the task and the supervisor. He then sought to apply his theories further up the hierarchy. In contrast, Fayol's 'top down' analysis concentrated on universal concepts and principles which were to be applied from the managing director downwards.

Although Fayol admitted the difference in approaches which they took in their research, he was quite complimentary about Taylor's work which he did not view as incompatible with his own work on the activities and principles of management.

3.2 Fayol's 14 principles of management

Fayol proposed **14 principles** which he believed would show managers how to be successful. This was contrary to the then popular opinion that managers were 'born' and not 'made'.

Although not completely applicable to some modern organisation structures, many of these principles are still regarded as fundamental 'common sense' rules. Looking at the principles gives us a further insight into the nature of management, and thinking about these principles Fayol identified gives any manager a better insight into the nature of management.

Fayol's 14 principles were:

1   division of work

2   authority

3   discipline

4   unity of command

5   unity of direction

6   subordination of individual interests to the general interest

7   remuneration

8   centralisation

9   scalar chain

10 order

11 equity

12 stability of tenure of personnel

13 initiative

14 esprit de corps

We consider each briefly and in relation to examples both from Fayol's own day and in modern times.

DIVISION OF WORK (1)

'The object of **division of work** is to produce more and better work with the same effort. The worker always working on the same part, the manager concerned always with the same matters, acquire an ability, sureness, and accuracy which increase their output.

It is not merely applied to technical work, but without exception to all work involving a more or less considerable number of people and demanding abilities of various types, and it results in specialisation of functions and separation of powers.' (Fayol, 1949)

A good example of such division of work or **specialisation** in an industrial context was the assembly line which Henry Ford introduced in his factory in the early twentieth century. He had the idea of pulling partly assembled cars along on bogies past a succession of workers who then worked on the cars in a pre-determined sequence, each worker having a specific task to perform. This might be, for instance, to affix a door, headlight or wheels.

ACTIVITY 18

Give two advantages of specialisation for management. Give two disadvantages for the workers.

Division of work plays an important part in many modern industrial situations but its disadvantages as well as its advantages are readily apparent. Typical advantages include:

- increase in production
- ease of training workers
- use of semi-skilled workers that are cheaper than craftsmen.

Typical disadvantages that specialisation of functions may bring in an industrial context include:

- boredom – automatic response
- loss of autonomy – management controls the operation
- stress – speed dictated by the line
- fatigue.

AUTHORITY (2)

Fayol's second principle recognises the importance of **authority** and discipline in any business organisation. Authority is the right to give orders and the power to exact obedience . . . Responsibility is its natural consequence . . . Application of sanction to acts of authority forms part of the conditions essential for good management' (Fayol, 1949, p. 21).

Fayol also distinguished between official and personal authority. **Personal** authority is derived from intelligence, experience and ability; **official** authority is derived from position within the organisational hierarchy.

Note that in discussing authority, Fayol links it to two other requirements – **responsibility** and **sanction**.

- Responsibility: with the exercise of managerial authority comes managerial responsibility. It cannot be avoided, Fayol says. But fear of responsibility can, he says stifle initiative.
- Sanction: the disciplinary power of authority 'to exact obedience' in Fayol's words. But its use depends upon judgement and 'demands high moral character, impartiality and fairness'.

ACTIVITY 19

Note down the differences you see between the authority, responsibility and sanction of a sergeant over a private soldier and the authority, responsibility and sanction of the leader of a mountaineering expedition over an expedition member.

Remember that Fayol distinguishes between official and personal authority. The sergeant has official authority which derives from his rank and position; the mountain expedition leader (unless it is army led!) has personal authority which derives from intelligence, experience, ability to lead and past successes.

Both carry the responsibility of ensuring the safety of their team. However, the sergeant also has a responsibility to ensure completion of the task, for example, taking a bridge, and this may be considered more important than safety of the individual. (See subordination of the interest of the individual later.) It is hoped that the expedition leader considers individual and group safety as paramount to the successful ascent of the mountain!

Sanction depends upon the action and the situation. A sergeant could order a man to be court-martialled, and if guilty, executed, for treason. The expedition leader's ultimate sanction would probably be to order the individual to leave the expedition.

DISCIPLINE (3)

Fayol defines the **discipline** necessary for management of an organisation in the following terms: 'Discipline is in essence obedience, application, energy, behaviour and outward marks of respect observed in accordance with the standing agreements between the firm and its employees, whether these agreements have been freely debated or accepted without prior discussion, whether they be written or implicit, whether they derive from the wish of the parties to them or from rules and customs' (Fayol, 1949, p. 22).

The need for discipline if a business undertaking is to be successful is just as important now as in Fayol's day, though its defining characteristics might be identified somewhat differently or given different emphasis.

ACTIVITY 20

1 Using the characteristics of Fayol's discipline, how would discipline have been observed on board a Royal Naval vessel in his day?

2 Would any of these defining characteristics be seen differently in modern business situations?

---

1 In Fayol's day, and today also in an armed services situation, discipline would show itself as the following:

● obedience: orders are to be obeyed

● application: the ordered and practised manner in which duties are carried out, for example, guns manned, decks cleaned

- energy: the way in which duties are carried out, for example, with vigour and not half heartedly

- behaviour and outward signs of respect: salutes and verbally acknowledging captain and other officers.

2   In modern business or industrial situations, outward signs of respect might be shown less formally and unquestioning obedience would not be expected or desired in many situations. However, the underlying need for mutual respect and ultimately, obedience to what a successful outcome requires, would still be recognised.

UNITY OF COMMAND (4)

Essentially Fayol advocates in his principle of **unity of command** that a person has only one boss. He says 'As soon as two superiors wield their authority over the same person or department , uneasiness makes itself felt . . .' Dual command he says '. . . wreaks havoc in all concerns, large or small . . .' (Fayol, 1949)

ACTIVITY 21

What are some of the potential problems if unity of command is not maintained? Have you met any organisational structures that do not follow this principle?

You might have noted problems concerning:

- two bosses unknowingly duplicating work

- two bosses unknowingly missing a task which they believed the other was supposed to do

- conflict between the bosses over the allocation of:

  - tasks

  - personnel under their control

  - physical and financial resources

- workers 'playing off' one boss against the other

- confusion amongst workers about which boss to report to on specific tasks or functions.

Given these potential problems, it is not surprising that in many organisations this principle is still revered. However, in a modern **matrix** organisational structure a subordinate can have two bosses: one is 'functional' and the other 'product' or 'project'. Indeed, this form of organization is often used by civil engineers and others involved in large projects. For example, a design engineer reports to his functional boss, the design director, regarding the technical aspects of designing. He is also a member of the project team(s) for the project he is currently working on and he reports to the project manager in this role and interacts with the other members of the project team, for example, construction, purchasing, quantity surveying, finance, etc (Figure 4).

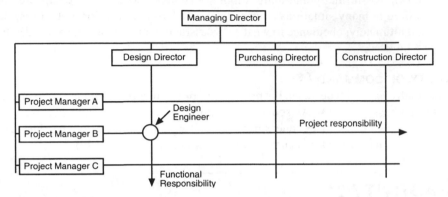

Figure 4: Matrix structure

In Figure 4, the design engineer reports to two bosses – one is his function or design boss, and the other is his project boss. Hopefully the needs of these bosses will complement each other rather than conflict.

Modern organisations do not always follow the unity of command principle, although it is then even more important that roles do not become confused and the next principle we look at – unity of direction – becomes paramount.

UNITY OF DIRECTION (5)

Fayol emphasises the distinction between unity of direction as a management principle and unity of command. **Unity of direction** means 'one head and one plan for a group of activities having the same objective.' The intention is to unite and co-ordinate activities for a common goal.

ACTIVITY 22

Think of an example in modern management of Fayol's unity of direction principle at work.

You might have thought of a wide variety of examples from the corporate mission and objectives that give direction to the departments of a large company to the co-ordination of functions required in any single project. It is, perhaps, when it is lacking that the need for unity of direction is most obvious. How many times have you noticed a new housing estate's recently laid roads being ripped up to install cabling or pipes because of a lack of co-ordination between housing contractor and services providers? Clearly the 'one head and one plan' has been violated here.

SUBORDINATION OF INDIVIDUAL INTEREST TO GENERAL INTEREST (6)

Through greed, laziness or short-sightedness individuals can inadvertently or deliberately put themselves or their department on a higher ranking of importance than the organisation to which they belong.

- Workers in a company which is under severe pressure for its survival might go on strike for better pay, despite the fact that this may hasten the company's demise.

- Sales managers might boost their own income, based on sales commission, through selling inappropriate or unnecessary products to unsuspecting customers, who may not renew later contracts when they realise that they have been duped.

For the organisation to run at its optimal effectiveness, the organisation's importance needs to prevail over that of the individual person or department. Fayol suggests that this can be brought about in the workplace by:

- good example from superiors
- seeking fair agreement as far as possible between conflicting interests
- instant supervision to ensure that individual interests are not taking priority.

REMUNERATION (7)

Fayol was concerned here with the principle of a fair day's pay for a fair day's work and how both parts of this equation can be achieved. He describes different methods of payment such as individual and group schemes, piece rates and profit sharing. He admitted that none were entirely satisfactory.

CENTRALISATION (8)

By the principle of **centralisation,** Fayol meant the need for information to flow to a central higher authority for key decision-making. Commands from this central point are then sent back down to subordinates. **De-centralisation** occurs when decision-making ability is given to subordinates.

Although Fayol believed that in general, centralisation was an important principle for effective control, he recognised that in some circumstances de-centralised authority might be necessary. He argued that the degree of centralisation was dependent upon specific situations such as the size of the organization, for example, in a small organization absolute centralisation was possible, and the abilities of managers and employees. 'It is a problem to be solved according to circumstances, to the best satisfaction of the interests involved' (Fayol, 1949, p. 33).

In fact, it is this approach that has prompted the observation that perhaps Fayol was ahead of his time by, in effect, proposing an approach to management similar to modern **contingency theorists** who argue that control and management approaches should be varied according to particular task and personnel involved.

ACTIVITY 23

What are the advantages of centralisation and de-centralisation?

Centralisation focuses decision-making, for example, in one person or department. It thus gives the decision-maker an overall perspective of what is happening in the organisation. It allows decisions to be taken quickly. And, it allows for a standard approach. The decision-makers are likely to be specialists.

De-centralisation allows for decision-making to be made at lower levels in the organisation. There may be a point in an organisation's growth when there is a need to start de-centralising due to the sheer overload of decisions which have to be made centrally. Local variations may be dealt with more efficiently by those closest to them. De-centralisation also gives the opportunity for people to become involved in and own the decision-making process and is good training for aspiring senior managers.

SCALAR CHAIN (9)

The **scalar chain** is the hierarchical chain in an organisation through which communication flows and authority is exercised. Fayol acknowledges the need for this chain if, for example, unity of command is to be maintained. He remarks upon the incredibly long chains prevalent in his day amongst the French governmental departments and the accompanying deterioration in communication. He was to severely criticise the French Post and Telegraph department and other government institutions in his later writings. You cover communication in more detail in Unit 10.

ACTIVITY 24

What are the likely problems in organisational communication when authority and communication are organised in a hierarchical scalar chain?

Problems include:

- distortion of the message at each link in the chain can detract from the intended communication – even to the point of a contrary meaning being understood by the final recipient

- long time required for a message to reach someone distant from another person in the chain

- possible redundancy of the information for people who are intermediate links in the chain as they don't need to know the information.

Fayol advocated a gang plank solution to the communication problems of the scalar chain in which horizontal communication could take place between individuals in different sections or departments, so long as agreement could be reached between the two subordinates (Figure 5). These subordinates had to keep their immediate superiors informed and they could only act within prescribed limits. In Figure 5, C is communicating with M directly rather than up and down through the route BAL.

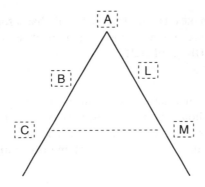

Figure 5: Gang plank

ORDER (10)

Fayol advocated the principle that there should be 'a place for everything and everything in its place'. This maxim applied equally to materials as to people. In the workshop, materials had to be stored in clearly pre-designated areas and tools had to be returned to a neat and ordered store. Dirty, unkempt working areas did not observe this requirement.

People, too, had to have a 'place' in the organisation with defined duties which fitted in with overall corporate objectives. Fayol advocated that an organisation chart should be drawn up to facilitate this process. Such charts are readily accepted in modern businesses and are usually given to new recruits along with their job descriptions to give them a sense of place and function in the organisation. A new employee in the oil distribution company in Review activity 2 might, for instance be given a chart like the one shown in Figure 6.

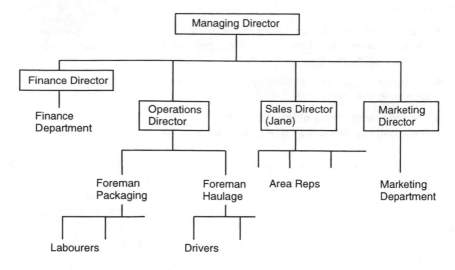

Figure 6: Organisation chart

Management readily makes use of organisational charts for planning its strategic use of staff, for example, for new positions as it expands its operations or for promotions and 'reshuffling' of staff.

EQUITY (11)

By **equity,** Fayol meant essentially creating a sense of fairness within the organisation. People should be treated equally well. It is distinguishable from justice; justice attempts to carry out the letter of the 'law', that is, company rules, and policies and procedures, whereas equity attempts to carry out the 'spirit' of the 'law'.

ACTIVITY 25

Read the following scenario. Can you apply Fayol's principles 6, 7 and 11 to it?

Case study

A company which manufactures furniture has been desperately trying to avoid going out of business during the recession. The senior management team now considers that the worst is over and is now congratulating itself for surviving this latest trauma. The team feels that it is only because of its exceptional drive, initiative and sheer hard work that the company has survived. Like the rest of the employees in the company its members have not taken a pay rise for the last three years. However, they are now considering awarding themselves a pay rise of 15% to put themselves back in line with management in other companies of their type. There is only sufficient money to award a rise of 4% for the rest of the employees.

The remuneration (principle 7) of employees and senior management continues to be a hot area of debate. What is a fair day's work? Does it equate to effort or to the current market price for an individual's labours?

The argument for awarding the large pay increase is that good senior management:

- is a rare commodity
- ensures the survival and prosperity of the organisation
- results, over time, in benefits which 'trickle down' to everyone in the organisation
- if they are not paid at a level comparable with managers elsewhere they will leave the organisation.

The counter argument could be:

- it is morally unjust, that is, it is against Fayol's equity principle 11, for senior management to reward itself large pay rises and not its workers
- managers are free to leave and seek higher paid jobs in other organisations if they so wish.

But even if we accept (and you may not!) that senior management can award itself large pay rises, what about the effect that these rises might have on the morale of the rest of the employees and thus to the organisation as a whole? Should management subordinate its rights in this instance for the common good of the organisation? Remember this is principle 6.

STABILITY OF TENURE (12)

This principle of **stability of tenure** sets out the need for continuity in a manager's job and is linked to job security. Although Fayol talked about managers, the principle and his reason for advocating it are valid for all workers.

ACTIVITY 26

Why do you think Fayol may have advocated stability of tenure as a management principle?

A manager needed time to get to grips with his job and the tasks required of him, and to get to know the various people he interacted with. Continuity provided the opportunity for this to happen. It was far better in Fayol's view to have a 'mediocre' manager who stayed, than a rapid succession of 'good' managers who left. And apart from the time element, the training process of the manager was also expensive.

From a human perspective, people were likely to feel anxious and perhaps perform less well if they felt they might be replaced. However, in some circumstances this would have to happen, because of old age or sickness, and so Fayol suggested that stability of tenure must be a balance against other organisational requirements.

INITIATIVE (13)

Fayol's principle of **initiative** encouraged everyone within the organisation to contribute towards ideas and plans and then attempt to ensure that these are carried out successfully. 'It is,' he wrote, 'one of the most powerful stimulants of human endeavour' (Fayol, 1949, p. 39).

ACTIVITY 27

How does this principle compare with Taylor's ideas about planning and doing within an organisation?

In this respect, Fayol appears to be at odds with Taylor who advocated that all of the planning and thinking should be done by managers and that workers were paid to produce, not to think! Fayol's views are much closer to modern management thinking with its encouragement of initiative and discretion, in order to make better use of its human resources.

Fayol admitted that it required a confident manager to welcome initiative and acknowledge the ideas and plans of his subordinates, but insisted that this manager was to be preferred to a manager who through his own insecurity stifled the enthusiasm of his workforce.

ESPRIT DE CORPS (14)

The principle of **esprit de corps** concerns the need for harmony and teamwork in an effective organisation. Workers should be encouraged to work for the common good of the company. Fayol scorns the 'divide and rule' policy whereby management deliberately encourages conflict between worker groups on the basis that a divided workforce will cause them no trouble. Communication should be encouraged and it should be verbal, where possible for 'speed, clarity and harmony'.

In Unit 9, you discuss teams and cohesiveness – the 'togetherness' of a team's members. You will see that cohesiveness is a property that can act either 'for' or 'against' management. Here, Fayol is advocating the encouragement of positive aspects of this collective will and, again, this is very much in tune with modern management ideas.

ACTIVITY 28

If we consider the British motor manufacturing industry, we can see that a great deal of change has occurred in the way in which companies operate today as opposed to, say, twenty years ago. These changes have followed the Japanese way of doing things to some extent.

Do you think initiative and esprit de corps play a part in this industry?

Initiative is positively encouraged amongst all personnel in today's motor industry. There are individual suggestion boxes. Rewards can be as great as a company car for a suggestion which saves sufficient money for the company. There are also **quality circles** which are groups of volunteers who choose problem or development areas in their immediate work environment; improvements are made and problems solved.

Esprit de corps is important. Although identifying with the company to the degree that the Japanese do may not be accepted, teamwork is strongly emphasised. Competition between teams can be fierce as they strive to achieve better status. Section teams are briefed and operate according to master plans and schedules. Considering the complexity of a modern car plant it is soon apparent that such teamwork is essential. Again, quality circles are another example of teamwork.

THE 14 PRINCIPLES AND OTHER THEORISTS

Apart from the continuing relevance of many of Fayol's principles, particular management theorists such as Brech (Brech, 1965) and Urwick were heavily influenced by Fayol. Urwick published his own set of 29 principles of administration (Urwick, 1943).

3.3 Fayol's managerial activities

Fayol identified **planning, organising, command, co-ordination** and **control** as essential elements of management. We now consider each, in turn.

PLANNING

'The plan of action is, at one and the same time, the result envisaged, the line of action to be followed, the stages to go through and methods to be used' (Fayol, 1949, p. 43).

For Fayol the general features of a good plan include:

- **unity** – one plan, although it may be split into others, Fayol talked of annual and ten-year forecasts for the mining industry, featuring:
- **continuity** – it must continuously guide
- **flexibility** – it must meet unforeseen occurrences
- **precision** – it must be as accurate as possible.

Fayol said that good planning was difficult; it required managers who were competent. In an attack on the French state administration, he blamed its poor quality administration on instability of tenure and on the French ministers. He questioned the ability of ministers to gain sufficient competence to make decent plans given their short period in office and also their level of responsibility and commitment to long-term plans. The essentials of good planning – unity, continuity, flexibility and precision – were therefore frequently lacking.

ACTIVITY 29

The world of industry and commerce today is a much faster changing world than the one in which Fayol worked. Are his features of a good plan still relevant in your view, or are different qualities required?

In today's world, there is a greater emphasis on flexibility, for example, the ability to employ additional staff as and when required, and less on continuity. Nevertheless, Fayol's features for a good plan are essentially just as relevant.

ORGANISING

'To organise a business is to provide it with everything useful to its functioning: raw materials, tools, capital, personnel' (Fayol, 1949, p. 53). Fayol concentrated on human organisation and many of his recommendations reflected his 14 principles of management.

ACTIVITY 30

Look at the following Fayol's stated requirements concerning organisation. Which of his 14 principles do you think are being obeyed?

- 'See that the human and material organization is consistent with the objective, resources and requirements of the concern.'

- 'Fight against excess of regulations, red tape and paper control.'

The first statement is consistent with the principles of division of work, order and unity of direction. The second statement is consistent with his 'gang plank' solution to communication difficulties and to a sensitive approach to centralised flow of information and directives.

Fayol also discussed organisational structure. For example, he looked at spans of control that concern the number of subordinates reporting to a manager. He used examples which ranged from an organisation consisting of one craftsman up to the biggest organisations of the day. Using as a base, 15 workers reporting to one foreman, and four foremen reporting to one manager, and so on, he showed that the number of levels of rank in the largest business organisation of up to one million employees need be no more than eight or nine. He was a great advocate of the use of organisation charts – you met these earlier under principle 10 – to depict organisational structures.

Fayol's writings on organising were broad in scope; one issue, we briefly discuss, concerned the qualities desirable for managers. The second issue, the importance of good selection and training, is very much at the top of the modern industrial agenda, for example, National Vocational Qualifications (NVQs). It is worthwhile to note these, but they are beyond the scope of this unit.

ACTIVITY 31

What sort of qualities do you think a good manager possesses?

Compare your answers with Fayol's list below. You may note the interesting sequence of the list which Fayol ranked in the correct order of importance. For example, he insisted that 'bad health may nullify all other qualities taken together' – an example of yet another argument which indicates just how close Fayol's views were compared with modern thinking.

Fayol's list of managerial qualities:

1   health and physical fitness

2   intelligence and mental vigour

3   moral qualities: steady persistence, thoughtful determination, energy, dash if need be, courage to accept responsibility, sense of duty, care for the common good

4   sound general education

5 managerial ability to plan, organise, command, co-ordinate and control

6 general knowledge of all the essential functions

7 widest possible competence in the specialised activity characterising the concern (Fayol, 1949, p. 73).

COMMAND

'The organisation, having been formed, must be set going and this is the mission of command' (Fayol, 1949, p. 97). Fayol's term 'command' has military connotations today and is rarely used in current management theory. Instead, we talk of 'leadership' as being a central activity of managers. In a business sense, a leader is someone who provides direction to his or her followers for the purpose of achieving the organisation's goals.

Again, Fayol proposed a series of guidelines for managers who were to lead or exercise command successfully. These were:

1 have a thorough knowledge of their personnel

2 eliminate the incompetent

3 be well versed in the agreements binding the business and its employees

4 set a good example

5 conduct periodic audits of the organisation and use summarised charts to further this

6 bring together their chief assistants by means of conferences, at which unity of direction and focusing of effort are provided for

7 avoid becoming engrossed in detail

8 aim at making unity, initiative and loyalty prevail among the personnel.

ACTIVITY 32

The implication of Fayol's command guidelines is that managers can make themselves more effective as leaders by developing the skills and qualities necessary. Do you think that leaders are born or made?

This question has been a bone of contention among management theorists for many years.

(a) Some would argue that someone either is, or isn't, a good leader and that is simply the end of the story.

(b) Others argue that leadership is like any other skill and that it can be learnt.

(c) Yet another view is that there must be some crucial 'spark' of leadership ability already in an individual but that this can be developed. This last approach is the one which has gained most currency in recent years.

Considering Fayol's principle of command, above, items 1-7 fall into category (b); they are skills which can be developed by the majority of people. We would suggest that item 8 is not so easy to achieve; gaining unity, initiative and loyalty is not subject to a simple prescription and indicates a category (c) approach. However, all theorists agree about the central part that leadership plays in effective management.

CO-ORDINATION

'To co-ordinate is to harmonise all the activities of a concern so as to facilitate its working, and its success' (Fayol, 1949, p. 103).

ACTIVITY 33

Note down an example of work activity or an event which you have been involved in which was run 'in a disorganised way'. Analyse briefly what the causes and characteristics of the 'disorganisation' were. Note down an activity or event which was well organised and analyse briefly how this good organisation showed itself. Compare your ideas with Fayol's analysis given below.

Your examples will almost certainly have highlighted the central parts played by unity of direction and good communication in well-organised activities. Conversely, the 'we were never told' syndrome is a frequent cause of poor co-ordination and disorganised activity.

For Fayol good co-ordination was characterised by:

1   Each department, for example, finance, production, maintenance, carrying out its function in an orderly and competent fashion.

2   Each part of a department knowing exactly what 'communal' tasks are required of it.

3   Departments adjusting their work schedules according to circumstances and to the needs of the whole company operation.

Conversely, he saw poor co-ordination as characterised by:

1   Each department ignoring the others and operating solely for its own goals.

2   Barriers existing within departments themselves and people hiding from responsibility behind 'pieces of paper'.

3   Lack of initiative or loyalty towards the company as a whole with all interests being self-centred.

Fayol stressed that co-ordination had to be positively encouraged; it did not happen of its own accord. His solution – recognising the crucial needs for unity of direction and good communication – was to have a weekly conference of departmental heads. If departmental heads could not attend every week they should be represented by liaison officers, for example, the general manager.

CONTROL

The final crucial management activity postulated by Fayol was control. 'Control consists in verifying whether everything occurs in conformity with the plan adopted, the instructions issued and principles established' and points out 'weaknesses and errors in order to rectify them and prevent recurrence' (Fayol, 1949, p. 107).

This was the **feedback** loop. If plans had been sensibly drawn up, resources organised, command suitably exercised and all departments worked as one, then – given that unforeseen circumstances did not intrude – the control mechanism should show that the aims and objectives of the plan had been met and that no rectifying action was required for this or future plans. You will probably recognise from our discussion in Section 1 of Child's control model that this is essentially a control systems approach.

Typical operations that could be subjected to control, that is, measured in order to monitor progress, included:

- incoming and outgoing materials checked for quantity, quality and price
- stores records
- progress of operations
- maintenance of plant and equipment
- 'working' of men and machines
- financial and management accounts.

To be effective, Fayol noted that control had to be:

- timely

- acted upon

- responsible and impartial with limits not to be exceeded

- in the hands of the right people, Fayol favoured inspectors for when operations became 'too numerous'

- inspectors had to have 'competence, sense of duty, judgement and tact'.

Do you think Fayol's control is relevant today?

3.4 Fayol's relevance today

Although the world in which management takes place has changed immeasurably and although management theory has developed considerably, Fayol's work is still relevant today. His approaches continue to influence theorists.

MANAGERIAL FUNCTIONS APPROACH TO MANAGEMENT THEORY

Fayol's management activities or 'functions' are still used in management theory to introduce the way in which organisations carry out their operations.

- Peter Drucker, a contemporary management guru, put forward his functional model in which the managerial functions are specified as:
  - sets objectives
  - organises
  - motivates and communicates
  - measures
  - develops people (Mullins, p. 372).
- Brech talked of management as a social process and identified four elements:
  - planning
  - control
  - co-ordination
  - motivation (Mullins, p. 370).
- In almost all of them, the influence of Fayol's work can be traced directly or indirectly. A modern management text like *Management* by Stoner and Freeman (1989) uses the model of planning, organising, leading and controlling and they hang their discussion of management on this framework.

It is possible to detect many similarities in all of these and other models. In many instances, the same functional elements are described although they may belong to different functional categories, depending upon the model. Thus Drucker has a separate function for developing people; Fayol talked about training and education in his discussion of organisation.

RELEVANCE OF THE PRINCIPLES AND MANAGERIAL ACTIVITIES

In addition to Fayol's general approach, his principles of management and managerial activities focused on issues which are still central to management theory whether or not his specific views or principles are accepted as holding good in today's management environment. We have already noted the continuing relevance of many of his management principles. A brief review of his managerial activities indicates that they are still central to the managerial function today.

Planning

Any modern company has a whole array of plans, varying from the grand strategic plan in which a company may be planning what markets it will be attacking over the next five or ten years (the Japanese tend to have longer time scales such as this) to the yearly and more immediate operational plans.

Organising

It is well recognised that good organizational structure (Child, 1984) is essential for an organization to achieve its goals. This so-called basic structure incorporates the organizational charts held in such esteem by Fayol. The theory of organisations has developed enormously but it is refreshing to note that there is still a place for his classical ideas.

Command

Environmental changes have all played a part in significantly altering the styles of leadership which many companies aspire to today. Fayol's leaders demanded and got loyalty and respect. Today that loyalty and respect can no longer be assumed but has to be won. The authority of position is much reduced. And, of course, the 'workforce' itself has changed radically. Heavy manufacturing (shipyards, steel production, mining) has been replaced by 'high tech' manufacturing industries (car and electronics), service industries (insurance, banking) and a growth in retailing. The workforce is more educated and aware of its importance. Managerial roles have become blurred as the expertise of the specialist has increasingly turned 'subordinates' who needed directing, into 'colleagues' who require only briefings and to whom many previous managerial responsibilities are now delegated.

It is for these reasons that Fayol's rather military guidance on leadership is sometimes said to be outdated. Nevertheless, it is accepted without question that the function of leadership and how it is exercised is central to good management.

Co-ordination

Good co-ordination is as essential now as in Fayol's day, in fact, even more so for flexibility. Of course, in some organisations, for example, the matrix structure mentioned earlier, it is even more important and the detailing of functions even more significant.

Technology has made communication easier and quicker but the principles remain the same. Breaking down the barriers between individuals and departments remains a challenge for management; yet modern philosophies, such as total quality management, demand that people work together and that communication flows down to all levels. It also demands that communication flow is upward with delegation from below; this is definitely not in Fayol's scheme of things!

Control

Fayol's principles regarding control are still very relevant. He would no doubt be delighted by the development of them through sophisticated systems devised to ensure that processes are running within operational limits and that management's plans have been acted out.

- Quality control, for example, now uses statistical analysis to check the acceptability or otherwise of incoming and outgoing goods.

- Quality assurance systems, for example, ISO9000 involve functions such as sales, production, personnel and finance. Essentially, such systems document work procedures and then audit them to check for compliance in practice. It is this compliance which 'assures the quality' of the product to the customer.

One major shift away from Fayol's ideas, however, has been the introduction of quality as being a responsibility not of 'inspectors' but of everyone in the organisation. Each individual is responsible for his or her contribution to the product. We may well assume, however, that with his espousal of initiative and flexibility Fayol would have welcomed such a development.

IMPACT OF ENVIRONMENTAL CHANGES

Of course, what has changed over the intervening years since Fayol's day is the managerial and business environment. Businesses do not operate in isolation but are affected by the world around them. There have been great social changes which have affected managerial function and styles.

ACTIVITY 34

Note down changes in the social and business environment, noting briefly any changes you think they required in management functions and styles.

- People no longer accept authority without question. They often resent the paternal attitude of management over worker that was so often used in the past. Discipline is now more difficult to enforce.

- Our attitudes have changed. We like to be treated more as equals; to be informed of decisions which could affect our working lives; to participate in the decision-making processes.

- Customers are more ready to complain or buy elsewhere; they demand and they receive. Competition is now on a global basis.

- Economies have expanded; individuals have more buying power.

● And, of course, there is technology, changing at an ever-accelerating pace, bringing new products, new processes and ever-decreasing product life cycles. In Fayol's day, the Model T Ford was supreme. Introduced in 1908, it was in production for almost 20 years. Today, Nissan produces a new model every five years; some 'adventure' vehicles such as the small 4 x 4 Japanese 'jeeps' have a life from drawing board to phase-out of only two years (*Top Gear,* BBC, Nov 1994).

What does all of this mean? Quite simply it means **change**. For change, we could read lack of stability. It is argued by modern theorists that, however central the factors Fayol and the other classical theorists identified, their management models were perhaps appropriate for **stable** companies, such as Ford in its early days, but have simply become outdated in today's fast moving world in which flexibility is so often the key.

REVIEW ACTIVITY 3

Suggested time: 45 minutes.

Read the case study and then answer the questions that follow it.

Mike Lewis and Widgets

Mike Lewis, the production director, sat back and considered his plan for his company's manufacture of widgets. He had conveniently ignored the corporate plan which he believed to be unworkable. He was pleased with himself; he was using every bit of equipment, some of it virtually irreplaceable, to its maximum capacity. '100% utilisation', he mused, 'and we'll need that in the next 18 months if my forecasts are correct'. Indeed, every process had been meticulously studied to determine the optimum output, each operation timed to the split second. There was no room for error in this business – time was money. When Bob Short, the works manager asked about coverage for maintenance of the machines or holiday periods for the operators Mike had replied that 'we'll tackle that when we have to!'

Bob Short, the works manager, wasn't pleased with the planning arrangements but he got on with the job in his usual down-to-earth fashion. He prided himself at having worked his way up from an apprentice to his current position. He knew all of his workers and encouraged them to come to him if they had problems, whether they were of a work or a domestic nature. Each day he would make a routine tour of the various workshops; he liked to be seen to be 'leading from the front'; there wasn't a job in the factory he couldn't do himself and he was better than most at that. He held a meeting each week with all shop floor staff; he gave feedback from senior management and encouraged their ideas (and heard their complaints!). He was respected rather than liked; he could be tough when he needed to be and didn't suffer fools gladly. He had no room in his factory for shirkers or incompetents. He knew exactly when to push his staff if, for example, he required overtime to be worked but he rewarded his staff well. He tried to generate in them his own enthusiasm for the job via the meetings and the suggestion box. Posters on the walls declared the best idea of the month. Not always popular when urgent orders had to be met, staff were at least quite clear of the end results required of them even in the midst of 'rush jobs' and they knew that Bob wouldn't take 'no' for an answer.

Making use of Section 3.3, answer the following:

1 List Fayol's four features of good planning; discuss Mike's plan in the light of Fayol's features.

2 Identify in Bob's approach, instances of Fayol's guidelines for successful command in operation.

3 Give briefly three examples of co-ordination (or lack of it).

4 List four areas of control, as given by Fayol, that Bob Short could use in his factory.

Summary

This section has introduced the management writings of Henri Fayol. In particular we have looked in some depth at his '14 principles of management' and his 'managerial activities'. As you have explored each principle and managerial activity, you can see that although Fayol lived in a time when control could be exerted in a more autocratic style than is usual now, many of his ideas are still of value to the modern manager.

SECTION 4
Human Relations

Introduction

The aim of the section is to introduce you to the philosophy of early human relations and its association with the work of Elton Mayo. You look at Mayo's work at the Western Electric Company – the illumination studies, the interviewing programme and the bank wiring room studies. You look at its implications for management thinking and organisational study in the 1930s and its relevance in a modern managerial setting.

4.1 Elton Mayo (1880-1949)

George Elton Mayo's contribution to early management theory lay in increasing our understanding of individual and group behaviour at work and was in stark contrast to the so-called classical theories of management exemplified by Taylor, the Gilbreths and Fayol. It was to form the basis of early human relations theory.

Unlike Taylor and Fayol, Mayo was not an engineer or an industrialist. He originally trained as a philosopher and became an industrial psychologist. He left his native Australia for the USA in 1922, where, in 1924, he became a professor at Harvard Business School, specialising in industrial research.

4.2 The Hawthorne plant

The series of experimental studies which were to make him world renowned were carried out between 1927 and 1932 at the Hawthorne plant, near Chicago, of the giant Western Electric Company (Mayo, 1949). In 1927, this factory employed 29,000 people. It produced telephone equipment for companies using the Bell system. Thousands of men and women were employed at the Hawthorne plant alone. Many different types of work were carried out, often of a semi-skilled and sometimes a skilled nature, in a factory environment. For instance, workers had to assemble relays or electro-magnetic switches, construct wiring 'banks' with units containing over 3000 terminals, and split mica that was used as an insulator.

INDUSTRIAL RELATIONS AT HAWTHORNE – THE PATERNALIST APPROACH

The Western Electric Company prided itself on being at the forefront of technology and having management philosophies to match. It recognised the importance of the worker to the extent that it had established, before the experiments, 'industrial relations' as one of the eight functional organisational branches at its Hawthorne plant. The others were accounting, operation, production, inspection, technical, specialty products and public relations.

The industrial relations branch ensured that a whole range of services and obligations were carried out for and on behalf of the workers. These included assistance with insurance, building loans, benefit plans for sickness, accident and death, provision of a restaurant and of a 'fully equipped hospital' as well as recruitment and training. A very full social and sports calendar was also arranged for all employees.

A statement of the company's employee relations policy set out the following ten intentions:

1   to pay all employees adequately for services rendered

2   to maintain reasonable hours of work and safe working conditions

3   to provide continuous employment consistent with business conditions

4   to place employees in the kind of work best suited to their abilities

5   to help each individual to progress in the company's service, for example, promotion in-house

6   to aid employees in time of need, for example, benefit schemes

7   to encourage thrift, for example, workers buying company stock

8   to co-operate in social, athletic and other recreational activities

9   to accord to each employee the right to discuss freely with executives any matters concerning his or her welfare or the company's interest

10 to carry on the daily work in a spirit of friendliness.

ACTIVITY 35

If acted upon by management, this policy should ensure fair wages and work conditions and, indeed, appears to offer only advantages for the worker. Can you see any possible disadvantages?

his paternal attitude might become rather irksome. In fact, the evidence available, admittedly from the supervisors only, is to the contrary. Supervisors found only advantages in the benefits system and their only 'moan' was that their stocks had declined in price!

Item 10, carrying on the daily work in a spirit of friendliness, seems more of a 'wish' than a policy. It is unclear how this might be effected and what the intention of the policy is. 'Co-operation', perhaps? Is it possible to assist this 'friendliness'?

What happens if policies regarding hours of work and continuity of employment cannot be maintained? In fact, even Western Electric was to feel the effects of the depression which meant that during the early 1930s it reduced hours of work. It had begun to lay off its older staff and unproductive workers and the remaining staff were in daily fear of losing their jobs.

The policy does not consider any sort of work group. All items appear to relate only to the individual. There is no mention of unions or the right of an individual to join one. Nevertheless in essence, the company was very sophisticated for its day and strove to operate along paternal lines, according a great deal of attention to the welfare of its workers. In this respect it was following the example established earlier by people like Robert Owen in the Lanarkshire mills in Britain where he was committed to improving working conditions and providing housing, education and other benefits for the workers.

The paternalistic approach was seen as being in the interests of the company as well as those of its workers. Well treated, secure and 'happy' workers would be better motivated and more productive. And this dual concern for good working conditions and good productivity and quality was also reflected in the company's research into worker productivity and the different work conditions factors that might affect this.

Before Elton Mayo became involved at the Hawthorne plant, the company's own research department had already engaged in considerable research in this area. It was because of their puzzlement at results shown in some early studies – the so-called illumination experiments of 1924-1927 – that Mayo was called and asked to do further experiments at the plant. These, carried out over a five-year period, were to involve thousands of people and to radically influence the development of human relations as a management theory.

4.3 The Hawthorne experiments

To see how these developed we look in chronological order and in detail at the original 'illumination experiments' and then at a series of experiments carried out subsequently at the plant by Mayo. These were:

- **relay assembly test room studies,** 1927-29
- **interviewing programme,** 1928-30
- **bank wiring observation room experiments,** 1932.

There was a further interview programme in 1936 but we do not consider this.

Out of these experiments came a growing realisation of the importance for work motivation, productivity and organisational commitment of factors such as:

- a worker's sense of being valued in the workplace, through their treatment, attention to their needs, consultation and so on

- effects of human factors outside an individual's work circumstances, involving social and emotional factors, and not susceptible to simple scientific management

- effects of social and group organisation within the workplace, particularly in relation to: development of informal group rules; stronger than financial incentives; group pressures to conform; and importance of status within and between groups.

These factors were in addition to the original purpose of his experiments which was the investigation of how particular physical working conditions affected worker productivity.

ILLUMINATION STUDIES (1924-27)

The illumination studies set out to look at the effect of various intensities of light on productivity amongst workers at the Hawthorne plant. At about this time, there was widespread industrial interest in trying to determine through research the effects of fatigue on worker productivity and the factors likely to induce fatigue. The illumination studies were a part of this general interest.

Much of the work at the Hawthorne plant was fiddly and dexterous. It was work which required good eyesight, for example, mica was split into thicknesses of a few thousandths of an inch or masses of small wires were wired to terminals. The researchers postulated that there was an optimum quality and intensity of light which would reduce fatigue and thus increase output and quality.

THE EXPERIMENTS

A total of three lighting experiments were carried out. The first used three different departments; when lighting levels were increased production went up in two but not in the third. This result was confusing and the suspicion was that either the work or workers were different in some way

A second series of experiments was therefore carried out - this time in one department but using two different groups, one of which was a 'control' group in which lighting levels were kept constant. Again, another confusing result showed both groups increased productivity! The researchers thought that, perhaps, this was due to seasonal variation in light and the presence of natural as well as artificial light.

In order to overcome this 'problem', a third set of experiments were carried out, this time solely in artificial light. Again, the output for both groups went up during the course of the experiments, even when the intensity was lowered again and restored to its original value.

From a scientific point of view, the experiments were a failure. They had demonstrated that productivity increased with increasing illumination, as expected but also that productivity increased when illumination levels remained the same and even when they were progressively lowered!

Hawthorne's own research staff were baffled and this led Western Electric to call in Mayo from the Harvard Business School. His brief was to investigate these and other fatigue-related factors at the Hawthorne plant. In particular, he was to begin investigating the effect of the length of the working day and rest breaks on fatigue and productivity.

RELAY ASSEMBLY ROOM TESTS (1927-1929)

First relay assembly room group experiment

In the previous illumination studies, there had been objections raised about the validity of the tests because of their rather uncontrolled nature. This time productivity was to be measured for a specific task – the assembly of relays. Output in this job was thought to be largely a function of the individual worker as it did not involve an assembly line where machine speed dictated output. Tests were devised to answer the following questions:

1   Do employees actually get tired out?

2   Are rest pauses desirable?

3   Is a shorter working day desirable?

4   What are the attitudes of employees towards their work and towards the company?

5   What is the effect of changing the type of working equipment?

6   Why does production fall off in the afternoon? (Landsberger, 1968, p. 8)

A typical shift pattern in the relay assembly room was for a 48-hour week to be split as follows:

Monday-Friday: 7:30-12:00; 12:45-5.00
Saturday: 7:30-12.00

The experiment was conducted in various stages but essentially consisted of altering the length of the working day and introducing rest and tea breaks in the morning and afternoon.

Six women were chosen for the experiment, with two friends selecting the others. They were taken from their regular department and placed in a separate test room. They were told to work at their own pace; their supervisor was one of the researchers. They were consulted about the experiments themselves. At all times, the researchers attempted to keep the group co-operative.

Results were again surprising. For every change introduced, there was a resultant increase in productivity; this even applied when the length of the working day was increased and when conditions were returned to previous ones.

ACTIVITY 36

What might have caused this?

Mayo's inference from this was to mark a milestone in management thinking. He postulated that the reason for the increases in productivity was as much to do with the attitude of the women themselves as the actual physical benefits of the breaks, etc. They were responding to the attention and interest shown in them by high-ranking officials They had been made to feel special by being selected and placed in the test room. They were being consulted rather than being just told what to do by their normal supervisor and they liked this too.

This response became widely known as the 'Hawthorne effect'. The further inference we are tempted to make is that the illumination studies were submitting to the same effect. However, Mayo did not refer back to these earlier, crude studies as they were flawed in his opinion by the presence of too many variable factors.

Second relay assembly room group experiment

However, interviews with the women in the first experiment also suggested other possible reasons for the results. The most significant of these and one which seemed to offer an alternative reason was that the method of payment had been altered from a group-based one to an individual piece rate.

A further experiment, the second relay assembly group, was therefore conducted to test this hypothesis. However, although productivity was subsequently found to rise because of this (13%), it was not considered as significant as the rise in productivity of the original relay assembly room group (30%) and therefore Mayo asserted that his original inference was valid.

Clearly, reasoned the researchers, there were factors at work which they had hitherto not considered. At this point, their research moved away from the measurably scientific, that is, the task and working conditions, towards the people involved in the work itself.

They decided to investigate some of the social issues further and accordingly amended an 'interviewing programme'. This was intended to discover what employees saw as sources of satisfaction and dissatisfaction at work and the information was to be used to supplement training courses for new supervisors.

INTERVIEW PROGRAMME

We will not go into detail here. Suffice to say that over 10,000 interviews were carried out, and these could last up to an hour and a half! However, a useful summary of the results is shown below:

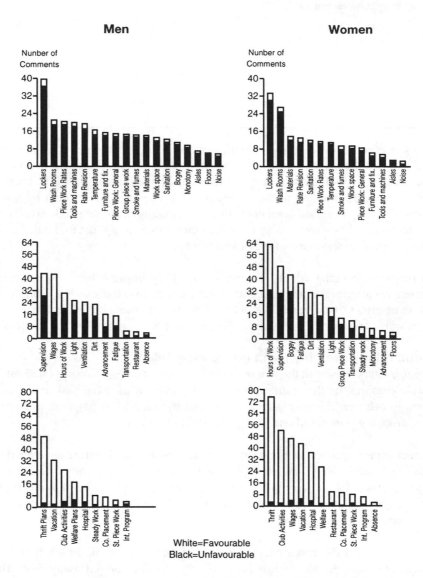

Figure 7: Industrial topics arranged according to tone, based upon 10,300 interviews
Source: Roethlisberger & Dickson, 1966, p. 247

However, just as important as these, perhaps unsurprising, findings were the questions thrown up by the interview data and the important influence they had on the direction of Mayo's work at the plant. It seemed to Mayo from the interviews that as well as specific factors apparently causing satisfaction and dissatisfaction – such as physical aspects of the working environment – there were other 'irrational' and 'social' factors in the background which the interview programme did not go far enough to explore fully. Let's look at both these aspects in turn.

PHYSICAL WORKING ENVIRONMENT

In analysing the interview responses, Mayo had, of course, to consider how reliably the stated causes of satisfaction or dissatisfaction could be considered the actual causes.

As Roethlisberger and Dickson (1966) point out:

- there was much less dissatisfaction over conditions expressed among office workers than among shop floor workers

- in these kinds of surveys workers tended to only talk of working conditions in negative terms; they fail to mention good working conditions which they take for granted

- Hawthorne compared favourably in its conditions with other industries.

However, as Roethlisberger and Dickson also recognise, parity with working conditions elsewhere might be irrelevant. Workers don't compare their working conditions with other industries or factories.

We might certainly have expected that in a new industry such as telephone components, unlike traditional heavy industry, poor hygiene and unhealthy working conditions would have been eradicated. Management should have been able to:

- install more lockers

- maintain sanitary washrooms

- eradicate some of the noise and dust pollution by using various guards and extractor fans.

However, this was not the prime management consideration at the time and poor working conditions were as Roethlisberger and Dickson stated, the norm. For example, the new Ford Motor Company plant, established to build the Model T, suffered from the same (or worse!) work environment.

Many of the complaints about a poor working environment, and the piece rate system, could therefore be seen as having a rational basis in the actual conditions. Although, it might be difficult to determine exactly the effects upon productivity, it was clear that they were a significant cause of worker dissatisfaction.

IRRATIONAL RESPONSES AND 'SENTIMENT'

However, some aspects of the responses made Mayo feel that other factors were involved and that the interviewing programme, although it was useful in providing supervisory trainers with case study material, did not delve deeply enough into the causes of satisfaction or dissatisfaction at work:

● Many of the complaints or answers were too vague to give reliable or useful information on specific causes of satisfaction or dissatisfaction at work. For example, 'too hot' did not define what temperature was too hot.

● There was also a great deal of inconsistency in the replies; he wondered why were some favourable and others not. He had deduced that the supervisors did not have the same complaints regarding conditions as shopfloor workers did, so perhaps the complaints had something to do with the 'social organisation' of the company.

● Mayo was also intrigued to note that when respondents in interviews were allowed to make their own comments, sources of satisfaction and dissatisfaction were influenced it seemed by factors outside their immediate work situation. Interviews recorded conversations concerning the individual's home circumstances (married, living alone, bereaved, living with one's parents), state of mind (depressive, obsessive) and culture (there were many immigrant workers). In this respect, the workers' answers were not always 'rational' and were often linked to 'sentiment'.

These different, even contradictory, reactions to the same working conditions suggested that other factors might be affecting responses. If attitudes could be influenced irrationally by cultural and social factors outside the workplace it seemed reasonable to conclude that the dissatisfactions expressed might also have something to do with the social organisation in the work situation and the feelings of workers about it.

As outlined by Watson (1987), Vilfredo Pareto (1848-1923) an active member of the Harvard sociological society to which Mayo belonged, had already put forward the idea that the systematic soldiering recorded by Taylor was the result of irrational fears and anxieties linked to the need to be loyal to group members and was thus not open to solution through scientific management. He had also talked of the need for a system, suggesting that the worker could not exist in a vacuum, as an individual, but needed to be integrated into the industrial organisation which functioned as a living, organic whole.

As stated by Roethlisberger and Dickson (1966, p.375): 'the relation of the individual employee to the company is not a closed system . . .The ultimate significance of his work is not defined so much by his relation to the company as by his relation to the wider social reality. Only in terms of this latter relation can the different attitudes of satisfaction or dissatisfaction of individuals who are presumably enjoying the same working environment and occupational status be understood.'

During his analysis, Mayo realised that he had spread his net too wide with his questionnaires. He had masses of information but insufficient depth, particularly regarding social organisation. He also suspected that the interviewees weren't always giving truthful answers to the questions in case they displeased their superiors.

To combat these shortfalls, he was to embark on a further investigation – one of detailed observation. The forum for this work was the bank wiring room.

ACTIVITY 37

How might the following social factors affect an individual's work performance?

The worker is:

● a young woman

● living at home in the USA in Mayo's time

● with her immigrant parents

● who are poor

● and strict.

The young woman is likely to be an important breadwinner in the family. Perhaps the family depends on her in other ways, for example, as an interpreter and an expert in the American way of life. She may see her role as essential to the family's well-being and yet feel burdened because of this. As a breadwinner, she may wish to please her bosses at work; there will be pressure for her to achieve high productivity if she is working on piece rates.

Living at home with her immigrant parents might also cause problems which are transferred to the work situation. Her parents are strict and they know that she is important to the family as the breadwinner. They may insist that she works overtime and may restrict her social life, and not allow her any friendships. All these pressures from her personal and social situation could lead to feelings of apathy or resentment at work and affect her performance.

BANK WIRING OBSERVATION ROOM STUDY (NOVEMBER 1931-MAY 1932)

By this stage, Mayo was doggedly trying to design an experiment which was as free as possible from extraneous factors. In his original studies, he attempted to determine the effects of the physical conditions on worker productivity – an active role in which he altered controlled factors such as rest breaks and measured the results. In the bank wiring studies, his emphasis had changed to one where he was trying to maintain a stable environment and then observe the workers and their social organization – a passive role. He then tried to interpret these observations.

THE EXPERIMENT

A group of 14 men were chosen, consisting of:

- three subgroups of three wiremen
- three solderers (one per subgroup of wiremen)
- two inspectors (shared between the three subgroups).

The wireman's job was to attach wires to a bank of terminals. Some 6600 attachments per day was considered a good rate. The solderman's job was to solder these connections. The inspectors had the job of testing the finished 'equipment' for quality.

The payment system operated on a so-called bogey system. The bogey was the management's target rate of work, for example, 6600 connections per day. The group as a whole was paid according to the number of 'equipments' it produced. This was the pot of money available. Individuals were paid from this pot according to the number of hours they worked and their own hourly rate which was determined by their individual output. It thus differed from other systems such as individual piece work.

For the experiment, the group was put into a separate room away from the rest of the department. There was to be no special treatment for the group, unlike with the relay assembly room. The observer was to adopt as unobtrusive a role as possible and to act in a casual manner.

ACTIVITY 38

What factors of social organisation do you think might affect the group's behaviour, interactions and productivity?

There is a range of possibilities. Check whether any of yours relate to the actual findings which identify important facts about groups and the influence they have on individuals in them. Note:

- importance of status within and between groups
- development and influence of informal group rules
- pressures to conform to group norms.

FINDINGS

Wiremen, soldermen and inspectors

Wiring was considered a higher ranking job than soldering with most wiremen starting as soldermen, and the wiremen could, unofficially, tell the soldermen what to do. For example, they would 'trade jobs', although this was something which they were not supposed to do. Inspectors had an occupational status higher than both. However, it was soon apparent that one of the rules of the group was that no-one was supposed to maintain social distance; so the inspectors were not to act in an officious manner.

Cliques
A 'front room' and a 'back room' mentality evolved in which two distinct cliques established themselves. Clique 'A' considered itself to be superior to clique 'B'.

Supervision
The first line of supervision was the group chief (GC). As the experiment was located in a separate room, the GC did not spend all of his time there. In fact, the GC's attitude was more in tune with the workers than with management. For instance, there were certain rules and procedures which he did not perceive to be important and he would 'turn a blind eye' as required. The employees had their own 'rules and logic'.

Straight line output
The researchers very quickly noticed that output per man varied only slightly; when a man had finished what he considered to be his daily output, say two units per day, he would effectively stop working.

Workers felt that to go above this norm would somehow bring trouble. Perhaps management would decide that the workers were capable of greater output and would reduce the hourly rates or increase their demands for production output. The end result was that when the output for each man was graphed, the resultant 'curve' was approximately a straight line at a constant level. In fact, the group was acting to restrict output:

- those who worked above the agreed norm were called 'rate-busters'
- those who worked below the norm were called 'chiselers'
- this norm was not the management 'bogey'
- pressure was put upon these workers to conform or be subjected to group scorn and isolation.

In fact, some of the more productive workers did not report all of their work! And, they could easily maintain an almost dead-straight line of output, day after day. Another worker did not have good relations with the rest of the group and used his high output to antagonise the others! However, the most disliked member of the group was neither a rate-buster nor a chiseler but a squealer – someone who informed on the group to management.

Conclusions
The conclusion drawn from these experiments was that:

- the group could exert considerable social pressures on its members to the extent that it could over-ride financial incentives
- the group had its own set of rules and norms which included everything from setting output rates to methods of group discipline.

ACTIVITY 39

Answer the following questions:

1 What were the conclusions drawn by Mayo in his relay assembly room tests of 1927-30?

2 What were the experimenters' original aims in the interviewing programme?

3 What sort of responses did the interviewing programme yield?

4 What were the main findings of the bank wiring room studies?

1   Mayo proposed that the changes in productivity in his experiments – concerning the length of the working day and rest breaks – were as follows:

- changes were as much to much to do with the attitude of the women themselves as the actual physical benefits of the breaks

- productivity improved even when conditions were returned to previous ones

- the women were responding positively to the attention and interest shown in them by the experimenters and high ranking officials, the so-called 'Hawthorne effect'; they were made to feel special by being selected and placed in the test room; they were asked for their opinions.

2   The original aims were to investigate sources of satisfaction and dissatisfaction at work as they were considered to be possible hidden factors affecting productivity.

3   The responses can be grouped into two areas:

- In the area of 'working conditions', it was clear that the piece rate system and the lack of washrooms were a concern but thrift and welfare plans were liked.

- It was clear that 'social' factors affected their responses and that people were affected by their backgrounds and home situation. In effect, they brought their problems (or lack of) to work. The experimenters called this 'sentiment'. Moreover, because of this it appeared, on the surface, that workers often held irrational views.

4   Cliques were formed amongst the 14 men. These cliques exerted considerable influence over group members, to the extent that even financial incentives to individuals could be nullified; productivity was tied to group norms of productivity. Those members who consistently flouted these norms (too high or low) were liable to sanctions and exclusion from the group.

THE GREAT DEPRESSION

We need to note that the experiments took place during the time of the depression and that this was likely to result in effects on the group such as:

- people are fearful for their jobs

- people actually work harder in the belief that by doing so their company will survive due to their efficiency, however, where sales orders are restricted people may take the view that by working more quickly they will simply work themselves out of a job

- morale can be heightened in the 'we're all in this together' mould

- morale can be weakened as people resign themselves to what they see as their inevitable fate

- decisions on who is to be sacked next may preoccupy people's minds and cause fear, mistrust and conflict.

4.4 Mayo and anomie

Before reviewing the significance of Mayo's work at Western Electric's Hawthorne plant for the development of human relations theory, we note briefly also a link between his work and that of Durkheim. As you will recall from Unit 1, Durkheim saw unrestricted individual aspirations, pursued without regard to discipline, principle or guiding norms, as a threat to the organic integration of a society and of organisations. This danger he called **anomie**.

At the Hawthorne plant, there was a fertile seedbed for anomie, with its large numbers of new immigrant workers in the 'land where anything was possible' if an individual worked at hard enough. Mayo, acknowledged this concept and felt that industrial management had an important role to play in countering anomie by fostering group affiliation and sentiments in the work place. The interview programme and personnel approach can be seen as very much directed towards this end. Ignoring the role of other institutions like the churches and trade unions in creating social integration, his belief in the social value of creating workplace affiliations and loyalties made him very much a 'management man'. He has been criticised on this account.

Other factors, however, suggest that the practical significance of the concept of anomie to Mayo's experimental and theoretical contributions should not be overstressed.

- Landsberger (1968) believes that Mayo's acceptance of the concept of anomie was 'of some, but only tangential, relevance' and may have been based on only two cases where maladjusted workers resolved their out-of-work conflicts and worked effectively for the first time in their careers. Social data for the whole Hawthorne workforce rather than for selected groups was lacking.

- We should note again that Mayo's initial experiments at Hawthorne did not focus on issues of social integration or the social needs of individuals and groups, but it was directed to rational, scientific factors and their supposed effect upon worker productivity.

4.5 Human relations – implications and relevance today

The Hawthorne experiments acted as the cornerstone for the development of what became known as **human relations**. This fresh approach contributed immensely to the study of organisational behaviour by identifying:

- Hawthorne effect
- bank wiring room and its group phenomena
- concept of social system
- idea of irrational response and sentiment.

All of these factors above combined to indicate that an individual:

- does not work just for economic reward
- is not necessarily rational in his or her thinking.

Work and home conditions have a bearing on a individual's attitude at work as does the nature of his or her social interaction at work with colleagues, subordinates and management. Man has social as well as economic needs and in some way these factors affect productivity in the workplace, as they appear to affect individual and group performances. It is management's job to elicit these social needs and attempt to satisfy them in the work situation, resulting in a dual benefit for management and workers.

Initially in the 1930s, companies used this new awareness of human relations in managing people largely as an assistance to managerial control and in a rather simplistic way. The underlying thrust behind Mayo's work was, as Watson (1987) says, to integrate the work group into the organisation in order to better control it. Indeed, the interview programme and personnel approach at Hawthorne were intended to:

- tease out the underlying, non-rational fears and anxieties of individual workers
- alleviate any fears the workers had
- provide case study material for their personnel trainers so that managers and supervisors could better understand their workers and so handle them more effectively.

Early human resource management essentially consisted of supervisors listening to workers' grievances, taking an interest in their social needs, and recognising the power of the group. These supervisors required training so that they could attune themselves to their charges. Human relations was used essentially by management as a counter to the increasing power of the unions.

Today the underlying principles of social and group needs are used in supervisory and junior management training, particularly in the areas of communication and handling of people. The idea, for instance of 'group norms', is part of training in group behaviour.

Also, in a broader sense, we may detect some of Mayo's views in modern management thinking. For instance, the following two schemes – although one is primarily quality driven and the other politically motivated – embody the principle that managers care for their people. The underlying message is that they appreciate the contribution which all staff can give to the work situation:

- *Investors in People* – a nationally recognised award which organisations now may receive for demonstrating commitment to the training and developmental needs of all staff; it recognises the contribution and importance of all of its members.

- *Opportunity 2000* – a national initiative to increase the quality and quantity of women's participation in the workforce so that at all levels, women have the opportunity to make progress according to their abilities.

Of course, it is possible to adopt a more cynical stance. Thus, in the factory situation, according to Watson, 'existing structures have been marginally humanised' (1987). In other words, some of the rough edges of the harsh and often scientific approaches in the workplace have been knocked off; but the underlying emphasis is still on task, method and output.

Whether we see Mayo's work as helping to shift the emphasis in management from task control to a more human-orientated approach to work, or as extending management control mechanisms into the area of the workforce, there is no doubt that his ideas acted as a catalyst and fed further work by industrial psychologists and sociologists in areas such as motivation, group dynamics and leadership. These are all areas of immense relevance both to researcher and practitioner.

REVIEW ACTIVITY 4

Suggested time: 30 minutes.

Consider the case study and then answer the questions that follow it.

Shopquick Supermarket Chain

Shopquick (UK) Ltd is a major supermarket chain with stores predominantly in England and Scotland. It is one of a number of newer supermarkets on the scene which have the policy of 'piling them high and selling them cheap', no-frills shopping. Its stores compare in size with those of its competition: Food Giant, Aldi and Kwiksave.

Recruitment and training

Reginald Homeworthy is general manager of the new Sunderland outlet based in Hendon. A Yorkshire man in his late forties and having worked his way 'up through the ranks', he was personally involved in recruiting all of the store's staff of 22. Staff are expected to be able to function in any area of the store, from shelf stacking to working at the check-out tills. They have all been especially trained in-store by the company's training manager. Later recruits will be 'shown the ropes' under the careful guidance of one of the two supervisors. Reginald also has a deputy manager, Sheila, to assist him. Sheila has a degree in French and marketing and this is her first 'proper' job since graduating, although she did spend 6 months of her placement year with Shopquick at one of its London sites.

Store layout
As is common in many modern stores, the arrangement of food and other items in the store, as well as storage, check-out and access details was well planned. Reginald was insistent that the store had its own bakery. ('Its the smell – makes customers think of bread their Granny used to bake . . .') He has been closely involved with getting the lighting levels right: intensely bright in the cold storage areas and nicely mellow in the bread and cakes section. And of course, he has quotas to meet for the company's own brand products so he has had to think about where to position these. Like all modern supermarkets all of the products have a bar code and the check-outs act as EPOS (electronic point of sale) which means that at any one time Reginald knows how well particular lines are selling and what the stock levels are. He is prompted by the computer for re-order quantities.

Of course, competition is fierce and Shopquick runs a lean operation. This means there are the fewest personnel for any situation and only at peak times are all of the check-outs staffed.

Staff – attitudes and perceptions
Sandra and Barbara were recruited as 'operative staff' from the closely-knit Hendon council estate. Sandra is in her late teens and still living at home whilst Barbara is a single parent with a two-year-old son, Wayne. They were asked to give their views on various aspects of their jobs. Whilst they are grateful to have a job they both think that their take-home wage is inadequate. Barbara says that if it was not for her mother looking after Wayne she would not be able to afford the necessary childcare and would not be working at all.

'Its OK, I suppose', says Sandra guardedly, 'although Mr Homeworthy can be a bit strict at times. I prefer it when Sheila is in charge – she lets the supervisors decide in which order to do jobs, as long as things get done. Whereas, for instance, Mr Homeworthy gives us a print-out from his computer and highlights the stock replacements for us.'

Barbara has different views 'I'm not really bothered about that', she says, 'but it would be nice if I could be allowed to leave early on Tuesday nights to pick Wayne up. Its my Mum's bingo night and heaven knows, she's got little other pleasures in life.'

They both agree that the physical working conditions can be tough. 'Have you seen the size of some of the pallets we're expected to pull around – massive! They're designed for gorillas, not us!' complains Sandra. 'And the rest breaks – only half an hour for lunch, if you can get it. Do you know that last week both Dawn and Sarah were down with the 'flu and we both had to cover for the whole week? We hardly got a lunch break between us! At this rate we'll be on sick soon.'

And then there's the issue of smoking, or rather lack of it. Both women readily admit to being nicotine addicts and yet there is a strict no-smoking policy within the store and the rest room. As Barbara explains, 'Mr Homeworthy has said that he will sack anyone caught smoking on the premises. By break time, we're desperate and we used to go in the toilets but now Mr Homeworthy has installed smoke alarms there and so we have to go outside to the car park. Someone told me that he was even thinking of making us change out of our uniform if we needed a smoke but I suppose he realised we'd probably be late getting back so he didn't go ahead with that one.'

Both women have had worse bosses. Reginald is courteous, always greeting his staff with a friendly 'Good morning'. But he doesn't really appear to appreciate their problems, nor is there any mechanism by which he may be made aware of them. In his eyes 'an efficient store is a happy store', as he so often tells his staff.

'I do enjoy working here, for all that', says Sandra. Barbara agrees, 'Yes, I know that the money's just as poor as most places around here, but a job's what you make it, isn't it? I mean, at least we can have a good 'crack-on' [lively gossip] here with the other girls. If any of us has a problem, we can talk about it here. And old Reggie – he may think he can make us work our socks off but he doesn't have a clue really. We do enough to keep him happy most of the time though, although he can't expect miracles for the money he pays us!'

1   How are Mayo's experiments and findings relevant in this case study?

2   How could Reginald Homeworthy improve human relations at Shopquick?

Summary

In this section, you were introduced to the work of Elton Mayo at the Hawthorne plant and you looked at a series of his experiments:

- illumination studies
- relay assembly room tests
- interview programme
- bank wiring room.

We considered the concepts of fatigue in the workplace, the so-called 'Hawthorne effect' and Mayo's ideas on 'irrational responses', 'sentiment' and 'anomie'.

We concluded in our discussion of the Hawthorne experiments that individual and group social needs of workers exerted considerable pressures in the work place. They could over-ride individual, rational needs and threaten management's control.

In the closing remarks, we discussed the relevance of human relations today and concluded that the ideas of Mayo were implicit in modern managerial thinking and still directly relevant to management training.

Unit summary

In this unit, you have met some of the early experiments and theories relating to management's efforts to increase its effectiveness and efficiency in the workplace by implementing new control methods.

These control methods, in the case of scientific management and principles of administration focused on work tasks and relied upon:

- control systems
- administrative frameworks
- use of economic rewards.

We suggest that, although scarred by obvious deficiencies, these ideas and methods are still significant in today's workplace, at least in terms of job design and methods, even if their basic assumption that management and worker can work in harmony is more arguable.

In the latter part of the unit, you were introduced to ideas relating to the significance of the human individual and the social group in the workplace. The inference from these ideas was that management should beware of concentrating primarily on task and systems. Human beings are not machines, they have 'irrational' needs! Management was urged to attune itself to these needs and somehow attempt to satisfy them, this is a change in management thinking of quite fundamental proportions.

We suggest that these ideas also still have value today, especially in the light of further studies which have increased our knowledge of what motivates the person in the work situation.

We have used the word 'introduced' twice . This is quite deliberate, the unit should have explained for you the origins of some of the theories we examine in more detail in later units.

References

Brech, E F L (1965) *Organization: The Framework of Management,* second edition, London: Longman.

Child, J (1984) *Organizations,* London: Paul Chapman Publishing.

Cole, G A (1990) *Management Theory and Practice,* London:DP Publications.

Conlin, J & Renshaw, P (1978) *The Growth of American Trade Unions* (audio tape & booklet), 84 Queensway London: Audio Learning.

Farquhar, H H (1919) 'Positive Contribution of Scientific Management'. In Del Mar, D & Collons, R D (1976) *Classics in Scientific Management: A Book of Readings,* Birmingham, AL: The University of Alabama Press.

Fayol, H (1959) *General and Industrial Management,* London: Pitman.

Fox, A (1985) *Man Mismanagement,* London: Hutchinson.

Gantt, H (1919) *Organizing for Work,* New York: Harcourt, Brace and Hove.

Gilbreth, F B (1908) *Field System,* New York: Myron C Clark.

Gilbreth, F B & Gilbreth, L M (1916) *Fatigue Study,* New York: Sturgis and Walton.

Gilbreth, F B & Gilbreth, L M (1922) 'Superstandards – Their Derivation, Significance and Value', *Bulletin of the Taylor Society,* June.

Huczynski, A & Buchanan, D (1991) *Organizational Behaviour,* Englewood Cliffs, NJ: Prentice Hall.

Landsberger, H A (1968) *Hawthorne Revisited,* New York: W F Humphrey Press Inc.

Littler, C R (1983) *The Development of the Labour Process in Capitalist Societies,* London: Heinemann.

Mayo, E (1949) *The Social Problems of an Industrial Civilization,* London: Routledge.

Mullins, L J (1993) *Management and Organisational Behaviour,* London: Pitman.

Parker, S R, Brown, R K, Child, J & Smith, M A (1978) *The Sociology of Industry,* London: George Allen and Unwin.

Roethlisberger, F J & Dickson, W J (1966) *Management and The Worker,* Cambridge, MA: Harvard University Press.

Rose, M (1988) *Industrial Behaviour: Research and Control,* second edition, Harmondsworth: Penguin

Schermerhorn, J R, Hunt, J G & Osborn, R N (1991) *Managing Organizational Behaviour,* Chichester: Wiley.

Sheldon, O (1924) 'Taylor the Creative Leader'. In Del Mar, D & Collons, R D (1976) *Classics in Scientific Management: A Book of Readings,* Birmingham, AL: The University of Alabama Press.

Stoner, J A F & Freeman, R E (1989) *Management,* Englewood Cliffs, NJ: Prentice Hall.

Taylor, F W (1947) *Scientific Management,* New York: Harper and Row.

Urwick, L (1943) *The Functions of Administration,* New York: Harper and Row.

Watson, T (1987) *Sociology, Work and Industry,* London: Routledge and Kegan Paul.

Answers to Review Activities

Review Activity 1

1   The early theorists were interested in keeping a tight rein on all elements of the production processes; in particular items (c), (e), (f) and (g) which all belong to Child's second operational level of control.

   All of the statements reflect our present understanding of management control. Note that (a), (b) and (d) belong to the strategic level of control.

2   See Figure 1.

3

- Scientific management is a rather mechanistic approach to control and concentrates on improving the efficiency and effectiveness of the work situation. Control is centred around setting standards, breaking processes down into their basic parts, it requires little initiative from workers.

- Human relations is a people-orientated approach to control. It considers the needs of individuals and groups and the way in which they interact socially. Management attempts to make itself aware of these factors and use them to influence activities at work.

- Fayol's principles of administration are concerned with organisational policies and guidelines. Management attempts to control work by establishing a structural framework in line with these guidelines. 'Control' is singled out as one of the principles; however, it is related to business administration in general.

4   (b) and (d) are correct.

Review Activity 2

Using the Taylor's framework, your answers should include the following points

1   'Develop a science' for each element of a man's work:

- Jane asks 'first-class' reps for good practice and uses this to develop a standard format of reports and sales procedures

- routing of calls on computer to minimise dead-time

- Jane develops the communication system: area reps must report in via downloading from their laptop once per week; messages to be sent via modem to laptops.

2   'Scientifically select then train':

- Jane is considering a 'careful programme of recruitment of younger, more 'professional' representatives'

- Selection of the 'first-class' reps is based on scientific principles; Jane will use the criteria on the standardised forms – number of customers visited, etc – to choose good performers.

3   'Heartily co-operate with the men':

- The increase in communication, both the reporting in and the monthly meeting, indicate that Jane is attempting to foster co-operation, particularly in the implementation of the new systems.

- Additionally, Jane hopes that she will receive co-operation from the first-class reps to review best practice and to assist in training.

4   'There is almost equal division of work and the responsibility between the management and the workmen':

- Essentially, she intends to do the planning – abdicated by the previous sales director – in co-operation with the sales reps who should now be more efficient at doing their sales rounds.

- She will not do all of the planning herself, but it will be much more under her control than under the previous regime. For instance: routing of calls has been taken away from the sales reps and is now done under management control by computer; information is no longer collated in an individual way by the sales reps, but is now very strictly laid down on the new forms and with the laptop inputs, again this is management controlled; and even the sales reps' time for meeting each other is coming under increasing management control, with the monthly meetings being controlled by management.

5   Incentives; higher wages for workers and lower labour costs for management.

Bonuses are on offer. These are not arbitrary, although there will be an initial period in which Jane will try out her 'points system'. This is intended to assist in the establishment of the level of bonus with regard to effort and reward. Bonuses are thus set scientifically.

Jane believes that she can set the bonuses to be of mutual benefit for sales reps and the company which will benefit from increased sales.

Review Activity 3

1   The four features of Fayol's planning are:

- unity of plan, including regular forecasts of, say, five and ten years
- continuity
- flexibility
- precision

One plan
There clearly is not one plan but two. No matter how much Mike dislikes the corporate strategy, he should attempt to either put his views forward with the purpose of amending it or he should amend his own plan to be in line with it.

Forecasts
Mike's forecast is for the next 18 months. Time scales depend upon the rate of change of the environment, for example, technological change (personal computers, etc.) and fashion. The corporate plan probably has longer time scales, for example, the next five years.

Continuity

Mike's plan appears to have 'holes' in it. It does not allow for covering maintenance of machines or holiday breaks; it is not 'continuous'. Provision should be made to cover these definite items.

Flexibility

Mike's plan does not seem very flexible. He may achieve almost 100% utilisation of the equipment but what happens if a machine breaks down? After all, these machines are 'virtually irreplaceable'. Also, if his workforce is also working flat-out what will he do if people are ill?

In order to work in practice, plans must be flexible enough to cope with the 'unexpected' to some extent. Although if we think of machines and workforce working flat out for 18 months, it is more likely than not that something will go wrong to upset the plan. Mike needs to have a plan which allows for such contingencies.

Precision

Operations have been meticulously studied. It is implied, although, we are not told, that Mike's plan goes down to precise details in accordance with these studies. If Mike's plan is precise then we can expect that it will be carefully detailed so that those actions he planned will be carried out.

Note: be careful not to mistake precision for accuracy. The plan may be carried out to Mike's way of thinking but it may still 'miss the target'.

2   We list the items in the case study against Fayol's eight guidelines for command. Bob Short, works manager, wasn't pleased with the planning arrangements but he got on with the job in his usual down-to-earth fashion. He prided himself at having worked his way up from an apprentice to his current position.

1   He knew all of his workers and encouraged them to come to him if they had problems, whether they were of a work or a domestic nature.

5   Each day he would make a routine tour of the various workshops;

4   He liked to be seen to be 'leading from the front'; there wasn't a job in the factory he couldn't do himself and better than most at that.

6   He held a meeting each week with all shopfloor supervisors; he gave feedback from senior management and encouraged their ideas and heard their complaints! He was respected rather than liked; he could be tough when he needed to be and didn't suffer fools gladly

2   [He had no room in his factory for shirkers or incompetents.]

3   He knew exactly when to push his staff if, for instance, he required overtime to be worked but he rewarded his staff well.

8   He tried to generate in them his own enthusiasm for the job via the meetings and the suggestion box. Posters on the walls declared the best idea of the month.

7   He was not always popular when urgent orders had to be met, but staff were quite clear of the results required of them even with 'rush jobs', and they knew that Bob wouldn't take 'no' for an answer.

3

Poor co-ordination: almost inevitable between departments, for example, production and sales if Mike ignores the corporate plan and operates solely for production goals.

Good co-ordination: in Bob Short's department, all of the workers know exactly what they should be doing.

Good co-ordination: work schedules are adjusted 'according to circumstances'; Bob Short will ensure that production continues during holiday breaks and illnesses.

You might have included Bob Short's managerial style. He certainly isn't one to 'hide from responsibility' behind pieces of paper!

You might have thought that the use of suggestion boxes and meetings showed initiative and loyalty, and hence good co-ordination.

4   You could have described areas of control as follows:

● Incoming and outgoing materials checked for quantity, quality and price

● Stores records kept

● Progress of operations

● Maintenance of plant and equipment

● 'Working' of men and machines

● Cost control (management accounts).

Review Activity 4

1   Mayo's experiments and findings are of some relevance when we consider the work situation:

● Like the work observed in the Western Electric Company, repetitive and boring tasks are carried out by semi-skilled staff.

- It is clear that the women's motivation to work is affected by their home circumstances – Barbara is a single parent with a young son, Sandra is in her teens and still living at home. This was a factor picked up by Mayo in his interviewing programme.

- The women admit that they enjoy the job because they can talk to and joke with each other. They need social interaction – they don't work just for the money. Mayo talked about these needs and described the cliques established in the bank wiring room experiments. Also, the relay room assembly experiments had a group of women selected on the basis of friendship.

- The women workers in Shopquick set their own group norms – 'old Reggie doesn't have a clue' they say – in spite of all of Reginald's latest managerial ideas.

- It appears that when Sheila takes an interest in the staff through involving them in the tasks, they appreciate it. Although no proof of performance improvement is mentioned in the case study.

2   To answer this question, we first need to pick out the human relations aspects of the case study.

Essentially, problem areas in human relations are summed up in the phrase in the case study concerning Reginald 'But he doesn't appear to appreciate their problems, nor is there any mechanism by which he may be made aware of them'.

Reginald needs to take an interest in his employees, or alternatively to leave Sheila to manage them, as she appears to have a much better rapport with the employees. The forum for this interest could be:

- weekly staff meetings to give out company information and to receive feedback from employees

- 'open door' policy – Reginald inviting staff to discuss their problems with him

- staff suggestion box

- employee of the month or year, with perhaps a photograph in store and some award

- company newsletter including features from and about employees

Specific issues which currently need to be addressed include:

- Barbara leaving early to collect her son. Could Reginald consider flexitime?

- staff coverage for holidays and illness

- no-smoking policy – a controversial issue! Should Reginald consider a smoking room?

Reginald should accept that his staff are from a closely-knit community and that they will form cohesive, informal groups within the work situation. He might wish to foster these bonds through, for example:

● company social gatherings

● training events.

Note that the lighting intensities mentioned are directed at customers and their buying behaviour, not the staff. Studies have shown that lighting intensity affects what people buy; finding the optimum lighting conditions involves a systematic, scientific management, approach to the best way of eliciting the customer's favourable response to buy.

UNIT 2

TECHNOLOGY AND FLEXIBILITY

Introduction

Technology as a means to facilitate the production of goods and services has always been with us. **Technology** describes systems of production on which all human beings depend, to a greater or lesser extent. These systems range on a continuum from the very primitive basic tools to the very sophisticated micro-electronics.

Our focus in this unit is on technology and technological change during the twentieth century within industrialised societies. We look at the dominant production systems and their effects upon people who work with them. In particular, we examine some of the debates concerning the major twentieth century technological development within the workplace. This is the system of **mass production,** or extreme specialisation, and its implications for workforce and management. We look at the technological developments which may supersede mass production and the controversies concerning these developments.

We start with the problem of definition and then move on to a consideration of Fordism. We look at the concept of alienation in relation to technology and the important contribution of the American researcher, Blauner. We then go on to deal with post-Fordism and flexible specialisation. Finally, we examine new technology and its impact upon manufacturing and the office.

Objectives

By the end of this unit, you will be able to:

- define technology and identify different types of mechanisation.
- identify some of reasons for technological change.
- describe what Durkheim identified as the fundamental differences in technological and social organisation between a pre-industrial and an industrial society.
- describe the impact of division of labour upon an industrial society.
- define Fordism and outline its production system.
- identify the advantages, drawbacks and limitations of Fordism.
- relate Marx's concept of alienation to work in modern technological settings.
- describe the work and conclusions of Blauner on alienation, along with some assumptions and limitations of technological determinism.
- explain the relationship between control, de-skilling and technological change in labour process theory, and identify some of the theory's limitations.
- identify in a contemporary industrial example the characteristics of post-Fordism.

- describe how work and technology are developing in the view of flexibility theorists, the reasons they see for this, and the likely effects for employees and organisational management.

- describe some criticisms of flexibility theory and outline some of the drawbacks and limits to flexibility.

- describe the characteristic features of new technology.

- explain how new technology can increase skill requirements and improve the quality of working life.

- describe convergence theory and its implications in basic terms.

SECTION 1

Technology at Work and Technological Change

Introduction

In this section, we look at:

- the definition of technology and the different types of mechanisations

- how the forces that drive technology also produce effects in the social and economic organisation of society

- the division of labour associated with the move from pre-industrial to industrial societies with its shaping influence on both work and the norms and values of societies

- how early managerial efforts developed to produce control systems that would avoid inefficiency or breakdown in industrial processes and would maximise productivity and economy.

1.1 Technology: definitions and perspectives

In general lay terms, **technology** can include a wide range of different things such as tools, instruments, machines, organisations, methods, techniques. It is an umbrella term which we use to denote any or all of these things.

Winner (1977) gives us a more precise indication of what technology is and identifies three distinct uses of the term:

- **Apparatus:** physical and technical devices such as tools, instruments, machines, appliances, gadgets and weapons that are used to perform a variety of tasks. They have a purpose.

- **Technique:** technical activities such as methods, skills, procedures or routines that people perform to achieve specific purposes.

- **Organisation:** social arrangements such as factories, bureaucracies, armies, research and development teams, etc, that are created to achieve technical, rational productive ends.

McLoughlin and Clark (1994), focusing particularly on Winner's apparatus dimension, look at technologies as engineering systems and define them in the following terms: '. . . rather than just being pieces of hardware and software, 'technologies' are also conceptualised as systems based on certain engineering principles and composed of elements which are functionally arranged [configured] in certain specific ways' (McLoughlin & Clark, 1994, p. 132).

They applied their definition to examine:

- how the introduction of electronic telephone exchanges has affected maintenance work

- how computer-aided design has affected the job of the draughtsman.

You will note how their definition of technology focuses upon Winner's apparatus dimension since they found that dimension particularly useful for the purpose of examining how technological change in terms of changing apparatus affects jobs.

The approach that we adopt in defining anything depends on why it is being studied in the first place. This is an important point. Huczynski and Buchanan (1991), for example, argue that the interests of engineers are different to those of social scientists:

- Engineers are not concerned with social relationships in the workplace when designing new machinery. They are concerned with the machinery itself as a technical fact.

- Social scientists are not deeply concerned with design intricacies of machinery. They are concerned with looking at the machine in relation to human labour with the emphasis on group interaction and individual behaviour.

Our interest here is in the social scientific approach to technology and how, for example, machines have increasingly replaced human effort and skills. Using this approach, we do not look at technological development in terms of speed, complexity and size of operations as the engineering perspective might. We look instead at the levels of mechanisation required in the search for more speed, precision, standardisation, efficiency, etc, and at the changing user-machine relationships this involves. This change involves the relationships between what the apparatus can do and what is required of the user in terms of muscle power, mental processes, judgement, etc.

ACTIVITY 1

The American, James R Bright identified 17 levels of mechanisation and their relationship to the sources of power and control (Bright, 1958). His scheme is illustrated in Figure 1.

Examine his analytical table and note down some of the things it tells us about how the apparatus is controlled at the various levels identified and the user-machine interaction.

From man				From a control mechanism that directs a predetermined pattern of action				From a variable in the environment									Initiating Control Source
Variable				Fixed within the machine				Responds with signal			Responds with action: Selects from a limited range of possible pre-fixed actions			Responds with action: Modifies own action over a wide range of variation			Type of Machine Response
Manual		Mechanical (Non-Manual)															Power Source
1	2	3	4	5	6	7	8	9	10	11	12	13	14	15	16	17	Level Number
Hand	Hand Tool.	Powered Hand Tool	Powered Tool, Hand Control	Power Tool, Fixed Cycle (single function)	Power Tool, Program Control (Sequence of fixed functions)	Power Tool System, Remote Controlled	Actuated by introduction of work piece or material	Measures characteristic of work	Signals preselected values of measurement. (Includes error detection)	Records performance	Changes speed, position, direction according to measurement signal	Segregates or rejects according to measurment	Identifies and selects approriate set of actions	Corrects performance while operating	Corrects performance while operating	Anticipates action required and adjusts to provide it	Leve of Mechanization

Figure 1: Levels of mechanisation
Source: Bright, 1958

Apparatus from levels 1 to 4 in Bright's scheme are human operated and controlled; that from levels 5 to 8, the machine movements follow a fixed pattern; and that from levels 9 to 17, the machine is controlled by information coming from outside the apparatus.

The important general observation you should have noted about the user-machine relationship is expressed in comments made by Huczynski and Buchanan (1991): 'Bright's scheme emphasises the way in which operations of the machinery are controlled. The key element is therefore the way in which the relationship between the machine and the user changes. This relationship depends on developments in the machine's capability to determine and control its own cycle of operations. This is one central aspect of the changing relationship between user and the 'engineering system' identified by Mcloughlin and Clark earlier.'

Such a capability obviously changes significantly the skills and capacities needed from users and the kind of work they are required to do.

Bright's type of analysis and perspective is fundamental to the social scientific approach to technology focusing on the effects of developing technology in relation to human labour and the changes that are brought about by the 'imperatives of technology'.

1.2 Imperatives of technology

It was Galbraith (1971) who coined the term the **imperatives of technology**. He argued that the very pursuit of rational means to maximise profitability and efficiency, which was the driving force of nineteenth-century capitalism, led to the development of new types of technology which drastically changed the organisation of work processes, the form of financial investment and ownership and the social class structure of industrial society.

- Technology breaks down the process of production into component parts, each of which relates to an area of specialised knowledge.

- The division of labour, which we discuss in more detail later, becomes more elaborate and encourages a high degree of specialisation, not only in terms of technologists, technicians and manual skills, but also in terms of co-ordinators and planners of the production process.

- The search for increased efficiency and economy has led to two main developments: (i) the rise of large-scale production and distribution, combined with complex organisational bureaucracies; and (ii) the increased involvement of the state throughout the twentieth century (notwithstanding the Thatcher years). This was because only the state could take the risks attached to certain spheres of industrial society by, for example, financing, through the education system, the necessary knowledge and skills in a country's workforce.

We now consider the most important economic and social development that has itself determined the nature of technology and the work process – the **division of labour**.

1.3 Division of labour

The sociologist, Emile Durkheim, was optimistic about the process of specialisation in industrial society in his book *The Division of Labour in Society* (1947). His ideas concerning the division of labour are still highly relevant today and are summarised below.

PRE-INDUSTRIAL SOCIETY

The first point we can make here is that Durkheim saw a fundamental difference between pre-industrial and industrial society. He saw pre-industrial society as based on uniformity in that:

- labour is relatively unspecialised, that is, people made the products they consumed such as clothes and food

- members of society share the same beliefs and values and this uniformity binds everyone together in a close-knit community, usually a rural community.

This type of uniformity is what Durkheim calls **mechanical solidarity**.

INDUSTRIAL SOCIETY

Industrial society, according to Durkheim, is based not on uniformity but on difference. This type of society is one which is characterised by **organic solidarity**. Durkheim calls it this because just as in a physical organism, the various parts are different yet work together to maintain the whole organism.

- In an industrial society, in order to produce goods and services more efficiently, members specialise in particular roles.

- At the same time, specialisation requires co-operation as members of society are dependent on each other's specialised skills, and this interdependence forms the basis of an industrial society's unity.

ANOMIE

The division of labour within industrial society, therefore, for Durkheim at least, is potentially beneficial to society and its members provided that the relationship between citizens and state, and employees and employers can be governed by contract and underwritten by a system of social, moral and legal obligations. This is called a **normative framework**. 'Normative' refers to how society expects us to behave. If we breach the 'norms of behaviour' then we may be punished depending on the gravity of the action.

The normative framework is a form of control and is based on:

- moral obligations that the state expects of its citizens and vice versa in terms of how to behave and conduct ourselves by conforming to recognised and accepted expectations

- legal obligations as citizens to conform to legislation, and as employees and employers to observe in a reciprocal way the contract of employment

- social obligations which individuals have to each other within the family and community, for example.

The normative framework as a means of control is essential to the maintenance of organic solidarity and integration in modern society. Durkheim argues that there is an ever-present danger that material advancement and sectional interests may lead to a breakdown of parts of the normative framework and result in moral confusion and lack of purpose. He conceptualised this as **anomie**.

Durkheim regarded anomie as a pathological state, a social disease, which exists at individual, group and societal levels and shows itself in certain behaviours and conditions.

- At **individual** level, anomie may show itself as deviant behaviour, for example, the pilfering employee or the sexual harasser.

- At **group** level, anomie may manifest itself by the existence of cults in society and conflicting work groups in organisations.

- At **societal** level, anomie may be present during periods of rapid industrial change.

For example, in the USA during the mid-nineteenth century there was considerable industrial unrest as trade unions flexed their muscles. There were few mechanisms in place to deal with widespread disruption and sections of the population became restless and dissatisfied as social and legal controls were largely ineffective to deal with this new situation.

In summary, Durkheim argues that the division of labour in industrial society gives rise to a wide variety of activities and occupations which depend upon each other and which are integrated through organic solidarity. Organic solidarity is maintained by a normative framework as a system of control. However, there is always the potential danger of anomie occurring at different levels within society because of the complexity of the division of labour and the increasing pace of technological and social change. Within the organisational context as within society itself, the nature of the system of control and how to prevent it breaking down and giving rise to anomic behaviour becomes an important focus of study.

We look next at some developments that took place to counter the dangers of such a breakdown in control, at least in the industrial sphere of society, but you should first complete the following activity.

ACTIVITY 2

Explain Durkheim's view of the fundamental differences in technological and social organisation between an industrial and a pre-industrial society.

You should have included the following points:

Pre-industrial society:

- based on mechanical solidarity
- its unity comes from a shared culture based on tradition and face-to-face relationships
- social relationships based on close personal ties centred on the family, neighbourhood and church

- people have a sense of belonging to the community in which they have been born and raised

- people are united in a social group because they are basically similar

- technology is primitive and work is labour intensive

- many crafts are based on cottage industries.

Industrial society:

- based on organic solidarity

- its parts are different but each is necessary for the functioning of society – just like the different parts in a petrol engine or in the human body

- industrial society has a specialised division of labour with each occupational group being dependent on the others

- people become increasingly different, fewer aspects of culture are shared and life is centred on the individual rather than the community

- specialised divisions of labour arise as a result of the mechanisation of technology.

Although Durkheim welcomed this change, feeling that it would provide more freedom for people to live their own lives, he feared its consequences. In particular, he saw the rapid social change of the nineteenth century producing a situation of anomie. Traditional norms and social controls were breaking down and yet had to be replaced by new ones. As a result, individuals were becoming increasingly rootless, isolated and dissatisfied. Anomie and the breakdown of social controls was seen in the rising rate of suicide, crime, industrial unrest and social disorder in urban society.

1.4 Scientific management: contributions of Adam Smith and Charles Babbage

The transition from pre-industrial to industrial society was marked, aside from other developments, by the division of labour which Durkheim generalised to the whole of industrial society. However, Adam Smith, one of the founders of modern economics, had already identified various advantages which the division of labour provides in terms of increasing productivity.

His most important work, *The Wealth of Nations* (1910) opens with his famous description of the division of labour in a pin factory paraphrased as follows:

'A person working alone could perhaps, make twenty pins a day. By breaking down the task into a number of simple operations, however, the workers carrying out specialised jobs in collaboration with one another could produce 48,000 pins per day'.

Charles Babbage (1835) extended Smith's analysis. According to the 'Babbage principle', technological progress in production can be measured by the degree to which the tasks of each worker can be simplified and integrated with those of other workers. This process:

● reduces the price employers have to pay for hiring workers and the time needed to learn each job

● weakens workers' bargaining power and thus keeps wage costs down.

1.5 Contribution of F W Taylor

Sixty years or so after Babbage's contribution, these ideas reached their most developed expression in the work of F W Taylor (1947). Taylor's approach, to what he called scientific management, involved the detailed study of industrial processes in order to break them down into simple operations that could be precisely timed and organised.

We will not describe the detail of Taylor's contribution here as you were given a comprehensive account in Unit 1. We need simply say that Taylor's scientific management, 'Taylorism', established the mechanisms whereby traditional controls over the work or labour process were transferred from the workers to line management.

The USA, at the time Taylor was writing his principles of scientific management, was witnessing a major industrial reorganisation as you saw in Unit 1. Scientific management was considered to be a reasonable approach to managing the technical, economic and social problems of that country.

REVIEW ACTIVITY 1

Suggested time: 30 minutes.

Individually or in a small group, outline the impact the division of labour has had upon industrial society, using what you have learned in this section and from Unit 1 where appropriate.

Summary

In this section, we have defined technology and identified various levels of mechanisation. We have also noted how the search for increased economy, efficiency and profitability and the development of technology have led to important developments in industrialised societies in the organisation of work, economic activity and social structures. You have identified the basic differences set out by Durkheim between industrial and pre-industrial societies, and the primary part played by the division of labour in an industrialised setting. You reviewed the impact of the division of labour on an industrial society in Review Activity 1.

SECTION 2
Emergence of Fordism

Introduction

Taylorism had a widespread impact on the organisation of industrial production and technology in many countries; he was concerned with improving industrial efficiency. However, Taylorism gave little consideration about how products should be sold unlike the next major development in industrial organisation that took place – **Fordism**. We examine this now.

Mass production using the division of labour needs mass markets, and the industrialist Henry Ford was among the first to see and exploit this fact. His name was given consequently to the large-scale assembly-line industrial system which he developed and which others copied. 'Fordism is the name used to designate the system of mass production, tied to the cultivation of mass markets which Henry Ford himself developed' (Hounshell, 1984). Fordism, then, concerns manufacturing carried out in large plants, producing mass market materials using assembly-line processes.

2.1 Henry Ford's system

Ford established his first plant at Highland Park, Michigan, in 1913. It made only one product, the Model T Ford car, thereby allowing the introduction of specialised tools and machinery designed for speed, precision and simplicity of operation.

One of Ford's most significant innovations was the construction of a moving assembly line, apparently inspired by Chicago slaughter houses, in which animals were 'disassembled' section by section on a moving line.

Each worker on Ford's assembly-line had a specific task, such as fitting the left-side door handles as the car bodies moved along the line. Before 1929, when production of the Model T ceased, fifteen million cars were made.

PROBLEMS, PROBLEMS
Having apparently maximised productive efficiency, Ford began to discover problems with assembly-line production. The main problem was with rates of absenteeism and labour turnover which soon became extremely high. Annual turnover, for example, was more than 50,000 workers and total annual training costs amounted to $2 million.

Ford tried to deal with this by offering workers wage incentives to change personal and work habits. Bonuses and other incentives depended on employees behaving soberly and respectably, and limiting their alcohol consumption. The company even set up its own 'sociological department' to investigate and report on workers' private lives (Meyr, 1981).

WORK ON THE ASSEMBLY-LINE

Fordism eventually became central to the automobile industry worldwide, and was also adopted in other industrial settings. A vivid picture of work on the assembly line is provided by an employee in a Citroen factory in the 1970s. 'Each man has a well-defined area for the operations he has to make, although the boundaries are invisible. As soon as a car enters a man's territory, he takes down his blow torch, grabs his soldering iron, takes his hammer or his file and gets to work. A few knocks, a few sparks, then the soldering is done, and the car is already on its way out three or four yards from this position. And the next car's already coming into the work area. And the worker starts again. Sometimes, if he's been working fast, he has a few seconds respite before a new car arrives; either he takes advantage of it to breathe for a moment, or else he intensifies his efforts and 'goes up the line' so that he can gain a little time. If, on the other hand, the worker's too slow, he 'slips back', that is, he finds himself progressively behind his position, going on with his work when the next labourer has already done his. Then he has to push on fast trying to catch up. And the slow gliding of the cars, which seems to me so near to not moving at all, looks as relentless as a rushing torrent which you can't manage to damn up – sometimes its as ghastly as drowning' (Linhart, 1981, pp. 15-16).

ACTIVITY 3

Put yourself in the position of the worker providing the above quote. From an employee's point of view, what are the disadvantages of working within a Fordist production system?

There are a number of disadvantages:

- repetition of task
- boredom and monotony
- speed of line determines how long is spent on each task
- slower workers have problems in keeping up with the speed of the line.

LIMITATIONS OF FORDISM

Despite its drawbacks from the employee perspective, Fordism had at one time seemed the likely future of large areas of industrial production. However, according to Sabel (1982), the high point of Fordism has already passed. In fact, it only became prominent in some industrial sectors, most notably the car industry itself.

The reasons for this lie in the fact that it has many drawbacks besides those for employees. The specific drawbacks of Fordism as a production system include:

- Fordism can only be developed in industries producing standardised products for large markets; to set up mechanised production lines is enormously expensive.

- Once a Fordist system is established, it is quite rigid. In order to alter a product, for example, substantial re-investment is needed.

- Fordist production is relatively easy to copy if sufficient funding is available to set up the plant, and firms in countries in which labour-power is expensive find it difficult to compete with those in areas where wages are cheaper. This was a factor involved in the first successes of the Japanese car industry and more recently that of South Korea.

- Under Fordist production systems where jobs are sub-divided into monotonous tasks, they offer little scope for creative involvement of employees (Salaman, 1986).

- Because of this, it is difficult to motivate workers to do more than the bare minimum necessary to get by, and levels of job dissatisfaction are often high (Wood, 1982).

While these drawbacks are very important, we must also recognise that Fordism had its advantages, particularly for the employer and consumer in terms of economies of scale. This means that the larger the unit of production, the greater the potential output of goods at cheaper unit costs. In order to take full advantage of these economies, the factory must produce at its maximum capacity. This in turn means that there must be a ready market for the goods. The consumer is, therefore, part of this equation, and the consumer also derives benefits from Fordism by being able to afford to buy the goods produced in this way.

REVIEW ACTIVITY 2

Suggested time: 20 minutes.

Read the extract from Beynon's *Working for Ford* (1975) which describes the conditions at the Halewood plant during the late 1960s, and the short piece by a senior manager. Answer the questions that follow.

Working for Ford

Working in a car plant involves coming to terms with the assembly line. 'The line never stops you are told. Why not? . . . Don't ask. It never stops'. The assembly plant itself is huge and on two levels, with the paint shop on the one floor and the trim and final assembly departments below. The car shell is painted in the paint shop and passed by lift and conveyor to the first station of the trim assembly department. From this point, the body shell is carried up and down the 500-yard length of the plant until it is finally driven off, tested and stored in the car park.

Few men see the cars being driven off the line. While an assembly worker is always dealing with a moving car it is never moving under its own steam. The line stands two feet above floor level and moves the cars monotonously, easily along. Walking the floor of the plant as a stranger, you are deafened by the whine of compressed air spanners, you step gingerly between and upon the knots of connecting air pipes which writhe like snakes in your path, and you stare at the moving cars on either side. This is the world of the operator. In and out of the cars, up and over the line, check the line speed and model mix. Your mind restlessly alert, because there's no guarantee that the next car will be the same as the last. But still a blank – you keep trying to blot out what's happening. 'When I'm here my mind's a blank. I make it go blank'. They all say that. They all tell the story about the man who left Ford to work in a sweet factory where he had to divide the reds from the blues, but left because he couldn't take the decision-making. [. . .]

The history of the assembly line is a history of conflict over speed-up – the process whereby the pace of work demanded of the operator is systematically increased. This can be obtained in a number of ways, the most simple involving a gradual increase in the speed of the line during a shift. The worker gets suspicious after a bit because he finds that he can't make time on the job. He can't get those few stations up the line which allow him a break and half a ciggie now and then. The long-serving stewards and workers at Halewood insist that plant management made frequent use of this type of speed-up in the early days of the plant. Production managers out to make a name for themselves can only do it through figures – through their production and their costs. They abuse their supervision to this end. To service the god of production is also to serve yourself and in this climate a few dodges are part of the game. (Beynon, 1975, pp. 109, 138-9)

A Senior Manager
We are here to make a profit and that's the bottom line. If we don't succeed, we all go down. The assembly line is efficient and workers know the score. I'm sick of these hairy-arsed sociologists who go soft on the workers and blame management for everything that goes wrong.

Define Fordism and indicate how the scenario illustrates a Fordist production system. Comment on the scenario in the light of the advantages, limitations and drawbacks of Fordism.

Summary

In this section, we have identified the emergence of Fordism as a system of production, have offered a definition of Fordism and outlined its production system. You have noted the drawbacks to Fordism from an employee perspective and we have considered other drawbacks and advantages for the employer and consumer. In the next section, we consider two concepts, alienation and de-skilling, which have been closely linked with the development of industrial technology and with Fordism.

SECTION 3
Alienation and De-skilling

Introduction

The concepts of **alienation** and **de-skilling** have been developed to describe two central effects of the industrial process associated with technological development, Taylorism and Fordism.

Whether these were inevitable effects of technological development or of the employer's drive for control over production – and whether future development in technology and industrial organisation will diminish or even remove their effects – are questions of considerable debate.

In this section, we look at what we mean by these concepts and how they developed. We analyse the drives behind technological change and the likely effects of future change on industrial organisation and on employee alienation and de-skilling.

We begin by looking at the historical development of the alienation concept and the contribution of Marx.

3.1 Marx and alienation

We should emphasise that Marx was commenting upon the changing industrial and technological circumstances of the nineteenth-century British context and that his analysis precedes the development of mass production on Fordist lines.

Marx was one of the first writers to grasp that the development of modern industry would reduce many people's work to dull, uninteresting tasks (Marx, 1963). He points out that in traditional societies, or pre-industrial societies, while work was often exhausting:

● agricultural workers had a real measure of control over work with some application of knowledge and even skill

● the work of the skilled artisan was even more rewarding.

By contrast, workers in an industrial society:

● have little control over the nature of their tasks

● in a machine-minding technology like that emerging in the nineteenth century when Marx was writing, they contribute only a fraction to the creation of the overall product

● they have no influence over how, or to whom it is eventually sold.

Work thus appears as something alien, a task which the worker must carry out but which is of itself unsatisfying.

Marx sees a major paradox at the heart of modern societies. On the one hand, the development of industry generates enormous wealth, but on the other hand, large numbers of those whose labour is the very source of this wealth are denied any effective control of the work and are in receipt of subsistence-level wages.

For Marx, alienation not only refers to feelings of indifference or hostility to work, but to the overall framework of industrial production within a capitalist setting. Alienation expresses the material lack of control workers have over the settings of their labour.

ACTIVITY 4

Read the following extract from Marx describing alienation in graphic terms, then identify four examples from modern industry which demonstrate the relevance of his view of alienation.

Alienation

'What constitutes the alienation of labour? First that work is external to the worker, that it is not part of his nature; and that, consequently, he does not fulfil himself in his work but denies himself, has a feeling of misery rather than well-being, does not develop freely his mental and physical energies, but is physically exhausted and mentally debased. The worker, therefore, feels himself at home only during his leisure time whereas at work he feels homeless. His work is not voluntary but imposed, forced labour. It is not the satisfaction of a need but only a means for satisfying other needs. Its alien character is clearly shown by the fact that as soon as there is no physical or other compulsion it is avoided like the plague. We arrive at the result that man (the worker) feels himself to be freely active only in his animal functions – eating, drinking, and procreating, or at most also in his dwelling and personal adornment – while in his human functions he is reduced to an animal. The animal becomes human and the human becomes animal! (Marx, 1963: pp. 124-25)

Obviously most examples do not fit all the features of Marx's account, but there are many to choose from, and you might have included:

● The assembly-line worker from Review Activity 3.

● Examples of work which are physically tiring and heavy such as construction labouring and where leisure time is seen as recuperative by having a few pints in the pub which leads us on to the important point concerning:

● A division in the worker's mind between work and non-work where the latter is time spent on activities which help the worker forget the time spent in work.

3.2 Alienation after Marx

Where Marx focussed on alienation in the objective nature of the work situation, more recent sociological studies of alienation have concentrated on workers' feelings and attitudes, that is the subjective dimension of the work situation.

An important example of such a study is a report produced by the US Department of Health, Education and Welfare entitled *Work in America* (1973) which covers a wide variety of industrial and organisational settings at a time when Fordist assembly-line production processes were, in general, the industrial norm. Unlike most official reports, this study attracted much media and public attention.

It found that many work settings involved: 'dull, repetitive, seemingly meaningless tasks, offering little challenge or autonomy thereby causing discontent among workers at all occupational levels'.

Other findings of the report were:

- blue-collar or manual workers felt they had:
  - little control over their working conditions
  - could not influence decisions about their jobs.
- Their work schedules were fixed and they were subject to close and continuous supervision.
- Levels of dissatisfaction with work were also high among those in white-collar or non-manual jobs.
- Amongst white collar workers:
  - those in lower-level office work found their jobs routine and boring, providing little scope for initiative,
  - many middle managers expressed similar dissatisfaction and felt called upon to put into practice, policies they had no influence in setting up.
- Those in higher management positions were more likely to be satisfied with their work, considering themselves to have a measure of independence, challenge and variety.

No wide-ranging survey of this type has been carried out in Britain, but the fragmentary research that does exist suggests parallel conclusions. Many people enjoy their work in spite of the tasks they are called upon to perform rather than because of them, and often value social contact with others, for example, more than their actual jobs.

ACTIVITY 5

● Explain briefly the objective nature of alienation of labour according to Marx.

● Summarise the factors in the workplace which give rise to subjective feelings of alienation amongst workers.

● Comment on how technology and Fordist production processes are likely to influence the level of subjective alienation felt by those involved with them.

Marx argued that alienation is an objective condition which stems from capitalist exploitation of the workforce. This implies that even if you don't feel alienated, you nevertheless are; you are merely a 'happy robot'.

Alienation is a **subjective** feeling state which arises as a result of certain features of the workplace such as boring, tedious and repetitive tasks, close supervision and lack of any control over the work process itself and over decision-making concerning tasks and jobs.

Technology itself is an important factor which influences levels of alienation, and the Fordist system of production with its subdivision of tasks and its emphasis upon assembly-line mass production accentuates feelings of boredom, lack of control and general job dissatisfaction. Fordist production lines give rise to high levels of labour turnover and absenteeism and are therefore costly to the employer in terms of replacing and retraining labour.

3.3 Technology and alienation: the Blauner study

A very influential study by Blauner (1964) attempted to demonstrate empirically that it is precisely those assembly-line, Fordist production processes which give rise to the highest levels of alienation.

Basically, Blauner was interested in finding out the extent to which the technology which defined the production process actually caused or determined those negative subjective feelings which define alienation. He set out to do this through the following steps.

Step one: The conceptual framework

Blauner developed a framework which enabled him to test workers' feelings of alienation. In other words, he attempted to breakdown the concept of alienation so that he could study it empirically by isolating what he considers to be its four essential components. These components he called: **powerlessness, meaninglessness, isolation,** and **self-estrangement**.

ACTIVITY 6

What you think he meant by these terms in the light of the characteristics of alienation we have already discussed? Compare your ideas with the component descriptions that follow:

Powerlessness

A person is powerless when he is an object which is controlled and manipulated by other persons or by an impersonal system such as technology, and when he cannot assert himself as a subject to change or modify this domination.

Meaninglessness

A person experiences alienation of this type when his individual acts do not seem to have any relation to the wider context in which the person operates. In the work context therefore, a person's individual work task may seem to have little or no meaning when the end product is very complex and sophisticated – such as car production.

Isolation

This happens when a person has a feeling of being in, but not belonging to, a community, an organisation or a workplace. There is a feeling of remoteness and an absence of loyalty. In the work situation, the person may be isolated from colleagues by distance, noise and sheer 'aloneness' on the assembly line.

Self-estrangement

A person experiences this when his work activity becomes a means to an end rather than an end in itself, as, for example, when workers feel that it is the financial rewards (the pay) rather than the job itself that is important. In addition, work does not contribute to personal identity and satisfaction but is damaging to self-esteem. There is also a lack of interest and involvement in the work or job.

ACTIVITY 7

Individually or in small groups, identify a number of real-life work situations in which you have experienced or witnessed one or more of these alienation states. If possible, discuss these experiences with other members of the group, and/or with your tutor. Discuss how these alienating feelings were or might have been remedied. A commentary is inappropriate here as you will all have different experiences.

STEP TWO: THE SURVEY FRAMEWORK

Blauner then devised specific questions and other measures to test the four alienation components by questionnaire and interviews.

STEP THREE: SELECTION OF THE RESEARCH CONTEXTS

This was an extremely important stage as, in order to test whether technology was the main, if not the sole cause or determinant of alienation, he needed data from a wide cross-section of organisatons and industries which used different types of technology.

This cross-section of industries could also be linked with technological development over time. The four industries he settled on covered:

● craft technology

● machine-minding technology

● assembly-line Fordist technology

● continuous process (automated) technology.

Printing – 'craft' technology

Traditionally, a craft technology required skill, judgement and initiative. Workers were free from much external supervision. They saw the finished product. They were not socially isolated but well integrated into their local community. They were involved in their work.

Textiles – machine-minding technology

Workers were largely machine minders. They experienced powerlessness and were subject to strict supervision. The product was standardised and required little skill in manufacture. However, the workers were involved in a small, closely-knit community united by ties of kinship and religion. This accounted for low levels of self-estrangement. Subjectively, they were not dissatisfied.

Car manufacture – assembly-line Fordist technology

The assembly-line gave workers little or no control over their work. The work was routine and fragmented. The product was standardised and workers had little identification with it. They were socially isolated and had no social community outside work. There were high levels of self-estrangement. They were dissatisfied with their lot.

Chemicals – continuous-process technology

Here there are high levels of automation which reverses the trend towards further division of labour. Workers have a sense of control over their technological environment usually absent in mass-production factories. The result is meaningful work in a more cohesive, integrated industrial climate.

ACTIVITY 8

On a scale of low, intermediate and high, what levels of alienation would you expect to find in the four industrial contexts chosen by Blauner? Figure 2 summarises the results of Blauner's research.

Industry	Levels of Alienation		
	Low	Intermediate	High
Printing			
Textiles			
Car Manufacture			
Chemicals			

STEP FOUR: THE RESULTS AND THEIR INTERPRETATION

Figure 2 summarises the results of Blauner's research.

Type of work	Craft minding	Machine line	Assembly	Process
Type of Production/Product	No Standardised Product	Mechanisation and Standardisation	Rationalisation/ Standarised Product	Rationalisation Uniform Product
Level of skill	High	Low	Low	Responsibility and Understanding Needed
Level of Alienation	Low	High	Highest	Low

Figure 2: Results of Blauner's research

As Blauner suggests, we can interpret the results of the research in two ways. Firstly, we can take a 'snapshot in time' approach and argue that in 1964, when Blauner published his results and when the dominant mode of production in manufacturing was the Fordist-type assembly-line, alienation levels generally were at their highest. Whereas, say, in 1804 when craft technology was predominant, alienation was at its lowest.

Secondly, we can take a historical perspective on alienation, and as Blauner states: 'Because secular developments in technology, division of labour and industrial social structure have affected the various dimensions of alienation largely in the same direction, there is a convergence of long-range trends in the relation of the factory worker to his work process. Alienation has travelled a course that could be charted on a graph by means of an inverted U-curve.' (Blauner, 1964)

The results then are:

1   In the early period, dominated by craft industry and technology, alienation is at its lowest level.

2   The curve of alienation, especially powerlessness, rises sharply in the period of machine-minding industry and technology.

3   The alienation curve continues upward to its highest point in the Fordist assembly-line industry and technology of the twentieth century. In car production, the combination of technological, organisational and economic factors has resulted in the simultaneous intensification of all dimensions of alienation.

4   Finally, in the automated process industry, there is a counter-trend which can be expected to become more important in the future. The case of the continuous-process industries, particularly the chemical industry, shows that automation increases workers' control over the work process and checks the further division of labour and growth of large factories. The result is meaningful work in a more cohesive, integrated industrial climate. The alienation curve begins to decline from its previous height as employees in automated industries gain a new dignity from responsibility – hence the inverted U curve.

IMPLICATIONS OF BLAUNER'S FINDINGS

The main implication Blauner drew from his research, taking the historical perspective, was that while the worker may not always be satisfied and integrated, the future trend will lead in that direction. In other words, there is an optimistic view of the future which will be dominated by automated continuous-process technology and a non-alienated workforce with higher skills and greater autonomy in their work.

Blauner's work is important because of its central emphasis upon technology. He regards that changes in technology and production systems follow an evolutionary logic independent of the role of employers and managers. According to him, it is only technology and its process development that can directly influence workers' attitudes and feelings, and so determine levels of alienation. For this reason, Blauner has been called a technological determinist.

Other theorists strongly dispute this. They see changes in technology and production sytems as being determined not by some natural process of technological development, but by the desire of employers and managers to control the production process and the people involved in it as fully as possible. They consider that this essentially involves the de-skilling of jobs and processes, and they would dispute Blauner's view that future continuous-process developments will create a workforce for whom the effects of technology are fulfilling rather than alienating.

ACTIVITY 9

Read the case study and then answer the following questions. With reference to Blauner's work on alienation, comment briefly on where you see this scenario falling in his historical perspective of technological development. Do you think this scenario supports or refutes Blauner's conclusions?

Electric light bulb manufacture

Factory X manufactures electric light bulbs for a major DIY chain. Production was 800 bulbs an hour, of the type having a metallised reflector and the components of the glass envelope were made elsewhere. They travelled on a chain conveyor around the plant, which occupied an area of about 30 feet by 10 feet and was quite new. It was noisy, and the large room which housed it was drab but conditions otherwise were not unpleasant.

The plant was almost completely automatic. Parts of the glass envelope, for example, were sealed together without any human intervention. Here and there, however, were tasks which the designer had failed to automate, and workers were employed, mostly women, mostly middle-aged. One picked up each glass envelope as it arrived, inspected it for flaws, and replaced it if it was satisfactory, once every 4 seconds. Another picked out a short length of aluminium wire from a box with tweezers, holding it by one end. Then she inserted it delicately inside a coil which would vapourise it to produce the reflector, repeating this again every 4 seconds. Because of the noise, and the isolation of the workplaces, and the concentration demanded, conversation was hardly possible.

This scenario could be matched by countless examples from any industrialised country. The jobs were obviously bad ones, and something should have been done about them, however, the situation is far from unusual.

The scenario does not fit neatly into Blauner's scheme. We have a combination of full automation in some parts of the factory which corresponds to the fourth phase of technological development identified by Blauner, and in other parts of the factory, women work with Fordist production methods. This scenario does not suggest a linear evolutionary progression to full automated technology and so does not fully support Blauner's view of the historical evolution of technology.

We could reasonably assume that the women experience a degree of alienation because of their relative isolation and the monotony of their tasks. We could also reasonably argue that the women's work is subject to a high degree of managerial control, although we do not know how close the supervision of tasks is.

3.4 De-skilling: technological development as a means of control

Blauner assumed that there is some sort of inevitable internal logic which propels technological change and which is not influenced by human agency alone. Others, however, have argued that the search for new and 'better' production technologies and processes and their introduction into the work and labour process are part of a conscious decision on the part of employers to exert greater control over work and the people performing work tasks.

We now examine the concept of de-skilling of work as part of labour-process theory. This is very important in that it helps us to understand the motives and interests which lie behind the introduction of technological change.

LABOUR-PROCESS THEORY

In contrast to Blauner's work, labour-process theory seeks to uncover the social and economic interests which lie behind technological change. Labour-process theory has its origins in the work of Karl Marx, but its relatively recent re-emergence can be attributed to the publication of a book, written by Harry Braverman called *Labor and Monopoly Capital,* in 1974.

Braverman set out to challenge what he saw as the technological determinist assumptions of writers such as Blauner. Braverman instead offered a model of evolution of modern enterprises which identified:

● capitalist search for increased profitability; and

● management concern for increased control over work,

as the driving forces behind technological change.

The conclusions which Braverman arrived at contradicted Blauner's view that technological development through automation would inevitably raise the levels of skill and autonomy of the workforce. Rather, Braverman argued, automated technologies were introduced by management with the intention of de-skilling, that is, reducing the skill content of jobs in order to increase management control over the labour process.

We now look in more detail at the two interconnected themes that Braverman explored to arrive at his conclusions:

- Firstly, he examined the relationship between management control and the labour process.

- Secondly, he examined how management sought to gain control over the labour process through scientific management or Taylorism, de-skilling and technology.

MANAGEMENT CONTROL AND THE LABOUR PROCESS

Braverman makes the assumption that there is a fundamental conflict underlying the relationship between capital and labour, and that relations between management and workforce and the question of technological change need to be seen in the light of this basic fact.

For Braverman, the employment relationship begins when the employer buys the services of an employee in the labour market. In entering into a contract of employment, the employer and employee have only agreed the terms and conditions of the employment relationship. The detail of what work employees do, when they do it, and how it is done have to be resolved day-by-day in the workplace.

Braverman argues that, in order to get the maximum return on their 'investment' in human labour, employers have to maximise their control over the behaviour of employees, whatever the type of technology currently in use. 'The essential function of management in industrial capitalism is control over the labour process' (Braverman, 1974).

Braverman's view of management control is, therefore, in direct contrast to that of Blauner, and Woodward (1970) who did similar work to Blauner within the British context. Blauner and Woodward saw the problem of management in terms of how to develop control systems most appropriate to the type of technology within the organisation and assumed that employers, managers and workforce would have a common interest in establishing appropriate control systems to achieve efficient production and commercial success. Whereas, Braverman believed that management control systems were one aspect of the wider class conflict between capital and labour, and that the introduction of automated technologies and control systems was part of a more general attempt by management to achieve greater control over the workforce.

ACTIVITY 10

Identify two or three examples of management control over the workforce. One example mentioned above is control through the contract of employment which places obligations and duties upon the employee.

Other examples of control include:

- **technological:** work is controlled by machinery and the assembly line. As we have noted, the Fordist assembly-line imposes the greatest degree of management control over the workforce, and craft technology the least degree of management control.

- **bureaucratic:** workers are controlled by rules and procedures and the detailed specification of work content and method. It is also to some extent technology-related.

- **financial:** concerns issues like investment decisions (what particular plant and machinery to buy), and remuneration decisions (determining levels of pay for the workforce).

In addition, Thompson (1990) argues that control of work within capitalism involves three elements:

- mechanisms by which employers direct work tasks

- procedures whereby they supervise and evaluate performance in production

- apparatus of discipline and reward.

The question we must ask ourselves now is: How has management sought to gain control over the labour process?

SCIENTIFIC MANAGEMENT, DE-SKILLING AND TECHNOLOGY

Braverman argued that in the early days of industrial capitalism, workers, who were largely craft workers, were initially in control over the labour process by virtue of the skill brought to their work. However, this degree of job control represented a direct challenge to the employers' drive for greater efficiency and profit.

According to Braverman, the most important response to the challenge was the development, at the turn of the century, of the theory and practice of scientific management or Taylorism which advocated the pursuit of industrial efficiency by the complete separation of conception from execution. The mental labour of planning and decision-making was separate from the exercise of manual labour.

The objectives of this Taylorist approach were two-fold:

- firstly, job content was to be de-skilled progressively as work was broken down into fragmented tasks requiring little mental ability and only physical effort

- secondly, the functions of planning and decision-making required to direct and control the execution of work were to be increasingly concentrated in the expanding ranks of management and managerial functions.

Consequently, the general skills of craft workers were reduced to job-specific ones, largely as a result of mechanisation. During the first quarter of the twentieth century, jobs were broken down allowing companies frequently to dispense with skilled labour, and, through Taylorism, to exert greater management control over the workforce.

ACTIVITY 11

Read the following extract about the electrical equipment industry. Then answer the following questions. Does this example illustrate Braverman's thesis? What would be the different interpretations of Braverman and Blauner of the change to a semi-automated process?

'Electrical employers transformed the work of making lamps. The jobs were simplified and divided into minute segments with the former skills built into specialised machines. This allowed the companies to cut costs, increase production, and eliminate skilled workers. The craftsmen, who had used their own specialised skills and knowledge to produce the lamps, were replaced by workers – predominantly women – who performed only one special operation and required little training to do the job'. (Thompson, 1990)

In this example, we have:

- de-skilling process which transforms, or degrades craft work into unskilled work

- implicit transfer of control from craft worker to management.

This follows Braverman's view. Braverman did not see the use of automation to de-skill jobs as an expression of the inevitable impact of technology itself whereas Blauner would have seen it in that way. It is seen entirely as a product of the need to control the labour process in order to increase profits. Braverman's views are based on a model of the implications of technological change which derives directly from management's attempts to seek control over the labour process.

SOME CRITICISMS OF BRAVERMAN'S DE-SKILLING ARGUMENT

We are now in a position to identify a few important criticisms of the de-skilling argument:

1 Braverman assumes that the drive for profit requires management to take control over the labour process away from the workforce, and that one particular strategy, Taylorism, is the most appropriate way of achieving this.

   This argument has been questioned on the grounds that:

   - there are other strategies available for management to control labour

   - these may not involve a de-skilling of jobs and reduction in worker autonomy.

Friedman (1977), for example, has argued that a Taylorist strategy of 'direct control' may be appropriate for semi-skilled or un-skilled 'peripheral' workers, but that a strategy of 'responsible autonomy', which delegates a certain amount of discretion to workers in order to gain their commitment to management's goals, is more appropriate for skilled 'core' workers (for example, skilled engineers) who are strategically important to the production process.

2   A second criticism is that Braverman presents a picture which suggests that the workforce passively accepts the de-skilling of its jobs and offers no resistance to, or at least makes little attempt to influence, management plans.

3   A third criticism of Braverman's analysis is his insistence on a model of the employment relationship between management and workforce as always being in conflict. This leads to the conclusion that the workforce always needs to be controlled by management and ignores the possibility of common interests that exist between management and the workforce. For example, a common interest in the survival of the firm, or a common interest as shareholders in the organisation or industry could exist.

These criticisms suggest that the effects of technological change may be more complex and ambiguous than Braverman and his followers indicate. However, the points we noted earlier suggest that Braverman is correct in his criticism of technological determinism as put forward by Blauner, especially where it leads to the conclusion that the introduction of automated technology will inevitably raise the general level of skill and autonomy of the workforce.

But the argument that the effects of technological change can be explained largely, if not wholly, in terms of the management strategies to de-skill work seems equally flawed in the light of these criticisms.

REVIEW ACTIVITY 3

Suggested time: 10-15 minutes.

Read the following two short cases describing work re-structuring involving technological change. Then answer the following questions. Comment on both cases using the perspectives of Blauner and of Braverman. How do these cases expose the limitations of their respective approaches?

Case 1: Re-organisation of work at Volkswagen

An experiment was set up by Volkswagen in one of its German engine plants in 1975. Car engines are usually built on an assembly line, with each worker having one or two minutes to complete a standard task. Volkswagen instead set up four groups each of seven workers. Within each group, four worked on assembly, two on testing, and one was in charge of supplying materials. The members of each group were trained so that they could carry out all the team jobs, and were allowed to rotate job assignments as they wanted. The group had to meet a quota of making seven engines a day. Surveys revealed that motivation and job satisfaction levels were higher after the change than before. Absenteeism and labour turnover declined. Levels of production, however, were not high enough to satisfy the Volkswagen management (although the groups met their quotas), and in 1978 the experiment came to an end.

Case 2: Re-organisation of work at Saab-Scania

An experiment was set up by Saab-Scania in their engine factory at Sodertalje. The new factory layout consisted of an oblong conveyor loop which moved the engine blocks to seven assembly groups each with three members. Each production group had its own U-shaped guide track in the floor beside the main conveyor loop. Engine blocks were taken from the main track, were completely assembled by the group and were then returned to the main track. The engine blocks arrived with their cylinder heads already fitted and the groups dealt with the final fitting of carburettors, distributors, spark plugs, camshafts and other components. Each group assembled a complete engine and decided themselves how their work was allocated. The guide track of each group was not mechanically driven. The group was simply given 30 minutes to complete each engine and they decided how that time should be spent. Individual jobs on the conventional assembly line had a cycle time of less than two minutes. As a result of these changes, productivity increased, costs were reduced, product quality improved and labour turnover was cut over 4 years from 70 to 20%. In addition, co-operation between management and workers improved.

Summary

In this section, we have looked at the concepts of alienation and de-skilling in relation to technological change at the workplace. The ideas of Marx on alienation were related to modern technological contexts.

You then examined the work of Blauner which looked more closely at the relationship between technology and alienation. The conclusions of his research were explained and some criticisms of his approach were offered.

You then considered the whole area of de-skilling, control of work and technological change within the labour-process theory and the limitations of this approach, especially with regard to the contribution of Braverman.

SECTION 4

After Fordism

Introduction

So far, we have considered technology at work in terms of:

- how it can influence or determine workers' feelings of alienation about their work
- how it can be used to exert greater control by management over the workforce through de-skilling and de-grading work.

These effects are associated with technology and technological change in the industrial environments of both Taylorism and Fordism. However, an influential body of theory and writing has sought to demonstrate the breakdown of production systems based on Fordist assembly-line methods (Piore & Sabel, 1984; Piore, 1986). Piore believes that capitalist countries have entered a **post-Fordist** era. He claims that much work is now organised according to the principles of what he calls **flexible specialisation**. Other writers see organisations developing more flexible internal labour forces on similar principles.

In this section, we look at:

- what post-Fordism and flexible specialisation mean
- what technological, production and consumption changes are seen as driving and characterising them
- their perceived effects on work organisation, and on employees and their skills
- criticisms against claims that work and technology are moving in the direction of post-Fordism and flexibility models
- some drawbacks and limitations that organisations might encounter.

We look first at post-Fordism and flexible specialisation.

4.1 Post-Fordism

Post-Fordism represents a movement beyond Fordism. It signifies a qualitative shift in the organisation of production and consumption. Post-Fordism is essentially optimistic as an ideology. Like Blauner, the breakdown of the assembly-line and the introduction of new work technologies are seen as creating opportunities for re-skilling the workforce and offer the prospect of a multi-skilled labour force operating flexibly in a less hierarchical work environment.

There have been production changes over the last two decades associated with post-Fordism and we can summarise these as:

- changes in product life and product innovation, with shorter, flexible runs and a wider range of products on offer

- changes in stock control, with just-in-time methods removing the need to hold large amounts of costly stock

- changes in design and marketing, such as the development of niche marketing, in response to an increasingly diverse pattern of consumer demand

- changes in consumption with increased emphasis upon niche markets, market segmentation and rapidly changing consumer tastes.

POST-FORDISM AND FLEXIBLE SPECIALISATION

Figure 3 summarises the differences between Fordist and post-Fordist systems. Look carefully at the features identified then read through the 'example of McDonalds', the fast-food chain, that follows and answer the questions.

	Fordist	Post-Fordist
1. Technology	fixed, dedicated machines	micro-electronically controlled multi-purpose machines
	vertically integrated operation	sub-contracting
	mass production	batch production
	for a mass consumer market	diverse, specialised products
2. Products	relatively cheap	price variable
	variable quality	high quality
3. Labour Process	fragmented	integrated
	few tasks	many tasks for versatile workers
	little discretion	some autonomy
	hierachial authority and technical control	group control
4. Contracts	collectively negotiated rate for the job	payment by individual performance
	relatively secure	dual market, secure core; highly insecure periphery

Figure 3: Fordist and post-Fordist systems contrasted

ACTIVITY 12

The Example of McDonalds

McDonalds' secret recipe for success comes not from the Big Mac sauce, but from a new production process, using a combination of the Fordist conveyor belt with a Japanese emphasis on flexibility.

Each store is a factory where workers' skills have been kept to a bare minimum. No chefs, no apprentices wanted on this burger-line; everyone has been levelled down to the uniform 'crew member' rushing between stations to perform tasks learnt in a day. From Oxford Street to Manila, McDonalds' workers follow identical steps to produce identical burgers.

Labour costs should never exceed 15% of an outlet's sales. 'It is very tight' said one manager. 'If sales are down, labour costs must come down. You have to cut the staff and make those remaining work harder'. Workers hired for busy sessions are later shown the door.

Such flexible working practices are as contagious on the high street as on the industrial estate. By employing part-timers, stores can cover unsociable hours without paying overtime, and adjust workers' hours on a weekly, or even daily basis as sales and staff numbers fluctuate. As one manager put it: 'We don't have full and part-timers here. Everyone at McDonalds works flexible hours'.

The new tribe of so-called 'peripheral workers' is becoming increasingly central to the economy. Today, one in four British workers are part-time and 90% of them are women. (Adapted from Lamb & Perry, 1987)

1   What characteristics does the McDonalds operation show of a post-Fordist organisation in each of the four areas of technology; products; labour process; and contracts?

2   Does McDonalds fulfill all the criteria for post-Fordist organisations? If your answer is 'no', explain briefly why not.

1   ● The technology employed is a mix of Fordist and post-Fordist. Catering is certainly for a global mass market but within fairly small units of individual outlets. The technology is standardised but relatively small scale within the individual outlets, and is batch rather than mass production.

   ● The products are relatively cheap and the quality is relatively satisfactory. This is more Fordist than post-Fordist.

- The labour process again is a mix of Fordist and post-Fordist with relatively few tasks, little discretion and control mechanisms. There is, however, some versatility of task, and workers are part of a 'crew'.

- The contracts show evidence of a post-Fordist system in operation with part-time working, flexible hours, etc.

2   The answer to this question is 'no'. Figure 3 shows us why.

4.2 Flexible specialisation examined

As we have just seen, McDonalds is a good example of what Piore and others argue is a post-Fordist organisation. It shows a number of the specific characteristics that indicate a move to **flexible specialisation** in work processes and management that Piore identified as the main characteristic of post-Fordist systems.

In broad terms, we can characterise some of the primary features or principles of flexible specialisation under four headings:

- greater specialisation of product

- changed patterns of work and management

- more flexible organisation structures

- different training needs.

GREATER SPECIALISATION
According to Piore (1986), manufacturers have used new technology to make manufacturing more flexible. For example, computer numerical controlled machine tools can frequently be re-programmed to perform different tasks:

- this enables manufacturers to make goods in small batches economically

- it no longer costs vast amounts to shift from the production of one product to another.

Piore suggests that this process helps industry to meet changing demands as consumers are increasingly demanding more specialised products.

CHANGED PATTERNS OF WORK AND MANAGEMENT
These developments have resulted in changes in patterns of work and management:

- as companies become more flexible they require more flexible and skilled workers

- a new employment structure is being evolved in which low-skilled repetitive tasks are reduced, but the highly skilled work involved in designing products or in shifting from one product to another remains

- management tasks similarly follow the same pattern.

More flexible organisation structures

More flexible working requires a more flexible organisation structure. Firms are organised;

- less hierarchically with
- more communication between departments.

Many companies, for example, have adopted the Japanese 'Kanban' or 'just-in-time' system whereby large stocks or parts are no longer held in reserve. Instead, they are delivered just before they are needed to the appropriate workers. Apart from cutting costs, this allows the product to be changed very quickly.

Different training needs

Workers in companies which are changing along these lines need to be more broadly trained as their work becomes increasingly varied. This core group of workers enjoys more job security and management makes greater attempts to enlist their co-operation through, for example:

- quality circles
- worker representation on company boards
- profit-sharing schemes.

Some implications of flexible specialisation: an overview

What implications would flexibility theorists draw about the direction that work and technology are moving in, and the impact of the new technology and environment upon employees and the management of organisations? Flexibility theorists would argue that flexible specialisation allowed by the new technologies increases the skills needed by the workforce, and unlike industries where Taylorist scientific management techniques are used, workers may co-operate with management in organising the labour process. By implication, they would argue that job satisfaction increases and alienation and industrial conflict decreases.

In fact, flexible specialisation can be regarded as a new form of skilled craft production made easily adaptable by programmable technology to provide specialised goods which can supply an increasingly fragmented and volatile market.

With such a view, we can see how it might be suggested that the future for job design is based on flexibility and multi-skilling, driven by a market imperative and fostered by intense marketing and advertising. With this in mind, we could also argue that workers respond best and most productively when they are not highly controlled by hierarchical layers of management and are provided with opportunities to move beyond narrowly defined and prescribed jobs.

4.3 The flexible firm

The British economist, John Atkinson, in his theory of the **flexible firm** (1988), shared similar views with Piore about the direction of technology, work processes and work organisation. Atkinson believes that a variety of factors have encouraged managers to make their firms more flexible. These factors include:

- recent economic recessions
- weakening trade union powers
- technological changes
- reductions in the working week.

According to Atkinson, flexibility takes two main forms:

- **Functional flexibility** is the ability of managers to redeploy workers between different tasks. It requires the employment of multi-skilled workers who are capable of operating in different areas within a firm. Such flexible workers form the **core** of a company's workforce. They are employed full-time and have considerable job security. The core usually comprises managers, designers, technical sales staff, quality control staff, technicians and craftsmen.

- **Numerical flexibility** is provided by peripheral groups and is the ability of firms to reduce or increase the size of their labour force. There are two peripheral groups:

  - The **first peripheral group** have full-time jobs but enjoy less job security than core workers. They comprise, for example, clerical, supervisory, component assembly and testing staff, and are easier to recruit than core workers as their skills are common to employment in many different firms.

  - The **second peripheral** group are even more flexible. They are not full-time permanent employees and many work part-time, on short-term contracts, under temporary contracts, or under a government training scheme. The peripheral group can be quickly called in and disposed of in response to fluctuations in the product market. They can be regarded as labour 'on call', providing a 'buffer' stock of resources enabling the organisation to 'organically' expand and contract.

Atkinson believes that flexible firms are making increasing use of external sources of labour or **outsourcing**. More work is sub-contracted and the self-employed and agency temporaries are also used.

Atkinson does not go as far as Piore in believing that the trend towards flexibility increases the skills and autonomy of all the workforce. He certainly believes that core workers benefit from the changes in terms of greater variety of skills and greater opportunity to participate in decision-making, whereas peripheral workers have little opportunity in these areas.

ACTIVITY 13

Identify three main differences between the Fordist organisation or firm and the flexible organisation or firm. Provide one reason for each of these differences.

Figure 3 identifies some significant differences. Sub-sections 4.2-4.3 also provide you with answers to this question.

4.4 Criticisms and evaluation of theories of flexibility

Theories which see an increasing flexibility of work have become controversial because they contradict the widely held belief among sociologists that work is becoming less satisfying and less skilled. Anna Pollert(1988), one of the strongest critics, has even tried to 'dismantle' the theory of flexibility and she believes that the theory is over-simplified and inaccurate. We now consider the specific criticisms.

PRODUCTION METHODS

Pollert does not believe that Fordist production methods have ever been as dominant as flexibility and post-Fordist theories imply:

- Small-batch production has been important throughout the twentieth century and companies with the flexibility to produce specialised products are nothing new.

- Pollert does not believe that there has been any marked reduction in the importance of mass production.

- She points out that the success of Japanese business is largely the result of producing cheap, well-designed and reliable products rather than specialist products in small numbers.

- The spread of more flexibility in industry is, she argues, in any case limited by the cost of new technology.

FLEXIBILITY AND SKILL LEVELS

Pollert questions the views that flexibility, where it has been introduced, has led to the workforce requiring more skills. Basing her argument on a number of empirical studies, she claims that flexibility can have a wide variety of effects upon work:

- She says that more flexible production may lead to 'continuing dependence on traditional skills, de-skilling, skill increases and skill polarisation'.

● Management and workers may come into conflict as a result of the introduction of new technology or management proposals for new working practices (Pollert, 1988).

SKILL LEVELS AND NEW TECHNOLOGY

Wood (1989) also criticises Piore and Atkinson. Like Pollert, he questions the view that changes associated with flexibility have led to workers needing greater skills. His own study of two British steel-rolling mills found that new technology did help to increase the range of products produced but it did not increase significantly the skills needed by workers.

He suggests that many of the workers who do highly skilled jobs with the new technology were skilled workers to start with and have not had their skills increased. In other cases, flexibility for workers means little more than having to move between semi-skilled jobs which require little training.

Wood accuses supporters of theories of flexibility of greatly exaggerating their case. He questions the degree to which there has been a move towards specialised production by asking, 'What proportion of the cars of even the British royal family or president of the USA are custom-built?'.

Wood attacks Piore and Sabel for ignoring the negative consequences of changes in work for the British workforce in the 1980s. These include job losses, unemployment, tightening of performance standards, labour intensification, changing employment contracts and reduction of the power of trade unions and workers' representatives.

ACTIVITY 14

Briefly summarise Pollert's and Wood's criticisms of theories of flexibility.

Sub-section 4.4 deals with the specific criticisms. Pollert argues that there has always been a degree of flexibility in production methods, and that there are cost factors which limit the spread of flexibility in industry. Mass production methods will always be required. She also questions whether flexibility always leads to new skills acquisition. Wood's own specific criticisms support Pollert's last point.

4.5 Further evidence on flexible labour approaches

We have seen that there has been considerable criticism of flexibility theory and claims that there is relatively limited evidence of a move to a flexible firm with a core and peripheral groups. Nevertheless, there is ample evidence that in Britain, organisations are seeking to move towards the flexible firm at least in relation to part-time workers. The numbers of part-time workers have increased, as has the proportion of part-time work within the economy as a whole. We explore this issue more fully in Unit 5.

There is also evidence that organisations have sought changes in working practices which involve demarcations between jobs and allow for easier redeployment of workers across tasks. The third workplace industrial relations survey (known as WIRS) conducted by Millward et al (1992) found that 36% of all workplaces in the sample reported changes in working practices aimed at increasing flexibility.

An earlier survey of 600 organisations carried out by the Advisory, Conciliation and Arbitration Service (ACAS, 1988) found that 34% had introduced flexibility between groups of craft workers during 1984-7; 25% introduced changes allowing production workers to perform minor maintenance tasks; and 21% introduced new payment systems rewarding the acquisition of new skills.

ACTIVITY 15

Read the following scenarios concerning Burton and Ferodo, two firms seeking greater workforce flexibility. Then answer the questions which focus upon employment patterns and policies in relation to the flexible firm model.

Case study 1: The Burton Group
The Burton retail group have dismissed some 2,000 full-time sales staff in their shops and offered them redeployment on part-time contracts. They have also offered 'nil hours' contracts to some workers whereby they are offered work as and when required. This is to enable staffing levels to be adjusted in line with customers' shopping patterns.

Case study 2: Ferodo deal on changes in working practices'
Management and unions at Ferodo, the brake lining maker, have reached agreement in principle on widespread changes in working practices at the company's Derbyshire plant. The changes are likely to include multi-skilling, the elimination

of demarcation between grades, a job evaluation system, and site performance-related pay.

A series of joint working parties, with representatives from management and the trade unions, have been set up to make specific proposals for change at the Chapel-en-le-Frith plant. They are expected to take some months to prepare their proposals and the changes will come into effect gradually.

The negotiations have been going on since last November and have encountered stumbling blocks. In December, shop stewards representing the 1,600 workers were told that the company would consider closing the plant and moving operations to a greenfield site in the north-east if they did not accept more flexible practices.

Ferodo said yesterday the objective of the plan was to optimise the use of expensive capital intensive equipment by learning new skills and becoming more flexible.

At the moment, the company has many types of machines and numerous job levels for each machine. The company wants to both reduce the number of operating levels and eliminate the present system whereby a man operating a grinding machine, for example, would never operate a drilling machine.

There will be a review of working practices in all departments. Present job definitions, grading, pay structures and production agreements would all have to be changed. (Source: *Financial Times*, 21 February, 1989)

1   What are the main forms of labour flexibility?

2   What different forms of flexibility are illustrated in each case?

3   Explain the differences in the approach of the two companies to the question of flexibility.

4   To what extent do you see either Burton or Ferodo as examples of organisations moving in the direction of the flexible firm model?

1   The main forms of labour flexibility are:

●   numerical

●   functional

Additionally, flexible firms are distancing by replacing employees with sub-contractors and outsourcing. Section 4.3 deals with these types.

2   The Burton Group's emphasis is on increasing numerical flexibility by converting full-time jobs into part-time ones. By contrast, Ferodo has emphasised a move to greater functional flexibility by developing multi-skilling through training and job redesign.

3   The following factors explain the different forms of labour flexibility sought

in the two firms:

- differences in the nature of product or service
- differences in patterns of demand for product or service
- differences in technology
- different workforce characteristics.

The Burton Group operates towards the lower end of the retail clothing market. Competition is based largely on price rather than quality of products or service. This places a priority on reducing operating costs rather than on investing heavily in staff skills and expertise. Cost control very much focusses on labour costs. The increased use of part-time and casual labour reduces both wage and non-wage costs in the following ways:

- staff are only paid when their services are needed
- depending on the number of hours worked each week, part-time staff qualify for fewer statutory rights such as sick pay, paid maternity leave and protection against unfair dismissal
- given the high levels of labour turnover and absenteeism in retailing, 'nil hours' contracts can provide a pool of labour to cover temporary gaps among full-time and permanent part-time staff.

The pattern of demand fluctuates with stores being busier at certain times than at others. Variations in customer activity according to the time of day, day of the week and seasonal fluctuations provide a rationale for adjusting staffing levels in line with fluctuations in levels of customer activity.

By contrast at Ferodo, the desire to operate costly capital equipment more cost-effectively is a major factor behind the flexibility drive. Improvements may be made by:

- reducing downtime resulting from delays in effecting minor repairs and maintenance work caused by existing rigid demarcation between operators and maintenance workers
- providing better coverage from within the workforce for gaps in staffing caused by absences
- reducing overall staffing levels.

These improvements can be made by introducing multi-skilling and redeploying workers from one machine to another. Functional flexibility permits the intensification of work by combining tasks so that workers can move from one task to another in response to the production flow.

The emphasis on functional flexibility combined with the nature of the various skills demanded of workers precludes consideration of the employment of part-time or temporary workers on any scale. This is because of Ferodo's need to invest in training workers in the plant-specific combinations of skills that functional flexibility requires. This investment is recouped most certainly and quickly from full-time, permanent employees.

4   From question 3, it appears that in the case of the Burton Group, there is a move towards numerical flexibility but this trend is not matched by a corresponding move towards functional flexibility. We can, therefore, conclude that the Burton Group does not equate with the flexible firm model provided by Atkinson.

As we noted earlier, government policies which encourage greater labour market flexibility would tend also to encourage those organisations such as the Burton Group to introduce greater numerical flexibility within their own internal labour markets.

On the other hand, Ferodo is moving towards greater functional flexibility but without seeking to convert its full-time workers into part-time workers. The emphasis is very much on multi-skilling and training for multi-skills. Again, the Ferodo example does not equate with the Atkinson model.

4.6 Limits to flexibility

In practice, there are limits to flexibility. As we have seen, the flexible firm means that there are many changes in relation to work and the number and type of employees required. It is likely, for example, that greater labour flexibility can only be achieved in some cases at the expense of other aspects of the employment relationship which are valued by employers.

ACTIVITY 16

Note down any possible drawbacks for employers in the type of labour flexibility envisaged by the flexible firm theory.

The disadvantages in using non-standard labour include:

- costs to the employer in staff commitment and manageability
- training, integration and other problems
- conflicts with existing arrangements and agreements which limit the actual flexibility achievable.

COSTS TO THE EMPLOYER

Organisations often perceive that there are significant costs attached to the use of non-standard labour. Surveys conducted by Hunter and MacInnes (1991, 1992) for the Department of Employment reveal that:

- temporary workers are seen to be less committed and reliable than permanent staff
- part-time workers employed on a permanent basis are seen as reliable but more difficult to manage than full-time workers because they spend less time at work.

There is, as Claydon (1994) points out, a possible paradox – the inflexibility of the flexible workforce! He goes on to state: 'This not only restricts the uses to which non-standard workers are put: it has also meant that some organisations have moved away from non-standard contracts. This is because initial cost savings were seen to be outweighed by additional costs arising from lower commitment' (Claydon, 1994, p. 109).

TRAINING, INTEGRATION AND OTHER PROBLEMS

The extensive use of non-standard labour can also pose other problems for organisations. A study of US-owned electronics plants in Ireland (Geary, 1992) found that local managers were keen to minimise their use of temporary workers despite certain advantages they provided in terms of the exercise of managerial control. The reasons for this are:

- problems in providing necessary training for temporary workers within the period of their employment
- widespread use of temporary workers led to reduced commitment from permanent staff and they suffer lower morale and motivation
- conflicts between permanent and temporary staff impede the development of good working arrangements
- difficulty of terminating temporary workers once they become integrated within the workforce and the organisation
- a fear that being seen to operate different standards of treatment for temporary and permanent staff, for example, in terms of non-wage benefits such as sick pay, might undermine management's claim to be following enlightened human resource management policies for the workforce as a whole. This in turn could threaten the basis of trust and cooperation between managers and permanent staff.

The study concluded that: 'management would have preferred to attain a requisite level of control over their labour force by engendering their cooperation and commitment to the organisation' (Geary, 1992, p. 267).

CONFLICTS WITH EXISTING AGREEMENTS AND OTHER ARRANGEMENTS

In other cases, management's efforts to increase labour flexibility may conflict with other work arrangements and with existing agreements between management and trade unions. This is illustrated by the example of British Rail's introduction of **flexible rostering** (Pendleton, 1991).

FLEXIBLE ROSTERING AT BRITISH RAIL

Flexible rostering was an attempt to increase the proportion of the time on their shift that train drivers actually spent driving trains. While management succeeded in moving from fixed eight-hour shifts to a work rota which provided for shifts varying from seven to nine hours, this increase in labour flexibility actually obstructed flexibility in both work scheduling and in day-to-day labour deployment. This was because of the need to reconcile management's aim of flexibility with existing agreements with trade unions regarding working hours and arrangements. The nature of the compromise was such that while flexibility of hours worked was increased, this detracted from, rather than improved, operational flexibility.

4.7 Flexibility: the future - a review of the post-Fordist debate

We have looked now in some detail at the notion of post-Fordism and at the debate on:

- whether there is a significant trend to flexible specialisation which will grow in the future

- what the effects of continuous-process technologies are likely to be for employees and organisational management.

Let's now summarise in very broad terms the positions taken in the debate and what the evidence may suggest about current trends and possible future developments. Braverman's theory of the degradation of work, and Piore and Atkinson's theory of flexible specialisation reach very different conclusions about the direction that work and technology are moving in, particularly in terms of their impact upon employees and the management of organisations. Braverman adopted a Marxist approach and was very pessimistic. Piore and Atkinson used more conventional economic theories and reached predominantly optimistic conclusions.

Nevertheless, criticisms of the theories suggest that they share a common fault. All three writers claim that work is developing in a particular direction. Critics suggest that they ignore evidence which shows that work may develop in different ways, in different industries and different types of employment. While much work is becoming less skilled and more tightly controlled, other work is retaining or increasing its skill content and becoming more flexible. We examine this issue further in section 5 when we deal with the impact of new technology upon manual and office work.

Moreover, we have argued that the balance of research evidence relating to the flexibility debate suggests that while organisations have made efforts to increase flexibility in numerical and/or functional respects, these efforts do not conform very closely to the model of the flexible firm. In particular, there is little evidence that core and periphery strategies are being employed by organisations. More broadly, this may reflect the relative absence of any form of strategic thinking about company employment patterns among managers.

This short-term approach concerning employee and labour matters also suggests that organisations' labour policies may be influenced by the general labour market environment. Government policies aimed at increasing general labour market flexibility together with recession may encourage some organisations to cut costs by reducing standards of employment and taking advantage of workers' vulnerability to intensify work. While this may be presented within the context of the flexibility thesis, it is debatable whether such actions contribute to the long-term health of organisations or that of the economy.

Fortunately, some managers appear to recognise this and, in particular, that there may be significant costs attached to both numerical and functional flexibility initiatives if they weaken the basis for worker co-operation in production and discourage training and the development of improved skills.

REVIEW ACTIVITY 4

Suggested time: 40-50 minutes.

You have encountered some very important issues concerning post-Fordism, flexible specialisation and some criticisms of the flexible firm theory. By answering the following questions, you will consolidate your knowledge in each of these areas.

1 Briefly summarise the notions of post-Fordism and flexible specialisation.

2 Evaluate the technological and production changes which characterise post-Fordism and flexible specialisation.

3 Identify the perceived effects of post-Fordism and flexible specialisation on work organisation, employees and their skills.

4 Criticise the claims that work and technology are moving in the direction of post-Fordist and flexibility models.

5 Summarise the drawbacks and limitations that organisations might encounter in moving towards a flexible firm situation.

Summary

In this section, we have looked at post-Fordism, flexible specialisation, the flexible firm, and you have identified important criticisms of the flexible firm theory. We have identified the characteristics which have given rise to the notion of post-Fordism by reference to McDonalds.

We then went on to look at flexible specialisation and the flexibility theorists such as Piore and Atkinson, how and why work and technology are developing in these theorists' views and the likely effects of these changes upon employees and organisational management. Finally, we dealt with important criticisms, limitations and drawbacks of flexibility theory and the flexible firm model.

We examine the specific issue of new and advanced technology and its effects upon work organisation in Section 5.

SECTION 5

New Technology and Work Organisation

Introduction

Some types of work are becoming less skilled while other work retains or increases its skill content. One important reason for this, as we have seen, is the degree to which flexible specialisation can influence employment patterns within the work organisation. Another important reason lies in the introduction of new or advanced technology and how that technology is used within the work organisation.

In this section, we look at:

- what new technology means
- the argument that new technology in both manufacturing and in the office can increase rather than decrease skill requirements
- the extent to which new technology can improve the quality of working life.

We begin by examining the characteristics of new work technology.

5.1 Evolution of new work technology

There is nothing really new about computers as they have been around since the 1940s. Mcloughlin and Clark (1994), citing research by Friedman and Cornford (1989), identify three phases in the development of computer systems:

- *phase 1* focussed on the development of large mainframe computers used in defence and university research applications. The hardware was relatively unreliable and costly. This phase lasted from the 1940s until the mid-1960s.

- *phase 2* concentrated on improvements in software as the hardware became more reliable. The 'information technology revolution' became a media catch phrase. This phase lasted until the mid-1980s.

- *phase 3* lasting from the mid-1980s to date is concerned with the problem of matching the supply of computer hardware and software with the demands and needs of users.

ACTIVITY 17

We look at the problem of matching the supply of hardware and software with the needs of the user. Read the following extract and suggest what sort of problems both supplier and user can face in the work situation.

Do systems designers understand their users?

Instead of manning the bridge with helmet and heavy binoculars, the skipper of a $1 million Aegis cruiser exercises command from the hi-tech CIC or Combat Information Center, a windowless room linked to the outside world through glowing computer and radar screens. Never before has a warship's captain had access to so much instant and accurate information. Even so, the skipper and his crew are not immune to confusion – the 'fog of war'. A horrified world learned precisely that in July (1988), when the *USS Vincennes* shot down an Iranian airliner, killing 290 civilians.

The tragedy marked the first time an Aegis cruiser had fired its missiles in combat. And it should rekindle efforts to tame the complexity of weapons systems – especially with programs such as *Star Wars* looming. Ever since the Aegis was designed in the late 1970s, critics have worried that its sytems are too complex for mere mortals to comprehend. In its recently released investigative report, the US Navy touched on the issue of breakdowns between man and machine. But the inquiry team found that the highly sophisticated computer and radar systems aboard the *Vincennes* had performed flawlessly.

The real lesson of the *Vincennes* is that electronic systems can produce far too much data for human beings to digest in the heat and strain of battle. Engineers who design such systems often forget this . . . A review board did recommend some changes in the Aegis. One culprit was a hard-to-read computer display that doesn't show an aircraft's altitude beside its radar track. Investigators called for a redesigned screen and better training . . .

The loss of 290 innocent lives is too high a price for working out a new weapon system's bugs. (Griffiths, 1988, p. 28)

Identifying the demands and needs of users is a difficult and complicated process:

- users can have little understanding of the possibilities and constraints of computer systems

- users can fail to realise all the opportunities of such systems

- users can make unrealistic demands on the system

- systems designers often have limited understanding of the actual conditions under which users operate their systems. These conditions can include: noise or interference from the user's environment; and giving confusing information via a visual display terminal

5.2 Information technology and its uses

After looking at the phases of development of computer technology, we are now in a position to define what it is. The following definition is taken from Huczynski and Buchanan (1991). You will note that they prefer to use the term 'information technology' for the purposes of their definition: 'Information technology is the term now used for all types of computer hardware (machines) and software (programs that tell computers what to do), telecommunications and office equipment' (Huczynski and Buchanan, 1991, p. 329). Information technology has a wide variety of uses and impacts across a large number of fields. Characteristics, uses and impacts of information technology, both actual and potential, are listed below. Some factors are beneficial and some are non-beneficial to the organisations operating the technology or to those who are at the receiving end of it.

Government

- facilitation of tax collection

- auto-monitoring of traffic to facilitate road-use tolls

- improved citizen participation

Crime and justice

- computer crime, costly and difficult to trace

- use of robots for prison security

- foolproof electronic voiceprinting and fingerprinting

- improved surveillance technology and property protection

Economy and work

- informed decisions and improved productivity
- robots to do hazardous and boring work
- improved employee monitoring

Health and health care

- computer-assisted diagnosis and cost analysis
- smart card health and medical history recording
- computer as home health advisor

Education and knowledge

- expert systems for everyone; mind extension
- information overload
- mass information storage on compact disk
- individual computer-based tutoring and improved learning

The individual

- friendly machines liberate people
- human-machine interaction as isolating and dehumanising
- sense of time accelerated and confused
- social interaction not based on locality, loss of sense of place.

The reasons for introducing new technology usually concern potential or perceived benefits to the organisation. These might include greater economies, efficiency gains, and more effective control over processes, etc.

In most cases, the benefits to the organisation, as a result of introducing new technology, also provide benefits to those who are at the 'receiving end' – the hospital patient, the student and the employee. The benefits to the organisation and to the recipient usually considerably outweigh the possible non-beneficial effects.

However, taking the example of 'Economy and work', we could argue that information technology and automation improves the quality of decision-making and increases productivity, but replacement of workers by machines creates unemployment, and the greater monitoring and control of employees does not necessarily benefit them.

TO INFORMATE AND AUTOMATE

It is important to note that the introduction of new information technologies does not have to mean the total replacement of human labour in the control of work operations if the implications of this technology are to be properly understood and its benefits realised.

This point is reinforced in the distinction made by Zuboff (1988) between the **automating** and **informating** capabilities of information and computing technologies. She states that: 'Information technology is characterised by a fundamental quality that has not yet been fully appreciated. On the one hand, the technology can be applied to automating operations according to a logic that hardly differs from that of the nineteenth century machine system – replace the human body with a technology that enables the same processes to be performed with more continuity and control. On the other hand, the same technology simultaneously generates information about the underlying productive and administrative processes through which an organisation accomplishes its work. It provides a deeper level of transparency to activities that have been either partially or completely opaque. In this way, information technology supersedes the traditional logic of automation. The word that I have coined to describe this unique capacity is informate. Activities, events, and objects are translated into and made visible by information when a technology informates as well as automates.'

ACTIVITY 18

As Zuboff's distinction is very important, describe the term informate in your own words.

According to Zuboff, one of the main effects of computer technology is to informate the workforce, that is, it greatly increases the amount of information available to workers and managers.

INFORMATION HANDLING CAPABILITIES

Zuboff identifies the ability of new technology to informate as well as automate. Buchanan and Boddy (1983b) identified four informating capabilities which make computing systems different from 'old' mechanical technologies. We now look at each of these:

Information capture

Computing systems gather, collect, monitor, detect and measure. Some devices gather information through sensors without human intervention. Computerised equipment that monitors and controls shows active information capture.

Information storage

Computing systems convert numerical and textual information into digital form and retain it in memories from which it can be retrieved when required. Computers also store their own operating instructions and software.

Information manipulation

Computing systems can rearrange and perform calculations on stored information. Manipulation means organising and analysing, especially where repetitive calculations are involved as in:

- calculating the monthly payroll

- generating standard accounting figures for an organisation.

As the size and cost of storage media continues to fall, it has become possible to develop fast and flexible ways of manipulating text and graphical information.

Information distribution

Computer systems can transmit and display information electronically on video screens and on paper. A numerically controlled machine tool can tell a central computer that it has finished a particular task. Sensors can be used to give operators displays of production process information.

According to McLoughlin and Clark (1994), these capabilities provide computing and information technologies the capacity to automate the control of production and service operations. This can happen in three ways:

- equipment can give operator feedback information to make operator control of the equipment or process more effective

- equipment or process can be taken under computer control through a predetermined sequence or cycle of operation

- deviations from equipment or process standards can be measured and corrective action initiated by the computer.

5.3 Replacement or compensation

So far, we have considered the characteristics of new technology and its uses enabling us to arrive at a definition of information technology.

We have also looked at Zuboff's important automate and informate idea and the information handling capacities of advanced technology. Before we move on to examine the effects of information technology on the shop floor and in the office, there is an important issue for us to consider. It concerns:

- human replacement effects of new technology

- compensatory mechanisms associated with technological change.

The human replacement effects are not straightforward, because various compensatory and limiting effects come in to play in many situations.

REPLACEMENT EFFECTS

The popular image, reinforced by information technology salesmen, claims that the new devices will increase productivity through replacement effects. These claims are based on the assumption that as machines do more and more, people will be required to do less and less. This kind of productivity increase will therefore reduce job opportunities and create unemployment.

Replacement would then involve the substitution of intelligent, or at least clever, machines for people at work, in manufacturing and in offices. This view implies that offices and factories of the future will be fully automated and with minimal human supervision.

The evidence on the so-called factory and office of the future shows that this is not the case. Forester (1989), for example, claims that only 10% of automated manufacturing applications have achieved returns on investment, and that some have been disasters. Forester offers the following explanation: ' . . . people got carried away with the utopian visions of automated factories overlooking the high cost of high tech and the enormous complexity of factory operations. Robots were absurdly over-hyped: it was conveniently ignored that they were both much more expensive and less flexible than humans . . . Much can be achieved by improving quality and product inventory flow without resorting to this expensive high tech 'fix' . . . a total machine takeover in factories no longer seems to be the goal. Rather it is a common sense partnership between machine and man' (Forester, 1989, p. 10).

Or consider this extract entitled 'Book your place in cyberspace': 'How many times have you woken up wishing that your office would just disappear? In the 'wired' future this might just happen; desks and filing cabinets will be replaced by serene meeting rooms and open spaces, office workers superseded by techno-literate secretaries. The office as we know it will cease to exist. That is the theory. In practice, moving from the actual to the virtual office is a logistical nightmare that few have the incentive to tackle. Organisations which have to move or rebuild premises may tweak office organisation but to date there are few operational 'offices of the future'.' (*The Observer,* 28 May, 1995)

The overall effect of technical developments may thus depend on the operation of a number of compensatory mechanisms.

COMPENSATORY MECHANISMS AND LIMITING EFFECTS
Compensatory and limiting mechanisms are processes that can offset the replacement effects of technical change. There are a number that can operate:

New products and services
- Technical innovation generates new products and services (personal computers, video recorders, commercial databases).
- These innovations change the pattern of demand for goods and services.
- This leads organisations to invest in factories and offices to make new products and services which in turn leads to new employment opportunities.

Lower costs increase demand

- Higher productivity means producing the same output with fewer resources or more output with the same or fewer resources.

- Therefore, lower costs can be passed on to the consumer resulting in lower prices.

- Consumers will have more money to spend which may increase demand for other goods and services in the economy.

Time lags

- It takes time to incorporate new devices into existing systems.

- Organisations do not adopt innovations as soon as they become available; it is expensive to replace existing facilities completely.

- In many organisations, the 'state of the art' technology may simply be inappropriate for the work as well as too costly.

Risks

- It is sensible for organisations when they do adopt new, untried technologies to introduce them incrementally to avoid risks.

Expectations of demand

- Expensive investment in new technology is not likely unless an organisation expects the market for its goods and services to grow.

- In that case, the organisation may need to employ more people to handle the increase in business.

Technical limitations

- New technologies do not always live up to the claims of salesmen.

- New technologies may not be able to do everything the 'old' technology was capable of doing.

- Existing jobs, skills and machinery may be required to work alongside the old devices for some time.

We have looked at the characteristics of new technology. Next, we examine fairly briefly the impacts of technologies upon manufacturing and the office environment.

5.4 Impact of new technology upon manufacturing

In contrast to Braverman's thesis of technological change being used to de-skill work, the argument has been put forward that advanced technology in manufacturing can upgrade skill requirements.

ACTION-CENTRED AND INTELLECTIVE SKILLS

Earlier in this section, we made a distinction based on Zuboff's work, between the automating and informating capabilities of information technologies. The automating effects involved the substitution of technology for human labour, while the informating effect involves the generation of new and deeper levels of information about work operations.

These technical influences have direct effects upon:

- nature of work tasks
- skills required to perform them
- subjective experience of work

In order to explore these effects, Zuboff makes a further distinction between **action-centred** and **intellective** skills.

Action-centred skills

According to Zuboff, skilled manual workers had traditionally used skills based on the physical experience of manipulating things and they developed 'experience-based knowledge'. These skills only have meaning within:

- the context in which the associated physical activities can occur
- through the act of physically performing the task.

Action-centred skills are therefore closely associated with the physical performance of work tasks – 'acting on' or 'acting with' raw materials, work pieces or technical artifacts, etc.

Intellective skills

The automating effects of information and computing technologies involve computerising tasks based on action-centred skills thereby making labour of this type redundant.

In this changed situation, employees:

- work with information provided by these new technologies – the data interface
- input information into the new system.

Work with a data interface requires new and more abstract 'intellective skills'. This involves:

- the performance of mental tasks, or 'procedural reasoning'
- an understanding of the internal structure of the information system and its functional capabilities
- an understanding of what actions at the data interface lead to appropriate outcomes
- an ability to interpret new data as feedback on the results of responses.

The performance of work tasks is therefore experienced in an entirely different way. According to Zuboff, thought is removed from the action context, 'absorption, immediacy and organic responsiveness are superseded by distance, coolness and remoteness' (Zuboff, 1988, p. 75).

ACTIVITY 19

Read the case study. Is it relevant to the move from action-centred to intellective skills that Zuboff sees?

Biscuit baking

Buchanan and Boddy (1983*a*) compared the implications of computerisation on two occupations, those of doughmen and ovensmen, in a Glasgow biscuit factory. In the case of the doughmen, action-centred skills were reduced, but they had no opportunity to use intellective skills. The case of the ovensmen was different, as we now see.

The ovensman was responsible for baking biscuits that had the correct bulk, weight, moisture content, shape colour and taste. This was a complex operation as action to correct a defect affecting one of these features could also affect the others. The period of training was 12-16 weeks.

The old electro-mechanical system was replaced by a microprocessor-controlled check weigher which recorded and displayed the weight of each packet as it passed over the weigh cell. The computer also gave summary information on packet weights to the ovensman through a video display unit. This display was frequently updated and information presented in digital and graph form; it also produced management reports.

The information from the new system indicated errors but did not show what was causing the problem or what action to take to correct it. The ovensman had to consider the properties of the flour being used and the dough that it made. In other words, the ovensman had considerable responsibilities to make informed decisions; he had become a 'process supervisor'.

You should be clear about the distinction between 'action-centred' skills – related to physical performance of work tasks – and 'intellective' skills which require mental reasoning, understanding of the information system and actions required, and interpretive abilities concerning feedback data.

In the case study:

- There is the absence of any opportunity for doughmen to use intellective skills which demonstrates that some jobs cannot be transformed in this way.

- There are increased opportunities for ovensmen to demonstrate newly acquired intellective skills.

Buchanan and Boddy (1983a) argue that the introduction of computerised packet weighing technology complemented the skill and knowledge of the ovensman and created a role in which he:

- got rapid feedback on performance

- had discretion to monitor and control the process more effectively

- had a good understanding of the relationships between process stages

- had a visible goal that could be influenced

- felt that the job had more interest and challenge.

This, and other studies of advanced technology applications in manufacturing, suggest that intellective skills and informating capabilities actually increase for many workers whose jobs are affected by computerisation. As Mcloughlin and Clark state: '. . . new computing and information technologies require increased informed human intervention to interpret information and monitor the process and to be able when required to make decisions and solve problems (McLoughlin & Clark, 1994, pp. 149-150).

ADVANCED MANUFACTURING TECHNOLOGY AND THE QUALITY OF WORKING LIFE

Advanced manufacturing technology (AMT) has the capacity for informating and developing intellective skills. A related issue raised by Mcloughlin and Clark is concerned with:

- the extent to which AMT should be 'human-centred'

- whether the various work redesign techniques that have been developed in the past might enjoy a new and more successful lease of life if combined with the human-centred design of computing and information technologies.

Human-centred design principles, according to Badham (1990) typically involve:

- design and use of technology in a way which complements rather than replaces human skills

- adoption of forms of work organisation which enhance rather than constrain operator discretion and which encourage the integration of separate organisational functions

- provision of a work environment which maximises social communication and promotes healthy, safe and efficient working.

Work redesign principles concern the upskilling of various aspects of job content and focus upon:

- ways in which individual jobs can be altered to extend the range of tasks carried out and to expand the scope for workers to exercise discretion and expertise

- relationship between work design and production technology so that workgroups can be allocated the responsibility for deciding how work is to be organised and executed in particular areas, or 'production islands'.

The combination of human-centred design principles and work redesign principles may provide the optimum form of job content and work organisation which, as Buchanan (1985) argues, gives workers:

- more and faster information feedback on performance

- meaningful, interesting and challenging goals

- control over workflow

- discretion over methods of task allocation

- opportunities to develop skill and knowledge through work.

ACTIVITY 20

In small groups, discuss whether the principles of human-centred design and work redesign could be combined with AMT in manufacturing operation. Identify some possible examples.

You may have considered some of the better known experiments in work design such as the Volkswagen and Saab experiments which we mentioned in section 4. Another example you might have thought of is the Volvo plant at Kalmar, Sweden which was the first to be designed around the concept of team-based assembly and regarded as a model of what can be achieved with advanced technology and self-managing groups.

We can conclude that the principles of human-centred and work design can be effectively applied to many manufacturing contexts, thereby improving the quality of working life.

There are also research projects which point to a relatively optimistic future in this respect; two examples are:

- European Strategic Programme for Research in Information Technology (ESPRIT)

- Forecasting and Assessment of Science and Technology (FAST) programme.

The aim of both of these European projects is to design software and hardware which is geared towards the development of skills of human operators rather than their erosion or elimination.

In addition to these projects, there is ongoing research into 'human-centred' system design in Sweden, where the Swedish Centre of Working Life has been working on various projects to democratise the design of computer-based systems since the late 1970s (Scarborough & Corbett, 1992).

5.5 Impact of new technology in the office

We have argued that advanced technology in manufacturing can, in many cases, encourage the upgrading of skills, the acquisition of new ones and teamwork. There are similar trends and developments in office settings. We now consider the impact of new office technologies upon:

- word processor operators
- senior management grades
- middle management grades.

WORD PROCESSOR OPERATORS

Word processing applications are many and varied. They include:

- spreadsheets
- database enquiry systems
- electronic mail
- facsimile transmission
- management information support systems
- management decision support systems.

All levels of staff from office clerk to chief executive are potential users of information technology in the office. Unfortunately, there are some organisations where word-processing technology was introduced, often as part of a wider system of information technology, but the effects of the new technology were not particularly beneficial to, or had a neutral impact on, the operator.

An early study by Buchanan and Boddy (1982) which analysed the effects of word processing in a large marine engineering consultancy found that video typing:

- reduced task variety, meaning and contribution to the company's end product
- increased control over typing quality, skill and knowledge requirements, in some respects, and pay and promotion prospects
- reduced the overall quality of the typing service.

Buchanan and Boddy argue that the word-processing system would have been used more effectively if the work had been organised in such a way that the new technology complemented the existing skills, capabilities and knowledge of the typists . This is the same argument as for the manufacturing context. In other words, in order for the operator to derive maximum benefit from what new processing technology can potentially offer, it is important to design a human-centred office system. Successful operation of such a system depends upon:

- proper planning
- high level of technical management skills
- adequate user training
- stability to identify and solve the teething problems of new systems.

A human-centred office system will also seek to avoid many of the office automation hazards.

ACTIVITY 21

The more common office automation hazards together with some possible causes are listed below. If you were designing a human-centred office system, what ergonomic and organisational solutions would you suggest?

Hazards include:

- reproductive disorders – male infertility, abnormal pregnancy, miscarriage, still birth
- upset domestic life
- eye strain, blurred vision, flickering lids
- stiff neck and shoulders
- arm and wrist pains
- backache
- headache
- repetitive strain injury (RSI)
- stress from concentration

Possible causes are:

- repetition
- static loading
- work pace
- intense concentration
- poor posture
- inadequate desk and chair
- badly designed keyboard
- poor lighting
- radiation
- screen glare and flicker

Ergonomic solutions include:

- good lighting
- desk and chair design
- good displays
- properly designed and placed keyboards
- check posture and movement.

Organisational solutions include:

- job enlargement
- increased task variety
- multi-skilling
- more rest breaks
- planned job rotation
- exercise programmes.

A human-centred office system: the Citibank example

One example of a study of an attempt to introduce a human-centred office system is that by Matteis (1979). Matteis investigated an organisational restructuring programme in Citibank, a large American organisation.

To help the organisation cope with an increasingly diverse market, Citibank decentralised with divisions concentrating on particular customer groups. This also involved decentralising the technology from mainframe computers to mini- and micro-computers in a distributed network.

Matteis gives as an example the processing of a letter of credit. The bank switched from a 'production-centred' approach in which all letters, from whatever source, were dealt with in a common processing system, to a 'market-centred' approach. This meant that one group now handled all operations with respect to one letter, with different groups dealing with different types of customer. In addition, a detailed analysis was made of the work which had to be carried out to complete a transaction. This was used as the basis for the design of a new computer system, and the design of individual work stations.

The intention was to reorganise tasks so that each person could process the entire letter of credit transaction using the new system.

SENIOR MANAGEMENT GRADES

A study by Martin (1988) examined the potential value of management information systems to senior management as sources of information and as decision support tools. The conclusions of this research are rather pessimistic.

Martin looked at how senior managers spent their time. He found that many senior management decisions are based at least in part on judgement and partly on experience. These decisions are not entirely dependent on data and analyses from an information system.

Despite some enthusiastic individuals and some limited achievements, Martin concludes that:

- computer-based information systems have little to offer senior executives
- the nature of the top executive job prevents extensive computer use
- many recent design features make such systems even less practical.

Martin suggests that senior managers should:

- limit the 'learning time' they allocate to their systems
- spend more time with system designers to make sure they get the management information they need.

A more optimistic picture of the impact of information technology on middle management emerges as we now see.

MIDDLE MANAGEMENT GRADES

Huczynski and Buchanan (1991) argue that some middle managers can benefit from the introduction of computer-based systems. They cite a study of a business hotel in Glasgow undertaken by Buchanan and McCalman. Buchanan and McCalman (1988) show how applications of computer-based systems for handling customer reservations and billing, and for dealing with restaurant and bar orders, captured and analysed information not available to hotel management with a conventional manual system.

They argue that these developments were beneficial to managers and to decision-making, and claim that computer-based systems have five implications:

- computerised information systems encourage managers to share information previously protected in manual systems
- better, shared information increases the motivation and confidence of managers
- shared management information increases the visibility of the personal work performances of individual managers
- better information, increased confidence and increased visibility increase the pressure on managers to react rapidly and appropriately to exploit business opportunities and resolve problems
- shared information, shared confidence, shared visibility and shared pressure encourage a co-operative approach to management decision-making, reducing opportunities for power struggles and interdepartmental conflicts.

REVIEW ACTIVITY 5

The following questions will help you to review your knowledge of advanced technology and its impact upon work situations in manufacturing and office contexts:

1   What are the defining characteristics and uses of new work technology?

2   Explain Zuboff's ideas about the impact of new technology.

3   Discuss how new technology can upgrade skills and improve the quality of working life in both manufacturing and office contexts.

Summary

Our objectives in this section are to identify the characteristic features of new technology, and to argue that in many situations within manufacturing and office environments, information technology can result in skills upgrading and in improvements in the quality of working life.

Zuboff's ideas concerning the informating capabilities of new technology, together with the intellective skills that it might generate are relevant to our discussion of the effects of new technology in manufacturing and office contexts.

We should bear in mind that new technologies open up new areas of management choice for products, processes and organisational arrangements. The capabilities of a new technology are more like enabling characteristics. They do not 'determine' organisation functions or structures, but open up new opportunities while creating constraints. They encourage some forms of organisation while inhibiting others.

Unit Summary

In this unit, we have considered technology as a dynamic phenomenon which is very much related to the more general process of industrial and social change. The process of technological development has been considered by using the Blauner study to illustrate and exemplify the evolution of technology from craft technology which was predominant in pre-industrial societies to assembly-line technology which was prominent in the industrial society of the mid-twentieth century.

Within this context, we looked at the notion of Fordism and scientific management which are associated with assembly-line or mass production methods and which are in turn related to attempts by employers and managers to tighten up controls over the labour process through, amongst other things, the de-skilling of the labour force.

We then examined the ideas concerning the emergence of post-Fordism which is concerned with new methods of working and new computer-based technologies. In relation to this development, the debate about flexibility was highlighted and emphasised.

CONVERGENCE

Finally, we considered more specifically the nature and characteristics of new technologies and their up-skilling potential. To conclude this unit, and to put what we have learnt so far into perspective, it is helpful to draw attention to the notion of convergence that has preoccupied many sociologists. In the introduction to this unit, we mentioned that the so-called imperatives of technology are accompanied by major changes in the structure of work and industry, and the effects of these changes have, according to some sociologists, changed the nature of society itself.

For example, during the late 1950s and early 1960s, American sociologists argued that all societies 'converge' as they reach an advanced stage of industrialism. The term 'industrialism' is taken to mean the process of industrial change which includes, of course, technological change. One of the main proponents of the 'convergence thesis' were Clarke Kerr et al and their conclusions were published as *Industrialism* and *Industrial Man* (1962). This thesis held that industrialism in itself generates the same problems for all societies in which it occurs and that the solutions to them are necessarily similar.

These solutions impose certain changes on major social institutions and processes such as the education and occupation systems, the class and status systems, industrial relations and the family so that they become uniform. These changes produce a socially, geographically and occupationally mobile and flexible society characterised by the values of individualism and achievement. Any remaining political or cultural differences between such countries are almost irrelevant to the long-term pattern of convergence.

The convergence thesis may well be more appropriate today than in the 1960s as a result of the development of a global technological or information village assisted by optical fibre information highways. Also changes in the global political configuration such as the decline of communism and the establishment of market economies in former communist countries and the adoption of market forces within China and Vietnam support the convergence thesis.

We can conclude, therefore, that industrial and technological changes have implications far beyond the individual worker and the individual nation state. The focus is increasingly upon the global economy and the shifts and transformations within it.

References

Advisory, Conciliation and Arbitration Service (1988) *Labour flexibility in Britain: The 1987 ACAS Survey,* Occasional Paper 41, ACAS.

Atkinson, J (1988) *Flexibility, Uncertainty and Manpower,* IMS Report No. 189, Brighton: Institute of Manpower Studies.

Babbage, C (1835) *On the Economy of Machinery and Manufacturers,* London: Charles Knight.

Badham, R (1990) *Beyond One-Dimensional Automation: Human-Centred System Design in European Manufacture.* In Karwowski, W & Rahimi, M (eds), *Ergonomics of Hybrid Automated Systems II,* Amsterdam: Elsevier.

Beynon, H (1975) *Working for Ford,* Harmondsworth: Penguin.

Blauner, R (1964) *Alienation and Freedom,* Chicago: University of Chicago Press.

Braverman, H (1974) *Labor and Monopoly Capital: The Degradation of Work in the Twentieth Century,* New York: Monthly Review Press.

Bright, J R (1958) *Automation and Management,* Division of Research, Harvard Business School reprinted in Huczynski and Buchanan (1991) p. 272.

Buchanan, D A (1985) 'Using the new technology', In Forester, T, (ed) *The Information Technology Revolution,* Oxford: Blackwell.

Buchanan, D A & Boddy, D (1982) 'Advanced Technology and the Quality of Working Life; The Effects of Word Processing on Video Typists', *Journal of Occupational Psychology,* 55, (1), pp. 1-11.

Buchanan, D A & Boddy, D (1983a) 'Advanced Technology and the Quality of Working Operators', *Journal of Occupational Psychology,* 56, (2), pp. 109-19.

Buchanan, D A & Boddy, D (1983b) *Organisations in the Computer Age: Technological Imperatives and Strategic Choice,* Aldershot: Gower Publishing.

Buchanan, D A & McCalman, J (1988) 'Confidence, Visibility and Pressure: The Effects of Shared Information in Computer Aided Hotel Management', *New Technology, Work and Employment,* 3, (1), pp. 38-46.

Claydon, T (1994) 'Human Resource Management and the Labour Market', in Beardwell, I and Holden, L, *Human Resource Management: A Contemporary Perspective,* London: Pitman.

Durkheim, E (1947) *The Division of Labour in Society,* New York: The Free Press

Forester, T (1989) ed. *Computers in the Human Context: Information Technology, Productivity and People,* Oxford: Blackwell.

Friedman, A (1977) *Industry and Labour: Class Struggle at Work and Monopoly Capitalism,* London: Macmillan.

Friedman, A & Cornford, D (1989) *Computer Systems Development: History, Organisation and Implementation,* Chichester: Wiley.

Galbraith, J K (1971) *The New Industrial State,* Harmondsworth: Penguin.

Geary, J F (1992) 'Employment, Flexibility and Human Resource Management: the Case of Three American Electronics Plants', *Work, Employment and Society,* 6, pp. 251-270.

Gilbert *et al.*

Griffiths, D (1988) 'When Man can't Keep up with the Machines of War', *Business Week,* 12 September, p. 28.

Hounshell, D A (1984) *From the American System to Mass Production 1800-1932: The Development of Manufacturing Technology in the United States,* Baltimore MD: John Hopkins University Press.

Huczyinski, A & Buchanan, D A (1991) *Organisational Behaviour: An Introductory Text,* Englewood Cliffs, NJ: Prentice Hall.

Hunter, L C & MacInnes, J (1991) 'Employers' Labour Use Strategies – Case Studies', *Employment Department Research Paper* 87. London: Employment Department.

Hunter, L C & MacInnes, J (1992) 'Employers and Labour Flexibility: The Evidence From Case Studies', *Employment Gazette,* June, pp. 307-315.

Kerr, C, Dunlop, J T, Harbison, F H & Mayers, C A (1962) *Industrialism and Industrial Man,* London: Heinemann.

Lamb, H & Perry, S (1987) 'Big Mac is Watching You', *New Society,* 9 October.

Linhart, R (1981) *The Assembly Line,* London: John Calder.

Martin, C (1988) *Computers and Senior Managers: Top Management's Response to Interactive Computing,* Manchester: NCC Publications.

Marx, K (1963) 'Alienated Labour', in T Bottomore (ed), *Karl Marx: Early Writings,* Harmondsworth: Penguin.

Matteis, R J (1979) 'The New Back Office Focuses on Customer Service', *Harvard Business Review,* 57, March-April, pp. 146-159.

McLoughlin, I & Clark, J (1994) *Technological Change at Work*, Milton Keynes: Open University Press.

Meyr, S (1981) *The Five Dollar Day: Labour Management and Social Control in the Ford Motor Company, 1908–1921*, New York: State University of New York Press.

Millward, N Steveur, M, Smart, D. and Hawes, W R (1992) *Workplace Industrial Relations in Transition*, Aldershot: Dartmouth.

Millward, N (1994) *The New Industrial Relations*, London: Policy Studies Institute.

Pendleton, A (1991) 'The Barriers to Flexibility: Flexible Rostering on The Railways', *Work, Employment and Society*, 5, pp. 241-257.

Piore, M (1986) 'Perspectives on Labour Market Flexibility', *Industrial Relations*, 45, (2).

Piore, M & Sabel, C (1984) *The Second Industrial Divide: Possibilities for Prosperity*, New York: Basic Books.

Pollert, A (1988) 'Dismantling Flexibility', *Capital and Class*, 34.

Sabel, C (1982) *Work and Politics; The Division of Labour in Industry*, Cambridge: Cambridge University Press.

Salaman, G (1986) *Working*, London: Tavistock.

Scarborough, H & Corbett, J M (1992) *Technology and Organisation: Power, Meaning and Design*, London: Routledge.

Smith, A (1910) *The Wealth of Nations*, London: Dent.

Taylor, F W (1947) *Scientific Management*, New York: Harper and Row.

Thompson, P (1990) *The Nature of Work*, London: Macmillan.

US Department of Health, Education and Welfare (1973) *Work in America.*

Winner, L (1977) *Autonomous Technology: Technics-Out-Of-Control as a Theme in Political Thought*, Cambridge MA; MIT Press.

Wood, S (1982) (ed), *The Degradation of Work*, London: Hutchinson.

Wood, S (1989) ed, *The Transformation of Work?* London: Unwin Hyman.

Woodward, J (1970) ed, *Industrial Organisation; Behaviour and Control*, Oxford: Oxford University Press.

Zuboff, S (1988) *In The Age Of The Smart Machine*, New York: Heinemann.

Recommended Reading

You are advised to read the following material:

SECTIONS 1 AND 2
Thompson, P (1990) *The Nature of Work,* London: Macmillan, Chapters 1, 2, and 3

SECTION 3
Beynon, H (1975) *Working for Ford,* Harmondsworth: Penguin, Chapter 1 and Conclusion.

Blauner, R (1964) *Alienation and Freedom,* Chicago: University of Chicago Press, Chapter 1.

Thompson, P (1990) *The Nature of Work,* London: Macmillan.

SECTION 4
Wood, S (1989) ed, *The Transformation of Work?* London: Unwin Hyman, Chapter 1

SECTION 5
McLoughlin, I & Clark, J (1994) *Technological Change at Work,* Milton Keynes: Open University Press, Chapters 1, 2, and 5.

Preece, D (1995) *Organisations and Technical Change,* Chapters 3 and 4. London: Routledge.

Answers to Review Activities

Review Activity 1

Listed below are a number of points which you may have made. The list is not exhaustive and you may have come up with other related ideas.

- The transition from pre-industrial to industrial society as noted by Durkheim was marked by the decline in cottage industries and the rise of the factory system.

- The factory system resulted in a concentration of labour and it then became possible to organise (design, subdivide) their work to achieve a division of labour which allowed more productive use of power, machinery and space to generate increased output.

- Generation of increased output as a result of the division of labour required the development of management and organisation; divided work must be designed, co-ordinated and integrated.

- Once work was divided, each contributor to the process became interdependent with every other and the flow of work required a disciplined and reliable workforce.

- Two major objectives of the new activity of management within the factory system were:

  (i) the achievement of control and discipline

  (ii) the development of management structures.

- Taylorism arose as a direct consequence of these objectives (or needs), and with its underlying principles of job fragmentation, tight job boundaries and the separation of mental and manual labour, became the dominant ideal for job design in Britain and the USA.

Review Activity 2

The answers to these questions are contained in the section. You will have noted that particularly from the employee's point of view, there are few advantages to the Fordist production system. You should also have noticed that there is a basic conflict of interest between the shop floor workers and their managers, particularly when you take into consideration the senior manager's quote.

Review Activity 3

Before work restructuring at the Volkswagen and Saab-Scania plants took place, the perspectives of Blauner and Braverman would have some validity. Blauner would argue that prior to the changes, both plants had an assembly-line production technology and this would give rise to high levels of alienation. As a technological determinist, Blauner would also argue that assembly-line technology based on Fordist principles would inevitably give way to automated production systems which would be less alienating.

Blauner's analysis would be less convincing after work restructuring. He was not familiar with the ideas of job design. The 'new' situation at the two plants was still based on mass-production technology and yet the new technology and working arrangements meant that workers in teams would be less alienated and more motivated.

With regard to the contribution of Braverman and the control and de-skilling debate we examined, we would accept the idea that motives and interests on the part of employers guided the choice of technology which resulted in greater controls over, and the de-skilling of, the workforce under assembly-line conditions. This, as you know, contrasts with the determinist view of Blauner. However, as a result of work restructuring at both plants, the trend towards de-skilling and greater management control was reversed, and so the Braverman analysis becomes less valid under these conditions.

So why did the experiment at Volkswagen, and later at Saab, come to an end? The answer is that while these experiments yielded benefits to the workforce and management alike, in the longer term, the search for greater productivity, and profitability, meant that a reversion to assembly-line production would, despite the inherent problems associated with such technology, produce more predictable results.

Review Activity 4

1   Sub-section 4.1 deals with the characteristics of post-Fordism and flexible specialisation.

2   Sub-sections 4.2-4.3 deal with a number of changes such as specialisation and technology, production and organisation structures, training needs and so on.

3   Sub-section 4.3 deals with the Atkinson model in terms of employment patterns and the two different types of flexibility.

4   Refer back to sub-section 4.4.

5   The two examples of Burton and Ferodo provide evidence of drawbacks and limitations to the flexible firm theory. Sub-section 4.6 deals with limits to flexibility in terms of costs, training and conflict issues.

Review Activity 5

Question 1 focuses upon the content of sub-sections 5.1 and 5.2. Question 2 is concerned with the theoretical framework of this section and deals with the informating capabilities of new technology. Sub-section 5.4 introduces the idea of intellective skills. Information concerning question 3 is contained in sub-sections 5.4 and 5.5.

UNIT 3

CONTINUITY AND CHANGE

Introduction

In this unit, we consider change and transition and the reasons for this process of change, particularly as it affects the organisations and institutions of our society. If we were somehow transported in time back to the mid-nineteenth century, we know that many things would be unfamiliar, strange or unusual. While nineteenth-century Britain would be unmistakably 'British', many things such as transport, patterns of behaviour and other structures and processes would be virtually unrecognisable.

Similarly, if we were projected into the twenty-third century, many of the current institutions, structures and processes with which we are familiar would have changed beyond all recognition or have ceased to exist altogether.

Try this experiment for yourselves! Get a few members of your family, or your friends, or your study group together for the following activity.

ACTIVITY 1

You are probably familiar with the following institutions or structures of our society: democracy, technology, monarchy, work organisations and trade unions. Discuss, within your group, how these institutions or structures might be different, either (i) one hundred years from now, or (ii) in the mid-nineteenth century.

This kind of exercise also raises the questions of how changes will take place and what factors will influence their nature. In this unit, we are concerned with answers to these questions.

We look at change in general terms, the role of individual action or agency and structure in bringing about change and the development of social movements. We also examine the transition from industrial to post-industrial society and from modernism to post-modernism.

Objectives

When you have completed this unit, you should be able to understand why change occurs in a society and to illustrate the process of change by examples from trade unions and work organisations. You should also be able to appreciate the major change processes affecting organisations and society as well as being able to identify and explain 'post-industrialism' and 'post-modernism' as central concepts of change.

By the end of this unit, you will be able to:

- define change.
- identify significant features of two theories of social change – social evolutionism and historical materialism.
- discuss and give examples of the influence upon social change of the physical environment, political organisation and cultural factors.
- describe the origins and implications of the 'agency' and 'structure' approaches of social change.
- indicate the limitations of both 'agency' and 'structure' approaches to social change and illustrate how the two can be seen as complementary.
- explain what we mean by a social movement and give examples of different types.
- discuss the features, development and dynamics of social movements and their relation to change with reference to the work of Smelser and Touraine.
- identify the features and dynamics of post-industrialism and discuss what evidence there is of change towards post-industrialism in current British society.
- identify some common features shown by post-Fordist manufacturing and marketing developments, and the cultural ideas and philosophy of post-modernism.

SECTION 1
Change

Introduction

In this section, we examine what **change** is. A definition of change is provided and two important theories of change – **social evolutionism and historical materialism** – are outlined. We end with an overview of the main influences upon change.

Human beings have existed for about half a million years. Agriculture is only about 12 000 years old. Civilisations date back to no more than six thousand years or so. If we think of the entire span of human existence as a day, agriculture would have been invented at 11.56 p.m., and civilisations would have come into being at 11.57, while the development of modern societies would start at 11.59.30! Yet more change has probably occurred in the last thirty seconds of this 'human day' than in the whole of the time leading up to it.

The pace of change in the modern era is easily demonstrated by reference to rates of technological development. Let us consider the following statement by Landes: 'Modern technology produces not only more, faster; it turns out objects that could not have been produced under any circumstances by the craft methods of yesterday. The best Indian hand spinner could not turn out yarn so fine and regular as that of the mule; all forges in eighteenth-century Christendom could not have produced steel sheets so large, smooth and homogenous as those of a modern strip mill. Most important, modern technology has created things that could scarcely have been conceived in the pre-industrial era; the camera, the motor car, the aeroplane, the whole array of electronic devices from the radio to the high-speed computer, the nuclear power plant, and so on almost ad infinitum . . . The result has been an enormous increase in the output and variety of goods and services, and this alone has changed man's way of life more than anything since the discovery of fire: the Englishman [the Englishwoman] of 1750 was closer in material things to Caesar's legionnaires than to his own great-grandchildren.' (Landes, 1969, p. 5)

ACTIVITY 2

Landes' statement about the pace of change and what we have read has given us a good idea of what change actually is. Define change in your own words.

Your definition of change may vary from those of your colleagues. In sub-section 1.1, we look at a more detailed definition.

1.1 Defining change

The Greek philosopher, Heroclitus, pointed out that a person cannot step into the same river twice. On the second occasion, the river is different, since water has flowed along it and the person has changed in subtle ways too. While this observation is in a sense correct, we do of course normally want to say that it is the same river and the same person stepping into it on two occasions. There is sufficient continuity in the shape or form of the river, and in the physique and personality of the person with wet feet to say that each remains the 'same' throughout the changes that occur.

Identifying significant change involves showing how far there are alterations in the underlying structure of an object or situation over a period of time. In the case of human societies, to decide how far, and in what ways, a system is in a process of change, we have to show to what degree there is any modification of basic institutions during a specific period.

All accounts of change also involve showing what remains stable, as a baseline against which to measure alterations. Even in today's rapidly moving world, there are continuities with the long-distant past. Major religious systems, for example, like Christianity or Islam, retain their ties with ideas and practices initiated 2000 years ago. Yet most institutions in modern societies clearly change much more rapidly than those of the traditional world.

1.2 Theories of social change

Two general approaches have been more influential than any others in attempts to understand the general mechanisms of change through human history. The first approach is called **social evolutionism,** and the second is called **historical materialism**.

EVOLUTIONARY THEORIES

If we compare different types of human society in history, it is clear that there is a movement towards increasing complexity. Hunting and gathering societies found at the earliest stage of human development are relatively simple in structure compared with the agricultural societies which emerged at a later period. Industrialised societies are more complex than any that have existed before and involve many separate institutions and organisations.

The development of increasing complexity has often been analysed using the concept of **differentiation**. As societies become more complex, areas of social life that were once mingled become clearly differentiated and separate from each other.

One of the evolutionary theories most influential today was put forward by Talcott Parsons (1964, 1966). Parsons suggests that social evolution is an extension of biological evolution. Both types of evolution can be understood in terms of what Parsons calls evolutionary universals. These are any types of development which occur on more than one occasion in different conditions, and have great survival value.

Vision is an example of an evolutionary universal in the natural world; it emerged not just in one part of the animal kingdom, but developed independently in several species. The ability to see allows for a much greater range of co-ordinated responses to the environment than is possible for unsighted organisms, and hence has great adaptive value. Vision is necessary to all animals at higher stages of biological evolution.

ACTIVITY 3

Can you think of any other evolutionary universals in human culture?

Communication is fundamental in all human culture, and language is the basis of communication. **Language** is thus the first and most significant evolutionary universal for social evolution; there is no known human society that does not possess a language. Three other evolutionary universals found even in the earliest forms of society are **religion, kinship,** and **technology**. These four universals concern such essential aspects of any human society that no process of social evolution could proceed without them.

Parsons claims that social evolution can be analysed as a process of progressive differentiation of social institutions as societies move from the simple to the more complex. We can identify four levels of evolution that characterise societies, and these are:

- Societies characterised by constitutive symbolism. These are the earliest forms of society where the symbols are largely religious in character and which permeate all aspects of social life, as, for example, the aboriginal societies of Australia. These types of society are also known as **hunter-gatherer.**

- The next level of evolution is the **advanced primitive society**. These societies are based more on hierarchy and develop a definite productive system, involving agricultural production and settled places of residence.

- Further up the scale we find what Parsons calls **intermediate societies**. These are what most other writers have termed civilisations or traditional states such as ancient Egypt, Rome or China, and are associated with the emergence of writing and literacy. Religion undergoes further elaboration; political leadership develops in the shape of government administrations headed by aristocratic rulers. Several new evolutionary universals come into being in all societies at this stage including bureaucratic organisation, monetary exchange and a specialised system of law.

- **Industrialised societies** stand at the highest point in Parson's evolutionary scheme. They are far more internally differentiated than societies of the intermediate type. The economic and the political systems become clearly separated from one another, and both are distinct from the legal system as well as from religion. The development of mass democracy provides a means of involving the whole population within the political order. Industrialised societies have much higher territorial unity than earlier types, being distinguished by well-defined borders. The superior survival value generated by the institutions of industrialised societies is well demonstrated by the spread of industrialism worldwide, leading to the more-or-less complete disappearance of the earlier types of society.

ACTIVITY 4

From the paragraph about industrialised societies, identify at least two evolutionary universals and briefly explain their importance for that type of society.

One evolutionary universal for industrial society is the system of mass democracy. The representative system of democracy that exists in Britain and other western societies serves important functions which include:

- representation of interests of individuals by their parliamentary representatives

- periodic change of government as a result of general elections which enable the main political parties to assume power and pass legislation which reflects party policy.

Another evolutionary universal is the existence of a distinct economic system. For Britain and other western societies, capitalism is the economic driving force. The central importance of market forces and how they can influence consumer choice and organise research, innovatory and production processes is the main economic characteristic of these societies.

HISTORICAL MATERIALISM

Our second interpretation of change is based on the work of Karl Marx (1971). This interpretation has something in common with evolutionary theories in that both regard the major patterns of change as being brought about by human interaction with the material environment. We can summarise this theory of change in the following points:

- According to Marx, every society rests on an economic base or **infrastructure**, changes in which tend to govern alterations in the **superstructure** – political, legal and cultural institutions.

- Social change can be understood through the ways in which, in developing more sophisticated systems of production, human beings progressively come to control the material world and subordinate it to their purposes.

● Marx refers to this process as one of the expansion of the **forces of production,** in other words, the level of economic advancement a society has reached.

● According to Marx, social change does not occur only as a process of slow development, but in the shape of revolutionary transformations. Periods of gradual alteration in the forces of production and other institutions alternate with phases of more dramatic revolutionary change. This has often been referred to as a **dialectical interpretation of change.** The most significant changes come about through tensions, clashes and struggles.

● Changes that occur in the forces of production set up tensions in other institutions in the superstructure; the more acute these tensions become, the more there is a pressure towards an overall transformation of society. Struggles between classes become more and more acute, ultimately producing either disintegration of existing institutions or the transition to a new type of social order through a process of political revolution.

● As an illustration of this theory, we can take the changes involved in the replacement of feudalism by industrial capitalism in European history. The feudal economic system was based on small-scale agricultural production, the two principal classes being aristocrats and serfs. According to Marx, as trade and technology (forces of production) developed, major changes began to occur in the infrastructure. These led to a new set of economic relations centred on capitalist manufacture and industry in the towns and cities. A series of tensions developed between the old, land-based, agricultural economic order and the newly emerging capitalist manufacturing system. The more acute these tensions became, the greater were the strains on other institutions. Conflict between aristocrats and the newly developing capitalist class ultimately led to a process of revolution, signalling the consolidation of a new type of society. In other words, capitalism had come to replace feudalism.

ACTIVITY 5

Select two revolutionary changes from those listed and discuss briefly the extent to which Marx's ideas concerning historical materialism can explain the changes:

● French revolution

● Russian revolution

● 'rock' revolution (music)

● information revolution.

The French and Russian revolutions can be examined using the historical materialism perspective. Both revolutions had the following aspects in common:

- well-established monarchies prior to revolution representing the 'established order'
- both revolutions resulted in the end of monarchy; the overthrow of the Romanov dynasty in Russia and the execution of Louis XVI in France
- both revolutions resulted in the establishment of leadership purporting to represent the 'masses'.

Using the interpretation of historical materialism, these revolutions resulted in a transfer of control of the superstructure of society from monarchy to the masses as a result of conflicts between opposing forces (the dialectical process).

The 'rock' and information revolutions, on the other hand, cannot be analysed in the same way. In these examples, the term 'revolution' is used loosely to denote major changes that have evolved from earlier forms. Using the example of the rock revolution, we can see that rock music, which takes many forms, has its origins in American blues music and is a development of that tradition. In other words, rock music is part of a process of evolution of modern popular musical form. and as such can be considered as evolutionary rather than revolutionary change. Indeed, rock music can be regarded almost as an evolutionary universal! We can say the same about the information revolution.

We now go on to look at the influences on change.

1.3 Influences on change

We can summarise the main influences on social change under three headings:

- **physical environment**
- **political organisation**
- **cultural factors.**

PHYSICAL ENVIRONMENT

As evolutionists have emphasised, the physical environment often has an effect on the development of human organisation. Obviously, peoples in polar regions necessarily develop different habits and practices from those living in sub-tropical areas. Less extreme physical conditions also affect society. The native population of Australia never stopped being hunters and gatherers since the continent contained hardly any indigenous plants suitable for regular cultivation, or animals which could be domesticated to develop pastoral production.

Yet the direct influence of the environment on social change is less than might be supposed. The evolutionists' emphasis on adaptation to the environment is less illuminating than Marx's stress on the importance of productive relations in influencing social development. As we saw above, and in our previous discussions of the social changes and changes in the relations of production of the industrial revolution, there is no doubt that the types of production system strongly influence the level and nature of change which goes on in a society even if not to the extent that Marx suggests.

POLITICAL ORGANISATION

A second factor strongly influencing social change is the mode of political organisation. In hunting and gathering societies, this influence is minimal, but in all other types of society the existence of distinct political agencies – chiefs, lords, kings and governments – strongly affects the course of development a society takes. For example, rulers or monarchs can initiate processes of territorial expansion which increase the economic wealth of those societies they control. On the other hand, a monarch who tries and fails to take over other lands may bring a society to economic disruption or ruin.

Quite different types of political order may exist in societies which have similar production systems. For example, even though we suggested earlier that mass democracy is an evolutionary universal, some industrial societies have experienced fascism while still remaining essentially capitalist in nature, while others with similar production systems have experienced centralised state socialism. Military strength, however, is an important aspect of political influences over social change. Military power played a fundamental part in establishing most traditional states and influenced their subsequent survival or expansion in an equally basic way.

CULTURAL FACTORS

Cultural factors that influence social change include the effects of religion, styles of thought and consciousness. However, religion may be either a conservative or innovative force in social life. Many forms of religious belief and practice have acted as a brake on change, emphasising the need to adhere to traditional beliefs and values. Yet, religious convictions frequently play a mobilising role in pressures for social change.

Other cultural influences include the nature of communications systems, for example, the invention of writing, and the influence of leadership.

ACTIVITY 6

Give one example of change that might be linked to each of the three factors – physical, political, cultural.

Physical: societies cut off from others by mountain ranges, impassable jungles or deserts often remain relatively unchanged over a period of time, for example, Tibet.

Political: a good example of a society which developed as a result of political organisation and military strength is the rise of the Roman Empire.

Cultural: the invention of writing allowed records to be kept, making possible increased control of material resources and development of large-scale organisations.

1.4 Change in the recent past

We noted earlier the enormous changes that have occurred in the recent past. How do we explain why the last two hundred years, the **period of modernity,** has seen such a tremendous acceleration in the speed of social change? While this is a very complex issue, it is not difficult to identify some of the factors involved which again fall broadly into the economic, political and cultural spheres.

ECONOMIC INFLUENCES

The most far-reaching influence here is the impact of **industrial capitalism.** Capitalism differs in a fundamental way from the production systems existing before it because it involves:

- constant expansion of production

- ever-increasing accumulation of wealth.

Capitalist development promotes the constant revision of the technology of production, a process into which science is increasingly drawn. The rate of technological innovation fostered in modern industry is vastly greater than in any previous type of economic order as the examples of the motor industry and computer technology suggest.

Looking at the car industry, we see that almost every year the major manufacturers bring out new models or new varieties of existing models. The increased importance of the car in our lives has resulted in the development of an entire motorway system to serve it. This in turn has brought about major changes in travel patterns.

The development of industrial capitalism thus fundamentally altered people's ways of life. Ours is the first type of society in which the large majority of the population do not either live in small rural communities, or gain their livelihood from the land. The changes associated with urbanism and the development of new work environments have affected most other institutions as well as having been affected by them.

POLITICAL INFLUENCES

The second major type of influence on change during the period of modernity consists of novel political developments such as the struggle between nations to expand their power, develop their wealth and triumph militarily over their competitors.

Governments now play an important role in stimulating, and sometimes retarding, rates of economic growth, and in all industrial societies there is a high level of state intervention in production, the government being the largest employer.

Military power and the industrialisation of war have had far-reaching consequences. The military strength of western nations allowed them to influence all parts of the world and provided an essential backing to the **globalisation** of western life-styles. For example, the economic and military domination of the USA has allowed the global expansion of McDonalds, the fast food chain, so that if you consume a McDonalds burger in Moscow, you are also consuming part of American global culture.

CULTURAL INFLUENCES

Two other primary influences throughout the period of modernity have been:

- development of science
- secularisation of thought.

Each influence has contributed to the critical and innovative character of the modern outlook. We no longer assume that customs or habits are acceptable merely because they have the authority of tradition. On the contrary, our modes of life in modern societies are increasingly required to have a 'rational' basis. They have to be constantly defended, and if necessary changed, according to whether or not they can be justified on the basis of persuasive arguments and evidence.

For instance, we could make the rather bold claim that a design for building a hospital would not be based mainly upon previous tastes (irrational), but upon its ability to serve the purposes to which a hospital is put – effectively caring for the sick. Note that there are cost implications here.

It is not merely alterations in how we think that have influenced processes of change in the modern world; ideals have also changed. Ideals of:

- self-betterment
- freedom
- equality, and
- democratic participation

are very largely creations of modernity. These ideals have served to mobilise far-reaching processes of social and political change, including revolutions and social movements. Although they were initially developed in the west, such ideals have become globalised, promoting change in most regions of the world.

REVIEW ACTIVITY 1

Suggested time: 45 minutes.

1 Among the important factors in modern social change that we have discussed are the expansion of industrial capitalism, the development of centralised nation-states, the industrialisation of war and the emergence of science and 'rational' or critical modes of thought.

   Taking the example of the modern work organisation, in a group, if possible, discuss how the above factors have influenced its development and functions.

2 Identify and discuss how modern social change might be seen as illustrating features of social evolutionism and/or historical materialism.

Summary

In this section, you have identified what social change is and have looked at two important theories of social change – the evolutionary theory and historical materialism. You have identified a number of evolutionary universals found in industrial societies and discussed some revolutionary changes in the light of historical materialist ideas. We then considered the important influences upon change with particular reference to physical, political and cultural factors. Finally, we looked at change within industrial society from economic, political and cultural perspectives.

SECTION 2

Action versus Structure

Introduction

We have looked at change and reasons for change. This is crucial to our understanding of how modern society and its institutions and structures work. However, this is not the whole story, because within all modern societies, there is an ongoing debate about how these changes take place. To appreciate the nature of this debate, we can ask two questions:

- Do individuals, we can call them actors or agents, by themselves cause change, and if so, to what extent?

- Or, is it the interplay between individuals and the larger structures within our society, such as political, economic and cultural structures and organisations, that result in change?

In this section, we briefly address these issues.

A major theme pursued by Durkheim, one of the 'founders' of sociology, and subsequently by many other sociologists is that the societies of which we are members exert social constraint over our actions. Durkheim argued that society has primacy over the individual person (Durkheim, 1982). Society is far more than the sum of individual acts; when we analyse social structure, we are studying characteristics that have a 'firmness' or 'solidity' comparable to structures in the material environment.

For example, think of a person standing in a room with several doors. The structure of the room constrains the range of his or her possible activities. The siting of the walls and doors, for example, defines the routes of exit or entry. Social structure, according to Durkheim constrains our activities in a parallel way, setting the limits to what we can do as individuals. It is 'external' to us just as the walls in the room are.

This point of view is expressed by Durkheim in a famous statement: 'When I perform my duties as a brother, a husband or a citizen and carry out the commitments I have entered into, I fulfil obligations which are defined in law and custom and which are external to myself and my actions . . . Similarly, the believer has discovered from birth, ready fashioned, the beliefs and practices of his religious life; if they existed before he did, it follows that they exist outside him. The system of signs that I employ to express my thoughts, the monetary system I use to pay my debts, the credit instruments I utilise in my commercial relationships, the practices I follow in my profession, etc. – all function independently of the use I make of them. Considering in turn each member of society, these remarks could be made for each single one of them.' (Durkheim, 1982, pp. 50-1)

ACTIVITY 7

Can you think of any possible criticisms of Durkheim's view that social structures are external to us as individuals and constrain us in the same way that 'solid structures' in the material environment might?

Although the type of view Durkheim expresses has many adherents, it has also met with sharp criticism from advocates that stress the influence of individual action on society.

- What is 'society', the critics ask, if it is not the composite of many individual actions?

- If we study a group, we do not see a collective entity, only individuals interacting with one another in various ways.

- 'Society' is only many individuals behaving in regular ways in relation to each other. According to the critics, as human beings, we have reasons for what we do, and we inhabit a social world permeated by cultural meanings. Social phenomena are precisely not like 'things', but depend on the symbolic meanings with which we invest what we do. We are not the creatures of society but its creators.

2.1 Basic premises

It is unlikely that this controversy about action and structure will ever be fully resolved. It has existed since modern thinkers first started systematically to try to explain human behaviour. Moreover, it is not a debate confined to sociology only but concerns all areas of the social sciences. There are, however, a number of points that can usefully be made before we look at it in more detail later.

- The differences between the views can be exaggerated, and while both cannot be wholly right, we can fairly easily see connections between them. Durkheim's view is in some respects valid. Social institutions do precede the existence of any given individual; it is also evident that they exert constraint over us.

  Consider Giddens' example of the monetary system: 'I did not invent the monetary system which exists in Britain. Nor do I have a choice about whether I want to use it or not, if I wish to have the goods and services which money can buy. The system of money, like all other established institutions, does exist independently of any individual member of society, and constrains that individual's activities.'(Giddens, 1989)

- On the other hand, it is obviously mistaken to suppose that society is 'external' to us in the same way that the physical world is, for the physical world would go on existing whether or not any human beings were alive, whereas it would be quite absurd to say this of society. While society is external to each individual taken singly, by definition it cannot be external to all individuals taken together.

● As human beings, we do make choices, and we do not simply respond passively to events around us. Giddens (1989) argues that the way forward in bridging the gap between 'structural' and 'action' approaches is to recognise that we actively make and remake social structure during the course of our everyday activities. For example, the fact that you use the monetary system contributes in a minor, yet necessary, way to the very existence of that system. If everyone, or even the majority of people, at some point decided to avoid using money, the monetary system would dissolve.

ACTIVITY 8

Choose one example from your own experience to illustrate the bridging of the gap between structure and action approaches in the same way that Giddens does with his example of the monetary system. Indicate how your example might be interpreted by structure and action approaches respectively and how they might be reconciled through the approach taken by Giddens.

A topical example in the UK is the National Lottery. The National Lottery exists independently of us as individual members of society. We, as individuals, can choose whether or not to participate in it by purchasing 'scratch cards' or lottery tickets, or not. This is the 'action' aspect.

In practice, our choice may not only be the result of our own particular views of the lottery, but also the result of other influences or structures that lie outside our individual domain.

If we decide to buy a ticket, this may be due to:

● our own individual preference (action)

● influence of family and peer groups (action)

● pressures of advertising (structure).

If we decide not to buy a ticket, this may be due to:

● individual preference (action)

● to avoid becoming a gambler (action)

● pressures of institutions such as the church or anti-gambling lobby (structure).

As with the money example, we can see that reasons for participating or avoiding the lottery are derived from both structure and action factors. The important point remains that if everyone or the majority of people stopped participating in the National Lottery, then the National Lottery would cease to exist.

We have considered the basic premises underlying the action and structure debate. We now examine these aspects in more detail.

2.2 Agency or structure: the essential question

We begin by looking in more detail at the fundamental question implied in our introduction to the action and structure debate. Can individuals or groups of individuals determine their own goals or are those goals determined by the underlying forces of society as a whole? The answer we give to this question is controversial and not everyone will agree with it.

Here are some other, more concrete, ways of posing the essential issue:

- Was the second world war the outcome of Hitler's deliberate intentions, or was it the consequence of underlying social forces?

- Would the Russian revolution have taken place without Lenin's personality and skills?

- Would the morale of the British people during the second world war have been sustained without Winston Churchill?

There are two very different ways in which these questions can be answered. One stresses the importance of the individual or group agency. The second world war, for example, could be explained as the outcome of Hitler's agency, of his consciously intended actions. A structural view, however, would draw attention to the background and underlying social factors shaping and constraining the conflict between nations.

These two very different views can be seen to be derived from two different images of society and its relations which we now examine.

2.3 The first image of society

The origins of the agency view lie in the seventeenth century with the work of Thomas Hobbes who wrote a book called *Leviathan* in which he challenged the established structures of medieval society. Hobbes, whose work provoked the opposition of supporters of the church, offered an explanation of society based on consent and contract. He thought of society as something which individuals, in a sense, 'contract into'. It is not imposed on them against their will, and their membership of society isn't just the outcome of tradition. Rather, society is the outcome of the individuals' desires to live and to interact with one another in the pursuit of their own personal goals.

Our purpose in looking at Hobbes' work has been to establish that there is a very strong tradition in the social sciences which stresses the view that individuals and the action or agency of individuals are the basis of the social order, and that it is society or the state that exists to promote and defend individual ends, rights and liberties. The individual has the freedom, or free will, to determine his actions, and society in this sense is not constraining, but enabling.

We can summarise the action or agency view in the following:

● For individualists, the way society is organised is taken to be the outcome of individual will and choice.

● For individualists, the way society is organised is the outcome of the interactions and negotiations between many individuals each seeking to pursue their own goals.

This is the **first image of society** which is embedded in much social theory, and which is reinforced by the fact that we actually do live in a society in which individual interests and rights are highly valued and in which the commercial and contractual relations of the market are widespread.

ACTIVITY 9

Think of an example of this first image of society in operation.

You might have suggested any one from many examples of this first image of society in operation. Let us look at two:

Example one
This example of the **agency view** of society is derived from classical economics. This view of the economy and what happens in it derives from the view that the economy is the outcome of individuals choosing how to maximise their utility, hence the economy is the result of many individuals making decisions about, say, what to buy. If we all decided to buy bicycles instead of cars, what would happen to the car industry? Or if most people decided to go to France to buy cheap French beer what would happen to the off-licence and supermarket trade in beer?

Example two
This example is taken from political theory and is called the **liberal democratic view** of the state. In this view, the individual is perceived to be relatively free and independent. Individuals clearly perceive their own interests and devise ways and means of satisfying them. Interests are satisfied through the mechanisms of democratic politics which link people to the government and make government responsive to the needs of individuals.

In the heyday of Thatcherism, when Margaret Thatcher was the British Prime Minister, there was, as you may know, the media phenomenon of the 'Essex man'. This phenomenon arose as a result of the Conservative election victories of the 1980s and coincided with brief periods of relative prosperity for certain sections of the population. It was believed that voters in the south of the country changed their voting behaviour because they, as individuals, believed that the Conservatives could bring prosperity to them. Voters in Essex and elsewhere clearly perceived their interests in relation to how the Conservative government could respond to their interests and their conscious actions in pursuit of those interests were shaping political and social factors.

ACTIVITY 10

Just how convincing is this first image of society; does it convince you? Are the economy, politics and the state, and society generally, just the outcome of individual choices?

Compare your ideas with the sub-section that follows.

2.4 The second image of society

It is difficult to make much sense of society without understanding the way it defines our actions, and without understanding the structures and processes within which each individual action is located. If this is the case, then it is easy to see that there are going to be important respects in which society constrains and determines our actions. What we do, and the choices we make must be understood as, in some measure, the outcome of society. This is the **structural** approach.

So what does this structural approach offer us that the individualist, action or agency, approach doesn't? We have already seen that one of the main contributors to the structure debate was Durkheim (1982).

Durkheim, above all, expressed the importance of the social dimension of experience and the respects in which it presses upon us. In contrast to Hobbes, Durkheim conceived individual and group actions as the outcome of social influences, pressures and constraints rather than society as the outcome of individual and group actions. He thought of society as a complex of external and constraining forces which together both defined and determined individual and group action.

We can now summarise the first and second images of society, the action or individualist and the structural approaches, in the following simple statement. For individualists (action or agency), society is the outcome of individual actions and choices. For structuralists, individual actions and choices are the outcome of society.

STRUCTURAL INFLUENCES AT WORK IN SOCIETY

We look now at two examples of the second image of society at work, but first, complete the following activity in which you look at some of the influences on an organisation in a society.

ACTIVITY 11

What influences an organisation to produce what it does?

Your list should include some of the following influences:

- profit motive
- market influences and conditions
- production system: technology
- structure of the organisation: tall, flat, bureaucratic, etc.

You may not have come across the terms 'tall' or 'flat' in relation to organisation structures. Remember the organisation chart that you met in Unit 2. The chart will show, amongst other things, all the levels of responsibility from chief executive down to routine supervision. An organisation with a tall structure has many levels of responsibility and authority, while the organisation with a flat structure has relatively few levels of authority and responsibility and has a much flatter shape.

Think about the influences identified here, and about the points made in the Durkheim quotation you read earlier in sub-section 2.1, in relation to the following examples. The first is an account of events in the late 1970s when the British National Health Service was unusually short of kidney machines.

Example 1: The British economy and Lucas Aerospace

At that time, Lucas Aerospace, a division of Lucas Industries, put forward a plan to close a number of its plants around the country. When the workers found out about the plan, they were naturally concerned and a group of senior convenors of Lucas Aerospace developed a strategy which, they believed would keep the plants open by producing socially useful products such as kidney machines. However, when this plan was put to the senior management of Lucas, it was eventually rejected for the following reasons:

- The product mix was unsuitable: technology etc could not be adapted for such products.

- Apart from the proposed kidney machines, there was no assured market for any of the other products.

- As there was no assured market, profit levels would be squeezed, and even for kidney machines, profit margins would be tight.

- Manufacturing components for aircraft lay within the company's expertise which did not extend to other products.

- The whole company structure was geared towards the aerospace industry, and could not be changed.

Therefore, kidney machines could not be produced, because the structural constraints of the economic system, both within and outside the organisation made it impossible for the firm to produce them and continue to survive in the economic market.

Example 2: The British economy and the steel industry

During the 1960s, the then nationalised British Steel Corporation made a strategic decision to concentrate all sheet steel production in a few large integrated steel plants. This seemed to make economic sense at the time because most steel production took place in a large number of relatively small plants. Plans went ahead for the construction of four large plants in Scotland, south Wales and the north-east of England

It was thought that with this degree of modernisation, Britain's steel industry could successfully compete in terms of price and quality with those industries in mainland Europe, and more importantly, with those in Japan and the Far East, taking advantage of economies of scale and new production processes.

However, global recession during the 1970s meant that there was a global surplus of sheet steel and prices were driven down. The problem was compounded for BSC owing to long delays in building the new integrated plants. As the new plants were eventually completed, it was found that because of recession and the global glut, there was not enough demand in the market for these plants to operate economically. The new plants were operating well below capacity, and it was felt that BSC had committed a lot of financial and other resources to no avail.

When BSC was privatised during the 1980s, important decisions had to be made if the new company – now British Steel – was to be viable. As part of the new strategy, 50% of the workforce were to be made redundant, many traditional steel plants were to be closed (Corby and Consett, for example), and a number of the new integrated plants were to be mothballed.

ACTIVITY 12

1 In a group, if possible, identify the structural constraints which led to British Steel making some unpalatable decisions.

2 Can you see any aspects in either of the two examples which suggest that people are not just passive creatures of social structures – despite the structural constraints you may have identified in responding to question 1.

3 Can you think of other examples where individuals have changed social, political and economic structures? You can comment on how they did it through, say, working together, creating structures to counterbalance other structures they were fighting, and what their goals, aspirations and beliefs were.

1 The structural constraints you may have identified include:
   - unfavourable market conditions
   - global competition
   - profit motive
   - outdated production processes.

2 You may have chosen the first example of Lucas where the senior convenors developed a strategy for keeping the plants open. This illustrates the point that within structural constraints, there is the potential for individuals to influence events even if they are not successful.

3 A good example here is the victory of Greenpeace over Shell in June 1995. The following quotes are taken from *The Guardian,* 21 June, 1995: 'Greenpeace last night claimed its most sensational victory in 25 years of environmental campaigning after the international petrol giant Shell was forced to abandon its decision to dump an oil rig in the Atlantic Ocean. Greenpeace took on one of the world's largest oil companies and the government, and forced a fundamental policy change with a few weeks' direct action. Greenpeace's campaign was last night described by British environmental activists as a triumph for the growing grassroots direct action movement which, they said is becoming a major policy force.'

Greenpeace is an environmental direct action lobby which enables individuals to work together to fight established interests and structures. Members of Greenpeace also share individual aspirations and beliefs about the environment which have an important influence on their interaction with and impact upon society.

2.5 Summary propositions

From our discussions so far, we can now make a number of summary propositions as follows:

- The individualist, agency or action view holds that society is the outcome of the interaction between an aggregate of individuals each pursuing their own goals. The emphasis is placed on the power of individuals to choose for themselves and to determine their own goals. The primacy of individual choice and action is stressed. Our examples suggest that, in fact, there are considerable limitations on these.

- Structural views, on the other hand, stress the respects in which individual action is the outcome of underlying social processes, structures and relations. They stress the aspect of constraint as opposed to choice. And they stress the way in which we are born into a society which already exists and which is resistant to the will of any particular individual within it. In addition, they draw attention to the ways in which individual behaviour requires some external structuring in order for organised action to take place and in order to make possible the intermeshing of the actions of a large number of individuals.

- While we have presented these two images as contrasting ones and in competition with each other, it is important to understand that they are not necessarily opposed. Do you think that the course of your life is largely snaped by factors beyond your control, or do you think that you really can determine your own goals and perhaps, in association with others, have some influence on how society is organised? Or is it a bit of both? We would suggest that it is, in fact, a bit of both, which leads on to the next point.

- We can't understand social relations, structures and processes without reference to the values and beliefs of those involved. The extreme 'structural' perspective implies the view that an extreme 'passive' conception of social actors as just the outcome of social processes is not adequate since it does not take account of how the values, beliefs and aspirations of individuals and organisations can change the social relations, structures and processes of a society.

- If social actors aren't just passive objects thrown up by social forces, an account of social change will have to involve reference to the aspirations, goals, and struggles of those involved, although, of course, what they do is heavily constrained by circumstances.

REVIEW ACTIVITY 2

Suggested time: 30 minutes.

1 Explain and discuss the differences between structure and action and agency as explanations of social change.

2 Examine the limitations of the agency and structure approaches to social change.

Summary

We have discussed the origins of the agency and structure views of social change and looked at their contrasting implications. In discussing examples through each perspectives, we have noted limitations to each approach. It is possible to see them as complementary as we actively make and remake the social structures that affect our lives. You have identified examples of both structural constraints and individual agency at work and can now explore the relationship between action and structure and their influence upon social change.

SECTION 3

Social Movements: an Introduction

Introduction

We have looked at social change and the role played by both the individual as actor and the structures and processes which both influence and are influenced by the individual. Our understanding of these aspects is essential before we consider the important functions in promoting social change. These have become known as **social movements**.

In this section, we begin with a definition and classification of social movements and then go on to consider two theories of social movements – those of Smelser and Touraine. We conclude with the specific example of British trade unions.

3.1 Definition

A social movement may be defined as a collective attempt to further a common interest, or secure a common goal, through collective action outside the sphere of established institutions.

This definition needs to be wide-ranging because of the variations between different types of movement. Examples of social movements can range from the relatively small, such as the temperance movement, to the relatively large, such as the trade union movement. The following points help to clarify the definition.

- Many social movements are very small, numbering perhaps only a few dozen members; others might include thousands or even millions of people.

- Some movements carry on their activities within the laws of society while others operate as illegal or underground groups.

- Often laws are altered partly or wholly as a result of the action of social movements. For example, groups of workers that called their members out on strike used to be engaging in illegal activity. Eventually the laws were amended, making the strike a permissible tactic of industrial conflict.

- The dividing lines between social movements and formal organisations are sometimes blurred, because movements which become well-established usually take on bureaucratic characteristics. Social movements may thus become formal organisations, while, less frequently, organisations may devolve into social movements. The Salvation Army, for example, began as a social movement, but has now taken on most of the characteristics of a more permanent organisation. An example of the opposite process would be the case of a political party which is banned, and forced to go underground, perhaps becoming a guerrilla movement.

- Similarly, it is not always easy to separate social movements from **interest groups** – associations set up to influence policy-makers in ways that will favour their members. An example of an interest group would be the Automobile Association, which lobbies Parliament to defend the interests of motorists. But was the Campaign for Nuclear Disarmament which regularly lobbied Parliament about matters to do with nuclear weapons, an interest group or part of a more wide -ranging mass movement? There is no clear-cut answer in such cases. Social movements often actively promote their causes through organised channels while also engaging in more unorthodox forms of activity. A Mexican terrorist group actually uses the Internet as a means of communication!

> ## ACTIVITY 13
>
> 1 Define social movements in your own words.
>
> 2 Identify three social movements and briefly state what their aims are.

1   Refer back to the definition we provided earlier. The essential points to include are common interest or aims, collectivity of action and that the group is not part of established institutions.

2   Social movements do vary in size and composition and the distinction between a social movement and an interest group is often blurred. Don't worry about this now. Possible examples include:

   ● Campaign for Real Ale which acts as a lobby to promote the spread of cask-conditioned ale

   ● Greenpeace set up to campaign for environmental issues

   ● women's rights movements which tackle discrimination against women.

3.2 Classifying social movements

Many different ways of classifying social movements have been proposed. Perhaps the neatest and most comprehensive classification is that developed by Aberle (1966), who distinguishes four types of movement as follows:

1   **Transformative movements** aim at far-reaching change in the society of which they are a part. The changes their members anticipate are cataclysmic, all-embracing, and often violent. Examples are revolutionary movements, or some radical religious movements.

2   **Reformative movements** have more limited objectives, aspiring to alter only some aspects of the existing social order. They concern themselves with specific kinds of inequality or injustice. Examples include the Women's Christian Temperance Union and anti-abortion groups.

Note, transformative and reformative movements are concerned mainly with securing changes in society. Aberle's other two types are each mainly aimed at changing the habits or outlook of individuals.

3   **Redemptive movements** seek to rescue people from ways of life seen as corrupting. Many religious movements belong in this category as they concentrate on personal salvation. Examples are Pentecostal sects which believe that individuals' spiritual development is the true indication of their worth.

4   Finally, there are the somewhat clumsily entitled **alterative movements** which aim at securing partial change in individuals. They do not seek to achieve a complete alteration in people's habits, but are concerned with changing certain specific traits. Alcoholics Anonymous is an example.

ACTIVITY 14

By referring to our four-fold classification of social movements, give four further examples of social movements and identify which type each is.

By referring to our classification, you should not have too much difficulty in coming up with examples. You may have thought of Gamblers Anonymous as an example of an alterative movement, or Outrage as an example of a reformative movement.

3.3 Theories of social movements

Two theoretical perspectives are particularly important in helping us to understand the development and dynamics of social movements and their relation to social change. These are the approaches of Neil Smelser and Alain Touraine. Smelser is broadly associated with a structural approach (Smelser, 1963) and Touraine with an agency view of change (Touraine, 1974).

NEIL SMELSER: SIX CONDITIONS FOR SOCIAL MOVEMENTS

Condition one: Structural conduciveness

This concerns the general social conditions promoting or inhibiting the formation of social movements of different types. For example, in Smelser's view, the American socio-political system leaves open certain avenues of mobilisation because of the relative absence of state regulation in those areas. Thus there is no state sponsored religion, for example, people are free to choose the religious groups to which they wish to be affiliated, if any. Such conditions are favourable for the development of some sorts of social movements; they do not, as such, bring them into being.

Condition two: Structural strain

This concerns tensions which produce conflicting interests within societies. Uncertainties, anxieties, ambiguities or direct clashes of goals, are expressions of this tension. Sources of strain may be general or specific to particular situations. For example, sustained inequalities between ethnic groups give rise to overall tensions; these may become focused in the shape of specific conflicts when, say, blacks begin to move into a previously all-white area.

Condition three: Spread of generalised beliefs

Social movements do not develop simply as responses to vaguely felt anxieties or hostilities. They are shaped by the influence of definite ideologies which crystallise grievances and suggest courses of action that might be pursued to remedy them. Revolutionary movements, for instance, are based on ideas about why injustice occurs and how it can be alleviated by political struggle.

Condition four: Precipitating factors

These are events or incidents that actually trigger direct action by those who become involved in the movement. The incident when Rosa Parks refused to move to the part of the bus reserved for blacks in Montgomery, Alabama, in 1955, helped to spark off the American civil rights movement.

Condition five: Co-ordinated group

The above four conditions might occasionally lead to street disturbances or outbreaks of violence, but such incidents do not lead to the development of social movements unless a co-ordinated group mobilises to act. Leadership and some kind of means of regular communication between participants, together with a supply of funding and material resources, are necessary for a social movement to exist.

Condition six: Operation of social control

Finally, the manner in which a social movement develops is strongly influenced by the operation of social control. The governing authorities may respond to the challenge by intervening in the conditions of conduciveness and strain which stimulated the emergence of the movement. For instance, in a situation of ethnic tension steps might be taken to reduce some of the worst aspects of ethnic inequality that had initially generated resentment and conflict.

ACTIVITY 15

Smelser's model is useful for analysing sequences in the development of social movements, and collective action in general. According to him, we can understand each stage in the sequence as 'adding value' to the overall outcome, each stage being a condition for the occurrence of the subsequent ones. However, critics have pointed to some problems with his theory. What might these be?

You might have suggested the following:

- A social movement may become strong without any particular precipitating incidents – in the sense of public confrontations – being involved in its growth.

- Conversely, a series of incidents might bring home the need to establish a movement to change the circumstances which gave rise to them.

- A movement may open up social strains, rather than just developing as a response to them. For example, the women's movement has actively sought to identify and combat gender inequalities where before these had been unquestioned.

- Smelser's theory treats all social movements as 'responses' to situations, rather than allowing that their members might spontaneously organise to achieve desired social changes. In this respect, his ideas contrast with the approach developed by Alain Touraine.

ALAIN TOURAINE: HISTORICITY

Touraine's theory of social movements can be summarised in the following points (Touraine, 1974).

1   Touraine emphasises that social movements reflect the stress placed in modern societies on activism in the achievement of goals. Modern societies are marked by what Touraine calls **historicity**. This is an outlook in which knowledge of social processes is used to reshape the social conditions of our existence. For example, identifying the nature and distribution of inequalities in schooling was one of the factors which promoted the rise of the civil rights movement in the USA.

2   Touraine has been less interested in the background conditions that give rise to social movements than in understanding the objectives which social movements pursue. Social movements do not just come about as irrational responses to social divisions or injustices; they develop views and strategies about how these can be overcome.

3   Social movements, Touraine suggests, cannot be understood as isolated forms of association. They develop in deliberate antagonism with other groups – usually with established organisations, but sometimes with rival movements.

4   All social movements have interests or aims which they are for and against. In Touraine's view, other theories of social movements, including that of Smelser, have given insufficient consideration to how their objectives are shaped by their encounters with others who hold divergent ideas – as well as the ways in which they themselves influence the outlooks and action of their opponents.

For example, the objectives and outlook of the women's movement have been shaped in opposition to the male-dominated institutions which it seeks to alter, and have then shifted in relation to its successes and failures. They have also influenced the perspectives of men. These changed perspectives in turn have stimulated a re-orientation in the women's movement – and so the process continues.

5   Touraine argues that social movements should be studied in the context of what he calls **fields of action**. The term refers to the connections between a social movement and the forces of influences against which it is ranged. The process of mutual 'negotiation' involved in a field of action may lead to a change in the circumstances the movement sought to contest, but also to a merging of the perspectives held by each side. Either way, the movement may evaporate – or become institutionalised as a permanent organisation.

For example, trade unions became formal organisations when the right to strike and modes of bargaining acceptable to both workers and employers were achieved. These were forged out of earlier processes of confrontation involving considerable violence on both sides. Where there are continuing sources of conflict, as in relationships between employers and employees, new movements still tend sporadically to re-emerge.

ACTIVITY 16

Read the following brief scenario of the green movement in Britain. Then identify features of Touraine's analysis relevant to that movement.

The green movement in Britain

There are a large number of groups which together have put green arguments on the political agenda. They range from small nature conservation groups like the Marine Conservation Group, or groups for bats and dolphins through to the Royal Society for the Protection of Birds and the National Trust committed to heritage as well as wildlife conservation. There are also amenity and landscape groups and the well-known campaigning bodies such as Friends of the Earth and Greenpeace.

Greens take our current ecological problems very seriously, arguing that we must take immediate steps to decrease our consumption of energy and raw materials, and to reduce drastically our polluting behaviour. In their view, we must lower our expectation of material goods and learn to enjoy simpler sustainable lives. We must begin to decentralise our societies and learn to live predominantly with the resources of our local region.

We can look at some of Touraine's points noted above and relate them to the green movement.

1   Touraine's first point regarding historicity is relevant. The greens have looked at the extent to which pollution and general degradation of the environment have continued apace during the twentieth century and have decided to do something about it.

2   Green groups have clear strategies for overcoming environmental problems (Touraine's point 2).

3   Touraine's point 3 suggests that green groups develop in deliberate antagonism to established organisations such as governments, protesting about nuclear testing, and specific organisations such as ICI, protesting about polluting the Mersey.

4   Touraine's point 5 is important. Our previous example of Greenpeace and Shell where Shell backed down has led to a merging of perspectives between Shell and Greenpeace as to the best method of disposal.

Touraine's approach lacks the clarity of Smelser's, although it is important to stress that social movements develop through a process of mutual shaping and redefinition alongside opposing groups and organisations. Such an analysis can be applied to movements concerned primarily with individual change even though Touraine says little about them.

For example, Alcoholics Anonymous is a movement based on medical findings about the effects of alcohol on people's health and social activities. The movement has been shaped by its opposition to advertising designed to encourage alcohol consumption, and its attempt to confront the pressures alcoholics face in a society in which drinking is seen in a tolerant light.

3.4 Structural and social action approaches

As you will probably already have realised from our discussion of the work of Smelser and Touraine, the study of social movements and their relation to change is approached differently by those who emphasise a structural view of change and those emphasising the importance of individual agency in social change.

However, just as we saw that there is a complementary nature of their different approaches to social change in general, so we can see that the questions upon which they focus in regard to social movements are also complementary.

In its study of social movements, the structural approach addresses two questions:

- What broad changes do social movements reflect?
- What broad changes might they bring about?

Behind these questions is a view of social movements as responses to and agents of fundamental social change. The focus of attention is on the nature of their response (especially the movements' ideologies) and possible outcomes (the stakes involved).

In contrast, social action approaches address the following questions:

- What are the reasons for, and barriers to, our involvement in collective action?
- What must a social movement do to secure that involvement and pursue its aims?

The complementary nature of these issues is obvious in the questions themselves. In Review activity 3 you look at the trades unions as an example of a social movement and its relation to change, and you will find a number of these issues need to be examined.

3.5 Some conclusions

Other significant points to note in finishing our discussion of social movements and change concern:

- importance of their role as agents of change and the opportunities for change they help to create
- nature of their role and the different ways they achieve their effects.

We should consider the following points:

Social movements achieve their effects in a number of ways:

- Firstly, they are a source of cultural innovation. Here, their effects are far-reaching. From dress style, through linguistic innovation, to their impact on gender relations, social movements have provided a central generator of new values and lifestyles. This has an indirect effect on political institutions such as parties because it changes the cultural environment in which they operate.
- Secondly, social movements have a more direct impact upon politics and other decision-making institutions through the absorption of their demands. One prime effect of social movements here is to challenge and move the boundary between state and civil or private society. For example, in the case of feminism, the contested borders between public and private, evident in changes in everyday life at home and at work, were beginning to find a political language in the late 1960s. Wages for housework is an example of altering boundaries between private and public.

The course and outcome of social movements is determined not exclusively by their ideological content, that is the 'view' of change expressed by the movement and to which its members subscribe, but also by their organisational features and the resources which they come to command.

Some social movement analysts have argued that social movements have a definite career or life-cycle. For instance, the career of a social movement may go through a series of stages starting with high levels of mobilisation around specific issues and ending, potentially, at least, with the incorporation of the movement and its issues into mainstream decision-making institutions, particularly those of the state. The relationship between the trade union movement and the Labour party is an example.

Some social movement analysts have also argued that social movements present the state, political parties, and other social institutions with an opportunity to change or 'modernise'. For example, they may alter their policy base and thereby broaden their appeal in order to widen their electoral base. Do you think that this is happening to the Labour party in Britain in the 1990s? The incorporation of green issues into the programmes of social democratic parties in Europe demonstrates both of these aspects. It can be viewed as an attempt to move away from a traditional 'working class' policy base and thereby appeal to potential supporters within 'the new middle class'.

REVIEW ACTIVITY 3

Suggested time: 60 minutes.

This review activity concerns British trade unions. The example is in two parts; answer the questions at the end of each part.

Industrial conflict between workers and employers in the first half of the nineteenth century was frequently only semi-organised. Where there was confrontation, workers would quite often leave their places of employment and form crowds in the streets. They would make their grievances known through their unruly behaviour or by engaging in acts of violence against the authorities. Workers in some parts of France in the late nineteenth century retained the practice of threatening disliked employers with hanging!

Part One: The development of unions in Britain

Use of the strike, which is now associated with organised bargaining between workers and management, developed slowly and sporadically. The Combination Acts passed in Britain in 1799 and 1800 made the meeting of organised workers' groups illegal, and banned popular demonstrations. The acts were repealed some 20 years later, when it became apparent that they stimulated more public disturbances than they quelled.

Trade unionism soon became a mass movement, that is, a social movement, and union activity was legalised in the last quarter of the nineteenth century, after which membership increased to cover 60% of male manual workers in Britain by 1920. The British trade union movement is co-ordinated by a central body founded in 1868, the Trades Union Congress (TUC), which developed strong links with the Labour party.

The development of the union movement has varied considerably between countries, as has the influence of the unions over the workforce, employers and government. In Britain and the USA, unions have been established for longer than in most European societies. The German unions, for example, were largely destroyed by the Nazis in the 1930s, and set up afresh after the second world war. The development of the French union movement did not, in fact, occur until the 1930s, when freedom to organise unions and negotiate collective labour contracts was formally recognised.

Less than 50% of the labour force in Britain today are union members, compared to under 20% in the USA. Most European countries are below the British figure in terms of membership levels; but Belgium and Denmark have rates of around 65%, while in Sweden, membership is as high as 90%. The decline in trade union membership in all these countries is of interest in the context of this example.

Sweden provides a good example of a country in which the labour movement plays a major and direct part in influencing government policies. In that country, there is continuous consultation between union representatives, employers and government at national level.

The existence of unions

Although their levels of membership, and the extent of their power, varies widely, union organisations exist in all western countries. All such countries, and now even in Eastern Europe, legally recognise the right of workers to strike in pursuit of economic objectives. Why have unions become a basic feature of western societies? Why does union-management conflict seem to be a more or less ever-present feature of industrial settings?

Some have proposed that unions are effectively a version of medieval guilds – associations of people working in the same trade or craft – re-assembled in the context of modern industry. Frank Tannenbaum, for example, has suggested that unions are associations built on the shared outlook and experience of those working in similar jobs (Tannenbaum, 1974). This interpretation might help us to understand why unions often emerged first amongst craft workers, but it does not explain why they have been so consistently associated with wage-bargaining and industrial conflict. For a more satisfactory explanation, we must look to the fact that unions developed to protect the material interests of workers in industrial settings in which they hold very little formal power.

In the early development of modern industry, workers in most countries were without political rights, and had little influence over the conditions of work in which they found themselves. Unions developed in the first instance as a means of redressing the imbalance of power between workers and employers. Whereas workers had little power as individuals, through collective organisation their influence was considerably increased. An employer can do without the labour of any particular worker, but not without that of all or most of the workers in a factory or plant. Unions were originally mainly 'defensive' organisations, providing the means whereby workers could counter the overwhelming power over their lives which the employer enjoyed.

Workers now have rights in the political sphere, and there are established forms of negotiation with employers, by means of which economic benefits can be pressed for and grievances can be expressed. Yet union influence, both at the level of the local plant and nationally, still remains primarily **veto power**. In other words, using the resources at their disposal, including the right to strike, unions can normally only **block** policies or initiatives of employers, they cannot help formulate them in the first place. There are various partial exceptions to this, as in cases where unions and employers negotiate periodic contracts covering conditions of work. There is an increasing tendency for these to include 'no-strike' agreements for the duration of the contract. Internationally, union officials may have a significant role in formulating economic policies, especially in Scandinavia.

Yet unions in some countries have faced a constant battering from some employers and governments. The rights of industrial negotiation that workers hold have had to be won in the face of much bitter opposition, and once achieved have frequently been subjected to further attacks. Employers in some industries have consistently refused to employ union members or allow company union branches to be established. The employers' resistance to the unions has been especially pronounced in the USA – one factor in the low incidence of union membership in the country. For instance, in the 1920s and 1930s, under the slogan of the 'American plan' the National Association of Manufacturers fought against some of the key bargaining rights claimed by unions. 'Yellow-dog' contracts, under which employees agree not to join a union, were promoted, together with more positive schemes, like profit-sharing, designed to show workers that rewards could be achieved without unions.

In groups, if possible, use the example of trade unions to illustrate the formation and functions of social movements. Is the trade union movement really a social movement? Refer to the ideas of Smelser and Touraine.

Part Two: Trade unions: recent developments

Unions themselves have altered over the years. Some have grown very large, and as permanent organisations, they have become bureaucratised. This means that they have undergone a transition from social movements to stable organisations.

Unions are staffed by full-time officials, who may themselves have little direct experience of the conditions under which their members work. The activities and views of union leaders can thus become quite distant from those of the members they represent. Shop-floor groups sometimes find themselves in conflict with the strategies of their own unions.

Most unions have not been successful in recruiting a high level of women workers; although some have initiated campaigns to increase their female membership, many have in the past actively discouraged women from joining.

In current times, unions in western countries are facing a threat from three connected sets of changes:

- ● Recession in world economic activity, associated with high levels of unemployment which weakens the unions' bargaining position.

- Decline of the older manufacturing industries, in which the union presence has traditionally been strong.

- Increasing intensity of international competition particularly from Far Eastern countries, where wages are often lower than in the west.

- Under Mrs Thatcher, the Conservative government in Britain followed policies designed to give fuller play to market forces. The Conservatives believed that the unions were too powerful, and introduced a range of measures designed to reduce the scope of their activities. The unions, it was argued, drive wages up to levels where British products become uncompetitive in world markets. Union power prevented firms from laying off workers when they needed to do so in order to maximise efficiency. Consultations between government ministers and union leaders became much less frequent than they had under the preceding Labour administrations.

- Employment Acts passed in 1980 and 1982 introduced new limitations on the legal rights of unions. The official definition of a 'trade union dispute' was tightened up, to include such activities as picketing the suppliers of an employer. The Trade Union Act of 1984 required that unions hold a ballot of members before undertaking industrial action, as well as introducing other restrictions on union rights. The civil servants employed at the government communications centre (GCHQ) were deprived of their right to belong to a union, a move which was justified by arguing that industrial action at GCHQ could represent a threat to national security. These measures have certainly had considerable effects on the union movement, nationally and locally. Subsequent measures and legislation up to and including 1993 have continued to reduce drastically union influence.

Given recent developments concerning trade unions, would you say that trade unions still represent a social movement? Justify your answer.

Summary

In this section, we provided an overview and definition of social movements. We then attempted to classify social movements into four types. You defined a social movement and identified examples of four types of movement using Aberle's classification. You then examined Smelser and Touraine's theories of social movements, the former representing a structural approach, and the latter an agency approach to change. Having noted some criticisms of Smelser's views and identified some features of Touraine's analysis in a contemporary example of a social movement, we noted the different but complementary questions posed by the two approaches about social movements. Finally, we reviewed other important effects and features of social movements and at factors which influence how these effects came about, how successful movements are, how they develop and so on.

SECTION 4

From Industrialism to Post-Industrialism

Introduction

We have looked at social change, its effects and causes, and theories about how it occurs. We also considered social movements as manifestations of such change, using the example of trade unions to illustrate this.

The period we concentrated upon was the period of industrialisation which can be traced back to the eighteenth century. So far our analysis has been confined to this period, the period characterised by modern society, or industrial society, a period increasingly being called **modernism**.

However, most commentators would agree that something significant is happening now. We are currently in a period of rapid technological change which is also witnessing some fundamental work transformations.

In this section, we attempt to identify and analyse what is happening in general terms, and we also focus upon technology, work and organisations.

4.1 Directions of change

There are a number of sound reasons for stressing the importance of identifying the direction of change.

Firstly, those who argue that modern industrial economies have undergone major changes in recent times are not necessarily suggesting that a total transformation of the economy has occurred. The changes so far are incomplete or uneven. At best, we can distinguish the lines of direction – the direction in which an economy faces and is moving towards.

Secondly, it should be possible to detect changes which are interconnected, to see how what happens in one part of the economy has affected the rest of the economy. For example, look at some of the recent trends in the UK economy (Units 2 and 5): the growth of service jobs and the decline in manufacturing employment; the introduction of new technologies based on the microchip; the shift in the structure and composition of the workforce from a male, full-time workforce towards a female part-time workforce; a change in consumption practices, with a greater emphasis placed upon choice and specialisation; and so on. Which changes, if any, are interconnected? And if they are interconnected, what kind of economy is taking shape?

Thirdly, a radical economic shift implies that a different set of dynamics is driving an economy. So identifying a shift of this nature is not simply a question of tracing the connections between a variety of changes; it also involves an identification of which elements are key to the direction of change. For example, in our discussion of the contours of post-industrialisation which follows, the movement beyond industrialism is not only marked by a sectoral shift in an economy from manufacturing to services; but it is also defined by the generation of knowledge and information which act as dynamics of change. As we see, the transformation of office work by information-processing technology is regarded by some as equivalent to the radical shift in industrial society from craft-based, factory production to a system of mass manufacture.

ACTIVITY 17

Why is it important to identify the direction of change in a modern industrial economy?

The important point concerns the interconnected nature of the economy and the fact that change in one sector brings about change in another. We can look at the basic key factors to see their influence on the direction of change.

4.2 From industrialism to post-industrialism and beyond

Industrialism has a long-standing imagery attached to it, one that conjures up heavy machinery, smoke-stacked factories and large workforces. The dominant role of machinery in the manufacture of goods, driven first by coal and steam and then by oil and electricity, gives a more precise focus to this industrial imagery.

With the rise of post-industrialism, a new kind of dynamic is said to have displaced the centrality of manufacturing technologies and the making of things. This we have referred to as the generation of knowledge and the control of information, a less tangible form of economic power organised around the 'clean' technologies of information and microelectronics (Units 2 and 5).

In common with such phenomena as rationalisation and bureaucratisation, post-industrialism is seen to cut across capitalist economies, radically re-shaping the social structure and patterns of work (Units 1 and 4). Here, we explore the context in which such claims have been advanced, and the different emphases that these claims have been given by writers on post-industrialism.

POST-INDUSTRIAL POSSIBILITIES

The idea that we may be moving towards a post-industrial society first took hold in the US in the 1960s against a background of rising prosperity and increased automation at the workplace. The image of post-industrialism was given a certain currency by a popular belief that an age of economic plenty was just around the corner and a general expectation that technology would solve the problem of mind-numbing jobs.

Commentators from across the political spectrum in the US spoke about the emergence of a new kind of society, although the clearest statement of what society might look like is attributed to Daniel Bell. In *The Coming of Post-Industrial Society,* published in 1973, he outlined the nature of the transition that industrial societies had embarked upon.

BELL'S VIEW OF POST-INDUSTRIALISM

Bell adopted a model of development which identifies three successive phases of economic progress:

Phase 1: is dominated by agriculture
Phase 2: is dominated by manufacturing
Phase 3: is dominated by services

In this scenario, historical progress involves a march through these three sectors. The movement refers to historical shifts in the bulk of the workforce, with the majority moving first from agriculture to manufacturing, and then on to the service sector. Today, for example, the USA, Japan and all the major European economies have more than half their workforce in the service sector.

According to Bell, the general direction of economic change within the western economies is therefore clearly towards a service economy. He also argues that each successive economic phase is organised around what he calls **axial principles**. Bell refers here to the mechanisms or dynamics that give shape to an economy. The axial principles are its driving force.

ACTIVITY 18

What can you identify as the axial principles or driving forces of Bell's Phase 2 and Phase 3 economies?

In an industrial society, the driving forces are seen as production and profit, the rational pursuit of economic growth through the application of energy and machinery. In contrast, the dynamic forces of post-industrial society are taken to be those of knowledge and information. In this view, it is the generation of knowledge and the processing of information that stimulate economic growth. They act as a source of innovation in the organisation and management of the economy and also take the form of a final product. Alongside the new technologies that are transforming and automating goods production we find a different product – information.

There is a wide range of changes in the social structure that Bell points to as a consequence of this new economic dynamic, of which three aspects are particularly significant (Bell, 1976). These changes relate to:

● kinds of work people do in society

● its occupational structure

● control of vital resources in the economy.

ACTIVITY 19

What sort of changes would you expect to see in each of these aspects of a society moving into a post-industrial economy?

You probably identified many changes and we now look at some of the most important ones.

The first aspect concerns a shift in the kinds of work that people do.

● Work is transformed, as knowledge leads to a fall in the number of manual, manufacturing jobs.

● At the same time, the growth of the service sector is represented as a source of non-manual work which involves at least some degree of creativity and sociability. Instead of working on things, people work with other people to deliver a service, which for some provides a more rewarding and interesting form of work.

The second, related aspect concerns the change in the occupational structure as manual jobs give way to white-collar and professional occupations. Old skills requiring strength and physical dexterity have given way to new forms of 'think' work.

Finally, Bell's emphasis upon knowledge and information as the key resources of a post-industrial society alert him to the significance of those who actually control these resources, the knowledge elites, as he calls them. The entrepreneurs who held sway in industrial society are giving way under a post-industrial ethos to the new technicalities in the universities, government institutions and economic enterprises.

Moreover, as intellectual work becomes more specialised, Bell sees the emergence of new hierarchies of technical elites alongside the increased professionalisation of work, and a shift towards the bureaucratisation of 'think' work within the advanced western economies.

TOURAINE'S VIEW OF POST-INDUSTRIALISM

The emergence of a post-industrial society was not something that was hailed only in the USA. In France, in the 1960s, against the backdrop of a radical student movement, Alain Touraine in *The Post-Industrial Society* (1971) spoke about a move from one kind of society to another.

Although less explicit than Bell about the economic characteristics of the new society, he also gave central place to the disposal of knowledge and the control of information, and stressed the importance of technology in what he termed the **programmed society**. Like Bell, he too identified the agents of change with the control of knowledge and called them, among other terms, a **technocracy**. The following points summarise Touraine's view:

- Central to Touraine's analysis of post-industrialism is the formation of a new social divide between, on the one hand, technocrats and bureaucrats, and, on the other, a range of social groupings, including workers as well as students and consumers.

- The principal opposition between social classes does not stem from the ownership and control of private property but from access to information and its uses. To speak of a dominant class in this context is thus to refer to those who have power over the livelihood and lifestyle of social groups within and beyond the sphere of economic production.

- This view represents a shift away from the more conventional Marxist views of social conflict held at that time, which located class tensions at the point of production, in the factory or workplace.

- The lines of protest may now take a variety of forms which have little connection to industry or particular material needs, and thus generate new social movements that are quite distinct from the older forms of class conflict. In the 1960s, the student movement and the women's movement were among the best known examples and, today, it is probably the environmental movement which is taken to represent the move beyond class politics.

POST-INDUSTRIALISM

Apart from the differences of emphasis among post-industrial writers, there is considerable agreement over the idea of post-industrialism and the economic direction in which it faces. The general thesis attracted much criticism in the 1970s, partly from those who mistook Bell to be saying that post-industrialism heralded the demise of capitalism as a competitive economic system, but also because the advanced economies had begun to experience a more sustained downturn in the pattern of post-war economic growth.

Nonetheless, the term **post-industrial** proved to be quite resilient and slipped into popular usage in a largely uncritical manner, until it resurfaced in the 1980s in the midst of a new, but related, set of debates.

ACTIVITY 20

Look again at the views of Bell and Touraine on post-industrialism. In a small group, if possible, discuss whether British society can now be described as 'post-industrial'. Identify specific features of British society, either from what you have read and also from your own experience, to support your discussion.

According to Bell, all western societies are at Phase 3 where the economy is dominated by services. The axial principles of Phase 3 societies are the generation of knowledge and the processing of information. Phase 3 societies are also known as 'post-industrial' societies. These societies are undergoing transformations in work, in the occupational structure and in the nature of control of key resources.

Touraine, like Bell, emphasises the shift from one type of society, the industrial, to another, the post-industrial. For Touraine, the 'post-industrial' society is characterised by the growing dominance of knowledge and information driven by technology. The post-industrial society means the formation of a new social divide based on technocrats and bureaucrats and shifts away from old class conflicts.

British society can most certainly be described as 'post-industrial' according to the analyses of both Touraine and Bell, and you may have identified the following characteristic features:

- decline of traditional manufacturing (shipbuilding, heavy engineering, steel industry)
- growth in the service sector (retailing, financial and information services)
- growing importance of information technology industries and services
- changes in patterns of working (more part-time work, more women employees, particularly in the service sectors).

4.3 Contributions of Castells and Gorz

Both Manuel Castells and Andre Gorz are post-industrial theorists and build upon the work of Bell and Touraine, but in different ways which we identify now.

CASTELLS: THE AGE OF INFORMATION

Castells' *The Informational City* (1989) analyses the rise of the information society and we can make two important points here.

Firstly, Castells argues that knowledge is used to generate new knowledge which itself acts as a catalyst for further economic development. In other words, because information is both a raw material, (a resource to be worked upon), and the outcome of the process of production, (a commodity in its own right), it is regarded as a central means of improving economic performance. It intensifies the process of economic innovation, and can be used to transform a wide range of economic activities – as a technological process or as a product embodied in a variety of manufactured goods and services.

For example, the new information technologies, according to Castells have:

● enhanced productivity by the introduction of microelectronics-based machines that transform the production process

● made possible the decentralisation of production while maintaining management control over various organisational activities

● enabled management to automate those processes using high cost and low skilled labour.

Secondly, one of the more interesting changes identified by Castells is that the new technologies have also enabled firms, especially the large multi-nationals, to operate in new ways, two examples are:

● The first is by using the combined advances in communication technologies, systems of management and technologies of production to operate in more 'footloose' fashion while retaining their links with markets and production complexes. The term 'footloose' as used here describes operations such as switching production easily to centres in order to take advantage of cheaper labour, better resources, state subsidies and tax breaks.

● The second example is related and concerns the growth of multiple networks between corporations. These networks enable firms to develop products jointly or to serve specific markets, and thus represent a different economic strategy from the establishment of multi-national 'empires'. For example, recent co-operation between Ford and Volkswagen has led to the joint development of an identical people carrier car, the Ford Galaxy and the Volkswagen Sharan. Joint airline ventures are another example.

These examples concern power, especially in relation to the kinds of labour employed by these large corporations. In relation to the workforce, Castells identifies:

● move towards the core-periphery model of the labour market where organisations increasingly employ two types of labour – part-time, relatively unskilled 'peripheral' workers with little security and a core of full-time, skilled workers relatively secure in their jobs

- concentration of 'information power' among a knowledge elite in the corporations

- automation of low-skilled jobs, especially among the unionised workforce in manufacturing.

ACTIVITY 21

What aspects of Castells' work do you see relating to the post-industrial themes we looked at earlier in the section?

Overall, many of the trends that Castells identifies do accord with earlier post-industrial themes. The focus upon the activities of multi-national corporations is different, but the priority given to knowledge and information as the driving forces of the coming society is there, as is the stress upon technology. What is absent from Castells' age of information, however, is the historical optimism which was present in some of the early post-industrial accounts.

GORZ: THE DIVIDED SOCIETY

A related debate around the future shape of the post-industrial society is found in the work of Andre Gorz. In *Farewell to the Working Class* (1982), Gorz develops a set of arguments concerning the changing **role of work** in post-industrial economies. The following points summarise his argument:

- The strong claim advanced by Gorz is that the new technologies are altering the structure of employment within society, and that this has led to a social division between an 'aristocracy' of secure, well-paid workers, on the one hand, and a growing mass of unemployed on the other. In between, the majority of the population are said to belong to a post-industrial working class, for whom work no longer represents a source of identity or a meaningful activity.

- Automation at the workplace has created 'jobless growth' and its rapid extension will, he argues, progressively undermine the quality and status of the remaining working-class jobs. Work, in this scenario, thus becomes an instrumental activity for the majority, undertaken solely to earn a wage with little or no satisfaction or skill content attached to it.

- A casualised and disorganised working class is in the foreground of Gorz's account, with a privileged minority – similar to Bell's knowledge elite – occupying the positions of power and influence.

- In a later text, *Critique of Economic Reason* (1989), Gorz intensifies this vision by referring to a society polarised between an emergent 'servile' class and a securely employed professional class.

- He stresses a growing social inequality as a marked feature of post-industrialism, and this places his views closer to those of Touraine's post-industrial vision and Castells' information age rather than to Bell's optimistic information society.

4.4 Post-industrialism: conclusions

Despite differences of emphasis and the range of aspects stressed among post-industrial writers, the arrival of post-industrialism can be signalled on a number of economic and social fronts. Above all, the writers we have considered so far, seem to agree on one thing: that there has indeed been a shift away from industrialism. In broad terms, this movement can be identified with a shift in the balance of the western economies from a manufacturing to a service base, primarily in terms of employment, although it is often extended to include the output of an economy. The following areas are a bit more contentious as there is some disagreement amongst the writers we consider.

OCCUPATION AND CLASS

On the occupational and class fronts, it becomes harder to identify common post-industrial themes. At best it could be said that Bell and Gorz focus on different aspects of the same transition.

Where Bell sees the growth of white-collar occupations and the formation of knowledge elites, Gorz emphasises the irrelevance of work to the majority and the fate of a de-skilled working class forced to serve those elites. Where one offers the prospect of an end to harsh manual labour, the other holds out for a better world outside of, rather than within, work.

Even so, it is evident that both Gorz and Castells see social and economic polarisation as part of the general direction of change.

NEW SOCIAL MOVEMENTS

Although we considered social movements earlier, it is important to reinforce the argument that one of the main features of post-industrial society is not its simple lines of division, but rather the cross-cutting nature of these new social movements that is stressed by both Touraine and Castells.

We could argue that one of the characteristics of post-industrial society is the emergence of these social movements, such as the women's movement and the green movement, which go beyond the 'old' industrial forms of class politics.

KNOWLEDGE AND INFORMATION

There is, nevertheless, complete agreement on one principal feature of the coming society among all the writers: namely, the central importance of knowledge and information in the transition, especially as a source of technological innovation.

Information and its uses is regarded as a major resource, which has already begun to reshape activities in manufacturing and state sectors as well as in the private services such as finance and commerce. Strong claims have also been advanced for the importance of information technology as a 'heartland technology'; that is, one capable of generating further innovations at the workplace and beyond.

To convey the importance of this dynamic, we need only to remind ourselves of the observation by Castells that information generation and processing is to office work what mass production was to craft-based manufacture – a radical shift in the structure and organisation of the economy.

GOING BEYOND

If Castells' observation is valid, then the question as to what exactly it is that we have gone beyond becomes important. We know that we have not gone beyond capitalism, for instance. In the west, a competitive economic system based on the purchase and sale of commodities is still intact, as are the social relations which underpin this system.

But we also know that there is agreement over the passing of industrialism. If post-industrialism, or 'informationalism' as Castells calls it, is therefore a new phase of capitalism, have we then also moved beyond the modern economy and its associated idea of progress?

If mass manufacture and mass markets may be regarded as the height of modern industrial progress, how should we regard the dynamic of information and the emergence of a more divided society? Should we consider these characteristics as a new form of economic modernity, or as something that takes us beyond the modern economic era, perhaps into an era of post-modernism. In Section 5, we briefly explore the notion of **post-modernism** in relation to change.

REVIEW ACTIVITY 4

Read the following brief case scenario of a major British bank which is currently undergoing a major organisational restructuring programme. Then identify any post-industrial features of its operations.

Bank Co

Like most other organisations, banks have had to come to terms with changes in the economy and society generally. Bank Co is one of the 'big five' banks in Britain. Its operations, principally in the provision of services to business and domestic customers has been affected by automation since the 1960s. The advent of the micro-electronics revolution in the 1970s and 1980s provided the opportunity for storing and processing information in ways that were more compact, flexible, dispersed and cheaper than hitherto. When combined with other new technologies such as laser scanning, fibre-optic cabling, satellite transmissions and two-way television systems – these developments have opened up further possibilities for major changes with far-reaching implications.

The main problem for Bank Co is to provide an improving service for the customer while ensuring optimal use of ever-developing new technologies.

The re-organisation plan contains the following elements:

- greater emphasis upon the bank's international interests and holdings,
making optimal use of global information highways
- reduction of its branches in the UK from 55,000 to 23,000
- 25% of the remaining branches to be minimally staffed but with state-of-
the-art customer technology
- rapid expansion of telephone and computer banking
- internal restructuring to include:
  - less hierarchical management structures
  - centralisation of expert and knowledge functions
  - greater flexibility and multi-skilling of staff

Summary

In this section, we considered change in relation to the shift from an industrial to a post-industrial society. You have identified the nature of the change towards post-industrialism, together with the characteristics of post-industrial society. You have also related these changes to the British context. You have examined the major contributions to post-industrialism, and you will now be familiar with the ideas of Bell, Touraine, Castells and Gorz.

SECTION 5

From Modernity to Post-Modernity

Introduction

In Section 4, we were concerned with the shift from an industrial to a post-industrial society. This shift represents the major change now occurring within the industrial sphere in the advanced societies of Europe and North America. The move towards post-industrialism is also being accompanied by important parallel developments in the cultural sphere. The term used to describe these developments is **post-**

modernism. As within the industrial sphere, society is moving from industrialism to post-industrialism, so within the cultural sphere, society is moving from modernism to post-modernism.

As we see, these parallel developments are not self-contained. There is a considerable degree of overlap between the two sets of changes. It is therefore more realistic and appropriate to argue that there are important links between cultural change, that is, changes in philosophy, ideas, art and music, and social change generally, including industrial change.

In this section, we explain the meaning of modernism and post-modernism, and identify some common features shown by post-Fordist manufacturing and marketing and the cultural ideas and philosophy of post-modernism.

5.1 Modernism

Modernism is a term used to describe developments of the modern, industrial age in relation to, for example,

● **technology**
● **work and organisations.**

Technology
The system of mass production and assembly-line technology, which developed during the early twentieth century and which is now known as Fordism (Unit 3) is regarded as part of the modernist phenomenon.

Work and organisations
A central modernist assumption is that the work organisation is based on rational principles of management, such as scientific management, and that the attainment of the goals of the organisation can promote human progress.

Modernism is also concerned with movements on a large scale, whether these movements are derived from culture, architecture, economic, political and social organisation or philosophy.

The philosophy underlying modernism is largely optimistic and embraces the idea that the human condition can be changed by big political movements, for example, Marxism, by Fordist mass-production technology, by large-scale high-rise high density housing, and by emphasising the active role of the state in people's affairs.

Modernism, therefore, relates to much of what we have been dealing with in this unit, that is, change within industrial society. But we also need to recognise that the concept of change helps to explain transitions from one type of society to another, for example, from industrial to post-industrial society.

5.2 Post-modernism

Post-modernism is an all-embracing umbrella term which incorporates or subsumes the major transitions that we have analysed so far in this unit and also in other units of the module. Thus, for example, post-modernism will incorporate:

- transition to post-industrial society
- transition to post-Fordist technology and work
- changes in organisation structure to less bureaucratised forms.

The emergence of new social movements of the 1980s and 1990s, such as those concerned with green issues, women's and gay rights may also be considered as part of the post-modern tradition.

Post-modernism represents a reaction to the ideas of modernism, initially mainly within the cultural sphere in art, architecture and literature. Within the industrial and organisational context, as we see, post-Fordism has been equated with post-modernism.

The following examples will help clarify more specifically the nature of post-modernism:

- In architecture, post-modernism prefers the popular styles, symbolised by Las Vegas, rather than the modernist soul-less buildings like the Manhattan skyscrapers or the residential tower blocks of post-war urban planning. In this sense, post-modernism does not represent one style of architecture but many different styles, ranging from the reconstruction of ancient Egypt within one Las Vegas hotel to the impressive functionality of the Lloyds building in London.

- Post-modernism seems to revel in fragmentation, ephemerality and discontinuity, preferring difference over uniformity. This contrasts with modernism, which emphasises uniformity, continuity and wholeness. An example of post-modernism in popular music would include recurrent waves of nostalgia and the fragmentation of 'dance' music into 'house', 'rave', 'techno' and 'jungle'.

- There is an emphasis in post-modernist thinking on looking for 'local' factors or partial explanations such as the micro-politics of power relations in different social contexts. This would emphasise, for example, multi-issue community politics and local pressure groups.

- Also in the political sphere, post-modernism is engaging in multiple, local autonomous struggles for liberation, rejecting the 'imperialism' of those who presumed to speak for others, for example, colonised peoples, blacks and ethnic groups, religious minorities, women, and the working class, with a unified voice.

- In the post-modernist context, high-brow authority over cultural taste collapses and is replaced by popular culture and consumerism. Various groups, such as youth and ethnic groups, develop their own sub-cultures by using consumer culture and fashion to construct a sense of their own public identities.

● Post-modernism entails changes in the way work, technology and organisations are structured, taking post-Fordism as an example.

ACTIVITY 22

Either individually or in a group, if possible, define modernism and post-modernism in your own words. Using some examples, identify three or four main differences between modernism and post-modernism.

You should be able to deal with both questions by referring to sub-sections 5.1 and 5.2. The statement reproduced below by Richard Gott, a journalist with *The Guardian,* concerning modernism and post-modernism will re-inforce your answers.

'The first half of the twentieth century was dominated by Modernism – a movement that rejected the legacy of the past, that was caught up in the early enthusiasm for technological progress and sought to create the world anew. It accompanied and may even be seen as the cultural equivalent of the Russian revolution. Rejecting tradition, it was the culture of innovation and change.

Fifty years later, however, by the second half of the century, this dramatic, daring and innovative trend had become the cultural norm accepted by Western Establishments. The revolutionary impulses that had once galvanised politics and culture had clearly become sclerotic. The Brave New World was in retreat. In its place has emerged a new movement that seeks to recover tradition, a world that seems to prefer stability to change. Just as the whole socialist idea has gone into retreat, so too the great modernist project has been largely abandoned.

Into this vacuum steps post-modernism, an eclectic movement of parody and pastiche that fits happily into a world where conservation has become the rage, where new pubs can be built with Victorian fittings, where modernist tower blocks are replaced with 'vernacular' retreats into the archaic. Post-modernism, of course, can also be portrayed in a progressive light. Some advocates of the post-modern believe modernism to have been a phallocentric, imperialist affair. In this light, post-modernism appears as a form of liberation, a fragmented movement in which a hundred flowers may bloom. Such people might also argue that while Modernism was the product of a particular Western culture, post-modernism heralds the recognition of a plurality of cultures.' (Gott, 1986)

In the remainder of this section, we deal with the example of post-Fordism in relation to post-modernism.

5.3 Post-Fordism and post-modernism

Some writers such as Murray (1989) equate post-Fordism with post-modernism. Murray provides us with two examples of post-Fordist, post-modernist forms of organisation. In Unit 3, we examined Fordism and post-Fordism within the context of technological change, so you should be familiar with the two notions. Post-Fordism, however, has wider ramifications than the immediate context of the organisation of work. Consider the following extract from an article by Hebdige (1989):

'One of the features of post-Fordist production is the leading role given to market research, packaging and presentation. While it doesn't literally produce the social, it's nonetheless the case that marketing has provided the dominant and most pervasive classification of social types in the 1980s (the yuppie is the most obvious example). We use these categories as a kind of social shorthand even if we are reluctant to find ourselves reflected in them.

We live in a world and in bodies which are deeply scored by the power relations of race and class, sexuality and gender but we also live – whether or not we know it consciously – in a world of style-setters, innovators, sloanes, preppies, empty nesters (working couples with grown up families), dinkies (dual-income-no-kids), casuals, sensibles, the constrained majority, and today's prime targets, the pre-teens and woofies (well-off-older-folk).

These are the types outlined in commercial lifestyling and 'psychographics' – forms of research which don't present descriptions of living, breathing individuals so much as hypothetical 'analogues' of 'aspirational clusters'. In other words, the new, intensive but speculative forms of market research are designed to offer a social map of desire which can be used to determine where exactly which products should be 'pitched' and 'niched'.

ACTIVITY 23

Can you identify any post-modern features in Hebdige's description of post-Fordist marketing and possible effects on the organisation of production?

The post-modern features of fragmentation, ephemerality, locality of markets and consumerist drives are obvious. Hebdige's quote draws attention to the new marketing categories necessary to the operation of post-Fordist technology, production methods and information networks. It enables organisations, whether they are in retailing, manufacturing or in other services, to target certain groups and adapt their manufacturing and other processes accordingly.

TWO OTHER EXAMPLES

Murray (1989) provides two other examples of the post-Fordist, post-modernist connection. The first of his examples is in the retailing sector, and the second is in manufacturing.

The example of retailing

Since the 1950s, retailers had been using computers to transform the distribution system. All mass producers have the problem of forecasting demand. If they produce too little, they lose market share. If they produce too much, they are left with stocks which are costly to hold or have to be sold at a discount. Retailers face this problem not just for a few products, but for thousands. Their answer has been to develop information and supply systems which allow them to order supplies to coincide with demand.

Every evening, Sainsbury's receives details of the sales of all 12,000 lines from each of its shops; these are turned into orders for warehouse deliveries for the coming night, and replacement production for the following day. With computerised control of stocks in the shop, transport networks, automatic loading and unloading in warehouses. Sainsbury's flow-line make-to-order system has conquered the Fordist problem of stocks.

They have also overcome the limits of the mass product. For, in contrast to the discount stores which are confined to a few fast-selling items, Sainsbury's, like the new wave of high street shops, can handle ranges of products geared to segments of the market. Market niching has become the slogan of the high street. Market researchers break down market by age (youth, young adults, 'grey power'), by household types (dinkies, single-gender couple, one-parent families), by income, occupation, housing and increasingly by locality. They analyse lifestyles, correlating consumption patterns across commodities, from food to clothing, and health and holidays.

The point of this new anthropology of consumption is to target both product and shops to particular segments. In modern shops, the emphasis has shifted from the manufacturer's economies of scale to the retailer's economies of scope. The economies come from offering an integrated range from which customers can choose their own basket of products. There is also an economy of innovation, for the modern retail systems allow new product ideas to be tested in practice, through shop sales, and the successful ones then to be ordered for wider distribution. Innovation has become a leading edge of the new competition. Product life has become shorter, for both fashion goods and consumer durables.

A centrepiece of this new retailing is design. Designers produce the innovations. They shape the lifestyles. They design the shops, which are described as 'stages' for the act of shopping. With market researchers, they have steered the high street from being retailers of goods to retailers of style.

These changes are a response to, and a means of shaping, the shift from mass consumption. Instead of keeping up with the Joneses there has been a move to be different from the Joneses. Many of these differences are vertical, intended to confirm status and class. But some are horizontal, centred around group identities, linked to age, or region or ethnicity. Whatever our responses, the revolution in retailing reflects new principles of production, a new pluralism of products and a new importance for innovation. As such it marks a shift to a post-Fordist/post-modernist age.

ACTIVITY 24

With reference to the retailing example, identify the changes that have taken place, and what these changes are a response to, under the following headings:

● demand, distribution and stocks

● marketing, product life and innovation

● design and lifestyle.

Retailers no longer need to retain large supplies of stock as post-Fordist production and distribution systems using computerised control ensures that supply is equated with demand.

An organisation using post-Fordist technology is flexible enough to focus upon particular markets. This is partly a response to consumer demand and partly due to the 'discovery' that niche marketing is potentially very profitable. The post-modern aspect to this is the fragmentation of the consumer market as identified in our example.

Design and lifestyle factors also serve to emphasise difference. The last two paragraphs of our example illustrate this very well.

The example of manufacturing

Manufacturers have also been adopting retailers' answer to stocks. The pioneer is Toyota which stands to the new era as Ford did to the old. Toyoda, the founder of Toyota, applied the just-in-time system to his component suppliers, ordering on the basis of his daily production plans, and getting the components delivered right beside the line. Most of Toyota's components are still delivered on the same day as they are assembled.

Toyota has used design and materials technology to simplify complex elements, cutting down the number of parts and operations. It adopted a zero defect policy, developing machines which stopped automatically, when a fault occurred, as well as statistical quality control techniques. The complex web of processes, inside and outside the plant, were co-ordinated through computers, and as a result, Toyota turned over its materials and products ten times more quickly than western car producers, saving material and energy in the process.

The key point about the Toyota system, however, is not so much that it speeds up the making of a car. It is that in order to make these changes (JIT, zero defects and total quality) it has adopted quite different methods of labour control and organisation. Taylorism did not work and quality could not be achieved with de-skilled manual workers. Taylorism wasted what they called 'the gold in workers' heads'.

Toyota, and the Japanese more generally, having broken the industrial unions in the 1950s, have developed a core of multi-skilled workers whose tasks include not only manufacture and maintenance but the improvement of the products and processes under their control. Each breakdown is seen as a chance for improvement. Even hourly paid workers are trained in statistical techniques and monitoring, and register and interpret statistics to identify deviations from the norm – tasks customarily reserved for management in Fordism. In post-Fordism, the worker is designed to act as a computer as well as a machine.

As a consequence, the Taylorist contract changes. Workers are no longer interchangeable. They gather experience. The Japanese job-for-life and corporate welfare system provide security. For the firm, it secures an asset. Continuous training, payment by seniority, a breakdown of job demarcations, are all part of the Japanese core wage relation.

The EFTPU (elecricians' union) still leads in pioneering new relationships with companies such as Toyota with single union and sometimes 'no-strike' deals which also embrace private pension schemes, BUPA, internal flexibility and union-organised training. These developments are all consistent with this type of post-Fordist industrial relations.

ACTIVITY 25

These points and developments concern Toyota, but they could apply equally to similar companies, particularly Japanese companies. Do you see any dangers in such developments?

The obvious danger is that it further hardens the divisions between the core and the peripheral workforce. The cost of employing lifetime workers means an incentive to subcontract all jobs not essential to the core. The other side of the Japanese notion of jobs-for-life is a majority of low paid, fragmented peripheral workers, facing an underfunded and inadequate welfare state. The duality in the labour market and in the welfare economy, could be taken as a description of Thatcherism. The point is that neither the EETPU's policy nor that of Mrs Thatcher should be read as purely political. There is a material basis to both, rooted in changes in production.

There are more general points concerning post-Fordist manufacturing which we need to emphasise:

● There are parallel changes in corporate organisation. With the revision of Taylorism, a layer of management has been stripped away. Greater central control has allowed the de-centralisation of work. Day-to-day autonomy has been given to work groups and plant managers. Teams linking departments horizontally have replaced the rigid verticality of Fordist bureaucracies.

● It is only a short step here to sub-contracting and franchising. This is often simply a means of labour control. But in engineering and light consumer industries, networks and semi-independent firms have often proved more innovative than vertically integrated producers. A mark of post-Fordism is close two-way relations between customer and supplier, and between specialised producers in the same industry. Co-operative competition replaces the competition of the jungle. These new relationships within and between enterprises and on the shopfloor have made least headway in the countries in which Fordism took fullest root, the USA and the UK. Here, firms have tried to match continental and Japanese flexibility through automation while retaining Fordist shopfloor, managerial and competitive relations.

● Yet in spite of this, we can see in this country a culture of post-Fordist capitalism emerging. Consumption has a new place. As for production the keyword is flexibility – of plant and machinery, and of products and labour. Emphasis shifts from scale to scope and from cost to quality. Organisations are geared to respond to rather than regulate markets. They are seen as frameworks for learning as much as instruments of control. Their hierarchies are flatter and their structures more open. The guerrilla force takes over from the standing army. All this has liberated the centre from the tyranny of the immediate. Its tasks increasingly concern the promotion of the instruments of post-Fordist control systems, software, corporate culture and cash.

ACTIVITY 26

With reference to our manufacturing example, identify the changes that post-Fordist manufacturing exhibits under the following headings:

● design and materials technology

● industrial control and organisation

● employer/employee union relationships.

You should be able to identify all the above features in the example. We give three suggestions.

- Design and materials technology facilitates production and makes production cheaper and more efficient.

- Taylorism is no longer relevant to the multi-skilled core workforce. The need for supervisory control diminishes and the worker assumes control and responsibility for quality of product together with his team. The old lines of authority and bureaucratic control that characterised many organisations organised on Taylorist principles give way to flatter structures based on teams linking departments horizontally.

- The nature of the employment relationship changes. Where unions are involved, it is on the basis of a single union agreement. The union is seen as one of the representative bodies that can share in joint consultation with management, and the traditional view of conflict gives way to one which emphasises co-operation.

REVIEW ACTIVITY 5

Suggested time: 30 minutes.

Summarise the features of post-modern industrialism and point out some related features of the post-modernist culture and society.

Summary

In Section 5, you dealt with change in relation to some of the ideas of post-modernism. We explained the nature of modernism and post-modernism. In the remainder of the section, we concentrated mainly on the industrial and organisational aspects of post-Fordism, linking these to the cultural ideas and philosophy of post-modernism.

Unit Summary

In this unit, we have considered the concept of change. Change is, of course, ongoing and is central to our understanding of organisations and the actors within them. We live in a society in which the pace of change is accelerating for a variety of reasons. Change also affects every society of a particular type more or less evenly. Western societies, for example, are undergoing the same transition from, for example, an industrial to a post-industrial society. These transitions do not happen of their own accord; they are heavily influenced and determined by the actions of individuals and groups within a given society. The debate concerning structure and action is therefore extremely important in this context, and within it the debate about whether individuals, or actors, influence structures or whether structures influence action.

Of course, individuals can do very little by themselves to change things, so they co-ordinate their individual activities within groups and collectivities, such as trade unions. Many of these groups and collectivities also become known as social movements which, through collective action and mobilisation, facilitate change.

Finally, we identified two major changes that are taking place in late-twentieth century western society; the transition from industrial to post-industrial society, and the move from modernism to post-modernism. These two types of change are fundamental to our understanding of, amongst other things, how organisations develop into the next century.

References

Aberle, D (1966) *The Peyote Religion Among the Navaho,* Chicago: Aldine Press.

Bell, D (1973) *The Coming of Post-Industrial Society,* New York: Basic Books.

Bell, D (1976) *The Cultural Contradictions of Capitalism,* New York: Basic Books.

Castells, M (1989) *The Informational City,* Oxford: Blackwells.

Durkheim, E (1982) *The Rules of Sociological Method,* London: Macmillan.

Giddens, A (1989) *Sociology,* Cambridge: Polity Press.

Gorz, A (1982) *Farewell to the Working Class; An Essay on Post-Industrial Socialism,* London: Pluto Press.

Gorz, A (1989) *Critique of Economic Reason,* London: Verso.

Gott, R (1986) 'The crisis of Contemporary Culture' *The Guardian.*

Hebdige, D (1989) 'After the Masses', in Hall, S & Jaques, M (eds) *New Times*, London: Lawrence and Wishart.

Hobbes, T ([1651]1962) *Leviathan,* (ed), Piamentaz, J, London: Foutana

Landes, D (1969) *The Unbound Prometheus,* Cambridge: Cambridge University Press.

Marx, K & Engels, F (1971) *The German Ideology,* edited and introduced by C J Arthur, London: Lawrence and Wishart.

Murray, R (1989) 'Fordism and Post-Fordism', in Hall, S. & Jaques, M, (eds) *New Times,* London: Lawrence and Wishart.

Parsons, T (1964) 'Evolutionary Universals in Society', *American Sociological Review,* 29.

Parsons, T (1966) *Societies: Evolutionary and Comparative Perspectives,* Englewood Cliffs, NJ: Prentice Hall.

Smelser, N (1963) *Theory of Collective Behaviour,* New York: Free Press.

Tannenbaum, A (1974) *Hierarchy in Organisations,* San Francisco: Josey Bass.

Touraine, A (1974) *The Post-Industrial Society,* London: Wildwood.

Touraine, A (1981) *The Voice and the Eye: An Analysis of Social Movements,* Cambridge: Cambridge University Press.

Recommended reading

FOR SOCIAL CHANGE AND POST-INDUSTRIALISM

Boudon, R (1986) *Theories of Social Change,* Cambridge: Polity Press.

Kumar, K (1978) *Prophesy and Progress: The Sociology of Industrial and Post-Industrial Society,* Harmondsworth: Penguin.

FOR SOCIAL MOVEMENTS

Wilson, J (1973) *Introduction to Social Movements,* New York: Basic Books.

FOR POST-MODERNISM AND POST-INDUSTRIALISM

Hall, S, Held, D & McGrew, T (1992) *Modernity and its Futures,* Cambridge: Polity Press, Chapters 4 and 5.

Answers to Review Activities

Review Activity 1

1 You will find sub-sections 1.3 onwards relevant to question 1. The first point that you could make is that the development of capitalism was initially linked with the emergence of the modern nation-state, the industrialisation of war and developing rational modes of thought.

The modern work organisation, particularly within the private sector of the economy, has been influenced by each of the above developments. Capitalism introduces the profit motive and the notion of market economics and free enterprise. Firms began to emerge, competing with each other within the same industry and technological innovation provided further impetus to competition. Section 1.4 – *Economic influences,* is relevant here.

The modern organisation was also influenced by the further development of the modern nation-state. As nations became wealthier, governments could afford to subsidise certain important industries such as shipbuilding and armaments within a mixed economy context. Also the growing economic and military influence of some nations such as the USA helped to create favourable conditions for the development of the modern multi-national organisation. Section 1.4 – *Political influences,* is useful in this respect.

Finally, the development of science and rational ways of thinking helped the modern organisation to develop through the creation of rational (bureaucratic) structures and rules, highly efficient methods of working, etc. Scientific management is a case in point. See Section 1.4 – *Cultural influences.*

2 The relevant section is here 1.2. You may have given examples of modern social change such as the computer revolution, mass production and so on. If you have confined yourself to changes within the modern British context, it is likely that these changes could be explained through social evolutionism rather than historical materialism.

Review Activity 2

1 You will find the relevant material in sub-section 2.1 which looks at the differences in basic terms. You can also refer to sub-section 2.2 for additional material.

The main points to highlight here are:

- that 'structure' is external to the individual and yet influences the individual. This is very much the position taken by Durkheim.

- structures, then, do influence us as individuals, but on the other hand, we, as individuals can influence structures through our own actions.

- it is this interplay between 'structure' and 'action' that gives rise to social change.

2   The limitations of the agency and structure approaches to social change are found in sections 2.3–2.4. They are demonstrated by the two examples of Lucas and the steel industry.

The power of individuals to determine their own goals and make their own choices is, in practice, severely restricted. By the same token, these examples also demonstrate that individuals are not just passive recipients of structural change.

Review Activity 3

1   You should have included some of the following points in your answer:

You will notice that the definition of a social movement provided in section 3.1 is relevant to trade unions, particularly in the early years of their formation:

- they are mass movements

- they are organisations that pursue collective goals through collective action

- they started off as illegal organisations.

Trade unions are largely reformative movements, being formed to improve the pay and working conditions of working people. Reform aims also extended to the political sphere with strong links to the Labour party.

The theories of both Smelser and Touraine are useful in explaining the development of trade unions. For example, Smelser's condition one (structural conduciveness) can explain why trade unions developed in the first place (no legislation to improve workers' conditions), Smelser's condition three is relevant as it is valid to argue that trade unions were at least partly influenced by the political ideology of socialism. Finally, condition five of Smelser concerning co-ordination and mobilisation through leadership is vital for social movements to exist and thrive. Trade unions satisfy this criterion.

Touraine concentrates on agency, focusing upon the aims of individuals as well. The aims of individuals coincide with the aims of the movement, that is, they are indistinguishable. Indeed, the movement's leadership should reflect individual aims and aspirations. Sometimes these aims may conflict and strains between individual and organisation occur.

2   We could argue that even with recent developments in legislation etc, trade unions, according to our initial definition, still represent a social movement. However, we could also argue that the initial conditions which gave rise to the formation and development of trade unions as a social movement no longer exist. Workers enjoy basic rights at work which trade unions originally fought for.

The European Union, with the exception of Britain, has adopted the Social Charter which gives both full and part-time workers comprehensive employment rights.

In addition, changes in work patterns, new technology, and the changing nature of society itself – towards post-industrialism and post-Fordism – may make trade unions less relevant to workers' experiences than they used to be.

You may therefore have concluded that while trade unions still represent a social movement, the potency of the social movement has declined as a result of these changes.

Review Activity 4

Not all the features of post-industrialism are relevant to Bank Co's operations. Bell has commented upon the rapidity of technological change and the generation of knowledge and information which are important factors influencing the banking sector. The banking sector is part of the service sector of the economy and has witnessed considerable growth since the 1950s. There has, however, been some employment reduction in the banking sector, and with further organisational restructuring, more redundancies are inevitable.

Castells has commented on the rise of the 'information society' and the role of knowledge in improving economic performance and efficiency. Banks such as Bank Co are very good examples of organisations which use information technology for this purpose.

Finally, Gorz argues that new technology alters the structure of employment – flexibilisation of labour. He also contends that automation creates 'jobless growth'. Both of these contentions are relevant to the banking sector, and in particular, to the restructuring plan of Bank Co.

Review Activity 5

You need to identify the features of post-modernism as explained in section 5.2 and then look at the two examples to identify both the industrial and cultural features of post-modernism in order to link them.

Some points of particular importance which you should have identified are:

- move towards post-industrial society
- adoption of post-Fordist technology at work
- less bureaucratised organisational structures.

These developments represent a reaction to the ideas of modernism as we argued earlier in the section.

UNIT 4

THE NATURE OF ORGANISATIONS

Introduction

In this unit, we have set the stage for more detailed investigation of organisations and how they exist in today's business environment. You have looked at the background of industrial sociology and how current administration and control mechanisms and ideas about work have developed in the context of technology and change. With this basis we can now look at the functioning of organisations and relate these ideas back to those early researchers and theorists.

In this unit, we help you to explore the nature and purpose of organisations and to understand and identify different organisational structures. We aim also to give you an understanding of the factors that must be considered when an organisational structure is designed.

Key choices and issues concerning organisational structure design include:

- how jobs and departments should be differentiated and grouped
- how organisational activities should be co-ordinated and controlled.

Perhaps you can now see why you have covered the historical development of work and how it is organised and controlled. By looking at the factors that influence decisions on these issues of differentiation, co-ordination and control, you will be able to evaluate the appropriateness of particular organisational structures for different organisations in their particular circumstances, and to participate actively in the design of organisation structures to meet identified needs.

Objectives

By the end of this unit, you should be able to:

- define an organisation.
- distinguish between the formal and informal elements of organisational life.
- identify the importance of organisation structures and what they do.
- identify the key processes that take place in the structuring of an organisation.
- analyse and evaluate in practical examples
    - the extent to which jobs or departments within the organisation are specialised or differentiated
    - the ways in which the organisation's jobs and departments are grouped together, and
    - the appropriateness of those groupings
    - the integrative processes at work within the organisation

- the forms, levels and spans of managerial control used within the organisation.
- explain the nature of organisational missions and goals.
- evaluate the relevance of particular organisational goals and missions and their importance for organisational effectiveness.
- identify the use and value of organisation theory.
- evaluate the influence of size, technology and environment on an organisation's structure.

SECTION 1

Organisations and their Structures

Introduction

In this section, we look at the essential nature of organisations and their defining characteristics. We examine what we mean by the terms **formal** and **informal** in relation to organisations, and look at two classifications of organisations. One classification is based on their primary purposes, the other is based on the intended beneficiaries of an organisation's activities.

We also look at the nature and consequences of organisation structure. We note how it provides the framework of activities, relationships, hierarchy and lines of communication within which the co-ordination and control of an organisation's activities can take place. Finally, we examine the two key processes of differentiation and integration that are needed in creating an organisation structure.

1.1 Definition

We see evidence of organisations around us everyday – schools, universities, churches, sports teams, youth clubs, supermarkets, bus companies, garages, and so on. All of these are organisations whose goods and services we have purchased, for whom we may have worked, or of which we have been members.

ACTIVITY 1

What features do these bodies have in common that makes them organisations and which distinguishes them from other forms of social entity?

An organisation is a clearly bounded group (or groups) of people interacting together to achieve a particular goal (or goals) in a formally structured and co-ordinated way. This definition picks out certain key features of organisations, which distinguish them from other social groupings, such as a crowd or a group of friends.

- An organisation has clear boundaries. We can tell who is a member and who is not, for example, the army, the police, supermarket staff.

- An organisation involves people collaborating together with one another, for example, a detective may collaborate with a uniformed police officer to investigate a crime.

- An organisation has a defined goal (or goals). It exists to achieve a particular purpose (or purposes). For example, the police exist to protect the public from crime, amongst other reasons.

- An organisation has a formal structure. Its various tasks are clearly defined and grouped together into jobs and departments. For example, in a police force, the criminal investigation department is separate from the traffic department.

- An organisation's activities are formally co-ordinated. Rules and procedures exist governing how the people performing the organisation's tasks will collaborate to ensure its purposes are achieved. For example, a local police force will have procedures setting out how to deal with an emergency, such as an explosion in a city centre. These will include both the duties of the CID – to investigate the causes of the blast – and of the Traffic Department – to minimise traffic disruption.

ACTIVITY 2

List the organisations with which you have had dealings in the last seven days.

It would be surprising if you cannot find at least seven to ten examples. Organisations are part of your daily life; they might include bank, building society, post office, petrol station, supermarket, library, local government office, leisure club, your place of work, cinema, restaurant, insurance broker, motoring organisation, hospital, church, sports team, etc.

1.2 Formality and informality

Our definition of an organisation indicates that certain of its key features are not left to spontaneity or to chance. There are rules about who is and is not a member. When you join a university as a student you must enrol. When you join a firm as an employee you sign a contract of employment.

The key purposes of the organisation will have been agreed and written down by its senior management. For example, your university or employing organisation almost certainly has a mission statement. Your particular department may have one too.

The people who perform tasks in an organisation are likely to have those tasks defined in writing, as job descriptions. This applies even when the tasks are performed on an unpaid, voluntary basis, for example, the secretary of a youth football team.

Finally, those performing tasks for an organisation are instructed by rules to whom they are responsible and when and how they should report on their activities. These rules and procedures, formally laid down by those responsible for running an organisation, make it clear that an organisation can be distinguished from other social groupings because it is a formal entity.

ACTIVITY 3

Define in one or two sentences what we mean by formality in an organisation.

Formality in an organisation means that it has been created with a declared and agreed purpose (or purposes), that its membership can be clearly defined, and that its tasks are defined and coordinated according to rules and procedures set out by those responsible for its management.

This does not mean, however, that organisations are only formal social entities. When people meet together at work, or in other organisations, much interaction takes place that is outside the formal rules and procedures of the organisation. Some people like one another and form friendships. Others do not. Some people bring common experiences to the organisation and so may share a particular outlook towards their work. For example, they may have undertaken the same training course or have the same professional qualification. Again, others do not. Hence there is great scope in an organisation for informal patterns of behaviour also, without reference to the formal aspects of its existence.

ACTIVITY 4

What type of behaviour do we refer to when we talk about informality in an organisation?

Informality within an organisation refers to those behaviours that take place without direct reference to its declared purposes, rules and procedures, but that arise from the spontaneous social interactions of its members.

It is possible, of course, for the formal and informal aspects of an organisation's life to be in conflict. For example, different sections or departments may develop animosities that prevent working together effectively. Nevertheless, the informal parts of an organisation can also be very beneficial and help the organisation better achieve its mission. Friendships within organisations help people enjoy their work and encourage them to collaborate closely with colleagues. Working groups with a common training and professional pride may well set informal norms or standards for their work that are higher than those formally required by the organisation. When new and unique problems arise, for which no formal rules or procedures exist, informal processes and collaboration can often ameliorate them in the short term, whilst highlighting the need for formal steps to resolve them in the longer term.

Managing the formal and informal aspects of organisational life, to ensure that the two are at least compatible, is not easy.

ACTIVITY 5

What key formal rules and procedures are you subject to in your student or working life? What informal behaviour do you engage in as a student?

As a student, you are almost certainly subject to rules and procedures concerning matters such as enrolment, attendance, library use, handing in assignments, and so on. As a worker, you will have agreed your working hours and job description. In either case, perhaps you socialise with colleagues, or discuss your work with fellow students and so on.

1.3 Types of organisations

As you will have realised, organisations are everywhere in society and vary greatly. Some are large; some are small. Some are very formal; others are more informal. Some serve their members; some serve others; and some serve both. Some are public, that is, owned by government; others are private, owned by individuals and groups in society. Some have voluntary membership, like a university; others do not, like a prison.

This variety means that there is not a single, universally accepted, way of grouping or classifying organisations into different types. Mullins (1993) classifies organisations on the basis of their primary purposes, distinguishing between:

- **economic organisations,** whose primary purpose is to sell goods and services in a market – such as business firms

- **protective organisations,** whose primary purpose is to defend the interests of a particular social group or groups or society at large – such as a police force, or trade union, or some charities

- **associative organisations,** whose primary purpose is to bring people together to pursue some common leisure interest or purpose – such as a youth club or sports club

- **public service organisations** which provide a government service – such as hospitals or roads

- **religious organisations** – such as churches or mosques.

An alternative typology, proposed by Blau and Scott (1966), divides organisations into different types according to who is intended to be the primary beneficiary of their activities. They distinguish four types of organisation:

- **mutual benefit associations,** intended primarily to benefit their own members, like a trade union

- **business concerns,** intended primarily to benefit their owners, like a company

- **service organisations,** intended primarily to meet the needs of an external client group, like many charities

- **commonwealth organisations,** intended primarily to meet the needs of the public at large, like many public services, such as the police or the army.

ACTIVITY 6

Taking the list of organisations with whom you have dealt in the last seven days in Activity 2, try to classify them using Blau and Scott's four categories.

If you cannot clearly classify each into one of the four categories, do not worry too much. A problem with almost any system of classification is that not all organisations will fit neatly into it. You may find some other ways used to group or classify organisations as you study organisations further. For the moment, you only need to be aware that:

● organisations are very varied

● different methods of classification can be used to emphasise different aspects of their variety.

1.4 Nature and consequences of organisation structure

Organisations bring together a variety of people, with different backgrounds, education, skills and experiences. Their collective task is to work together, doing a range of different jobs, to achieve a set of common, organisational goals.

What would happen if all these people simply 'did their own thing'? They could do whatever work they felt like doing, when they felt like doing it, in the way they thought best. The result might well be chaos.

ACTIVITY 7

Do this activity on your own or compare your answers with a small group. List three things you would do differently at work or at university, if allowed to 'do your own thing'.

You might have included some of the following points in your list(s). Answer them now, if you have not already covered them.

1 Would you still arrive as early and go home as late?

2 Would you spend as much time on the less pleasant aspects of your work or study as you do presently?

3 Would all aspects of your work or study be done to the same standard as they are now?

4 Even if you can answer 'Yes' to the above questions, do you think that everyone in your workplace or university (students and lecturers) would do the same?

Unless you, and all your colleagues, are very well motivated and able to act independently, and so are able to answer 'yes' to the four questions, then your workplace or university needs an organisational structure.

Among other things an organisational structure will:

- create a hierarchy giving someone or some people the duty of setting out rules about time-keeping
- will allocate both pleasant and unpleasant tasks to various people in the organisation according to their job descriptions
- will allocate to some people the task of checking that work or study is carried out to a sufficiently high standard.

An organisational structure provides an essential framework for the efficient running of your organisation. It ensures that the rules and procedures exist, and are obeyed, that are necessary for the smooth running, and even the continued existence, of the whole organisation.

WHAT ORGANISATIONAL STRUCTURES DO

An organisation's structure sets out formally:

- how tasks will be grouped together into jobs – for example, a counter clerk in a bank or building society may deal with initial customer queries, take in and pay out cash, make up accounts for customers, and make up till balances.

- how jobs will be grouped together into sections, departments and divisions – for example, an organisation may group together all its typists and word processor operators into a typing pool.

- who reports to whom – for example, at the end of his or her beat a police constable will report to a sergeant at the station any significant events that have occurred.

- who has authority over whom – for example, at the beginning of a shift the same police sergeant may instruct constables which beat each is to take.

Note, however, that the organisation's structure does *not* tell us anything about the informal, or unofficial, side of the organisation.

In summary, we can say that an organisation's structure sets out the formal framework of relationships within an organisation; the grouping together of its activities; its lines of communication; and its hierarchy. Within this framework, the co-ordination and control of the organisation's activities can take place.

ACTIVITY 8

Are the following statements True or False? Circle the correct answer in each case.

An understanding of an organisation's structure will tell us:

1 which managers have authority over which activity, for example, who is responsible for approving an expenses claim. *True / False*

2 to whom we should report a serious problem we have concerning the organisation, for example, when a hotel guest finds that its bedroom has not been thoroughly cleaned. *True / False*

3 who is likely to get on well with whom among the staff, for example, which staff are likely to have rows in front of customers. *True / False*

---

1 *True.* An organisation's structure embodies the hierarchy of formal authority amongst its staff.

2 *True.* An organisation's structure sets out its channels of communication and, hence, where and to whom particular problems should be reported.

3 *False.* Friendship and social contacts may be facilitated by the formal side of an organisation, but are more a function of its informal social groups and activities.

1.5 Organisational design: differentiation and integration

To create an organisational structure, two key processes must take place: differentiation and integration. **Differentiation** is the process of allocating the tasks that need to be done in an organisation to a series of sets or groups (jobs, teams, sections, departments) that make sense because they contain a range of tasks that have important elements in common, for example, common knowledge, common skills, the same type of customers.

This differentiation can be **horizontal,** that is dividing up people into groups who are at the same level in the organisation. For example, a university may have departments of business studies, engineering and humanities to divide up its lecturers into groups according to their ability to teach different subjects. Similarly, a large car show room will have a department that deals with sales and a department that deals with car spares and servicing.

Such differentiation can also be **vertical,** that is dividing up people who may share similar skills, knowledge, etc. into different managerial levels in the organisation's hierarchy. For example, the department of business studies in our university example may contain a head, a deputy head, a number of course managers and, below them in the hierarchy, the remainder of the lecturers. Similarly, in the car show room, the sales department is likely to have a sales manager in charge of a group of salespersons.

Integration is the process of ensuring that the activities of the various work groups in an organisation are linked together harmoniously, so that each group makes its maximum contribution to achieving the organisation's goals.

Like differentiation, integration can be both horizontal or vertical. **Horizontal** integration concerns activities that go on at the same hierarchical level in an organisation to make sure members of staff co-ordinate their activities. For example, in an electricity company, customer account staff dealing with customer telephone enquiries will share a common computer database so that they can deal with any customer who telephones. Similarly, in a university, a group of lecturers who teach a particular module jointly will meet periodically to discuss its progress and any changes to be made.

Vertical integration concerns the activities that go on at different hierarchical levels within an organisation to ensure that members of staff co-ordinate their activities. For example, at the end of each day at a bank's regional head-office, information will be collated and presented electronically to allow regional managers to assess the business done by each branch. Similarly, the bank's national head-office will send out standard operating instructions about how branches should deal with particular kinds of transaction, such as foreign currency exchange or sale of traveller's cheques.

In the next section, we explore further the questions that arise when we are trying to decide on the optimum degrees of differentiation and integration for an organisation's structure. For the moment, we conclude by noting that designing an organisation's structure involves these two processes: differentiating the various aspects of an organisation, and integrating them.

REVIEW ACTIVITY 1

Suggested time: 25 minutes.

Read the extract from the *Comfortable Shoe Company* case study and answer the questions that follow it.

Comfortable Shoe Company

It is 8.45 on a Monday morning and Mark Green, a salesperson with the Comfortable Shoe Company has just set out to visit a number of stores that stock his company's shoes in the nearby market town of Mapplethorpe. Mark is a member of the Comfortable Shoe Company's north west regional sales team. The other members are Bill Battersby, the north west regional sales manager, Sue Long and Jane Sutcliffe. Bill has divided the region into three districts, and Mark, Sue and Jane are each responsible for one of them. Before setting out Mark had telephoned Bill to say that he would call into the regional sales office, where Bill works, on his way home from Mapplethorpe to let Bill have a detailed breakdown of his district's sales figures for last month. This pleased Bill as he is about to compile the north west regional sales report for last month and send it to head office in London. Here it will be compared with other regions' sales figures for the month. Bill is also anxious to compare the north west's performance against that of other regions.

Just before Mark rang off Bill had said, 'Good luck at Campbell's, and don't go offering them more than the company's standard discounts. You know it drives head office wild'. The thought of visiting Campbell's after lunch worried Mark. It was Mapplethorpe's largest departmental store and had been the north west's biggest outlet for Comfortable Shoes. Over the past year, however, it had begun to stock fewer and fewer of them, and had replaced them with imported shoes from South America. Mark believed that the problem lay in his company's introduction of a standard discount policy which, in a memorandum from head office, instructed regional sales teams exactly what levels of discount they were allowed to offer to customers. Prior to this, the sales staff had been pretty free to determine what discounts they offered, and major customers had often obtained much larger discounts than were possible under the new standard discounts policy.

Mark cheered up at the thought of lunch. He had agreed to eat with Sue Long. She had promised to bring with her some samples of the company's latest shoe designs, which Mark thought would be of particular interest to Campbell's.

Campbell's customers were especially fashion conscious. He reflected that working in the north west sales team was not really so bad. They really were a team and their monthly team meetings were one of the best parts of the job.

List any examples you can find of: (i) horizontal differentiation; (ii) vertical differentiation; (iii) horizontal integration; and (iv) vertical integration.

Summary

In this section, we have defined the nature and characteristics of organisations, and distinguished between their 'formal' and 'informal' elements. You have applied one classifying typology to some organisations of which you are a member.

You have examined the purpose of organisational structure and have seen how it enables an organisation's activities to be co-ordinated and controlled, through the framework of activities, relationships, hierarchy and lines of communication that it provides.

Finally, we have seen how creating an organisation structure requires processes of differentiation and integration, and Review activity 1 enabled you to demonstrate how these key processes are reflected in a practical example.

SECTION 2
Understanding an Organisation's Design

Introduction

This section will prepare you to explore practically and in much greater depth the issues raised in Section 1. You examine the five key choices in organisation design regarding differentiation and integration, and of their relation to questions of managerial control. You will conduct wide-ranging interviews with two members of an organisation, and build up an information base that will help you to analyse how the key choices have shaped the organisation's structure.

2.1 Differentiation and integration

You met John Child's work in Unit 1 when you looked at his framework for management control. Here we examine five key questions that need to be answered if an organisation is to be well structured. Child (1988) draws the organisation designer's attention to the following questions:

- **To what extent should the work of an organisation be broken down into small parts, creating rather narrow, specialised jobs?** These jobs can then be combined to form narrow, specialist departments. For example, should a production worker perform the same task on a production line perhaps thousands of times per day, or be moved to other tasks periodically? Remember this too from our earlier discussions on production lines.

- **How many levels should an organisation have in its hierarchy and for how many people should each manager be responsible?** This, clearly, can be broken down into two questions but, as you see later, they are different sides of the same coin. For example, at the Comfortable Shoe Company Bill Battersby manages a staff of three and reports to a sales director at head office, who in turn reports to the managing director. Does Bill manage too many, too few or the right number of staff? Are there too many steps between the managing director and the ordinary salespersons, like Mark Green?

- **How should jobs and departments be grouped together?** For example, at the Comfortable Shoe Company, the north west sales team has been created partly because the staff concerned perform the same task and partly because they work in the same region.

- **How closely do the various parts of an organisation need to be integrated?** For example, in a hospital it is sometimes important for catering staff to know about the medical condition of patients, so that they can provide an appropriate diet. A high level of co-ordination between medical staff and those who actually prepare the meals is, therefore, needed.

- **How much control should management exercise over the activities of an organisation?** For example, at the Comfortable Shoe Company, sales staff are now controlled in the levels of discount they can offer by the company's standard discounts policy. In the past, they were less controlled.

We now analyse each of these questions in turn, but we emphasise at the outset that they are questions without single 'right' answers.

The organisation structure of your workplace or university may be remarkably different from that of other seemingly similar organisations nearby. This does not mean that your organisation has got it right and the others have got it wrong, or vice versa. What it shows is that even apparently similar organisations can be markedly different and, quite possibly, equally successful. The appropriate structure for a particular organisation depends on both the characteristics of the organisation itself and its relationship to its environment.

ACTIVITY 9

Suggested time: 2 hours 30 minutes.

Your Chosen Organisation

Before looking for answers to Child's five questions, you would find it helpful to find out more about an organisation with which you are already familiar. We call this your 'chosen organisation'. When you have done this, you analyse it in various ways while considering Child's questions.

The first thing you need to do is to decide upon your chosen organisation. If you are in full-time employment, you will probably gain most from the activity if you choose the organisation for which you work. You will already possess much useful information and developing your knowledge further will be of value both to you and to your employing organisation. If you are not in full-time employment, find an organisation with which you are already familiar. This will help you understand what you find out and contextualise it. You could choose a place where you work part-time, or have worked in the fairly recent past. You could choose an organisation whose services you use regularly, for example, a supermarket, a leisure centre, or a bus company. You will need to contact the organisation and obtain its approval to conduct the interviews.

Within your chosen organisation, you need to select two persons to interview. Choose two persons who you think will be knowledgeable about the organisation and who will each be willing to speak to you for about an hour. You will interview them on the basis of the questionnaire given below. Try to select people who work in different parts of the organisation and who do different jobs, so that you obtain varied points of view in answer to your questions. At least one of your interviewees should be in a supervisory or managerial position, as certain of the questions relate to the interviewee's supervisory responsibilities.

The questionnaire asks your interviewees a number of key questions about their work and their organisation. Treat the interview schedule as a whole and the questions themselves as guidelines. Before or during the two interviews, you may be able to think of more precise ways to phrase particular questions, as you know more about your chosen organisation than we do. Feel free to do so. The aim is to get the most informative and accurate answers to the questions.

Do not worry too much if your interviewees' replies are not wholly consistent. If possible, ask supplementary questions to clarify matters whenever it seems useful. Space is given with each question for you to fill in your interviewees' answers.

Do not forget at the beginning of each interview to:

● reassure the interviewee that everything he or she says during the interview you will treat as confidential

● explain why you are conducting the interview

● explain that you will return to give the interviewee a report on your findings

● thank the interviewee for giving up their time to see you.

INTERVIEW SCHEDULE ON YOUR CHOSEN ORGANISATION

Part 1 Your organisation

1   What is the name of the organisation?
Answer

Inte. viewee 1

Interviewee 2

2   How many staff does your organisation employ?
Answer

Interviewee 1

Interviewee 2

3   How many sites or branches does your organisation operate from?
Answer

Interviewee 1

Interviewee 2

4   On which site or branch do you work?
Answer

Interviewee 1

Interviewee 2

Part 2 Your job

5   What is your job title?
    Answer

    Interviewee 1

    Interviewee 2

6   What are the major responsibilities of your job?
    Answer

    Interviewee 1

    Interviewee 2

7   Does your organisation require that persons doing your job possess any
    particular qualifications or undertake any particular training? If your answer
    is 'yes', please specify the requirement(s).
    Answer

    Interviewee 1

    Interviewee 2

8   Are the requirements of your job set out in a formal, written job specification?
    Answer

    Interviewee 1

    Interviewee 2

9   Does your organisation have rules or procedures that lay down how you
    should go about performing particular tasks, for example, standard operating
    procedures, or are you fairly free to choose how you go about your work?
    Please give examples of any rules or procedures.
    Answer

    Interviewee 1

    Interviewee 2

10 Is the output of your work measured in any particular way to see if it is up to the standard your organisation expects? Again, please give examples of any forms of measurement.
    Answer

    Interviewee 1

    Interviewee 2

11 On the site or at the branch where you work is your job unique, or are there other people with the same or very similar title and job descriptions, or who perform the same or very similar tasks?
    Answer

    Interviewee 1

    Interviewee 2

    If the interviewee answers that his or her job is unique, go directly to question 13.

12 Do you work independently from the other person(s) on your site or at your branch who have the same or very similar job to you, or do you work as a team with them, sharing tasks and responsibilities?
    Answer

    Interviewee 1

    Interviewee 2

13 In carrying out your work to what extent are you dependent upon the work of other colleagues doing different jobs to your own?
    Answer

    Interviewee 1

    Interviewee 2

14 In carrying out their jobs, to what extent are other people in your workplace dependent upon the way in which you do your job?
    Answer

    Interviewee 1

    Interviewee 2

Part 3 Supervision at work

15 Do you supervise the work of anyone else in your organisation?
Answer

Interviewee 1

Interviewee 2

If the interviewee answers 'no' to question 15, please go directly to question 22.

16 How many members of staff report directly to you?
Answer

Interviewee 1

Interviewee 2

17 What jobs are done by the staff who report to you?
Answer

Interviewee 1

Interviewee 2

18 Are the staff who report to you responsible to you for all of their work, or do they report to another supervisor for some aspects of their work?
Answer

Interviewee 1

Interviewee 2

19 Is your supervision of your staff's work mainly a matter of you instructing them what tasks to perform and how to perform them, or it is more a matter of discussion and negotiation about how tasks should best be performed?
Answer

Interviewee 1

Interviewee 2

20 Do you feel that you are able to give adequate support and attention to the staff whose work you supervise? If your answer is 'no', please try to identify reasons why this may be so.
Answer

Interviewee 1

Interviewee 2

21 Where do the persons who report to you fit into your organisation's management system? Do they also supervise staff? If so, how many staff, doing what jobs, are they responsible for?
Answer

Interviewee 1

Interviewee 2

22 To whom are you directly responsible for your work in your organisation's management system?
Answer

Interviewee 1

Interviewee 2

23 How many other people, doing what jobs, does this person supervise?
Answer

Interviewee 1

Interviewee 2

24 In ascending order of seniority, what are the job titles of the managers who have direct authority over you? Start with your own supervisor and finish with the chief executive.
Answer

Interviewee 1

Interviewee 2

25 Do you feel that your supervisor instructs you how to do your work, or
    discusses with you the best way to do it?
    Answer

    Interviewee 1

    Interviewee 2

26 Do you feel that your supervisor has the knowledge and time to assist you as
    fully as you would like in your work?
    Answer

    Interviewee 1

    Interviewee 2

27 Many organisations have attempted to reduce their numbers and levels of
    managers in recent years. Has yours done so?
    Answer

    Interviewee 1

    Interviewee 2

    If an interviewee answers 'no' to this question, proceed directly to question 30.

28 Why did your organisation attempt to reduce its levels of management?
    Answer

    Interviewee 1

    Interviewee 2

29 What do you believe the consequences have been of your organisation's
    attempts to reduce its levels of management?
    Answer

    Interviewee 1

    Interviewee 2

Part 4 Departments in your organisation

30 What are the key tasks performed at your site or branch?
Answer

Interviewee 1

Interviewee 2

31 Are these various tasks performed in separate departments? If so, which?
Answer

Interviewee 1

Interviewee 2

32 Are other key tasks for your organisation performed on other sites or at other branches? If so, please specify which and where they are performed.
Answer

Interviewee 1

Interviewee 2

33 Does your organisation produce different products at different sites? If so, please specify which and where they are produced.
Answer

Interviewee 1

Interviewee 2

34 Does your organisation have a regional or district structure? If so, which are the regions or districts?
Answer

Interviewee 1

Interviewee 2

35 Does your organisation serve different types of customers, for example, wholesale and retail, on different sites or branches? If so, please specify which types of customers are dealt with at which places.
Answer

Interviewee 1

Interviewee 2

Having completed each interview, read your answers carefully both to refresh your memory about what you have discovered, and to make sure that what you have written reflects accurately and completely what you were told.

Summary

In this section, you have noted Child's five questions that are central to the design of organisation structures:

- degree of specialisation in jobs and departments
- number of hierarchical levels and the span of managerial control
- grouping of jobs and departments
- degree and closeness of integration between an organisation's parts
- degree of managerial control to be exercised over the different parts.

In Section 3, you look at these questions in detail and in relation to your chosen organisation and for which you have also gathered considerable information about the structure and processes of an organisation.

SECTION 3

Key Decisions in Designing an Organisation's Structure

Introduction

In this section, we examine in much more detail Child's five key questions about organisation structure and the issues they involve. Using our discussion and the information you have gathered about your chosen organisation, you analyse how the key questions and issues are reflected in its structure.

3.1 Specialisation of jobs

To what extent should the work of the organisation be broken down into small parts, creating narrow specialised jobs? Any organisation will have a number of tasks that need to be performed if its work is going to be properly accomplished and its objectives achieved. These may range from deciding whether or not to build a new factory, to controlling a piece of machinery on a production line, to answering customer complaints, to making the tea. In a very large organisation, such as a major engineering company like GEC, whose products range from simple fuses to advanced radar, there may be many thousands of these tasks. It is a key part of the organisation designer's role to group these tasks into the sets or collections that we call jobs.

ACTIVITY 10

Is this grouping of tasks into jobs a process of differentiation or of integration?

The correct answer is differentiation, because the organisation's tasks are being divided up into a series of separate jobs, each of which is in some respects different from the others. This process of designing jobs is very important because it:

- tells each of the organisation's employees what their responsibilities are

- tells each employee how and where they fit into the organisation as a whole, for example, to whom they report and, if they have managerial responsibilities, who reports to them

- helps customers and suppliers to know from whom they should seek help or advice, if they want something performed by the organisation.

ACTIVITY 11

Look back at your chosen organisation interview schedules and answer the following questions for both interviewees:

1 To whom are Interviewees 1 and 2 each responsible for the quality of their work?

Interviewee 1

Interviewee 2

2 If you were a customer or client of your chosen organisation, in what ways might Interviewees 1 and 2 each assist you, either by performing a task for you, or giving you advice?

Interviewee 1

Interviewee 2

---

1   Unless one of your interviewees is the boss and owns the organisation, each must be responsible to some person or group, for example, the shareholders.

2   If one of your interviewees was a shop assistant in a supermarket, he or she might be able to assist a customer by locating where a particular product is kept in the store, or telling them the price of an item, or telling them to whom they could complain, and so on.

If you cannot think of any ways in which either, or even both, of your interviewees could help a customer, it is likely that their job is so defined that they have little regular contact with the public.

SPECIALISATION AND JOB ENRICHMENT

In dividing up an organisation's tasks into a series of jobs for employees to perform, two key choices have to be made. These concern:

● choice between **work specialisation** and **job enrichment**
● choice between tight and looser job descriptions.

ACTIVITY 12

What do you understand by the terms work specialisation and job enrichment?

Work specialisation is the extent to which an organisation's tasks are divided into individual jobs. Job enrichment is the process of designing jobs so that the employee has increased levels of interest, achievement and recognition to motivate him or her in the workplace.

The first key choice posed by job design, therefore, is to what extent each particular job should consist of a small number of similar tasks which the employee performs repeatedly, so increasing his or her expertise (work specialisation); or to what extent each job should consist of a wide range of varied tasks, so that employees have increased interest in their work and a broader range of skills (job enrichment).

The case for specialisation in job design was recognised as early as 1776 by the economist Adam Smith in his book *The Wealth of Nations*. He wrote that if a person is able to concentrate on one task, or a small number of specific tasks, then as they work they will become more knowledgeable, dexterous and efficient, working faster and making fewer mistakes (Smith, 1910).

However, there are dangers if specialisation is taken to extremes. The worker may become bored with repetitive tasks, work less hard, pay less attention and make more mistakes. Jobs involving only a few repetitive tasks are also often poorly valued and carry low status in organisations, which again can demotivate those who perform them. In Unit 3, you looked in detail at division of labour in relation to technology and Fordism.

A good example of how important the choice is between specialisation and job enrichment can be seen in the motor industry. You saw this earlier in Unit 3 and particularly in Review activity 3, and also in the post-Fordism and Fordism comparisons.

Since the late 1980s, the British motor industry has seen major changes in the ways that the jobs of production workers are defined. Traditionally, the motor car industry has been one in which cars were made in a long series of small individual steps, on a long production-line, starting with a basic chassis or sub-frame and ending with a painted, polished car. Each step in the process would be carried out by one or a few workers, performing a task that might last seconds or at most, a few minutes. Workers performed these repetitive tasks again and again, as each new car came down the production line. They certainly knew their jobs well, but also sometimes became bored and demotivated, did not always work efficiently, and so required close supervision to avoid substandard work.

By the late 1980s, it was clear that British motor manufacturers faced a major competitive threat from Japanese car manufacturers such as Nissan, Toyota and Honda, whose cars were generally built to higher standards and were often cheaper, not least because Japanese motor industry workers were more productive. In response, firms such as Rover and Vauxhall (part of General Motors) have looked radically at production workers' jobs. They are engaged in a process of multi-skilling – that is, they are trying to give production workers a range of skills. This means that workers can perform several tasks upon a car as it passes their production line workstation and also that they can be moved from one workstation to another on the production line. Although it involved a great deal of money in training costs, workers are better motivated, raise their productivity, make fewer mistakes and require less supervision.

The second key choice in job design is whether each employee in an organisation should be given their own discrete job description, which is exclusive to them, so that their work overlaps as little as possible with that of their colleagues, or whether the organisation should deliberately define each person's job so that it overlaps significantly with that of their colleagues?

ACTIVITY 13

What do you think are the relative advantages and disadvantages in each of these choices?

Clear, discrete job descriptions have many advantages. They ensure that each person knows clearly what his or her job is, and for what he or she is responsible. People have a tendency to become demotivated if they do not know what is expected of them. Equally other people inside and outside the organisation, customers, for example, can find out who is responsible for what. It can also avoid the disagreements that sometimes occur between colleagues about who is responsible for what tasks. For example, in a bank, if a customer account manager is allowed to approve loans only up to £10,000 and all higher loans need the branch manager's approval, then the job is clear and disputes are unlikely to occur.

However, tight job descriptions can also lead individuals only to take an interest in their own job, to ignore its impact upon colleagues and their work, and not to feel a responsibility for the work of the organisation as a whole. For example, our customer account manager at the bank may take great care advising a customer requiring a loan of £8,000, because it is 'his' or 'her' customer, but spend less time trying to help a customer seeking a £150,000 loan, knowing that this will eventually have to be dealt with by the branch manager. Yet the customer requiring the larger loan may need more advice and may prove a more profitable customer for the bank as an organisation!

Issues of this sort have led some organisations to conclude that, whilst employees need to know clearly what their jobs are, it may be useful for groups of workers performing related tasks to have overlapping job descriptions, and hence shared responsibilities. Such overlapping needs designing with great care to avoid duplication of work and disputes over responsibilities. It needs to be accompanied by team-building activities, in which groups of colleagues working on related tasks are encouraged to work together harmoniously, and to recognise their responsibility for the work of the group as a whole, not just for particular tasks they happen to perform at any given moment. Such team-building can improve workers' motivation and cut costs also, as individuals try to ensure their work is done in harmony with that of colleagues and take time to help any colleague with a problem.

Again a useful illustration of the advantages of overlapping jobs and team-building can be seen in the motor industry.

As well as the working practice changes we discussed earlier, British motor manufacturers such as Vauxhall and Rover have re-organised production so that workers now work in teams who share overlapping job descriptions. Previously, parts of the British motor industry were notorious for tight lines of job demarcation where workers were very reluctant to do anything outside their particular narrowly defined job. Consequently, a simple machinery breakdown on a production line might bring the whole line to a stop while a maintenance person came to repair it, although the production worker was capable of repairing the machine himself or herself in seconds. Today such restrictions have been largely set aside. A production worker can recognise that the responsibility for repairing minor breakdowns is that of the team, not just of the member specifically appointed to do maintenance work. A simple breakdown can be repaired on the spot by the production worker with a minimum halt to production.

Clearly, in this case, the planned overlapping of jobs is closely integrated with the process of job enrichment we mentioned earlier. Simple maintenance is part of the production worker's wider and more interesting responsibilities.

3.2 Hierarchy and span of control

How many levels should an organisation have in its hierarchy and how wide should be the spans of control of its managers? The hierarchy of an organisation is the number of levels of seniority it contains from its chief executive to its least experienced operative. It tells us who reports to whom and who is responsible for whose work.

It is often the case that organisations attempt to present their hierarchies, their departmental structures and the jobs that have been defined within these, in pictorial form using an organisation chart. It is quite common now to see such diagrams displayed at the entrance to buildings or departments, and including names and pictures of the members of staff who hold various posts. You met this idea in Unit 1.

Organisation charts can be very useful to give a snapshot of the key elements of an organisation's structure. However, like maps, charts are abstractions from reality and exclude much information about an organisation's structure. They commonly include job titles, but not job descriptions. They tell you about the formal side of the organisation, but not its informal side, so they can give a misleading impression of how things really work. Hence we should recognise their value but use them with care. A number of organisation charts are used in this section. They do not cover the whole organisation depicted, only those parts of it about which you need to know.

Figure 1 shows an organisation chart with an extract from the hierarchy of a manufacturing company that works a 24 hour day and so operates a three-shift system. It illustrates the number of steps in the hierarchy from the managing director to the operatives who make the company's products in its factory. Normally the steps in an organisation's hierarchy are presented diagrammatically as being spaced vertically and linked by vertical lines. As a consequence, hierarchical relationships, that is, relationships of seniority, in an organisation are frequently referred to as its **vertical** relationships.

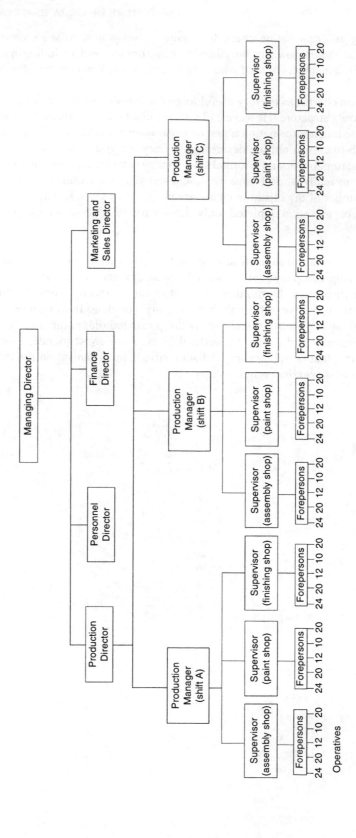

Figure 1: Organisation chart of ACME Manufacturing Company

ACTIVITY 14

Looking at the organisation of the ACME Manufacturing Company in Figure 1, how many steps are there in its hierarchy between the most senior and least senior of its employees?

There are five steps: from managing director (most senior) to production director (one step), from production director to production manager (two steps), from production manager to supervisor (three steps), from supervisor to foreperson (four steps) and from foreperson to operative, the least senior employee (five steps).

Organisations need hierarchy because of the range of tasks that they have to perform and the variety of different people with varying skills that they employ. ACME Manufacturing needs skilled operatives to assemble, paint and finish its products, but it also needs a production manager to ensure that the flow of work proceeds smoothly on each shift, a production director to ensure that the factory is equipped with modern machinery, and a managing director to ensure that the whole operation runs smoothly and that strategic plans are drawn up for its future development.

However, it is generally thought more efficient for organisations to have as few levels as possible in their hierarchies. The more levels there are in a hierarchy, the more steps that information has to pass through to move from top to bottom, or vice versa. Hence at ACME Manufacturing, a message from the managing director must pass through five stages to reach the operatives. Each stage is likely to add to the time the message takes to reach its destination. There is also the danger that it will be distorted through interpretation and re-interpretation at each stage, so that the operative will not receive precisely the message that the managing director intended.

The more steps there are in an organisation's hierarchy, the taller it is said to be. The fewer stages there are in an organisation's hierarchy, the flatter it is said to be (Figure 2).

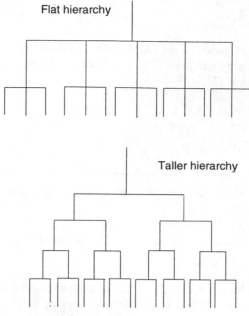

Figure 2: Flat and tall hierarchy

ACTIVITY 15

Look again at the interview schedules for your chosen organisation and see if
you can determine how many levels it has in its hierarchy. Present your
answer as a vertical chain linking each level in the hierarchy. For the ACME
Manufacturing Company this would be:

Managing director

|

Production director

|

Production manager

|

Supervisor

|

Foreperson

|

Operative

To do this, you will need to see how many levels of hierarchy there are above
and below each of your interviewees. For example, if you had interviewed a
supervisor at ACME Manufacturing he or she would have told you that there
are three levels of hierarchy above them and two below, giving six levels in
the hierarchy, with five steps between them. Use the different answers of your
two interviewees to confirm the number of levels you identify.

If your chosen organisation is a large one, it is possible that your interviewees may not have been aware of or indicated the full extent of the hierarchy. If so, you should have presented the hierarchy as fully as you can.

To have an adequate understanding of an organisation's structure we need to understand not only how many levels there are in its hierarchy, that is, whether it is tall or flat, but also how wide the supervisory responsibilities of its employees are, that is, the number of subordinates who report to an employee and for whose work that employee is responsible. The width of a person's supervisory responsibilities is called his or her **span of control**.

At ACME Manufacturing each production manager has a span of control of three supervisors, thus:

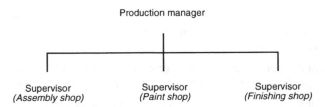

Note, the production manager's span of control does not include all of the 94 people below him or her in the hierarchy. The five forepersons and 860 operatives do not report directly to the production manager and so are not part of his or her span of control.

ACTIVITY 16

Select one interviewee from your chosen organisation and, using the interview schedule, determine the span of control of the supervisor or manager to whom he or she reports.

Your interview schedule should tell you how many other people report to your interviewee's supervisor. If you then add your interviewee himself or herself to that number, you will have the supervisor's span of control.

There are dangers associated with having too wide or too narrow a span of control. If a supervisor's span of control is too wide, then he or she may be unable to devote sufficient time to the various subordinates in the span. He or she may be unable to co-ordinate the subordinates' activities thoroughly, or to advise them when they face difficult problems. As a consequence early organisation theorists, for example, Graicunas (1937), concluded that spans of control should generally be quite narrow, generally not more than ten. In practice, organisations frequently exceed this figure. For example, at ACME Manufacturing the maximum figure is 24, for one of the forepersons in the assembly shop. This is not least because narrow spans of control can lead to 'over-supervision' in which subordinates' work is overseen so closely that they feel they have insufficient scope to use their own judgement and initiative, feel under-utilised and so become demotivated.

Equally, if supervisors are responsible only for a narrow body of work, then there may be inadequate attention paid to the need to co-ordinate the work of the organisation as a whole. Finally, it follows logically that in any given organisation, the narrower its spans of control, the taller its hierarchy must be.

In practice, spans of control are likely to vary according to a number of considerations, such as:

- complexity and variety of the jobs performed by the subordinates, for example, at ACME Manufacturing the managing director has only a four-person span, but one assembly shop foreperson has a 24-person span

- abilities of the supervisor and the subordinates, because good supervisors and subordinates can both operate in broad spans of control

- range of the supervisor's own responsibilities, for example, at ACME Manufacturing, the finishing shop supervisor has only a one-person span, but this is because he or she also acts as inspector of the quality of finished products and this is a time-consuming task.

THE FLAT ORGANISATION

In recent years, many organisations have devoted a lot of attention to shortening their hierarchies. You met this idea in earlier units. For example, in 1994, the government asked police forces in Britain to reduce their hierarchies by removing one rank from among their senior officers, probably chief inspector. The reasons put forward for creating flatter organisations are generally concerned with cutting costs and enriching the jobs of employees:

- Costs are cut because, as hierarchies are shortened, fewer people are employed as managers and supervisors.

- Jobs are enriched because the fewer managers who remain have wider spans of control. They are able to supervise their subordinates less closely, so the subordinates are empowered to do more for themselves.

If ACME Manufacturing decided, for example, to remove the grade of supervisor, the production manager for each shift would have a span of control of five, instead of only three. Each of the foremen might be expected to take decisions and responsibilities previously taken by a supervisor. Given the broader remit of the foreman, the operatives might then be expected to do things previously done for them by a foreman. For example, they may take more responsibility themselves for the quality of their work with less close inspection. Taking on broader responsibilities means a more varied, richer job for employees and can help to make them better motivated.

However, it is a mistake to believe that simply cutting the length of a hierarchy will produce beneficial effects. Those who take on increased responsibilities will need to be trained to do so, or they may become over-worked and stressed, and the quality of their work may fall. They may also become demotivated as their promotion opportunities diminish. For example, at ACME Manufacturing, an ambitious foreman no longer has nine supervisors' jobs to aspire to, but only three, much more senior, production managers' jobs. Finally, wider control spans can mean that the supervisor has less time to spend with subordinates, so that the organisation's communications deteriorate.

ACTIVITY 17

Looking back at the interview schedules for your chosen organisation, do your interviewees indicate their organisation has attempted to introduce a flattened hierarchy in recent years?

If your answer is Yes, do their answers indicate that their organisation has experienced any of the suggested benefits or disadvantages of a flatter hierarchy? Circle the correct answers.

Possible benefits

1   Cutting costs? *Yes / No*

2   Broader responsibilities and more enjoyable work for employees? *Yes / No*

Possible disadvantages

1   Over-work and more stress among employees? *Yes / No*

2   Poorer promotion prospects for employees? *Yes / No*

3   Poorer communications in the organisation? *Yes / No*

Whatever answers you have discovered, this activity, and those preceding it, should have helped you appreciate that the levels of hierarchy and the spans of control associated with them are important questions for any organisation.

3.3 Grouping activities

How should jobs and departments be grouped together? The way in which an organisation chooses to group together its activities to form units, sections, teams, departments or divisions (the names may vary from organisation to organisation) should reflect its strategic or fundamental goals, and the ways in which it expects those goals to be achieved. For example, during the 1980s many pharmaceutical companies created biotechnology research teams or departments in anticipation of major product range changes with the development of genetic engineering techniques.

The choice an organisation makes when grouping its activities together is also important for its staff, as it will determine which colleagues are to be supervised by a particular manager, to share a common set of objectives and to draw upon a common pool of resources. Staff in a particular department tend to identify with one another and to build up bonds of loyalty, common purpose and achievement with one another. For example, at the Comfortable Shoe Company the regional sales teams had their monthly sales figures measured, and compared with one another. Organisations can foster loyalties between team colleagues in these ways. They can also foster competition between teams to achieve the best results. Such rivalries can be constructive for the team and for the organisation as a whole, provided they are carefully managed and do not lead team members to hinder the performance of rival teams.

When deciding precisely how to group jobs together to form departments, the organisation needs to decide exactly what common characteristics or logical links between its activities it regards as being paramount. These should then be the basis for the formation of its departments.

ACTIVITY 18

Can you suggest any common characteristics around which organisations might choose to build their departmental, section or team structures?

There are three key characteristics of work around which organisations may build their teams, units, departments and so on:

- activities, processes or functions jobs share in common that might lead to their being grouped together – this is often called the functional principle and it creates a **functional structure**

- outputs, products, goods or services that groups of colleagues work together to produce – this is often called the product principle, and it creates a **product structure**

● customers that groups of colleagues work together to serve – this is often called the customer principle and it gives rise to a **customer structure**.

We now look at each of these in turn to see what they look like; to find out when they are used; and to find out what advantages and disadvantages they may have.

FUNCTIONAL STRUCTURE

This is the most common form of structure. Using the functional principle, jobs are grouped together to form departments because they involve similar or related sets of activities or skills which provide a key service to the organisation and to the achievement of its goals.

ACME Manufacturing has a functional structure. It has four functional departments: a production department; a personnel department; a finance department; and a marketing and sales department. Each has its own director who reports directly to the managing director (Figure 3).

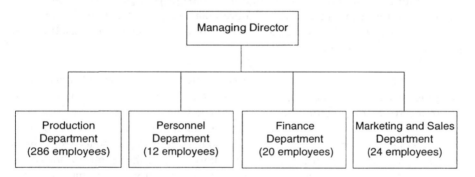

Figure 3: Extract from the structure of the ACME Manufacturing Company

Each department provides an essential service for ACME Engineering:

● production department assembles and paints its products, and checks each to ensure it is manufactured to customer standards

● personnel department ensures that the company has the right staff with the right skills in all four departments to do all the jobs that need doing; it also ensures that staff are appropriately rewarded, that they are trained and that their legal rights as employees are respected

● finance department ensures that ACME Engineering has the funds necessary to carry on its activities, that its bills are paid, that staff wages are paid correctly and on time, that proper accounts are kept, and so on

● marketing and sales department ensures that the company knows what is happening in its markets, that potential customers are kept informed about the company's products, that salespersons visit customers to take orders, and that those orders are delivered on time.

Notice that the departments do not have to be of equal size. The production department is larger than the other three. What is essential is that each department has an important, coherent and logically-related set of tasks to perform.

A functional structure has generally been found to be effective for small and medium-sized companies because:

- it helps ensure that each key function in the company is performed by specialists who concentrate on particular tasks, so gaining experience and using and developing their skills (in marketing, book-keeping and so on)

- it can help cut costs by enabling smallish organisations to make the best use of expensive equipment (note how ACME Engineering maximises use of its production machinery with three shifts) and of expensively trained staff, by allowing them to concentrate upon their particular specialisms.

Functional structures, however, do pose problems of horizontal co-ordination between the various functional departments. In relatively small organisations, like ACME Engineering, such problems can be overcome because managers often know one another well, see one another frequently and have sufficient opportunities to deal with common problems. As organisations grow larger, such possibilities may become fewer, because there are more managers, perhaps on different sites, and a functional structure may become less satisfactory. Then the organisation will need to consider restructuring.

A similar problem may occur if the environment outside the organisation is changing in ways that require new responses and ways of working from several departments at once. For example, ACME Engineering might find that technological changes require it to make and market new products. This would need close collaboration between the production and marketing departments. Companies with functional structures often find it difficult to organise the necessary horizontal collaboration. Again, a reorganisation may be necessary for the company to solve its problem.

ACTIVITY 19

Looking back at the interview schedules for your chosen organisation, can you see some of the key functions that it has to perform? Examples might include research product development, production, marketing, sales, distribution, finance, and personnel.

Are these key functions located in separate departments or are closely related functions together, for example, research and development, marketing and sales, sales and distribution?

If you have answered 'Yes', list the functional departments you have identified:

Although you may have identified some functional departments, note that it does not necessarily mean that your chosen organisation has a functional structure. It may use another of our three organising principles, as well as the functional principle.

PRODUCT STRUCTURE

The product principle groups together in a department, all the jobs necessary to the development, manufacture, marketing and sales of a particular good or service, or closely related group of goods or services.

A product structure brings together all of the functions, marketing, production, and so on, needed to bring a particular product to the consumer. So it tends to be particularly well suited to meeting the needs of the product. The focus for everyone, whatever his or her function and training, is on the needs of the product. If consumers indicate that they want the product changed in some way, then everyone in the department can concentrate on bringing about the necessary changes.

Large organisations producing a variety of products often favour a product structure. It means they can focus their efforts on changing consumer needs in a range of markets.

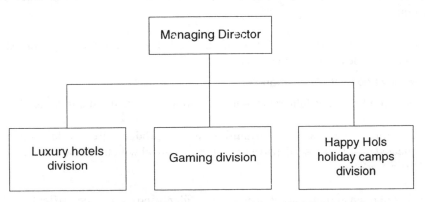

Figure 4: Extract from the structure of PFM Leisure plc

Take PFM Leisure plc as an example. The company is fairly large with 6,000 employees. It has three distinctive product lines: a small group of 12 luxury hotels, a chain of betting shops and six Happy Hols Holiday Camps.

Management of each product line involves different considerations:

- The luxury hotels provide a year-round service, including conference facilities, largely to businesses and senior business executives.

- The Happy Hols Holiday Camps provide a seasonal service, as it is closed from October to March, to families on tight budgets wanting a wide range of entertainment facilities for children.

- Customers at the betting shops usually drop in briefly to place a bet, then leave. However, although betting shops were previously allowed to provide only the most basic customer facilities, in 1994 the law was changed to allow them to be made more attractive and comfortable. PFM Leisure will need to respond to this change or their betting shops will lose custom to other companies who offer greater comfort to customers placing bets.

Given PFM Leisure's structure it is relatively well placed to meet this challenge. Responsibility for the betting shops lies completely in the gaming division. Its staff, no matter what their specialism, will be well aware of the implications of the legal changes. Finance staff will know that money will have to be found to upgrade the betting shops. Personnel staff will know that betting shop managers may have to be trained to manage a wider range of services, possibly catering services, for example, and new staff may need to be employed to provide them. Marketing staff will want to market the new, improved facilities, and so on, throughout the gaming division.

The need for such changes might be missed in a solely functional structure where, for example, marketing staff must monitor changes in the everyday market, and so might miss significant changes in small or unusual markets. Furthermore, once the need for a change has been identified, it may be difficult to bring together all those with the required skills and focus their attention on what is needed to bring the change about, unlike the situation at PFM Leisure with its product-based structure.

However, although a product structure is good at identifying changes in existing markets, it is less good at identifying:

- development of new markets
- related changes taking place in more than one market at one time.

The result can be missed opportunities, as new products are not developed, and duplicated efforts, as two departments attempt to deal with the same change in each of their markets.

Even where changing market needs can be identified, it may be difficult within a product structure to get close collaboration between two or more different departments to meet them. For example, an engineering company with product divisions might waste time, effort and money developing two very similar components for products manufactured within two different departments, when a single component might have been developed that was suitable for both of the products. Or a major fashion retailer, with divisions that specialise in mail-order retailing and in high-street retailing in stores, might easily miss the growth of tele-shopping because neither of them is directly involved in the market already. Some years hence, a failure to enter this market might seriously affect the company's prospects.

ACTIVITY 20

What are the key advantages of a functional structure and a product structure?

For a functional structure, the sorts of advantage you should be able to identify are:

- it concentrates the organisation's efforts on its key functions
- it allows staff to specialise and gain expertise in these key tasks
- it enables the fullest use to be made of specialist staff and equipment.

For a product structure, the sorts of advantage you should be able to identify are:

- it concentrates the organisation's efforts on particular products and markets
- it allows the organisation to be responsive to changes in existing markets
- it focuses staff loyalties on the product so that different specialists work closely together.

CUSTOMER STRUCTURE

The customer principle groups together in a department all the jobs necessary to service the needs of a particular group of clients or customers. A customer structure will bring together all the functions needed to serve a particular group of customers – marketing, sales, production and so on. It requires an organisation to decide what is the key feature of its customers, so that activities can be grouped together sensibly in ways that best serve their needs. One commonly used criterion for grouping customers is geography, that is, where they live, work and so on. Organisations adopt local or regional structures or, if they are transnational, have national structures.

Take, for example, Union Dairies Ltd, a national manufacturer and distributor of dairy products. Because customers for dairy products vary from place to place and because bulky raw materials, such as milk, are expensive to transport over long distances, the company has adopted a regional structure as follows:

Managing director

Northern and Yorkshire region   North west region   Midlands region   Southern region   South west region

Each region has all the functional specialisms needed to serve its market, so that it can meet its particular needs, for example, for local cheeses.

Some local authorities in the UK, such as Middlesborough and Tower Hamlets Borough Councils, have gone a long way towards a geographically-based customer structure. They run most council services through a series of local offices. This allows them to co-ordinate services at a local level and vary them to meet the needs of a particular locality.

An organisation can choose some other criterion than geography for grouping customers. Age can be a criterion. Political parties, for example, usually organise separate sections for young people and older members. Hospitals are often divided into departments which treat people with different kinds of illness.

ACTIVITY 21

What potential advantages and disadvantages can you see in a customer-structured organisation?

A customer structure has many of the advantages of a product structure. In particular, it allows all the staff in a department, district or region to focus their attentions upon the needs of a particular group of customers. Again it is of particular value to large organisations with a variety of rather different client groups, in different countries, and so on.

Like a product structure, however, the customer structure can lead to:

● missed opportunities, if they arise among previously unserved groups of customers

● duplication of effort, if different departments work on the same problem arising in different customer groups.

HYBRID STRUCTURE

Sometimes an organisation may choose not to organise itself according to one of the three function, product and customer principles, but it may combine two of them. Doing this gives rise to one of two other forms of organisation structure: a **hybrid structure** or a **matrix structure**.

A hybrid structure occurs when an organisation adopts a structure that uses two of the functional, product and customer principles as a basis for its design.

Take for example the case of Merritt Chemicals plc in Figure 5.

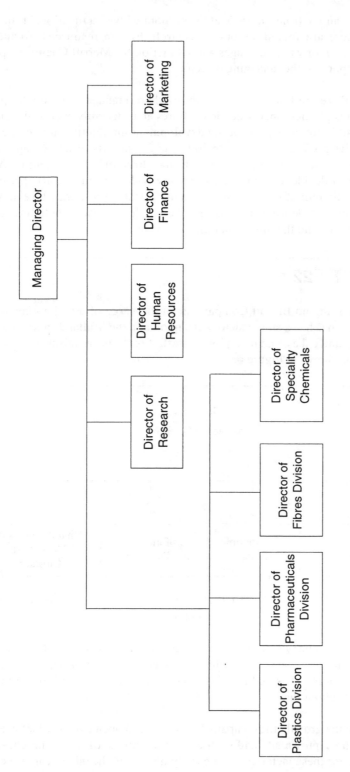

Figure 5: Extract from the structure of Merritt Chemicals plc

Here, as you can see from Figure 5, at the corporate level, a functional principle is adopted. There are four directors – research, human resources, finance and marketing – each of whom manages a key function for Merritt Chemicals plc as a whole and reports to the managing director.

In addition, there are four directors each of whom manages a particular product division, that is plastics, pharmaceuticals, fibres and speciality chemicals. They are each responsible for all aspects of the development, production and marketing of their particular product ranges, but within the constraints of any company-wide policies set by the four corporate functional directors. For example, Merritt Chemicals may decide to introduce a company-wide system of staff appraisal. In this case, the director of human resources and his staff at corporate level devise an appraisal system to be carried out across the whole company, including the four product divisions and the three functional divisions.

ACTIVITY 22

The Tasty Bun and Biscuit Company is on the verge of a major expansion. Until now it has had a single factory at Tiptown in the Midlands making all of its biscuits and cakes, and it employs a staff of 600. Its organisation structure has been as shown in Figure 6.

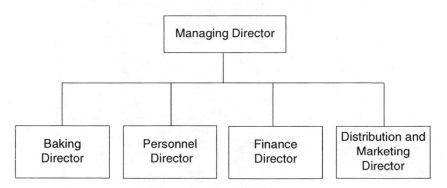

Figure 6: Extract from The Tasty Bun and Biscuit Company's organisation structure

However, the company has recently won two major new contracts, each with a national supermarket chain. These will necessitate a 200% growth in the company's production of both cakes and biscuits, and daily deliveries of all the company's products throughout the UK.

To cope with the growth, the company has decided to open two new factories, each as large as the Tiptown site and each employing 600 staff. It has purchased two suitable sites for these factories, one near Plymouth and the other near Manchester. The organisation now has to decide how to organise itself to cope with expansion.

Biscuits and cakes have always been produced using different production lines, processes and machinery at the Tiptown factory. Some economies could be gained by having one of the new factories concentrate on biscuits and the other one on cakes. This would allow each factory to develop a very large production line and a high level of expertise in producing one of the two product-lines. The company feels that the gains of so doing would be beneficial but small, as it has been able to develop its two smaller existing production lines at Tiptown to a very high level of efficiency already. The problem with this approach would be that at least some products would have to be shipped very long distances daily from Plymouth and Manchester to meet the supermarkets' national requirements. The alternative would be to build production lines for biscuits and cakes at each of the new factories and divide the country into three regional markets, each served by a single factory. This would have the advantage of allowing each factory to deal with the variations in regional demand that exist, which are significant, although not overriding.

The Tasty Bun and Biscuit Company wishes to know how it should organise production in the two new factories and, whatever decision it makes, how this should affect the company's organisation as a whole. What advice would you give?

As you will probably realise, there is no single, perfect solution to The Tasty Bun and Biscuit Company's problem. Taking the issue as a whole, it is probably best to locate production of biscuits and cakes at both of the new factories and distribute the product regionally. This will reduce distribution costs and allow the company to provide more easily for variations in regional tastes. Significantly this also ensures that all three factories have a consistent structure, which makes it easier for the organisation to decide upon its overall structure. Deciding what structure to adopt for the whole organisation would be more complex if the chosen structure had to incorporate three factories, each with its own unique production operation. The alternative, having one new factory manufacture cakes and the other biscuits, would reduce manufacturing costs, but would add to distribution costs. On balance, then, the decision to produce both cakes and biscuits at the new factories seems the most advantageous.

Should it involve the company in a change from its existing structure? As you will have noticed, the existing structure is functional. This will work satisfactorily whilst the company is organised on one site. It may be much more difficult to organise each function efficiently if they are situated on three factory sites a long way apart and with three times as many staff. The logical answer would probably be to re-organise to a hybrid structure, with a headquarters based upon the functional principle, to look after major, company-wide issues, and a customer structure based on three geographical regions each served by one factory as in Figure 7.

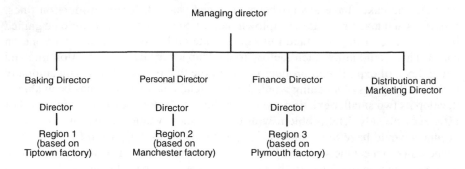

Figure 7: Suggested new structure for The Tasty Buns and Biscuits Company

The structure shown in Figure 7 would have the added advantage of focusing each region on its own particular customers, whose tastes vary.

If the company were to adopt the alternative production system of having a factory for cakes, a factory for biscuits, and both being produced at Tiptown, it would probably still find the functional structure inadequate, for the reasons we outlined above. It might then adopt a product structure with two departments, one for cakes and the other for biscuits. The difficulty for each department would be that each would have to operate on two widely separated sites, Tiptown and one of the new factories (Figure 8).

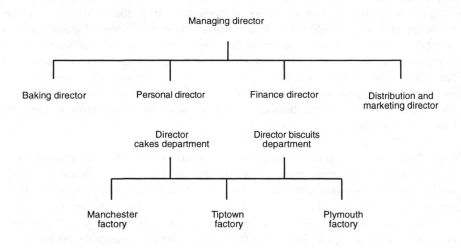

Figure 8: Alternative structure for The Tasty Buns and Biscuits Company

This exercise illustrates that organisation structures must be adapted to meet the practical needs of the organisation and that frequently there is no single straightforward answer to organisational problems.

The hybrid structure at Merritt Chemicals is a common one in large corporations. Similarly, such organisations frequently adopt a structure that combines functional departments or divisions at corporate level with a customer-based structure for providing its goods or services to customers. This happens, for example, at XYZ Tyres and Exhausts plc, a national company with over 100 service centres throughout the UK replacing car parts such as exhausts, tyres, batteries and brake linings. Its structure is shown in Figure 9.

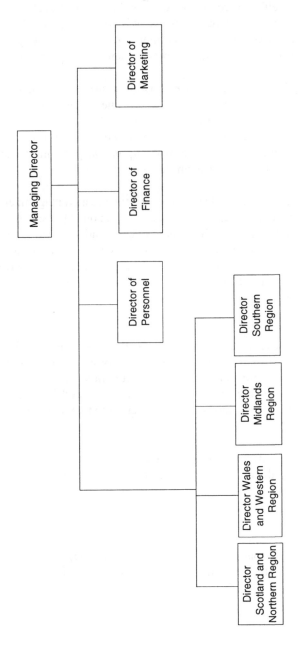

Figure 9: Extract from the structure of XYZ Tyres and Exhausts plc

Here there are three functional directors at a corporate level, personnel, finance and marketing, and four directors at a regional level. The latter are organised on a customer basis with geography being the criterion upon which customers are grouped together.

The advantage of this kind of hybrid structure is that it allows an organisation to concentrate the efforts of most of its staff on the production and delivery of its goods and services on either a product or customer basis, whichever is deemed most advantageous. Thus, at Merritt Chemicals and at XYZ Tyres and Exhausts, staff in the product-based divisions, at Merritt, and in the customer-based regions, at XYZ, can focus their efforts on their particular product and regional markets.

As we noted when looking at product or customer structures, each of these can foster innovation at market level. At the same time, each company's structure allows certain functions to be performed corporately. This can avoid duplication of effort in the product- or customer-based departments, and allow the functional specialists, at headquarters to concentrate upon the personnel, finance and marketing needs of the business as a whole.

For a company like Merritt Chemicals, there is a further advantage in employing a hybrid structure, in that its success is very dependent upon expensive research. This is too costly to be duplicated in each product division and also frequently relates to the work of more than one division. Organisations often find that certain important but costly functions, relevant to a range of their markets, are best performed centrally, even though a product or customer function may be appropriate to serve each market individually.

MATRIX STRUCTURE

A matrix structure uses the functional and product principles simultaneously to create an organisation structure with a dual hierarchy. In this dual hierarchy, one group of managers is responsible primarily for functional-related issues and the second group is responsible primarily for product-related issues. In a matrix structure, many staff will be responsible to and report to two managers, one in each hierarchy.

This is a complex form of structure often used when an organisation is trying to provide a range of products in changing markets. The organisation sees itself as under a number of conflicting pressures, so that neither the functional, nor product, nor customer principles can be applied satisfactorily across the whole organisation.

You may be familiar with this kind of organisation, as it is often adopted in universities and colleges, particularly for managing large departments and modular programmes. The Brightpool Business School chart illustrates this in Figure 10.

Management group	Head of Human Resource Group	Head of Accounting and Finance Strategy	Head of Marketing and Business Group	Head of Information Management Group
BTEC courses manager				
Undergraduate degrees manager				
Professional courses manager				
Postgraduate degrees manager				
Short courses manager				

Figure 10: Matrix structure at Brightpool Business School

Here there are two hierarchies: one with four heads responsible for managing groups of staff who teach the same subjects – the **vertical hierarchy;** and one with five managers each responsible for controlling a group of related courses – the **horizontal hierarchy**.

The vertical hierarchy is based upon the functional principle as each of the staff groupings reflects the particular expertise of its members. The horizontal hierarchy is based upon the product principle as each manager is responsible for a group of closely related products.

In a matrix structure like this, the teaching staff will find themselves responsible to two managers. For example, a lecturer in accounting and finance, teaching on the undergraduate degree programme is responsible to the undergraduate degree courses manager for various aspects of his or her work on the programme, for example, teaching the agreed syllabus, marking assignments on time and so on. At the same time, he or she will be responsible to the head of accounting and finance for seeing that his or her lectures are accurate and up to date and hand-outs are of an acceptable quality. The head will be responsible for deciding which staff from the accounting and finance group teach on the undergraduate degree programmes, whilst the undergraduate degree courses manager is responsible for ensuring that all of the lecturers on the undergraduate degree courses work together as a team to provide a good service for students.

Whereas, in all the other organisation structures, authority lies in the vertical hierarchy and any horizontal links represent co-ordination between people of the same rank, here the horizontal links represent a horizontal hierarchy of equal authority to that of the vertical hierarchy.

ACTIVITY 23

Look back over section 3.3 on the hybrid structure. What do hybrid and matrix organisations have in common? How do they differ?

Hybrid and matrix organisations are both based upon the application of two structural principles in the same organisation. They differ in that matrix structures involve the application of both principles to the same parts of the organisation at the same time, and hence give rise to a dual hierarchy. In a hybrid structure, each principle can be applied to different parts of the organisation at the same time. For example, in XYZ Tyres and Exhausts plc, the functional principle is applied to the senior and head office staff, whilst a geographically-based customer principle is applied to the remainder of the staff.

A matrix structure can provide very high levels of horizontal co-ordination, because the organisation's horizontal linkages, as well as its vertical ones, are represented by their own hierarchy. It can also give a high degree of flexibility, which is valuable when serving very varied markets. At Brightpool Business School, the needs of a student on a three-year full-time undergraduate degree programme are likely to be quite different from those of a senior manager wishing to attend a one-day short-course for updating on the latest management thinking in a particular field. The undergraduate degree courses manager and the short courses manager can ensure that each student receives a properly designed programme, whilst the heads of the staff group can see that capable staff are appointed to teach each programme.

The matrix structure is closely associated with the idea of the project team. This is when a group of staff is brought together from both hierarchies to deal with a particular project or problem. The flexibility of the matrix structure allows the organisation to call easily on a team of people with the right mix of skills to handle the project successfully. For example, if Brightpool Business School decided to set up a new undergraduate degree in accounting and information management, the undergraduate degrees courses manager could lead a team of suitably qualified colleagues from the accounting and finance group and the information management group to set it up.

ACTIVITY 24

Do you see any potential problems with the matrix approach? Or any specific circumstances where it may have advantages?

A number of large organisations, such as Monsanto Chemicals, ICI and Prudential Assurance, have adopted a matrix structure, at least in part. However, matrix structures do pose some problems:

- it can take a long time to arrive at decisions because staff from two hierarchies have to agree on them
- disputes can arise between the two hierarchies, as each has different priorities and concerns
- employees can become confused, having to respond to two different managers, whose wishes may not always be consistent.

Given these difficulties, and the extra costs of employing two sets of managers, an organisation will only find it worthwhile to set up a matrix structure in quite specific circumstances. These are:

- when it faces varied external pressures, for example, to run courses of high quality to satisfy students and qualification-awarding bodies and to run them at low cost to satisfy central government which provides the funds to run most courses
- when it serves a variety of changing markets, so that it constantly has to adjust its services to meet their needs
- where the organisation lacks the resources to provide for each of its markets separately, so that resources have to be shared between the various markets, for example, the lecturers teaching on Brightpool Business School's undergraduate degree courses are likely to be teaching on a range of other courses as well.

Even then, the organisation must put considerable effort into ensuring managers in each hierarchy are clear about their responsibilities and those of colleagues in the other hierarchy, if they are to avoid disputes and confusion. It must also ensure that its organisational culture stresses teamwork, so that staff will work together closely in an effective way.

SUMMARY

As you will have realised, the grouping of jobs into departments and departments into divisions, regions and so on, is a key choice in the structuring of an organisation. It can be made using the functional, product or customer principles, or by using two of them to form a hybrid or matrix structure. Whatever choice is made is unlikely to be easy or ideal, with costs as well as benefits for the organisation and its staff. The departmental structure finally chosen should be one that best reflects the objectives and purposes of the organisation.

3.4 Integration

Our next question is: 'How closely do the various parts of an organisation need to be integrated?' So far, in exploring the first three of Child's five questions, we have discovered that:

- organisations need to divide their various tasks up into jobs
- jobs are bound together into divisions and departments
- organisations normally create hierarchies in which some employees are responsible for and manage the work of others.

Furthermore, we have discussed several times the need for co-ordination, for example, between departments in a functional structure. This is a key issue for organisations. Having divided employee tasks into separate and specialist jobs, usually grouped into specialist departments, whether by function, product or customer, the organisation needs to ensure that these employees and departments work together efficiently for the good of the whole organisation.

Co-ordination is the process whereby the different tasks of individuals and departments are dovetailed or fitted together, so that the organisation can work smoothly and achieve its objectives efficiently.

Henry Mintzberg (1979), the American writer on management and organisations, identifies the three key ways in which co-ordination occurs as:

- mutual adjustment
- direct supervision
- standardisation.

Mutual adjustment is an essentially informal process whereby individuals adapt their understanding of a particular issue and their behaviour in respect of it, in the light of how others understand, react or propose to react to that issue.

For example, a maintenance worker on a factory assembly line faced with a new and particularly difficult breakdown on a piece of machinery might ask advice from a number of people before attempting to repair it. These might include fellow maintenance workers, and the maintenance supervisor. Production workers familiar with the machinery, and their supervisor, might also be asked, to see if they have useful suggestions and also to assess the likely consequences for the production process of the steps he or she proposes to take to repair the machine. The maintenance worker's final decision about what to do will reflect his or her adjustment to all the pieces of information and advice received.

Notice though that the process of adjustment is mutual. The production line workers and their supervisor are likely to approach their work differently as a consequence of the maintenance worker's decision about how to tackle this problem.

ACTIVITY 25

What co-ordination do you see taking place in this example of a mutual adjustment process?

The co-ordination that has taken place, in this process of mutual adjustment, has been both horizontal – between maintenance worker and other maintenance workers and the production workers – and vertical – between maintenance worker and the production and maintenance supervisors.

Reliance upon mutual adjustment alone as a means to co-ordination is generally only possible in a small organisation, because it is informal and often relies significantly upon people's social relationships. Larger organisations can utilise mutual adjustment within small working groups, but need to supplement it with other mechanisms for larger-scale co-ordination, such as direct supervision and standardisation.

Direct supervision occurs when one person is given formal responsibility for the work of another. This responsibility is defined, so that the person being supervised has a clear job description setting out his or her work and the supervisor is held responsible for the work that falls within that description.

Direct supervision tends to be used in organisations as they grow. They can no longer rely solely on the informal co-ordination provided by mutual adjustment. Hence, when jobs are created, some people are required to undertake supervisory tasks as part or all of their job descriptions. The creation of a system of direct supervision can therefore be related to the process of specialisation and the division of work.

It also involves the creation of a hierarchy in the organisation, where those in the supervisory positions are hierarchically superior to the people they supervise, and the people being supervised report to those supervising them. If you look back at Figure 1, the ACME Manufacturing Company, you will see that the managing director supervises the work of the production director (among others), who supervises the work of the production managers, and so on.

Managing director

Production director

Production managers

Supervisors

Foreperson

Operators

Figure 11: Extract from the structure of the ACME Manufacturing Co

According to Mintzberg (1979), when an organisation grows too large and complex to be adequately co-ordinated using both mutual adjustment and direct supervision, then it needs to standardise.

Standardisation is the process of defining a set of performance criteria to which some persons, things or processes are required to conform. It involves determining:

● what the important features are to which the measured item must conform

● level of performance to be expected for each feature.

Mintzberg suggests that organisations co-ordinate their activities by standardising skills, output and work processes. Standardisation allows employees to know clearly what the organisation expects of them, and allows those in supervisory positions easily to identify divergences from the organisation's agreed standards.

Using direct supervision and mutual adjustment, a supervisor in a craft workshop that makes high quality wooden furniture might reasonably oversee the work of, say, ten experienced carpenters. Each carpenter makes whole pieces of furniture individually and approaches each job in his or her own way. The foreperson may proceed partly through giving advice (mutual adjustment) and partly by instruction, for example, by instructing a carpenter which job to do first to meet an urgent order awaiting delivery (direct supervision).

This would not be possible, however, for a foreperson at ACME Manufacturing. There a foreman may supervise as many as 24 operatives, whose work must be closely co-ordinated with that of other workers in the manufacturing process, if production is to proceed smoothly, and where the products need to be consistent. Here it is likely that:

● skills will need to be standardised, so that employees in a particular job can reasonably expect to work at a particular speed and to a particular standard

● output will need to be standardised, so that those responsible for inspecting items or batches in the finishing shop can tell by performing a few speedy checks whether they conform to the laid down performance criteria

● the work process will need to be standardised, so that each worker performs an agreed task or set of tasks in an agreed way; thus each operative's work will be completed in precisely the way required for the next operative in the production process to undertake his or her work, and it will be ready at the right time so that the next operative does not have to stand idle waiting for work to do.

ACTIVITY 26

Looking back at the interview schedules for your chosen organisation, can you determine to what extent the interviewees' activities are co-ordinated by mutual adjustment; direct supervision; and standardisation? You may find the answers to Questions 9–15 and 19 helpful.

Unless your chosen organisation is a small one, it is likely that you will have identified all three forms of co-ordinating activity in the interviewees' answers.

STAFF AND LINE RELATIONSHIPS

One further aspect of co-ordination is worth noting. The form of vertical hierarchy associated with direct supervision, as at the ACME Manufacturing Company, is sometimes called a line relationship (Figure 11). Here there is a chain of command from the managing director to the operatives concerned with one of ACME Manufacturing's primary purposes of making its products.

However, many organisations are complex and have functions performed in them that are subsidiary to the organisation's primary purposes. People performing these secondary tasks usually have their own hierarchy and are often only able to advise rather than to instruct colleagues performing the primary functions. These secondary functions are often called staff functions and people performing them are said to have a staff relationship to those in the line management of the organisation. For example, at the ACME Manufacturing Company, the personnel director and departmental employees may perform a staff role for the company, giving advice about employment issues to managers in the line departments such as production, sales and marketing.

Finally it is worth noting that the concepts of staff and line, though sometimes useful in helping us to understand organisations, are not always easy to apply in practice. It can sometimes be difficult to determine whether a particular department, or everyone in it, is staff or line.

3.5 Control

How much control should management exercise over the activities of an organisation? As we have discovered, organisations need to ensure that employees' activities are co-ordinated so that one person's work dovetails with that of colleagues whose work is dependent upon his or her efforts. However, organisations need also to ensure that what employees do and how it is done is controlled in the more general sense and that it is consistent with the needs of the organisation.

So organisational control can be defined as the process whereby management regulates the behaviour of employees so that their work activities are consistent with the organisation's objectives. The key issue in this regulation of employees' activities is the extent to which such control should be exercised. This is the balance between **centralisation** and **de-centralisation**.

Centralisation occurs when all, or nearly all, of the significant decisions in an organisation's life are taken at, or near, the top by senior managers. De-centralisation occurs when many of the significant decisions in an organisation's life are taken by more junior staff in the organisation's hierarchy. Much modern management theory tends to stress the benefits of de-centralisation. For example, Rosabeth Moss Kanter (1984) has emphasised the benefits of empowering employees to enable them to take more control over their work and to take more decisions themselves.

De-centralisation:

- enriches people's work and so improves their motivation
- is essential if an organisation is to develop a flatter structure
- can give relatively junior staff experience of managing tasks and of taking decisions, so training them for more senior posts and responsibilities
- allows decisions to be taken close to the field of operations, so that they are more likely to take account of the practical problems of staff who will have to carry out the decisions, and of the customers whose needs are to be served.

However, despite the current emphasis on de-centralisation, all organisations must exercise a measure of control over their employees. They must strike a balance between centralisation and decentralisation.

Centralisation has its merits:

- it ensures that employees carry out a common policy and do not go their own way
- it allows quick decision-making as decisions are taken by a few senior managers, rather than through negotiation with a larger group
- it can reduce costs and increase specialisation as employees can work in more specialist units reporting to top management, rather than having to spread expertise more widely through the organisation to serve a larger group of decision-makers.

ACTIVITY 27

In striking the right balance for an organisation between centralisation and de-centralisation, a number of factors are likely to be influential. Read the case study about *Greatwear plc,* a worldwide chain of fashionable clothes for young women, with over 200 branches, and answer the questions that follow.

Greatwear plc

Greatwear plc began in the early 1980s as a single store run by an entrepreneurial retailer, Geoff Smith, who made all decisions himself. By 1985 Greatwear had 20 stores throughout Britain.

Smith still preferred to back his own judgement, rather than trust his managers to take any but the least important decisions, and among his decisions in that year was one to expand into the European market with 20 more stores, in France, the Netherlands and Germany. In the short-run this proved disastrous, as Smith's judgement about the kinds of clothes young French, Dutch and German women would buy proved to be wrong. The company made a loss for the first time in 1986.

Consequently, at the end of the year, the shareholders voted to replace Smith as managing director with Arthur Brown, a less flamboyant figure with a long career in fashion retailing. Brown vowed to continue the company's international expansion, hence its growth to 200 stores by 1994, but he said its style and philosophy must change to put its people first. Decision-making must be devolved as far as possible to store managers. New communications technologies would be introduced to keep them fully informed about what stock was available and which fashion lines were selling well or badly in which markets.

This strategy worked well in the late 1980s, hence, the company's rapid growth. However, during the early 1990s, as world recession took hold, expansion slowed and new investments became much more risky. Even well-established branches lost money. Arthur Brown therefore decided to use the company's advanced information technology system to monitor weekly sales in each branch and to take greater control over what lines were stocked in each store.

What key decisions were made at Greatwear plc about centralising and de-centralising control within the company? What factors influenced these decisions?

You will probably have recognised that Greatwear plc decentralised in 1986 as it had grown too large and varied to be controlled by a single person. This decentralisation was facilitated by the use of new communications technology, which enabled branch managers to be kept better informed. Arthur Brown's policy of putting staff first would motivate them and reflected a need to change the company's culture. Greatwear then centralised its control in 1991, again with the assistance of new technologies, in order to reduce risks and to cut the costs of loss-making branches.

The Greatwear plc case illustrates a number of the key influences that lead companies to centralise and decentralise. It also illustrates the very important point that the best balance between centralisation and de-centralisation is likely to vary with circumstances over time.

REVIEW ACTIVITY 3

Suggested time: 3 hours.

You now have some good interview data on your chosen organisation, and are aware of the key questions and issues that arise in designing an organisation.

1 Using this information and what you have learned about organisational design write about 300 words describing the key elements in the design of your chosen organisation, together with an organisation chart. If you are unable to construct an organisation chart for the whole organisation, do not worry, simply make it clear that your information did not allow you to cover the whole organisation and explain which part of the organisation, for example, a district, a division, a factory, your chart covers. You should think seriously about including in your account issues such as job design, hierarchy, spans of control, the departmental structure, co-ordination, the balance of centralisation and decentralisation, and management control.

2 Return to each of your interviewees and, using your description and chart, give them a 10-minute oral presentation on their organisation as you see it. Make notes on their reactions, so that you can correct any errors you have made, and record any new information they give you.

3 Amend your description and organisation chart in the light of what you have discovered.

There is no answer to this Review activity, but after your discussions with the interviewees, you may find it helpful to discuss your overall analysis with colleagues and/or your tutor.

Summary

In looking at how organisations are designed we have seen that in structuring any organisation two key processes take place: differentiation, the process of breaking up the work of an organisation into a series of tasks, jobs and departments that form the building blocks of the organisation; and integration, the process of building these various entities together, so that the organisation functions as a whole and not as a series of unrelated parts. You have identified aspects of differentiation and integration in the real example of your chosen organisation.

We have examined John Child's five key questions for organisational designers and have discovered, among other things:

- how job designers must balance job specialisation and job enrichment
- the balances that needs to be struck between length of hierarchy and span of control, and the need to take care when flattening hierarchies
- the functional, product and customer principles upon which departmental structures can be based, including hybrid and matrix structures
- the need for organisations to co-ordinate the activities of their members, and the informal and formal means whereby this can be done
- the need for managerial control in organisations
- the need to achieve the right balance between centralisation and de-centralisation, and how the required balance can alter over time.

Overall in the section, we have indicated how organisational design issues are usually not simple, but involve balancing a variety of competing claims. Hence there is rarely a single way of resolving an organisation's design challenges. You have examined the five key questions that must be asked in designing an organisation structure. You have used case study examples and your chosen organisation to:

- explore and evaluate the extent to which jobs and departments are specialised
- analyse and evaluate the grouping together of jobs and departments in an organisation
- identify and evaluate the integrative processes in an organisation
- identify and evaluate the forms of managerial control used in an organisation.

SECTION 4

Organisational Goals and Organisational Effectiveness

Introduction

In this section, we identify the nature of organisational missions and goals, and look at their importance for organisational effectiveness. We also examine the bases of organisational effectiveness, efficiency and economy on which the relevance and importance of particular organisational goals and missions should be assessed.

4.1 Goals and mission statements

In our discussions so far about organisations and their structures, we have implicitly assumed that they want to achieve certain things and not others. For example, in talking about Greatwear plc, we assumed it was a bad thing when the company began to make losses and a good thing that it was able to increase its market share by opening new stores around the world.

These are probably reasonable assumptions, but how can we know that these criteria are good measures of Greatwear plc's performance? A key way for us to find out is by examining Greatwear plc's organisational goals to see whether or not these criteria are relevant measures of what the company says it wishes to achieve.

An organisational goal is a state of affairs that an organisation says it wishes to achieve and in pursuit of which it directs its efforts. Without goals an organisation will tend to drift, having no particular targets to aim at. Senior managers will tend to take decisions in an inconsistent way, following whatever course seems to be appropriate at the time and changing course whenever a new piece of information, or even a change of mood, makes a change seem desirable.

For many lower down in the organisation's hierarchy, this is likely to become confusing. They will not know what they are expected to achieve. Lack of clear guidance from the top may be taken as an opportunity to go their own way, and do what is good for them personally, or for their particular part of the organisation.

ACTIVITY 28

Read the following case study, *Campbell's departmental store,* and then answer the questions that follow.

Campbell's departmental store

Campbell's departmental store in Mapplethorpe is a family-owned store which was run for 50 years by Tobias Campbell until his death seven years ago. Tobias Campbell was a somewhat autocratic man, who liked to give firm, clear leadership. He had declared that the store's motto would be, 'The best store with the best selection of quality merchandise available in Mapplethorpe, in every department'. Under his leadership, departmental managers and the store's buyers knew that they had to stock a very full range of articles from the best known manufacturers. If they did not do so, they would be severely reprimanded by Tobias Campbell and possibly lose their annual bonus. Campbell's prices were not the lowest, but under Tobias Campbell's leadership it certainly became the premier store in Mapplethorpe. It was consistently profitable, and when the town's two other department stores were taken over by national chain-stores, Campbell's remained proud and independent.

After Tobias Campbell's death, the managing directorship was taken over by his nephew, Cecil Campbell. Cecil had, up to then, taken relatively little interest in the business, preferring to spend his time on his country estate, 50 miles away. He had not got on well with his uncle, Tobias, and each of them had heartily disliked everything about the other. On the day he became managing director, he had been asked if he wished the company still to follow Tobias Campbell's motto. He had replied, 'Definitely not'. When asked what the store's new motto should be, he had said, 'I haven't thought of one yet, but I'll let you know.'

Seven years on he still had not announced what the new motto would be. During this time departmental managers and store buyers had begun to go their own ways. Most no longer stocked a full range of the best lines from all the well known manufacturers. Some even filled their departments with cheap, rather shoddy items sold at discount prices. Campbell's traditional customers had become disgruntled, but new customers had not been attracted in large numbers and the company's profits had fallen. During the last three years, it had recorded losses for the first time in its history.

1   What was Campbell's organisational goal under Tobias Campbell's leadership?

2   Does the store have an organisational goal under Cecil Campbell's leadership?

3   How did Campbell's benefit from having Tobias Campbell's organisational goal?

1   Under Tobias Campbell's leadership the organisation's goal was to be the best quality departmental store in town. This can be summarised in the words of his motto, 'The best store with the best selection of quality merchandise available in Mapplethorpe, in every department.'

2   No. There is no apparent organisational goal under Cecil Campbell's leadership.

3   Departmental managers and buyers knew clearly what was expected of them. Their success in ensuring that each of the store's departments was the best in Mapplethorpe in its particular field acted as a key criterion in measuring their performance, both for themselves and for Tobias Campbell. We might also expect that a determination to be the best in town would act as a motivator both for managers and staff, and even attract people to want to work at the store.

As the Campbell's case illustrates, goals can be very useful for an organisation. Tobias Campbell's motto is, in fact, a particular kind of organisational goal. It is what is called a mission statement or **mission**. An organisational mission is the long-term or overall goal of an organisation. It is a statement that sets out why the organisation exists and what it is for.

Today many organisations, including all, or almost all, colleges and universities, have mission statements. For a mission statement to be of real value as a guide and motivator for staff, and for it to be of value in informing the organisation's customers or clients, it must be both relevant to their needs and readily accessible.

ACTIVITY 29

Consider either your workplace or your university or your chosen organisation, what is its mission?

If it was difficult and time-consuming to discover the mission statement for the organisation you selected, it is likely that its effectiveness in giving direction to the organisation's activities is questionable. The central statement of why the organisation exists should lie behind all its activities.

Usually, however, an organisation will not find it enough just to have a mission statement. Mission statements tend to be rather broad and general, about the long-term. An organisation also needs shorter-term goals which can be related to its key activities and which can be measured to check that the organisation is performing well enough in each of them.

Richard Daft (1992) refers to the longer-term, broader goals included in a mission statement as an organisation's official goals. He refers to the shorter-term, more task-related goals – the way-stations on the route to achieving an organisation's mission – as an organisation's operative goals. Examples of these are profitability, market share, development of a new product within a particular time period, and so on.

An organisation's operative goals then are specific measures of achievement, usually covering particular key organisational tasks. Successive organisational goals over time act as steps towards the achievement of an organisation's mission.

4.2 Formal and informal goals

So far we have tended to assume that an organisation's formal goals will be shared equally by everyone in the organisation, but this is not necessarily always the case.

In general, it is the responsibility of an organisation's senior management to set its goals. However, it is also its task to see that such goals are achievable and shared by colleagues throughout the organisation. If goals are set that staff feel are not achievable, then far from being motivated to greater effort, they are likely to be demoralised.

Equally, it is important that an organisation's staff as a whole feel that its goals relate to them and their work. They must feel ownership of the goals – that the goals relate to them. Hence, if an organisation's mission highlights some departments and workers, but appears to ignore others, this can demotivate the staff and departments who feel ignored.

The process whereby goals are set is also important. A new mission statement is more likely to be acceptable if staff throughout the organisation – from different levels in the hierarchy and different departments – are consulted about its content. Clearly in a large, possibly transnational organisation not everyone can be consulted, but a wide consultation process is likely both to help the drawing up of an appropriate mission statement and to facilitate its acceptance. Similarly, the manager of a department is more likely to accept and be motivated by an operative goal, for example, to achieve a 15% profit next year, if he or she is consulted before it is set. Finally, however, senior management need to take responsibility for the organisational goals they set, whatever the process of consultation that has taken place.

In practice, the key influence upon an organisation's goals is likely to be that of a dominant group of its senior managers. The organisation's goals are likely to be espoused with different degrees of enthusiasm in different parts of the organisation. One of the consequences of the process of differentiation we discussed earlier is that different departments, divisions, or other groups of staff, in an organisation are quite likely to develop goals and values of their own, not officially approved by the organisation. These are **informal goals**.

Informal goals are measures of achievement developed by groups of staff within an organisation without the formal approval of its senior management. These goals can even be at variance with the officially approved organisational goals. For example, an organisation may specifically declare itself to be an equal opportunities employer in its mission statement, but a group of staff in a particular department may decide it does not want to work with women or with members of racial minorities. It could then develop informal processes to prevent their appointment, or to make working in the department uncongenial so that such persons do not stay long even if appointed. Of course, informal goals need not always be bad for the organisation. A group of craftsmen might, from pride in their craft, agree among themselves to work to higher standards than the organisation normally requires.

This process whereby an organisation's formal goals are set aside by informal ones is called **goal displacement**. To make sure that the organisation's official goals are not being displaced in this way, it is important that formal goals are kept under review to see that they remain relevant and accepted by staff.

The process of reviewing formal goals may itself lead to changes, of course. Where an organisation reviews its official goals and amends or replaces them with new officially approved goals, the process is called **goal succession**.

ACTIVITY 30

You know now that organisational missions should be relevant to those affected by them. Looking back over the mission statement you wrote down earlier, from either your employing organisation or your university, assess its value to you as an employee or a client.

If the mission statement truly encapsulates the business and purposes of the organisation, you should have had no difficulty, either as an employee or as a client, in identifying its relevance to you.

4.3 Goals and effectiveness

An effective organisation is one that achieves its goals. The Brazilian soccer team which won the 1994 World Cup was an effective organisation. It achieved what it set out to do.

Organisational effectiveness can be defined, therefore, as the extent to which an organisation is able to achieve the goals which have been set for it or which it has set itself. Effectiveness is the broadest, most significant measure of an organisation's achievements and managers of an organisation have a duty to try seriously to achieve its goals, unless they are illegal or immoral. Aiming for effectiveness, highlights the importance for an organisation of setting its goals with sufficient care. If this does not happen, an organisation may achieve its operative goals and even its mission, and still not make the best use of its resources and its people.

ACTIVITY 31

Can you think of ways in which poor goal setting might make achieving effectiveness very difficult?

Under-achievement can occur where an organisation's goals are insufficiently ambitious, so that staff are not encouraged to try hard enough, or over-ambitious, so that staff become demoralised.

Equally an organisation's goals may simply be misguided or misplaced, leading an organisation into markets or products to which its resources and capacities are not truly suited, so that it does not fully utilise its capacities. For example, returning to the case of *Campbell's departmental store,* even if Cecil Campbell were to set a new mission for the organisation, to stock a narrower range of cheaper products appealing to a wider range of Mapplethorpe shoppers, this might not secure the company's future. It might be that the two national chain stores operating in the town could pursue this approach better, as they could buy in bulk, more cheaply, and use national marketing to publicise their bargains. In this case, it would be very difficult for Campbell's staff to achieve the goal set for them and be effective. Even if they were to do so, it might be argued that they were not making the best use of the company's resources, in particular its long-established reputation for high quality.

As well as effectiveness, two narrower measures of an organisation's achievements are sometimes used:

- efficiency
- economy.

Organisational efficiency is defined as an organisation's capacity to produce goods or services at the lowest possible cost per unit of output – that is, with the lowest possible amount of its resources, human and material, going into each unit of output.

Efficiency is usually measured by putting a cash value on each organisational resource used in the production of a particular item and then aggregating these to arrive at a unit cost. For example, if Eco-Pumps plc, a small manufacturer of water pumps, rents a factory for £100,000 per annum, employs 20 staff at a cost of £400,000 per annum and uses materials at a cost of £500,000 per annum, its total costs are £1,000,000 per annum. If the company produces 2,000 pumps per annum, the unit cost of each pump is £500.

However, if Eco-Pumps plc were to expand its production to 2,500 pumps per annum, but, by making much better use of its resources, to keep rent and staff costs the same, and increase material costs by £100,000, then its total costs would be £1,100,000. The unit cost of each pump would fall to £440 per pump. Eco-Pumps plc would have become markedly more efficient.

Organisations are concerned about efficiency, and most will include efficiency targets in their operative goals. Many will make some mention of efficiency-related matters in their mission statements. Nevertheless, efficiency goals are essentially internally focused on the organisation's use of its resources – they do not tell us what an organisation's customers think of its products. For example, Eco-Pumps plc will not have improved its market position if customers find that, when production rises to 2,500 pumps per annum, quality falls and that pumps break down more often, so sales decrease.

Economy is an even narrower internal measure of an organisation's use of its resources. **Organisational economy** is the total value of the resources used by an organisation. So to become more economical, an organisation must use fewer resources than it used formerly. Becoming more economical may not, however, result in greater efficiency and, equally, becoming more efficient may not make an organisation more economical. For example, when Eco-Pumps plc expanded its production to 2,500 pumps per annum, its total costs grew from £1,000,000 to £1,100,000. Therefore it became a less economical organisation (by £100,000 per annum) even though it became a more efficient one.

Effectiveness, efficiency and economy, sometimes called the three Es of value for money, are all important to an organisation. However, there are potential conflicts between them. It is quite possible for organisations to become more economical and even more efficient, but less effective. Effectiveness, being the broadest of the three criteria and the only one that directly relates an organisation's activities to the needs of its customers or clients, is the most important of the three. Indeed, elements of the other two can be included within it via the organisation's goals. However, if an organisation is to be effective and to make the best potential use of its resources, much will depend on the care with which its goals are set.

REVIEW ACTIVITY 4

Suggested time: 15 minutes

1 What is the relation between an organisation's mission and its operative goals?

2 What do we mean by the terms 'informal goals' and 'goal displacement'?

3 What do we mean when we use the term 'organisational effectiveness'?

4 What factors in the goal-setting process are important for organisational effectiveness?

Summary

In Section 4, we have looked at the significance of organisational missions and the relationship between these and an organisation's operative goals. We have noted the dangers of goal displacement where formal organisational goals are not relevant or appropriate to groups and individuals implementing them.

We have identified what is meant by each of the terms 'effectiveness', 'efficiency' and 'economy' and noted some potential conflicts between them. You have seen how relevant and well drawn up missions and goals contribute to organisational effectiveness, and observed how organisational effectiveness is the basis on which the relevance and importance of particular missions and goals should be evaluated.

SECTION 5

Key Influences upon Organisation Structure

Introduction

In this final section, we examine the use and value of organisation theory, and evaluate the influence of size, technology and environment upon an organisation's structure.

5.1 Organisation theory

It is very common for people to think of organisations with which they are heavily involved, such as their workplace, as being unique. This may be so in certain limited respects but, as we have already established, organisations have many common features. Similarly, people frequently explain issues or problems that arise in the workplace in terms of individuals, their attitudes and behaviour. 'My boss doesn't spend any time with me, developing my skills and solving my problems, because she doesn't like me.' Again, there may be some truth in this, but it is usually far from being the whole truth. The boss may well dislike our complaining subordinate, but is unable to spend sufficient time with him or her because her span of control is too wide. Organisational theorists attempt to look at organisations in a clear-headed way searching for the common underlying patterns that lie beyond individual organisations, their structures, the behaviour of the people in them and their particular problems.

Organisation theory attempts to explain how organisations work by defining the common features that organisations, or groups of organisations, share, by collecting data about them, and by analysing them. You have, of course, been using organisation theory already, throughout this unit, though you may not have realised it. We have regularly defined and examined common features of organisational life, such as formality and informality, integration and differentiation, and so on. You have collected extensive data about your chosen organisation, and you have analysed it. In analysing the data, you have both attempted to explain how your chosen organisation works, and you have been trying to fit it into some of the common features and broader patterns of behaviour that organisation theorists believe to be important in explaining how organisations work.

WHY WE STUDY ORGANISATION THEORY
Organisation theory is especially useful for people who manage organisations, or who aspire to do so in the future. It enables the manager to see that his or her

organisation and its problems are rarely wholly unique. Usually, much of value can be learned from the behaviour of other organisations in broadly similar circumstances. It can help us to explain what is happening in our own organisation and to identify possible solutions to its problems.

Even if you do not aspire to be a manager, organisation theory should be of interest to you. We live in a world of organisations – work, university, clubs, shops, and so on. Organisation theory can help explain how they work and why they work in the ways they do. It may even enable to you to get the best out of each of them.

5.2 Key influences upon organisation structure

THE 'ONE BEST WAY'

Throughout this unit, we have been careful to point out that creating an organisation structure involves choices that are frequently not clear-cut. Organisational designers frequently have to make decisions on balance, trying to arrive at a workable and satisfactory structure in the face of competing priorities.

ACTIVITY 32

Look back briefly at the ACME Manufacturing Company organisation chart in Figure 1, and consider what the results might be if the company were to introduce a flatter hierarchy.

If the company introduced a flatter hierarchy this could certainly cut costs and enrich workers' jobs, but it might also increase stress, decrease motivation and worsen communications. The decision to go ahead and create a flattened hierarchy would involve reaching a balanced judgement of the likely advantages and disadvantages of such a course of action given the particular circumstances of the company at the time. There is no guarantee that a beneficial decision to flatten ACME Manufacturing's hierarchy now, would create a structure that would still be satisfactory in, say, five years' time. Nor would it indicate that ACME Manufacturing's success in flattening its hierarchy would necessarily mean that other organisations should do the same

The view we have taken is that, whilst organisation theory enables us to make judgements about what features and issues different organisations have in common, and even what the range of options is that they may share in trying to solve their problems, the appropriate structure for any particular organisation must be designed on the basis of its own particular needs and circumstances.

As you saw earlier in this module, this was not the view taken by the writers who founded management and organisation theory in the early part of this century, such as Henri Fayol, (1949) V A Graicunas (1937) and Max Weber (1964). Fayol and Graicunas belonged to what is often called the administrative principles or classical school of management theorists. They tried to devise rules or principles applicable in any organisation. If these principles were adhered to by organisation designers, they would uncover 'the one best way' to structure their particular organisation. You will remember from Unit 1 that Fayol's principles of administration included:

- division of work – an organisation's tasks should be grouped together into specialised jobs

- unity of command – no employee should report to more than one manager

- scalar chain – there should be a chain of command extending from the chief executive to the most junior employee in an organisation.

Graicunas, for his part, was very concerned with spans of control, and set out mathematically-based rules indicating the limits on how many subordinates should report to a manager.

ACTIVITY 33

Where in this unit have we so far utilised each of the following administrative principles in our study of organisations:

1 Division of work

2 Unity of command

3 Scalar chain

4 Span of control

---

1   We looked at the issues concerned with specialisation in job design in answering the first of Child's five questions.

2   We looked implicitly at the need for unity of command in answering Child's second and third questions. Of the various structures considered only the matrix structure explicitly moved away from this principle.

3   We looked at this principle in answering the second of Child's questions, in particular at the length of hierarchies.

4   We discussed spans of control specifically when answering Child's second question.

These principles are not out-moded, but we no longer regard them as providing absolute answers to our organisational questions.

Max Weber, writing from a broader sociological rather than a strictly managerial perspective (1964), was concerned with defining clearly the key elements of a **bureaucratic organisation**. According to him a bureaucracy would possess, among other things:

- a clear hierarchy
- clear job descriptions, with an emphasis on specialisation
- clear written rules
- appointment and promotion based only on skills and knowledge.

We might define a bureaucracy then as an organisation whose structure and management are based upon skills, knowledge, hierarchy and rules. In our everyday language, we frequently use the words 'bureaucracy' and 'bureaucratic' as terms of abuse for organisations, departments and colleagues that are slow, or inefficient, or who are more concerned with obeying the rules than getting the job done. However, this was not what Weber meant by bureaucracy. Weber believed that it was crucial to the efficiency of any organisation that its formal side, its rules and structures, conformed to the principles he laid down.

If you read over the earlier part of this section, you see the great extent to which organisation theory is still influenced by Weber's precepts. For example, our discussion of centralisation and decentralisation is fundamentally one about what rules should be made at what levels to govern an organisation. Yet, as with the administrative principles school, we do not regard these precepts as setting out unchallengeable principles for structuring all organisations no matter what their circumstances.

5.3 Contingency theory

From the late 1950s, a new approach to organisation theory was developed which became known as **contingency theory**. This theory argues that there is no 'one best way' to structure an organisation. An organisation will face a range of choices when determining how it should be structured. Successful organisations adopt structures that are an appropriate response to a number of variables, or contingencies, which influence both the needs of the organisation and how it works.

Contingency theorists have found that three contingencies are particularly important in influencing an organisation's structure. These are:

- its size
- the technology it uses
- its operating environment.

In this section, we conclude with an examination of each of these contingencies and the ways in which they can influence organisational structures. First, however, we draw your attention to two significant implications of contingency theory:

- if there is no 'one best way', then even apparently quite similar organisations, for example, two nearby colleges, may choose significantly different structures and still survive, be reasonably successful in achieving their missions, and so on

- if different parts of the same organisation are influenced in different ways by the contingencies bearing upon them, then it may be appropriate for them to be structured differently, for example, one university department may have a functional structure, whilst another may have a matrix structure.

5.4 Influence of size

Organisations can grow in two ways: they can simply grow larger, employing more people, using more machinery, utilising more buildings, and so on; or they can grow more complex – that is, more varied – in the work they do, in the types of people they employ, in the goods and services they provide, and so on. Of course, the two kinds of growth go hand-in-hand, but for convenience we look at them separately here.

GROWING LARGER
We have seen earlier that simple growth in size often leads to a need for both increased **formalisation** and **decentralisation**. In looking at the need for integration in organisations we concluded that, as organisations grew, they tended to rely on different forms of integrative activity or formalisation.

ACTIVITY 34

What kinds of development in the form of integrative activity take place as organisations grow bigger? Look back at the problems of Greatwear plc as it grew, to refresh your memory.

When organisations are small they can rely on mutual adjustment; as they grow they will adopt direct supervision, and, finally, as they grow larger still they adopt standardisation. Standardisation involves the setting of rules and procedures by the organisation's management for the conduct of key activities.

Formalisation is a closely related concept. Again it involves the setting of rules and procedures, but it also entails the setting down of rules, procedures and instructions in writing. Equally it involves the writing of reports by subordinates to tell their managers how the subordinates' work has been proceeding. As an organisation grows, it needs rules, instructions and procedures, expressed in writing, if its managers are to retain effective control of it and if its activities are to be well integrated. You will recall that the use of rules and of written communications are a key feature of bureaucracy. Child (1988) found that as successful organisations grew they tended to adopt greater formalisation.

Formalisation then involves the setting down by management of rules and procedures to govern important aspects of an organisation's activities. It further involves the use of written media to communicate significant rules, procedures or instructions, and for the presentation of reports.

You will recall that decentralisation occurs when many of the significant decisions in an organisation's life are taken by more junior staff in the organisation's life. Look again at Greatwear plc. As the corporation grew up to 1986, it became more and more difficult to control through a single leader. Many important decisions had to be decentralised to store managers, rather than authority to make them being retained at the top of the organisation's hierarchy.

It is common for organisations to decentralise as they grow larger, because those at the top:

● cannot know in sufficient detail about all of an organisation's activities

● cannot respond quickly enough to the many issues requiring a decision.

However, organisational growth is not accompanied by an inevitable and inexorable process of decentralisation. As Greatwear plc in 1991 illustrated, circumstances can arise when large organisations may choose to re-centralise aspects of their decision-making.

GROWING IN COMPLEXITY

The Greatwear plc case also illustrates that increased organisational size is frequently accompanied by increased complexity. The company's expansion into France, the Netherlands and Germany involved it in trying to meet the fashion needs of a much wider range of potential customers than those in Britain alone.

Complexity also arises because, as an organisation grows, its departments, divisions and so on also grow. As they grow, they become too difficult to manage as single entities, so they divide into more specialist units. Such specialist units may acquire great expertise, but their work may also become less familiar and more difficult to understand than before. Equally, when a unit splits, its two parts may require a specialist unit to co-ordinate them. So growth can mean that the organisation's hierarchy becomes both wider and longer.

For example, Greatwear plc's structure might have changed as in Figure 12.

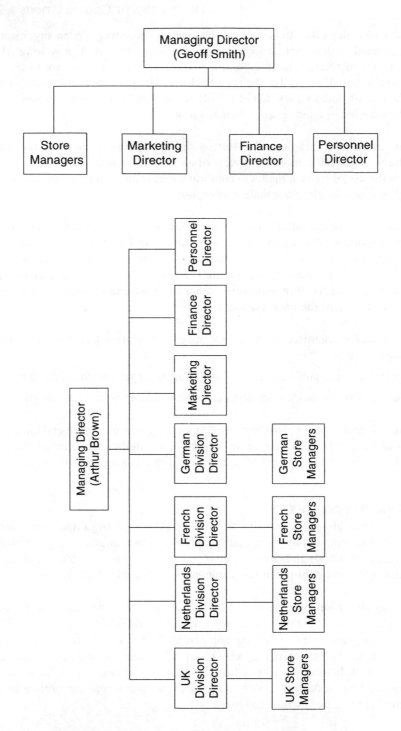

Figure 12: Greatwear plc structure before and after 1986

Notice that the more complex, wider and longer post-1986 hierarchy does not of itself preclude Arthur Brown's declared intention to increase de-centralisation. If the new national divisional directors and the store managers are able to take decisions that in the past would have been taken at headquarters, and possibly by Geoff Smith personally, then de-centralisation will have taken place.

5.5 Influence of technology

We looked at technology in some detail in Unit 2. Every organisation produces some goods or services that its clients or customers value, or it could not obtain the funds necessary to buy the resources it needs, such as staff, buildings, machinery, to continue to exist.

ACTIVITY 35

What goods or services are provided by the following organisations?

1   Arsenal Football Club

2   Church of England

3   Coca Cola Company

4   Your university or college

---

1   Arsenal Football Club provides entertainment.

2   Church of England provides teaching about Christianity, reinforcement of faith, various forms of social service, and so on.

3   Coca Cola Company provides various soft drinks.

4   Your university or college provides education, and possibly research and consultancy.

In order to provide such goods and services, an organisation employs a technology, or even a range of technologies.

An organisation's technology consists of the knowledge, equipment, techniques and processes that it uses to transform its various inputs into goods and/or services. Two key dimensions of an organisation's technology can influence the organisation's structure significantly:

- complexity of the technology employed
- predictability of the technology employed and its susceptibility to analysis.

In Unit 3, you looked at the use of technology and the development of Fordism, post-Fordism and post-modernism. Here you examine some specific approaches that affect organisational structure.

TECHNOLOGICAL COMPLEXITY

In a famous study of a hundred manufacturing companies in south east Essex, Joan Woodward (1980) concluded that between them they employed three types of technology. These were:

1   **Unit and small batch production,** where the goods were produced singly or a few at a time. Each unit or small batch would be unique and would be made to meet the needs of a particular client. Such production involved high levels of skills to make goods such as made-to-measure clothing, space satellites and so on.

2   **Mass production,** where large volumes of identical goods were produced and would be sold in a mass market to customers expecting a standardised product, such as boxes of washing powder. Here machinery does most of the work, with employees in a subordinate role.

3   **Continuous process production,** where the manufacturing process never stops and is conducted entirely by machines. Here the human beings do not make the product (the machines do) but simply monitor and control it. Examples are the chemicals and oil-refining industries.

Woodward concluded that each type of technology set different challenges for the organisation. For example, different steps will need to be taken to control the flow of work and motivate the staff in a craft furniture workshop than in an oil refinery. This in turn had consequences for the organisation's structure. In particular, as the technology employed became more complex, so the organisational structure became more complex. For example:

● hierarchy grew longer, not least because of the need for managers in integrative roles

● chief executive's span of control widened

● numbers employed in indirect, staff roles grew

● number of managers grew, to supervise and integrate the more complex processes involved.

TECHNOLOGICAL PREDICTABILITY AND SUSCEPTIBILITY TO ANALYSIS

In another study, Charles Perrow (1970) concluded that the key features of a technology were:

● the extent to which it behaved predictably, so that few problems arose and those that did were familiar

● the extent to which the technology could be analysed, divided up into a series of steps and standard procedures, especially when dealing with problems.

He found that organisations using predictable and easily analysed technologies, where there tended to be few exceptions such as breakdowns, and those that did occur could be solved using standardised procedures, tended to:

● have discrete job descriptions

● have little interdependence between different groups of workers

● lay down many precise rules

● set out precise procedures for dealing with problems

● set out precise plans, in order that activities are co-ordinated

● allow little discretion to people low down in the hierarchy.

These rather bureaucratic organisations he called **routine organisations**.

In organisations where the technology behaved unpredictably, with many exceptions, variations and breakdowns, Perrow found that:

● job descriptions were not discrete, but overlapped

● there were high levels of interdependence between different groups of workers

● high levels of discretion were allowed, even at quite low levels in the organisation

● co-ordination took place through good co-ordination and feedback between different groups of workers.

Taking the Woodward and Perrow studies together, we can see that the technology employed within an organisation is likely to have a significant effect upon management's choice of an appropriate structure.

5.6 Influence of environment

Organisations do not exist in isolation. Every organisation exists in an environment with which it interacts in order to survive and prosper. Organisation theorists often find it helpful to think of organisations as 'open systems'.

An open system is a set of interacting elements which takes inputs from its environment, transforms or changes them in some way, and produces outputs (goods or services) which are used by individuals or other organisations in its environment (Figure 13).

Figure 13: The organisation as an open system

An organisation consists of structures and processes which use people, technologies, machinery, raw materials and so on taken from its environment to produce goods and services needed in its environment. Therefore, an organisation is likely to be influenced by both:

● the provision of inputs from its environment

● its need to produce goods or services required within its environment.

For example, the age of the population, its education, its skills, and its values, will all influence the kinds of people an organisation can employ. The capabilities of the labour force will in turn influence both the quality and quantity of products an organisation can produce.

The key to understanding the influence of an organisation's environment upon its structure is to analyse the level of uncertainty or unpredictability in that environment. An environment can be uncertain because it is complex and varied, so that different elements of it may behave in different ways at the same time. It may also be uncertain because it is unstable, that is, it is subject to rapid and major changes. A famous study by Burns and Stalker (1966) led them to conclude that organisations in stable environments tend to adopt what they called a **mechanistic structure** in which, among other things:

● jobs were clearly defined and specialised

● there was a clear hierarchy

● communications tended to be vertical, up and down the hierarchy

● decisions were made near the top of the hierarchy and issued as instructions and rules.

Notice the similarity between a mechanistic structure and some of the prescriptions of early writers on management and organisations, such as Fayol and Weber. You should remember their work from Unit 1.

Burns and Stalker (1966) also found that organisations in more unstable and unpredictable environments tended to adopt a less rigid approach, which they called an **organic structure**. In an organic structure:

● authority tended to be based upon knowledge and expertise, not upon rank in the hierarchy

● jobs were not clearly or permanently defined, but allowed to develop and change with circumstances

● communication tended to be horizontal, across the hierarchy

● few instructions were given, rather colleagues gave one another advice.

This kind of structure enables the organisation to respond more quickly and flexibly to changes in its environment.

A later study by Lawrence and Lorsch (1969) found that, even within companies, different departments might well face different environmental conditions. A department facing a stable environment might need a mechanistic structure, whilst a company facing a changing environment might require an organic structure. Hence the company as a whole might need to emphasise differentiation in its structural decisions. However, such an organisation will also require a high level of integration, as the various departments will need to work closely together in a flexible way if the organisation as a whole is to meet the changing needs of its clients or customers.

REVIEW ACTIVITY 5

Suggested time: 20 minutes.

Read the case study, *Jonathan's Pizza Company,* and answer the questions that follow.

Jonathan's Pizza Company

Jonathan Pescatore set up a wholesale pizza business in 1979. He worked from a small factory unit on an industrial estate and by 1985 employed a staff of 12, one of whom was a driver. Jonathan undertook all management roles, including sales and marketing personally. The dough for the bases of his pizzas was mixed in a mixing machine, but the remainder of the production process was carried out by hand, each craftsman baker making, baking and wrapping his own batches of pizzas using the skills handed down during his apprenticeship. The pizzas were sold in 20 delicatessens in neighbouring towns.

By the late 1980s, demand for good quality pizzas had grown markedly, and Jonathan Pescatore had been approached by a number of supermarket chains to see if he could make a brand of luxury pizzas for their stores. To meet this demand, production would need to rise from about 2,000 pizzas per day to about 20,000 per day.

Jonathan was attracted by the potential growth in the business. However, he was concerned that the supermarkets were unwilling to order only one or two types of pizza, but they wished to be able to order large batches of often new flavours of pizza at short notice, to maintain a mass public interest in the product. He quickly realised that this would require not only a larger factory, but a totally different method of production. Batches would need to be much larger and each stage of the production process would need to be mechanised. The dough bases would need not only to be mixed, but also formed into circles by machine. Tomato sauce would need to be extended by a machine onto the bases, and grated cheese sprinkled over them by another machine. Only the final decorating with ingredients such as ham, mushrooms, anchovies, and so on, could be conducted by hand, so as to give the final article a hand-finished appearance that would justify a premium price. The 80 workers in the new factory would therefore not be highly skilled, but for the most part they would be semi-skilled machine operators.

Advise Jonathan's Pizza Company about the following aspects of organisation in their new factory:

1   need for clear job specifications

2   need for written rules and procedures

3   need to employ other people in managerial roles

4   need to employ a marketing specialist.

Summary

In Section 5, we have discussed the use and value of organisation theory and you have identified how key questions about organisational structure design relate to questions raised by earlier management theorists.

We have also looked at the influence and significance of size, technology and environment upon an organisation's structure. In Review Activity 5, you demonstrated your understanding of the significance of these factors upon organisational structure in a practical example.

Unit Summary

In this unit, we have examined fundamental questions about the nature of organisations and why organisational structures are important.

We have used organisation theory to analyse the five key questions that have to be answered when structuring any organisation. We have explored some of the main influences on organisation structures that will help us determine how we answer the key questions on structure for any particular organisation.

Having completed the unit, you should now be able to:

● describe the structure of an organisation

● present it on an organisation chart

● analyse the significance of key elements of that structure

● assess the appropriateness of the organisation's structure for its particular circumstances

● present your findings in a coherent and convincing way to colleagues.

References

Blau, P & Scott W (1966) *Formal Organisations,* London: Routledge and Kegan Paul.

Burns, T & Stalker, G (1966) *The Management of Innovation,* London: Tavistock.

Child, J (1988) *Organisation: A Guide to Problems and Practice,* second edition, London: Paul Chapman Publishing.

Daft, R (1992) *Organization Theory and Design,* West, St Paul, MN: West Publishing.

Fayol, H (1949) *General and Industrial Management,* London: Pitman.

Graicunas, V (1937) 'Relationship in Organization' in *Papers on the Science of Administration,* New York: University of Columbia Press.

Kanter, R (1984) *The Change Masters,* London: Allen and Unwin.

Lawrence, P & Lorsch, J (1969) *Organisation and Environment,* Homewood, IL: Irwin.

Mintzberg, H (1979) *The Structuring of Organizations,* Englewood Cliffs, NJ: Prentice-Hall.

Mullins L (1993) *Management and Organisational Behaviour,* third edition, London: Pitman.

Perrow, C (1970) *Organisational Analysis,* London: Tavistock.

Smith, A (1910) *The Wealth of Nations,* London: Dent.

Weber, M (1964) *The Theory of Social and Economic Organization,* London: Collier Macmillan.

Woodward, J (1980) *Industrial Organization: Theory and Practice,* second edition, Oxford: Oxford University Press.

Answers to Review Activities

Review Activity 1

This case illustrates a number of examples of each form of differentiation and integration.

(i) Horizontal differentiation can be seen in Mark, Sue and Jane's each taking responsibility for a district and in the division of the country into regions.

(ii) Vertical differentiation can be seen when comparing Bill's job, which is office-based and managerial, with those of Mark, Sue and Jane, who are highly mobile and deal directly with potential customers.

(iii) Horizontal integration can be found in (a) Bill's wish to compare his region's sales with those of other regions; (b) Mark and Sue's lunchtime meeting to co-ordinate the sales drive on Campbell's; and (c) the north west sales team's monthly meetings.

(iv) Vertical integration can be seen in (a) Mark's delivery of sales figures to Bill; (b) Bill's preparation of a monthly regional sales report for head office; and (c) head office's comparisons of regional performance. It can also be seen very clearly in the company's standard discounts policy, which amounts to a standard operating procedure. Finally, Bill's participation in his region's monthly team meetings will provide an occasion for vertical integration.

Review Activity 4

1   Where an organisation's mission refers to the long-term or overall goal of an organisation, its operative goals are the specific steps or measures of achievement in key organisational tasks that are set as goals in order to achieve the mission goals successfully.

2   Informal goals are measures of achievement developed by individuals or groups of staff without the formal approval of senior management. Where these replace the specified, formal goals of a team or department, the process is known as goal displacement.

3   Organisational effectiveness is the extent to which an organisation is able to achieve the goals that have been set for it, or which it has set for itself.

4   For organisational effectiveness to be achievable, it is important that goal-setting is carefully carried out:

- if goals are insufficiently ambitious, staff will not try hard enough to utilise the resources and efforts of the organisation fully

- if goals are over-ambitious and unachievable, staff are likely to be demoralised and to stop trying

- if organisational goals are inappropriate to its environment, markets, capacities, resources and so on, its ability to be fully effective will be reduced.

Review Activity 5

Jonathan's Pizza Company is growing considerably, moving from craft-based small batch production, to much larger batch, more mechanised production, and from a rather stable to a more unstable environment. This will tend to dictate the need (1) for clear job specifications and (2) for written rules and procedures.

This formalisation helps create a more mechanistic structure in which the larger numbers of semi-skilled workers will know clearly what their jobs are and how to do them. Jonathan Pescatore is unlikely to be able to control the 80 workers directly himself and so (3) will need to lengthen the hierarchy and create supervisory and junior managerial jobs, for example, a production manager, within the factory. Finally, the move into a larger, more unstable market is likely to entail the employment of a marketing specialist, so that a process of differentiation will take place (4).

UNIT 5

THE NATURE OF WORK

Introduction

In this unit, you are introduced in detail to the concept of work, with our main focus upon paid work within the employment relationship. In Section 1, we look at the meaning of work, both historically, when we revisit the ideas of Weber and Marx, and within contemporary British society. We then go on to look at how jobs and occupations are categorised, the characteristics of the labour market and the role of women workers within it.

In Section 3, we examine the meanings given to work by workers themselves, and the concept of 'work orientations' is introduced. This is followed, in Section 4, by an analysis of the emerging 'information economy' and the impact of new technologies upon work and organisations. You have already covered the implications of technology and change in Unit 2, and the changing and flexible patterns of employment that we are now experiencing.

Finally, we deal with trends and prospects concerning unemployment, the service sector of the economy, working time and work outside employment. As you can see, you have covered many ideas in this unit in previous units, but here we put them into context using slightly different contemporary perspectives.

Objectives

By the end of the unit, you will be able to:

- define work and differentiate between intrinsic and extrinsic rewards.

- indicate how the meaning of work and human attitudes towards it are affected by cultural and social factors and give some historical examples.

- explain how Weber's protestant work ethic and Marx's concept of alienation are relevant to modern attitudes to work and have meaning for the individual.

- describe in basic terms some models used to describe the structure of work and list the groups or categories identified in the hierarchical occupational model.

- explain through examples the concept of occupational mobility and some of the factors that may affect this.

- examine two significant features of the labour market, the dual labour market and the sexual division of labour, and discuss the reasons put forward to explain them.

- list some broad occupational groups into which work has been divided and give examples of how the market power and status of occupational groups may change as society changes.

- define the concept of 'work orientation' and critically discuss some important studies of it.

- illustrate how work orientation is a dynamic rather than a static quality and identify some of the influences inside and outside work that may determine how people give meaning to their work.

- describe some current changes in UK work and job patterns and in the economy, and identify social and economic factors influencing their development.

- describe a range of developments in information technology and explain their importance in relation to global competitive and economic developments.

- discuss the impact of new technologies on work, particularly in relation to flexibility, work design, and organisational structure and employment patterns.

- identify some of the changing patterns of work, employment and unemployment and discuss in an informed way possible future trends.

SECTION 1
Work, Meaning and Culture

Introduction

In this section, we look briefly at what work is, at how it has been seen by people at different times in history, and at some of the cultural and social factors that have affected the meanings given to it. Let's begin by considering what we mean by work.

ACTIVITY 1

In a small group, if possible, attempt to define what work is. Confine your definition to one or two sentences!

As you know from our previous look at industrial sociology, there is no universal agreement among social scientists about the definition of **work,** however, we offer two for you to consider.

The first point to note is that work cannot be defined solely in terms of the activities to which it refers, but must include reference to the purposes for which such activities are performed and the context within which they are performed.

For example, for some people, to work is to play games to entertain spectators, games such as soccer, tennis or snooker, which many others play for pleasure or relaxation. Reading a book for interest is a different activity from reading it to prepare a lecture or write a review; the significance of digging a garden or driving a car all vary depending on the purpose for which they are done, or whether they are done for their own sake or in order to produce a good or service.

Work activities are **instrumental activities,** that is, the work is seen as a means to produce an end, such as pay. This does not mean that these activities cannot be enjoyable, but whatever **intrinsic** rewards they offer to those who perform them, they are carried out in order to achieve some **extrinsic** purpose and not just for their own sake.

Within that limitation, however, almost any activity can be work. Brown offers the following broad definition of work: 'Any physical or mental activities which transform materials into a more useful form, provide or distribute goods or services to oneself or others and/or increase or improve human knowledge and understanding of the world' (Brown, R, 1984).

ACTIVITY 2

In talking about work as an instrumental activity, we made a distinction between **intrinsic** and **extrinsic** reasons for pursuing the activity.

1   What aspects of work do you think we mean in referring to: (a) extrinsic rewards; and (b) intrinsic purposes?

2   Can you identify occupations which may be seen by the worker in either: (a) mainly extrinsic terms; and (b) mainly intrinsic terms?

1

(a) By extrinsic purposes, we mean those aspects of work which are external to it but which are extremely important. Examples are pay, supervision and social relations. These aspects may contribute little to job satisfaction.

(b) By intrinsic rewards, we mean those aspects of work which individuals performing it find interesting in themselves. Work is seen as an end in itself. For example, workers who experience very high levels of job satisfaction also achieve high levels of intrinsic rewards from their work.

2

(a) Many examples of manual work fall into this category. For example, assembly-line workers doing boring and monotonous work, construction labourers and street sweepers may derive very little intrinsic rewards from their work. Some non-manual workers such as clerical workers may also fall into this category.

(b) Some manual jobs which provide the worker with plenty of variety and responsibility such as craft work (cabinet makers, for example) are relevant here. Many higher grade non-manual occupations such as senior management grades, researchers and scientists feature prominently here.

1.1 Culture and work

A second definition of work, which may be very similar to that which you came up with in your first activity, is given by Watson (1987): 'Work can be defined as the carrying out of tasks which enable people to make a living within the environment in which they find themselves.

This definition of work can be readily understood within the culture of western industrial society. But the meaning of work and attitudes towards it also changes according to the culture of different societies. Culture basically means: the system of meanings which are shared by members of a human grouping and which define what is good and bad, right and wrong and what are appropriate ways for members of that grouping to think and behave.

In order for us to appreciate the particular ways in which modern industrial cultures encourage us to approach work and evaluate its place in our lives, it is both useful and necessary to look briefly at how previous cultures have done this.

WORK IN GREEK, ROMAN AND MEDIEVAL SOCIETY

The ancient Greeks regarded the most desirable and only 'good' life as one of leisure. Work, in the sense of supplying the basic necessities of life, was a degrading activity which was to be allocated to the lowest groups within the social order, and especially to slaves. As Hannah Arendt (1959) explains, 'slavery was the social device which enabled the Greeks to maintain their view of work as something to be avoided by a full human being; what human beings shared with all other forms of animal life was not considered to be human'.

The Romans tended to follow the Greek view, whilst the Hebrews had a view of work as unpleasant drudgery. A modification of the Greek view can be seen in early Christianity which recognised that work might make one healthy and divert one from sinful thoughts and habits. Leading thinkers of the Catholic church, such as Aquinas, were influenced by the Greek view, but a doctrine did emerge which gave a role for work in the Christian scheme of things whereby it was seen as a penance arising from original sin. As Peter Anthony (1977) adds, 'it also contributed to the virtue of obedience but was by no means seen as noble, rewarding or satisfying'.

REFORMATION AND THE PROTESTANT ETHIC

It was with the reformation and the emergence of Protestant Christianity that we see work coming to be treated positively within western cultures. Within Protestantism, it was Calvinism which was at the forefront of this near revolutionary re-appraisal of work.

The Protestant ethic, as this new movement or ideology became known, encouraged hard work, not just in order to meet basic needs or to produce short-term capital gain, but as a virtue or duty in its own right (Weber, 1965).

We can summarise Weber's main points about the Protestant ethic as follows:

- the Protestant ethic suggests that hard work and application should be seen as a vocation
- the Protestant ethic suggests that a person is serving God by performing tasks in a self-disciplined and efficient way
- the Protestant ethic also demands that a person should combine hard work and self-discipline with an 'ascetic' or 'frugal' form of existence and by doing so this will encourage the accumulation of capital by individuals
- if a person works hard and lives frugally, then that person will achieve his salvation.

Such beliefs made a radical difference to the meaning which was attached to work. As Robertson (1984) states: 'In the course of time many Protestants came to believe that God helps those who help themselves. They came to assume that work could actually contribute to their salvation, not just give them confidence that they were already saved' (p. 57).

WORK IN THE INDUSTRIAL ERA: THE PROTESTANT ETHIC

ACTIVITY 3

How do you think the effects of the protestant work ethic might show themselves in societies that followed its beliefs, and how might they lend themselves to the development of industrialism?

The protestant ethic had a tremendous impact upon subsequent developments. With the growth of industrial capitalism, these influences spread further and wider as hard and effective work becomes the essential prerequisite of personal and social advancement, of prestige, virtue and self-fulfilment.

Whereas 'not to work' had once been an indicator of prestige and the 'good life', it is now associated with failure, a poor life and even disgrace. Perhaps one of the best examples of the success of the protestant work ethic is in the USA where the ideology of the 'American dream' emphasises hard work and self-reliance as keys to future success. The initial ideas concerning the protestant ethic are found in Max Weber's study *The Protestant Ethic and the Spirit of Capitalism*.

The protestant ethic justified the profit-making business activities of nineteenth-century entrepreneurs, thereby laying the foundations for the development of large-scale industrial capitalism. At the same time, the ethic also justified regular, specialised work for the employee.

WORK IN THE INDUSTRIAL ERA: ALIENATION

Associated with the notion that people can achieve self-fulfilment or self-actualisation in their work and their careers is its opposite – work **alienation**. This notion, which is derived from Karl Marx's analysis of capitalist society, has been very influential in sociology.

The basic idea underlying the concept of alienation is 'separation'. The main characteristics of alienation are briefly identified below. You had a more detailed discussion of alienation in relation to technology in Unit 2.

● Firstly, individuals become alienated or estranged from other people as relationships become merely calculative, self-interested and untrusting.

● Secondly, individuals become alienated from the product of their efforts since what is produced is taken from them and is not conceived by the workers themselves to meet their own ends or needs.

- Thirdly, individuals are alienated or separated from their own labour in that they do not derive the satisfactions or the delights that is possible in labour since that labour is forced upon them as a means of meeting other needs and because they put themselves under the control of other people in the work situation.

- Finally, the work of an individual becomes an alien thing which oppresses them and here we have the essential element of the Marxian notion of alienation: people can be alienated from themselves.

Marx's conception of human nature is one in which it is assumed that people realise their essential nature as a species – through productive work that is carried out for their own purposes and not under the control and exploitation of others. What this suggests, and we must emphasise this point, is that alienation is basically an objective state. Alienation is not necessarily reflected in job dissatisfaction or frustration.

For example, a person may be very happy sitting at a desk in someone's factory five days a week sorting pieces of paper which mean little to him, in return for a wage. Yet, in the Marxian conception of alienation, this person is alienated: he is not fulfilling himself in the way he might be if he was working under different conditions.

People are alienated, therefore, when they are not being what they possibly could be. For people to become what they could be, that is, to fulfil themselves or to achieve self-actualisation, they must create a society which, although taking a different form from capitalism, is still one in which work, as a source of fulfilment in its own right, is central.

ACTIVITY 4

1 What do the protestant work ethic and the Marxian concept of alienation have in common?

2 Identify two main differences between the protestant work ethic and the Marxian concept of alienation.

1   The main point here is that both the Protestant work ethic and the Marxian concept of alienation assume that work is a central activity of human life which distinguishes humans from other creatures.

2   One main difference between the two is that while the Protestant ethic regards work as a means of salvation, the Marxian view is that under capitalism, work for most people is a brutalising activity, unrewarding and unfulfilling.

Another main difference is the assumption of Marxists that work has the potential to be fulfilling only when the capitalist system of exploitation is removed and workers finally control and own the means of production under socialism. It is only in the 'real' world that things can be changed in this way, according to the Marxian view. The Protestant ethic, on the other hand, holds that work, however harsh and unremitting in the material world, nevertheless serves to increase the glory of God. Wealthy and poor alike had a duty to work and worldly work came to be seen as the purpose of life, ordained as such by God.

REVIEW ACTIVITY 1

Suggested time: 20 minutes.

Below are three quotes by workers about their work. Read the quotes and then answer question 1.

Quote 1
'I was at the ripe age of 25 when I started with the London General Omnibus Company – I am now 66 years of age . . . If I were 25 years of age today, you could stick this job on the buses where a monkey is reputed to stick his nuts!' (A bus driver)

Quote 2
At the end of the shift we'd run for the clock. I don't know why we did . . . it just meant we had to wait on the bus. Well one day I run to the clock, grab for my coat and its tied up in knots. It was Clarkey. He was a strong bastard and he'd really tied it up tight. I couldn't move it. So the next day I took some boxes of those very small tacks into work. I made a tiny hole in the pocket of Clarkey's coat, tipped the tacks in and then gave the coat a shake. When he came to pick it up it was like a ton weight' (Beynon, 1984).

Quote 3
'Work is my life, I live for my work and I want to get on and better myself. The pay is not great, but then you shouldn't judge work by how much you earn, should you? These days you should be grateful for whatever work you get. It should be everyone's right and duty to work'. (A senior bank clerk)

1   Which of these quotes are relevant either to an interpretation based on the Protestant ethic or to an interpretation based on the concept of alienation? Explain fully your choice.

2   Describe briefly some cultural views of work and its value.

Summary

In this section, you have studied important introductory aspects of work. We have considered definitions of work and have understood the distinction between intrinsic and extrinsic factors relating to work.

We have also identified the major ways in which work has been regarded throughout the ages.

We then went on to consider the influential Protestant work ethic which is one of the main ideological building blocks resulting in the evolution and development of modern industrial society.

Finally, we briefly talked about the Marxian concept of alienation which is useful in helping us to understand many people's views about their work within a modern industrial setting.

SECTION 2

Occupations and the Structure of Work

Introduction

In this section, we deal with how jobs and occupations are arranged and structured within British society, both vertically, or hierarchically, and horizontally. We also look at how people can progress in their jobs and careers, and why some people move downwards. We also examine the labour market and its characteristics, particularly in relation to part-time workers and women workers.

In order to understand work, we need to identify a pattern underlying the work which people do in modern societies. According to Watson (1987), there are two principles which underlie this pattern:

- structuring of work on a bureaucratic, administrative or 'formal' organisation basis
- structuring on the basis of occupations.

The first principle reflects how we think of work in an organisational perspective. We see it in terms of organisational roles, status, and structures, in terms of how tasks are designed by certain people who then recruit, pay, co-ordinate and control the efforts of others to carry out these tasks.

However, the second principle of looking at work is based on the fact that in society there are groups of people regularly doing similar tasks or following occupations (driving a bus, decorating a house, running a business, etc). This allows us to analyse work in society on the basis of the occupations people follow and to see the social and economic patterns, issues and implications that emerge from examining the society's occupational structure. It is with this second perspective on work that we are primarily concerned in this unit.

Before we move on, there are a number of points to note concerning the sociological study of occupations which constitute important defining characteristics of occupations:

- The study of occupations is based on the fact that work in any society is a socially desired activity and is fundamental to our understanding of social behaviour.

- Occupations go beyond a mere description of work tasks within a particular society. Occupations are roles within society that are defined by the nature of the work that individuals perform.

- Occupational status is achieved by most individuals in the majority of industrialised societies.

- Because occupational status is achieved, we are led to ask questions such as why individuals choose one occupation in preference to another and to examine the constraints placed on individuals in the choice process.

- Once in an occupation, we can ask questions about movement and career progression within the occupation, and what comprises an occupational career.

- Occupations vary in the degree of cohesion or unity they display and the extent of control that they can exert over their members.

- Occupations have different amounts of prestige and status conferred upon them by society, and many occupations and professions struggle to achieve and maintain levels of status and reward which their members enjoy (Dunkerley, 1975; Hall, 1975).

2.1 Occupational structure

Occupational structure is a way of describing and analysing the field of work and is used by sociologists to refer to the wider pattern in society which is created by the distribution of the labour force across the range of existing types of work.

The concept of occupational structure is very useful in helping sociologists to study important trends and patterns in work and changes in the distribution and composition of the labour force.

There are two patterns that are used in studies and which we should be aware of if we are studying the nature of work. The first we can call **horizontal patterning** and the second, **hierarchical patterning**.

HORIZONTAL PATTERNING

We can identify two examples or types of horizontal patterning. The first example involves the division of the work force into primary (agricultural and extractive industries), secondary (manufacturing), and tertiary (service) sectors, and is frequently used to show the horizontal differentiation of work in a society. This type of distribution, which is widely used by economists, has been used by sociologists mainly to study the impact of industrialisation processes upon these sectors.

The second example is called occupational situs. A situs is a category that is placed at the same level as other categories such that all categories are given equal weightings. It is best to think of situs categories as occupational families. Examples of occupational families could include political, professional, business, military, etc. It is then possible to compare occupations within each of these families.

HIERARCHICAL PATTERNING

It is far more common, however, for the hierarchical structuring of work to be emphasised in studies of occupational structure. This hierarchical pattern relates occupation to class and status which are concepts generally used inside and outside of sociology. We can, therefore, talk about high and low status occupations, and we can readily contrast the status of a senior management job with that of an assembly-line job.

The grading of occupations within a hierarchy ranges from high status and prestige at the top of the hierarchy to low status and prestige at the bottom of the hierarchy. In most, but not in all cases, the material reward of work, such as pay, is highest at the top end of the hierarchy, and lowest at the bottom end. There is also a correlation between high pay, status and intrinsic rewards from work which contribute to job satisfaction. A senior manager will have high status, high pay and considerable intrinsic rewards, while a street sweeper will have low pay, low status and few intrinsic rewards.

In the creation of a hierarchical structure to analyse work patterning, occupations are classified and grouped together in such a way that we can expect those individuals in any single group to share in broadly similar market and work situations. These are taken to be the two major components of class position. A simplified classification of occupational groupings based on the work of Goldthorpe et al (1980) using hierarchical patterning is given below.

Class I   higher-grade professionals, administrators, managers and businessmen

Class II   lower-grade professionals, administrators and managers; higher-grade technicians and supervisors of manual employees

Class III   routine non-manual, largely clerical, workers; sales personnel and other rank and file service workers

Class IV   small proprietors; self-employed artisans and other non-professional own-account workers

Class V   lower-grade technicians and supervisors of manual workers

Class VI   skilled manual wage workers

Class VII semi- and un-skilled workers.

ACTIVITY 5

Think of some examples of how the hierarchical classification of work can enable us to discover more about features of work and the social and economic issues surrounding it.

Studies using such a classification as a basis to analyse the profiles of work can identify features and trends in work that are of great social importance.

These categories, often called socio-economic groups or categories, are used to do certain things such as:

- examine the numbers of people covered by certain sectors or socio-economic groups
- look at the mobility of people between different categories
- consider the characteristics of people in various positions in terms of criteria such as gender, race and age, and especially the way these patterns change over time.

MOBILITY

Mobility is the movement of people between the different socio-economic categories during their occupational lifetime. This is sometimes called **occupational mobility**. But because this movement also involves classes, it is also called **social** mobility. For our purposes, though, we use the term occupational mobility.

Mobility also refers to movement of people across the socio-economic categories over generations. For example, you can compare the socio-economic position or occupational status of your grandfather at the end of his working life with that of your father. The first type of mobility is called **intra-generational** and the second type of mobility is called **inter-generational**.

The purpose of the next activity is to apply your understanding of hierarchical occupational structure and the concept of occupational mobility, and to help you reflect on what may affect mobility.

ACTIVITY 6

1 Assume that you start your occupational life in category VII as an unskilled worker, and that, during your occupational life you experience considerable occupational mobility and end up in category I. Identify at every stage of this process the important factors which might have influenced your rapid progress. Give examples of the type of work which you undertake within each category. Note that you do not necessarily have to move into each successive category; you can miss out one or two of them.

2 Repeat the same exercise starting from category I and finishing in category VII.

---

1   Factors which affect upward mobility during a person's working lifetime include:

- educational qualifications gained
- marriage, especially for women
- re-training for skilled jobs
- promotion
- strong work ethic.

2   Factors which affect downward mobility include:

- lack of motivation to re-train
- unacceptable life-style (for example, alcoholism, drug addiction)
- medical problems
- redundancy
- ongoing marital/family problems.

2.2 Work and occupations

Here, we look at examples of three major occupational groupings in a little more detail. They have been the subject of study by sociologists and we can therefore identify some of the important changes that have taken place within them. The groupings or categories we look at are:

- managerial and administrative occupations
- professional, supervisory and clerical occupations
- manual occupations.

As you will notice, these occupational categories are drawn from the hierarchical classification of occupations that we identified in sub-section 2.1.

We now consider these three categories in turn together with some issues relating to each which have been the subject of sociological debate.

MANAGERIAL AND ADMINISTRATIVE OCCUPATIONS

These occupations have been seen by many commentators as forming part of a new 'technocracy' and as playing an increasingly important role in the control of enterprises as the **separation of ownership and control** increased since the nineteenth century. The separation of ownership and control or the 'managerialist' thesis as it became known is based on the work of James Burnham (1945). He argued that the specialist knowledge and skills of managerial experts had become crucial to the successful running of increasingly large and complex organisations. The dominance of the owners of wealth is therefore undermined and a new class of professional salaried managers is said to be exercising significant control. Burnham calls this the 'managerial revolution'.

Subsequent research by Nichols (1969) and others has subjected the managerialist thesis to closer examination and has demonstrated that the claims made by Burnham were largely exaggerated. The basic conclusion of this research is that managers in large business enterprises are more oriented to and concerned with profit seeking and are more capable of obtaining it, than the traditional owner-managers. This research does not refute the basic argument of Burnham, but it does suggest a greater emphasis upon the increasing importance and power vested in the new breed of professional managers.

The growth of importance and power of managerial and administrative occupations throughout the twentieth century is, therefore, one of the significant developments within advanced industrial capitalist societies.

PROFESSIONAL, SUPERVISORY AND CLERICAL OCCUPATIONS

These three occupational sub-categories are often discussed sociologically in similar terms and, especially in terms of whether or not they are becoming 'proletarianised'. This concerns whether they are, or are not, moving downwards in the class and status hierarchy so that their members are finding themselves located in a position more like that of working class rather than middle class people.

ACTIVITY 7

Can you think of any factors which suggest that professional, supervisory and clerical occupations are becoming 'proletarianised'?

In the case of **professionals,** the sociological evidence (Perkin, 1989. Reed, 1989) is inconclusive and there are two views:

- On the one hand, we are moving to a 'knowledge' or 'information' society where that society is becoming increasingly 'professionalised' as power moves from commercial organisations to those occupations upon whom society is more and more dependent for specialised knowledge and its application.

- On the other hand, there is arguably an opposing trend. Professional work is increasingly devalued as increasing fragmentation of work associated with an extensive division of labour brings 'experts' more under administrative control and hence treats them more like the traditional wage worker.

Whether or not we agree with these assumptions, they do alert us to the different kinds of change that can occur to any occupation or branch of an occupation as a result of wider changes occurring in our society. For example, certain branches of the accountancy profession might be downgraded through, say, the computerising of routine operations whilst other branches might retain traditional advantages through their continued exercise of discretion and expert judgement at a strategic level in the management of capital.

When we look at **clerical** workers, research such as that of Abercrombie and Urry (1983) suggests a pessimistic conclusion and white-collar work generally is seen as liable to proletarianisation in two ways:

- as it gets more involved in the actual processes of production rather than the purchasing of labour power to carry out that production

- as its involvement in buying labour power itself becomes a routine pattern, de-skilled and restricted by bureaucratic controls.

Evidence for this is to be found in the growing numbers of white-collar workers who joined trade unions during the 1970s and 1980s. Membership of trade unions was traditionally regarded by most white-collar workers as something to be avoided owing to their higher social and occupational status *vis-a vis* manual workers, and because of their relatively higher wages, better conditions of work and more favourable market situation.

Foremen and **supervisors** are another group which is problematic in terms of position and status within work organisations. As Littler (1982) shows, the industrial foreman emerged out of the role of the independent labour contractor or piecemaster in the late-nineteenth and early-twentieth centuries. The process of emergence was not a straightforward one, however: some contractors became integrated into the organisation as a directly employed foreman, whilst others simply became workers or ended up as chargemen or leading hands. In spite of being a paid employee rather than a contractor, the traditional foreman hired, fired, set wages, planned and allocated work. This made him the undisputed master of his own shop.

However, the power of the foreman's role soon began to decline owing to the influence of technical experts, inspectors and rate-fixers. His power was also eroded by production engineers, personnel managers and the rest, so that supervisors became reduced to a role as 'man in the middle' in which they owe loyalty to both management and work force and yet are part of neither. Alternatively, the supervisor has been seen as the 'marginal man' of industry, that is, the one who is held accountable for work carried out but who is excluded from managerial decision-making.

More recently, the supervisor role has been further eroded and in an increasing number of cases, has disappeared altogether. For example, in many Japanese owned companies and in other companies using 'Japanese-style' production methods the supervisor has become a thing of the past. You saw this earlier with the 'team' approach.

MANUAL OCCUPATIONS

In theory, manual occupations have in common, a type of work and market situation which locates them in an inferior position to that of middle and upper class people. However, it has been widely recognised that manual workers, in common with the other groups we have considered, do not, in practice, form a particularly homogenous group. They are differentiated by skill, for example.

ACTIVITY 8

With reference to manual occupations, name three occupations which fall into 'skilled' and 'un-skilled' categories. What factors contribute to the defining characteristics of each of the six occupations, and have their market situations changed?

Examples of skilled manual occupations include coal miners, vehicle mechanics, some electricity supply workers, electricians, and bricklayers.

Examples of un-skilled manual occupations include agricultural labourers, construction labourers, canteen assistants, shop assistants, street sweepers and office cleaners.

Skilled workers' occupations share a number of characteristics which set them apart from un-skilled, and to a lesser extent, semi-skilled workers' occupations. Generally speaking, the following characteristics apply:

- **Apprenticeships:** many skilled occupations require a period of training before the worker becomes a fully-fledged specialist.

- **Specialist knowledge:** this is essential not only to 'learn the ropes' but also on a continuous basis as the demands of jobs change for a variety of reasons, changing technology being one of the main ones.

- **Control, autonomy, responsibility and discretion:** these factors relate to work performance. Skilled workers, in general terms, have considerable degrees of control over what they do, high levels of autonomy, responsibility and discretion which involve them making decisions about their work without necessarily having to get permission from superiors.

Un-skilled workers perform routine tasks which require little or no expertise. There is no apprenticeship system, no technical expertise or specialist knowledge and hardly any control, discretion, autonomy or responsibility.

MARKET SITUATION

Market situation is a term used to refer to people who share a similar position in a market economy. Factors such as market value, or pay and skill levels are important. The more skilled the worker, the better his market situation. However, certain factors can and do change market situation. For example, coal miners' market situation has changed because of pit closures causing many redundancies. The privatisation of pits has resulted in a deterioration in conditions of work and remuneration. In the case of print workers, their skills have been made virtually useless as a result of advances in print technology.

Even un-skilled workers' market situations change. Factors such as recession cause lay-offs and redundancies, for example, in the construction industry, and conversion of full-time un-skilled jobs into part-time jobs .

2.3 Types of work: labour market segmentation

As we saw earlier, the occupational structure of work is structured on the basis of occupational status which is hierarchically ordered and patterned. The labour market includes all those workers within the occupational structure, that is, all employees. Fevre's book *The Sociology of Labour Markets* (1992) looks at the workings of the labour market in greater detail. The term 'market' is important because it means that there are ongoing transactions between those who wish to buy the services of people (the employers) and those who sell, or wish to sell those services to employers (the employees). However, this definition of the labour market needs to be qualified in two ways:

- **Character of the labour market** is determined by the requirements of employers, and is based on needs for part-time workers as well as full-time workers, and workers meeting different and constantly changing skill criteria of employers.

- **Composition of the labour market:** apart from the status categories we have already considered, the labour market comprises broader categories based on:
  - gender
  - race and ethnicity.

CHARACTER OF THE LABOUR MARKET: THE DUAL LABOUR MARKET

The concept of the **dual labour market** first emerged in the USA as an attempt, within the context of the American occupational structure, to understand racial discrimination in employment, but is now used to embrace a wider range of issues.

We can divide labour markets into two sectors: the primary and the secondary.

In the **primary sector,** work is characterised by:

- good working conditions and pay levels
- opportunities for advancement
- fair treatment at work
- stability of employment.

In the **secondary sector,** workers in this sector are worse off in all the respects identified for the primary sector. Their work is associated with considerable instability of employment and a high labour turnover rate. The members of this secondary labour force will tend to be people who:

- are easily dispensed with
- possess clearly visible social differences
- are little interested in training or gaining high economic reward
- tend not to organise themselves into trade unions.

Given these features and the social and cultural characteristics of the wider society, we tend to find recruitment to the secondary labour force drawing to a disproportionate extent on women, blacks, immigrants, unqualified teenagers, students seeking part-time work, disabled and handicapped persons.

Most people have had experience of the secondary labour market. For example, you may have been served a burger at McDonalds by a part-time student, or have been served by an part-time assistant at your local supermarket. In terms of numbers of people employed on a part-time basis, this sector is certainly expanding.

But why has the dual labour market come about? The two main reasons for the secondary sector's expansion are related to:

● employers' reactions to the recessions of the 1980s and 1990s

● the continual struggle for control that goes on between employers and employees.

Employers' reactions to the uncertainties generated in economic life by the two major recessions have been:

● to develop an internal labour market and to create a stable and well-rewarded labour force having opportunities for promotion and training resulting in a skilled and motivated work force. This corresponds to the 'core' work force of the **flexible firm** we discussed in Unit 2.

● in firms less technologically advanced or which have less stable markets, adopting more typical hire and fire approaches towards the less skilled and organised employees who are more suitable to the employer's purposes. This obviously encourages the growth of the secondary sector.

● a reaction to organised (unionised) labour on the part of employers is also important here with an attempt to restore the flexibility lost with highly organised groups by using the 'buffer' of a weaker secondary labour group.

As we noted above, the continual struggle for control which goes on between employers and employees has been another important factor influencing the development of the secondary sector. Worker's strategies to secure advantaged work situations for their own particular groups are as important as the employer's strategies of divide and rule. For example, highly unionised groups of skilled core workers may seek, through their union, and by taking advantage of their relatively secure and privileged position within the organisation to gain improved working conditions and better pay for themselves. Employers, on the other hand, may wish to expand their part-time workforce, but they will need to bear in mind the possible reactions of the existing full-time workforce. These strategies are based upon a complex and ongoing interaction between technological factors, product markets, labour supply conditions and attempts to control the labour process itself. Remember these ideas from Unit 2.

It is much easier nowadays for employers to expand their 'peripheral' workforce because of high levels of unemployment within the economy, and government policies concerning the de-regulation of employment. For example, the abolition of the wages councils has meant that employers can offer extremely low wages to potential employees. Employers can increasingly take advantage of the secondary labour market to provide them with cheap, temporary labour which they can control.

Research by the Cambridge Labour Studies Group reinforces these points and has shown that, although the pattern of jobs available is largely a matter of technological and structural factors independent of labour supply, there is an important part played by social processes when it comes to supplying labour for secondary sector employment (Craig et al, 1982). It is factors such as the socially influenced low expectations of women, youths, black and immigrant workers which encourages the pattern whereby the secondary types of occupation are disproportionately filled by people in these categories. And it is also the outcome of patterns of stereotyping and discrimination on such grounds as race or gender.

ACTIVITY 9

1 Identify three types of work that a person employed in the secondary sector could do.

2 A major retail firm has decided that, in order to restore declining profit levels in the face of depressed consumer demand, it can make payroll savings by:

● reducing the number of full-time store employees from 25,000 to 12,000 nationally

● taking on around 12,000 employees on a part-time, temporary basis.

In addition, the company, at the request of the main trade union which represents shop workers, Union of Shop, Distributive and Allied Trades (USDAW), is negotiating a package which will provide better conditions of employment for its full-time workers.

What relevant points from sub-sections 2.3 and 2.4 would you use to explain why this company is choosing this particular strategy?

---

1 There are many types of work which a person employed in the secondary sector could do. A number of service industries stand out with extensive part-time working:

Cleaning services (55% men; 85.9% women working part-time)

Hotels and catering (43% men; 71.9% women)

Retail (26.2% men; 65.4% women)

Education (25.5% men; 55.5% women)

Medical and health services (20.8% men; 51.6% women)

(Source: Employment Gazette, December 1993.)

2   The concept of the dual labour market is the focus of this question, and there are a number of points you should have identified:

- the firm wishes to expand its secondary labour market because it is better suited to its purposes; it can keep labour costs down and hire and fire more readily
- all the part-time jobs are unskilled and this will keep training costs down
- part-time workers are less likely to join trade unions than the full-time workers
- part-time workers are more likely to be women rather than men, younger rather than older
- remaining full-time workers may have greater job security as a result of the re-structuring, will retain their union membership and enjoy better conditions of work.

The number of part-timers in Britain is now at an all-time high. Of the 21 million employees in the UK, around 6 million or 30% work part-time and 80% of part-timers are women. These figures are based on those in the *Employment Gazette* for 1993 and the *Labour Force Survey, 1992*.

COMPOSITION OF THE LABOUR MARKET: SEXUAL DIVISION OF LABOUR

Another important aspect of work revealed by study of the structure and segmentation of the labour market relates to the increasing number of women in the labour market and the continuing influence of stereotypical assumptions and discriminatory attitudes in the division of labour.

Apart from stereotyping and discrimination on the grounds of race within the labour market and in many work organisations, the gender aspect of discrimination is increasingly important as the proportion of women in the labour market rapidly increases. We now:

- review some salient patterns and features of women's employment
- review evidence of gender discrimination at work
- examine some different reasons put forward to explain why gender discrimination occurs.

2.4 Women's employment

There have been considerable increases in the proportion of women who work. From 1961 to 1981, the number of employed females rose by 2.7 million, while the number of working men actually fell by about 200,000. In 1961, women made up 32.3% of the labour force and by 1981, this increased to 39.5%. From 1984 to 1993, the number of women in employment increased by 16% while the number of men in work remained the same.

- Most of this rise has been due to the increasing numbers of married women who work. In Britain, at the end of the 1980s, around 50% of all married women were employed, compared to 20% in 1951.

- In the 1985-87 period, 78% of men and 67% of women of working age were in employment.

- However, it is overwhelmingly women who do part-time work. According to the 1993 *Labour Force Survey,* for example, there are now just under 21 million employees of which 5.88 million (28%) work part-time. and 80% of part-time employees are women.

There was a considerable increase in women's pay as a proportion of men's in the 1970s. In 1970, women earned 63.1% of men's wages and by 1977 this had risen to 75.5%. Since then, the upward trend has been reversed. Although women make up an increasing proportion of the labour force, they are not equally represented throughout the occupational structure.

- There is both horizontal and vertical segregation in men's and women's jobs. **Horizontal segregation** is the extent to which men and women do different jobs, while **vertical segregation** is the extent to which men have higher status and higher paid jobs than women.

- With regard to horizontal segregation, according to the *New Earnings Survey* of 1993, women held 60% of jobs in professional and related occupations in education, welfare and health, 74% of clerical and related occupations and 76% of jobs in catering, cleaning, hairdressing and other personal services. On the other hand, they held just 9% of professional jobs in science, engineering and technology and 11% of general management jobs. Moreover, women who have professional jobs tend to work in the lower professions, and many have routine non-manual jobs, and semi- or un-skilled manual jobs.

- Vertical segregation has actually increased this century. Although women have made small gains in some areas, for example, they have made some inroads into management, they now make up a much greater proportion of clerical workers than they used to.

- Within particular occupations, women are usually concentrated in the lowest reaches of the occupational structure. For example, civil service statistics indicated that in 1990, women made up 0% of the highest grade (permanent secretaries), 2.5% of the second (deputy secretaries) and 4.4% of the third (under secretaries). On the other hand, they made up 80% of the lowest category of staff (clerical assistants).

- Few women occupy elite positions in society. Currently, less than 10% are government ministers, MPs, ambassadors and army officers. Even in occupations in which women predominate, such as primary school teaching, they tend to miss out on the senior jobs. In 1990, over 90% of primary school teachers were women, but women held only 43% of head teachers' jobs.

GENDER DISCRIMINATION AT WORK

There is strong evidence of discriminatory behaviour in the workplace. Discriminatory attitudes among managers responsible for formulating and implementing personnel policies were shown to be widespread as studies by Hunt (1975) and Curran (1985) confirm. The latter study of a sample of 101 job vacancies in the north-east of England showed that there is widespread, blatant and potentially unlawful discrimination between men and women.

Discrimination occurs both in recruitment and in later years for women in all kinds of occupation. Lorber (1985) reveals that there are many 'ironic double binds' that virtually guarantee that women will not become fully accepted members of work communities which are dominated by men:

● if women are married, they are considered to be more committed to their family than to their career

● if they are unmarried, they are considered to be unreliable colleagues because other colleagues assume that their main consideration is a sexual relationship.

Davidson and Cooper (1983) have shown how prejudice and discrimination from both colleagues and corporate policy play a considerable part in keeping women out of upper middle and senior management positions. Another study of how women engineers are treated in the interview situation reveals the detail of discriminatory behaviour when women enter previously male preserves. Respondents reported such things as the smile on the interviewer's face when he asked 'And why do you want to be an engineer dear?' and another woman says that she was asked if she would cry if she did not receive an increase in salary.

ACTIVITY 10

Within a group, if possible, identify and discuss reasons for the existence of gender discrimination at work.

Check the reasons you have identified with those we give now.

REASONS FOR GENDER DISCRIMINATION

Having identified the main types of work which women do, and some examples of gender discrimination at work, let us now review the main reasons for this discrimination and then examine one in some detail. The conventional sociological explanation provides us with five reasons:

● The primary status of women is perceived to be as mothers and housewives. As such, their careers are discontinuous because they move out of the labour market to produce and rear children.

● Traditionally, women have been regarded as 'secondary breadwinners' compared to the male family head. This encourages the attitude that it is right and proper that women should be paid less than men.

- Women are less geographically mobile than men because of the mother/housewife role which ties them to their husbands. The family is much more likely to move house to follow the husband's career than that of the wife. This helps to explain the link between women and low status jobs, since a successful career often requires residential mobility.

- There is a large reserve of employable women which usually means that the demand for work will exceed its supply. As a result, employers will not have to attract female labour with high wages, career opportunities and improved working conditions.

- There are some statutory regulations dealing with the employment of women. These regulations limit their hours of work and bar them from some occupations.

These reasons are derived from Caplow's *The Sociology of Work* published in 1954 and are still applicable to contemporary Britain. The British experience shows that limited impact can be made through changes in legislation, for example, with the Sex Discrimination Act.

Many sociologists and feminists today place particular emphasis upon one of the factors mentioned by Caplow and this concerns the reserve of employable women. Marxist feminists believe that identifying women as a 'reserve army of labour' is the key to explaining their disadvantages. There are two aspects to this view which we briefly consider below:

De-skilling and the labour process

As we have seen in Unit 2, the work of Braverman (1974) is important here and we discussed it in relation to technological change. Braverman suggested that capitalism produced a progressive de-skilling of work, including clerical work, service sector work and retailing. According to Braverman, women have been drawn into these areas of work as the service sector has expanded, while the mainly male manufacturing area has declined. He explains women's entry into work in the following way:

- Women are no longer needed to produce commodities such as food and clothing for their families since these items can now be more easily purchased.

- Women are able to move quite easily from providing services for their family to providing them for other members of the community in return for a wage packet.

- Women have had to become an increasingly important source of labour as the reserve supply of other types of labour, for example, migrants from rural areas, has dried up.

- Women are a particularly suitable source of labour in an economic system that increasingly wants to employ un-skilled workers. Braverman believes that women have been used to replace skilled male workers and so helped employers to de-skill their labour force.

ACTIVITY 11

Are there any points which might argue against Braverman's views?

It is important to note and emphasise that a major problem with Braverman's views is his exclusive emphasis on de-skilling. Not all jobs have been de-skilled, nor for that matter do all women work in un-skilled jobs. Furthermore, it is possible that some jobs attract low pay not because they require little skill, but simply because they are seen as women's jobs. Thus nurses get comparatively low wages despite the professional skills and training required.

Women as a reserve army of labour

The second strand of Marxist thought is that capitalism required a reserve army of labour, that is a spare pool of potential recruits to the labour force.

- According to Marx, because of their built-in contradictions, capitalist economies went through cycles of slump and boom such as the ones we experienced in the 1980s and 1990s, and it was essential to be able to hire workers during the booms, and fire them during the slumps (Marx and Engels, 1971).

- In their pursuit of 'surplus value', capitalists tried constantly to improve the efficiency of their machinery. This reduced the work force required to produce existing products, but new products were constantly introduced. Again, a reserve army provided the necessary flexibility to deal with these changes.

Beechey (1986) identifies a number of ways in which women in contemporary Britain are particularly suited to form part of this reserve army. These include:

- Women are less likely to be unionised and so are less able to resist redundancy than men.

- Women's jobs are least likely to be covered by redundancy legislation, so it is cheaper to make them redundant rather than men.

- Unemployed married women may not be eligible to receive state benefit if their husbands are working, and for this reason might not appear in the unemployment statistics. Beechey states 'Women who are made redundant are able to disappear virtually without trace back into the family'.

- Because of their position within the family and the primary importance placed on their domestic role, women are likely to provide a particularly flexible reserve labour force. They are more likely to accept part-time work and variations in their hours of work.

- Women are often prepared to work for less than men because they can rely on their husbands' wages as the main source of income for the family.

The reserve army of labour certainly seems to explain some of the changes that have taken place in the proportion of women working this century in Britain. For example, it would appear to account for the increased employment of women during the two world wars. However, the theory does have some serious drawbacks:

- It cannot explain horizontal segregation in the labour market, that is, why women are largely confined to certain types of work.

- We may question the assumption that it must serve the interests of capitalism if women are used as a reserve army of labour. Women can also benefit capitalist employers by producing 'use values' in the home since this reduces the amount they need to pay to male workers.

- It is also argued that it benefits capitalism more if women are allowed to retain their jobs in times of recession and rising unemployment since they can act as a comparatively cheap substitute for male workers. This argument is called the **substitution theory**.

Clearly the best way to test these last two theories is to examine what happens to women's employment when unemployment generally is rising. During the 1980s and 1990s, male employment fell substantially as traditional manufacturing and extractive industries declined. During this period, female employment increased substantially. This increase was largely due to more women working part-time, so women do form a relatively flexible labour force. Whether this is the substitution effect or the reserve army effect remains contested.

REVIEW ACTIVITY 2

Suggested time: 45 minutes.

This review activity is in two parts. In the first part, you analyse the data presented in the bar chart in Figure 1. In the second part, you focus on the sexual division of labour.

Part 1

Examine the bar chart in Figure 1 and answer the following questions:

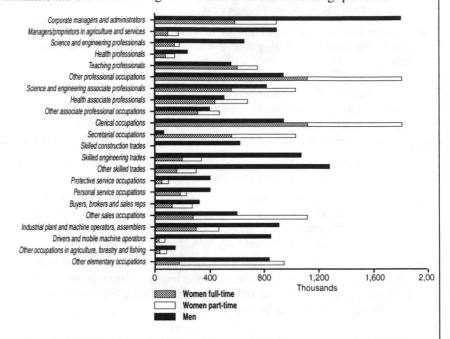

Figure 1: Numbers of women and men of working age in employment by occupation: Great Britain, Winter 1992/93 (not seasonally adjusted) (Soure: Employment Gazette Nov 93)

1   Figure 1 gives examples of both horizontal and hierarchical patterning of occupations:

- identify examples of horizontal patterning

- locate the occupational groups within each of the seven socio-economic categories of the hierarchical model given in the sub-section *Hierarchical pattering* on page 398.

2   What does the information tell us about dual labour markets?

3   Select two categories which show high levels of full-time and part-time women's employment and provide reasons for this distribution.

Part 2

4   In broad terms, compare the positions of women with those of men in the work force in terms of:

- full-time and part-time employment

- horizontal and vertical segregation in jobs

- pay.

5   Summarise the conventional sociological reasons put forward to explain why gender discrimination occurs

6   Summarise briefly the Marxist feminist reserve army of labour theory put forward to explain gender discrimination.

Summary

In this section, we have looked at the way that work is structured and have identified occupational groups and categories identified in the hierarchical occupational model. We also introduced the idea of social and occupational mobility and considered the extent to which people can either progress in their careers, upward mobility, or experience downward mobility.

We also considered some major occupational groupings such as managerial, professional and manual groupings and the reasons why the status and market position of some of the specific occupations within these groups have changed over the years.

Finally, we examined the concept of the dual labour market and the sexual division of labour and the reasons put forward to explain them. We looked particularly at the factors affecting women's employment.

SECTION 3

Work Orientations and Meaning

Introduction

We now move from reviewing the structure of work in our society and some of its important features, to look at how people feel about their work – the beliefs they hold about why they do it and the satisfactions they expect from it. If we put these together, they become the 'meaning' which individuals attach to their work. This meaning clearly affects their work attitudes and behaviour.

The concept of work orientation concerns the meaning attached by individuals to their work which predisposes them to both think and act in particular ways with regard to that work. The concept is used to investigate the various ways in which different individuals and groups approach their work and it takes, as its starting point, a basic distinction which we made earlier in the unit. This is the distinction between work meanings in which work offers intrinsic satisfactions to people, and meanings which recognise only extrinsic satisfactions. Figure 1 explains this distinction more fully.

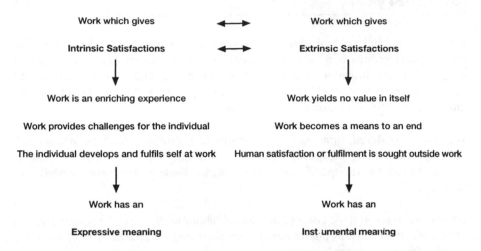

Figure 2: Meanings of work: a continuum

The main difficulty about this way of looking at what work means to people is that it has encouraged an 'either/or' type of debate. Much discussion of work attitudes and work motivation has focussed on the question of whether people generally are extrinsically or intrinsically oriented towards their work (see Figure 2). It is therefore frequently debated whether, on the one hand, people generally go to work 'just for the money' or 'basically for the company' or, on the other hand, they primarily want 'job satisfaction' or 'self-fulfilment'.

But this is simplistic and industrial sociologists have developed the concept of work orientation to go beyond this:

● to show ways in which people's approach to their work typically includes mixtures of these basic inclinations but nevertheless containing specific leanings in one or other of these general directions

● to help explain the factors, both individual and structural, which influence people's attitudes and behaviour with regard to their work.

ACTIVITY 12

The two quotes given below reflect expressive and instrumental work meanings. Comment on how each view of work may be expected to make these individuals act in a particular work situation.

Quote (a) – expressive
'I love my work. It is satisfying, challenging and motivating. The job I do has a lot of variety and I can pace myself and control what I do'.

Quote (b) – instrumental
'My work is boring and monotonous, but it pays well, and that's important these days. I can provide for my family and buy the luxuries that a lot of people can't'.

Quote (a)
The individual making this statement is obviously highly motivated, regards work as challenging and enriching, and sees his work as self-developing and fulfilling. He will act and behave in accordance with what his employing organisation requires of him, maybe serving the organisation in return for career progress, and will have a 'moral' commitment to his organisation. The meanings he gives to his work, and his actions and behaviour in accordance with those meanings will define his work orientation.

Quote (b)
The person making this statement has no job interest, is not motivated by his work, and sees work as a means to an end, that is, the pay packet. He works for high pay to satisfy needs that arise from outside the workplace. The meanings he gives to his work, and his actions and behaviour in accordance with those meanings will define his work orientation.

In this section, we look at types of orientation, at the factors affecting them, and at the question of whether orientation is constant or may change with circumstance.

3.1 Orientations to work: Goldthorpe et al

The research study which first introduced the notion of 'orientations to work' looked at workers in the car industry within the Vauxhall plant in Luton (Goldthorpe et al, 1980). This group of workers in the late 1960s was considered affluent. We should note that times have changed, and car workers in the 1990s are relatively less affluent than they were during the earlier period. However, this does not invalidate the study.

The main findings of the research were:

1   The workers did not appear to derive either intrinsic or social satisfactions from their work experience. **Social satisfactions** concern the quality of relationships with colleagues and co-workers both within and outside the work environment.

2   The workers did not express dissatisfaction with the jobs they were doing. It is important that we should note that the workers had knowingly chosen work with these deprivations in much the same way that today, highly paid oil rig workers choose their work in the full knowledge of the dangers and rigours of their work.

3   The Luton workers regarded their work as a means to a relatively good standard of living which could be achieved with the income made on the assembly line.

4   Because of this, the workers were said to have an instrumental orientation to work. The origins of this orientation were in the social class, community and family backgrounds of the employees and not in the workplace itself.

5   The technology of the Fordist work process did not appear to have a great deal of influence upon the workers' orientation. The motives, interests and extra-work background had to be taken into account, if not to be given a central emphasis. You met Fordism in Unit 3.

6   The researchers, as a result of their work at Luton, offered a typology of four possible work orientations. These characteristics are shown in Figure 3.

   ● The **instrumental** orientation reflects that found among the study's affluent manual workers.

   ● The **bureaucratic** orientation reflects patterns found among white-collar employees.

   ● The **solidaristic** orientation is inferred from the authors' understanding of more 'traditional' working-class employment situations such as coalmining and shipbuilding.

Orientation to work	Primary meaning of work	Involvement in employing organisation	Ego involvement	Work and non work relationship
Instrumental	Means to an end. A way of earning income	Calculative	Weak. Work not a central life interest or source of self-realisation	Spheres sharply dichotomised. Work relationships not carried over into non-work activities
Bureaucratic	Service to an organisation in return for career progress	"Moral" elements: some sense of obligation	Individual's position and prospects are sources of social identity	Not sharply dichotomised. Work identity and organisational status carried over
Solidaristic	Economic but with this limited by group loyalties to either mates or firm	"Moral" when identification is with firm. "Alienative" when this is more with workmates than with employer	Strong social relationships at work are rewarding	Intimately related. High participation in work-linked formal or informal associations
Professional		No details given		

Figure 3: Four possible orientations to work
Source: Adapted from Goldthorpe et al, 1968, pp. 38-41,
Cambridge University Press

ACTIVITY 13

Bearing in mind the Luton research, can you identify categories of worker who show an instrumental, bureaucratic and solidaristic orientation to work in the 1990s?

Instrumental: Examples of workers who might have an instrumental orientation in the 1990s include the oil rig workers we mentioned earlier, electricity supply workers, and workers who go abroad to the Middle East, for example, to get highly paid work. Workers who see their jobs intrinsically boring, such as assembly-line workers may have a predominantly instrumental orientation to work.

Bureaucratic: Examples here would include middle and higher levels of management, senior administrators, and those with high levels of professional expertise such as scientists.

Solidaristic: Examples of these workers are hard to find in the 1990s. This is because the traditional manufacturing and extractive industries in which they are found are in rapid decline. Coalmining, shipbuilding, dock work, steel manufacture and heavy engineering have either virtually ceased to exist or have experienced huge manpower reductions.

3.2 Subsequent research on orientations to work

The importance of the Luton study lay not only in the formulation of a typology of work orientations, but also in the finding that workers' prior orientations to work were largely shaped by factors outside of work such as class, family and community.

The workers actually came to Luton in the expectation of high extrinsic rewards and how they perceived these could be satisfied by the pay offered by their job. They were not concerned so much about workplace influences such as the technology employed (assembly line), the quality of the supervision or co-worker social influences. All they were concerned about was the pay packet at the end of the week.

By showing that the workers whom Goldthorpe and Lockwood studied in Luton acted at work and thought about their work in a particular way which was most strongly influenced by their deliberate choice to move into the car industry for extrinsic rather than intrinsic rewards, the authors did, however, tend to underplay the potential degree of influence which factors within work itself might have on work behaviours and attitudes generally.

To apply the notion of orientation to work to a wider range of work situations, we need to take into consideration the arguments which have been made by researchers subsequent to the publication of the Luton study.

STUDY BY BEYNON AND BLACKBURN

Beynon and Blackburn (1972) made a detailed study of a factory involved in the manufacture of luxury foods. Their main conclusions were:

- Although employees tend, as far as possible, to select employment in keeping with their priorities about what they want from work, they nevertheless make important adjustments and accommodations once in work, as their experience is influenced by such workplace factors as work processes, pay levels and power structures. These adjustments and accommodations include:
  - trying to get on well with work mates
  - trying to get on well with supervisors
  - acceptance of work constraints such as the speed of the assembly line
  - joining a trade union to improve pay and conditions.
- Orientations are also shown to be influenced by biographical factors in the worker's life outside the factory. These factors include:
  - **age:** as a worker gets older he may develop more and deeper social relationships with colleagues. Older workers are also regarded as more dependable by workmates and employers alike.
  - **marriage:** may well have a stabilising effect upon workers, and this will also make them more reliable as colleagues and as employees.

- **crises:** events such as divorce, bereavement, mental breakdown are likely to have important consequences for work behaviour, work attendance and so on.

● Goldthorpe et al tended to concentrate upon factors outside of work such as:

  - social class
  - geographical community in which the worker lives
  - immediate and extended family.

They argued that these factors were important in shaping the prior orientations which workers bring to their work. Beynon and Blackburn argue that while these factors are important in determining orientations to work, it is still necessary to look at factors within the work organisation which are also likely to influence these orientations. Examples of these factors are:

  - production system and type of technology used
  - nature and quality of supervision
  - importance of co-workers.

STUDY BY WEDDERBURN AND CROMPTON

Wedderburn and Crompton (1972) who studied three chemical plants, made a similar point. These authors found that:

● the workers whom they studied generally displayed the instrumental orientations to work as described in the Luton study.

● within specific work settings, different workers displayed different attitudes and behaviour which emerged in response to the specific constraints imposed by the technology and control setting. For example, the study identified different types of technology within each plant ranging from chemical process production automation (partial automation) to large batch production (assembly line) and small batch production. It was found that attitudes and behaviour varied amongst individuals working with these different technologies.

STUDY BY DANIEL

Daniel was a major critic of the approach by Goldthorpe et al. He accused those authors of failing to recognise the complexities of what it is that workers look for in their jobs. We now look at each of these points of criticism in turn:

● Daniel (1973) suggests that the Luton researchers paid too much attention to the aspect of job choice and thus failed to recognise that, once in work, employees display varying priorities, attitudes and interests – depending on the context they are in.

● He suggests that different attitudes will prevail, for instance, in what he calls the bargaining context from those which are indicated in the work context.

● In the bargaining context:

  - priority is given to the material rewards (such as pay) accruing from the job

- negative aspects of the job are stressed; these justify appropriate compensation

- management are seen as being on the 'opposite side'.

● However, if we examine worker attitudes where the work content itself is the focus of interest, we find that:

- there is more concern about the quality of the work experience

- social rewards of contact and communication with others are stressed

- the relationship with management is 'more characterised by a sense of common interests'.

ACTIVITY 14

What significant conclusions could we draw about work orientation from Daniel's comments?

The importance of what Daniel is saying is considerable:

● It suggests that every employee is likely to have different priorities at different times and in different contexts.

● How workers may view and interpret their work situations vary according to the importance attached by them to those situations at any given point in time.

● The employee acting to improve his or her pay packet or salary is not likely to show much interest in job satisfaction at that point in time. However, once the individual returns to the machine or desk, the intrinsic satisfactions to be gained in that specific context may become more important.

A study by Cotgrove et al (1971) illustrates this tendency identified by Daniel. The researchers studied a nylon spinning plant within ICI. At the time of the research, ICI attempted to introduce a participation scheme for some of the semi-skilled work force in the plant. The improved quality of working experience was recognised and appreciated by the work force yet, as the authors comment: 'this does not extend to any radical change when it comes to the pay and effort bargain. On this there are still two sides facing each other over a table in collective bargaining'.

More recent studies, have identified other factors external and internal to the work context which influence work orientations. Two of these factors are:

● **Education:** it has been argued that people with different levels of educational qualifications also have differing orientations to work and employment (Brown, 1987).

● **Nature of first job entered:** the experience of a first job can influence the orientations to subsequent jobs within other organisations (Ashton et al 1990).

SOME CONCLUSIONS

The various studies on orientations to work and the meanings given by workers to their work demonstrate that in order to understand work behaviour, we must recognise the importance of dynamic orientations and that, instead of relating work attitudes and behaviour in a direct way to either fixed psychological needs or technological constraints, we must also acknowledge that individuals see things differently and act accordingly in different situations and at different times.

This may seem a fairly obvious point to make but, as with so many generalisations which emerge from sociological study, this insight is not always present in our everyday thinking.

The common practice of labelling individuals and then expecting them to behave in conformity to our mental labels in every situation illustrates how we often fail to recognise that the orientations of people at work are dynamic. We might characterise or label a certain apprentice as a 'poor worker', a foreman as a 'loyal company man', a graduate trainee as 'having no interest in the firm' and a shop steward as being 'very militant'. These characterisations or labels given are important since they influence the way the individuals are treated by other people. Our tendency is to assume that these characterisations are fixed qualities of the individuals. But it is quite possible that changes might occur in each individual as the circumstances of each individual changes. For example, the apprentice's girlfriend becomes pregnant, they marry and he not only settles to his training but applies himself to his work in a way which he hopes will help him achieve eventual promotion.

ACTIVITY 15

In a small group, if possible, discuss the other three individuals we have just mentioned – the foreman, the graduate trainee and the shop steward. Remember the labels attached to each individual and consider what changes might occur to each of these individuals as a result of changing circumstances. Give each individual a new label.

The following are possible suggestions about how each of the three individuals might be influenced and how they might change. You may have come up with similar or quite different ideas

The *foreman,* like many other 'loyal company men' among his colleagues, becomes increasingly angry at the erosion of supervisory authority in a period of rapid organisational and technical change and he encourages his colleagues to unionise and present a militant opposition to the management, the ferocity of which had previously been unimaginable. The foreman, therefore is no longer regarded as the 'loyal company man' but rather as one of the employees who will be affected by these changes. He may even become a 'shop steward'.

The *graduate trainee* finds himself in a training placement that can give him access to the type of advancement he had previously felt unlikely to occur. He therefore becomes committed to the organisation and eventually becomes a 'loyal company man'.

The *shop steward,* having effectively defeated a set of managerial proposals to which his shop were strongly opposed, becomes, in the eyes of the management one of the most 'reasonable' of all the stewards and is singled out for special promotion. He may then become a 'loyal company man'.

We can see in these examples, illustrations of the ways that the individual employee's attitudes and behaviour can shift as a result of contextual changes which occur both outside the workplace and within it.

They are, of course, by necessity, rather simplified examples. If we were to attempt to understand more fully what was happening in each of these cases it would be valuable to examine how and why each individual came into their job in the first place.

The workplace orientations and the way they changed have partly to be understood in terms of the prior orientations of each individual – the particular wants and expectations brought into work in the first place by each individual with their own particular social class and family background, education, community affiliations and so on.

REVIEW ACTIVITY 3

Suggested time: 40 minutes.

Scenario 1

Dave has a job as a maintenance worker on an oil rig in the North Sea. His main reason for applying for the job was the relatively high pay. On average he works on the rig for six weeks and then has 1-2 weeks off. He is saving his wages to buy a house for himself and his girlfriend. Dave is not too concerned about his working conditions and he finds his work dull and routine. While he gets on with his workmates, he does not regard them as friends. His main concern is with his girlfriend, whom he wishes he could see more often, his parents and his friends.

To what category in Goldthorpe et al's typology might Dave be assigned and what characteristics does he show that meet the four dimensions which they see as defining that orientation?

Scenario 2

Several months later, Dave's work and domestic situation has changed:

- He has married his girlfriend and there are far greater pressures on him to spend more time with his wife who is now pregnant.

- His mother has died and Dave is still getting over the shock of his bereavement.

- There has been a re-organisation of maintenance work on the rig which has resulted in some redundancies. As a result, Dave's job specification has changed and his job has become more difficult.

- Dave has finally decided to quit his job to be with his family and friends. He has also decided to embark upon a distance education course which will eventually improve his job prospects and in the meantime has accepted a lower paid job.

Summarise the criticisms that have been made of the Goldthorpe et al view of work orientation and indicate aspects of the scenario which support the criticisms.

Summary

In section 3, we have dealt with work orientations and meanings. We defined work orientation, and then examined orientations to work in greater detail by reference to Goldthorpe et al's pioneering study. Having identified four types of orientation, of which only three need concern us, we then went on to consider some of the later studies dealing with orientations to work. These studies have established the validity of the 'orientation' concept and have suggested that people's work orientations are subject to a number of different influences which are both internal and external to the work environment.

From a review of these studies, we have established that work orientation is not fixed and unchanging, but can change according to internal and external influences. Work orientation is therefore dynamic and not static, and we have, through examples such as Activity 14, applied this idea to specific cases.

In the remainder of this unit, we analyse current trends affecting work and look to the future.

SECTION 4

Changing Work Arrangements

Introduction

We begin the section with a descriptive general review of the current work and job scene, noting the movement of jobs away from manufacturing and the public service, the fewer jobs available and the growth in work within the informal economy.

A particularly significant change in the economy impacting on work has been the growth of the information sector. This is linked to the contraction of other traditional sectors, but more particularly to information technology developments contributing to and interacting with global economic and competitive developments.

We then look at how technological developments – in part at least driven by economic pressures and the need to compete globally – have impacted on work and employment and on every aspect of the production and sale of goods. These technological developments have influenced the organisational context of production in terms of variety, design, production, marketing, finance and retailing etc, that is on the nature of work done.

They have also had an impact, in conjunction with economic factors, on how people work. New technologies have resulted in job and organisational changes which have resulted in:
- de-skilling of some jobs and the multi-skilling of others
- ability of employers to make their organisations more flexible through:
  - ease with which core things can be centralised for predictability and other aspects can be decentralised for speed and flexibility of response
  - restructuring for labour flexibility.

You will have met some of these ideas in earlier units.

4.1 Setting the scene

During the 1970s, the familiar scenery of our working lives began to show visible changes. The large employment organisations, the source of full-time employment for so many, began to decline. Some famous names from our industrial past disappeared for ever. The names on the high-street shop fronts changed and the way of life behind many of them also changed.

This process has continued into the 1980s and 1990s. The tradition of a man going out to work to support, by himself, a family at home became a statistical rarity. 'Long-term unemployment', 'youth unemployment', and 'redundancy' became familiar words, words which increasingly affected all social groups. Jobs began to be a scarce commodity, and 'work' started to mean other things besides the conventional full-time job. Second and third careers, 'moonlighting' and the black economy became part of our language. Handy (1985) summarises the major changes:

- full-employment society was becoming the part-employment society
- 'labour' and 'manual skills' were yielding to 'knowledge' as the basis for new businesses and new work
- 'hierarchies' and 'bureaucracies' were going out, 'networks' and 'partnerships' were coming in
- 'industry' was declining and 'services' were growing in importance
- a one-organisation career was becoming rarer, job mobility and career changes were more fashionable
- 'third-age' of life, beyond the ages of growing up and of employment, was becoming important to more and more people
- sexual stereotypes were being challenged, at work and in the home, and roles were no longer rigid
- work was shifting southwards, inside countries and between countries.

We consider some of these changes more fully in the following sections, and begin by looking in general terms at the changing work and job scene in Britain.

ACTIVITY 16

In the following two examples, people have experienced changes to their employment over the past ten years.

Example 1: Jane

Jane is 32 years old. She had a full-time secretarial job for five years with a large manufacturing company. The company then introduced new information processing technologies which reduced the scope for secretarial work throughout the organisation. Jane was offered a part-time secretarial post with full employment protection within the company, which she accepted. She also decided to join an agency which 'contracted out' secretarial work to other organisations. Jane is quite happy working on this basis as she can organise her domestic life around her work, and she has greater variety of experience working for different companies.

> **Example 2: Tom**
>
> Tom is 45 and for most of his working life he was working full-time as a computer specialist for three organisations. When he was 40, Tom was made redundant and decided to start his own specialist computer company, providing services on a sub-contracting basis to other organisations. He works mainly from home and finds that he now has more time for his family. He also finds that his work is more enjoyable and that he can employ the services of a network of former colleagues etc. as and when required.
>
> What aspects of the changes Handy summarises are reflected in the cases of Jane and Tom?

In the case of Jane, the trend from full employment to part employment has benefitted her. While she no longer feels that she can progress in career terms within her original company, she appreciates the opportunities that the secretarial agency provides in the variety of different work contexts she now experiences.

In Tom's case, his redundancy reflects the increase in the importance of networking which is particularly useful to those with specialist skills in the information technology area, and by deciding to be his own boss, he finds that he can take advantage of these networking opportunities while working from home.

CHANGING WORK AND JOB SCENE

The reappraisal of work is dependent upon what is happening to jobs. Handy (1985) presents us with the 'the bare facts for the UK':

- There are fewer jobs than there were, but not that many fewer. In 1961, there were 24.5 million people in employment in the UK, including the self-employed. In 1980, there were slightly more (25.2 million), but by mid-1982 the total had fallen to a level of 23.5 million, where it seems to be staying. In other words, jobs, contrary to popular opinion, did not start disappearing until 1981, and there are still only 1 million fewer than in 1961.

- But the jobs have continuously been squeezed out of business. In the 20 years from 1961 to 1981, 2.5 million jobs (13% of all jobs) were squeezed out of the business sector (both public and private) in Britain, although output increased. Higher productivity has tended to mean fewer jobs.

- Jobs were picked up by the public sector, however, this doesn't happen any longer. From 1961 to 1981, all the jobs lost from the business sector were picked up by the state services sector, maintaining the total level of employment. This is no longer so. The state sector is now contracting in terms of jobs.

- In general, jobs have continuously moved from manufacturing to service. From 1961 to 1981, 3.3 million jobs left the traditional worlds of mining, agriculture and manufacturing, and 2.2 million jobs were added to the service sector with 1.8 million of them in the public sector.

● Meanwhile, the labour force has been expanding . . . The labour force grew by 2.2 million from 1961 to 1981. Therefore, even if employment grew marginally up to 1980, unemployment would still have risen, and, in fact, did rise. Statistically this increase in the registered labour force was entirely due to an increase in the number of working wives which was up by 2.7 million over the 20 years.

● . . and is going to go on expanding for the next 20 years. The baby boom of the 1960s is now grown up and is beginning to work its way through the labour force, greatly outnumbering those who would normally be retiring. Over the next 20 years, there will be an extra 1.5 million people of working age, most of them wanting jobs.

● Demand for jobs has consistently exceeded the supply and looks like continuing to do so. The demand for jobs has grown by 2.2 million people or nearly 10% over the last 20 years and will grow by a possible 1.5 million over the next 20. Meanwhile, the supply has contracted by 1.1 million. The gap is unemployment.

4.2 The informal economy

The informal economy has always been with us, but it has a much higher profile these days. It contains all the uncounted activity in which we engage. For example, if you serviced your own car, the labour content is the same as if you paid a professional mechanic to do it for you. It is a payment to yourself and therefore has no knock-on value. It does not become part of the currency of society, which is why government takes little interest in it. But, of course, if we all serviced our own cars, there would be no jobs for garage mechanics and less money circulating in society.

ACTIVITY 17

Think of three other examples of informal economy activities like car servicing. What implications for the economy would there be for your examples?

There are many possible examples including all sorts of DIY activities that would otherwise have to be paid for (plumbing, central heating, floor tiling etc).Implications for the economy would include the increase in DIY outlets, such as B&Q, as part of the growing service sector. This would be reflected also in the decline in demand for the services of plumbers, tilers and domestic heating engineers.

PARTS OF THE INFORMAL ECONOMY

We can now identify three parts of the informal economy:

- The **black economy,** the uncounted 'market' of the moonlighter or criminal. Although much talked about and much indulged in at the margin by all sorts of people, this part of the informal economy is probably not as large in Britain as many think. It is an estimated 3% of the formal economy and much less than the estimated 20% in Italy, for example. However, there are likely to be local variations and fluctuations owing to unemployment levels, opportunities, etc.

- The **voluntary economy,** the voluntary work which occupies many of us for at least an hour a week, perhaps around 18 million of us, is equivalent to 500,000 full-time workers.

- The **household economy,** the large part of the informal economy containing all our domestic work, cooking, gardening, household maintenance, child care and old people care. Estimates suggest that over half the nation's productive work hours are spent in the household or around it. If this work were charged for, it might be equivalent to 40% of the total economy

The contraction of the labour market and the expansion of the labour pool has meant that in 1990, for example, 3.2 million people were looking for work, with no room in the formal economy. It is not surprising that the informal economy becomes interesting and important. It is the only place left where there is a sort of work, but there are no jobs and not much money .

4.3 The changing economy

We have mentioned earlier that there are now fewer jobs in manufacturing and a declining number of jobs in the public service sector of the economy. The traditional formal economy is divided loosely into the following sectors:

- **agriculture, mining and fisheries,** all of which have fewer jobs than even 10 years ago

- **industry,** particularly manufacturing industry, where again jobs have declined

- **services** which includes public and private services, where jobs have contracted in the former.

To the traditional economy, we may add a fourth:

- the **information economy:** to include all those activities which process or transform information. It is really a sub-category of services, but important enough to be identifiable.

The service and information economies employ well over 50% of the employees in employment, and some commentators have argued that because of this trend, we have entered the so-called 'post-industrial' society. The notion of 'post-industrialism' we discussed fully in Unit 3.

The decline of the traditional manufacturing industries is a development common to most western economies. The reasons for this decline include:

- substitution of capital equipment for labour in agriculture, mining and manufacturing has allowed output to grow while jobs decline

- cheaper labour costs in the developing and newly industrialised economies have drawn traditional manufacturing industries away from Britain

- long-term economic cycles of the sort described by Kondratiev were probably exacerbated or accelerated by the jump in energy prices during the 1970s.

KONDRATIEV

Nikolai Kondratiev was a Russian economist who in 1926 pointed out that economic activity moved in 'long waves' of 50 years or so in duration. The first long wave was from 1789 to 1849 (going up until 1814, then down); the second was from 1849 to 1896 (up until 1873), and the third was from 1896 to 1945. Although Kondratiev only identified the upswing until 1920 and did not venture to predict the future. Carrying on his time sequence produces a fourth wave from 1945 to 1995. The 1970s are the years of decline, leading into the beginning of a fifth wave at the end of the century.

Kondratiev did not think that the waves were accidental; 'important discoveries and inventions' were made during the downswing and then applied in the upswings. In recessions, Kondratiev's thinking receives renewed attention perhaps because he offers the promise of light at the end of the tunnel. Others, however, have had difficulty in fitting technological discoveries to his timescales, perhaps because it is extremely difficult to be precise about dates and limits to technological invention. Did the computer start to be developed in 1834 with Babbage or with the first electronic computer in 1946? This was also the start of an upswing, incidentally.

What Kondratiev did not comment on, but which is of perhaps the greatest social importance, is the fact that the principal focus of industrial activity tended to change with each successive wave. The first wave, based on the steam engine, had its focus in England, which had, by the end of it, 40% of the world's industrial production. Compare this with less than 3% today. Activity then moved to Germany and northern Europe, with the development of chemicals, steel-making and oil, and on to the USA, in the third wave at the end of the nineteenth century with the development of the automobile and the telephone. The fourth wave, after the second world war, focussed on Japan and California and the emergence of electronics.

Meanwhile, as the waves of economic activity moved on, the societies and communities of the earlier waves had to adjust. Where will the fifth wave, if there is one, find its focus? (Handy, 1985, pp. 23-24)

So far, we have considered some of the important developments affecting work and work patterns within Britain and by implication within other developed industrial capitalist societies. Two major influences on this which we now examine further are changing economic circumstances and new information technologies.

4.4 Economic circumstances and information technologies

There is no doubt that the impetus for industrial change lies in technical and organisational innovation, competition and the pursuit of material human improvement. Because of the enormous promise of industrialisation, society after society has followed the lead taken by Britain in the late-eighteenth century until today, we have the emergence of the aggressively capitalist nations of the far east as industrial forces, Japan being still the most important. You discussed these changes in Unit 1 at length.

However, even quasi-communist countries such as Vietnam and, of course, China have awoken from economic dormancy and now pose a problem for established, but declining, western economies. Moreover, into the twenty-first century, the more robust economies of south and central America and possibly Africa, using the new South Africa as the potential dynamo for change, will play a significantly more important part than before.

The lessons that the Japanese have learnt, for example, means that the Japanese economy has taken advantage of the achievements of the older western economies and has avoided their mistakes. This has enabled them to construct a set of social institutions and priorities at state and organisational levels which gives them a massive commercial and technological thrust that has powerfully challenged western economies.

So how have the western economies coped with this formidable set of competitive challenges?

- They have attempted to deal with this through the medium of western-owned multi- and trans-national interests and corporations by moving resources and production efforts to foreign settings where cheaper and/or more flexible labour is available.

- Many western companies have introduced new production technologies based on Japanese ideas which encourage greater efficiency within the production process, more flexible working methods and practices and better quality of product. Oliver and Wilkinson's book *The Japanisation of British Industry: New Developments in the 1990s* (1992) provides evidence of the extent to which British companies have adopted these practices.

CONSEQUENCES FOR WORK AND EMPLOYMENT

International competitiveness and trade threats have forced both employing organisations and states to seek ways of not only increasing the cost-effectiveness of labour itself, but of increasing the overall capacity of the organisations. Labour is used to innovate at a rate which will enable organisations to produce goods and services which are competitive in the international context. It is in this context that we need to understand the role of new technologies and, especially the part played by information technologies.

ROLE OF NEW TECHNOLOGIES

The term 'new technology' can embrace a range of technical developments of which the new **information technologies** are just one type. Arguably it is information technology which has the greatest potential for changing peoples' lives.

The **key characteristic** of information technology is the linking of advances in micro-electronics with innovations in telecommunications which means that:

- more communicable information is available than ever before

- it can be processed much more efficiently and flexibly

- it can be transmitted and acted upon more rapidly.

What is also novel about micro-processor-based innovations is the actual and potential impact which they can have as a result of their cheapness, speed, reliability, smallness and, above all, breadth of application.

ACTIVITY 18

In a group, or individually, identify as many uses of computing and information technology as you can in the three areas of:

- design and manufacture

- administration

- finance and retailing.

Your list may include at least some of the examples given in Figure 4. As you can see from the figure, the range of applications and their impact in all these fields is very great. They impact upon:

- products which people can buy, from home computers through to 'chip-controlled' car engines or domestic appliances

- how goods are developed, since products can be speedily designed on computers and rapidly tested by electronic simulations

- how things are made through the use of robots and computer-controlled machine tools and transfer devices

- how work is administered through applications in word processing, information storage and retrieval, electronic mail and computerised data analysis

- distribution of goods, where, in the example of retailing, bar-coded products are priced at the point of sale and are stock-controlled and monitored by computers

- financial institutions where innovations ranging from cash dispensers to 'electronic funds transfer' are appearing

● legal and medical work where 'expert systems' can help the practitioner rapidly tap vast electronic banks of information and the accumulated recordable judgements and diagnoses of countless human experts.

DESIGN AND MANUFACTURE

Computer Aided Design and Drafting (CAD)
- quantitative analysis
- interactive computer graphics

Computer Aided Manufacture (CAM)
- computer numerical control (CNC)
- robotics
- flexible manufacturing systems (FMS)

Computer Integrated Manufacturing (CIM)
- CAD/CAM
- computer-aided production planning (CAPP)
- computer-aided measurement and test (CAMT)

ADMINISTRATION

Computing
- on-line processing
- real-time management information systems (MIS)
- word processors, desk-top computers
- intelligent knowledge-based systems (IKBS)

Telecommunications
- electronic mail
- viewdata and on-line databases
- private automatic branch exchanges (PABX)
- local area networks (LANS)

FINANCE AND RETAILING

Finance
- automated teller machines (ATM)
- electronic funds transfer (EFT)

Retailing
- electronic point-of-sale machines

Finance and retailing
- electronic funds transfer at point of sale (EFTPOS)
- integrated circuit cards (smart cards)

Figure 4: Examples of computing and information technology in design and manufacture, offices and administration, and finance and retailing.
Source: McLoughlin and Clark, 1994, p. 16.

ACTIVITY 19

Identify one actual work-based example (type of organisation, type of work) from each of the three categories indicated in Figure 4.

1   Examples from this category include most types of manufacturing processes ranging from automated to assembly line. For example, within car manufacture, robotics and flexible manufacturing systems are used. Design teams, for example, in the design of engineering components, use CAD.

2   There are many examples here. Nearly all organisations use at least one application. The most obvious example is the use of word processors in offices. Similarly, electronic mail use is widespread. Organisations in telecommunications such as BT, Mercury, etc use most of these applications in exchanges and offices.

3   You may have identified organisations such as banks, building societies, insurance companies and the stock markets. In addition, many large retail outlets now use EPOS and EFTPOS.

4.5 Impact of new technologies upon work

The development of these new technologies has considerable implications for how people work. Perhaps the main development here arises from the integration of what previously have been considered separate areas.

For example, electronic networks and optical fibre 'information highways' can:

- connect together different organisations nationally and globally and link their component parts so that the processes of learning, research, design, manufacturing, administration, product and service delivery can be closely linked

- abolish existing distinctions between office and factory, works and staff, training and doing, and even home and work, through the development of electronic 'outworking'; it can also, in certain fields, undermine the distinction between worker and manager.

In fact, a large proportion of managerial and administrative jobs could disappear, and are, disappearing as machines are used for the co-ordination and the monitoring of tasks and the processing of information.

We can now look at some work and organisational-based aspects which have been influenced by both economic and technological factors. These aspects do overlap as they are so interrelated, but for convenience we look at them under the headings 'flexibility', 'work design' and 'organisational structures and employment patterns'.

FLEXIBILITY

As a result of the increased global economic pressures and competition we discussed earlier in this unit, the managements of employing organisations can be expected to seek greater predictability and tighter control over their circumstances. At the same time, and for the same reasons, they are increasingly going to see a need for adaptability and flexibility. We can expect them to pursue two basic types of flexibility. We dealt with these two types of flexibility more fully in Unit 2.

1   The first type involves staffing policies and structures which will enable labour to be taken on, dispensed with or moved about to suit changing circumstances. Remember the 'flexible firm'.

2   The second type of flexibility will involve the encouragement of those people whose work involves either technical complexity or the handling of crises to 'think for themselves' and take initiatives without waiting for orders – a sort of 'empowerment'.

The emphasis on one type of flexibility or another and the balance of the mix attempted in any organisation will vary with the circumstances and policies of each employing organisation. The use of new information technologies will certainly play a part in attaining the desired flexibility but the precise role of new technologies is partly a matter of choice and negotiation.

ACTIVITY 20

Can you suggest possible ways new technological developments might contribute to either of these types of flexibility?

The more important points you might have identified include:

● New technology may enable managers to bring about reductions in overall employment levels by eliminating and de-skilling jobs.

● New technology may also encourage reductions in employment levels and increases in the 'external' workforce by allowing some 'core' and 'peripheral' work to be sub-contracted or carried out on a different contractual basis from home through 'tele-working'.

● The erosion of skill demarcations when new technology is introduced suggests an increase in the second type of flexibility (functional flexibility) through a 'multi-skilling' of core workers.

WORK DESIGN

We have mentioned before the contribution of Henry Braverman (1974) who sees a logic of de-skilling in the trends of work design in capitalist societies. We also discuss this more fully in Unit 2. It is true to say that considerable flexibility of the first type identified above can be achieved if new technologies are used to reduce the work efforts of employees to ones involving machine-minding and machine-feeding.

Considerable flexibility can be achieved if the old ideals of the scientific management movement are approached and much discretion is given to the managers who tightly control a limited workforce which can be cheaply employed, easily trained, readily recruited or dispensed with and who have limited bargaining power. But here we have a dilemma, because to do this would, in many circumstances, risk compromising the second type of flexibility referred to above, whereby employees are encouraged to think for themselves and to take initiatives to cope with crises or technical problems which cannot be designed out of the work context.

Studies of the introduction of information technologies to work places show that there is no one clear direction being taken, either towards de-skilling or its opposite. However, Salaman (1992) has argued that recent studies on the impact of information technology on core work have failed to support the de-skilling thesis, while Thompson (1990) states that as far as the core workforce is concerned, multi-skilling is clearly a reality for a growing proportion of manufacturing employees.

The following examples illustrate the point as well as indicating how technological change may impact upon work design in different sectors of work.

Example 1: Use of Computer Numerical Control (CNC) technology

CNC technology enables the removal of control over machine processes from worker to management. This option could support Braverman's view. Alternatively, managements may choose to involve the operators in the implementation of the new system and can choose to re-train and re-skill them so that they play a part in programming the machines which they use. Managements therefore have a clear choice in deciding whether to de-skill or enrich these jobs. Of course, such decisions depend on the contingencies, needs or issues raised in each particular situation so the impact of the technology will depend on their decision. For example:

- if management decides to negotiate and arrive at an accommodation or agreement with the work force, would the final agreement be a different outcome from that originally intended by management?

- if the work process involves frequent batch changes, a high incidence of new work and where variability in materials or physical conditions creates a requirement for flexibility at the point of production, then a greater degree of initiative might be given to those workers in these situations.

Example 2: The service sector

In those parts of the service sector which are highly unionised, for example, local authority, some workers are better able than others to resist degradation of their work. This can be due to:

- collective union organisation itself

- scarcity of labour factors

- important key positions held within the work process.

Consumer preferences also come into play within certain occupations. For example, doctors, whether in general practice or within hospitals may be able to sustain claims that they have an exclusive right to conduct certain activities because consumers expect this and because of their professional expertise.

But we must nevertheless be wary about making these generalisations seem valid in all situations because they are not. They would not be true, for example, in the case of:

- the GP who now finds that he has more paperwork to deal with and delegates routine surgery to a nurse

- former local authority binmen who are contracted out to a private waste disposal company and are now experiencing deteriorating conditions of work, lower pay, shorter holidays etc.

Example 3: The office

This is one area where the impact of information technology is particularly great, and while the possibility for upgrading or de-skilling work is there, evidence suggests (Crompton & Jones, 1984) that the office, with its heavy concentration of women workers and all that this implies for any ability to resist managerial and male initiatives, is the site of considerable efforts to de-skill work. Lane's (1985) review of the German experience shows that a range of more challenging tasks do come about with computerisation but that such high discretion jobs are fewer than was the case before the change and tend to be filled by men. The routine office work was largely done by women, who complained of an increase in both mental and physical strain after office computerisation.

ACTIVITY 21

Individually or in a small group, describe the main ways by which work has been re-organised as a result of organisational and technological change.

This activity focusses on the issues of flexibility, de-skilling, re-skilling and up-skilling. You also met these issues in Unit 4. McLoughlin and Clark (1994, Chapter 6) make a few valuable points in relation to technological change:

- new technology replaces certain manual routine tasks and skills.

- new technology also creates new task and skill requirements that enable the technology to complement human problem-solving and decision-making abilities.

They comment: 'However, case study evidence also suggests that the absence of a detailed consideration of job content and work organisation in management strategies can lead to outcomes which allow workers to exercise considerable influence over job content. In some instances, this facilitates the informal clawback of skills by workers and workgroups who are able to re-negotiate the content of their jobs so that the technology could be operated in a way which complemented rather than replaced their skills and abilities . . . it does appear to be the case that (in these instances) skills have not been significantly eroded by the introduction of new technology. Indeed, this evidence points towards up-skilling, although the extent to which this has resulted in greater flexibility consistent with a broader trend towards flexible specialisation is questionable'.

ORGANISATIONAL STRUCTURE AND EMPLOYMENT PATTERNS

Both economic pressures and the opportunities provided by developments in information technology have resulted in new thinking about how organisations should be structured, together with the development of the work patterns to be associated with these new structures. We discussed these ideas concerning organisational structure in Unit 5 and so we only briefly deal with them here.

Basically, for an organisation to cope with environmental challenges, they have to balance:

- predictability
- innovative flexibility.

This may involve organisations in decentralising their structures whilst retaining a high degree of centralisation in some important respects. This fits in with the analysis of Peters and Waterman (1982) and subsequent contributions. These authors suggest having a simple basic structure, say a divisional one, together with autonomous units which deal with, for example, problem-solving and policy implementation.

We must note, however, that information technology which makes decentralisation ever more feasible also allows for 'recentralisation'. Recentralisation means that comprehensive and current information gets directly to senior management, management structures are simplified and senior managers' spans of control reduced. Decentralising tendencies can exist at the same time in the same organisation. Information technology can allow more effective delegation through putting sub-units into an information network with other sub-units, enabling them to make acceptable decisions without checking with the centre.

A final issue which we need to remember is the reality that exists in many organisations where work is restructured according to labour flexibility criteria. You dealt with this largely in Unit 2, and within a broader context, in Unit 3. It is concerned with the maintenance of a core group of permanently employed workers, a first peripheral group of less secure workers and a second peripheral group who are part-timers, people on short-term contracts or job-sharers.

In addition to these categories, a range of specialised tasks like systems analysis and simple ones like cleaning are likely to be 'put out' through the use of temporary agencies, sub-contracting and other 'outsourcing' practices such as 'tele-working' or 'networking'. In these, people work from home and are linked by computer into the organisation. All of these developments have implications for the overall pattern of work which is likely to prevail in society as a whole, as we shall see in the concluding section.

REVIEW ACTIVITY 4

Suggested time: 30 minutes.

1 Summarise what you see as the most significant current changes in UK work and job patterns in the economy, and identify some of the social and economic factors influencing their development.

2 Review the impact of new technologies on flexibility, work design, and organisational structure and employment patterns.

Summary

In this section, you have covered the changing patterns of work in contemporary British society. The important changes concern the declining manufacturing sector of the economy, the rise of the service sector, and the changing pattern of jobs within these sectors. We then considered the growing importance of the informal economy and the emergence of the information economy.

You looked in some detail at the nature of new technologies employed in industry today, and at the impact of these new technologies upon such important areas as working practices and flexibility, de-skilling and re-skilling, work design and organisational structure.

SECTION 5

Changes in Work, Employment and Unemployment

Introduction

In this brief section, we look at unemployment, changes within the service sector, and changes concerning working time and work outside employment.

5.1 Unemployment

Levels of unemployment have been on the increase in western societies ever since the maintenance of full employment as an economic policy goal was seen to be unrealistic in the 1970s. The causes of the increase in unemployment are due to:

- technological change
- structural factors such as the long-term decline in traditional manufacturing industries and de-industrialisation generally
- 'long-wave theories' such as those of Kondratiev may also account for increased unemployment during both upswings and downswings of an economic cycle.

The future levels of unemployment are difficult to predict, but one scenario suggests that overall employment levels of the future will depend partly at least, on developments in service industries. Some commentators see this as offering employment and potentially replacing much of that lost in manufacturing.

We now turn to the service sector.

5.2 The service sector

Jobs in manufacturing have fallen considerably during the past decades, while service sector jobs have increased. The increased importance of the service sector is crucial to the vision of a post-industrial society as espoused by Bell (1974) and others. You had a more detailed discussion of this in Unit 4.

It is not necessarily the case, however, that a move from secondary sector employment (manufacturing) to tertiary sector employment (services) indicates a basic move from an interest in producing goods to an interest in consumption, or that Bell's post-industrial service-sector dominated economy is the pattern for the future. The picture is more complex and perhaps less hopeful.

● Distinguishing between jobs 'belonging to' or provided by the manufacturing and service sectors is often rather arbitrary, as the second and tertiary sectors are increasingly intertwined and the old 'categories' no longer apply as rigidly as they used to.

Service requirements are often met by increased production by the manufacturing industry, rather than leading to increased employment in the service sector itself. For example, we do not take washing to a laundry so creating laundry service employment; instead we purchase washing machines thereby putting demand on the manufacturing sector.

Even in the service sector itself, we can see that in some areas, jobs may be replaced by technically supplied service 'products' used directly by consumers themselves, for example, computer-aided learning and distance education materials in the education sector. Thus, there is a developing self-service economy that affects both manufacturing and services alike.

● One claim that is often made is that in areas like retailing, distribution, state employment, leisure, telecommunications and financial services, there will be an increase in work. But in many instances it is a spurious claim because each of these areas is subject to a competitive environment and is vulnerable to the impact of information technologies so may either lose or increase jobs in the future.

For example, recent pressures on state employment, the civil service for example, have led to employment reduction. Add to this the applications of new technology to administration, tax collecting and the education sector, as you saw earlier, then there is still considerable potential for job reduction in the service sector.

Nor will increased activity in these areas necessarily benefit service sector employment primarily. In telecommunications, for example, we might reasonably expect that increases in work will arise more from the production of various devices than from new jobs based on their use in the service sector.

We cannot, therefore, escape from the conclusion that recent job reductions in many parts of the service sector are set to continue for the foreseeable future and that an unrealistic very high level of business growth would be needed on a sustainable basis to ensure present levels of employment. This now raises the issue of what alternatives exist for those within paid employment and we explore this next.

5.3 Working time and work outside employment

Here we consider the two important issues of working time and work outside employment.

WORKING TIME

Charles Handy (1985) suggests that the trend in hours worked over a person's lifetime is moving from 100,000 hours (47 hours a week including overtime for 47 weeks per year for 47 years) towards 50,000 hours (35 hours for 42 weeks per year for 35 years). This trend, evidence suggests, is not going to provide a larger number of jobs. In all cases where hours have been reduced, employers have sought and achieved increased productivity. In the British case, overtime working has also tended to increase.

European studies show that the general reductions in working hours made across Europe are widely linked by employers to attempts to respond to competitive market pressures. This is done by:

- reorganising the working week so that there is no loss in operating time

- introducing new and more flexible working arrangements so that operating time can be increased

- introducing innovations in shift patterns and the combining of full and part-time staffs to give increased flexibility as well as lower contractual working hours

- creating more flexible working patterns through increased part-time working and more temporary work.

Most part-time jobs are low-status jobs filled mainly by women, and this is a function of the dual labour market. Given the domestic tasks expected of women workers, it is unlikely that such employment patterns will free people to engage in wider activities in society away from the work place.

People's patterns of employment in the future are likely to be increasingly heavily influenced by the requirements of employers to achieve the two types of flexibility we discussed earlier. This means that there will be a growing gap between people in 'core' jobs and those in 'peripheral' work. This is not a particularly optimistic scenario.

WORK OUTSIDE EMPLOYMENT
The number of self-employed workers has increased substantially during the past 20 years or so, and now comprises around 12% of the total working population. A significant proportion of these are engaged in 'outwork' from organisations, who, instead of employing them, act as their 'clients'.

It is widely forecast that home-working arrangements will increase as more people engage in 'tele-working', 'tele-commuting' or 'networking' where computer links are used to link the home and the client organisation.

Another aspect of work outside employment is the growth of the informal economy which we have already considered. This is what is variously known as the black, hidden, subterranean or irregular economy where economically valuable work, legal or illegal, is done for gain but is not officially 'declared' for tax purposes. The informal economy includes both employed and unemployed people and studies such as those undertaken by Pahl (1984) have shown that it is the employed person who often plays an active part within the informal economy.

A final scenario is that of the 'two-job' economy where part-time workers may have two part-time jobs of similar status. This largely affects women workers in families where the former male earner is now unemployed, or people who are single parents.

REVIEW ACTIVITY 5

Suggested time: 30 minutes.

1 Set out the arguments against the idea that the service sector will generate sufficient jobs to compensate largely for the loss of manufacturing jobs.

2 Review briefly some of the likely features of employment and work outside employment, in the future.

Summary

In this section, you have covered the following aspects:

- changing patterns of unemployment and reasons for these changes
- reasons for job reduction in the service sector of the economy
- trends in working time
- work outside employment and the prospects for the future.

Unit Summary

In this unit, we have sought to provide an overview of work both as a concept and as an activity. Our main emphasis has been upon paid work within the employment relationship.

As we have seen in section 1, work has not always been regarded by society as a source of self-fulfilment. The ancient Greeks and Romans, for different reasons, regarded work as a demeaning activity, and it was not until the post-reformation period and the evolution of the work ethic that work began to be regarded as a potentially dignified activity capable of becoming a source of intrinsic value and satisfaction. This view of work has been with us throughout the nineteenth and twentieth centuries, and indeed has formed one of the justifications for the establishment and continued prosperity of capitalist economies.

In section 2, we dealt with occupations and the structure of work, together with horizontal and hierarchical patterning of occupations. We then looked at types of work and the evolution of the labour market in late-twentieth century Britain, concentrating upon the dual labour market and the role of women workers within it.

The important area of work attitudes and behaviour was then examined in Section 3. This helped us to understand the meanings which people give to their work, together with the sources of prior work orientations and how these orientations can change. Much of the evidence we examined derived from the studies of work attitudes undertaken during the 1970s and 1980s. This body of evidence contradicts much of the rather prescriptive studies undertaken by industrial and organisational psychologists such as Herzberg et al.

In section 4, we dealt with changing work arrangements, the emergence of the informal economy and the information economy. We then concentrated upon the impact of new technologies upon work, work flexibility and skills. Its effects upon work design and organisational structures were also considered.

We finally looked at how patterns of work, working time and work outside employment are changing, together with their likely future prospects. Future scenarios suggest a continuation of current trends well into the twenty-first century. The rest is science fiction!

References

Albercrombie, N and Urry, V (1983) *Capital Labour and the New Middle Class,* London: Allen and Unwin

Anthony, P (1977) *The Ideology of Work,* London: Tavistock.

Arendt, H (1959) *The Human Condition,* New York: Doubleday.

Ashton, D, Maguire, M & Spilsbury, M (1990) *Restructuring the Labour Market: the Implications for Youth,* Basingstoke: Macmillan.

Beechey, V (1986) 'Women and Employment in Contemporary Britain', in Beechey, V & Whiteleg, C (eds) *Women in Britain Today,* Milton Keynes: Open University Press.

Bell, D (1974) *The Coming of Post-Industrial Society,* London: Heinemann.

Beynon, H (1984) *Working for Ford,* Harmondsworth: Penguin.

Beynon, H & Blackburn, R (1972) *Perceptions of Work,* Cambridge: Cambridge University Press

Braverman, H (1974) *Labour and Monopoly Capital,* New York: Monthly Review Press.

Brown, P (1987) *Schooling Ordinary Kids,* London: Tavistock.

Brown, R (1984) 'Work, Past, Present and Future', in Thompson, K (ed) *Work, Employment and Unemployment,* Milton Keynes: Open University Press.

Burnham, J (1945) *The Managerial Revolution,* Harmondsworth: Penguin.

Caplow, T (1954) *The Sociology of Work,* New York: McGraw Hill.

Cotgrove, S, Dunham, J & Vamplew, C (1971) *The Nylon Spinners,* London: Allen and Unwin.

Craig, C, Rubery, J, Tarling, R & Wilkinson, F (1982) *Labour Market Structure: Industrial Organisation and Low Pay,* Cambridge: Cambridge University Press.

Crompton, R & Jones, G (1984) *White Collar Proletariat: Deskilling and Gender in Clerical Work,* London: Macmillan.

Curran, M (1985) *Stereotypes and Selection; Gender and Family in the Recruitment Process,* London: HMSO.

Daniel, W W (1973) 'Understanding Employee Behaviour in its Context', in Child, J (ed) *Man and Organisation,* London: Allen and Unwin.

Davidson, M & Cooper, C (1983) *Stress and the Woman Manager,* Oxford: Blackwell.

Dunkerley, D (1975) *Occupations and Society,* London: Routledge.

Fevre, R (1992) *The Sociology of Labour Markets,* Hemel Hempstead: Harvester Wheatsheaf.

Goldthorpe, J H, Lockwood, D, Bechhofer, F & Platt, J (1968) *The Affluent Worker: Industrial Attitudes and Behaviour,* Cambridge: Cambridge University Press.

Goldthorpe, J H, Llewellyn, C & Payne, C (1980) *Social Mobility and Class Structure in Modern Britain,* Oxford: Clarendon Press.

Grint, K (1991) *The Sociology of Work: An Introduction,* Oxford: Polity Press/Blackwell.

Hall, R (1975) *Occupations and the Social Structure,* Englewood Cliffs, NJ: Prentice Hall.

Handy, C (1985) *The Future of Work,* Oxford: Blackwell.

Hunt, A (1975) *Management Attitudes and Practices Towards Women at Work,* London, HMSO.

Lane, C (1985) 'White Collar Workers in the Labour Process, the Case of the Federal Republic of Germany', *Sociological Review,* 33.2, 298-326.

Littler, C (1982) *The Development of the Labour Process in Capitalist Societies,* London: Heinemann.

Lorber, J (1985) *Women Physicians, Careers, Status and Power,* London: Tavistock.

Marx, K & Engels, F (1971) *The German Ideology,* edited and introduced by C J Arthur, London: Lawrence and Wishart.

McLoughlin, I & Clark, J (1994) *Technological Change at Work,* Buckingham: Open University Press.

Nichols, T (1969) *Ownership, Control and Ideology,* London: Allen and Unwin.

Oliver, N & Wilkinson, B (1992) *The Japanisation of British Industry: New Developments in the 1990s,* Oxford: Blackwell.

Pahl, R R (1984) *Divisions of Labour,* Oxford: Blackwell.

Perkin, H (1989) *The Sociology of Management,* Brighton: Harvester.

Peters, T J & Waterman, R H (1982) *In Search of Excellence,* New York: Harper and Row

Reed, M (1989) *The Sociology of Management,* Brighton: Harvester.

Robertson, J (1984) *Future Work,* Aldershot: Gower.

Salaman, G (1992) *Work Design and Corporate Strategy,* in Allen, J, Braham, P & Lewis, P, *Political and Economic Forms of Modernity,* Oxford: Polity Press/Blackwell.

Thompson, P (1990) *The Nature of Work,* London: Macmillan.

Watson, T J (1987) *Sociology, Work and Industry,* London: Routledge.

Weber, M (1965) *The Protestant Ethic and The Spirit of Capitalism,* London: Allen and Unwin.

Wedderburn, D & Crompton, R (1972) *Workers' Attitudes and Technology,* Cambridge: Cambridge University Press.

Recommended reading

SECTION 1

Anthony, P (1977) *The Ideology of Work,* London: Tavistock.

Beynon, H (1984) *Working for Ford,* Harmondsworth: Penguin.

Grint, K (1991) *The Sociology of Work: An Introduction,* Oxford: Polity Press/Blackwell, Chapter 1.

Salaman, G (1992) *Work Design and Corporate Strategies,* in Allen, J, Braham, P & Lewis, P, *Political and Economic Forms of Modernity,* Oxford: Polity Press/Blackwell.

SECTION 2

Fevre, R (1992) *The Sociology of Labour Markets,* Hemel Hempstead: Harvester Wheatsheaf, Chapters 1 and 2.

Thompson, P (1990) *The Nature of Work,* London: Macmillan, Chapter 7.

SECTION 4

McLoughlin, I & Clark, J (1994) *Technological Change at Work,* Buckingham: Open University Press.

Oliver, N & Wilkinson, B (1992) *The Japanisation of British Industry: New Developments in the 1990s,* Oxford, Blackwell.

Thompson, P (1990) *The Nature of Work,* London: Macmillan.

SECTION 5

Handy, C (1985) *The Future of Work,* Oxford, Blackwell.

Answers to Review Activities

Review Activity 1

QUESTION 1

Quote 1

This quote is very revealing. The bus driver is looking back over the 40 years of his employment and is basically suggesting, or at least implying, that, in retrospect he has regrets. Reading between the lines, we can conclude that this older worker feels that his job has not been self-fulfilling, and we could also argue that he has regarded work, at least in part, as an alienating experience .

Another aspect to this which is particularly relevant to older workers is that over time, views of work can change and workers can develop psychological methods to cope with perceived frustrations of work. Nevertheless, workers may not always learn to accept their work situation and may well blame themselves for their relatively low position. If work is experienced as boring or alienating, then it would be irrational to consider it as self-fulfilling. On the other hand, if you do not expect much from work you will not be disappointed and may, in fact, remain 'happy' with your lot.

Quote 2

This quote, taken from Beynon's *Working for Ford*, is attributed to an assembly-line worker. Studies such as Beynon's have established that assembly-line work is routine, boring and monotonous, and workers performing such work experience high levels of alienation. Although alienated, these workers often create diversions to alleviate their boredom.

Any satisfactions gained by these workers can be generated at work without being directly related to any particular aspect of work. As this worker explained to Beynon, there is more to work than work!

Quote 3

In order to explain the clerical worker's view, it is worth re-reading sub-section 1.1. Here we could argue that work is seen as a vocation, and while there appears to be a high degree of commitment to work, there is also the aspiration to progress through the career hierarchy.

Also expressed in this quote is the view that workers should have an almost moral commitment to work, irrespective of the type of work being done.

QUESTION 2

This question is concerned with the subject matter of sub-section 1.1. You should have made the point that work has been viewed differently through the ages. There is a certain similarity of views with regard to the Greek and Roman conceptions, where work was considered to be demeaning and relegated to slavery. This view of work tended to persist through the middle-ages up to the reformation.

Work in the post-reformation period, partly as a result of the protestant work ethic became elevated in status and was seen in a positive light as an activity which bestowed dignity to work and the people doing it. The value of this ideology to society is demonstrated by the rapid advance of industrialisation and the emergence of powerful modern economies.

Review Activity 2

Part 1

1   Horizontal patterning concerns the location of similar occupational activities and grouping them together within that broader occupational or professional category. Not all of the occupations identified in the chart can be classified in this way. Of the ones that can be classified, the main examples are:

- Industrial, plant and machine operators, assemblers
  Drivers and mobile machine operators

- Buyers, brokers and sales reps
  Other sales occupations

- Protective service occupations
  Personal service occupations

- Clerical occupations
  Secretarial occupations

2   We can also locate the occupational groups within the seven socio-economic categories identified in the sub-section hierarchical patterning. Examples are:

Class I   Corporate managers and administrators
             Science and engineering professionals

Class II   Science and engineering associate professionals
             Health associate professionals

Class III Clerical occupations
             Secretarial occupations
             Buyers and sales representatives
             Other sales occupations

Class IV   None identified

Class V   Supervisors in construction and engineering trades

Class VI   Industrial plant and machine operators
             Drivers

Class VII Other elementary occupations

The concept of the dual labour market was examined in sub-section 2.3. The dual labour market comprises:

- primary sector where jobs are skilled and the pay is good

- secondary sector where jobs are unskilled and semi-skilled and where pay and conditions are markedly inferior.

Within the primary sector, the chart indicates that with the exceptions of the teaching and health professions, the other professional categories have much higher proportions of male and full-time professionals. This also applies to the skilled trades and machine operations occupations.

Within the secondary sector, occupations such as personal services and secretarial and clerical occupations have relatively high proportions of part-time workers and sub-contracted workers who are mainly women.

3 The two categories which you might select are clerical occupations and personal service occupations (cleaning, etc). Reasons for the high levels of full- and part-time women's employment within these categories can be found in sub-section 2.4 and would include:

● employers' requirements for cheap and flexible labour

● explanations relating to the operation of the dual labour market and to the sexual division of labour.

Part 2

Check your review of the material against the relevant text to make sure that you have identified all the important points correctly.

Review Activity 3

Scenario 1

Dave has an instrumental orientation to work. Work is seen by Dave as a means to an end, and he has obviously chosen this work because of the relatively high pay. He does not find his work self-fulfilling and he makes a clear distinction between his work and non-work activities.

Scenario 2

Sub-section 3.2 deals with some of the criticisms of the Goldthorpe et al view.

● Within the work context, there has been some job re-structuring which has made Dave's job more complex. The job has therefore become less attractive as Dave is still on the same pay. This is certainly a contributory factor in making him decide to quit.

● His marriage and bereavement are very important external factors which have affected his work orientation.

● Both internal and external factors have in turn influenced Dave's decision to better himself by taking a distance education course and to do a less financially rewarding job within his locality.

Orientations to work are, therefore, dynamic and subject to the sort of influences and factors that Dave has experienced.

Review Activity 4

(i) This question covers the content of sub-sections 4.1-4.3. You should have referred to Handy's summary, mentioned the factors associated with changing work and jobs, with particular reference to the characteristics of the informal economy and the emerging information economy discussed in sub-sections 4.2 and 4.3.

(ii) This question covers the content of sub-sections 4.4 and 4.5. You should have defined new technology and made a note of the various applications of new technology in industry, perhaps with reference to Figure 4. You should have discussed flexibility and work design and focussed upon the impact of new technologies on these areas and in relation to organisational structure and employment patterns. You should have identified issues concerning centralisation/decentralisation and recentralisation, together with core/periphery aspects.

Review Activity 5

1   You will find the relevant information in sub-section 5.2. Although the service sector has assumed greater importance over the past four decades, both manufacturing and service sectors (secondary and tertiary sectors) are becoming more inter-related as the self-service economy affects both sectors in the following ways:

● many 'service' jobs are within the manufacturing sector

● information technology affects both sectors and is likely to result in an increased rate of job reduction (full-time)

● competitive market environments continue to exert pressures for greater efficiencies within both sectors.

2   Section 5.3 deals with this question.

UNIT 6

PSYCHOLOGICAL PERSPECTIVES ON WORK AND ORGANISATIONS

Introduction

Psychology as a body of knowledge is used by a large proportion of industrial, business and commercial organisations in the private sector and also many areas of the public sector. The application of psychology in organisations can range from situations where large overall programmes are in place to smaller departmental initiatives where psychological techniques, such as aids to selection and promotion procedures, are used.

Within the discipline of psychology, personality is a field of study rather than a particular aspect of the individual. No other area of psychology covers as much ground as the field of personality, which overlaps extensively with neighbouring areas.

Many theories support our current understanding of personality. In this unit, you examine five broad theoretical areas. Theorists conceptualise personality in a variety of different ways and it is important for you to appreciate these in order that you can find ways that you think about yourself and others.

Theories provide an orientation and perspective that stimulate different types of research. They also lead to different approaches for assessing personality, testing and to thinking about people in organisations. Trait and biological theories have provided the basis for many modern psychometric tests for personality in organisations.

Perception is another field of study within psychology. This overlaps with personality. We examine the processes involved in perception and the importance of social perception in organisations.

Characteristics of individuals explained by personality theories can be used in selection procedures and in post-selection situations (promotion and appraisal). Ensuring the right people are selected for organisations is vital to their success, therefore you will examine approaches to selection processes and associated methods that can be used to aid rational selection of candidates for jobs in organisations.

The approaches to selection are linked to general and psychometric testing, and we pay particular attention to the rationale for tests in areas of personality and intelligence.

Objectives

At the end of this unit, you will be able to:

- explain and describe five theoretical approaches to personality.
- give examples of a range of different types of personality traits which may be exhibited by individuals.

- outline the processes involved in perception.
- explain the importance of social perception in organisations.
- describe why it is important to assess certain personality traits for the work place.
- explain the organisational processes involved in selecting an interview candidate for employment.
- use and describe methods for the rational selection of interview candidates for employment.
- demonstrate familiarity with certain dimensions of personality and how they may be quantified.
- explain and describe a range of tests and testing procedures employed in organisations and the selection of suitable candidates for employment and clinical evaluations.

SECTION 1
Individual Differences and Personality Theory

Introduction

In this section, you are introduced to historical theories of **personality** and their development and influence on current theories. We emphasise personality traits; these feature strongly in the application of psychology to people in organisations. You will also become familiar with the concept of dimensions of personality and some approaches used in their assessment.

To many people, personality means something different. One definition is: 'the total of the psychological, intellectual, emotional and physical characteristics, especially as others see them' (Longman *Modern English Dictionary,* 1980).

There are many complex and diverse aspects of human personality. In order to deal with some of the major theories, you examine five major approaches to personality that have emerged from over a century of research in psychology as a science and profession. These approaches are:

- **psychodynamic**
- **trait and biological**
- **humanistic**
- **behavioural**
- **cognitive.**

1.1 Psychodynamic approaches

The work place presents us with various problems, many of these are solved at a psychological level, through unconcious internal forces. To understand how we deal with unconscious wishes, Sigmund Freud (1933) developed the 'anatomy' of the mind. This led to the structural view of personality consisting of three agencies of mental personality: the id, the ego and the superego:

- **the id** – is that physical part of ourselves motivated by pleasure which can lead to unrestrained behaviour. The id contains everything inherited, it is the basis of personality, the energy source for the system and the basis from which the ego and superego later develop. The id lies in our unconscious.

- **the ego** – is a direct outgrowth from the id. The ego is more down to earth than the id and its task is preservation of the individual. Its function is governed by the reality principle, which requires it to test reality and delay discharge of tension until the appropriate conditions prevail. The ego lies predominantly in our conscious.

- **the superego** – is the conscience which imposes standards and has high demands. It is the judge of right and wrong. The superego develops in us at around the age of six after our long dependency on parents and/or care givers. The superego lies in both our conscious and unconscious.

The **conscious** is defined as: '. . . the realization or recognition of actions, emotions etc by the doer' (Oxford *Modern English Dictionary*).

The **unconscious** is defined as: ' . . . that part of the mind which is inaccessible by the conscious mind but which affects behaviour, emotions, etc' (Oxford *Modern English Dictionary*).

Carl Jung, an associate of Freud, developed his own differing theories based around the collective unconscious. This was quite different to the personal unconscious, whose contents were once conscious but have been forgotten or repressed. The contents of the collective unconscious, he proposed, had never been in consciousness. He also proposed that the collective unconscious contained archetypes (basic images). Their contents are not acquired but due to heredity. Jung's approach became known as **analytical psychology**. He detailed a conscious side to the psyche and an aspect that is unconscious which develops and unfolds to integrate with the rest of personality into a life pattern. He proposed that the unconscious of every female includes a masculine element (the animus) and that the unconscious of every male includes a feminine element (the anima). To be constructively masculine or feminine, individuals of each sex must integrate these opposite sex elements within themselves. (Jung, 1964)

Jung's work proved important in assigning the extent to which personality traits are exhibited. He described four ways of experiencing the world: sensing, intuition, feeling and thinking. He proposed that we differ consistently in the degree to which we place emphasis on each of the experiences we have. In addition, Jung suggested the dimension **extroversion-introversion**. Introverts withdraw into themselves especially when encountering stressful emotional conflict, they tend to prefer to be alone, avoid others and are shy. Extroverts, in contrast, react to stress by trying to lose themselves among people and social activity.

ACTIVITY 1

Look more closely at the degree to which an individual exhibits introversion or extroversion as initiated by Jung and consider how this differs in us all. What groups of people in organisations would be interested in the degree to which these characteristics are exhibited and how these characteristics can be assessed?

Managers and organisational psychologists are interested at different stages of employment history:

- in designing a job where the specifications for the person are important
- at interview to obtain the best candidate in terms of these characteristics and their requirements for a job
- whilst in the job to observe development, in line with perhaps changes in a job or for on-going assessment.

In all of these examples, the degree to which the characteristics are exhibited would be important, that is mildly extrovert or very extrovert, as opposed to say mildly introvert or very introvert.

In an organisational context, it is interesting to note that the extrovert is usually drawn into an occupation that allows them to deal directly with many people, such as sales, as they tend to be conventional, sociable and outgoing.

ACTIVITY 2

To what areas of our conscious or unconscious do the following agencies of mental personality, proposed by Freud, refer: the id, the ego and the superego.

The id refers to our conscious, the ego to our unconscious and the superego to both our conscious and unconscious.

There are four further major contributors to psychodynamic approaches:

- Alfred Adler's interests lay in the area of compensatory motivation. Central to his theories were physical weakness and sibling rivalry. He proposed that this biological vulnerability becomes the root for a psychological state that endures in us all, leading to feelings of inferiority. Failure to develop effective compensations can result in inferiority complexes. Mishel (1993) p.70.

- Erich Fromm (1947) differed from Freud in that he proposed that we are social beings to be understood in our relations to others. He proposed social orientation in contrast to Freud's biological orientation and went on to state that our character traits develop from experiences with others.

- Erik Erikson (1963) was interested in the problems of social adaptation. He proposed that as we develop, the solution of problems at eight psychosocial stages, rather than several psychosexual stages suggested by Freud, determines how adequate we will become as adults. At each stage of these developments, Erikson proposes an internal struggle or 'crisis'. This arises from our efforts to solve problems at the various stages. This can be applied to situations in the work place, in coming to terms and adapting to a new job, a promotion, competing with peers, meeting deadlines, developing expertise and many other areas which may prove problematic. In identifying these psychosocial stages, Erikson is credited with the term 'identity crisis' which describes certain stages in adolescence.

- Klein and Kohut (1984) – in recent years, object relations theory and the self have been recognised as transformations of psychodynamic theory. Supported and developed by Melanie Klein and Heinz Kohut, the theory is based on mental representations of the self and other persons. These mental representations are said to develop in our early relationship with the care giver. These representations are characterised by emotional splits into good or bad components.

The latter psychoanalysts placed more emphasis on the ego than on the id, promoting independent development of the ego. As neo-Freudians, they were more optimistic about the ability of humankind to change.

ACTIVITY 3

Examine, in basic terms, some principal differences between the psychodynamic approaches of Freud, Jung and Erikson. In your opinion, what relevance, if any, do these personality theories have in the work place?

Freud was principally concerned with the conscious and unconscious and his work had specific reference to clinical development situations. Jung's work developed from this and was concerned with the collective unconscious and characteristics of personality such as introversion and extroversion. These latter concepts have particular relevance in the work place. Erikson was concerned with social adaptation and developmental processes, again both have possible relevance and implications for the work place.

1.2 Trait approaches

The oldest and most enduring approach to individuality is known as the **trait approach**. Here we can be classified by the trait terms of everyday language, such as friendly or aggressive, to describe and compare our psychological attributes. Trait theories highlight properties, qualities or processes that exist in us all. They can be used to account for our behavioural patterns, and for our behavioural differences, in response to similar situations. Three major theorists have contributed to these approaches: Gordon Allport, Raymond B Cattell and Hans J Eysenck.

ALLPORT

For Allport (1937), traits are the mental structures that account for consistency in behaviour. He proposed three trait types:

- **Cardinal traits** which are organised around our achievement of goals and the attainment of excellence, for example, a successful sale, contract or promotion.

- **Central traits** which are generalised and provide a broad influence for us, for example, diplomacy and customer relations.

- **Secondary dispositions or attitudes,** which are specific narrow traits, for example, opinions on accuracy and precision approach to tasks.

He maintained that these traits operated uniquely within us all, with the pattern of operation determining our behaviour.

CATTELL

Cattell (1950, 1965) proposed a whole series of traits, many of which could be identified through statistical and other types of analysis. He distinguished between:

- **common traits** possessed by us all, and
- **unique traits** specific to individuals.

He also distinguished surface traits from source traits:

- **surface traits** include integrity, thoughtfulness, thrift and tidiness, which are overt or manifest trait elements; they can be determined through test responses or scores

- **source traits,** proposed many years after he proposed surface traits, include ego, strength, neuroticism (emotional stability), dominance and submissiveness; they can be determined for individuals only by using the mathematical technique of factor analysis.

Cattell's trait system also grouped traits into how they may be expressed:

- **dynamic traits** are triggered or guided by a goal or objective that we may have

- **ability traits** are concerned with our performance and effectiveness in obtaining goals

- **temperament traits** involve energy or emotion.

ACTIVITY 4

Examine the members of your immediate family, your student friends or colleagues at work. Identify in them some common traits and unique traits as proposed by Cattell.

Consider Allport's three trait types. List some of the traits you would expect to see demonstrated by a retail pharmacist.

The concepts of common and unique traits as separate entities are difficult to attribute. These suggestions serve as a guide. Generally, you can indicate emotion as a common trait, also optimism and pessimism. Unique traits could be intelligence, temperament, thoughtfulness and excitability which are clearly unique to individuals.

In applying the trait types to a retail pharmacist, you would expect to see cardinal traits in aiming for a successful business with a reputation for excellence. Central traits would involve the process of pharmacy gained probably from inner abilities and knowledge and additionally in attitudes towards dealing with the public. For secondary dispositions, this could be concerned with refinements and accuracy in preparing prescriptions, medicines and other services to the public.

EYSENCK

Eysenck attempted to measure our traits and group them into some overall categories of our personality type. He extended the work of Carl Jung on introversion-extroversion, but where Jung had identified these as two different personality types, Eysenck identified introversion-extroversion as one of two major dimensional traits of personality. These traits may be assigned a value on a scale and represented visually on a diagram (Figure 1) as axes in space. The second major personality dimension which he identified and also investigated was **emotional stability** or neuroticism.

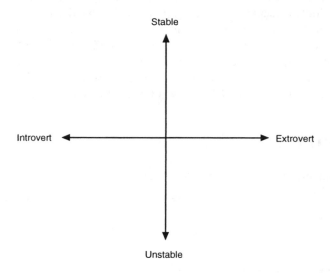

Figure 1: Dimensions of personality
Source: Eysenck & Eysenck, 1975

Eysenck promoted the use of questionnaires in attempting to measure the traits that we exhibit and which we can group to produce categories of our personality type.

Reflect on how identifying the degree to which a person exhibits such personality traits might be of value to a manager and in what work situations it might be useful. Look back to the commentary to Activity 1.

OTHER TRAIT-BASED APPROACHES

It is now widely accepted amongst trait researchers that there are five broad dimensions to personality: **neuroticism, extroversion, openness to new experience, agreeableness** and **conscientiousness**. These definitions help in capturing personality differences in terms of language description.

Other approaches to traits, focus on typical examples of particular categories about ourselves. An example of this is extroversion (sociable and outgoing). This highlights identification of trait trends as summaries of our behaviour. Each of these categories can include the level of personality characteristics on a bipolar scale (Figure 2).

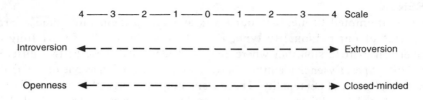

Figure 2: Bipolar scale representation

Eysenck looked at two major dimensions to personality as we have noted, however, it is now widely accepted that the gaps provided by the poles can be scaled (assigned values) or scored. The scale in Figure 2 serves as an example. We can be assigned a score or scale which could be used to highlight traits, and possibly the degree to which the traits are exhibited. For example, if you had a score of two, at the extrovert end of the scale in Figure 2, a person could be considered to be more of an extrovert than you if their score was four, at that end of the scale.

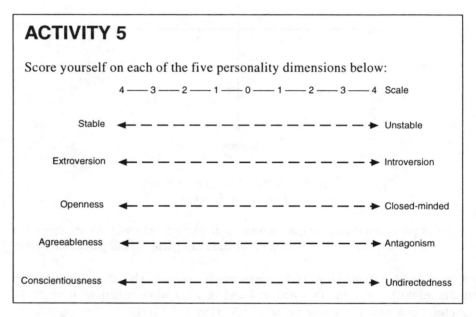

ACTIVITY 5

Score yourself on each of the five personality dimensions below:

If many of your scores were high at the left-hand of the scale, this may be considered as not desirable on the agreeableness-antagonism dimension in certain organisational roles. Similarly, this could apply on the introversion-extroversion scale. This process serves as a self-evaluation, however, it is usually the case that the appearance and arrangements of questions designed to assign your position on such scales, may not be as explicit as these here.

Examples of actual questions contained on the Eysenck Personality Questionnaire (answered with a 'yes' or 'no') are:

Question 16. Have you ever blamed someone for doing something you knew was really your fault?

Question 20. Are all your habits good and desirable ones?

Question 50. Do most things taste the same to you?

1.3 Humanistic approaches

These approaches are based on experiences of individuals as they perceive them. They are also known as self-theories.

Consider the following scenario:

Steve is a recent graduate in Business Administration. He is engaged to Louise. 'I've got my degree now, although it's only a second class degree. Mum and Dad were really proud of me at the graduation ceremony. Mum, Dad and Louise all expect me to now get a good job, I just made it through the course and now I've got an interview for a job. What will the interview be like, will they test me, if I don't get the job, will Louise be let down, because we really need the money for our engagement? I know I'll get really worried before the interview. So far things have gone my way, but now this is real life, can I deal with it?'

Steve's experiences are typical of those that provide the basis for theories that deal with the self, subjective internal experiences and personal concepts.

Perhaps the most influential theorists in humanistic approaches were Abraham Maslow (1968), George Kelly (1955) and Carl Rogers (1959). Maslow maintained that as humans we are innately good. Although he did not coin the notion of self-actualisation, he came up with a definition of a **self-actualiser** as someone who exhibits no neurotic or psychotic symptoms and was in the healthiest 1% of the population. These types of people experience transient self-actualisation comprising values such as perfection, uniqueness and self-sufficiency. Compared to Freud's theories, these are much more positive and optimistic, as Maslow maintained that none of our innate needs are anti-social. Maslow was a major contributor to motivational theories and he set out a five-tier hierarchy of needs. We discuss his approach in detail in Unit 8.

Kelly was an advocate of **personal constructs**. These constructs are ways in which we represent or view our own experiences. He maintained that trait psychologists try to find the subject's place on theoretical personality dimensions. He proposed that personal construct theory tries to see how we can see and align events on our own dimensions. This could, he maintained, enable us to assess, evaluate and better control our own behaviour. This work led to the formation of encounter groups which enabled many people to experience great personality changes later in life when their circumstances changed.

Carl Rogers believed that the way we see and interpret events in life determines behaviour and personality. He believed that personality was not due to a series of unrelated factors but a coherent whole which requires positive regard from other people. His theory is often referred to as the **self-theory of personality**. He proposed two systems: the self, composed of individual perceptions of the 'I' or the 'me' and their relationships to others and life in general; and the organism, that which functions as an organised whole. They can either be opposed to each other or in harmony. In an opposition situation, they can result in maladjustment – experiencing tensions and losing contact with the organism.

1.4 Behavioural approaches

The behavioural theories are synonymous with learning theories, which fall into three broad types:

- **Classical conditioning** pairs together a potent and neutral stimulus event. The potent stimulus is replaced to a large extent, eventually, by the neutral stimulus. This conditioned reflex is a basic type of associative learning and depends on learning.

- **Operant conditioning** is a situation where our behaviour patterns may be modified by changing the consequences or reinforcements, to which they lead.

- **Observational learning** is emphasised by recent social learning theories. Here complex and important potential behaviour can be acquired without external reinforcement to us as learners.

Reinforcements play a part in all approaches. They are particular events that strengthen the tendency for a response to be repeated. The social system can be regarded as a set of reinforcers, due to the fact that we respond to our peer groups, especially in working environments. Reinforcement in organisational situations – training situations, performance feedback, appraisal, etc – takes the form of praise and criticism in order to strengthen or discourage particular behaviours and actions.

Classical conditioning is a type of learning which was emphasised by Ivan Pavlov (1927). He noticed that a hungry dog salivated (unconditioned response) when presented with food (a potent stimulus). If a bell was sounded (neutral stimulus), alongside the presentation of the food (unconditioned stimuli), then eventually the dog could be made to salivate (conditioned response) in the absence of food by the sound of the bell alone. The condition that elicits a conditioned response, he called a conditioned stimulus. From this initial finding, he and other researchers developed specific theories on learning. This type of learning is now referred to as classical conditioning.

Skinner and his associates were interested in behaviour exhibited by individuals and examining the conditions that control it (Skinner, 1953). He concentrated on stimulus events and response patterns. He maintained that we all exhibit freely emitted behavioural response patterns, which he called operants. These operants allow us to operate in our environment. We can modify these operants and in turn we can be changed by these modifications.

The theorists who support operant conditioning propose that our behaviour patterns may be modified by changing reinforcements. In organisations, information, attention and recognition are typical reinforcements which can greatly influence behaviour by operant conditioning.

Learning without reinforcement is known as cognitive or observational learning. The learning can be acquired without undertaking the learned response, for example, we can learn a lot about disciplinary procedures in organisations without ever having been disciplined or acting as a trade union official.

Bandura is currently the leading theorist in the analysis of observational learning and its relevance in personality (Bandura, 1969). He emphasises how the observer attends to a modelled sequence of novel behaviour, which is essentially developmental.

ACTIVITY 6

Consider the three behavioural approaches, which of these would be best applied in the training of a marketer and retail manager?

You could answer classical, operant and observational approaches to both roles. However, you should consider that the answers concern the degree and emphasis to which they would be employed in training.

For the marketer, there would be elements of classical conditioning, as there would be with all trainees in business. For example, a permanent job after training would be a potent stimulus, supplemented with rankings or ratings. A neutral stimulus could be verbal praise or encouraging comments. However, the emphasis would be on operant and observational approaches – operant in terms of reinforcements, such as incentives and reward, and observational in terms of developing product awareness and being aware of design and customer requirements.

For the retailer, the operant and behavioural approaches would apply for similar reasons to those for the marketer, however, perhaps more emphasis would be placed on classical conditioning, because there is more emphasis on repetitive or routine approaches. This is influenced by the particular nature of retail chains and their management structures.

1.5 Cognitive approaches

Cognitive approaches question the theories of classical conditioning which traditionally relied on experimental work. The role of cognition arises out of the need to reinterpret how classical conditioning works. Theorists who support cognition feel that this has an effect on classical conditioning. Whilst the behaviourists put forward the idea that stimuli control behaviour, the cognition theorists reason that cognitive transformations and interpretations of stimuli determine the impact the stimuli have in observational learning and classical and operant conditioning.

Many studies have been made on how cognitive social processes influence behaviour. The processes and outcomes are necessary in supporting theories of personality. The theorist, Mischel, proposed a set of psychological variables enabling the analysis of our differences in cognitive social terms (Mischel, 1993). These served as alternatives to psychodynamics and trait approaches. They allowed theorists to study how we generate distinctive complex behaviour patterns in interacting with our environment and the processes of everyday life.

The first cognitive approach is to consider our encoding. **Encoding** is a procedure by which we categorise ourselves and situations. Cognitionists propose that our performance depends on how we see ourselves and others and the situation. How we react to things depends on our encoding, and in this we all differ greatly. This has many implications in the work place.

Consider the following scenario:

Paul is a manager in a sales department, where an organisational psychologist has undertaken a recent evaluation of management attitudes. The psychologist has made an assessment of Paul and found that he has encoded all of the administrative and clerical staff, that he manages, as being of low intelligence.

Clearly this sort of encoding can, and does, occur in organisations. Cognition has implications for self-esteem, self-evaluation and self-appraisal, that is, self-concepts, for individual and group processes in organisations. This approach also finds wide application in human resource development areas for training, career planning and goal setting.

ACTIVITY 7

Consider the following set of tasks. Indicate with a yes or no whether you can do them or not. For those you can do, give yourself a score between 10 and 100 on your possible confidence in carrying out the tasks. Score yourself high for the more confident you are. This is a self-evaluation.

<table>
<tr><td></td><td>Can do</td><td>Confidence Score</td></tr>
<tr><td>1 Go to lunch on your first day at work with a group of people you do not know</td><td></td><td></td></tr>
<tr><td>2 In your first work group meeting, discuss a controversial topic with people whose views differ greatly from yours</td><td></td><td></td></tr>
<tr><td>3 Work with a person whose behaviour you find obnoxious or irritating</td><td></td><td></td></tr>
<tr><td>4 Complain about poor work from a colleague</td><td></td><td></td></tr>
<tr><td>5 Reprimand an unco-operative subordinate</td><td></td><td></td></tr>
</table>

This activity highlights some ways in which a self-evaluation could be undertaken. A person with 20 years work experience might have answered yes ('can do') to all questions, and gave high scores for each. You could be exposed to questions of this sort. On interviews you may be asked to comment on hypothetical situations similar to those above. You may also be faced with such situations, in life or at work.

REVIEW ACTIVITY 1

Suggested time: 1 hour.

Read the article 'Personality Types and Business Success of Small Retailers' by Rice, G H & Lindecamp, D P, Item 6.1 in the Resource section.

The underlying implication of the research in this article is that managerial performance – and hence business success in organisations – can be linked to managerial personality types and traits. To what extent do you think this link between managerial personality type and organisational business success can usefully be made?

Does the failure of this research study to find support for its initial hypotheses suggest to you that it is unprofitable to pursue links between Jungian personality types and business performance, that is, that the outcomes of further research would be predictable? Or do you think that further research might find support for such links?

Summary

In this section, you have examined five theoretical approaches to personality. You have focused on trait theories and considered some dimensions of personality. You have attempted the assignment of some theoretical approaches to job function requirements and been exposed to a short, illustrative process of self-evaluation.

SECTION 2

Perception

Introduction

As part of your study of human personality, you should appreciate that our perceptions can influence our psychological base and the ways in which we interact with other people in organisations. In this section, we examine the ways in which personality adds to the psychological perspectives that we need to consider in relation to organisations. Perception is concerned with the ways in which we receive stimuli from the environment. Here, we are concerned essentiaily with those psychological processes which include how we select, how we may organise and how we may interpret these stimuli. In addition, we introduce social perception, in order to highlight the relevance of perception to organisations.

2.1 Elements of the perception process

Perception can be defined as: 'The faculty of perceiving [often followed by] the intuitive recognition of a truth, aesthetic quality, etc' (Oxford *Modern English Dictionary*).

In order to appreciate the processes surrounding perception it is important that you consider the selection and organisation of stimuli from the environment to provide a meaningful interpretation. By definition, a stimulus is any change in energy that causes an excitation of the nervous system, leading to a response. We are exposed to stimuli in the environment through our five senses:

- tasting
- smelling

- **hearing**
- **seeing**
- **touching.**

When you greet a new employee or colleague you would probably use the senses of smell, hearing, seeing and touching. If you were to meet a personal friend or partner, taste may also occur as a result of a kiss.

To help us make sense of our environment, we are selective with some stimuli and we filter out others. For example, if you are using a computer you can filter out voices and actions around you to pay attention to what you are doing. The screen and its contents stand out and the other stimuli blend into the background.

Once the selection process has occurred the process of organisation arranges the stimuli into meaningful patterns. Our perceptual process tends to organise stimuli so that they fit logical patterns and often filter out stimuli that are inconsistent or contradict our view of reality.

For example, you may have a friend or colleague who you like very much, however, you hear him or her being opinionated or bigoted on a particular subject. As this may not fit into your image, you may not incorporate this perception into your overall impression of him or her.

The process of interpreting stimuli is subjective and can vary considerably. For example, in a working environment one of the managers may smile at you, in conversation. You could interpret this as pleasurable or it could make you nervous. A colleague observing this may interpret the smile as the manager disguising boredom from being in your company.

The interpretation of sensory stimuli will probably lead to one of the following four responses:

- **behavioural**
- **experience of feelings**
- **attitudinal**
- **motivational.**

ACTIVITY 8

Generally, we are surrounded by many stimuli but focus only on a small number. As you are reading this section, list some stimuli that you are currently 'filtering out'.

The stimuli might include: pressure on the skin of your back from the chair you are sitting on; pressure on the skin of your fingers from holding a book or pencil; pressure on your arms from leaning on a table or chair; people talking; music playing; movement in an adjoining room or the same room; noise from traffic nearby; aroma from coffee, perfume, after-shave or food; visual distractions; and many more.

In the study of perception, we give special weight to sensations as the primitive elements out of which more complicated perceptions can be built, and on the basis of which inferences can be drawn about reality. Thus sensory processes are seen as simple and primary, whereas perceptual processes are complex and derivative. A leading nineteenth-century medical physiologist, Wilhelm Wundt adopted this view. However, Gestalt psychologists such as Max Wertheimer, Wolfgang Kohler and Kurt Lewin supported the belief that a complex perception cannot be explained as a linear sum of the sensations that its parts arouse. Miller (1975).

The notion that perceptions are built from sensations as an analogy to a wall being built from bricks is now generally recognised as being unsatisfactory. The step that carries perception beyond sensation is often called an unconscious inference, a term coined by perhaps the most prominent nineteenth-century physiologist, Herman Ludwig Von Helmholtz. The perception itself is termed an unconscious conclusion. To endorse this view of perception we need to further consider the selection, organisation and interpretation processes.

2.2 Selection

The selection process provides a range of factors which lead us to pay attention to some stimuli. They fall into two categories:

- internal factors
- external factors.

INTERNAL FACTORS

Internal factors relate to the individual and include their learning, motivation and personality. These factors are important in developing our perceptual set. These perceptual sets can be refined and modified by training and experience in order that we are 'set' to attend to some stimuli and to interpret them in uncertain situations. Our perceptual sets are affected by our learning, motivation and personality.

- Effects of learning on selection

One influence on our perception is past experiences and what we have learned from them. Our perception in a given situation is often conditioned by our learning.

For example, a sales person and a computer technology specialist demonstrate a computer to employees in an organisation. The sales person will emphasise the appearance, software, ease of use, user-friendly add-ons. The computer technologist will detail the technical specifications, interfacing and networking details. Each will pay attention to different aspects of the stimulus (computer) as a result of their experience and training. Differences such as these are common in organisations and can lead to problems in communication (Dearborn & Simon, 1958).

- ● **Effects of motivation on selection**

Dominant needs and desires can influence our perception. For example, if you are looking for a job, you are more likely to pay attention to job advertisements than someone who already has a job. Generally we are motivated to perceive those things which will satisfy our needs.

For example, when crossing a busy road where self-preservation is a dominant need, you would probably not be listening so attentively to the sound of a bicycle bell as for the sound of the horn of a truck or car.

- ● **Effects of personality on selection**

The relationship between personality and perception is complex. Personality can affect how and what we perceive, whilst our personality can be shaped by our perceptions.

For example, personality qualities such as active, optimistic or aggressive may be required in the selection of a financial portfolio, alternatively, controlled thoughtful and careful qualities may be required. In either case, these qualities would influence the selection process.

ACTIVITY 9

Consider the following scenarios:

1 French traffic police may be able to obtain promotion based upon increased conviction of speed offenders. A group of French officers are to visit Great Britain to observe British policing methods. Jacques, one of these officers, makes a point of attending a demonstration of an electronic speed detection system soon to be introduced into his force.

2 An experienced British police officer demonstrates an electronic speed detection system to visiting police officers from France.

Which of the three internal factors influencing selection are at work in the two scenarios?

1   Motivation on selection. Jacques is motivated by the opportunity of promotion in this scenario.

2   Learning on selection. The British police officer will pay attention to the stimulus (electronic detection system) based on his or her use of the detector, not necessarily the technical detail.

EXTERNAL FACTORS

Here the nature of the stimuli is important. **Nature principles** can influence the degree to which a stimuli can be perceived. Such principles can be used in marketing, design and commercial exploitation of products and services for organisations, these include:

- **Size principles,** which are related to the fact that something is more likely to be perceived if it is large. In organisations, the size of a person's office is often linked to their importance.

- **Intensity principles,** which are related to the fact that more intense stimuli are more likely to be perceived: You would be more likely to respond to a demand from a section leader or manager to attend a meeting, rather than a polite request for you to pop into one.

- **Contrast principles,** which highlight an increased likelihood of perception on stimuli that can 'stand out' from an array or set of background stimuli: Examples of these are bright colours, in a dull range; sweet, sour and pungent odours, in a range of background odours; particular sounds, such as music, in a range of background noise.

- **Motion principles,** which are based on the fact that a moving stimulus is more likely to be perceived than a stationary one: presentations in the work place are best facilitated with actions rather than a motionless delivery.

- **Repetition principles,** which are linked to conditioning in supporting the fact that repeated stimuli are better perceived than a single stimulus; this principle is employed widely in training, education and advertising.

- **Novelty and familiarity principles,** which support the fact that either a novel or familiar factor heightens perception; dressing informally in a formal working environment can be considered a novelty and may attract the attention of colleagues, this would appear perhaps 'normal' outside of the office. When starting a job in an organisation, you may perceive the face of a former undergraduate colleague, this could register familiarity.

External factors would not usually register individually, but they would cluster as a collective pattern of factors to form an overall perception.

2.3 Organisation

Organisation is the second process of perception and occurs after selection. It involves organisation of stimuli into meaningful patterns on the basis of four tendencies:

● **Proximity** is a tendency to perceive groups of stimuli, which may be closely related to each other; this can be applied visually. In an organisation, we could consider groups of people who work in close proximity, for example, accountants and marketers. They could be considered a group as a result of this proximity but they may, in fact, not be related at all.

● **Similarity** is a tendency to perceive like objects or functions as a common group. In hospitals, different groups such as doctors, nurses, ward managers, laboratory staff have different aspects or colours to their uniform or attire, but all are perceived as hospital staff. Differentiation is achieved by their uniforms.

● **Closure** is a tendency to complete an object or function so that it is perceived as an overall form.

● **Continuity** is a tendency to perceive objects or functions as continuous patterns. In an organisation, an employee who adheres to procedures to the exclusion of all other considerations may do so out of a need for continuity.

In all general situations, we seem to perceive our surroundings using the organising tendencies outlined above and using the simplest grouping patterns.

There is one further tendency which can be considered in the organisation of stimuli:

● **Figure-ground** is a situation which considers a scenario consisting of objects (figure) set against some background (ground). For example, the black writing on this page can be considered as figure and the white background, ground. Or vice-versa. The latter reversibility of the phenomena can occur quite frequently. This is linked to the fact that what one individual perceives is not necessarily what another perceives.

ACTIVITY 10

Observe the images in Figure 3 (a)-(d).

a)

b)

c)

d)

Which of the following tendencies do you think is visually represented by (a)-(d): continuity; proximity; similarity; closure.

(a) is proximity, the squares on the left are perceived as vertical columns and those on the right as horizontal rows.

(b) is similarity, the equally spaced dots are seen as falling into horizontal groups of two with similar units grouped together.

(c) is closure, both shapes are seen as a square and triangle even though both are incomplete.

(d) is continuity, the shapes are perceived as a continuous pattern.

In essence, we should realise through these illustrations that we are surrounded by a variety of stimuli which can be organised into simplistic or complex patterns, the organisation of which depends on our individuality.

2.4 Interpretation

This process involves the interpretation of what has been perceived and occurs after selection and organisation. Perceptions are placed into patterns, the patterns can be subject to errors in our overall perceptions. These errors can be due to:

- **Illusions** – false interpretations perceived by the mind of sense perceptions.

- **Stereotyping** – a categorisation of material with a certain set of assumptions or predictions based on limited information. Examples of these are 'older people are less ready to change' and 'overweight people are slow'. Stereotypes are known to be inaccurate, however, it does happen to be an easy way to think.

- **Halo effect** – results in people perceiving others through the 'halo' of a single striking attribute, such as, height, weight, manner or accent, and so seeing in them, or assuming that they will have, other qualities that the perceiver associates with that particular attribute.

- **Projection** – a tendency to reflect our own attributes in other people, such as, feelings, motives or attitudes.

- **Expectancy** – expectations bias how we perceive events; you may accept a job that prior to starting you are told that management is strict. Your perceptions on starting may be negative, based on your expectation of a strict environment.

- **Perceptual defence** – a process of blocking or screening threatening perceptual input stimuli to the eyes and ears. This blocking or screening may occur through rejection and ignoring stimuli.

ACTIVITY 11

Can you identify any work situations where it is useful to have an awareness of the possible perceptual pitfalls associated with interpretation?

Interviewing is perhaps the most important area where awareness is necessary. It is usually the case that a representative from a personnel or human resource management section is present at organisational interviews to raise interview panel awareness in these areas. Dealing with members of the public, in service sector organisations, usually requires training or instruction about how to avoid illusion, stereotyping and projection. Working in media organisations where it may be necessary to meet celebrities may introduce errors of illusion, stereotyping or expectancy. In almost all work situations where interaction with people occurs, there is the possibility of pitfalls associated with interpretation.

All of the above interpretation processes have particular relevance in the work place, especially in the selection and interview of candidates for jobs.

2.5 Social perception

Social perception is the process by which we interpret and understand people around us through perceptions of their behaviour, attitudes and motives. This process is more complex than our perception of inanimate objects and includes a range of influences and contributions from personality approaches. Therefore, in applying social perception we may employ trait and biological, humanistic and cognitive approaches. Any failure to accurately perceive a social situation could prove damaging to a social relationship. In organisations, there are many factors that can influence our social perception. These factors can be placed into three basic categories: the person being perceived; the person perceiving; and the situation.

THE PERSON BEING PERCEIVED
Our perception of people can be influenced in three main areas:

- **Appearance:** physical characteristics play an important part in influencing how we perceive other people. These can include sex, age, height and weight. The way people dress can also be an influence. All of these observations can be influenced by our self-concept (which we discussed in Section 1), stereotyping, the halo effect and expectancy.

- **Communication:** can occur verbally or non-verbally. Verbal influences can include accent, which may indicate a person's national or regional origins to us. This may in turn cause us to attribute certain characteristics to those people. Non-verbal influences can include such factors as facial expression, eye contact, body language and gestures.

- **Ascribed attributes:** are those attributes that we often attach to people when we first meet or prior to an initial meeting. They are usually based on their status or occupation.

ACTIVITY 12

Consider the film actor Richard Gere. How tall do you think he is?

The actual height of Richard Gere is irrelevant. As a result of his reputation portrayed in the cinema and his social life you would probably imagine him to be very tall, therefore our perception of his height is influenced by his status.

PERSON MAKING THE PERCEPTION
In perceiving others, we can experience various general and personality influences:

- **Self-concept** can be a major influence on how we perceive others. Accurate perceptions of ourselves can result in an ability to better perceive others accurately. Insecure people can often have inaccurate perceptions of other people.

- **Cognitive structure** is a means of using multiple traits in describing or encoding others. Frauenfelder (1974) has maintained that people who make more complex assessments of others also tend to be more positive in their evaluations. These people should also form more accurate perceptions of the strengths and weaknesses of others.

- **Response salience** is linked to the halo effect, based on perception of perceived noticeable factors. It is specifically concerned with those factors in the environment such as age, sex and abilities.

- **Prior experience** concerns how our historical experience of a person can influence our perception of that person's current abilities, traits or behaviours.

THE SITUATION

The environment in which we exist can influence our perceptions. Two aspects of this are:

- **Organisational role** concerns the person in an organisation who makes the perception. It has long been proposed (Dearborn & Simon, 1958) that the position we occupy in an organisation can influence our perceptions of work and the people at work. It is also the case that personality theories overlap with observations on perception in our understanding of social interaction as there is a core assumption of the cognitive social approach to personality. This provides evidence for the demonstration and usefulness of encoding strategies to represent events.

- **Location** of an event influences our interpretation of the behaviour of people surrounding the event. For example, singing, whistling and talking loudly may be acceptable behaviour in a staff common room, but not in someone's office or at a meeting.

2.6 Causal attribution

This area has been greatly influenced by Jones and Davis (1965) and Kelley (1973). In everyday relationships, judgements of a person's actions depends on the perceived intentions of the person carrying out those actions who is sometimes referred to as the actor or actress. Whether the actions seem deliberate or accidental can be important in the perception. All of us, as the observers of such actions, inquire into the causes of such behaviour. For example, why was my supervisor so off-hand with me? why did my colleague ignore me? The answers to these questions concern their attribution or cause of behaviour, and they influence our understanding and interpretation of the interaction. The meaning of each of these acts and hence their impact depends on the observer's inferences about the intentions motivating them.

Kelley's theory of causal attribution addresses why people behave in particular ways by considering three major factors:

- **Consensus** is the extent to which other people behave the same way as the actor or actress.

● **Consistency** is the extent to which the actor or actress behaves in the same way in the same situation at other times

● **Distinctiveness** is the extent to which the actor or actress behaves in the same way in other situations which will affect how a person interprets the behaviour of another person in such an interaction.

These factors can all vary in degree, and in Kelley's model, how these factors are combined and exhibited in any particular behaviour, is what leads us to decide whether the person's behaviour is attributable to internal causes or to reasons external to them. This can be represented diagrammatically (Figure 4).

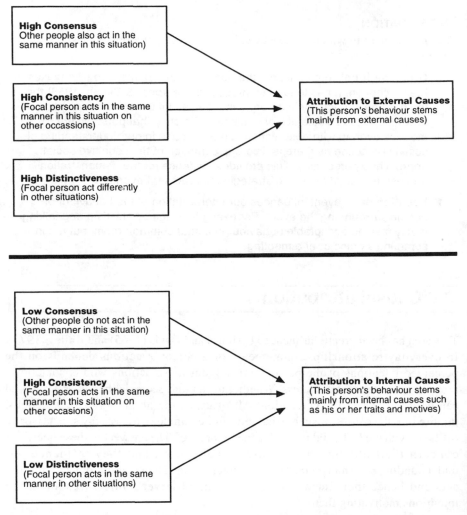

Figure 4: Kelley's theory of causal attribution

ACTIVITY 13

A colleague continues to behave in a noisy obnoxious fashion, disrupting the concentration of others. If you can understand the causes of this behaviour, you may be able to change it. Your colleague is the only one behaving in this way, the colleague frequently behaves in this way and you have observed that your colleague behaves in this way in other situations.

Use the representations in Figure 4 to identify whether the factors causing your colleague's behaviour are internal or external.

Your colleague is the only one behaving in this way (low consensus), the colleague frequently behaves in this way (high consistency) and you have observed your colleague behaving in this way in other situations (low distinctiveness). A logical conclusion would be that internal factors are causing the behaviour.

In contrast to this, you could have someone acting bloody mindedly in a situation of external pressure (for example, a redundancy threat) where others have acted similarly under the same pressures. This would show high distinctiveness, and high consensus.

REVIEW ACTIVITY 2

Suggested time: 30 minutes.

Read the extract from the article 'Counterfeits, Conceits and Corpses: The Failure of the Mask in Corporate Performance' written by Hopfl on the implications for organisational behaviour. This is Item 6.2 in the Resource section.

What aspects of perception, that we have looked at in this section, can you see in operation or being discussed, implicitly or explicitly, in the extract. You may consider that these will include social perception, perceptual selection, organisation and interpretation.

Summary

In this section, you have looked at a range of processes and factors involved in the perception of our environment and in social perception. You have seen how we select and organise stimuli received from the environment so as to provide meaningful interpretations of our experience. You have observed by your own practice, the process of filtering out sensory stimuli and noted how learning, motivation and personality affect which stimuli we focus upon and how we interpret them. You have noted also how external factors in the stimuli themselves affect how things are perceived – their size, intensity, motion etc – and you have used the four processes involved in perceptual grouping in a practical example. You have reviewed a number of possible perceptual errors and noted the relevance of these to work place situations.

You noted how personality factors may affect social perceptions and the consequent relevance of personality theory to the field of perception. The appearance of a person, the way they communicate and their ascribed attributes can all play a part in perceptions of them, and the personality of the perceiver can affect this also. Finally, we looked at a model about how we decide if the causes of a person's behaviour are internal or external to them, and you evaluated a practical example in terms of that theory.

SECTION 3

Development of Selection Procedures

Introduction

Selection procedures in organisations can range from simple ad hoc and informal approaches to extremely structured procedures which attempt to seek out particular specifications or traits in people and also attempt to rationalise the whole process. In this section, you examine some of these procedures and how they may contribute to selection processes in organisations.

The **selection procedure** can be broken down into four general stages:

● **Job analysis** is the systematic collection of information about the job and the person required to fill the job. The process can be divided into two parts, a job description which describes the job and an employee description or personnel specification, which outlines the characteristics of the person for the job.

- **Shortlisting** occurs after advertising, the process attempts to meet some of the requirements of the employee description.

- The **interview,** here the interviewers should be familiar with the job description and employee description. Interviewers should consider the environment, interviewee reception, the questions asked, listen attentively, respond to interviewee's questions, plan summaries and undertake assessment and fair comparison of candidates.

- **Assessment** of applicants can occur using judgement, ranking or grading techniques, the latter two presenting a more rational approach. The assessment can also incorporate testing for personality, aptitude and other traits.

3.1 Job analysis

This is the process by which the facts of each job are systematically identified and recorded. Information is obtained containing the tasks, procedures, responsibilities and personal requirements. In job analysis terms, a job is a collection of tasks which constitute the work of one person. A task is a major element of work intended to achieve a particular result.

Job analysis is a multi-purpose technique; it has other uses in addition to recruitment and selection. It can be used in connection with training and development, organisation and manpower planning, performance appraisal and job evaluation. In recruitment and selection, it is used to produce:

- **Job description** – This basic document provides an outline of the activities and responsibilities involved. It can include the job title, department, section salary, responsibilities (staff, money, machines or equipment), main duties and contacts. It could also include any special demands or unusual circumstances.

- **Employee description or personnel specification** – This document describes the main characteristics needed to perform the job at the required standard. The number of specifications can be quite large, in essence, there is a need to consider areas such as general impression, motivation, education, experience and adjustment, to various factors.

The employee description must be derived from the job description to produce complementarity. Additionally, it should be over-rigid in personality requirements as they are difficult to define. The human qualifications that could be included here are education, experience, training, judgement, initiative, physical skills and emotional and physical characteristics.

3.2 Shortlisting

Shortlisting selects the best candidates for interview according to the job and employee descriptions, avoiding discrimination. Procedures are probably laid down in the organisation's human resource guidelines. This is also probably the first opportunity to look at references for the candidate. It is usually the case that these may be distorted as the candidate would have chosen and briefed a referee. A team approach is usually favoured when shortlisting. Rational approaches can be used and you see an example of two of these approaches later in this section.

3.3 The interview

QUESTIONS
In all interviews there should be an allowance for a candidate to provide an input. You can formulate questions in various ways to include the following:

- **Open questions** could take the form of 'tell me a little bit about . . .' or 'what do you think of . . .' to give the candidate a chance to open up. On the other hand, closed questions usually require a prescribed answer and limit a candidate's response. The indirect question could be followed with a more probing question to develop the interview.

- **Leads** to keep the interview continuous, and avoid silence; you should have lists of items for discussion on specific topics.

- **Catch questions** introduce bias into interviews or can be used to further examine a candidate's expertise or performance under pressure. These could take the form of on-the-spot assessments. Unless they are absolutely necessary and to be fair, you should try to avoid questions which could upset the candidate or make them feel uneasy. Structured testing, at a different time in a controlled way, can be used as an alternative to on-the-spot assessments.

COMMON FAULTS AND PROBLEMS
Examples of faults and problems that can lead to false perceptions, a lack of reliability and which may invalidate interviews are:

- confused objectives – interviewer and interviewee need to be clear on what they want to achieve
- inadequate planning
- non-systematic approach has not established guidelines and procedures
- lack of coverage indicates bad planning and lack of relevant questions
- failure to establish rapport
- stereotypical pre-conceived ideas in the interviewer result in leading questions
- prejudice due to appearance, race or disability

- halo effect rating candidates high or low on a range of characteristics due to one striking characteristic
- negative information
- favourite catch questions
- over-talkative interviewer
- mannerisms can distract an interviewee.

To avoid such problems, most organisations now require staff to attend interview training courses before being allowed to sit on interview panels.

3.4 Assessment of applicant

GRADING APPROACH

In order to make the interview meaningful and to make a decision about the applicant, you can categorise interview requirements under the following five headings:

- **general impression** (GI)
- **motivation** (Mo)
- **education** (Ed)
- **experience** (Ex)
- **adjustment** (Ad).

This is known as the five-fold grading system advocated by Fraser (1958). The majority of areas within the system are self-explanatory with the possible exception of adjustment. This is the degree of pressure, pace and intricacy involved in a job. The assessment in the interview gauges how a candidate may respond to these factors.

With this set of grading criteria, an interviewer can compare candidates against each other and against the employee description. This can aid in selecting the most appropriate candidate for the job. An interviewer can place each of the five areas into a diagrammatic form of grading as shown in Figure 5.

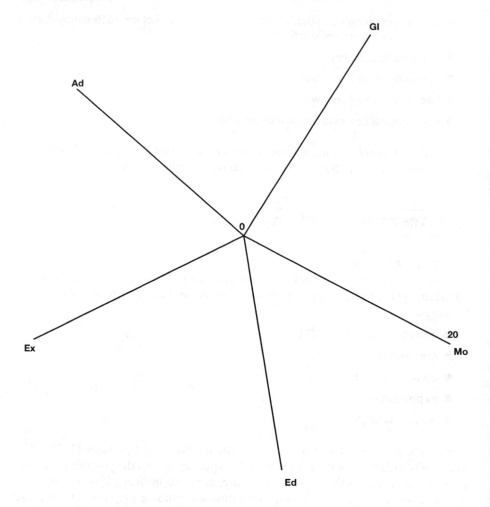

Figure 5: Pentagonal peg

Figure 5 shows the pentagonal peg which was developed by Fraser. Each point is represented by a line on a scale 0-20. If we consider motivation as an example, low marks indicate low motivation and high marks indicate high motivation. A score of 10 could represent average motivation. This rationalises what is essentially a subjective approach. The other factors can be considered in the same way.

Consider the following scenario:

Candidate 1 has received the following scores in an interview:

General impression	10
Motivation	12
Education	18
Experience	6
Adjustment	15

A pentagonal peg reflecting the candidate's grades can be demonstrated by linking the scores with lines as shown in Figure 6.

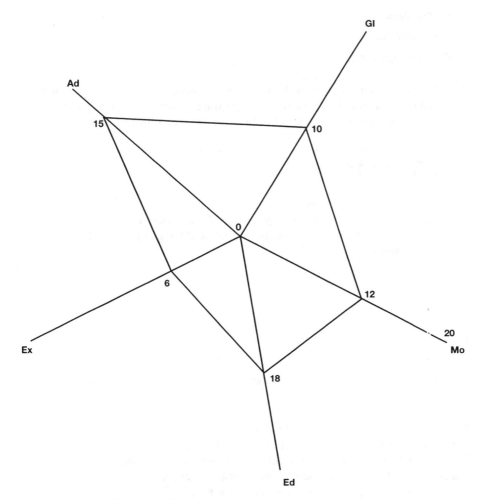

Figure 6: Pentagonal peg representing grading

This process can be followed for each successive candidate, producing a separate diagram for each candidate or all candidates can be superimposed on the same diagram for comparison.

Relying on memory is not usually sufficient for these processes, and in terms of rationalising a process and justifying selections you may make. This approach could serve as a visual analysis tool and record for a set of competing candidates.

Another set of considerations provides for a person specification when interviewing. This is advocated by Rodger (1951) and is known as the seven-point plan it includes the following:

- **physical make-up**
- **attainments**

- general intelligence
- special aptitudes
- interests
- disposition
- circumstances.

These focus areas are normally the major areas addressed when organisations get involved in recruiting. Both the five-fold grading system and seven-point plan are concerned with aspects of personality that you have examined previously.

ACTIVITY 14

Consider that someone you know is applying for a job as a police officer. Use Rodger's seven-point plan to prepare a brief person/employee specification, asking for desired candidate qualities which will be necessary to do the job's specified duties.

You should be able to identify with the role of a police officer and you might list the following specifications:

Physical make-up: fit, agile, no disabilities (mental or physical)
Attainments: good academic level (at least 'A' levels)
General intelligence: high, demonstrating resourcefulness and common sense
Special aptitudes: even-tempered, good judge of people, decisive
Interests: sporting, athletic, activity and team-based
Disposition: warm, friendly, detached and objective
Circumstances: stable personally and financially.

MULTI-ATTRIBUTE APPROACH

This approach is a complementary or alternative process to using the pentagonal peg. It can arise when considering selection with multiple attributes, you as the decision maker, may need to examine one or more of several alternative attributes. The attributes you need to consider may be quantifiable, qualitative, or both. It is also possible that representative values may vary widely or may be vague or fuzzy.

Several methods meet the eventualities that can arise in multi-attribute approaches. They stem from the need to present attributes in a form in which they can be evaluated as part of the process in a coherent and uniform way. They include contests, scoring, ranking, screening and evaluating fuzzy sets of information.

In observing two of the most commonly used multi-attribute methods, consider the following scenario:

The evaluation of candidates for the post of marketing analyst.

These evaluations are to be based on curriculum vitae and job interview evaluation. The attributes on which you will observe this evaluation are:

A1 = Salary
A2 = Highest qualification
A3 = Personality
A4 = Competitor knowledge
A5 = Experience (years)

The relevant sections of the curriculum vitae (cv) of five candidates for the post are given in Table 1. You will observe how to extract the required attributes and place them in a suitable evaluation table, known as a tableau.

Additionally attributes, not apparent from a curriculum vitae (personality and competitor knowledge), have been supplied at the end of each cv.

With a complete evaluation tableau, you can apply a range of multi-attribute approaches in turn, using suitable methods. Using this approach, you can familiarise yourself with the two popular methods.

Name:	Adams	Brown	Collins	Davey	Edwards
Age:	27	28	28	30	31
Salary required (pa):	£30,000	£36,000	£29,000	£33,000	£34,000
Highest qualification:	'A' levels	MBA	BA(Hons)	HND	BA(Hons)
Notes from interview:					
Personality:	Bad	Excellent	V.good	Good	V.good
Competitor Knowledge:	Excellent	V.good	Excellent	Good	V.good
Relevant experience (years):	8	4	5	6	5

Table 1: Extracts from Curriculum Vitae

Multi-attribute Evaluation

There are various multi-attribute methods that can be used to evaluate the optimal candidate. The two methods you will study are the **ranking method** proposed by Borda and a method known as **exclusionary screening**. Giocoechea et al (1982).

Remember the attributes you need to consider for the candidates are:

A1 = Salary
A2 = Highest qualification
A3 = Personality
A4 = Competitor knowledge
A5 = Experience (years)

RANKING

It is possible to transform the qualitative ratings to scores. The usual procedure is to rank the qualitative attributes, such that the highest rank is the best. Generally in converting to scores, it is usual to have scores ranked such that the highest score is the most preferred attribute, this facilitates a consistent analytical approach for a range of methods. There are anomalies that can arise when applying this rule. In the case of salary (**A1**), the highest amount is not the preferred amount for an employer. There is an approach that can overcome this:

Method

The highest value for a row can be identified (in this case £36,000) and the absolute difference (ignoring sign) with every value in the row is determined as follows:

A1	£30,000	£36,000	£29,000	£33,000	£34,000

can be transformed to:

A1	6	0	7	3	2

Using this scores transformation procedure results in the highest value becoming the lowest and vice versa. The rule of highest is the best has now been applied.

With the above ranking and scores transformation considered, the remaining scores can be assigned according to the following procedures:

A2 = Qualifications: MBA (4), BA(Hons) (3), HND (2), 'A' level (1)
A3 = Personality: excellent (4), v. good (3), good (2), bad (1).
A4 = Competitor knowledge: (as for **A3**)
A5 = Experience: years already ranked, but you may need to change the sign, depending on preference, as length of experience could be a disadvantage.

The scores matrix for the data would now read:

	Adams	Brown	Collins	Davey	Edwards
A1	6	0	7	3	2
A2	1	4	3	2	3
A3	1	4	3	2	3
A4	4	3	4	2	3
A5	8	4	5	6	5

With a scores matrix constructed, you are now in a position to undertake an analysis which is, in formal terms, **rational.**

Various rational methods are available and the choice of method may be influenced by your particular objective. The Borda method, derived in the late-nineteenth century, simply totals each attribute score – in this case for each candidate.

	Adams	Brown	Collins	Davey	Edwards
Totals	20	15	22	15	16

As the procedure of highest is best has been applied, best overall candidate would have highest score, in this case, Collins with a rankings score of 22.

EXCLUSIONARY SCREENING

This approach involves three steps, examining attributes using a set of exclusion criteria. In this method, conversion to scores is not usually required.

- **Step 1** – The minimum acceptable scores or attribute levels are specified.

- **Step 2** – Identify acceptable or unacceptable qualitative actions for each attribute, these can also be assigned by assessment or scores.

- **Step 3** – Acceptable actions can be placed in an optimal set, the highest number of acceptable actions is selected as the best alternative.

Establishing criteria can be the result of a series of evaluations which are themselves **decision-making criteria** (formulated by groups, for example) and the results of such an input are usually reflected in the subsequent ease of analysis.

Acceptable sets for the attributes are suggested as follows:

Attribute	Acceptable levels
A1 =	£32,000 (at most)
A2 =	BA(Hons) (at least)
A3 =	V. good (at least)
A4 =	V. good (at least)
A5 =	6 years (at least)

ACTIVITY 15

Using the extracts from curriculum vitae (Table 1) and the suggested exclusion criteria, assess which candidate has the largest number of acceptable criteria.

Attribute	Acceptable level	Suggested sets acceptable
A1 =	£32,000	
A2 =	BA(Hons)	
A3 =	V. good	
A4 =	V. good	
A5 =	6 years	

You can lay out your answer as below. Candidate C (Collins) has satisfied four criteria (more than any other), and is therefore the most acceptable candidate.

Attribute	Acceptable level	Sets acceptable
A1 =	£32,000	A, C
A2 =	BA(Hons)	B, C, E
A3 =	V. good	B, C, E
A4 =	V. good	A, B, C, E
A5 =	6 years	A, D

Using specified criteria has eliminated the least desirable candidates.

3.5 Assessing personality

The assessment of personality can occur prior to the selection process, during the process or after appointment as part of an ongoing evaluation or appraisal system in an organisation.

This type of assessment is considered as a complex area and is subject to many disagreements. Most of us believe that we are good at accurately establishing the personality of other people, when evidence shows that we are not as good as we believe.

Questionnaires have been developed, largely based on the beliefs of what personality means to the person developing the questionnaire. Two of the most frequently used are:

● **Eysenck Personality Inventory** (EPI) – The aim of the formal process is to assess the dominant traits of people who fall into one of four main quadrants (Figure 7). These result from a mixture of two of the main dimensions of personality:

  – stable introvert

  – stable extrovert

– anxious introvert

– anxious extrovert

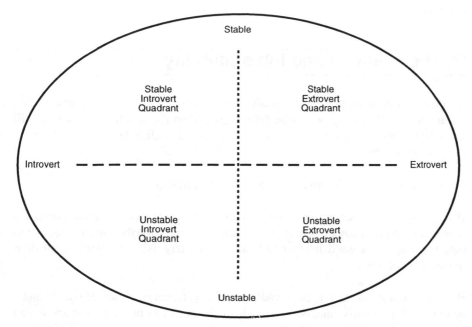

Figure 7: Dimensions of personality indicating dominant trait quadrants

Many of us do not fall clearly into any of these four quadrants, but may fall partially into one.

● **16 personality factor questionnaire** (16PF) (Cattell) – this questionnaire is designed to assess sixteen factors concerned with personality:

reserved	outgoing
less intelligent	more intelligent
affected by feelings	emotionally stable
submissive	dominant
serious	happy-go-lucky
expedient	conscientious
timid	venturesome
tough-minded	sensitive
trusting	suspicious
practical	imaginative
forthright	shrewd
self-assured	apprehensive
conservative	experimenting
group dependent	self-sufficient
uncontrolled	controlled

The ideas of Eysenck and Cattell have formed the basis for many personality tests. In this unit, you are presented with an over-simplified view to highlight the ideas behind assessing personality for selection. Details of these, and other tests are examined in the next section.

3.6 Personality and job suitability

If you consider what you have already read on personality, and look at Cattell's statement that 'Personality may be defined as that which will tell what a man will do, when placed in a given situation', you should realise how useful it can to measure personality.

Let us consider the following scenarios to highlight this:

If we analyse the occupation of a bank clerk, we realise that certain qualities are required for a good bank clerk. He or she must be scrupulously honest, attentive to detail, calm, and a good listener as bank clients may ask for advice about their monetary problems.

By contrast, a good sales person would require different qualities. He or she must be extrovert, persuasive and persistent. He or she must be optimistic and possess an unshakeable belief in themselves. We can well imagine that, if the bank clerk and the sales person changed places, they might both become completely frustrated.

We can see that personality tests, as well as aptitude tests, can be useful in career guidance. These tests are used to assess personality, aptitude and other traits and can be incorporated into a grading system or multi-attribute approach to further enhance the selection process.

A power station operative may have the necessary manual skill and succeed on a test for power station operatives but has he also the necessary personality characteristics to submit to a somewhat tedious routine day in and day out for the next 40 years?

In selection procedures, the application of aptitude tests and personality tests are attempts to substitute a scientific system or a system of trial and error. Organisations hold these tests at selection to increase the probability of selecting the correct person for a job.

If you would be allowed to try a job, to see if you like it, without any real guidance, much time and money would be wasted. People frequently change their jobs, and employers are forced to put themselves to the trouble and expense of training someone else.

Consider this statement: 'We are not, of course, saying that every individual within a certain personality type is exactly like every other individual within the same type, however there are a number of predictable characteristic reactions to situations within each type. Not only will the unstable introvert act differently in a given situation from the unstable extrovert, they will also act differently from the stable introvert. Sub-dividing both extroversion and introversion into stable and unstable, and both into characteristic reactions in specific circumstances, we are all the time seeking more and more precise information. To do this, we require more and more sophisticated tests' (extracted from Schofield, 1972).

From this, you can see that not only is some indication of personal occupational interest areas necessary for useful vocational guidance, but also some indication of where an individual lies on these two main dimensions of personality. This type of information, plus a measure of general intellectual ability, form the basis of sound guidance since they give a more comprehensive and rounded picture. Whilst guidance is never absolute, it seems reasonable that sounder judgements will be made if more information is available to those involved.

3.7 Management and candidate fit

One of the traditional philosophies surrounding the design of jobs is based on scientific management ideas, using rational economic man assumptions. The **job-centred philosophy** suggests that individual jobs should be specified by management, independent from particular job holders, to meet the goals of the organisation. Attached to these are the customary approaches of human resource departments which have vacancies within organisations – job analysis, shortlisting, interviewing, and assessment of applicants to match physical and psychological characteristics. With these approaches, the person is effectively fitted to the job. There is a view that this philosophy is too narrow in matching people to work, as it is purely job-centred. There may well be a need for different philosophies based on technological and social planning, which could cover a whole range of social, political and technological values. Some of these areas have found support in recent legislation, such as the race relations act and sex discrimination act.

Any push for the view expressed above will be met by resistance from some organisations due to the possible lack of concern for organisational objectives of profit and survival. There is perhaps, now, favour given to a middle ground approach, a **person-centred philosophy,** which recognises both the organisational and individual needs. In this approach, you would be selected for employment based on wider considerations than for one specific job. Instead the characteristics required would be flexible in order that they could be modified to suit or re-designed to accommodate the abilities, development and needs of the individual. This is perhaps a response to the changing educational, technological and social requirements of individuals.

'This supports the human relations movement, along with organisational theorists and behavioural scientists reacting against scientific management by advocating management practices based on a recognition of the importance of human psychological and social needs' (Torrington & Chapman, 1983).

An example of this approach is one adopted by some multi-national companies and is known as a **curve scheme**. Here exceptional graduates are usually employed by an organisation and placed on a planned career path, undertaking a variety of roles for short periods of time in order that they might develop and follow a path to management very quickly.

REVIEW ACTIVITY 3

Suggested time: 30 minutes.

Case Study – Treyt NHS Psychiatric Trust

Treyt NHS Trust Services is a large health and psychiatric service for a northern region in the UK. Its psychiatric service provides support in the community, for hospitalised patients and forensic patients, those that are capable of or have committed gross criminal acts. The psychiatric service in the trust has the following senior management structure:

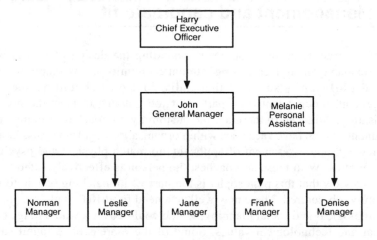

Figure 8: Treyt NHS Psychiatrist Trust

Harry is the chief executive officer, he is a qualified psychiatric nurse and general nurse (RMN and RGN) with 28 years' experience in the national health service (NHS) and two years' experience in the newly formed NHS trust.

John is the general manager for medium secure provision in the trust. He is 36 years of age, RMN qualified with a first degree in health management and an MBA. He has a personal assistant, Melanie who is 45 years old. His responsibilities include management of the psychiatric services within the trust, with a business emphasis. He is not a member of the trust board, but interacts with the following board members: chief executive, medical director, nursing director, information director, marketing director, estates director, quality director and human resource development director.

John has occupied the general manager's post for two years, during which time he has established the psychiatric services as a trust (as it was formerly NHS controlled). He has overseen the introduction of new, business-like services, which can also be 'sold' to other trusts. John has five managers for each of the different areas of the psychiatric service. All NHS trust management and senior management staff who interact with John consider him to be a competent and successful manager. This success has been complemented through his interaction with local authorities, the police, the press and the media (an essential part of his job).

A personality assessment of John places him in the stable extrovert quadrant of the personality dimension grid.

There are five managers of the different provisions within this area of the trust, who all report directly to John. These are:

Norman is 38 years of age. He has been a manager for 5 years and is due to complete his health service management degree at the end of the year. He is currently diploma qualified. Norman manages the sections service and John places a lot of trust in him. He is easy going and sociable and has demonstrated good leadership qualities. His responsibilities include management of three acute wards, some special care services, community services and five other hospital sections. He currently earns £27,000 per annum and would only consider a new role for an increase of £5,000.

Leslie is 33 years of age. He has been a manager for two years and has a diploma in health service management. He manages three community health centres and the psychology section. John has spent a lot of time guiding Leslie in management practices. Leslie is quite impulsive and excitable and has demonstrated some aggression when dealing with staff. He currently earns £25,000 per annum and if he were to seek promotion he would request a salary increase of £5,000.

Jane is 30 years of age and has held her post for four years. She is bright and academically very good, she has a degree in psychology and is currently studying for a masters' degree in human resource management. She has responsibility for day services, the physiotherapy ward, occupational therapy and community rehabilitation. Jane is single-minded, excitable and touchy, and although well qualified has experienced difficulties with subordinate staff, resulting in disciplinary action against some of them. Jane earns £22,000 per annum, she would welcome a move from her current position and would probably look for a salary increase of £4,000 per annum.

Frank is head of psychiatric nursing and the professional leader. He is 40 years of age and holds a degree in sociology and a masters' degree in health care ethics. He is in charge of eight nursing wards. He possesses a calm manner, is controlled and thoroughly reliable. He earns £30,000 per annum and he is happy in his work. He would not really like a more senior role and would only consider one for a substantial increase in salary of the order of £6,000 per annum.

Denise is the business manager. She is 45 years of age, holding a first degree in English literature and a master of philosophy degree by research. Her salary is £31,000. She has been in the post for five years and is responsible for administration, medical employment, five community teams and transcultural services. Denise is ambitious, shrewd, talkative and a natural leader. If promotion was possible, Denise would insist on a salary increase of at least £6,000 per annum.

John's success as a general manager has resulted in him being 'head-hunted' for a position on a trust board in a different region. He is due to resign in the near future.

Harry, the chief executive of the trust, has talked with John about a replacement. Harry intends to interview all five managers, in the first instance, for John's job and, if none of the internal candidates are suitable, he will seek an external appointment.

Harry intends to consider five major attributes in the appointment of John's replacement, they include: salary (which should not exceed £35,000) and relevant experience (which should be no less than four years at management level). The others include academic qualifications, which should be at least a first degree, a high level of competence in their previous work and preferred candidates should demonstrate a range of personality traits that show a tendency towards a stable extrovert.

Question 1

Construct a screening table for the managers, based on the following screening criteria and attribute labels:

A1 = Salary required (no more than £35,000)
A2 = Experience required (at least four years in management)
A3 = Qualifications required (first degree at least)
A4 = Competence level (at least good)
A5 = Personality (extrovert and stable)

Your table should highlight the candidate who would be most suitable for the post of general manager, based on the screening criteria specified.

Requirement 2

Consider that all internal candidates have been unsuccessful. Construct a person specification for the general manager position. As a guide, use

Rodger's seven-point plan. In this exercise, comment on the requirements of each area under two headings, essential and desirable, as follows:

	Essential	*Desirable*
Physical make-up		
Attainments		
General intelligence		
Special aptitudes		
Interests		
Disposition		
Circumstances		

Summary

In this section, you have been introduced to methods of selection employed by some organisations, you examined approaches to person-specification, and you examined some rational approaches to selecting candidates for jobs. Finally, you observed some approaches to assessing and assigning personality to people in organisations.

SECTION 4

Psychometrics: Traits, Aptitudes and Function

Introduction

So far in this unit, you have examined historical theories of personality, the dimensions of personality, the processes of perception and the development of selection methods. Assessment and the facilities of quantifying personality, perception and attitude can provide useful inputs to selection, and when people are already employed, through job assessment and appraisal. In this section, you look at the procedures and processes surrounding testing for personality traits and some aspects of perception, aptitude and intelligence.

4.1 Psychometrics

Psychometrics is defined as ' . . . pertaining to the measurement of that which is psychological. Hence: pertaining to mental testing in any of its facets, including assessment of its personality, evaluation of its intelligence, determining aptitudes etc.' (Reber, 1985, *Dictionary of Psychology,* Penguin)

The use of tests in selection is increasing and the range of tests available includes those to measure personality, intelligence, ability, aptitude, potential for training and values. In the UK, there are approximately 700 different types of test in use. In the UK, testing within or on behalf of organisations is usually undertaken by occupational psychologists, psychologists or people who have obtained a qualification in administering tests, which has been approved by the British Psychological Society. Other options existing for organisations include:

- employing psychologists or qualified consultants, as and when the need arises

- sending staff to qualified people for testing and confidential reports

- employing consultants to devise tailor-made tests for an organisation and training employees of the organisation to interpret the results

- buying ready prepared tests from agencies and sending results back to them for interpretation.

Intelligence tests give us an overall indication of mental capacity. However, early pioneers in this area were unclear about the concept of intelligence and the question of 'what is intelligence?' is still with us today. In the late-nineteenth century, Galton (1869) originated the subject of psychometrics. He investigated models and procedures, initially for intelligence measuring and developed this into areas of visual, auditory and other psychophysical variables. He also explored the idea of using the normal distribution curve as a model for the distribution of test scores.

We do not undertake a detailed examination of intelligence tests in this unit, but it is worth noting in passing that acceptance of the results of such tests can be problematic due to:

- many variables that contribute to intelligence

- societal differences in responses

- test bias

- debated moral validity of tests

- inherent limitations of tests

- ethics surrounding testing.

In the early part of the twentieth century, Spearman continued Galton's developments in mathematical areas such as chi-square tests, correlation and more complex correlation matrices to lay down the foundations of factor analysis, the method which was to be used by Cattell for determining source traits and which we look at later in this section.

Essentially, there are two models of psychometrics:

- **function** is concerned with occupational and educational testing, particularly the school, college and university examination systems
- **trait** is concerned with biological variation in personality and aptitude.

ACTIVITY 16

We might be exposed to the following tests. Classify them into function, trait, or a mixture of both models.

1 Civil Service entrance examinations

2 GCSE examinations

3 RAF flight assessment tests

4 Police initial recruitment test (PIR)

5 Police superintendent examinations (from chief inspector)

---

1   Function. These examinations seek to assess abilities in language, mathematics, logic and general knowledge.

2   Function. The GCSE system is a classic example of educational testing.

3   Mixture. Both academic and trait models would be used in terms of assessing a minimum knowledge base. Also abilities to respond under pressure and to particular problems would need to be assessed in terms of traits.

4   Function. A common misconception is that traits and personality are assessed on police entrance examinations. This is not the case as their general level of education is assessed through a series of 360 questions.

5   Mixture. At higher levels of the police force, in parallel with many other organisations, there is a need to assess certain aptitudes and personality traits. Police forces in the UK seek specialist help in constructing psychometric tests at this level as aids to their selection procedures.

We have dealt with theories supporting various traits, before continuing with psychometrics, we need to examine some concepts of aptitude:

APTITUDE

Aptitude tests give a measure of the potential of any of us to develop in specific or general ways. Aptitude concerns our abilities before we are subjected to training in a specific task. Therefore, aptitude depends on the abilities we develop through heredity and growth, and the extent to which these abilities can be improved through exercise and experience in general.

Aptitude tests are designed so that certain types of experience that we may gain do not influence the scores we attain. Intelligence tests, for example, are aptitude tests in the sense that education and experience have little or no effect on our scores.

4.2 Testing for traits

Psychometric tests were devised to measure traits which represented biological variation in personality or aptitude. Scores are used as a measure, and in general scoring for function or trait is based on a fundamental theorem of true scores.

FORMULATING AND SCORING TESTS

Most tests are composed of **items.** Items are questions initiating a response which can be rated, ranked or scored. These items can be linked to knowledge or persons:

- **knowledge** questions measure ability, aptitude or achievement, examples include educational and intelligence tests

- **person** questions measure personality, mood or attitude.

Knowledge questions usually elicit an empirical answer, where this may be known or not known. This could be regarded as a uni-dimensional approach. Person-based questions can indicate degree and range, in terms of scores or ranks:

- **True scores** consist inherently of two component parts, a subject's actual score, which is termed a true score (T) and some error of measurement (E). An observed score (X) links the two:

$$X = T + E$$

An actual score on its own has no value and therefore we require knowledge of the error term to gauge an observed score.

REFERENCING

Two types of referencing are considered in psychometric testing:

- **Norm referencing** notes your responses to a test and interprets them in terms of an average. This is usually with reference to a population. It uses the performance of a whole group of individuals as the standard against which individuals are judged.

- **Criterion referencing** measures your performance against some outside criterion of job effectiveness, for example, persuasiveness. Not only will this indicate how useful, say, personality questionnaires could be in predicting future job performance, but also which scales should be taken most notice of.

ACTIVITY 17

Which of the following assessments do you think are norm referenced or criterion referenced?

1 GCSE examinations

2 Undergraduate assessments

---

1 GCSE exams are norm referenced. The population of students is considered and the grading system ranges from A to F. Essentially, performances are compared against each other.

2 Undergraduate assessments are usually criterion referenced and aim to assess whether a set of learning outcomes has been achieved.

STANDARDISATION

Once a test has been devised it needs to be standardised.

For example, Kirsty, a recent graduate, undertakes a test as part of the interview for a job. She scores 20 on the introversion/extroversion test. Is this a high or low score?

What we don't know is what the score represents. We could obtain this from norm referenced information given by a general population mean and standard deviation for introversion scores. With this information, we could say how introverted or extroverted Kirsty is.

The score may be criterion related, there may be information in a handbook to inform us of the level of Kirsty's introversion, for example, a raw score of 20 could indicate that she is sober, rigid or anxious, or alternatively stable and introverted.

Usually norm referencing is more common than criterion referencing. If we are using the Eysenck personality inventory, a handbook could provide the mean and standard deviation score for introversion. These norms are given separately for males and females, for different ages and different occupational groups. There are many different types of scores used and therefore use is made of a standard score. This can be used to gauge your dimensional position on an inventory, in relation to a population average.

If you examine the diagrammatic representation of the dimensions of the Eysenck personality inventory (Figure 9), you should be able to relate the concept of norm and/or criterion scores to the assessment of particular personality traits.

Figure 9: Dimensions of personality (after Eysenck (1965))

To interpret the standard scores you should consider that any score can be placed within the first, second or third (outer) ring of the circle. If it is found to be in the first ring you would be in the normal and ambivert range. This represents you being placed within one standard deviation of the population mean score (above or below) and would account for 68% of the population.

If your score lies between the first and second ring, you would have a tendency towards the traits in the outer circle. This represents you being placed between one and two standard deviations from the mean (above or below), and would account for approximately 27% of the population.

If your score lies in the outer ring, you would be firmly placed at the extremes of a normal distribution curve and would be strongly introverted or extroverted, stable or unstable. This represents you being placed between two and three standard deviations from the population mean score (above or below) and would account for approximately 4% of the population.

In applying the normal distribution to this inventory or any other statistical evaluation, estimations with 100% certainty are not undertaken and cannot be achieved due to the nature of the normal curve.

OTHER SCORING METHODS

In addition to using this score approach, other scoring approaches can be used for a variety of situations. We look briefly at four of these:

- **Z scores** are standard scores and refer to a number of standard deviations away from a mean score. A person's raw score can be related, mathematically, to the mean and standard deviation score for the population of interest as follows:

$$\frac{\text{raw score} - \text{mean score}}{\text{standard deviation score}} = Z \text{ score}$$

The Z score can be positive or negative and lies between zero and plus or minus three.

ACTIVITY 18

Steve, our recent graduate, has scored 8 on the introversion/extroversion test. The mean score for the population is 14 with a standard deviation of 3, the Z score is $(8 - 14)/3 = -2$. This would place Steve in the second ring or in the tendency area of the personality inventory. He has been placed in the unstable extrovert quadrant. Indicate some of the traits that the assessment has shown that Steve may exhibit.

Steve may exhibit the following traits, observed on the Eysenck personality inventory: active, optimistic, impulsive, changeable, excitable, aggressive, restless and touchy.

- **Z scores** can also be produced for many other psychometric tests. Not all of these tests can have the Z score related to interpretation as easily as the example you have seen.

- **T scores** are used to avoid difficult interpretations of positive and negative Z scores. To avoid obtaining and interpreting negative numbers, a system has been devised where the Z score is normalised with a mean of 50 and standard deviation of 10. To apply these adjustments we can multiply Z scores by 10 and then add 50:

$$T \text{ score} = (Z \text{ score} \times 10) + 50$$

This always produces a positive value, as Z scores do not usually fall outside the range -4 to +4.

Another score that avoids use of negative values is the stanine score:

- **Stanine scores** transform Z scores to a scale that ranges from one to nine.

Another test is the intelligence quotient (IQ) test which was originally developed by Binet in the early twentieth century. The Stanford-Binet IQ scores have been modified and developed to produce IQ format scores.

- **IQ format scores** are transformed Z scores based on a mean of 100 and a standard deviation of 15 as follows:

$$IQ = (Z \times 15) + 100$$

If you were to receive a standard score of 2 on an IQ test, your IQ would be rated as:

$$IQ = (2 \times 15) + 100 = 130$$

This would place you in the 'very superior' band of between 130 and 140. Persons above 140 are regarded as 'near genius'.

Some IQ tests use different standard deviations, for example, Cattell uses 16 rather than 15 (Cattell 16 PF scale). You have observed the characteristics to which Cattell refers in Section 3.

One of the reasons for the use of T scores, stanine scores and IQ format scores is for ease of presentation to the person that has been tested. They are given a value which is positive and relates to an easier personal interpretation.

ACTIVITY 19

List some traits that may be exhibited by a stable introvert, and an unstable (anxious) introvert.

You could have included the following:

Stable introvert: calm, even-tempered, reliable, controlled, peaceful, thoughtful, careful, passive.

Unstable introvert: quiet, unsociable, reserved, pessimistic, sober, rigid, anxious, moody.

4.3 Other tests

Measurements of typical performance or personality tests have been devised both for research on personality and for use in practical situations. Serving both purposes are a great variety of written tests. The **Minnesota Multiphasic Personality Inventory** (MMPI) is the most thoroughly studied questionnaire and it has become the basis for investigating many personality traits and types. It comprises 550 mini-statements to which you can answer *true, false* or *don't know*. The test contains a set of self-report scales that were initially used to classify psychiatric patients into types on many psychiatric dimensions (Hathaway & McKinley 1942, 1943). The scales can be administered to a range of subject groups, students, organisational employees and psychiatric patients. Items are then examined to determine significant differences of particular diagnostic groups compared to 'normals'. In this way, it gradually becomes possible to devise scales that discriminate different groups of people. The MMPI has been sorted into ten basic scales:

- hypochondriasis
- hysteria
- depression
- psychopathy
- paranoia
- psychoasthenia
- schizophrenia
- hypomania
- masculinity - femininity
- social introversion.

These serve as short descriptions for scales which are further defined by their extensive associations with other indices of psychiatric ratings and correlations obtained through decades of research. They are continuously revised with statistical methods. The scales are, therefore, considered to be empirically validated.

In recent years, projective personality tests such as the **Rorschach** (inkblot) and **Thematic Apperception Test** (TAT) have found widespread use, especially in clinical work. They are also used for perception assessments. These tests are usually structured around a task which is ambiguous. The purpose of the test is usually disguised and you can respond in whatever way you choose. In these tests, the tester presents you with ambiguous stimuli (inkblots or pictures) and asks questions:

- for a Rorschach test, this could be 'what does this remind you of', when shown an inkblot
- for a Thematic Apperception Test, this could be 'can you suggest a story', when shown a picture.

4.4 Factor analysis

There are thousands of trait terms or types of traits and as a result, testers or psychometricians try to group responses from tests into basic clusters. To help with this, a technique known as **factor analysis** can be used. Interpretation of results from this analysis is linked to the five types of trait dimensions that we discussed in Section 1. The analysis is usually undertaken on responses to a questionnaire. It is used to reduce the questionnaire to those questions that are really measuring different personality traits of the respondent. The starting point of the analysis is to obtain a matrix of the correlations between variables, gained from answers to questions. The analysis identifies patterns from correlations. It does not indicate traits directly but offers guidance for the tester about what patterns predominate. A hypothetical matrix can be seen in Figure 10.

	X_1	X_2	X_3	X_4
X_1	1.00	0.85	0.35	0.20
X_2		1.00	0.95	0.15
X_3			1.00	0.75
X_4				1.00

Figure 10: Hypothetical matrix of correlations between variables (Xs)

We can see in the representation of Figure 10 that there is a high correlation between variables X2 (horizontal) and X3 (vertical) of 0.95. This would indicate that they are associated with the same underlying construct or factor, due to this high correlation. You should also observe that correlations of 1 are given for variables of the same type, this is expected and is ignored in a subsequent analysis.

4.5 Information technology

With developments in information technology the whole area of testing has become streamlined, resulting in data banks of questions, items and tests. Tests can now be widely administered on computer with instantaneous analysis leading to automatic reporting and recommendations, in other words, administration. Even the complex method of factor analysis (and other complex statistical methods) can be undertaken rapidly using computer-based approaches. Although interpretation of such applications requires expertise, current information technology developments in areas of 'expert systems' will greatly assist and support psychometric testers and an organisation in applying and using the information it can gain from such tests.

REVIEW ACTIVITY 4

Suggested time: 90 minutes.

Read the article 'Assessment Centre Dimensions, Personality and Aptitudes' by Bronach Crawley et al. This is Item 6.3 in the Resource section.

Comment on, and critically evaluate the approach undertaken by the author. Do you think the aims of this study have been met? How does this reflect on the validity and reliability of findings?

Summary

In this section, you have been introduced to the quantification of traits, aptitudes and intelligence using psychometric tests. You have observed some approaches to the referencing and standardisation of tests and test scores. You have been introduced to a variety of important tests, such as EPI, IQ, MMPI, Rorschach and TAT and have learnt about the recent impact information technology has had on testing. You have investigated some of the historic and current philosophies surrounding test design.

Unit Summary

In this unit, you have been introduced to five approaches to personality which have emphasised the relevance of trait theories and certain personality dimensions. In addition, you have been introduced to the processes of perception and social perception. With both of these psychological areas, you have examined the application and importance of them for people in organisations.

You have seen how personality and perception can play an important part in selection procedures, in contributing to decision making as specific criteria (perhaps being tested), or subjectively (through social interaction, opinion or observation). Selection procedures were examined with influences from the psychological areas, rationality and processes such as job analysis and person specification. The subject of testing was also considered and we concluded with a comment on management and candidate fit.

You examined the development of psychometric testing including the assessment of personality traits, perception, aptitudes and intelligence and its growing importance in organisations, for use in selection and appraisal. We discussed the processes of scoring, referencing and standardisation and observed the dimensions of personality in more detail. We also considered the impact of more sophisticated analysis and information technology in the area of testing.

The inter-relationship of psychology, selection and testing are important when considering people in organisations. It is essential that in considering any one of these areas, we acknowledge that the others play a key role. This fact has been implicit throughout the unit. In order for any one of the areas of psychology, selection and testing to develop there needs to be parallel developments in the two other areas.

References

Allpot, GW (1937) *Personality: A psychological interpretation,* New York: Holt Reinehart and Winston.

Catell, RB (1950) *A systematic theoretical and factual study,* New York: McGraw-Hill.

Catell, RB (1965) *The scientific analysis of personality,* Baltimore: Penguin Books.

Dearborn, D and Simon, H (1958) 'Selective Perception: A Note on the Departmental Identifications of the Executives', *Sociometry,* 21, 140-144.

Erickson, E (1963) *Childhood and Society,* New York: Holt, Reinehart and Winston.

Eysenck, HJ and Eysenck, S. B. G. (1975) *Eysenck Personality Questionnaire (Adult),* London: Hodder and Stoughton, Chigwell Press.

Fraser, JM (1958) *A handbook of employment interviewing,* MacDonald and Evans.

Freud, S (1933) *New Introductory Lectures on Psychoanalysis,* translated by WJH Sproutt, New York: Norton.

Frauenfelder, KJ (1974) 'Cognitive Determinant of Favourability of Impression', *Journal of Social Psychology*, 94, 71-81.

Gatton, F (1869) *Hereditary Genius*, London: Macmillan.

Goicoechea, A Hansen, DR and Duckstein, L (1982) *Multiobjective decision analysis with engineering and business applications*, Wiley.

Hathaway, SR and McKinley, JC (1942) 'A Multiphasic Personality Schedule. (Minnesota): III The Measurement of Symptomatic Depression', *Journal of Psychology*, 14, 73 – 84.

Hathaway, SR and McKinley, JC (1943) *MMPI Manual*, New York: Psychological Corporation.

Jones, EE and Davis, KE (1965) 'From Acts to Dispositions: The Attribution Process in Person Perception', in L Berkowitz (Ed.), *Advances in Experimental Social Psychology* (Vol. 2), New York: Academic Press.

Kelley, HH (1973) 'The Process of Causal Attribution', *American Psychologist,* 28, 107-128.

Kelly, GA (1955) *The psychology of personal constructs*, (Vols 1 and 2), New York: Norton.

Kohut, H (1984) *How does analysis cure?*, Chicago: University of Chicago Press.

Maslow, AH (1968) *Toward a psychology of being*, (2nd edition), New York: Van Nostrand.

Mischel, W (1993) *Introduction to Personality*, fifth edition, New York: Harcourt Brace.

Pavlov, IP (1927) *Conditioned Reflexes*, translated by G V Anrep, London: Oxford University Press.

Rodger, A (1951) *The seven-point plan*, NIIP.

Rogers, CR (1959) *Psychology: a study of a science*, (Vol 3), pp. 184-526, New York: McGraw-Hill.

Schofield, H (1972) *Assessment and Testing An Introduction*, London: Unwin.

Skinner, BF (1953) *Science and Human Behaviour*, New York: Macmillan.

Torrington, D and Chapman, J (1983) *Personnel Management*, second edition, Englewood Cliffs, New Jersey: Prentice-Hall International.

Recommended Reading

Anstey, E (1966) *Psychological Tests*, London: Nelson.

Lyman, H B (1963) *Test Scores and What They Mean*, Englewood Cliffs, New Jersey: Prentice-Hall.

Miller, G A (1975) *Psychology*, Harmondsworth: Penguin.

Rust, R and Golombok, S (1992) *Modern Psychometrics*, London: Routledge.

Warr, P B (ed) (1970) *Thought and Personality*, Harmondsworth: Penguin.

Answers to Review Activities

Review Activity 1

The second sentence of this article 'Very few field studies have examined the relationship between managerial performance and Jungian personality types' is an indication of past relevance and attention paid to this type of study. We could argue that the success of individual managers is not really the aim of organisations, but rather it should be organisational success through good management. To assess individuals when other factors such as customers and the environment contribute to their performance, can be considered as narrow and limited.

Traits that might lend themselves to this type of study could be, on the extrovert side: active, optimistic, aggressive, leader, impulsive; and on the introvert side: careful, controlled, pessimistic and rigid.

There appears to be a contradiction in the three hypotheses which covered a majority of eventualities, but none of the hypotheses were supported. Although any result should not be seen as negative, the results of this research do not really contribute to our knowledge of personality in organisations, rather it seems a weak attempt at supporting 'speculation'.

Review Activity 2

Seeing and hearing play an important part in the audience and actor interaction. Social perception, particularly in the area of location, seems to be particularly important, especially in paragraph one. We can also see examples of both actor and audience perceptions in the form of perception of others, through self-concept and prior experience.

Selection processes play a part in highlighting the effects of learning and personality from both actors and audience. In terms of perceptual organisation, there appears to be a tendency for the actor to exhibit similarity, where the audience is perceived as objects or functions as a common group.

There are numerous errors of perceptual interpretation by the audience: perceived illusion from the audience, stereotyping, projection, expectancy and perceptual defence. It is also possible that the actors demonstrate a range of these as well.

As you can see, just a small illustration of organisations (albeit an analogous situation), in this article, can generate a broad spectrum of observations. You should be aware that social perception and general perceptual processes are complex and require experienced interpretation, however, they are extremely important at various stages of organisational processes that involve people.

Review Activity 3

Question 1
You could construct the multi-attribute acceptable sets tableau, using the initials of each manager as follows:

		Acceptable sets			
A1	N	L	J		
A2	N		J	F	D
A3			J	F	D
A4	N			F	D
A5	N				D

Both Norman and Denise have the largest number of acceptable sets and are highlighted as being the most suitable, equal candidates for the general manager's post, based on the chief executive's criteria. However, don't forget that you could also use the Borda method to arrive at a rational selection.

Question 2
It is quite usual to list essential and desirable person-specifications. A list of minimum requirements follows but you may have gleaned more, or less, from the case outline.

Essential

Physical make-up	fit, good normal health, vision and hearing
Attainments	degree; at least four years' management experience in a hospital
General intelligence	above average
Special aptitudes	ability to interact with senior management, board members, police, media. abilities in report writing and public speaking, negotiating skills
Interests	wide and varied involving people
Disposition	adaptable to pressure, changing circumstances
Circumstances	able to travel, work and attend meetings out of hours

Desirable

Physical make-up	as for essential
Attainments	as for essential
General intelligence	analytical, high IQ
Special aptitudes	as for essential
Interests	knowledge of current affairs, political sensitivity
Disposition	not easily frustrated, open to other views, not argumentative
Circumstances	flexible

There is a tendency to place too much detail against these specifications. However, this plan forms the basis for a formal person-specification.

Review Activity 4

The stated aims of this study are to establish whether particular management competencies are the expression of underlying personal attributes in various types of work situation.

The conclusion within the article is self-critical of the areas examined. Having looked at these areas using the model and methodology on which current assessment centre design is based (job analysis to task areas to dimensions to exercises for the dimensions), the authors conclude from the results of the study that a more appropriate methodology would be to proceed as job analysis to task areas to job sample exercises with content validity. This type of self-critical approach to research is important for progress to be made in a complex field.

In all cases, where propositions or hypotheses need to be supported, findings such as the above (re-examination of method) are important contributions to our development of knowledge in the areas of personality and testing.

The methodological approach in this paper included using the multi-trait-multi-method technique. The results showed that generally there was little evidence of any significant relationships. Correlations for the Personality Questionnaire (PQ) and Myers-Briggs were all very low (less than 0.4), and more significantly the correlations of FIRO-B were lower. The correlations for the aptitude tests were also low (maximum of 0.44). These all indicated low predictive power of the tests and little support to the contention that personal attributes affect the competencies of management performance.

There are similarities here with the article, Item 6.1, you examined in Section 1. The processes and hypotheses, or propositions surrounding the linkage of personality to the work place are complex and difficult to establish. Indeed, they are so closely inter-related that, to ensure their validity and effectiveness, developments in testing will need to be made in parallel with developments in personality studies, and probably vice-versa.

UNIT 7

MOTIVATING THE WORKFORCE

Introduction

Delivering a good performance at work has been shown to be a function of ability, experience, reward and, above all, motivation. We are purposive beings and we continually select goals which are important to us and seek to achieve them. It is this goal-directed activity we call **motivation**. Given the importance of employees as an organisational resource, it is obviously crucial that managers should understand the nature of motivation so that they can better manage those forces, both internal and external to individuals, that lead some to apply only minimal effort to their work tasks while others expend much greater effort and consequently are much more productive.

However, motivation is a very complex subject, influenced by many variables. There is no *one* answer to what motivates people to work well but rather a number of sometimes competing theories, each subject to varying degrees of criticism. Collectively, however, these theories provide a valuable basis for study and discussion and a fund of ideas. Mullins (1993) argues that it is up to managers to judge their relevance and how they might be drawn upon and applied in their particular work situations. Before beginning to explore some of the more important of these theories, however, the first activity will help you to focus on those work-related goals which are important to you.

ACTIVITY 1

What do you want from your job?

When you apply for a permanent appointment, what job or job-related characteristics influence your choice? Several characteristics which have been shown to be important in influencing job choice are:

A	Leisure	–	short working hours and much free time
B	Salary	–	high income
C	Promotion	–	chances for advancement within the organisation
D	Security	–	little danger of being made redundant
E	Conditions	–	pleasant and safe working environment
F	Benefits	–	pension scheme and fringe benefits
G	Trade union	–	active union
H	Fulfilment	–	meaningful/stretching work
I	Training	–	opportunities for training and education
J	Prestige	–	job has high status within the community

Using the grid in Figure 2:

● Work your way down the list, each time comparing pairs of characteristics and entering, in the appropriate square, the letter denoting which of the two characteristics is likely to be the more important to you in influencing your choice of job. In this way, you will ultimately compare each characteristic with every other characteristic. To assist you here, have a look first at the example grid in Figure 1. When comparisons are being made between leisure and salary and the latter is seen to be of more importance, then the appropriate choice box is the one where we have entered B. Where we have placed C relates to comparisons between leisure and promotion, D to comparisons between leisure and salary and so on.

● List in column one, how many times each letter appears in the grid.

● Rank order the characteristics in column two. For example, if 'Training' has appeared the most often then '1' will head the column, and so on

● The final task of this activity, compiling a *group* ranking in column three, should obviously be carried out in small groups. In the process of doing this, you will find it interesting to discuss commonalities and differences and the reasons behind your choices. You can also compile a 'whole class' ranking to get a broader picture of the characteristics that individuals feel are more or less important in terms of job choice.

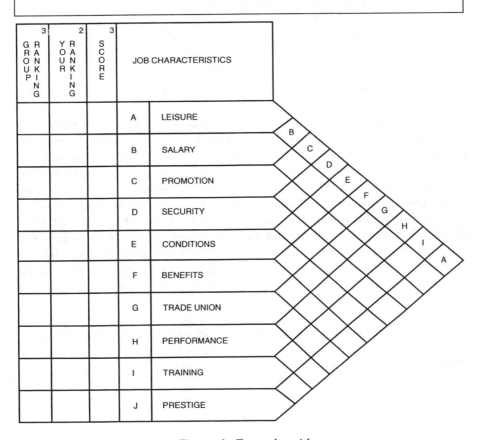

Figure 1: Example grid

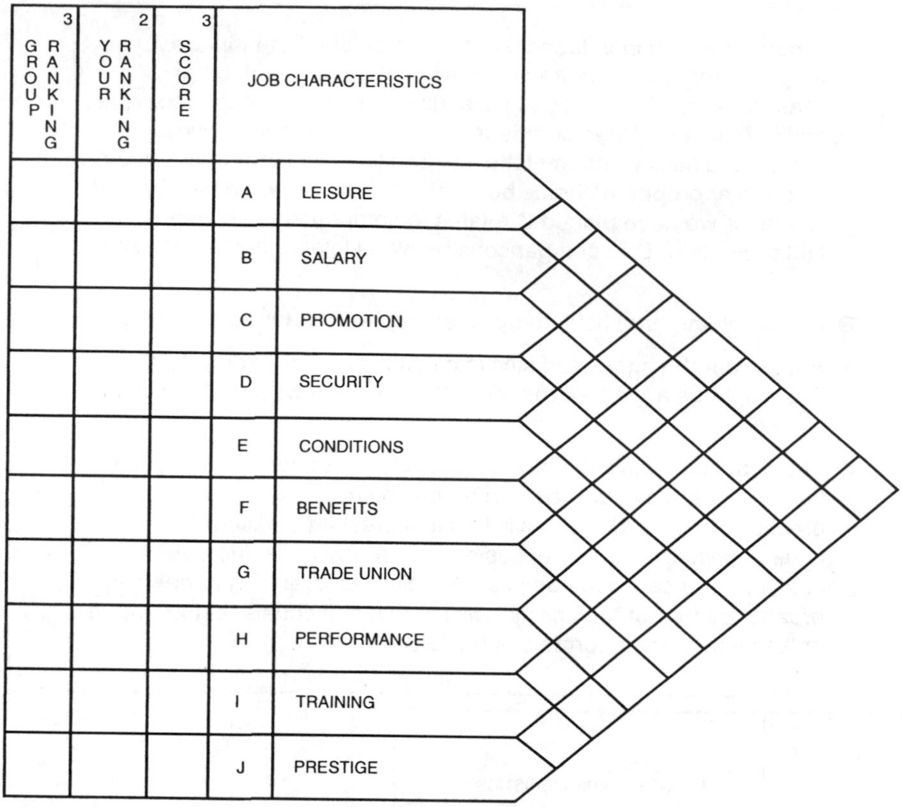

GROUPING 3	YOUR RANKING 2	SCORE 3		JOB CHARACTERISTICS
			A	LEISURE
			B	SALARY
			C	PROMOTION
			D	SECURITY
			E	CONDITIONS
			F	BENEFITS
			G	TRADE UNION
			H	PERFORMANCE
			I	TRAINING
			J	PRESTIGE

Figure 2: Characteristics influencing job choice grid

Obviously, there is no correct answer to this activity. We wanted you to think about what *you* desire from a job; what it is that leads you to seek one appointment and have little interest in another. We also wanted you to think about how far what *you* value is shared by others. When we discussed motivation, we mentioned that it was affected by 'forces both internal and external to the individual'. Given the 'down-sizing' ethos of the 1990s, it would be interesting, for example, to see where 'security' is in the rank order. It is likely that it will have been highly valued, while given the decline of trades unionism both in power and membership, it is likely that it will have been placed low in the rank order. There may have been exceptions to these examples due to 'internal' factors; this begins to reveal the complexity of this subject area. You will refer back to your choices when you develop certain motivation theories later.

Note that for Activity 11 in Section 3, you will need to obtain two job advertisements which you are or would be realistically interested in. It would be helpful if you start looking for suitable advertisements now.

Objectives

By the end of this unit, you will be able to:

- define motivation and explain the importance to managers of understanding it.
- explain how motivation theories are classified into content theories and process theories.
- describe the nature of human needs.
- explain Taylorism and its motivational implications.
- understand the motivational implications of the Hawthorne experiments.
- appreciate Maslow's hierarchy of needs and its motivational implications.
- set out Alderfer's ERG theory and its motivational implications.
- explain Herzberg's two-factor theory and its motivational implications.
- describe expectancy theory and its motivational implications.
- understand equity theory and its motivational implications.

Section 1

Motivation Theories

Introduction

In this section, we begin by distinguishing between content and process theories of motivation and then go on to examine a number of the more important content theories and their motivational implications.

1.1 Content and process theories: the distinction

We have already pointed out that there are many motivation theories and we examine a number of the more important ones here. They fall into two groups:

- **content theories**
- **process theories.**

Firstly, it is useful if we explore this distinction. We all have needs, whether they are for food, friendship, money or status. It may be that status or salary were significant characteristics that influenced your job choice. Now the fulfilling of such needs can be seen to lead to behaviour. Individuals feel a certain compulsion to do things in order to eliminate their physiological and psychological deficiencies. Figure 3 sets out a simple model in terms of the need for food.

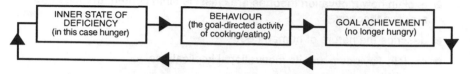

Figure 3: Modification of inner state

Motivation theories concerned with identifying the needs towards which behaviour is directed are referred to as content theories. These theories assume that individuals have a set or packet of needs and behave in ways which satisfy them. We say more about the nature of these needs in sub-section 1.2.

Process theories, on the other hand, are not concerned, with the static analysis of needs but rather with the dynamic, mental processes that lead individuals to pursue particular goals rather than any others. However, most need theories also concern processes in the sense that they make propositions about how and when particular needs become salient. They are concerned with need satisfaction and how needs become prioritised. The basic idea of process theories, that individuals are able to select goals and take appropriate paths towards them through a continuous process of calculation, is set out in Figure 4.

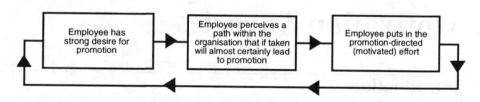

Figure 4: Process theories: a model of their underlying approach

We can say that content theories see motivation as a response to need deficiency. Process theories, on the other hand, are concerned with the processes that have led an individual to put effort into achieving a particular goal. We examine content theories first, starting with an examination of the nature of human needs.

1.2 Content theories: nature of human needs

Content theories explain why individuals behave in a particular way in terms of those individuals' pursuits of need fulfilment. In the context of Activity 1, it is likely that when you rank-ordered the characteristics that influenced your job choice, content theorists would argue that you were saying things about your need deficiencies. But what is the nature of human needs?

We could argue that biological factors are the basic determinants of our behaviour. We saw in Figure 3 that hunger drives us into behaviour and we certainly do not have to learn to be hungry! However, while hunger may well cease to 'motivate' us once we have eaten, it is likely that we have learnt to be hungry at culturally appropriate times and to eat in a socially acceptable way. It is even open to us to deliberately override our need for food by taking a decision to fast. What we are saying is that our motivational drives may be either innate, learned, or a mixture where innate, psychologically based drives are modified by socio-cultural conditioning or learning. Nevertheless, it is still useful to draw a distinction between:

- drives that have a **physiological** base
- motives that have a **socio-cultural** base.

Arguably, innate drives can be 'fully' met while learned drives tend to be never fully satisfied and lend themselves to continuous motivation. This distinction is worth bearing in mind, and it will become clear, as we explain the content theories. Certainly, the fact that 'learned' needs can never be fully met gives much scope for management practice.

One of the first modern commentators on motivation was Frederick Taylor, whose work you have already met in Units 1 and 5. Before looking at Taylorism, however, do the following activity.

ACTIVITY 2

What in broad terms do we refer to when we talk of motivation? Explain, with an example if possible, what it is about learned, as opposed to innate or physiologically-based needs, that makes them potentially useful for managers? Which of the two motivational theory types sees motivation as a response to need-deficiency and what does this mean?

When we talk about motivation, we refer to goal-directed activity and it is the content theories that see motivation as a response to need deficiency. The mainsprings of our behaviour are seen to be the drives to fulfil our needs.

Learned, as opposed to innate or physiologically-based drives, are potentially of more use to managers because they tend to be never fully met. For example, it is possible for managers to provide us with a non-threatening place of work and so satisfy, at least within the laws of employment, our need for physical and psychological safety. On the other hand, our need to develop our capacities and express them is 'limitless' and lends itself to continuing motivation.

1.3 The work of Taylor

As you saw from Taylor's work in Units 1 and 5, scientific management required workers to do things in the right way, to change their practices in accordance with science and in return to receive increases in pay (Taylor, 1947). The primary motive for high effort was to be high wages. This implies, of course, that Taylor's model of motivation was uni-dimensional, with employees seen as essentially economic animals. So scientific management can be seen to have implicitly incorporated an early need 'theory' within it and certainly the satisfaction of basic physiological needs is usually associated with money or, rather, with what money can buy. However, we have all heard about people who have no need of further money but who carry on working. Given this, it would seem that other needs are also being met at work. Taylor's 'theory' was deficient, but his focus on money as the key motivator was to influence later theories of motivation. Before saying something of the implications of Taylorism for managers seeking to motivate their employees, do the following activity that will help you to consolidate your understanding of the distinction between content and process theories of motivation. Schein, in 1988, describing the main models that managers use to explain the behaviour of their subordinates, referred to Taylor's rational economic model of the employee.

ACTIVITY 3

Individually, answer the following two questions about Taylor's rational economic man and then discuss with your group.

1 Why do you think this model was so-called?

2 Given the way that Schein has referred to Taylor's model of the employee, do you think that Taylor's motivation model sits happily with the content theories of motivation? Explain your answer.

---

1   Taylorism incorporates a view of the employee of being, at least to some degree, rational and calculative. To receive high rewards, workers must follow a certain path; they must learn to do things in the new 'right', scientific way.

2   While Taylor's model of motivation can be viewed as an early need 'theory', it also incorporates, at least to some degree, a view of the individual as rational and purposive. Given that choice is involved, and that it is concerned with the dynamic mental processes which lead individuals to pursue particular goals rather than others, then we could argue that it sits uneasily with other content theories.

We now look at the implications of Taylorism for managers seeking to motivate their employees.

1.4 Motivational implications of Taylorism

The essential aim of Taylorism was to design jobs to enable the maximum technical division of labour through job simplification. Work tasks, therefore, were fragmented and the workers de-skilled and since the analysis required that managers see the individual as an economic animal fuelled by money - it was money that was seen to be the incentive. When employees are paid a time rate, there is no direct and visible relationship between effort and reward, but when they are paid directly for effort, the assumption is that they will work harder. As Beardwell and Holden (1994) pointed out: 'It can be argued all payment by results systems reflect the traditions and principles of scientific management when tasks which could be measured would have standards of performance.'

Watson (1987) pointed out that scientific managers did not invent the logic of de-skilling, but just developed the principles of work organisation, first written about in a systematic way, in 1776, by Adam Smith in *Wealth of Nations*. As Watson observes: 'Smith recognised that enormous gains in efficiency were to be obtained if what might be seen as a 'whole' task such as the making of pins could be split up into a number of smaller scale and less skilled tasks or jobs. Each job would be easy to learn and each operation readily repeatable. The employer would benefit enormously from the increased dexterity of the worker, the reduction of time spent in preparation and changeover from one operation to another and from the possibilities which were opened up for further mechanisation.'

ACTIVITY 4

What other enormous benefit to the employer did Smith fail to point out?

Once you move beyond the craft principle to this kind of de-skilling, the cost of labour is also reduced. Later content theorists like Herzberg, who you will meet later in this unit, have argued about the illogicality of expecting high employee motivation in situations of job simplification. Such theorists were working with multi-dimensional models of motivation as you will see, and did not consider the pursuit of extra money as the main motivator. The next important development in terms of needs theories of motivation arose from the Hawthorne experiments of the 1920s and 1930s which have become associated with the name of Mayo.

1.5 Motivation theory and the Hawthorne experiments

You will remember from Unit 1 that in the initial stages of the Hawthorne studies, workers were seen as just responding passively to the right environmental mix. Once the productivity of the control group, working at a constant lighting level, rose in tandem with the productivity of an experimental group whose level had been increased, it was felt that psychological factors must be at work and Mayo was brought in to investigate matters further. He concluded that:

- working conditions were of less importance than the continuing attention that the employees were getting

- attitude changes had taken place at the individual and the group level so that for the first time employees felt part of the company

- the most important factor affecting productivity was the quality of inter-personal relationships. The high production teams were in fact self-governing to quite a large degree and they co-operated wholeheartedly with their managers – the teams had independently introduced job rotation.

Roethlisberger and Dickson, in an analysis of the Hawthorne experiments in 1939, were to further confirm the hypothesis that motivation, output and the quality of the output were primarily related both to the colleague and team relationships and to the broader relationship between workers and their managers. All of this work pointed firmly towards the importance for motivation of social needs being fulfilled through work and not just the economic need which Taylor had focused on. Schein has written of the 'social model' of the employee which assumes that:

- work people are motivated by social needs

- work people want rewarding relationships in their work situations

- individuals are more responsive to the pressures of their work teams than to managers.

ACTIVITY 5

Read the case study about *David Lane, Operations Manager*, answer the questions that follow and share your results with a group, if possible.

David Lane, Operations Manager

Patterson Transport is an independent road haulage company located in Warrington, north west England. The company operates 40 lorries with 46 drivers, 6 mechanics and 5 administration staff. Most of the company's work comprises transporting road-making materials for major construction firms.

Ted Patterson, the owner, makes all the management decisions and carries out all the management functions. He employs a bookkeeper to keep the accounts and administer the wages, two clerks and a shorthand typist. Most of Ted's time is spent negotiating contracts with construction firms or planning the operating schedules for the fleet of lorries. In the latter task, he is assisted by Reg Morris, age 35, a former driver who was transferred to administrative work 8 years ago when he suffered an injury to his spine, as the result of falling off a ladder while painting his house. Over the years, it has become the custom for Reg to prepare the operating schedule sheets and for Ted to merely sign them for issue to the drivers.

Ted recently decided that he could no longer keep in touch with all aspects of his business and needed to appoint someone to assist him in running the company. He created the post of operations manager, to take responsibility for all vehicle schedules and maintenance. When he heard about the new job, Reg asked Ted if he could fill the post but was told by Ted that he needed someone with management experience.

David Lane was appointed to fill the post. Twenty-seven-year-old David had a degree in business studies, specialising in transport studies, and previously worked as assistant manager of the contract department of one of Ted's customers. David was engaged to marry Ted's only child, Susan, and Ted hoped that he would eventually take over running the company so that he could retire. To provide an office for David, Reg was moved from the room he occupied and provided a desk in the general office, where the other administrative staff worked. Reg was assigned the task of maintaining the company's filing system.

During the first month in the post, David became aware that absenteeism among the drivers had increased. On 14 occasions, drivers had failed to work to the schedules David had issued, complaining that the schedules were impossible to follow and demonstrated an ignorance of the transport business. In fact, the schedules were identical to schedules that the drivers had followed, without comment, in the past. David decided to take no action, in the hope that the situation would improve as the drivers became accustomed to his appointment.

Two months later the situation had not improved: absenteeism and lateness among the drivers continued and schedules were not being kept. David convened a meeting of all the drivers and mechanics. He opened the meeting by outlining the present position on absenteeism and time-keeping, and explained that they were meeting to explore why the present situation had arisen and what could be done to improve matters. David voiced his belief in democratic management and said that they could best achieve the goals of the company through the co-operative efforts of the drivers, mechanics and himself.

David asked for comments on the issues of timekeeping, absenteeism and the work schedules but no comments were forthcoming. He attempted to provoke comments by mentioning that they now found it impossible to follow schedules which were the same as ones previously worked. He suggested increases in traffic and revised one-way systems as possible causes, but still no comments followed.

David felt frustrated by the lack of response. He asked everybody to give these matters some thought and said that he would call a meeting in a week's time to discuss them.

After the meeting ended, the drivers and the mechanics regrouped informally. The two recurrent themes in their discussions were that Lane had been foisted on them because he was marrying Ted's daughter and that the right person for the operations manager post was Reg.

1   Bearing in mind Schein's social model of the employee referred to earlier, how would you explain the events at Patterson Transport?

2   How do you think the crisis could be resolved?

1   It is likely that you will have highlighted the role of the informal group of drivers and mechanics and how its norms are obviously much stronger than any pressures that their new operations manager, David Lane, can bring to bear. Reg Smith, once a driver, has their loyalty and indeed may well be their informal leader. Certainly, with Ted Patterson, the owner, spending most of his time on the road negotiating contracts, Reg is effectively their manager. It is Reg who prepares and issues operating schedules to the drivers and presumably also liaises with the mechanics on lorry availability. The group is upset at the rupturing of the cosy set-up and relationships which appeared to have existed prior to David's appointment, and feel that 'their' Reg has been humiliated and was the right man for the job. All of this is compounded by the fact that they feel nepotism got David the post rather than ability.

2   Obviously the company is on the very edge of crisis and something needs to be done quickly. We could take the line that Ted should face his employees with the ultimatum that either the absenteeism, poor timekeeping and the breaking of schedules ceases or they will be sacked. The main problem with this strategy, of course, is that if the drivers and mechanics do not co-operate, in the short term at least, Patterson Transport will have to cease operations and this may mean the end of the company. On the other hand, Ted could recognise that it is his poor handling of the situation which has placed his firm in jeopardy. He has alienated his workforce, destroyed the social relations which had previously existed, and which apparently contributed to the success of Patterson Transport, and now he must begin to put things right.

David Lane must obviously retain his position: he is to marry Ted's daughter, but more importantly because the workers cannot be seen to have usurped Ted's right to appoint the operations manager of his choice. David would be better preparing for the take-over of the company by negotiating contracts with Ted and this is where his previous experience lies. This would allow Reg to return to his previous job, perhaps with a mollifying job title. David must obviously establish proper working relations with the workforce in the longer term and this process is likely to be facilitated by setting things right with Reg. We say more about group processes in Unit 9.

We now look at the management implications of the Hawthorne findings.

1.6 Management implications of the Hawthorne studies

In the first place, managers must obviously be very aware of the importance of social need satisfaction in the workplace. They must accept and co-operate with informal work groups, since it is these that provide the context within which many of their employees seek need satisfaction. However, this does not imply a passive role for management. They have an important role in creating team spirit at the micro-level, and indeed at the level of the work force as a whole. As Wickens points out in 'Steering the Middle Road to Car Production', item 8.1 in the Resource section: 'A team begins with individuals whose contributions are recognised and valued and who are motivated to work together to achieve clear, understood and stretching goals for which they are accountable. The best team results come with positive leadership and tough goals.'

Managers should not underestimate the ability of work teams to shape the motivation of individual workers. It has been shown that employees are often more responsive to the social 'forces' of their team than to the controls and the incentives of the wider organisation. We saw this, in fact, in the case study.

Given the importance of teams at work, first line supervisors obviously have particularly important roles and responsibilities. To a large extent, it is through them that the energies of teams are harnessed in the best interests of the organisation. Obviously, supervisory styles of leading are relevant here and we say more of this in Unit 9.

While Mayo is normally associated with the simple notion of meeting social needs at work, you will know from Unit 1 that his interests were much broader than this. Mayo was therefore concerned that employees should satisfy a whole range of needs in the work area which he considered would be beneficial to the cohesion and stability of society generally.

ACTIVITY 6

Mayo's broader concerns about social breakdown and industrial conflict were due to the influence of the writings of a French sociologist. Who was he?

Durkheim was a major influence on Mayo. Unlike Durkheim, however, you will remember Mayo saw the cure for the pathologies of industrial society as lying in the skills of management and good communications.

REVIEW ACTIVITY 1

Suggested time: 45 minutes.

Read the following case-study and answer the questions that follow it.

Production at Trevor Thompson and Sons

The Trevor Thompson Company specialises in making fishing rods. Trevor formed the company, with a staff of five, about ten years ago to produce a new style fishing rod which he had designed. The rod was a success and, gradually, the work force was expanded to accommodate an increase in demand for the rods. Most of the workers are women, recruited from the local comprehensive school.

They work in teams of four persons to assemble, inspect and package a fishing rod from start to finish. The whole of the production area is partitioned so that each team works in a separate area. The walls of the partitions are decorated with posters of personalities, pop groups, film actors and holiday postcards. The expansion has been achieved by forming new teams comprising one experienced worker, selected from a list of volunteers, and three newly-recruited employees. Workers receive a basic wage and a group bonus which increases with the number of rods produced. Newly-formed teams receive an additional learning bonus for the first three months after formation and the experienced worker setting up the team gets a one-off payment as a training bonus.

Each team takes charge of its own quality control and discipline. If the performance of a team member falls below standard, the team decides what, if any, action is to be taken. In extreme cases, the team might ask the production foreman to have an individual removed from the team. At work, team members chat mainly about their social life, and very rarely about the task or company matters.

Around 12 months ago, Trevor designed another rod specifically for night fishing. A market research survey, carried out by a consultant, revealed a market for the new rod and Trevor decided to put the night fishing rod into production as an addition to the company's range. Acting on the advice of the marketing consultant, Trevor decided to call in an engineering consultant to give expert advice on manufacturing the new rod. The consultant recommended a flow-line production process to manufacture both the old and the new rods. Trevor accepted the recommendation and secured a bank loan to finance the re-engineering of the whole production process.

To avoid a loss of production, the new manufacturing layout was introduced during the two weeks the company closed for the annual summer holiday. The workers were told that some changes would take place while they were on holiday and that there would be, in the words of Trevor, 'a nice surprise' awaiting them on return from holiday. Most of the workers assumed that the production area was going to be redecorated, and removed any postcards and posters they wished to keep.

Under the flow-line process, the manufacture of a fishing rod is broken down into five elements and each element is given to one worker to perform. Each worker sits in line alongside a track which is in continuous motion, at a constant speed calculated by the consultant. The basic rods are automatically fed onto the track and, in turn, each worker completes one element of the fishing rod. The finished rod is then carried to an inspection position, where it is checked for quality and then stacked. The track contains ten 5-person production units.

Together with the new manufacturing process a measured day work payment system was introduced, the specified level of performance which the workers had to achieve was calculated by the consultant. At Trevor's insistence, and against the advice of the consultant, a unit bonus was also paid for exceeding the level of performance. In addition, a special commissioning bonus was paid for the first two months following the introduction of the new process.

The new production process was explained to the workers when they returned from holiday. Training in the new methods of production proved difficult because the only experience that could be given was on the actual manufacturing track. This problem was aggravated by 12 newly-trained workers leaving within the first two months of the new process.

Three months after the introduction of the new manufacturing process, output of rods had stabilised at 16% below the performance level set by the consultant, and the amount of management time spent dealing with problems associated with the quality of the rods produced increased by 65%. After the significant level of wastage during the first two months, labour turnover returned to the previous employment pattern, but absenteeism increased by 20%.

1   Briefly re-state the fundamental assumption of content theories of motivation and then explain how what happened at Trevor Thompson and Sons could be seen to support this assumption.

2   Re-state what we have called the 'basic idea' of process theories of motivation. Then, with reference to Figure 4, suggest what Trevor was likely to have had in mind when he insisted that a unit bonus be paid for exceeding the specified level of performance.

3   How do you see the respective assumptions derived from the work of Taylor and Mayo relating to this scenario? Identify how Trevor could in part at least have managed the situation better had he possessed an appreciation of the Hawthorne findings.

Summary

In the unit introduction, we defined motivation in broad terms as goal-directed activity, explained its importance to managers and indicated that there are a number of motivation theories. In Activity 2, we reinforced your grasp of the concept, asserted that motivation theories could best be grouped into content and process theories and drew out the distinction between them. In the context of exploring Taylorism and motivation and its implications for managers, you consolidated your understanding of the distinction by answering whether or not his 'rational economic' model sat happily or not with other content theories. Activity 4 also required you to think through a key employer benefit of his approach.

We also discussed the nature of human needs generally and made a distinction between needs that have a physiological base and those that have a socio-cultural base. Learned, as opposed to innate needs, make them potentially more useful to managers. We then took a further look at the Hawthorne experiments in terms of the social model of motivation and examined the implications of its findings for management. You consolidated your understanding of how employees are often more responsive to the social forces of their group than to the controls and incentives of management. Finally, you linked what we said in Unit 1 about Mayo's broader concerns about societal cohesion and stability to what we examined here.

In terms of human needs, Maslow, an American psychologist, developed a theory that was the first comprehensive attempt to classify individual needs, and we examine his approach next.

SECTION 2
Maslow's Hierarchy of Needs

Introduction

Maslow developed a five-tier hierarchy of needs (Maslow, 1943). We look first at what Maslow said about the power of these needs and how they operate before looking in more detail at each of the need levels. Until a need level is satisfied, it is seen to remain the dominant need level. Once that need level is satisfied, the next need level up becomes the motivator, that is, a satisfied need no longer motivates. However, since when one need level is satisfied, the next level dominates, individuals are always in a motivated state. Thus, according to Maslow, individuals work their way up the hierarchy as the need levels below become satisfied. However, changing circumstances may bring a reversion to earlier need levels. If, for example, self-actualisation needs dominate but you lose your job, the basic physiological needs immediately become predominant. Figure 5 shows this hierarchy.

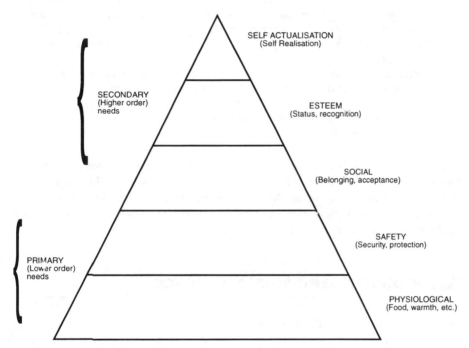

Figure 5: Maslow's hierarchy of needs

Now let us examine each need level more closely, noting how the hierarchy incorporates, and builds upon, previous thinking about motivation:

- **Physiological needs** are the basic biological needs essential for survival. They include drink, sleep and oxygen as well as food and warmth.

- Once these basic needs are satisfied, **safety and security needs** become dominant. We are seen to be motivated to protect ourselves from physical and psychological threats in the environment and to provide for the future. These first two levels are essential to existence and can be considered to be covered by the 'rational economic' model of the employee.

- When these are reasonably satisfied, then **social needs** fulfilment becomes the main stimulus to behaviour. Social needs include belonging, a need for love, friendship and social interaction. In the work situation, the need to belong and be accepted by our fellow employees predominates. Work, according to Mayo, is an essentially social activity and not performed by numerous, isolated beings, each rationally pursuing their own economic interests as Taylor would have wished to see it.

- Once satisfied, the need to belong becomes a need to more than belong. The **need for esteem** predominates and this includes, for example, the need for self-respect, for respect from others, recognition and status.

- When esteem needs are adequately satisfied then **self-actualisation needs** become more important. These include achievement, individual growth and the realisation of our potential. As Maslow pointed out, few people become everything that they are capable of becoming. So while managers seeking to increase their employees' motivation must consider their physiological and safety needs, the higher need levels which can be 'satisfied' in a greater variety of ways than the lower need levels, offer them even more scope.

  (Huczuski and Buchanan, (1991), point out that Maslow argued that we have in fact **Seven** innate needs, that is, beyond 'Self-actualisation' these are needs for *freedom of enquiry and expression* and for *knowledge and understanding*. These are usually viewed as having less relevance at work).

We suggested at the beginning of this unit that the various theories are subject to varying degrees of criticism. For example, we have already implied that approaches that only take account of basic physiological needs or even theories that 'add on' social needs are incomplete. It would be useful therefore to look at some of the main problems associated with Maslow's theory.

2.1 Problems with Maslow's theory

While it has had a significant impact on management approaches to employee motivation, Maslow's work is considered weak in many respects. However, to be fair, he always saw it as tentative; he did not originally intend it to be necessarily applied to the work place and he was worried at the way he saw it being 'swallowed whole' by many enthusiastic people. The main weaknesses that have been highlighted are:

- it has been argued that the theory is vague in that it is not clear, nor indeed is it measurable, just how much a need has to be satisfied before an individual can proceed to the next level

- there is evidence that the rigid demarcation of needs is suspect and that they can exist simultaneously and horizontally as well as sequentially and vertically

- it has been pointed out that the distinction between higher and lower order needs does not stand up to scrutiny, for example, while money, and what it can buy, can satisfy basic physiological needs, it can also satisfy status needs.

Certainly, Maslow's theory has deficiencies but, as we have pointed out, it nonetheless has been very useful in drawing attention to the fact that behaviour at work is influenced by the desire to 'eliminate' a number of needs. Also, it would appear reasonable to assume that needs often do operate in some sort of hierarchy even though the nature of this hierarchy may well vary from individual to individual. Maslow, however, would have accepted many of these criticisms. He was well aware of the complexity of motivation patterns and the fact that they alter according to circumstances. For example, when commenting on the possible rank ordering in Activity 1, we suggested that in the climate of today, job security, or perhaps more realistically relative job security, may be placed near the top; in a different climate, it might be seen as less important.

ACTIVITY 7

What does self-actualisation mean, and why are the higher level needs of individuals, such as self-actualisation, important to managers?

Maslow did not coin the notion of self-actualisation but he did define it. Self-actualisation, he wrote, '. . . refers to the desire for self-fulfilment, namely, to the tendency for . . . [an individual] . . . to become actualised in what he is potentially . . . the desire to become more and more what one is, to become everything that one is capable of becoming.' The higher level needs, like self-actualisation, are important to managers because, for example, while eating leads us to feel we have had enough food for the time being, when we have been stretched at work, have risen to the occasion and have gained self-esteem and recognition, our needs in these directions are still not fully satisfied. It is very unlikely that we feel that we have had enough positive strokes and self-fulfilment for the time being. The reverse is in fact likely. That is, we become actively motivated to seek further and continuing fulfilment of such needs and obviously our managers can make use of this.

We now examine further the motivational implications of Maslow's theory.

2.2 Motivational implications of Maslow's theory

- Managers should always bear in mind that:
  - employees are continually trying to satisfy needs
  - they should make use of this knowledge in ways appropriate to their particular work context.
- They should particularly bear in mind that it is the relatively unsatisfied needs that lead to motivation and that they must determine what they are and adapt their reward structure to them.
- They should recognise the particular importance of the higher order needs in terms of motivation.
- They must be keenly aware of individual differences, however, and the fact that different people may have different preferences in terms of rewards.

ACTIVITY 8

To help your understanding of Maslow's ideas, read the following case study and answer the questions that follow it.

Alfred Moran, Personnel Manager

Nineteen years ago, Alfred Moran, age 42, began working as a personnel assistant in the personnel department of Town Mills Limited. After spending five years in this position, he progressed to become recruitment manager for the company. After he had spent six years in this position he was promoted to personnel manager and has been working in this job for the past eight years.

Alfred was able to move upward in the personnel department much faster than most people of his age in the company, bypassing several managerial grades and individuals. Alfred possesses above-average intelligence and potential and at university he passed all his Institute of Personnel Management professional examinations with 'A' grades. Of all the managers on his grade at Town Mills, he is the youngest. Alfred's next possible advancement in the personnel department would be to personnel director. The present incumbent of this post is due to retire in about three years time.

Alfred has five managers reporting to him: recruitment manager, training manager, industrial relations manager, personnel services manager and organisational development manager. Alfred apparently did an outstanding job during his first years with Town Mills, as evidenced by his rapid movement upwards in the department. However, according to the personnel director and some of his subordinate managers, Alfred's performance has deteriorated during the past three years. Some of the complaints are: lack of interest in his job; absence from departmental meetings; failure to submit reports on time; and the loss of confidence of his subordinate managers.

As a result of economic conditions and the loss of three major government contracts six months ago, Town Mills was forced to reduce production and declare some redundancies. At this time, the recruitment manager prematurely retired because of ill health and the personnel director asked Alfred to return to his previous job, so avoiding managerial redundancy in the personnel department. Although Alfred had not worked in this job for eight years, the personnel director thought that he should have no problems in carrying out the duties of the post. Alfred's salary was unchanged, so he did not suffer a loss of earnings, and he was permitted to retain the company car which was attached to the post of personnel manager.

In the first month following his re-appointment as recruitment manager, Alfred was absent from three important departmental meetings, made several critical errors in his contribution to the company's long-term manpower plan, and failed to attend an industrial tribunal to represent Town Mills in a case concerning one of the company's former employees. The personnel director warned Alfred that his recent behaviour could not be tolerated.

The personnel director did not know that in his spare time, and at weekends, Alfred worked for a firm of management consultants, planning and teaching interpersonal skills development courses for supervisors. This spare time activity had been lucrative for several years and Alfred had invested this income in a garden centre, managed jointly by himself and his wife. Together, these two activities took up a lot of Alfred's time.

Business unexpectedly improved when Town Mills succeeded in procuring several important government contracts which guaranteed the continued functioning of the company for five years. This change in fortune had an immediate impact on the task of the personnel department, which was required to plan the re-structuring of the workforce, and the organisation, to meet the needs of the expansion in production. The Board authorised the re-appointment of a personnel manager to carry out these tasks.

Do the following tasks, and then discuss your ideas in a group, if possible.

1   Comment on Alfred Moran's career and performance patterns at Town Mills, and outside of it, in the light of Maslow's hierarchy of needs.

2   Would you reappoint Alfred Moran as personnel manager? Explain your

---

1   You will probably have commented on Alfred's talent and drive culminating in his appointment as personnel manager. His rapid upward movement would appear to testify to his very strong desire to meet his higher order needs and, especially, self-actualisation. Alfred's career trajectory, however, has reached a hiatus in that his next possible advancement within Town Mills is three years away when the personnel director retires. Could this type of individual put his drive for self-actualisation 'on hold' for three years? To make matters worse for Alfred, he then had to return to being recruitment manager, a post he had left behind eight years ago. Certainly, he retained his personnel manager salary and car, but he no longer had the status which went with that post.

You may have found it unsurprising if Alfred at this time had turned elsewhere to satisfy his self-actualising needs. However, we are told that 'for several years' he had already been 'turning elsewhere', and it says much for his drive and talent that perhaps for about half of this time he had been able to keep fully on top of his Town Mills post and work for a consultant and jointly manage a garden centre. For a long time, Town Mills had not been stretching him sufficiently, and presumably, as soon as this was the case, he had found himself unable even then to put his self-actualisation on hold. During the last three years, however, Alfred's performance had deteriorated and it is likely that you will have been clear that this was not due to the fact that he was not up to his Town Mills post but because, as it has been suggested, it was not in itself fully satisfying his needs. Increasingly, of course, his performance deteriorated as he invested more and more of himself into his stretching, outside interests. It was increasingly in these that his self-actualisation needs were being met, and seemingly, and unethically, he was just clinging to his salary from Town Mills for as long as he could get away with it.

2   It may be that in your group you found conflicting opinions on whether or not he:

- should be approached in terms of taking on the personnel manager post again

- would accept the position if offered.

Your discussions may have concerned whether Town Mills could afford to lose such talent, especially given the fact that had it provided the challenges Alfred obviously needed, he may have never turned elsewhere for his need fulfilment.

On the other hand, it has already been suggested that he has been acting unethically in taking his salary and delivering in return a performance, which he knows better than anybody, is unacceptable. Also, of course, it would send out all the wrong messages within the company were they to appoint a personnel manager who has visibly fallen down on his job and lost the confidence of subordinate managers.

It would appear very doubtful that Alfred would be considered for the position and in the unlikely situation that the Board discusses the matter with him, it is equally unlikely that he would accept it.

The next content- or needs-based theory that we examine is Alderfer's **Existence, Relatedness and Growth (ERG) Theory.**

2.3 Alderfer's ERG theory

While drawing upon Maslow's ideas, Alderfer developed them into something different and more complex (Alderfer, 1969). He re-structured Maslow's five need levels into three groups:

- **existence needs** which correspond to the first two levels of Maslow's hierarchy and include all forms of physiological and material needs

- **relatedness needs** which include Maslow's social needs level and those esteem needs which derive from other people

- **growth needs** which relate to self-actualisation.

He conceived these three groups of needs are more of a continuum than a hierarchy, that they are not necessarily sequential and that deprivation is not the only way to activate a need. For example, the more that growth needs are satisfied, the more they might increase in intensity. This, of course, we have argued, is implicit in Maslow's model.

He also accepted the idea that two needs could operate at once. For example, an employee whose promotion has been blocked may still continue to seek advancement but may also try to build better colleague relations.

He also distinguished between what he called **episodic needs** which are purely situational, and **chronic needs** which persist over time. For example, nurses may strike in a given situation while at the same time recognising that this may be at total odds with their long-term needs.

ERG theory takes up some of Maslow's points while, overall, it is more realistic. Certainly it is useful for managers to be aware that two needs can operate at once, that seemingly erratic behaviour can be explained in terms of episodic needs and that the more growth needs are satisfied, the more they assume importance.

ACTIVITY 9

Joan Penn, a committed infant teacher, is very concerned with growing class sizes in her region and is currently involved in a campaign to try and get her teacher's union to take a stronger line on the issue. She has recently applied for the deputy head post at a nearby school and feels very strongly that she is ready for it. At the shortlisting, a governor whose husband teaches at Joan's school comments that Joan is going to have to make her mind up – does she want to be a rebel or part of the establishment?

If you were the head, you knew of Joan and her abilities and wanted her shortlisted, how would you explain her behaviour so that the comment did not affect her chances?

You would argue that Joan is a very able and ambitious teacher whose ultimate goal is to be the head of her own school. Her current union activities only reflect her commitment to the children of the region and her concern that class sizes at the moment are not in their best interests. You might point out that she sees no clash between her situational concerns and her long-term career ambitions, that is, her union activities reflect purely episodic needs which in no way have bearing on, or deflect from her chronic, long-term motivations. Knowledge of Alderfer's work allows us to go beyond 'commonsense' reactions which point to erratic behaviour and analyse Joan's behaviour at a deeper level.

REVIEW ACTIVITY 2

Suggested time: 30 minutes.

1 Which two levels of Maslow's hierarchy are covered by the rational economic man model of the employee?

2 Explain what we meant when we said that the need to belong, once satisfied, becomes a need to more than belong.

3 Why does the distinction between higher and lower order needs not stand up to scrutiny?

4 Relatively unsatisfied needs lead to motivation. Explain.

5 Alderfer's growth needs relate to self-actualisation. What do you understand by self-actualisation?

6 Give an example of two needs operating at the same time.

Summary

Our objectives in this section were to give you an appreciation of both Maslow's hierarchy of needs and Alderfer's ERG theory and their motivational implications. You acquired a broad understanding of Maslow's model and focused specifically on the importance of higher order needs to managers. With terms of ERG theory, you clarified the difference between the episodic and chronic needs and identified the fact that more than one need can operate at any one time.

The next important needs theory we examine is that of Frederick Herzberg whose work in the 1950s was again a development of Maslow's hierarchy of needs.

SECTION 3

Herzberg and Motivation

Introduction

In this section, we begin by setting out Herzberg's **two-factor approach** and then go on to offer criticisms of it. We close by examining the motivational implications of Herzberg's work.

Note in this section, you will need the two job advertisements we mentioned to in the unit introduction. They should be for jobs that you are, or would be, realistically interested in.

3.1 The work of Herzberg

We have said that Herzberg's work represented a development of Maslow's (Herzberg, 1968). There were, however, two key differences between the ideas of Herzberg and those of Maslow:

- Herzberg made a much stronger distinction than Maslow between the lower and the higher order needs

- Herzberg's theory was based on empirical data derived from interviews with engineers and accountants.

What Herzberg did, in fact, was to ask his sample of professionals, two key questions. The first related to what made them feel particularly good about their jobs and the second to what made them feel particularly bad. On the basis of the responses, Herzberg developed his influential 'two-factor' theory of motivation:

- **Hygiene factors** – that is to say, acceptable company policy and administration, salary, quality of supervision, working conditions, relationships with fellow employees and job security. These factors all related to Maslow's lower order needs and, are extrinsic to the actual job. They were so-called because Herzberg argued that in their absence, employees would be dissatisfied. If the need for these factors is not properly met, then dissatisfaction will exist. But furthermore, Herzberg argued that their presence will not actually move employees to greater effort. High performance relates to the next set of factors.

- **Motivating factors** – it is these then, achievement, recognition, advancement, responsibility and the work itself, which create what Herzberg referred to as job satisfaction and which lead employees to perform well. He saw satisfaction arising only from the job content, while potential dissatisfiers related to the environmental or job context factors.

ACTIVITY 10

What implications do you see in Herzberg's view about what must happen if motivation to high performance is to be improved?

Herzberg identified that job content must allow people to satisfy their needs for achievement, recognition and responsibility and that the content of many jobs might have to be re-designed to allow for this.

Before we examine the measures that Herzberg specified through which the content of jobs could be changed to improve performance, it would be useful to look at the most important problems associated with this theory.

3.2 Criticisms of the two-factor approach

● Surely individuals are motivated when they are dissatisfied and believe that the undertaking of a certain activity will deliver greater satisfaction. According to Herzberg, in the absence of motivators, there is not necessarily any sense of the frustration of higher order needs. Obviously this may be true of certain individuals but clearly, in many cases, people will be frustrated where the possibility of meeting their higher order needs does not exist.

● There is a methodological criticism which raises doubts about the validity of the two, supposedly clearly distinguishable, factors. Just as footballers will attribute a win to their personal skills and losing to heavy going or a biased referee, so surely employees will perceive satisfying incidents as a favourable reflection on their job performance and dissatisfying incidents as being related to external (hygiene) factors. Certainly it has only been possible to replicate Herzberg's findings using his particular 'critical incidents' method of enquiry, where respondents were asked to report on occasions where they had particularly good or bad feelings about their jobs.

The following activity will help you to understand the distinction that Herzberg made between hygiene and motivating factors.

ACTIVITY 11

1 Go back to the list of characteristics in Activity 1 and identify each as a hygiene or a motivating factor.

2 How many motivating factors featured in your top three rankings? What were they?

3 Reflecting on your choices now, do you wish to change your ranking at all? *Yes / No.* If 'Yes', in what way?

4 You were asked earlier to collect two advertisements for jobs you are or would be realistically interested in. Stick them in the spaces provided. Read them again and answer the following questions:

JOB ADVERT NO. 1

Job advert no.1

How many hygiene factors were mentioned? What were they?

How many motivating factors were mentioned? What were they?

Note that the advertisement may express the same ideas in different ways. For example, 'self-actualising' jobs may be referred to as 'rewarding', and so on.

JOB ADVERT No. 2

Job advert no. 2.

How many hygiene factors were mentioned? What were they?

How many motivating factors were mentioned? What were they?

5 Has your analysis led you to re-think the attractiveness of these jobs at all?
Yes / No. If 'Yes', explain.

The characteristics listed in Activity 1, as you will have noted, are largely hygiene-orientated: leisure, salary, security, conditions, benefits, trade unions, training and prestige. Fulfilment and promotion are obviously motivating factors. Some would argue that 'opportunities for training and education' and 'prestige' are also motivating factors. What do you think? The case for the former characteristic appears the strongest, although it obviously does not fit neatly into Herzberg's categorisation. However, just considering its importance may be useful.

There is obviously no right or wrong answer to how many motivating factors featured in your top three rankings. You know best what your needs are but it may have been the case that reflecting on your choices in this context you wished to change them. Did you? It might be that 'salary' was everything to you and is still so, but you should note that while hygiene factors may initially draw people to jobs, job content subsequently becomes more important to them. We asked you to analyse the job adverts not only to get you to think about Herzberg's classification, but to encourage you to reflect further on your choices and the criteria which you used. These analyses might help you clarify what issues you need to address with prospective employers.

We now look at the implications of Herzberg's theory.

3.3 Implications of Herzberg's theory of motivation

As you know, scientific management or Taylorism, was one of the earliest attempts to design jobs with performance in mind. Given the uni-dimensional, money model of motivation, however, Taylor's principles ignored the fact that the work was so repetitive and boring that employees became dissatisfied, frustrated and apathetic. Deriving from his theory, Herzberg specified three ways by which job simplification could be revised:

- **job rotation**
- **job enlargement**
- **job enrichment.**

We look briefly at each of these.

JOB ROTATION
Employees exchange jobs periodically to break the monotony; they ideally learn new skills and are provided with fresh job challenges. The Hawthorne studies revealed the existence of this practice, although in that case it was unofficially organised within informal work teams. Note that:

- there is some evidence that this technique sometimes heightens satisfaction but it does not improve productivity

- if employees are rotating around highly repetitive tasks then there is little opportunity to learn new skills and hence an absence of challenge

- where jobs have previously been enlarged or enriched, and where the aim of management is multi-skilling, then job rotation may prove a more effective technique. This approach would appear to have effects when it is part of a larger package.

JOB ENLARGEMENT
In job enlargement, there is an increase in the number of operations which an employee performs. However, as Herzberg observed, and as we have already pointed out, if the added tasks are equally tedious, then the technique will be of limited value in motivating people. Again, there is some evidence that this technique may increase employee satisfaction but is does not go far enough and it is unlikely that motivation will be affected. Herzberg's third way, job enrichment, is likely to affect motivation.

JOB ENRICHMENT

This is the redesign of jobs incorporating Herzberg's motivators so that responsibility and challenge are increased. This technique may involve job enlargement, which is sometimes called horizontal loading. This is the expansion of the job through adding more varied tasks. Essentially , however, enrichment concerns vertical loading, that is creating a 'new' job involving greater responsibility and greater autonomy for the employee.

ACTIVITY 12

What kinds of things do you think might be done to achieve job enrichment?

What Herzberg suggested, for example, was:

● to allocate new and challenging tasks to employees to upgrade their skills and to develop them

● where this may not be possible, periodically to allocate them special assignments which involve challenge

● where possible, to assign employees to complete meaningful units of work rather than fragmented tasks

● to allow employees greater access to information, greater discretion and emphasise personally accountable results

● always to provide feedback as soon as possible on performance.

Managers must be aware, however, that the needs that job enrichment meets are not necessarily universal. Remember the 1968 study by Goldthorpe et al, which you met in Unit 5, where a group of workers were found to have adopted an 'instrumental orientation' to their jobs. Their main concern was economic rather than an interest in the content of their jobs. These workers would arguably have no interest in job enrichment. However, you also saw in Unit 5, Daniel's argument (1973) that orientations to work are dynamic. Daniel would hold that while economic instrumentality may draw certain people to well paid jobs, once in post other needs, for example, related to job content, may surface. The technique of job enrichment is, therefore, not unproblematic and managers must be aware of these potential problems.

ACTIVITY 13

Read the article by Wickens, Item 7.1 in the Resource section.

1 Find examples or facets of job rotation, job enlargement and job enrichment in the practices described.

2 Identify what Wickens sees as the paradox inherent in these practices.

3 Explain in what way job enrichment particularly, might be seen to heighten the paradox.

4 Indicate how Wickens envisages the paradox being resolved.

1   In terms of job rotation, for example, when discussing the teams at Uddevalla who complete the final assembly of four cars each shift on static platforms, Wickens points out that each team has a spokesperson, a role which is rotated between team members at intervals determined by them. It is the spokesperson who assigns work, guides the team, plans, reports, leads discussions and resolves individual and practical problems.

Job enlargement is also implicitly referred to in the quotation from *The Machine that Changed the World* by Womack et al. They say: 'We are very sceptical that this form of organisation can ever be as fulfilling as lean production. Simply bolting and screwing together a large number of parts in a long cycle rather than a small number of parts in a short cycle is a very limited vision of job enrichment.'

This is, of course, job enlargement rather than job enrichment. Job enrichment proper is mentioned at a number of points. Wickens writes of the operatives being given responsibility for 'standard operations'. There is also mention of them being involved in changes to the process and in a range of discretionary tasks.

2   Wickens perceives that the paradox inherent in these practices as two, seemingly opposed, objectives. On the one hand, management seeks to enhance the commitment and motivation of the workforce and to achieve this must seemingly loosen their control of the process, and on the other hand, such control is seen as crucial to long-term effectiveness.

3   Job enrichment, particularly, might be seen to heighten the paradox because the greater discretion advocated for employees reduces management controls.

4   Wickens envisages the paradox being resolved by moving to a position where employees are involved in changes to the process – 'control by the process changes to control of the process'.

Herzberg himself was well aware of the problem of the loss of control that his ideas on job enrichment involved and to counter it placed great emphasis on personal accountability, results and direct feedback on performance.

ACTIVITY 14

Consider again Wickens' resolution to the paradox of production. What are your views about it and about the general possibility of its resolution? Discuss your answers in a group, if possible.

Any disagreements with Wickens' resolution are likely to concern values and attitudes. On the one hand, for example, we could argue that his position is the only practical, realistic, human one to take, with all organisational members ultimately gaining. On the other hand, we could argue that in a capitalist society, the reality is that work people will never in any real sense control the process and that, for example, people-centred volume production is a contradiction in terms.

Despite the problems of the paradox that Wickens highlights, Herzberg's approach to job enrichment and work design is still in use. For example, a number of successful applications are reported by Huczyinski and Buchanan (1991). Indeed, the 1990s saw something of a resurgence of interest in it and in related approaches. We mention an advanced and much-applied scheme in the context of the motivational implications of expectancy theory.

Summary

The objective of this section was for you to gain an appreciation of Herzberg's two-factor theory and of its motivational implications. The theory was set out and using your job advertisements, you were able to distinguish between hygiene and motivating factors. Before outlining the implications of Herzberg's theory, you looked at what must happen if motivation to high performance is to take place. Activity 12 focused on his techniques for job enrichment. In the context of the Wickens article, you found examples of job rotation, job enlargement and job enrichment, to explain the paradox of production as Wickens sees it and to set out how job enrichment could heighten it.

The implications about motivating people that managers can draw from Herzberg's work are embodied in the three ways that he specified how job simplification could be revised. Firstly, job rotation involves the periodic exchange of jobs ideally to learn new skills. Secondly, job enlargement increases the number of physical operations which an employee performs. Finally, job enrichment which may involve job enlargement but which is essentially about creating new jobs with greater autonomy and responsibility.

SECTION 4
Process Theories of Motivation

Introduction

In this section, we begin by reminding you of the distinction that we have drawn between process and content theories of motivation and then go on to give you an appreciation of two important process theories. Firstly, we examine expectancy theory, together with a model of job enrichment which takes into account the implications of expectancy theory, and finally we address equity theory.

4.1 Process theories

We suggested at the beginning of this unit that there is no one overall theory of motivation but rather a number of theories which collectively provide a storehouse of ideas which management can draw upon and apply in their own particular work contexts. We also pointed out that these theories can be usefully grouped into content and process theories. Content theories attempt to determine the specific needs that motivate individuals, while the process theories seek to analyse, as Ivancevich and Matteson put it in 1993, 'how individual behaviour is energised, directed, maintained and stopped'. A study of two important process theories will help you to understand this complex subject. The first process theory we present is **expectancy theory**.

4.2 Expectancy theory

According to expectancy theory, as Pheysey (1993) says, '. . . people are able to create expectancies for themselves. The theory states that a person calculates the value of a certain benefit, or set of linked benefits, and then estimates the likelihood of acquiring them through his or her own efforts. The person is only motivated if there is a good chance of getting something that is wanted.'

ACTIVITY 15

If high productivity will alienate an employee from their team, and that employee especially values getting on very well with them, will the ultimate outcome be high or low productivity?

The answer, of course, is low productivity. In expectancy theory, employees are seen as behaving in ways instrumental to the achievement of valued goals.

Vroom produced the first systematic formulation of an expectancy theory of work motivation in 1964.

THE WORK OF VROOM

Vroom defined motivation as a process governing choices between alternative forms of voluntary action and argued that the strength of an individual's motivation is the product of:

- strength or valence of that individual's preference for a particular outcome

- expectation of the individual that certain behaviours will in fact lead to that desired outcome. Vroom used the notion of 'subjective probability' since it is only an 'expectation' dependent upon the individual's perception of the probable relationship that exists between the behaviour and the outcome.

Vroom developed an expectancy equation, that is, a way in which motivation could actually be assessed and measured, which in its simplest form is:

$$F = E \times V$$

Where F is the strength of the motivation to behave, E is the expectation or subjective probability that the behaviour will result in the desired outcome, and V is the valence or strength of the individual's preference for that particular outcome.

Let's look at some examples.

- Employees will not be motivated if, while perceiving a close relationship in their organisation between high performance and promotion, they do not want the extra responsibility. The valence of their preference for that outcome is nil or very low.

● Employees will be highly motivated if they want promotion – its valence has a positive value in that they do not view it neutrally, or wish to avoid it – and they perceive a very close relationship between high performance and promotion in their organisation.

ACTIVITY 16

Is it likely that individuals will be motivated if they want promotion but do not perceive any relationship between high performance and gaining promotion?

It is very unlikely that they will be motivated and this has obvious implications for managers as you will have recognised. This example looked at the expectancy equation in its simplest form where one outcome is expected for a given action. Reality is more complex and it may be that an individual desires promotion but worries about the inevitable extra stress and fears former colleague rejection. Vroom recognised that different outcomes are likely to result from a given action and his equation in its more complex form seeks to sum across the total number of outcomes to arrive at a single figure which indicates the attractiveness of the contemplated behaviour. Porter and Lawler have developed Vroom's model.

THE WORK OF PORTER AND LAWLER

Porter and Lawler point out that the level of an individual's motivational effort does not lead directly to a certain level of performance (Porter & Lawler, 1968). Certainly they would agree that an individual's motivation is a function of the perceived effort and reward probability and the value placed on that reward. However, they also see as relevant the individual's abilities and traits and role perception of the required direction and level of action necessary to effective performance. Porter and Lawler see motivation and performance, therefore, as separate variables which is something that is obscured in content theory. The basics of their model are expressed diagrammatically in Figure 6.

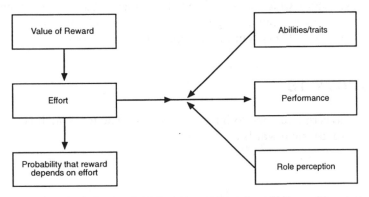

Figure 6: Porter and Lawler model

ACTIVITY 17

Porter and Lawler's position is that motivation and performance are separate variables and in pointing this out they have developed Vroom's model. Explain the difference as they see it between the variables and indicate how Figure 6 clarifies this.

Porter and Lawler drew attention to the fact that just because an employee is motivated, it does not necessarily mean that he or she will perform well. The individual may see a clear link between effort and reward and value that reward, but there are other things that affect effective performance. Does that individual have the necessary skills and abilities or, if relevant, the required level of persistence? The employee will need to have a full grasp of all that is entailed in being able to perform effectively in that task. Figure 6 shows how abilities and traits and role perception mediate between effort and performance.

In terms of rewards, Porter and Lawler also distinguished between:

- **intrinsic rewards** – for example, promotion or bonuses which tend to be given by others
- **extrinsic rewards** – for example, sense of achievement or sense of self-worth which are given by individuals to themselves.

They argued that job satisfaction is more likely to be produced where performance involves intrinsic rewards. Performance does not lead to satisfaction as traditional thinking held but rather, successful performance, the rewards that follow it and how these rewards are perceived, determine job satisfaction.

In terms of how rewards are perceived, Porter and Lawler hold that most of us have a sense of the level of reward we should fairly receive for a given performance so that one of the factors in the determination of satisfaction is getting rewards which meet and excel those which we perceive to be equitable. Satisfaction, therefore, is an effect, rather than a cause, of performance. It would be useful for us now to evaluate expectancy theory, but first complete the next activity.

ACTIVITY 18

Which Herzberg's factors do intrinsic rewards relate to? Which Herzberg's factors do extrinsic rewards relate to?

Intrinsic rewards are Herzberg's motivating factors while extrinsic rewards are his hygiene factors. Some textbooks still refer to the latter as maintenance factors. For example, the presence of good working conditions and good quality supervisors maintain an acceptable level of non-dissatisfaction.

EVALUATION OF EXPECTANCY THEORY

It is useful to remember that expectancy theory is only a model which seeks to mirror the complex, motivational processes of working life and their outcomes. It does not claim to describe actual, step-by-step, motivational decisions taken by individuals. Presented to managers as an analytical tool, it does not provide specific suggestions about what motivates employees nor specific solutions to motivational problems. What it does do, however, as Luthans (1992) put it, is to '. . . help management understand and analyse workers' motivation and identify some of the relevant variables'.

In making clearer the complexity of motivation, expectancy theory is sometimes more difficult to understand, and is certainly more difficult to apply, than the content theories whose continuing popularity evidences their simplicity. However, the Porter and Lawler model is more applications-orientated and the findings of two studies reviewed by Mullins (1993) produced results which were generally supportive of it. For example, it was found that:

- where pay was concerned, the value of the reward and the perceived effort-outcome probability did combine to influence effort

- those managers who believed that pay was closely related to performance outcome did receive a higher effort and performance rating from superiors

- a high level of performance was produced by the interaction of effort and role perceptions

- intrinsic rewards were found to contribute substantially more to job satisfaction and performance than extrinsic rewards.

Although expectancy theory is presented to managers as an analytical tool, it does indicate that they should give attention to a number of factors.

ACTIVITY 19

Can you identify any points that expectancy theory suggests managers should give attention to if they are to motivate their people to high performance?

Mullins (1993) has highlighted some of the more important motivational implications of expectancy theory:

- Managers need to bear in mind the importance of the appropriateness of rewards in terms of performance. The incentives for higher performance should be outcomes of high value for those concerned.

- Managers must seek to establish, in the individual's perception, clear relationships between effort-performance and rewards as perceived by the individual.

- Managers must establish clear procedures for the evaluation of individual levels of performance.

- Managers must attend to the intervening variables, abilities, traits, role perceptions, and also organisational procedures and support facilities, which may affect performance.

- Managers must seek to minimise undesirable outcomes which may be perceived to stem from high performance, such as accidents, group sanctions and lay-offs.

The ideas and principles of expectancy theory have also been used to develop a more sophisticated approach to job enrichment as a motivating tool than that initially suggested by Herzberg. We now look at a model of job enrichment which takes into account the implications of expectancy theory. This is the popular and comprehensive model developed by Hackman and Oldham in 1980.

4.3 Hackman and Oldham model of job enrichment

At the heart of Hackman and Oldham's approach is the notion that when individuals consciously or unconsciously work out the balance between expected rewards and effort which determine their motivation, their calculation is affected by how they experience their job. Put simply, if they see scope in their job to gain the rewards that they value, they will be more highly motivated than if they see little potential for this or if gaining the rewards will demand incommensurate effort. Given this, it should be possible, by re-designing their job, to change their perceptions and so create a different expectancy calculation. From management's view, the purpose of engineering the new 'calculation' is to enhance that individual's performance.

Let us look in more detail at the propositions involved in this process. Firstly, we examine some aspects of jobs which help determine how an individual sees the scope, or limitations, in them for higher level satisfactions.

Jobs can be analysed in terms of the employee's perception of the extent to which five core dimensions are present in their jobs. These dimensions are:

- **skill variety** – the degree to which the job is perceived to involve different activities involving a range of different skills and talents

- **task identity** – the degree to which the job is perceived to involve the completion of a 'whole' piece of work with a visible outcome

- **task significance** – the degree to which the job is perceived to have a meaningful impact on others, either internal or external to the organisation

- **autonomy** – the extent to which the job is perceived as involving independence and discretion in both planning and doing it

- **feedback** – the extent to which the effectiveness of job performance is perceived to be clearly and directly related back.

The questionnaire, found in Hackman and Oldman (1980), can be administered to employees which assesses how they perceive their job content along these dimensions. It also calculates an overall measure of experienced enrichment in the job, called, in the Hackman and Oldham equation, the motivating potential score *(MPS)*:

$$MPS = \frac{SV + TI + TS \times (\text{autonomy}) \times (\text{feedback})}{3}$$

Where *S* is skill variety, *TI* is task identity and *TS* is task significance. Note that the equation reflects that 'autonomy' and 'feedback' are seen to be the greater motivating influences.

Three psychological states, that are crucial to high motivation, high 'growth' satisfaction and high performance, are induced in those employees who perceive themselves to have enriched jobs in terms of the core dimensions and so they have a high *MPS*. These are:

- **experienced meaningfulness of the work,** related to skill variety, task identity and task significance

- **experienced responsibility for the outcome of the work,** related to the degree of autonomy

- **knowledge of the results,** related to feedback.

Note, however, that while the perceived presence of the core dimensions are seen to induce these three psychological states in employees, the model holds that how strongly they are felt is moderated by the employees' knowledge and skills, 'growth need' strengths and lack of dissatisfaction with the job context factors.

In order to increase motivation and performance, therefore, managers must re-design those jobs where the motivating potential score *(MPS)* is low.

ACTIVITY 20

Bearing in mind the core job dimensions that affect how people experience their work, can you suggest any principles that might be applied in re-designing jobs to improve their motivational potential?

Hackman and Oldham suggest five implementing concepts which can be applied to jobs to improve their motivating potential:

- combining tasks – to enhance skill variety and task identity
- forming natural work units – to enhance task identity and task significance
- establishing direct employee/client relationships, rather than mediation through junior management – to increase skill variety and autonomy
- vertical loading – to enhance autonomy
- opening feedback channels.

Figure 7 sets out the potential sequence of Hackman and Oldham's job enrichment strategy.

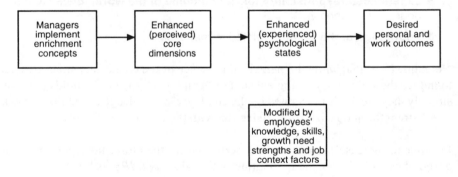

Figure 7: Hackman and Oldman's job enrichment strategy

Tests of this model have provided mixed results but generally it would appear that jobs which had a high score on the core dimensions were associated with high levels of both personal and work outcomes. Certainly expectancy theory has highlighted more factors which affect motivation. The second process theory which we examine is equity theory but first of all complete the next activity. You draw out the contrast between the implications for work organisation and management of a Taylorite 'economic rational' approach to motivation, and that influenced by job enrichment and expectancy models.

ACTIVITY 21

List the Taylorite opposites of the following eight job enrichment principles:

1 considerable discretion

2 considerable knowledge, planning and control

3 'large', visible transformations to product/service

4 'long' cycle time

5 pace varied

6 quality judged

7 skill challenge

8 social interactions built-in

Your answers should have been along the following lines:

1 minimal autonomy

2 minimal knowledge/planning/control

3 very small transformations to product/service

4 very short cycle time

5 pace constant

6 quality standard pre-determined

7 minimal skill

8 confined to individual work station.

We move now to a second process theory of motivation, equity theory. This can be seen as complementary to the expectancy theory we have just examined.

4.4 Equity theory

Equity theory has received increasing attention in recent years. It holds that a major input into job performance and satisfaction is the assessment that employees make of whether or not they are being equitably or fairly treated in terms of rewards. Employees are considered to make regular equity comparisons with others which may result in either:

- **perceived equity-balance**
- **perceived positive inequities** – where employees feel that they are receiving a relatively more-than-fair reward than others in proportion to effort
- **perceived negative inequities** – where employees feel that they are receiving a relatively less-than-fair reward, in proportion to effort, than others

Both of the latter states produce motivating states of mind.

The theory asserts that employees seek an equitable balance between perceived job demands and rewards. Where this is seen to exist, employees' feelings of equity are likely to foster high performance and satisfaction. In situations of inequity, however, employees experience discomfort. It is the level of this discomfort or tension that determines the strength of the motivation. Where the perceived inequity is in terms of under-reward, employees are likely to be motivated to move to an equity-balance by, for example:

- decreasing their inputs
- seeking to increase rewards
- leaving the situation either literally by resignation or informally, for example, by increasing their lateness and absentee rates
- change their comparison point by beginning to compare themselves with a less advantaged group within or outside the organisation.

ACTIVITY 22

Where employees perceive over-reward inequity how are they motivated to restore equity?

Just as in situations of felt, negative inequity, employees have been found to decrease the quality or the quantity of their work. In situations where they feel over-rewarded, they have been found to do the opposite. However, while equity may thus be restored in the short term, employees may not really want to put in this extra effort in the long term. Given this, they may leave the situation. Some research has also suggested that in such situations, employees may achieve equity by psychologically distorting the comparisons. For example, they may convince themselves that their current level of pay, which they perceived as involving an over-reward, does not in fact give them the buying power that they previously thought it did.

ACTIVITY 23

Do you see any potential problems and motivational implications for managers in what we have said about equity theory?

Problems which have been associated with equity theory are:

- Should rewards be commensurate with employee input or with the quality and quantity of work produced in that other factors may affect output?

- It is very difficult to measure the level of tension which is seen to determine the level of motivation since perceptions of inequities, that is, the feelings of employees about their reward levels, are by definition subjective.

- Again in terms of the importance of perception, it may be that some employees will not, for example, perceive under-reward inequity as motivating.

- Little is known about how employees select their comparison points.

Despite these and other difficulties, equity theory does help in the understanding of possible work dissatisfactions and does have certain implications for managers.

The following motivational implications of equity theory have been identified:

- Given that 'social comparisons' are important rather than the absolute amount of the reward, then managers must seek to develop reward systems which present a picture of equity both on an individual-to-individual and a group-to-group basis.

- Given that the employees act on the basis of their perceptions, managers must seek to get the reward system understood and accepted by all. This should include, of course, the comparison points considered appropriate.

REVIEW ACTIVITY 4

Suggested time: 45 minutes.

To help your understanding, re-read the *Production at Trevor Thompson and Sons* case study on page 528 and answer the questions that follow our brief review of the last part of it.

The new manufacturing layout introduced a Taylorised set-up with low motivation. Under the new flow-line process the manufacture of each fishing rod was broken down into five elements. The workers now sat alongside the continuously moving track with the basic rods fed automatically onto it with each worker in turn completing an element of the rod. Finished fishing rods were carried to an inspection position where they were checked for quality.

1 With the benefit of hindsight, what motivational implications of expectancy theory could you suggest Trevor should have borne in mind when considering introducing the new layout?

2 With the benefit of hindsight, which of Hackman and Oldham's implementing concepts could you suggest Trevor should have borne in mind when considering introducing the new layout?

3 With the benefit of hindsight, which implications of equity theory could you suggest Trevor should have borne in mind when introducing the new layout?

Summary

Our objectives in this section were for you to appreciate both expectancy and equity theories and their motivational implications. You gained a grasp of the basic ideas of expectancy theory, and developed this into Vroom's expectancy equation and then Porter and Lawler's approach. You clarified the distinction that they make between extrinsic and intrinsic rewards and related that distinction back to Herzberg's two-factor theory. You then considered the general, motivational implications of expectancy theory.

You moved on to the Hackman and Oldham model of job enrichment which, using ideas and principles of expectancy theory, involved a more sophisticated approach than that initially suggested by Herzberg. You contrasted the implications for organisation and management of job enrichment and expectancy models with their Taylorite opposites. You then evaluated equity theory and its relation to motivation.

Unit Summary

In this unit, you have looked at motivation, what it is and how various theories have developed. Then you looked in detail at several theories and their motivational implications in the work place.

We have mainly focused on the re-structuring of individual jobs in relation to motivation. However, in the context of the Wickens article, team working, an important development in job design, was also mentioned. You look again at groups and teams in Unit 8 and their motivational implications.

References

Alderfer, CP (1969) 'An Empirical Test of a New Theory of Human Needs', *Organisational Behaviour and Human Performance*, 4, pp. 142-75.

Beardwell, I and Holden, L (1994) *Human Resource Management: a Contemporary Perspective*, London: Pitman Publishing.

Daniel, WW (1973) 'Understanding Employee Behaviour in its Context' in *Man and Organisation*, Ed. Child, J. London: Allen and Unwin.

Goldthorpe, JH Lockwood, D Bechhofer, F and Platt, J (1968) *The Affluent Worker: Industrial Attitudes and Behaviour*, Cambridge: Cambridge University Press.

Hackman, JR and Oldham, GR (1980) *Work Redesign*, London: Addison-Wesley.

Herzberg, F (1968) 'One More Time: How Do You Motivate Employees', *Harvard Business Review*, 46, pp. 53-62.

Huczyinski, AA and Buchanan, DA (1991) *Organisational Behaviour: an Introductory Text*, second edition, Englewood Cliffs, New Jersey: Prentice-Hall.

Ivancevich, JM and Matteson, MT (1993) *Organisational Behaviour and Management*, third edition, Irwin Inc.

Luthans, F (1992) *Organisational Behaviour*, sixth edition, New York: McGraw Hill Inc.

Maslow, A (1943) 'A Theory of Human Motivation', *Psychological Review,* 50, (4), pp. 370-96.

Mullins, LJ (1993) *Management and Organisational Behaviour,* third edition, London: Pitman Publishing.

Pheysey, DC (1993) *Organisational Cultures: Types and Transformations,* London: Routledge.

Roethlisberger, FJ and Dickson, WV (1939) *Management and The Worker,* Massachusetter: Harvard University Press.

Porter, LW and Lawler, EE (1968) *Managerial Attitudes and Performance,* Homewood, IL: Irwin.

Schein, EH (1988) *Organisational Psychology,* third edition, Englewood Cliffs, New Jersey: Prentice-Hall.

Taylor, FW (1947) *Scientific Management,* New York: Harper & Row.

Vroom, VH (1964) *Work and Motivation,* Chichester: John Wiley.

Watson, T (1987) *Sociology, Work and Industry,* London: Routledge and Kegan Paul.

Wickens, P (1993) 'Steering the Middle Road to Car Production' in *Personnel Management,* June, pp. 34-38.

Womack, J Jones, D and Roos, D (1990) *The Machine that Changed the World,* Rawson Associates.

Recommended Reading

Huczyinski, JR and Buchanan, DA (1991) *Organisational Behaviour: an Introductory Text,* Englewood Cliffs, New Jersey: Prentice-Hall, second edition, Chapter 4.

Luthans, F (1992) *Organisational Behaviour,* New York: McGraw Hill, sixth edition, Chapters 6 and 7.

Mullins, LJ (1993) *Management and Organisational Behaviour,* London: Pitman Publishing, third edition, Chapters 14 and 15.

Wilson, DC and Rosenfeld, RH (1990) *Managing Organisations,* New York: McGraw-Hill, Chapters 5 and 7.

Answers to Review Activities

Review Activity 1

1   Content theories assume that individuals have a packet of needs and behave in ways which satisfy them. In the light of Mayo's work, it seems very likely that Trevor's workforce was motivated by social needs and this is reflected in its behaviour. Each team has a clear sense of territory and, for example, the employees talked mainly about their social life and very rarely about work-related matters. When the new manufacturing layout was introduced, work was individualised, the sense of territory lost and the outcome was an increase in turnover, a fall in output and a deterioration in quality.

2   Process theories assume that individuals are able to select goals and take the appropriate paths towards them through a continuous process of calculation. What Trevor was likely to have had in mind when he insisted on the introduction of a unit bonus to be paid for exceeding the specified level of production, appears to be an assumption that his employees had a strong desire for higher earnings and, having given them a clear route to this end, the expectation that they would put in 'increased financial reward'-directed effort.

3   Trevor failed to recognise that his employees were motivated by social needs and introduced job specialisation. He appears to have seen this primary motivation for high effort to be higher earnings via the unit bonus scheme. As we have already seen, the new layout undermined teamwork and inhibited social interaction. Had Trevor been familiar with Mayo's work, it is likely that he would have recognised the importance of social need fulfilment to his employees and sought a better balance between the new technical layout and their desired social interactions. Certainly, he would have insisted on the introduction of the unit bonus scheme which potentially directly undermined the sense of group.

Review Activity 2

1   Basic physiological needs and needs for safety and security.

2   The implication is that once we have gained entry into a group that is important to us, the relief at belonging is quickly superseded by, for example, a concern that we are given respect within that group.

3   Certainly, money can satisfy our hunger for food but it may also be used to satisfy our need for status and esteem. For example, a junior clerk may invest in a mobile phone and contrive to give the impression that he is making

important business calls. Money can also buy, of course, a Rolls Royce which almost invariably will generate interest and speculation about its occupant.

4   Look back at question (2); a yearning to belong to a valued group will continue to motivate us. It is our state of not belonging, our unsatisfied need, that activates us. Once we have gained entry, of course, the need to belong is satisfied and is soon replaced by our need for respect from other group members or the status of having an important role in the group which then motivates us.

5   The notion of self-actualisation involves the idea of 'fully' realising our potential. We 'grow' and become, as far as we are able, the person we are capable of becoming.

6   It is perfectly reasonable to assume that we may want to satisfy both social and esteem needs. Equally, a starving painter may be fully aware that he is producing his finest work but may also yearn for financial security or the recognition of his peers.

Review Activity 4

1   In terms of expectancy theory, Trevor could, for example, have established just what 'incentives' his staff valued. It is likely that they would have wanted as many social team orientated aspects to have survived the transition as possible. Given this, Trevor should have sought to minimise what his employees would have perceived as undesirable outcomes stemming from the new higher performance requirements. For example, given that the track contained ten five-person units, as much a sense of 'team' as possible should have been retained.

2   In terms of Hackman and Oldham's implementing concepts, Trevor could, for example, have considered allowing the five-person 'teams' to do their own inspection and hence enhance quality feedback.

3   You might have found that the motivational implications of equity theory were less relevant. This is perfectly reasonable. As we observed in the unit introduction, it is up to managers to judge the relevance of motivation theories and whether or not they can be applied in particular contexts.

UNIT 8

GROUPS AND GROUP EFFECTIVENESS

Introduction

As you have seen from your earlier studies of Taylor and scientific management, he suggested that workers were fundamentally economic animals. He also suggested that **systematic soldiering,** where workers came together to hold down production, would be cured when managers began to do their jobs properly, that is, to relate directly to each worker and satisfy his or her personal self-interest. For, as Watson (1987) put it, Taylorism suggests that each worker is '. . . a self-seeking, non-social individual who prefers the management to do their job-related thinking for them.'

You know from your knowledge of the Hawthorne experiments and, for example, from your work on motivation in Unit 7, that there has been a volte face in management thought on both counts. Indeed, it has been observed that the writings of Mayo created a *cult* of the group. We are now able, however, to put the importance of groups into their proper perspective while still recognising that they are an essential feature of organisational work patterns. One of our purposes in this unit is to make this clear. Work is a social activity. There are many organisational goals that *cannot* be achieved by members acting independently. Given this, most individuals spend a great deal of their organisational time working with others in groups. Before beginning to explore groups and group effectiveness, however, do the following activity which requires you to bring into focus groups that feature, or have featured, in your life.

ACTIVITY 1

The notions of groups and teams have already been referred to and by now you should have your own ideas about the meaning of these terms.

1 Make clear the difference, as you understand it, between groups and teams.

When you joined your study programme, it is likely that you became a member of a small discussion group of students that convened as and when required. We call this group, *Group 1*. It is also likely that you belong to other groups and we would like you to focus on one of these which we call *Group 2*. Answer questions 2 and 3 about *Groups 1* and *2* respectively and, if you also belong to a *Team* in some context of your life as distinguished by you earlier, then also answer question 4.

2 *Group 1*

We have referred quite unproblematically to this group actually *being* a group. Did you, however, get a real sense, over time, of actually belonging to a group? Explain your answer.

3 *Group 2*

What is/was the size of the group?

What circumstances gave rise to the group?

If you were not a founder member of the group, describe your experience of gaining acceptance.

4 *Team*

What circumstances gave rise to your team?

Do/did your team have any norms of behaviour which conflict/conflicted in any way with its 'official' norms? If so, explain.

---

1   It is likely that you will have distinguished between groups and teams by stressing the *formal* nature of the latter, brought together by management to accomplish a specific task. We say more about formal and informal groups during the unit.

2-4 There are obviously no *correct* responses to these questions. The overall purpose of this activity was for you to reflect on *your* group or team experiences. You will need to refer back to your responses at appropriate points in the unit.

Objectives

By the end of the unit, you should be able to:

● define a group.

● distinguish between formal and informal groups.

● list the types of formal groups.

● explain the main purposes for which individuals use groups.

● list the major organisational purposes of groups and teams.

● evaluate the notion that groups develop in stages.

● explain the major determinants of group effectiveness.

● understand Belbin's notion of team roles.

● identify the symptoms of groupthink.

● show an awareness of the importance of group task and maintenance functions.

SECTION 1

Groups

Introduction

In this section, we explore the concept of the primary group and then go on to examine types of groups. We mention secondary groups but the main emphasis is on the distinction between formal and informal groups at work. We close with an examination of the purposes for which individuals may use groups.

1.1 Definition of a group

Handy (1993) defined a **group** as '. . . any collection of people who perceive themselves to be a group.' So, when we use words like groups or group relationships, we refer to the existence of a psychological relationship. A collection of people then, who happen to find themselves in the same queue for the cinema are not a group – despite the existence of the spatial relationship. As Brown (1971) put it, the term group '. . . is reserved for those aggregates of people which have psychological effects on, and implications for, the individuals composing the group.' Becoming a group member, she stresses, '. .. implies a psychological process of affiliating to others and interaction with others'.

Groups, then, have an independent identity. This implies acknowledged behaviour which defines those who are 'in' and those who are 'out', and the loyalty of the former is expressed in their acceptance of the attitudes and standards of behaviour that bind the group together. The notion of loyalty, of course, always implies the possibility of disloyalty and the consequent use of sanctions against those who transgress against group norms.

In Activity 1, you looked at your own subjective awareness of actually belonging to *Group 1* and to describe your experience of gaining acceptance in your *Group 2,* if you were not a founder member. Remind yourself now of your answers to 2 and 3. Did you have a sense, over time, of 'bending' in the direction of the expectations of the group? And in terms of *Group 2,* were you aware of being processed into an acceptance of any group norms as you moved towards insider status? To help you appreciate what is meant by a group, do the following activity. Look out particularly for the impact of group membership on the machinists in the case study in terms of their acceptance of certain attitudes and standards of behaviour.

ACTIVITY 2

Read the case study *Joan Shaw, Production Manager,* then perform the tasks at the end and share your results in a group, if possible.

Joan Shaw, Production Manager

Joan Shaw was promoted from sewing machine shop supervisor to production manager of Swift (Wholesale Clothes) Limited nine months ago. Swift is a small company, manufacturing ladies' skirts, blouses and dresses. Joan had previously been appointed supervisor from outside the company, about five years earlier.

From the beginning, she noticed that most of the teenage, female machinists did not seem to be interested in working very hard, and took no pride in the quality of their work. As supervisor, her frequent attempts to improve this situation had been blocked by the former production manager, Joe Manners, whose retirement at the age of 65 had led to Joan's promotion. Joe's favourite remark to Joan was: 'Don't rock the boat; we've operated like this for as long as I can remember, and we've not gone broke yet.'

Joan is a self-confident, alert and energetic 45-year-old. She arrives for work every day at 7 am, an hour and a half before the official start time. She usually works through her lunch hour, and stays late every night. Other than bank holidays, she has not taken a holiday since she joined the company. It was this dedication to her work which led the general manager to promote Joan when Joe retired. No supervisor was appointed to replace Joan. The general manager felt that Joan would be able to supervise the day-to-day work of the 40 machinists and adequately perform the tasks associated with the production manager's job. Joe had contributed little during his last few years with the company and it seemed to the general manager that Joan carried out most of the production manager's work.

When she was promoted, Joan advised the general manager that she would make improvements to the manufacturing process by increasing the level of output and the quality of the garments. In an attempt to achieve these goals, she persistently harassed the machinists about their work. She regularly inspected their work and complained to them about the quality of their sewing, often taking over the machine to demonstrate the correct work methods. The machinists began to mimic Joan's much-used question, 'Am I the only one here who knows how to sew properly?'

The company recruited trained machinists and Joan would explain the work methods of the company before putting a new machinist to work alongside an experienced machinist. The experienced machinist was supposed to help if the new recruit had difficulties. The machinists referred to this induction period as 'breaking in a newcomer'. They did not wait to be asked for assistance, but would approach a new machinist and show her the 'easy way' to produce the garments. A typical exchange between a new and experienced machinist would be:

Experienced machinist:	No, that's not the way to turn a sleeve. Look, if you do it like this you don't have to double sew the seams.
New machinist:	But I'm doing it the way Miss Shaw said I had to.
Experienced machinist:	I know you are, but she's never had to sit sewing like that for eight hours a day. You do it my way, it's easier.
New machinist:	But she'll come round and see that I'm not sewing the way she said I had to.
Experienced machinist:	Don't worry about that; when she's here we do it her way. Sometimes she sees us taking the short cuts and just shows us the right way. Just slow down and do it our way.
New machinist:	But Miss Shaw says I have to do twenty a day. If I slow down I'll never get them done!
Experienced machinist:	I'm sure she did. You try to do one in thirty minutes, that way you'll do sixteen a day.
New machinist:	But Miss Shaw wants me to do twenty. I'll be able to do this many, and double sew the seams, when I get used to the machine.
Experienced machinist:	You'll wear yourself to a frazzle doing so many. Sixteen's a fair number for the pay we get.

Output has fallen since Joan became production manager, and there has been no improvement in the quality of the work produced. One reason for the fall in production is that on several occasions sewing has been held up when stocks of cloth ran out because Joan had not re-ordered in time. Also, the machinists' morale has dropped. One long-serving machinist summed up her feelings: 'Before she [Joan] came and Joe was here we were one happy family, working at a nice pace. Now we either sit around doing nothing because there's no cloth to sew, or we are being nagged to work harder.'

1   Make notes on the notion of 'breaking in a newcomer'.

2   Do you think it is possible for 40 machinists to be a group?

3   How do you think the situation could be resolved?

1   It is likely that you will have highlighted the role of the experienced machinist, both socialising newcomers into the 'easy' way to produce garments and into the unofficial, output norm of sixteen garments a day. The 'old hands' point out that sixteen is seen as 'a fair number for the pay we get'.

The experienced employees also point out that when Joan Shaw is about, they produce the garments according to her formally laid down standards, and that if she catches them taking short cuts, all she does is show them again the official way to do it.

2   Forty would appear too large for a psychological relationship to exist between them. It seems reasonable to assume that once the number exceeds, say, twelve members, sub-groups are likely to emerge. However, Mitchell and Larson (1987) would still consider twenty-member 'groups' as groups and argue that 'the frequent, face-to-face interaction and mutual influence that is characteristic of small groups is much less likely to occur when there are more than about twenty people involved.' Of course, at Swifts there may well be sub-groups with identical norms and certainly the fact that they are all doing similar work, are seemingly located in close proximity to each other and all face the common, external threat of Joan Shaw, would certainly enhance their cohesiveness.

3   Obviously, the general manager must address the situation with some urgency. Since Joan became production manager. output has fallen and there has been no improvement in quality. Also, of course, she is not adequately performing the tasks associated with her job. We could take the line that Joan Shaw has to go but it is likely that she is still well regarded by the general manager and, in many ways, she is an exceptional worker. The best strategy might be for the general manager to appoint an experienced supervisor from outside and to ensure that Joan sticks to her job and leaves the new supervisor to carry out her role. A group incentive scheme may also help in this situation, especially since performance is directly measurable.

It would be useful now to look more closely at the types of groups that are likely to exist in an organisation.

1.2 Types of groups

Our main interest here is in **primary** rather than **secondary** groups, that is, in what we have already identified as psychological groups where membership is small enough for all to have frequent, face-to-face contact and where feelings of loyalty, comradeship and shared values exist among members.

Entire organisations, on the other hand, are examples of secondary groups which are always formally set up, are usually larger and are impersonal. As Luthans (1992) has pointed out: 'Initially, the [term] primary group was limited to a socialising group, but then a broader conception was given impetus by the results of the Hawthorne studies. Work groups definitely have primary group qualities.'

Primary groups can either be **formal** or **informal**. Formal primary groups are those prescribed by the organisation. The teams at Uddevalla, referred to in Unit 7, and in Item 7.1, 'Steering the Middle Road to Car Production', are prescribed by the company. Clegg, in his article, Item 8.1, refers to Japanese quality circles where the work teams are joined by staff specialists such as engineers. Quality circles too, are examples of formal, primary groups. Such groups then will have certain roles and goals predetermined so that prior to member interaction, certain aspects of behaviour are already fixed. Japanese business organisations, of course, as Clegg points out, are premised on self-managing teams.

Where, of course, the formal organisation fails to provide for primary groups, informal primary groups will spring up. Even with formal primary groups, however, informal norms and forms of behaviour are likely to evolve which will often run counter to those of the formal organisation.

ACTIVITY 3

Read the article by Clegg, Item 8.1 in the Resource section. In what ways, do Japanese organisations seek to inhibit the evolution of norms and forms of behaviour which may run counter to the formal demands of the company?

You will probably have mentioned spiritual training which essentially involves socialisation to, and indoctrination in, company goals.

Other examples of formal primary groups would be committees that managements set up on either a temporary or a permanent basis, or the task forces they establish for fixed periods to accomplish specific work. In contrast to such formal groups, primary groups are seen to arise simultaneously.

Informal groups then, as Mullins (1993) puts it, are 'based more on personal relationships and agreement of group members than on defined role relationships. They serve to satisfy psychological and social needs not related necessarily to the tasks to be undertaken.'

However, roles, norms and goals do tend to develop in informal groups arising out of the current interaction of members. You saw something of this in the Joan Shaw case study. The Hawthorne studies, of course, which you examined in Unit 1, painted a more detailed picture of informal groups. As well as norms against producing too much, there were pressures not to produce too little and sanctions ranged from 'kidding rebukes' to ostracism. The membership of one informal group included the supervisor and an inspector. In this case, the official organisation of the company came to an end, in reality, above the primary group level.

This examination of the types of groups existing in organisations suggests that it would be useful to consider the purposes for which individuals use groups. We have already mentioned psychological and social need satisfaction. Before we elaborate on these purposes, however, complete the next two activities to help you consolidate your understanding of the distinction between groups and teams and to apply this understanding about groups and their types to a case study situation.

ACTIVITY 4

In question 1 of Activity 1, you distinguished between groups and teams. However, this was really distinguishing between informal groups and formal teams. Are you still happy with your answer? If you are not, amend it.

ACTIVITY 5

Read the case study, *Trouble at Mill Associates,* and then describe what you would do to sort out this situation if you were the managing partner. In doing so, reflect particularly on the nature of groups and the types of group.

Trouble at Mill Associates

Mill Associates is an accounting firm, which has grown in 30 years from a simple chartered accountants to a large national firm providing a broad spectrum of financial services and advice. The firm is a partnership with 17 partners and 15 offices located in major cities and towns. Each office is managed by a partner, who has direct responsibility for the work of the professional and support staff in his/her office. The cleaning, maintenance and caretaker service is provided by a contract firm.

It is the partners' policy to recruit fully qualified staff and currently the firm employs about 150 professional accountants. The accountants are placed in one of the three salary groupings termed 'accountant', 'senior accountant' and 'principal accountant'. Within each group, there is a ten-point scale. The size of the differential between each point on the scale is approximately £500 with considerable overlap between the groupings, so that the maxima of the accountant scale equates to the third point on the senior accountant scale, and the maxima of the senior accountant scale equates to the third point on the principal accountant scale.

The salary groupings are designed to reflect professional responsibility, and the number of scales within each grouping are designed to recognise salary growth as a result of experience. Staff progress automatically within their salary grouping up to the maxima for that group, selected staff are promoted to a higher grouping by the partners. There is no formal system of performance appraisal, but the partners consider that they know their staff 'pretty well'. The majority of newly appointed staff are placed on the accountant scale at a point appropriate to their qualifications and experience, very exceptionally appointments are made directly to the minima point on the senior accountant scale.

One of the firm's largest offices is situated in Birmingham. In addition to the managing partner, this office employs 38 professional accountants and 11 secretarial and administrative staff. The office accommodation is a three-storey block. Originally, the office space was allocated according to a salary grouping. The third floor accommodated the partner and the partner's secretary, and six principal accountants occupying the other three offices. The senior accountants, three sharing an office, occupied the second floor. The accountants and the administrative staff occupied the ground and first floors. Over the years, the allocation plan has become distorted so that some offices are now shared by members of all three salary groupings.

Gordon Gray, Alec Brown and Simon Andrews occupy one of the third floor offices. Gordon, the firm's only specialist in bankruptcy, was recruited as a senior accountant 17 years ago and promoted to principal accountant two years later. His colleagues attribute his rapid promotion to principal accountant to the fact that he belongs to the same masonic lodge as the managing partner.

Gordon is a nationally known fuchsia grower. He developed a collection of new hybrid varieties and is in great demand to show his plants, and to lecture on fuchsia cultivation and propagation. Alec and Simon believe that he devotes far more time to his hobby that he does to his job. Gordon prefers to work at home. He attends the office once or twice each week to pick up messages, most of which are taken down by Simon, who is continually interrupted in his work to answer Gordon's telephone.

Alec and Simon have been with the firm for ten years and seven years, respectively. Alec is one of the firm's five taxation specialists and Simon is the firm's only pension fund management specialist. During the past two years, the pension fund work has more than doubled and it is generally recognised by the accounting and administrative staff that Simon contributes more than any other member of the firm. Recent government legislation concerning occupational pension funds has added further major elements to the pension fund work.

This increase led Simon to ask the managing partner to employ another pension fund specialist to take over some of the additional work. The partner refused the request, telling Simon that he had no evidence that Simon was overloaded. When told of this decision, Alec commented to Simon, 'Your problem is that you are so competent at your job that it appears that you are never unduly pressed.'

Brenda Sykes was appointed in the accountant grade about twelve months ago, and was recently assigned to work with Alec on taxation matters. Her office was on the ground floor, for convenience of access to Alec, it was decided by Alec that it would be sensible for Brenda to move into his office on the top floor. Simon agreed. To create space for her, Gordon's desk was moved from its prime position by the window to a less attractive site near the door. When Brenda demurred at moving Gordon's desk without his agreement, Simon replied, 'Well he is never here anyway, so what does it matter? The only work he does is picking up his pay cheque – which amounts to yours and mine put together.'

When Gordon came into the office and saw the changes that had been made, he was furious. He stormed out of the office, fetched the caretaker, and had his desk replaced in its previous position. He then went to see the managing partner and told him what had happened. He insisted that Alec, Simon and Brenda should be moved from the office because, 'The top floor is supposed to be for principal accountants, and they should not be there.'

Gordon told Alec, Simon and Brenda the gist of his conversation with the managing partner. After discussing the situation among themselves, the three also went to see the managing partner and asked that Gordon be moved to another office. Simon said to the partner, 'He is never here anyway, so it doesn't matter where his desk is. Not only does he earn more than we do for doing less work, we have to spend a lot of our time taking his telephone calls and trying to deal with inquiries about bankruptcy.' They told the managing partner that if he moved them out of their office they would leave the firm to set up in business on their own account as pension fund and taxation consultants.

What would you do about this situation if you were the managing partner? Explain your answer.

It is likely that you will find another office for Gordon for whatever your relationship with him, you would not want to let it jeopardise the success of Mill Associates. The pressing problem is to avoid losing Alec, Simon and Brenda who are, if necessary, determined to set up their own business.

It is not clear from the case whether or not you were personally responsible for the original salary and status grouping of staff but it is clearly an outdated notion and one that now actually impedes rather than facilitates performance. The status group were by definition not teams, nor did the occupants of the third floor office in question comprise a cohesive group. In the interests of efficiency and effectiveness, natural task groups must be allowed to form. Indeed, you should now consider formalising this tendency throughout the company. Certainly, Alec and Brenda will be one such team and it is likely that you will have realised that Simon's over-work has contributed to this crisis and that it is now time to bring in another pension fund specialist to assist him. Taking a decision on task teams generally, and taxation and pension fund teams in particular, may make it easier for you to handle Gordon. Any office changes can then be 'sold' on the basis of being part of a larger plan and nothing personal, and you may well be willing to let Gordon have an office of his own with a secretary working for him.

1.3 Purposes for which individuals use groups

Obviously, individuals use groups for different reasons and, while for the purposes of our exposition, these reasons can be distinguished, there may in reality be a lot of overlap between them.

- Groups may be a means of reducing insecurity. It is likely that we arrive in organisations as quite isolated strangers and the group offers a haven of guidance, support and security.

- Groups are a means of satisfying our interaction and affiliation needs. We want to belong and we want to share in something.

- Groups are a potential means of satisfying status and self-esteem needs. The group can give the individual recognition and the fact that within the wider organisation that group may be quite highly valued may further enhance feelings of self-worth.

- Groups may assist individuals to establish a self-concept. It is often in the eyes of others, and in terms of their relationship to these others, that individuals can best define themselves. This implies, of course, a more active use of groups than just providing arenas within which security, affiliation and self-esteem are to be found. The next purpose is even more active.

- Groups may provide a means of satisfying power and goal achievement needs. For example, joining together with others may, as you have already seen, enable individuals to counter what they see as unfair organisational demands. The collective power of the group may enable individuals to achieve goals which may have been unattainable to individuals acting alone.

Groups capable of fulfilling such purposes do not develop instantly, of course, as we have already implied and as you will know from your own experience. Primary groups, whether formal or informal, become psychological groups over a period of time. We examine a popular model of group development which identifies four successive stages involved in this process, but first of all try the following activity to help you understand the purposes that group membership may serve for individuals.

ACTIVITY 6

In terms of the group(s)/team which you addressed in Activity 1, reflect on the purpose(s) they served for you:

1 List the potential purposes for which individuals may use groups which you feel apply/applied to you.

2 Did you use them for purposes other than those posited? If so, what were they?

3 If you belong/have belonged to a formally designated team as well as an informal group, are you able to distinguish in any way between respective purposes served?

Individuals use groups for a variety of purposes and those referred to in this section are standard but not exhaustive. To isolate and reflect on other purposes which you were/are able to serve will further your knowledge of groups and indeed of yourself. If you are able to distinguish in any way between the purposes for which you used informal groups as opposed to teams, then this may add to your knowledge of the differences between them. It could be argued, for example, that to be a member of a formally designated team further incorporates the individual into the organisation and hence limits the types of purpose for which that individual may wish to use their team membership.

REVIEW ACTIVITY 1

Suggested time: 20 minutes.

1 What do you see as the main difference between the way Handy and Brown defined groups?

2 In what kind of groups are certain aspects of behaviour already fixed prior to member interaction?

3 List as many types of formal group as you can.

Summary

In Section 1, we have been concerned with establishing the meaning of the concept 'group'; distinguishing between formal and informal groups; listing the types of formal group; and explaining the main purposes for which individuals use groups.

We sought to do this with discussion and definitions, but also by asking you to draw on your own group and team experiences both in terms of your sense of being processed by the groups and in terms of the purposes which group membership served for you. The *Joan Shaw Case Study* focused especially on the impact of group norms and the fact that these were at odds with the wider organisational purposes. To help you understand the restrictive nature of norms, you referred to the Clegg article which looked at a number of mechanisms by which Japanese workers are brought to align their group norms with the objectives of the enterprise as a whole. For example, the notion of spiritual training is referred to what essentially means socialisation to, and indoctrination in, company goals.

In Section 2, we examine Tuckman's model of the development of groups as they move from infancy, through adolescence and into the effectively performing adult stage.

SECTION 2

Tuckman's Model of Development

Introduction

In this section, we present a popular, four-stage model of group development. Having explored these stages, we make certain observations about the gap which may exist between the model and reality.

2.1 Stages of group development and maturity

Tuckman and Jensen (1977) suggest that groups go through a series of four developmental stages on their way to becoming an effective, psychological group:

STAGE 1 – FORMING

This stage commences, of course, with the bringing together of a number of wary and perhaps anxious and unsure individuals. There are as yet no ground rules and in this vacuum each seeks to find out about the others and make an impression. More specifically, each individual has an idea of the prospective role they would like to play and concerns about the broader, linked issues of hierarchy and leadership. Indeed, the very terms of reference of the group may as yet be unclear. This stage will only be transcended when there has emerged a certain sense of involvement and cohesiveness. The 'individuals' have started to think of themselves as members of a group.

STAGE 2 – STORMING

This is the period of disagreement and potential confrontation. Members now feel more confident and able to express their views more forcefully and more openly. Some may reject the tentative ground rules that had developed during the first stage or there may be a general reaction against all prior arrangements. If this stage is to be successful, there must be a move to a working through of conflicts and the initiation of purposeful discussions on structure, leadership and acceptable ways of operating.

STAGE 3 – NORMING

At this stage of development, there is a clear sense of group identity and a group cohesiveness; norms, procedures, roles and structure become formally established. The group is then ready to fulfil its purpose but it must be remembered that what is in place may not necessarily lead to effectiveness in management terms. In the Hawthorne bank wiring room experiment, as you are aware, group norms led to restrictions on production. It is this stage then that management must seek to influence since once groups are fully developed with an entrenched culture, it is much more difficult to alter their members' attitudes and behaviour.

STAGE 4 – PERFORMING

Given that the group has successfully progressed through the earlier stages, it is now fully functioning and able to concentrate on effective performance.

In terms of these stages, however, you should note the following:

- Different groups may process at different speeds through the stages.

- Certain groups may skip stages. For example, a hand-picked task team may be formed and be performing effectively almost from the outset.

- Certain groups may get 'stuck' before reaching the performing stage and so never be very effective. For example, disagreements and conflicts may never be worked through openly. The 'storming' stage then is initiated covertly and is never in fact completed. It continues 'off-stage' throughout the whole process and in such situations, performance will obviously suffer.

- Effective performance must be sustained both by self-monitoring and external feedback. Even with such monitoring and feedback, of course, effectiveness will only continue for as long as the group is able to maintain itself as a cohesive entity. Continuing effectiveness is consequent upon the continuing personal fulfilment of group members.

In the introduction, we argued that groups, whether formal or informal, are an essential feature of organisational life. Teams are created, informal groups emerge and, as we observed when discussing the stages of group development, managers must seek to influence them at the crucial norming stage if their objectives, and the wider organisational objectives, are to be aligned. Obviously we are implying that groups and teams are required to fulfil important purposes for organisations, as well as for other members, and we examine what these are in Section 3.

REVIEW ACTIVITY 2

Suggested time: 15 minutes.

1 Why is the storming stage of group development 'stormy'?

2 Why will a group never be fully effective if the storming stage is never completed?

3 Is it enough for a manager to help guide a group through to the performing stage and then leave it to its own devices?

Summary

In Section 2, we have been concerned with grasping and evaluating the notion that groups develop in stages. We introduced Tuckman's popular four-stage model and examined each stage. Review Activity 2 was aimed at reinforcing key aspects of the process and we made clear that, by definition, the model does not always match complex reality. Certain groups get 'stuck' at a stage and some groups will not necessarily follow the four-stage process.

SECTION 3

Organisational Purposes of Groups and Teams

Introduction

In this very brief section, we follow Handy in his listing of the major organisational purposes of groups and teams. We conclude by pointing out that to be effective in terms of particular purposes, groups must not attempt to perform any functions simultaneously. In specifically focusing on effectiveness, we set the scene for dealing primarily with the determinants of group effectiveness in Section 4.

3.1 Organisational purposes of groups and teams

Charles Handy (1993) identified the following major organisational purposes of groups to:

- distribute work, having brought together a particular set of skills, talents and responsibilities
- manage and control work
- facilitate the problem-solving process by bringing together all of the available capacities to apply to it
- pass on decisions or information to those who need to know
- gather ideas, information and suggestions
- test and ratify decisions
- co-ordinate and facilitate necessary liaison
- increase commitment and involvement
- resolve arguments and disputes between different functions, levels and divisions
- inquire into the past.

Handy argues that groups cannot successfully perform simultaneous functions. For each function, they behave differently and need to be organised and managed differently and, indeed, need to see themselves as a different group. Handy suggests that this can be accomplished by such simple devices as separating the different functions that they may have to perform by time, venue or even, for example, by committee title. Of course, more factors than this will determine the ultimate effectiveness of a group's performance, we examine some of the more important of these in Section 4.

REVIEW ACTIVITY 3

Suggested time: 15 minutes.

Read the following case study and then answer the question that follows it.

Marshall's Casing Ltd.

Frank Webb, the safety officer at Marshall's Casing was becoming increasingly worried about the company's poor safety record in recent months. He was particularly disturbed that while all of the managers paid lip service to accident prevention, when production pressure was on, it seemed that they were quite willing to suspend safety precautions. With the news of two major new orders in the pipeline and the next meeting of the Safety Committee still three weeks away, Frank decided to raise his concerns at the following Monday morning's production meeting.

Do you think that this was a sensible thing for him to do? Explain.

Summary

In Section 3, we have been solely concerned with the major organisational purposes of groups and teams. We listed the examples of the more important of these and as Review Activity 3 sought to stress, in terms of effectiveness, we must remember that groups cannot generally perform two functions simultaneously.

SECTION 4
Group Effectiveness

Introduction

In this section, we examine the determinants of group effectiveness in terms of three sets of variables. These variables are variously labelled by different writers but they all essentially refer to influences in the situation which are **given** in the short term, influences that can be adapted in the short term to **better fit** the givens, and finally the **outcomes** in terms of performance and satisfaction. In the course of examining these variables, we present Belbin's team roles, along with the notion of groupthink, group task and maintenance functions and communication networks.

4.1 Determinants of group effectiveness

There are a number of models which set out useful ways of thinking about the determinants of group effectiveness. The majority of these distinguish between three sets of variables which, however they are named, essentially reflect the same approach. Kretch et al (1962), for example, divided the determinants of group effectiveness into:

- **independent variables** – group, environmental and task variables
- **intermediate variables** – for example, leadership style and group task motivation
- **dependent variables** – that is the outcomes, productivity and member satisfaction.

According to the model of group effectiveness presented by Hackman et al (1979), group effectiveness is influenced by:

- **group design factors,** interpersonal processes and the environmental context which combine to influence
  - **intermediate criteria,** for example, group effort, which in turn determine
  - **work group effectiveness,** productive output and personal need satisfaction.

Handy, on the other hand, labels his three sets of variables:

- the **givens** – the group, the task and the environment
- the **intervening factors** – leadership style, processes and procedures, motivation
- the **outcomes** – productivity, member satisfaction.

In our discussion of the determinants of group effectiveness we use Handy's headings, but under them we also draw more generally from the other models to help us explore and highlight the more important factors.

Givens:	Group	Task	Environment
	● size	● nature	● physical setting
	● member characteristics	● effectiveness criteria	● cultural setting
	● hidden agendas		● leader/member status
Intervening Factors:	Leader style		
	Group functions		
	Interaction patterns		
	Member satisfaction		
	Group productivity		
Outcomes:			

Figure 1: Determinants of group effectiveness

The notion of the **givens** or the independent variables, is that there are certain aspects of the situation that will affect the outcome which in the short term are given constraints within which the group must operate. Obviously these givens can be altered in the medium or long term. The **intervening factors** or the intermediate variables, on the other hand, can be changed in the short term. However, as Handy points out, this division is not absolute. It may be, for example, that a so-called given like the nature of the task can be altered in the short term. As Handy puts it: 'The successful manager is the one who constantly appraises and challenges the constraints.'

ACTIVITY 7

Note down what sorts of thing in group situations you feel might be given constraints, in the sense we have just explained.

You might have listed a number of things but most are likely to be related to the givens that we now examine as significant influences on group performance. These are **group-related, task-related** and **environmental factors**.

Group-related factors are:

● size

● member characteristics

● presence of hidden agendas in the group.

Task-related factors are:

- nature of task
- how group effectiveness is measured.

Environmental factors are:

- physical setting
- cultural setting
- leader and member status.

4.2 The givens

GROUP-RELATED VARIABLES

Group size

The optimum size of a group in terms of its effectiveness is related to the nature of the task. In terms of problem-solving, for example, larger groups tend to do better since the range of skills and knowledge is wider. For tasks involving pooled interdependence between group members, such as cleaning the cabin of a jumbo jet, as maintenance crew size increases, the job gets done much more quickly. On the other hand, where effectiveness hinges on the quality of the group's interaction as in a research team, problems of co-ordination outweigh the enhanced skills and knowledge base as group size is increased.

Also, of course, by definition, as we go beyond the size compatible with having the characteristics of a psychological group, participation, involvement, cohesiveness and member satisfaction decreases. So, as Hogg wrote in 1990: 'With fewer members [than five] there is a danger that there will not be an adequate mix of skills and abilities. With more than 10-12, problems arise because the processes start to become difficult to handle, with team members starting to divide themselves into sub-groups. Other difficulties arise in that it becomes awkward to ensure the involvement of all members of the team. More people are less able to express themselves in large groups.'

If the group size is truly a given in the short term, it does not mean that chairpeople and leaders cannot do anything about the resultant constraints on their group's effectiveness. Once aware, for example, of group resources being neglected for whatever reason, they can take the relevant members on one side and still ensure that task accomplishment benefits from their contributions.

Member characteristics

Obviously, member ability is important in terms of effectiveness but so also is group compatibility. Research has shown that other things being equal, groups composed of members with a wide range of complementary abilities and skills out-perform those groups in which all of the members have essentially the same set of abilities and skills. As Hogg (1990) put it, like a good comedy act, [team members] should have compatible skills, experience and personality rather than being of the same mould. However, as she went on to say, 'members of a team do need to have the same values and principles, so that they start from a common base, can agree priorities and, most important of all, can start to build up a relationship of trust.'

The recipe for effective groups in terms of member characteristics then is variety and compatibility. Obviously 'likes' do attract, and cohesive and satisfying groups will form when members are, for example, similar in attitudes and values, but groups which are heterogeneous in certain characteristics are likely to be more productive, even though they are also likely to exhibit more conflict. Mullins has listed two of the characteristics of an effective work group in fact as:

● openly expressing feelings and disagreements

● resolving conflict themselves.

Belbin (1981) took further the notion of the most effective teams being heterogeneous when he discovered that successful management teams consisted of a mix of individuals, each performing a different role. These roles are:

● **chairperson** who co-ordinates efforts and does not have to be brilliant

● **shaper** who is strongly task-oriented, gives direction to the team and is extrovert

● **plant** who is the team's introverted creative thinker

● **monitor-evaluator** who is analytical and critically evaluates the work of the team

● **company worker** who transforms talk and ideas into practical steps

● **team worker** who is supportive and takes care of group harmony

● **resource-investigator** who networks and 'fixes' things

● **completer-finisher** who keeps the final goal in sight and checks and chivvies to that end.

Of course, group membership in organisations is normally pre-determined by technical function but as Makin et al pointed out in 1989, a knowledge of Belbin's roles helps group effectiveness in two ways:

● It draws our attention to the role preferences of individuals and through observation we may be able to judge the strength of those preferences. Obviously ideally, individuals should be given tasks which allow them to perform their preferred role, especially where strong preferences exist.

● It draws our attention to missing roles which are making the group less effective. Even if it is not possible to import someone to fill a missing role, we can at least try to find someone who would not find it too alien to adopt the role.

In terms of missing roles, Makin et al gave the example of certain quality circles that had ceased to meet and who were found to lack members whose preference was the completer role. It seemed that these groups had been good at problem- and solution-generation but could not carry their ideas through.

We now examine the final aspect of the group as a given: hidden agendas.

HIDDEN AGENDAS

When we discussed the storming stage of group development, we argued that at this period hostility is generated and that the false consensus of the forming stage is likely to be challenged. We also argued that if the disagreements of this stage are not openly and successfully worked through, they will just be driven underground and will always be there to affect performance. Ideally then, individual and group objectives will be aligned but where individual objectives are covertly promoted at the expense of the group, performance will suffer.

There is no simple answer to this problem, of course, except to say that the onus is always on leaders, and indeed all members, to stress the collective purposes of the group. Behavioural analysis can be a useful tool in diagnosing and dealing with hidden agendas, but it does require some specialist skills and knowledge. Tim Dickson, in the *Financial Times* (17 March 1995) reported how behavioural analysis helped eradicate what he described as the 'tricks and games' which were impeding the effectiveness of the board of Swiss Re, the world's second largest reinsurance company. This is Item 8.2 in your Resource section.

Of course, groups can be too cohesive but before we examine this phenomenon, do the following activity which highlights the negative impact on group effectiveness of hidden agendas.

ACTIVITY 8

Read the case study, The Housing Department, and answer the questions following it.

The Housing Department

John Whiteside, 27 years of age, had joined the local government authority as a trainee in the housing department 10 years ago. He was promoted to a section supervisor after five years and, two years ago, was appointed section office manager. He has line responsibility for a mainly female staff of 13, including two section supervisors, one male and one female.

The task of John's office is the maintenance of prospective tenant waiting lists for the houses and flats owned by the authority. This involves considerable personal contact with the public. The office is situated in a depressed inner-city area; as a consequence, John's staff are frequently called upon to deal with people with a range of social problems and often are subjected to abuse from the public. New staff, who receive no formal off-the-job training, find it difficult to cope with this aspect of the work and there is a high level of turnover during the first twelve months after employment.

John's immediate superior is the department deputy manager, Alan Downs, who in turn reports to the department manager. The post of department manager has been vacant for the past four months since the promotion of the incumbent to another authority, and Alan has been in temporary charge of the department for this period. Alan, in his present post for 24 months, age 31 years and married with two small children, expects to be promoted to the manager position in due course, and frequently expresses this ambition to John and to other members of the department.

It is common knowledge in the housing department that Alan and Sarah, a 25-year-old enquiry counter assistant who works in one of the two sections for which John is responsible, are having an affair. For the past six months, Alan and Sarah have frequently taken an extended lunch break of three to four hours and some mornings do not arrive for work until one or two hours after the official start time. Two weeks ago, while carrying out a routine check of unoccupied properties, a clerk from the department discovered Alan and Sarah in an empty flat at 10 am on a Monday morning. Alan explained to the clerk that they were inspecting the property; even so the occurrence led to some ribald comments when the clerk told the other members in the department what had occurred.

Because of Sarah's absenteeism, Sheila, the other counter assistant, often experiences job overload. John has discussed Sarah's absences with Sheila, with a view to reprimanding Sarah. Sheila asked him not to do this because she believed that this would make things difficult for her as Sarah would tell Alan that she had been making trouble. Against his better judgement, John agreed to this request because the enquiry counter assistants – the front line in dealing with the public – are crucial to the smooth operation of the section.

John and his two supervisors are sceptical about Alan's ability to be an effective department manager. The previous manager had been respected for his technical competence, hard work and human relations skills. Under his leadership, the department performed well. Since his departure, it has become apparent that absenteeism and lateness among the staff has increased, and the quality of the work has slackened considerably. John finds it difficult to correct the situation because of the example set by Alan. The junior members of the department resent the conspicuously favourable treatment afforded Sarah, which they attribute to her relationship with Alan.

The female supervisor in John's section has submitted her resignation and the local authority has advertised for a replacement. Alan advised John informally that he wants a female replacement because of the need for female representation in the supervisory and management positions in the department. It is local authority personnel policy that preference is given to suitable internal candidates when filling supervisory and management positions. Sarah is the only internal female candidate for the post.

Satisfaction and effectiveness are inexorably deteriorating in John's 13-strong, mainly female team. What hidden agendas are contributing to the team's poor performance? Suggest how John could tackle this difficult situation.

One hidden agenda concerns the fact that John is unhappy with Sarah's absenteeism but has promised her fellow counter assistant Sheila that he will not raise the issue with her. Sheila fears that Sarah will tell Alan that she has been making trouble for her and that he will make things difficult for her. There is also, of course, Alan's individual objective of making Sarah a supervisor which inevitably will be perceived to be based on his relationship with her rather than on grounds of merit. Sarah, we assume, is happy to go along with this and so again this is another individual objective at odds with the overall effectiveness of the housing department team. Finally, of course, and partly explained by these various hidden agendas, is the fact that John and his two supervisors are sceptical about Alan's ability to be an effective departmental manager. Alan's example is making it difficult for John to improve team effectiveness and John finds it impossible to talk to Alan about how his behaviour is progressively damaging performance.

In terms of tackling the situation, the ball is very much in John's court. What is hidden and damaging must be brought to the surface and, at present, however he feels and whatever he thinks, John is acquiescing to the situation. John's stance is only serving Alan's interests and certainly not those of the housing department team. The only route that would seem open to him is to go above Alan's head and reveal what is happening. Either he could go to a senior officer in the council or perhaps he might find it easier to initially talk to the relevant councillor.

GROUPTHINK

You have examined the issue of hidden agendas and the damage that they can do to effective team performance, now it is useful to introduce and examine the notion that groups can be too cohesive.

ACTIVITY 9

Note down briefly any potential dangers you see in a group becoming over-cohesive.

Over-cohesive groups tend to serve themselves rather than their organisation. Janis (1972) has highlighted the following symptoms of over-conformity in the concept of groupthink. You may have noted some of these, but perhaps in different terms in your answer:

- the **illusion of invulnerability** which leads groups to over-estimate their ability to be successful against very high odds and extraordinary risks mainly due to the fact that there are no discordant, warning voices

- **collective rationalisation** which leads groups to ignore shortcomings in plans and decisions, discount warnings and rationalise failure

- **belief in the inherent morality of the group** which means that the group is not only convinced of the logical correctness of what it is doing but also in its inherent morality

- **stereotypes and outgroups** are viewed as being less able than themselves; the outgroups, of course, will include their competitors

- **direct pressure on dissenters** in the sense that individual member doubts are immediately suppressed or at least not allowed to be pursued

- **mindguards** which prevent members discussing their doubts outside of their group which protects them from counter information or competing viewpoints

- **self-censorship** which means that members will screen out any misgivings that they may have about a particular decision

- the **illusion of unanimity** which stems from self-censorship and the operation of mindguards, in such a group, silence is likely to be read as strong agreement and lukewarm approval as genuine consensus.

As antidotes towards groupthink tendencies, Janis suggests that groups should, for example, specifically delegate one member to critically evaluate the contributions of the rest, ensure that doubts and uncertainties are fully discussed and should have leaders who can take criticism of their judgements.

Now before turning to the task-related givens, do the following activity. It will enhance your understanding of groupthink by drawing your attention to factors in a directors' meeting, which are actually preventing tendencies towards groupthink developing.

ACTIVITY 10

Read the following case study and answer the question that follows.

John Simpson, Fifty Cycle Sales Manager

John Simpson joined Allard and Davis Engineering Limited from school as a technical apprentice. The period of his apprenticeship was marred by a skin allergy, which was eventually attributed to a fluid used in the firm's manufacturing process. Despite this, John progressed well in both the academic and practical aspects of his studies and for two years in succession was awarded the 'apprentice of the year' prize by the professional engineering association that he was striving to join.

Shortly after John successfully completed his apprenticeship, he was forced to abandon an engineering career on the advice of his doctor and the company created a clerical job for him in its sales office. Within five years, he was appointed one of the company's sales managers, with responsibility for a major product line.

Allard and Davis is one of three companies in England manufacturing large vessels for holding and heating various types of liquid and material. The vessels, referred to as 'kettles' in the trade, are custom-made units designed and built to customers' specifications. The cost of a unit can range from around £200,000 to over £500,000. The company differentiates its products according to 'cycles', the term used to identify the temperature to which the things contained in a vessel are heated.

The company employs four sales managers, each responsible for a 'cycle' product line. Although designated as a sales manager, the role does not involve 'managing' people or other resources. The major task is to advise customers on technical specifications to ensure that a unit will satisfy the requirements of the customer. The sales managers work mainly at customers' premises and, collectively, receive administrative and secretarial support from a central sales office.

In the four and a half years that John has been fifty cycle sales manager, sales of the fifty cycle line have risen from 21% to 52% of the company's annual turnover.

The company's marketing manager is about to retire at the early age of 48. John has informed the marketing director that unless he is promoted to the marketing manager post he will leave Allard and Davis and join a competitor. A meeting of the company's directors has been called to decide whether to promote John or to call in a firm of recruitment specialists to find a new marketing manager from outside the company. None of the other sales managers are considered to be suitable for promotion because two are in their early sixties and will retire within three years, and the other has been in the post for only four weeks.

The managing director opened the meeting: 'We are here to decide whether to promote John or risk losing him to Ballards. I think that you will agree that he has been a very successful sales manager. You can rely on him to get a job done; the trouble is that he seems to rub people up the wrong way in the process. It seems that he is not well liked.'

The marketing director spoke next: 'I admit that, on a personal level, I dislike him, but that's not the point at issue. He is a very good sales manager. This is proved by the tremendous increase in sales of fifty cycle kettles. As marketing manager, he can get the other sales managers to do the same for the other lines. In any case, we just can't afford to let him go to Ballards and we have no option but to promote him.'

The personnel director replied: 'Well, I agree, John has done a very good job, but he's too competitive. He's too aggressive for his own good. He can't abide to lose and will do anything, no matter what, to win. He treats the office staff badly. When something goes wrong he makes sure that one of them takes the blame and never gives them credit for anything that goes well. I think that he is basically insecure. Deep down he is not really sure of himself, that's why he goes around treating everybody so badly and trying to intimidate people. I think . . .'

The production director interrupted: 'Look, forget the psychological clap-trap, John is trying to blackmail us into promoting him. He is an out and out swine. He uses people like I use machines. He's got no conscience and he's got no scruples. He causes more ill-feeling and more trouble, in this company than everybody else put together. Every time he comes into my department, he causes a row. Let's bring in somebody from outside.'

Marketing director: 'I agree he is a manipulator. He will do anything to get what he wants. If this involves using people, he doesn't seem to mind. He knows what he wants and goes all out to get it, and woe betide anyone in his way. But this doesn't alter the fact that we cannot afford to let him go to Ballards.'

Production director to marketing director: 'Well, if he's promoted you'd better watch out. Mark my words, he'll have you out of your job within a couple of years.' The other directors laughed. As the laughter subsided, the managing director said: 'Well, one thing seems sure, he's not very popular.'

What in the directors' meeting is preventing any tendencies towards groupthink?

In the first place, there is no illusion of invulnerability. The group realistically accepts the external threat of Ballards which will become even more dangerous if John joins it. Also, there is no pressure to withhold doubts at the meeting. All of the directors express their views and the only one that they all appear to share, as the managing director points out, is that John is unpopular. The marketing director is for his appointment, the production director is against it and the personnel director also appears to be building up to recommending that John should not get the job of marketing manager. It would also appear that mindguards are not in operation. All of the directors seem to be fully aware of the feelings of other employees towards John. We could possibly argue, of course, that they may be filtering out information which does not fit in with their view of him but this would appear unlikely. Finally, there is clearly no illusion of unanimity. There is disagreement, they are voicing this disagreement and there would appear to be no indications of a tendency towards over-cohesiveness. Despite the disagreement, there is a shared commitment to making a decision which is best for their organisation.

We now move on to examine the independent variables affecting group performance which relate to the task. We examine the nature of the task and the criteria of effectiveness.

TASK-RELATED VARIABLES

Nature of the task

Tasks make demands on groups and if these tasks are to be performed effectively, then these demands must be met. This was implicit, of course, in what we said earlier, about how confusing two tasks in the one group will undermine success.

As we then indicated, the performance of a research team, for example, is dependent upon a high degree of group interaction. The making of handmade leather goods, on the other hand, may well necessitate sequential interdependence among group members.

Some tasks then demand more group interaction than others and if the necessary level of interaction does not take place then group performance suffers. We have already mentioned problem-solving in the context of group size but, of course, the success of that task additionally requires that the group is supportive. Task type then affects the kind of group necessary for effectiveness.

Effectiveness criteria

The criteria by which performance is assessed is an important determinant of the operation of a group. Management must be precise about the standards they require and if, for example, they stress speed and quality, then group effectiveness is likely to be adversely affected.

ACTIVITY 11

Re-read the Activity 2 case study, *Joan Shaw, Production Manager.* What two criteria of effectiveness was Joan seeking to establish? These were not compatible with the group norms, so which suffered?

Joan advised the general manager that she would increase both output and quality but the experienced machinists resisted these twin demands and socialised the new machinists into their way of doing things. It was, furthermore, mentioned that the low morale of the machinists, presumably consequent upon the pressures they felt that they were under, also contributed to the fall in production levels.

The final givens which helps determine group effectiveness that we examine concern a group's organisational environment.

ENVIRONMENTAL VARIABLES

The physical setting

Physical settings can have significant effects on group interaction. You have only to compare, for example, the impersonality of a classroom with the teacher standing at the front facing fixed and separate rows of desks with a circle of students and their tutor in a small seminar room. Physical proximity increases interaction which, in turn, increases feelings of co-operation. The linear track of a Fordist factory could be said to individualise the operative and preclude group formation. Production lines in Japan, as you will know from the Clegg article, are organised to be more flexible and in some industries are U-shaped with a consequently different effect on operative interactions. In discussing team building, Hogg (1990) stresses the importance of physical location for team building. 'Proximity,' she writes, 'tends to increase interaction and positive feelings. Sharing facilities can increase cohesion.'

The cultural setting

Paul Bate (1992) has argued that organisations must find cultural solutions to certain basic organisational issues. One of these, he argues, is how emotionally bound up people become with others in the work setting. If the solution is seen to be a high level of unemotionality then this, as Bate argues, will 'influence specific norms such as . . . whether one shows feelings in a meeting, whether to handle a sensitive issue personally . . . and so on.' Now Bate argues that such cultural orientations, and their linked norms, will affect, for example, problem solving within the organisation. The adherence to norms whose establishment has been influenced by the wider culture, may be inappropriate for particular group tasks. Quality circles have been known to founder because culturally induced norms were at odds with the required ethos of such groups.

Leader and member status

The power of a leader to sell, for example, the product of their committee, affects team spirit and performance. The status of individual members has a similar effect. Group effectiveness, then, is also determined by the leader's power position and the standing of the group as a whole.

ACTIVITY 12

Re-read the *Production of Trevor Thompson and Sons* case study in Unit 7, page xxx and then answer the following questions.

1   What was it about the physical setting prior to the introduction of the new manufacturing layout that facilitated group interactions?

2   There were obviously certain cultural norms in the company which also facilitated team building. What were they?

1   The employees worked in four-person teams assembling, inspecting and packaging the rods, each within their own partitioned areas.

2   Aspects of the cultural setting include the acceptance by Trevor that the teams could decorate their own areas, that group bonuses were paid and that teams also had charge of their own inter-team discipline.

SUMMARY OF THE GIVENS

The givens which we have discussed relate to the group, the group task and the group environment variables. The group variables were three-fold: size, member characteristics and hidden agendas. We argued that group size in terms of effectiveness, is related to the nature of the task. In terms of member characteristics, we focussed attention on Belbin's team roles and the idea that heterogeneous teams are the more effective. Finally, in terms of the group variables, the issue of hidden agendas was explored and it was in this context that we introduced the notion of groupthink.

The two task-related givens, that is, the nature of the task and effectiveness criteria, were then explored. In terms of the task, we argued that to be effective, the demands that it makes on the group must be met. We then examined the criteria by which performance is assessed as an important determinant of the operation of the group.

Finally, we addressed the three-fold environmental 'givens': the physical setting, the cultural setting and leader and member status. We stressed the importance of the physical location and its effects on interaction and the influence of cultural norms as a 'given'. Finally, we mentioned the leader's power and the standing of the group as impacting on effectiveness.

We now examine the intermediate or intervening factors which also help determine group effectiveness. As such factors can be changed more easily than the givens, they are arguably of more importance to those seeking to improve group performance.

4.3 Intervening factors

We examine these factors under three headings:

- **style of the leader**
- **group functions**
- **interaction patterns.**

Each of these can be adapted or changed in the short term to take account of the givens and so make possible enhanced effectiveness. We briefly only mention leader style as we deal with leadership at some length in Unit 10 but we examine group functions and interaction patterns in more detail.

STYLE OF THE LEADER

The contingency approach to leader effectiveness is obviously relevant here since it advocates that group leaders must bring their style to fit other situational variables such as the nature of the task and the requirements of subordinates. For more detail on the contingency approach you should look at Unit 11.

GROUP FUNCTIONS

For a group to be effective, two sets of functions must be undertaken. These are the **task functions** and the **maintenance functions,** and unless there is an appropriate combination of these two sets of processes, successful performance is undermined. Task functions, as the name suggests, are processes concerned with the accomplishment of the group's task. The task processes which ought to happen in any group are, for example:

- **initiating** – defining a problem, proposing a task, etc
- **information seeking** and giving
- **opinion seeking** and giving
- **clarifying** – clearing up confusions
- **evaluating**
- **decision making.**

Now while it is the responsibility of the leader that these functions are done, they may be spread among a number of group members. Task-orientated processes lead to the second set of processes, the maintenance functions. Maintenance functions are processes concerned with maintaining the group as an entity so that the task is accomplished. The maintenance processes which ought to happen in any group are, for example:

- **encouraging**
- **expressing feelings** - sensing, sharing
- **harmonising** – reconciling disagreements
- **compromising** – to maintain cohesion
- **gate-keeping** – keeping all communication channels open
- **setting standards** – to achieve, to evaluate achievement.

Again, these may be spread among a number of members and indeed, some may carry out both task and maintenance functions. The key point is that these two functions must be performed by some member(s) of the group or team to attain member satisfaction and performance.

Of course, it is possible to observe and record individual member behaviour in groups in terms of their performance of these two sets of functions. Trained observers can chart their behaviour on pre-designed forms which distinguish between member behaviours in terms of the functions being performed. Such behavioural analysis can, of course, become very complicated, especially when non-verbal behaviour is included in the framework, but the principle behind it is straight forward. An example of a section of a form designed so that the observer can record the performance of certain task and maintenance functions is given in Figure 2.

Group I Date	C B D A E				
	Alan	Betty	Clare	Denis	Erica
Information seeking	II	I		III	II
Opinion giving	I	I	III	I	II
Clarifying	III	II	I	II	I
Decision making		I			III
Encouraring	II	IIII	II	I	III
Harmonising	I	III	II	II	II
Compromising	III	I	II	III	
Gate-keeping	I	II	I		

Figure 2:

The completed observation forms can be invaluable as a basis for discussing both individual and group performance in terms of the different functional behaviour inputs. These behaviours can be charted and discussed within the group over time so that an optimum balance can be arrived at. When we were discussing hidden agendas, we mentioned the behavioural analysis of the Swiss Re group's board meetings. In this case, the analysis aimed at making the board meetings more effective and the framework used looked at such factors as the length and style of contributions. Observer feedback and discussion helped shorten and better structure the meetings and the games were dealt with both at individual and board meeting level. A fuller report of what was done at Swiss Re is given in the article by Tim Dickson, Item 8.2 in the Resource section. The group can also influence its interaction pattern, as can the leader. Before we explore interaction patterns, however, that is the third intervening factor, try the following activity.

ACTIVITY 13

Re-read Activity 7 case study, *John Simpson, Fifty Cycle Sales Manager,* and answer the following question.

For a group to be effective, two sets of functions need to be undertaken. These are the task functions and the maintenance functions. Under these two headings, which functions do you feel were performed at the directors' meeting?

The task functions, that is those processes concerned with the accomplishment of the directors' task, include, for example, the managing director initiating and perhaps evaluating, the marketing director information and opinion seeking and giving, the personnel director clarifying, the production director evaluating, and so on.

The maintenance functions, that is those processes concerned with maintaining the group as an entity so that the task can be accomplished, include the majority of the directors expressing feelings. There was perhaps some compromising by the production director.

INTERACTION PATTERNS

The pattern of communication between group members affects both member satisfaction and performance. Shaw (1978) carried out a number of studies looking at the effects of different communication networks, classifying them into **centralised networks** and **de-centralised networks**. He identified three forms of centralised networks which are illustrated in Figure 3. These are:

- **the chain**
- **the wheel**
- **the 'Y' network.**

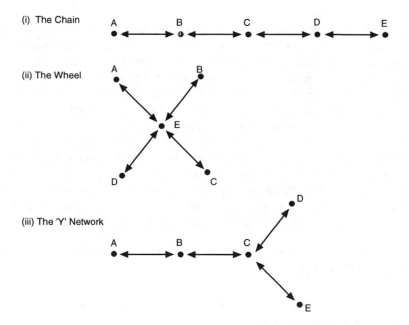

Figure 3: Centralised networks

In centralised networks, in order to communicate with others in the group, members have to go through one individual, usually the leader, who is at the centre. This means, of course, that the central individual has much more information than the rest and so these networks are associated with more autocratic styles of management.

In terms of the de-centralised networks, Shaw identified two main forms which are illustrated in Figure 4. There are:

● the **circle**

● the **all-channel network.**

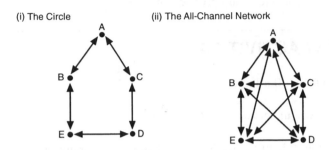

(i) The Circle   (ii) The All-Channel Network

Figure 4: De-centralised networks

In de-centralised networks, members do not have to go through a control individual and there is a free flow of information between them all. Democratic styles of management tend to be associated with these forms of network.

The relationship between network type and group member satisfaction is:

● satisfaction tends to be highest in decentralised networks where information and decision-making is shared

● in centralised networks, by definition, decision-making is located at the centre and those members outside of it do not feel involved. Overall member satisfaction is thus lower.

The effects of network types on task performance is:

● if tasks are simple, then centralised networks result in faster and more effective performance

● where tasks are complex, on the other hand, decentralised networks result in faster and more effective performance.

What we suggest then is that a knowledge of such feelings can be used to help adapt the group interactive patterns to fit the task in hand. There is no one best pattern of communication.

ACTIVITY 14

Again refer to the Activity 7 case study, identify the form of network being used by the directors and comment on its appropriateness.

The form being used was the all-channel network and for such a complex task as deciding whether or not John Simpson should be appointed to the post of marketing manager, it was entirely appropriate.

The givens then, and the intervening factors which can be changed in the short term to take account of them, determine the outcomes. As we have stated, they determine member satisfaction and group productivity.

REVIEW ACTIVITY 4

Suggested time: 30 minutes.

1   What do you understand by the givens?

2   Why is the style of the leader classed as an intervening factor?

3   What is the essential outcome in terms of group effectiveness?

4   What do you understand by mindguards and self-censorship as symptoms of groupthink?

5   Why are homogeneous groups less effective than heterogeneous groups?

6   Why is member satisfaction highest in de-centralised networks?

Summary

In this section, we addressed the fundamental and broad aim of making clear some of the major determinants of group effectiveness. Within this wider framework, we presented Belbin's notion of team roles, identified the symptoms of groupthink and drew attention to the importance of group task and maintenance functions.

Belbin's study was in fact long considered to be the authority on team-building and while we have not explicitly used that term here, our discussions of group effectiveness inevitably cover certain common ground, especially some team-building strategies. Makin et al (1989) have a useful section on such strategies including team-roles and also behavioural analysis to which we also refer. Mullins (1993) points out that the process of team-building especially focuses on the role of the leader and we have drawn your attention to Unit 9 where we cover leadership in more detail.

The main determinants of group effectiveness were set out and, having established that heterogeneous groups are the most productive, we drew attention to Belbin's discovery that successful management teams consist of a mix of individuals, each performing different roles. Hidden agendas, as one of the group 'givens' were explored further in the case study, *The Housing Department*. Then the notion that groups can be too cohesive was highlighted and a case study helped to reinforce our understanding of groupthink. Using the case study, *Joan Shaw, Production Manager,* you clarified effectiveness criteria as a task given. Then, having examined the environment givens, we turned our attention to the intervening factors and group functions and focused especially on communication networks. To aid understanding of behavioural analysis, we presented an observation sheet and visuals of communication networks, to highlight the final intervening factor, interaction patterns. The outcomes of the first two sets of variables, the givens and the intervening factors are member satisfaction and group performance.

Unit Summary

In this unit, we have been concerned with groups and group effectiveness. More specifically, we defined the concept of group. We stated that groups have an independent identity in that the term is reserved for those aggregates of people who have psychological effects on, and implications for, the individuals composing the group. We distinguished between formal and informal groups. Formal groups are those prescribed by the organisation in contrast to those which are based more on personal relationships and agreement of group members than on defined role relationships. Types of formal group were examined. These included work teams, quality circles, committees and task groups.

An appreciation of the main purposes for which individuals use groups was set out. We pointed out that these purposes may be active, power and goal achievement, for example, or they may be more passive. That is, groups may just provide arenas within which security, affiliation and self-esteem are to be found.

We looked at the main organisational purposes of groups and teams. Handy listed ten purposes and in examining these we pointed out that groups and teams cannot, however, successfully perform simultaneous functions.

We identified Belbin's notion of team rules and pointed out that successful teams consisted of a mix of individuals each performing a different role. The most effective teams are heterogeneous teams.

Symptoms of groupthink were identified. We stated that groups which are too cohesive do not serve the organisation.

The importance of group task and maintenance functions was explained. We pointed out that the task will only be accomplished if the group is maintained as an entity. We outlined and discussed the determinants of group effectiveness. We argued that there are three sets of relevant variables: the givens, the intervening factors and the outcomes which are, of course, productivity and member satisfaction.

References

Bales, RF (1950) *Interaction Process Analysis,* Reading, MA: Addison Wesley.

Bate, P (1992) 'The Impact of Organisational Culture on Approaches to Organisational Problem-Solving' in *Human Resource Strategies,* eds. Salaman, G. Cameron, S Hamblin, H Iles, P Mabey, C and Thompson, K London: Sage Publications in association with the Open University.

Belbin, RM (1981) *Management Teams: Why they Succeed or Fail,* London: Butterworth-Heinemann.

Brown, H (1971) Stability and Change in Social Groups in Open University *D100 Understanding Society: a Foundation Course,* Units 29-31, Stability Change and Conflict, Buckingham: Open University Press.

Clegg, SR (1992) 'Modernist and Postmodernist Organisations' in *Human Resource Strategies,* eds. Salaman, G Cameron, S Hamblin, H Iles, P Mabey, C and Thompson, K London: Sage Publications in association with the Open University, London.

Dickson, T (1995) 'Look, Listen, Learn then Alter' in *Financial Times,* 17 March, p. 14.

Handy, C (1993) *Understanding Organisations,* Harmondsworth: Penguin.

Hogg, C (1990) 'Team Building', *Factsheet 34,* October 1990, London: Institute of Personnel Management.

Janis, IL (1972) *Victims of Groupthink,* Boston: Houghton Mifflin.

Kretch, D Crutchfield, RS and Ballachey, EL (1962) *The Individual in Society,* New York: McGraw Hill.

Luthans, F (1992) *Organisational Behaviour,* New York: McGraw Hill.

Makin, PJ Cooper, CL and Cox, CJ (1989) *Managing People at Work,* Leicester: BPS Books.

Mitchell, TR and Larson, JR (1987) *People in Organisations: an Introduction to Organisational Behaviour,* New York: McGraw Hill.

Mullins, LJ (1993) *Management and Organisational Behaviour,* London: Pitman Publishing.

Shaw, ME (1978) 'Communication Networks Fourteen Years Later' in *Group Processes,* ed. Berkowitz, L New York: Academic Press.

Tuckman, B and Jensen, N (1977) 'Stages of Small Group Development Revisited', *Group and Organisational Studies,* 2, pp. 419-427.

Watson, TJ (1987) *Sociology, Work and Industry,* London: Routledge.

Wickens, P (1993) 'Steering the Middle Road to Car Production', *Personnel Management,* June 1993.

Recommended Reading

Huczynski, AA and Buchanan, DA (1991) *Organisational Behaviour: an Introductory Text,* London: Prentice-Hall.

Luthans, F (1992) *Organisational Behaviour,* New York: McGraw Hill, Chapter 12.

Mullins, LJ (1993) *Management and Organisational Behaviour,* London: Pitman Publishing, Chapters 6 and 7.

Answers to Review Activities

Review Activity 1

1   Handy defined a group as any collection of people who perceive themselves to be a group. Brown states that the term is reserved for those aggregates of people which have psychological effects on, and implications for, the individuals composing the group. The main difference between these two definitions lies in Brown's more explicit delineation. When a collection of people perceive themselves to be a group then this entity will in turn psychologically affect the individual's composing it with consequent implications for those individuals.

2   It is in formal, primary groups that certain aspects of behaviour are already fixed prior to member interaction. In that they are formal, certain roles and goals will inevitably be pre-determined. In contrast, of course, roles and goals in informal groups emerge from the member interaction which give rise to the group.

3   You may have mentioned work teams, quality circles, committees and task groups.

Review Activity 2

1   The storming stage is 'stormy' because it is at this stage that conflict emerges between individuals as they seek to come to terms with what they want from the group and the conflicts between their goals and the group goals. That which was beginning to develop at the formal stage is not yet accepted and may be challenged.

2   If the storming stage is not completed then important issues will never be confronted and blockages will not be worked through. Storming will, as it were, continue under the surface and the group will never be fully effective.

3   It is not enough to guide a group through to the performing stage: managers must sustain performance through feedback and encourage self-monitoring.

Review Activity 3

While appreciating Frank's worries about safety levels, especially in busy periods, it is likely that you will have felt that he was not going about things in the most effective way when he resolved to raise the issue of safety at a production meeting. It is perfectly reasonable to assume that all of the managers at Marshall's are committed to safety but inevitable they are also committed to the overall success of the company. It is unrealistic to expect them to usefully consider both the problems involved in meeting the new orders and the worsening company safety record at the same meeting. As Handy has argued, groups cannot successfully perform simultaneous functions. There is a best 'fit' between achieving a particular purpose and how the group is managed and organised and so on. Frank is likely to have been unwise in seeking to bring together the two functions in the one meeting. It may well have been better to request an emergency safety meeting as soon as possible if he really feels that the issue cannot wait.

However, Handy does give an example of functional managers at a top management committee having to speak to the first item on the agenda in terms of their departmental roles and to the next item as company managers. The managers, of course, found this very difficult to do and in this case they were only able to address these different types of items effectively when the agenda was divided into different types.

Review Activity 4

1   The givens are simply those independent variables that will affect group effectiveness but which in the short term are given constraints within which the group must operate.

2   The style of the leader is classed as an intervening variable since such variables can be changed in the short term and it is held that leaders are capable of changing their style in the short term.

3   The most fundamental outcome in terms of group effectiveness is, of course, group productivity.

4   Mindguards protect groups from counter information or competing viewpoints by preventing members discussing their doubts outside of the group. Self-censorship is the situation where members screen out their misgivings about a particular decision.

5   For groups to be effective, research has shown that certain roles must be performed. For example, efforts must be co-ordinated, ideas must be transformed into practical steps and so on. Belbin discovered that there are, in fact, such roles that must be performed if a group is to be effective. In that sense then, there must be a mix of individuals each performing different roles. Or at least, each role must be performed. Where there is no mix of individuals and, therefore, each of the different roles are not performed, that is to say, where the group could be termed homogeneous, then that group will be less effective.

6   Member satisfaction is highest in de-centralised networks because in them, information and decision-making are shared.

UNIT 9

LEADERS LEADING AND THE LED

Introduction

In this unit, we examine leadership in organisations. We first of all highlight that leadership is one of the key managerial roles and assert the importance to organisations of effective leadership. Leadership skills and the sources of a leader's power are then explored and we make clear that formal management position is just one of these.

The sources of a leader's power are, in fact, broken down into **personal power** sources and **organisational power** sources, and to help clarify this distinction, we discuss the notions of **transactional leadership** and **transformational leadership**.

Finally, we present and evaluate two important approaches to leadership effectiveness: the **universal traits approach** and the **situation-contingent traits approach**. In terms of the latter, we give an appreciation of Fiedler's extensive work in this area.

Objectives

At the end of this unit, you will be able to:

- define the basic process of leadership.
- understand the relationship between leadership and management.
- explain key leadership skills.
- identify the sources of a leader's power.
- distinguish between transactional and transformational leaders.
- appreciate the universal personality traits approach to leadership.
- appreciate the situation-contingent personality traits approach to leadership.

SECTION 1
Nature of leadership

Introduction

We begin this section, by defining leadership and stressing its importance to organisational effectiveness. We go on to distinguish leadership from management, set out the key leadership skills and examine the sources of a leader's power. Finally, we differentiate between transactional leadership and transformational leadership.

1.1 Definition

Leadership is the process of influencing others to work willingly and to the best of their capabilities towards the goals of the leader.

Leadership is a central process in facilitating group and organisational performance and effectiveness. It is therefore very important for us to understand the nature of leadership and what determines its effectiveness. Of course, leadership does not take place only within organisational structures but our interest here lies in this context. At top organisational levels, leaders have a long-term focus and are primarily concerned with strategic decision-making. At middle levels, the focus is shorter term with an emphasis on supplementing and developing the *given* structure. Lower level leaders, on the other hand, are concerned with *using* the structure to keep the organisation operating efficiently. The leadership role varies then according to organisational level but the common element is influence. However, this influence is subject to constraint even at the higher levels. Top leaders are constrained by internal and external factors though their role is clearly important in, for example, setting long-term objectives. As we move down the organisation, leader impact on the organisation reduces. Not all organisational leaders have the same priorities and at the different levels varying degrees of constraint operate. You should bear this in mind throughout this unit.

1.2 Leadership and management

As we have already suggested, leadership can have enormous influence on performance in organisations but since it is about how leaders carry out their role, rather than what tasks they perform, it is not a concept that can easily be pinned down. It is useful when beginning to think about the basic process of leadership to look at its relationship to management. Mullins (1993) has argued that 'To be an effective manager it is necessary to exercise the role of leadership'. Implicit in this statement, is the idea that it is possible to distinguish between a manager's potential leader role and other elements of management. In addressing the differences between leadership and management, Mullins summarises Saleznik's 1977 exploration of some of them. These are set out below and will help clarify the distinction being made.

MANAGERS	LEADERS
Managers tend to adopt impersonal or passive attitudes towards goals.	Leaders adopt a more personal and active attitude towards goals.
In order to get people to accept solutions, the manager needs continually to co-ordinate and balance in order to compromise conflicting values.	Leader creates excitement in work and develops choices that give substance to images that excite people. (Richard Branson, for example, obviously expanded consumer choice when launching Virgin Airways and did so with the compelling imagery of a Jack taking on a giant, in this case, British Airways. He himself gave further substance to this exciting representation by posing in mock-heroic stance at the launch in front of his rivals' logo.)
In relationships with other people, managers maintain a low level of emotional involvement.	Leaders have empathy with other people and give attention to what events and actions mean.
Managers see themselves more as conservators and regulators of the existing order of affairs with which they identify, and from which they gain rewards.	Leaders work in, but do not belong to, the organisation. Their sense of identity does not depend upon membership or work roles and they search out opportunities for change.

Source: Adapted from Mullins, 1993.

ACTIVITY 1

Individually, either:

1 Name a manager that you know, or have heard of, within or outside of your organisation, whom you feel has that 'special attribute of leadership'. What factors do you think contribute to this manager having this special attribute?

or

2 Think of any leader in any walk of life, whom you admire, or who is generally admired. List the qualities you feel this person has that makes him or her a leader

then

3 Work in small groups and share your ideas. List any leadership qualities or skills which are common to your lists. You may have used different words to describe the same thing. Discuss skills and qualities mentioned that were not shared. Can you now, as a group, add any to the common list?

There is are no one correct set of skills or attributes to list here. The activity's purpose was for you to explore what makes a good leader. However, according to Hellreigel et al (1989), the special attribute of leadership involves the four skills identified below. As you read, see if there is overlap between your lists, your group lists, and these skills.

1.3 Leadership skills

According to Hellreigel et al, there are four kinds of leadership skills:

- **Visionary skills:** people are willing to follow leaders because of their visionary skills. The led become committed to the leader's vision which involves values and goals and is, in itself, confidence-giving.

- **Communication skills:** following on from the above, successful leaders clearly have the skill to communicate this compelling vision that evokes enthusiasm and commitment.

- **Sensitivity skills:** effective leaders are both powerful and sensitive to the needs of others and so they allow their followers to share in developing goals and the satisfactions derived from reaching these goals.

- **Self-awareness skills:** effective leaders welcome feedback on their performance and continually take an inventory of themselves.

ACTIVITY 2

Was there any overlap between these four skills and your list or your group's list? Set out the common ground between them.

If your own examples of leaders were drawn from public figures in business or other spheres, it is likely that your lists of leadership qualities referred in some form to what Hellreigel et al categorise as visionary and communication skills. These are often more publicly visible than the sensitivity and self-awareness skills they list but which you may have identified also in some form in leaders of whom you have had personal experience.

The importance of a leader's visionary skills in influencing and gaining commitment from those led can readily be seen in operations such as Anita Roddick's Body Shop or Richard Branson's Virgin group and in the example which follows.

Roger Gowe, reporting on Glaxo's bid for Wellcome in *The Guardian,* 24 January 1995, wrote that its astounding success with the ulcer treatment Zantac, the world's best selling drug, was due to Glaxo's research and marketing skills and also 'because of another element of serendipity – the vision of the man who happened to lead the company through the 1970s and 1980s. Sir Paul Girolami, as he now is, retires this year after 27 years on the board. He is credited with setting the company on the route to the top, because he pursued a strategy very different to most British companies.

Firstly, while most were busy diversifying into business they knew little about, Glaxo opted to sell off everything except its prescription drug operation, including the baby milk business which had been its foundation.

Secondly, instead of concentrating on the UK and the Commonwealth, Sir Paul saw that drugs were truly international and successful drug companies would have to establish a global presence. Thirdly, Glaxo avoided the British trap of under-investment, pouring millions into research even in the knowledge that it would not pay off for a decade or more.

This visionary management, together with the good fortune of the once-in-a-lifetime Zantac 'discovery', rocketed Glaxo to the top of the tree.'

So far we have focused on the qualities which give leaders influence, but it is clear that the process of influence is a two-way matter. The leader obviously influences the followers, but the followers also explicitly or implicitly consent to the leader's influence. Given this, it is useful to investigate why followers consent to be influenced – that is, about the sources of a leader's power.

1.4 Sources of a leader's power

French and Raven (1968) have identified five sources of a leader's power.

LEGITIMATE POWER/AUTHORITY

This comes from the leader's formal position in the organisation, that is, because of their position, the leader has the right to expect or request subordinates to do certain things and they have an obligation to comply.

REWARD POWER

This comes from the leader's ability to provide the followers with something they want in return for the followers' desired behaviour. For example, the leader may be in position to provide more interesting assignments, increase pay or promote. Obviously the degree of reward power that a leader has is likely to depend upon their position in the organisation.

COERCIVE POWER

This comes from the leader's control over punishments. These may range from reprimands, failure to provide interesting assignments, promotions or even sackings. Obviously, coercive power must be used with discretion since there must be consent to the leader's influence and punishments could lead to the withdrawal of consent.

REFERENT POWER/AUTHORITY

This comes from the qualities that the followers associate with the leader. For example, the charisma or integrity of the leader may move the followers to admire the leader, want to be like the leader and want the leader's approval. This will obviously give the leader influence over the followers.

EXPERT POWER

This comes from the leader's expertise and knowledge. The leader, for example, is seen to have the 'know-how' to complete the task.

ACTIVITY 3

1 In terms of French and Raven's power sources, individually think about either the manager that you noted earlier who you felt had leadership attributes, or the leader that you admired and list what you perceive to be that leader's main sources of power and authority:

2 Work in a small group and pool the power sources each of you have listed and note how many times each power source is mentioned.

3 Either individually, or in your group, divide your power sources list into: organisational power sources which are prescribed by company rules and regulations; and, what might be termed, personal power sources.

Either individually, or still in your group do three more exercises:

4 Discuss whether or not you feel that a leader relying on organisational power alone is likely to bring forth from followers levels of performance well above the routine. Record your view and the group view here:

5 Look back at question 2 and see how many times each power source was mentioned and work out whether organisational or personal power sources were mentioned most frequently. Set out the scores.

6 In a group, discuss these scores. It is likely that personal power was mentioned most frequently. Why do you think that this was the case? If it was not the case, were there any reasons that might account for this?

Legitimate, reward and coercive power flow from organisational power sources; referent and expert power are personal power sources.

We would expect you to have taken the view that leaders relying on organisational power alone are unlikely to bring forth exceptional levels of performance from their followers.

considered the case of an acknowledged leader, or a manager you consider
leadership qualities, we would expect that personal power might have
ntioned most frequently. If personal power was mentioned most frequently
use we do rightly associate leadership with personal qualities. Of course,
power sources must be augmented by organisational power sources.

onship between these two power sources can be further illustrated by looking
at the notions of transactional leadership and transformational leadership. This distinction
was used by Burns, for example, in 1978 and as Arnold et al, 1991, have pointed out,
Bass developed a questionnaire in 1985 'to assess the extent to which subordinates feel
that their leader exhibits transformational and transactional leadership'.

1.5 Transactional and transformational leaders

Transactional leaders approach the leader-follower relationship in terms of an
exchange. The leader, on the basis of organisational power, does something for the
follower and in return the follower does something for the leader. The transactions
relate to short-term practical things and it is self-interests that are served. In this
way, such leaders gain simple compliance.

Transformational leaders can transact on a routine day-to-day basis but they
can also create vision and mobilise commitment to that vision. Personal qualities
are then not an end in themselves. Such leaders are able to persuade their followers
to work hard and accomplish the envisioned goals. They gain much more than
simple compliance.

Now where transactional leaders cannot also be transformational leaders we are
talking of personality trait deficiencies and certain approaches to leadership do
focus on the leader's personality traits. We look at one approach in Section 2.

REVIEW ACTIVITY 1

Suggested time: 30 minutes.

1 What do you understand by leadership?

2 How, according to Hellreigel et al, do effective leaders ensure their
necessary self-awareness?

3 Why must coercive power be used with discretion?

4 Transactional and transformational forms of leadership are not entirely
mutually exclusive. Is this true or false? Explain your answer.

Summary

In this section, we have defined leadership, highlighted its importance to organisations and differentiated it from management. We have also set out key leadership skills and explored the sources of a leader's power, distinguishing between personal power sources and organisational power sources. To help clarify this distinction, we also examined the notions of transactional leadership and transformational leadership.

SECTION 2

Leadership Effectiveness

Introduction

We examine two approaches to leadership effectiveness in this section. The first, the **universal personality traits approach** focuses on the personality traits of the leader. The second approach, the **situation-contingent personality traits approach,** stresses the importance of the situation. Remember that while each approach offers useful insights, we favour the situationalist perspective.

To help you focus on the issues raised in considering leader effectiveness and on the use and relevance of the two theoretical approaches, we begin with a case study activity which we re-visit at appropriate points in the section.

ACTIVITY 4

Read the following case study and then answer the questions that follow. Discuss your ideas in a group, if possible.

The Recreation Centre Manager

Andrew Rivers, aged 36, has been the manager of a local government-owned recreation centre for about six months. Prior to this, he resigned from the British army after serving for 18 years, his last posting being a company commander on operational duties in Northern Ireland. He enjoyed his military career. He successfully completed the military staff college course and his superior officers considered that he would have eventually reached general rank. His decision to leave the army was largely in response to pressure from his wife and children, who had become unhappy with service life.

Andrew's predecessor at the recreation centre, a former full-time tennis coach, had managed the centre for 12 years before moving to become the manager of a large leisure complex. For eight months between the departure of the former manager and the arrival of Andrew, the 56-year-old deputy manager had been in charge. The deputy had managed in the informal style of the previous manager, allowing great freedom of action to the five assistant managers, who supervised the day-to-day activities.

The centre opens seven days each week between 10 am and 9 pm from March to October, and 10 am and 6 pm from November to February. At least two assistant managers are always on duty: one in charge of the swimming pool and the other responsible for other activities. Each assistant manager learned all the tasks to be carried out and they organised themselves to ensure proper management coverage at all times. Although they were free to come and go as they pleased, the system worked well because on the few occasions when an assistant manager did not arrive for work, a colleague would readily substitute.

Morale at the centre has been low since Andrew became manager. In conversations with colleagues, all the managerial staff profess to being dissatisfied with the manner in which the centre is run. The organisational climate is cold, formal and stormy.

Andrew's working relationship with the deputy manager got off to a bad start. In preparation for Andrew's arrival, the deputy had the manager's office redecorated and had a plate bearing the name 'ANDREW RIVERS' attached to the office door. He also arranged a wine and cheese lunch party, to welcome Andrew and to enable him to meet all the staff. Andrew cancelled the party because 'he did not think it a good idea', and told the deputy that he wished that he had thought to consult him about the colour of the office decor as he did not like the cream paint on the walls. Andrew had the name-plate removed and replaced by a plate bearing the inscription 'MAJOR A D RIVERS, RA Retd'. The deputy, who had worked amicably with the former manager, avoids Andrew and, when asked a direct question, his answers are always brief and sometimes hostile.

Andrew told the assistant managers that he was 'shocked' by the 'informality' and the 'lack of discipline' in their attitude towards their work and the 'lack of proper procedures' for maintaining a roster showing which assistant managers were on duty. The assistant managers pointed out that the informal arrangements worked well, as evidenced by the fact that there had never been an occasion on which the centre was inadequately staffed. Andrew disregarded this evidence and informed the assistant managers that in future he would draw-up a roster detailing them for duty and they were not to exchange duties without his authority. The assistant managers ignored Andrew's instructions and made informal changes to his work roster. When Andrew inevitably realised that his instructions were not being carried out, he began to make periodic checks of which assistant manager was on duty. Andrew became angry when he discovered unauthorised changes, and heated conversations with the assistant managers followed. The assistant managers began to refer to Andrew as 'The Fuhrer'.

Ms Jean Morris, the county recreation manager, became aware of the problems that had arisen at Andrew's centre. During a coffee break at a routine meeting of managers of recreation centres in the county, she drew Andrew aside and explained that she had heard through the grapevine that the staff at the centre were dissatisfied with the way in which Andrew made all the decisions for the centre. Andrew was noticeably surprised, 'But I get paid to make the decisions,' he replied, 'it's my responsibility to decide how things should be done. I know morale is a bit low at the moment, but this is an initial reaction which will improve when the staff get used to the professional standards I insist on.' At this point the meeting reassembled.

1   Do you consider Andrew Rivers to be an effective leader? Explain your answer.

2   What do you think Ms Jean Morris, the county recreation manager should do if the situation continues?

---

1   If your answer was the product of group discussion, you may have had some conflicts of opinion over whether or not Andrew was an effective leader. Certainly, we could argue that it was necessary to put the rostering on a more formal basis. On the other hand, there is a lot of evidence to suggest that Andrew's stint was less than successful. More importantly your individual answer, or the discussions, should have touched on a number of concepts relevant to the understanding of leader effectiveness. For example,

● Was Andrew's leadership style, which appears to have been successful in the army, appropriate to the situation in the recreation centre? Implicit in this, is the idea that a leadership style has to be appropriate to a given situation if it is to be effective. The second theoretical approach which we are going to address, of course, explores the notion of contingency.

● Was Andrew able to vary his leadership style? You may have touched on two aspects of this issue. Was his style rooted in his personality so that he had 'no choice' but to be anything other than autocratic; or was it a product of eighteen years of socialisation into the army's officer class? And even if his leadership style was a result of his army experience, rather than personality traits, could he now change?

● Mention may also have been made of a phrase of Andrews quoted in the final paragraph. He is suggesting to Jean Morris that staff morale will improve after the negative initial reaction and talks of them getting 'used to the professional standards I insist on'. This remark could be interpreted to mean that Andrew believes that there is one best way to lead, that is, the way he insists upon and which appears to involve adhering to what he refers to as professional standards. To believe in a 'one best way to lead' approach obviously conflicts with the idea mentioned above – that a leadership style has to be appropriate to a given situation if it is to be effective.

2   If your answer was the product of group discussion then again you may have had some disagreements. At its simplest, Andrew either stays or goes. If he stays, it seems likely that the situation will only deteriorate further and even if Jean Morris monitors his performance as manager more closely, this would almost certainly further undermine his position. If Andrew is to 'go', then this would either be on a permanent basis involving a lot of problems which the county would have to resolve, or he could possibly leave on a temporary basis. For example, it might be considered appropriate that he attend a management course to help him adjust to managing in the civilian world generally, and in the world of county recreation centres more specifically. The assumption in this case would be that he is able to change. There is always the possibility, of course, that a person's personality and their conception of what management and leadership involve, will make it impossible for them to take a different approach.

2.1 Approaches to leader effectiveness

As we now look at two main approaches to the study of leadership, the **universal personality traits approach** and the **situation-contingent personality traits approach,** remember the Andrew Rivers case study and your answers and discussions. You will see how the approaches relate directly to the kinds of issues that the case study raised. The link between personality traits and leadership is important in both approaches, as their titles imply, and each offers useful insights into what effective leadership involves. However, we identify some limitations in the universal traits theory and we stress the value of the situationalist perspective – the view that leadership style must be varied appropriately to the particular situation if it is to be effective.

2.2 Universal personality traits approach

This approach derives from the 'great man' theory of leadership which can be traced back to the ancient Greeks. Leadership was explained on the basis of inherited traits so that certain individuals were born 'natural' leaders. Due to the presence of these traits, individuals were able to rise to the top in any situation and become great leaders. All leaders were seen to share common traits whose possession enabled them to be effective leaders irrespective of the circumstances in which they found themselves. These leadership traits then were seen to be universally effective across all situations.

Eventually, attention became focused on the universal traits possessed by all leaders irrespective of whether these were actually inborn or not. At its simplest, the research method was to study effective leaders, measure their personality traits, and then seek to establish which of their traits distinguished them from less effective leaders. However, while it is reasonable to assume that effective leaders do have personality traits and abilities which are different from those of less effective leaders, for example, initiative, decisiveness, drive and emotional stability, it is now generally accepted that it is not possible to adequately distinguish between them on the basis of traits alone. There are three main reasons why this is the case:

1   The list of research-generated 'relevant' traits is still growing, with every new piece of research attempting to demonstrate that these particular traits provide the key to leadership. The full list is now so long that it seems to call for a man or woman of almost extraordinary gifts to be an effective leader. You met some traits research and the theory underpinning it in Unit 6.

2   There is also disagreement over which traits are the more important. If you think back to the concepts of transactional and transformational leadership, it is obvious that they were developed within the framework of the trait approach to leadership. Where transactional leaders cannot also be transformational leaders, it is being suggested that this is due to personality trait deficiencies. For example, in the questionnaire developed by Bass which we referred to in Section 1, transformational leadership is seen to involve such traits as charisma and the ability to treat each of their followers on their own merits. And, of course, the traits which transformational leaders have and which distinguish them from transactional leaders are seen to be the leadership traits that really count.

3   Perhaps the most important problem with the universal personality traits approach is the failure to discover consistent trait patterns in terms of leader success or failure. For example, the possession of particular traits has been found to relate positively to successful leader performance in certain situations yet relate negatively to leader performance in others. In this regard, think of Andrew Rivers. While the universal personality trait theory has given certain insights into understanding leadership, it is only quite modest in its ability to actually predict which managers will be effective across many situations. What the approach misses out, of course, is that it does not take into account the situations in which leaders are operating. It is the characteristics of situations that account for the fact that the possession of particular traits are related to effective performance in one and negatively related to performance in another.

Your next activity helps you explore this important point and emphasises the need to see leadership qualities or traits in a situational context. We examine this approach next.

You will see that Activity 5 confirms what we said earlier about how we 'rightly associate leadership with personal qualities' but that it also implies that, generally speaking, leadership success or failure cannot be predicted on the basis of personal leadership qualities alone and without considering the situation. Andrew Rivers, though manager of his staff, was not their leader.

ACTIVITY 5

Consider, either individually or in groups, the appropriateness of Andrew Rivers' personal leadership qualities to his earlier career role.

1 What qualities or traits do you feel Andrew brought to his army role?

2 How you think these matched the military situation?

Obviously we do not have full information about Andrew and we must make assumptions based upon what we do know:

1 He may well have brought with him into the army a certain upbringing and education. Andrew may also have had the 'right' appearance as well as, perhaps, self-assurance, a cool head, a drive for achievement, aggressiveness and initiative. He commanded his men and he may also have had a certain aloofness which suited. You may have seen him slightly differently and used different words to describe his traits.

2 We know that he had had operational duties, at least, in Northern Ireland and it is likely that a cool head, self-assurance, aggressiveness and initiative would have been appropriate. Presumably Andrew also spoke and looked the part, and in the 'caste-system' of the army, inter-personal skills with fellow officers and a certain aloofness with other ranks may have fitted the situation.

2.3 Situation-contingent personality traits approach

This approach assumes that different situations require different sets of traits. It seeks then to find those personality traits that will improve leader effectiveness in specific situations rather than pursuing the somewhat fruitless search for traits that will improve effectiveness across a diversity of situations.

Fiedler (1967) has done extensive research in this area. He assumes that all leaders have fairly stable traits and that these lead them to having their own characteristic styles of leadership. Their style is seen to be rooted in their personality.

To establish what he sees as their key traits, Fiedler gets leaders to rate their 'least preferred co-worker' *(LPC)* on a scale. He asks leaders to choose that individual with whom task accomplishment has proved the most difficult in their experience and then measures the degree to which leaders are still able to favourably perceive that person. The resultant *LPC* score indicates the presence of one of two leadership styles in the leader:

- If the score is relatively high, then the leader is **relationship-orientated,** and has described their least preferred co-worker in both positive and negative terms. This style of leader, because of his or her personality traits, sees work in terms of people as well as task performance, so that even with someone with whom task accomplishment has proved the most difficult in all of their experience, they are still able to say positive things about them.

- If the score is low, then the leader is **task-orientated,** and has described their least preferred co-worker purely in negative terms. This style of leader, because of his or her personality traits, sees work paramountly in terms of task performance, and since they are describing someone with whom task accomplishment has proved the most difficult in all of their experience, they are unable to say positive things about them.

Since this approach seeks to match the leader style with the situation, and the leader style, stemming from the leader's traits, has been established, Fiedler next isolates three aspects of the situation which he sees as determining its favourability and so affecting the leader's influence. These three are, in descending order of importance:

- **Leader-member relations** – this is the group's willingness to accept the guidance of the leader and the degree to which that leader is trusted and liked.

- **Task-structure** – this is the degree to which the task can be carried out by standard procedures.

- **Position power of leader** – this is the power of the leader deriving from their position in the organisation. For example, how much influence the leader has over rewards or punishment.

2.4 Situations and leadership styles

Now let us look at what Fiedler's theory of leadership has to say about situations and appropriate leadership styles. When reading these propositions however, remember that while he built his influential theory from data collected over the previous 10 years, subsequent research by, for example, Peters et al (1985) and Bryman et al (1987) has only given it partial support. As Arnold et al (1991) observed: 'Laboratory-based studies have produced results more consistent with the theory than field studies.'

1   Where the situation is deemed good, that is, the leader-member relations are fine, the task is structured and the leader's position power is strong, then it is

desirable to have a **task-orientated leader** since it is not worth spending time on interpersonal relations. It is best that the leader just forges ahead with the task.

2   Where the situation is deemed bad, that is, the leader-member relations are poor, the task is unstructured and the leader's position is weak, then again it is desirable to have a **task-orientated leader** since things are so difficult anyway it just is not worth spending any time on interpersonal relationships. Again, it is best that the leader just forges ahead with the task.

3   Where the situation falls between these two extremes then keeping the group members happy becomes much more important. A **relationship-orientated leader** is needed to hold the members together so that the task can be tackled.

Fiedler in fact constructed eight combinations of group-task situations through which to relate leadership style (Table 1).

	Situation highly favourable							Situation highly unfavourable
	I	II	III	IV	V	VI	VII	VIII
Leader-member relations	Good	Good	Good	Good	Poor	Poor	Poor	Poor
Task structure	Structured	Structured	Unstructured	Unstructured	Structured	Structured	Unstructured	Unstructured
Leader position power	Strong	Weak	Strong	Weak	Strong	Weak	Strong	Weak
Desirable leader LPC score	Low	Low	Low	High	High	High	High	Low

Table 1: Fiedler's theory of leadership
Source: Arnold et al 1991

ACTIVITY 6

Identify by number which situations, according to Fiedler, relate to each of the three propositions, 1, 2, or 3 which we have just described.

1   In terms of this proposition, it is likely that you will have identified situation I.

2   In terms of this proposition, it is likely that you will have identified situation VIII.

3   In this case, you may well have identified situations IV or V which are moderately favourable with mixed variables. Leaders in such situations with interpersonal relationship orientations, that is high *LPC* scores, are likely to be more effective.

ACTIVITY 7

Think of any problems with the Fiedler model. Discuss your ideas in a group, if possible.

This is a difficult question, but you may, for example, have argued that:

- It appears to imply that leaders who are task-orientated are not concerned with group member relations.

- It is unreasonable to view leader-member relations as just a part of the situation. These two parties may change their relations over time.

This is not to say that the basic approach of the theory is not valid. Analyse the situation, specify the traits and orientation that a leader in that situation must have and then place an appropriate leader in charge.

To help your understanding of the situation-contingent traits approach it would be useful for you to apply it to the recreation centre situation. It is very likely that individually, or in your group discussions, you will have already decided that Andrew's traits and orientation, while seemingly highly appropriate in the army were much less so in the recreation centre. The implication of this is that different situations do appear to require different sets of traits and different orientations.

ACTIVITY 8

Look back over the Andrew Rivers scenario in Review Activity 1 and then answer the following questions. You can answer questions 4 and 5 in a group, if possible.

1 Did it appear that Andrew had fairly stable traits and that these led to his own characteristic style of leadership? Explain your answer.

2 Is it reasonable to assume that Andrew's style was rooted in his personality? Explain your answer.

3 If Andrew had rated his *LPC* do you think it likely that he would have had a low score and hence have been revealed to be a task-orientated leader? Explain your answer.

4 Either individually or in a group, analyse the situation in the recreation centre in terms of Fiedler's three main variables. Name each variable prior to analysing it:

5 Either individually or in a group, and remembering the three conclusions Fiedler reached about leader-orientation and situation contingency, discuss Andrew's suitability for the recreation centre manager post.

1   Yes, Andrew did appear to have fairly stable traits which led him to have a characteristic style of leadership. There was no attempt to modify his approach in this radically different context despite, for example, initial friendly overtures from his deputy. It would be useful to point out here that there is an approach to leadership which, while accepting that leaders are likely to have *preferred* styles or sets of behaviours, holds that they can be trained to change them to meet situation requirements. Hersey and Blanchard (1982), for example, developed a situational leadership theory which falls into this situation-contingent *behaviours* approach. They derived four leadership styles – **telling, selling, participating** and **delegating** – from the two behavioural categories of leader behaviour identified in the classic Ohio State University Studies which are now commonly referred to as task-oriented behaviours and people-oriented behaviours (Stogdill & Coons, 1957). According to Hersey and Blanchard's theory, and using scales which they developed, the level of maturity of followers can be established and then the leader can match this level with an appropriate style. Their theory points up the fact that there are situational factors which Fiedler did not consider.

2   Yes, it would seem reasonable to assume that Andrew's style was rooted in his personality. Again, his approach was totally unwavering and he was 'noticeably surprised' when confronted by the county recreation manager. We could argue, of course, that his personality had been formed by eighteen years in the army. You may have made this point earlier. Obviously this is something that we have no information about but even if it was so formed, it is now his personality.

3   From what we know of Andrew, it seems very likely that he would have scored low on the *LPC* scales. He would clearly appear to be a task-orientated leader in his approach to his team, the work and to his own manager. For example, Andrew cancelled the welcoming party arranged by his deputy saying that he 'did not think it a good idea' and when asked direct, work-related questions his answers were 'always brief and sometimes hostile'. Andrew also expressed shock at the informality of his staff's attitude to work. Then, when his manager raised the issue of his team's discontent with the way he made all of the decisions, his response was that it was he who was paid to make them. Andrew added that their morale would improve when they got used to the professional standards that he insisted on.

4   **Leader-member relations:** Andrew is disliked, to say the least and his team is not willing to follow his guidance.

   Task structure: From what is known from the case study, the task is likely to be quite clearly defined and standard procedures will be in evidence. The task is structured.

   Position power: The recreation centre is not privately owned and so Andrew's team will be government employees. Given this, despite being manager, his position power will be fairly weak. It is this that makes his team so ready to defy his authority.

5 The situation at the recreation centre relates most closely to the third statement
   in Fiedler's theoretical model in that it 'falls between the two extremes'. So:

   ● leader-member relations are poor

   ● task is structured

   ● leader-position is weak.

Keeping the group members happy then becomes much more important and so
a relationship-oriented leader is needed to keep the group members together so
that the task can be tackled. Andrew is a task-orientated leader and is obviously
unable to perform this role.

REVIEW ACTIVITY 2

Suggested time: 30 minutes.

1 What is the key difference between what we have referred to as the 'great
   man' theory of leadership and the universal personality traits approach?

2 The concept of transformational leadership was developed within the trait
   approach to leadership framework. Give examples of traits possessed by
   transformational leaders which are likely to be absent in transactional
   leaders.

3 We have suggested that it is the characteristics of situations that account for
   the fact that the leader's possession of particular traits is related to effective
   performance in one setting and ineffective performance in another. What
   three aspects of situations does Fiedler isolate as determining the
   favourability or otherwise of situations and hence leader influence?

4 Fiedler holds that the characteristic styles of leaders are rooted in their
   personality. Is this true or false?

5 How does Fiedler establish the key traits of leaders?

Summary

In this section, we have examined two approaches to leader effectiveness: the
universal personality traits approach and the situation-contingent personality traits
approach. Both of these approaches linked traits and leadership and both offered
insights into what is involved in leading effectively. Having highlighted some
problems with the first, however, we present the situationalist perspective as being
potentially the most useful.

Unit Summary

Our purpose in this unit has been to clarify the importance of effective leadership as a key managerial role and to assert its importance to organisations. Leadership skills were explored, as were the sources of leaders' power, and we divided them into personal power sources and organisational power sources. We also discussed transactional and transformational leadership to clarify this distinction. We then presented and evaluated two important leadership approaches. These were the universal traits approach and the situation-contingent traits approach. Finally, to help you understand the latter approach, you were given an appreciation of Fiedler's comprehensive research in the context of that perspective.

References

Arnold, J Robertson, IT and Cooper, CL (1991) *Work Psychology: Understanding Human Behaviour in the Workplace,* London: Pitman Publishing.

Bass, BM (1985) *Leadership and Performance: Beyond Expectations,* New York: Free Press.

Bryman, A Bresnen, M Ford, J and Keil, T (1987) 'Leader Orientation and Organisational Transience: an Investigation using Fiedler's LPC scale', *Journal of Occupational Psychology,* 60, pp. 13-19.

Burns, JM (1978) *Leadership,* New York: Harper Row.

Fiedler, FE (1967) *A Theory of Leadership Effectiveness,* New York: McGraw Hill.

French, JRP and Raven, B (1968)'The Bases of Social Power', in Cartwright, D and Sander, AF (eds), *Group Dynamics: Research and Theory,* third edition, New York: Harper and Row.

Gowe, R (1995) 'The Ultimate Drug Deal', in *The Guardian,* 24 January.

Hellreigel, D Slocum, JW and Woodman, RW (1989) *Organisational Behaviour,* West Publishing.

Hersey, P and Blanchard, KH (1982) *Management of Organisational Behaviour: Utilising Human Resources,* Englewood Cliffs, New Jersey: Prentice Hall.

Mullins, LJ (1993) *Management and Organisational Behaviour,* London: Pitman Publishing.

Peters, LH Hartke, DD and Pohlmann, JT (1985) 'Fiedler's Contingency Theory of Leadership: an Application of the Meta-analysis Procedures of Schmidt and Hunter', *Psychological Bulletin,* 97, 274-285.

Stogdill, RM and Coons, AE (1957) (eds) *Leader Behaviour: Its Description and Measurement,* Ohio: Ohio State University.

Recommended Reading

Arnold, J Robertson, IT and Cooper, CL (1991) *Work Psychology: Understanding Human Behaviour in the Workplace,* London: Pitman Publishing, Chapter 13.

Huczynski, JR and Buchanan, DA (1991) *Organisational Behaviour: An Introductory Text,* second edition, London: Prentice-Hall, Chapter 19.

Mullins, LJ (1993) *Management and Organisational Behaviour,* third edition, London: Pitman Publishing, Chapter 8.

Costley, DL and Todd, R (1991) *Human Relations in Organisations,* fourth edition, West Publishing, Chapter 10.

Answers to Review Activities

Review Activity 1

1   You could have answered the question in a number of ways. For example, you could have stated that it is a central process in facilitating effectiveness, you could have defined it as the process of influencing others to work willingly and to the best of their capabilities towards the goal of the leader or, following Saleznik, you could have distinguished it from management. You may also, of course, have argued that leaders are those with vision, communication, sensitivity and self-awareness skills.

2   Hellreigel et al see leader self-awareness as being ongoingly renewed via follower feedback, reinforced by the leader constantly taking a self-inventory.

3   The process of influence involved in leadership is two-way in that the followers consent to the leader's influence. Given this, while coercive power is an important source of a leader's power, it must be used with discretion because punishments could lead to the followers withdrawing their consent.

4   It is true that transactional and transformational forms of leadership are not mutually exclusive. We pointed out in this section that while transactional leaders can transact on a day-to-day basis they can also create vision and mobilise commitment to it and so gain much more than simple compliance.

Review Activity 2

1   The 'great man' theory of leadership held that certain individuals were born 'natural' leaders. The ability to be an effective leader was due to the presence of certain inherited traits. The universal personality traits approach, on the other hand, focuses on the 'universal' traits possessed by effective leaders irrespective of whether these are innate or not.

2   Transformal leaders have charisma and the ability to treat each of their followers on their own merits.

3   **Leader-member relations** – this is the group's willingness to accept leader guidance and the degree to which the leader is liked and trusted.

   Task-structure – this is the degree to which the task can be performed via standard procedures.

Leader position power – this is the power of the leader deriving from their position in the organisation. You will remember that we argued that Andrew Rivers' position power was fairly weak in the council-owned recreation centre.

4   Fiedler does assume that all leaders have fairly stable personality traits and that these lead to their own characteristic style of leadership.

5   To establish the traits of leaders, Fiedler gets them to rate their least preferred co-worker on a scale. In this way, he is seeking to establish whether or not they are able to perceive that person favourably despite that fact that with them, task accomplishment has proved the most difficult in their experience. If the *LPC* score is relatively high, indicating that the leader is still able to say positive things about this co-worker, then the leader is seen to be relationship-orientated. If the *LPC* score is low, indicating that the leader is unable to say positive things about this co-worker, then the leader is seen to be task-oriented.

UNIT 10

ORGANISATIONAL COMMUNICATION

Introduction

In this unit, we introduce theoretical frameworks of communication which can be applied to people in organisations. Also we establish the importance of communication at all levels and within all areas of organisations. 'Why don't you people communicate?' is far too often the exasperated outburst from customer to supplier, from supplier to customer, from subordinate to manager, from manager to subordinate and from colleague to fellow colleague. If the most common saying for failure is one of 'I was never told', perhaps the next most common saying would be 'But I was never asked!'.

The problem with organisations is that they consist of more than one person. Without them there would be perfect linkage between operations; the sort of ideas given by theorists such as Fayol would be faultlessly carried out via principles such as unity of command and direction. Agreed goals could be worked towards unerringly.

There would be a sharing of perfect knowledge on product and technical information. Customers would provide unambiguous specifications; suppliers would provide goods and services which exactly fulfilled these requirements. The results of actions undertaken would be effortlessly carried back and further action taken as appropriate. There would be clarity of understanding of thoughts, feelings and emotions.

However, often this doesn't happen by the very nature of ourselves as human beings, the tasks which are to be accomplished in the work situation, and in our increasingly complex living environments.

We can, therefore, look at communication as being an enabling factor which allows us to perform the work of the organisation. We can look at effects on and barriers to this process. Clearly it is extremely important for us to understand how these might arise, if we are to take a determined look at improving organisational effectiveness and efficiency. We also consider how organisational structure impacts upon the flow of information required for co-ordination, decision-making and awareness.

But, does communication go further than this? Is it good enough to just remove barriers? Such corrections may be seen as somewhat limited in scope; certainly barrier removal is an essential requirement but at the same time, communication can be used to positive effect in the organisation. Thus, for instance, we consider its use as an intrinsic element of the organisation's identity when we consider the communication of culture.

The term **communication** covers a vast field of study. There are many books you can consult on specific skills such as report writing, presentations and interviews and body language. Our aim here is to cover basic concepts which offer insights into the world of communication at work. We include communications theories and models, barriers to communication, formal and informal communication and communicating culture.

Objectives

By the end of this unit, you will be able to :

- explain what organisational communication means and its importance as a function of management.

- identify types and examples of verbal and non-verbal communication.

- demonstrate an understanding of the basic features of some models of communication.

- analyse barriers to communication and recognise them in case study situations.

- explain how communication occurs within formal organisation structures.

- explain the role of communication in decision-making and its relation to centralised and decentralised systems.

- discuss the advantages of both formal and informal communication networks in the organisation.

- demonstrate an understanding of the communication of the organisation's culture.

Section 1

Communication Theories and Models

Introduction

In this section, we look at definitions of communication in organisations; purpose and importance of communication; verbal and non-verbal communication; and models of communication

1.1 Definitions

Communication has many definitions. This is not because theorists are being deliberately awkward but simply that the field of communication includes a wide range of activities and that the act of communication indicates a number of processes taking place. Communication is an all-pervasive factor in our lives.

In what ways do you think you can communicate? At this early stage of the unit, your answers to this general question are likely to be very diverse and un-focussed. We use the case study, *Shopquick Supermarket Chain,* to focus our ideas. You may recall this case study from Unit 1. Read through it again and then answer the questions which follow in the activities throughout the section.

Shopquick Supermarket Chain
Shopquick (UK) Ltd is a major supermarket chain with stores predominantly in England and Scotland. It is one of a number of newer supermarkets on the scene which have the policy of 'piling them high and selling them cheap', no-frills shopping. Its stores compare in size with those of its competition: Food Giant, Aldi and Kwiksave.

Recruitment and training
Reginald Homeworthy, is the general manager of the new Sunderland outlet based in Hendon. A Yorkshire man in his late forties and having worked his way 'up through the ranks' he was personally involved in recruiting all of the store's staff – 22 in total. Staff are expected to be able to function in any area of the store, from shelf stacking to checking out shopping at the tills and they have all been specially trained in store by the company's training manager. Later recruits will be 'shown the ropes' under the careful guidance of one of the two supervisors. Reginald also has a deputy manager, Sheila, to assist him. Sheila has a degree in French and marketing and this is her first 'proper' job since graduating, although she did spend 6 months of her placement year with Shopquick at one of its London sites.

Store layout
As is common in many modern stores, the arrangement of food and other items in the store, as well as storage, check-out and access details is well planned. Reginald was insistent that the store had its own bakery –'Its the smell, makes customers think of bread their Granny used to bake' – and has been closely involved with getting the lighting levels right. This is intensely bright in the cold storage areas, and nicely mellow in the bread and cakes section. And, of course, he has quotas to meet for the company's own brand products so he has had to think of where to position these.

Like all modern supermarkets all of the products have a bar code and the check-outs act as EPOS (electronic point of sale) which means that at any one time Reginald knows how well particular lines are selling and what the stock levels are as well as being prompted by the computer for re-order quantities.

Of course, competition is fierce and Shopquick runs a lean operation which means using the fewest personnel possible at any one time. Thus only at peak times are all of the check-outs staffed.

Staff – attitudes and perceptions

Sandra and Barbara were recruited as 'operative staff' from the closely-knit Hendon council estate. Sandra is in her late teens and still living at home whilst Barbara is a single parent with a two-year-old son, Wayne. They were asked to give their views on various aspects of their jobs. Whilst they are grateful to have a job they both think that their take-home wage is inadequate. Barbara concedes though that if it was not for her mother looking after Wayne she would not be working at all.

'Its OK, I suppose', says Sandra guardedly, 'although Mr Homeworthy can be a bit strict at times. I prefer it when Sheila is in charge – she lets the supervisors decide in which order to do jobs, as long as things get done whereas, for instance, Mr Homeworthy gives us a print-out from his computer and highlights the stock replacements for us.'

Barbara has different views 'I'm not really bothered about that,' she says, 'but it would be nice if I could be allowed to leave early on Tuesday nights to pick Wayne up – its my Mum's bingo night and Heaven knows, she's got little other pleasures in life.'

They both agree that the physical working conditions can be tough. 'Have you seen the size of some of the pallets we're expected to pull around – massive! They're designed for gorillas, not us!' complains Sandra. 'And the rest breaks – half an hour for lunch – if you can get it. Do you know that last week both Dawn and Sarah were down with the 'flu and we both had to cover for the whole week; we hardly got a lunch break between us! At this rate we'll be on sick leave too.'

And then there's the issue of smoking, or rather lack of it. Both women readily admit to being nicotine addicts and yet there is a strict no-smoking policy within the store and the rest room. As Barbara explains, 'Mr Homeworthy has said that he will sack anyone caught smoking on the premises. By break time we're desperate and used to go in the toilets but now Mr Homeworthy has installed smoke alarms there and so we have to go outside to the car park. Someone told me that he was even thinking of making us change out of our uniform if we needed a smoke but I suppose he realised we'd probably be late getting back so he didn't go ahead with that one.'

Both women have had worse bosses. Reginald is courteous, always greeting his staff with a friendly 'Good morning'. But he doesn't really appear to appreciate their problems, nor is there any mechanism by which he may be made aware of them. In his eyes, 'an efficient store is a happy store', as he so often tells his staff.

'I do enjoy working here, for all that', says Sandra. Barbara agrees, 'Yes, I know that the money's just as poor as most places around here, but a job's what you make it, isn't it? I mean, at least we can have a good 'crack-on' [lively gossip] here with the other girls. If any of us has a problem we can talk about it here. And old Reggie – he may think he can make us work our socks off but he doesn't have a clue really. We do enough to keep him happy most of the time though, although he can't expect miracles for the money he pays us!'

ACTIVITY 1

Identify some ways through which Reginald might communicate with his staff.

You might have included:

- speech
- gestures (fist shaking, thumbs-up sign)
- facial expressions (smiling, frowning, quizzical, etc)
- grunts, groans, sighs
- silence
- written words
- pictures, diagrams, graphs

All of these carry some form of message. You might have gone further and included some of the following:

- the way he dresses
- his manner, posture, behaviour, for example, obsequious, domineering
- use of status symbols such as a title or salary, large office or car

You might have interpreted 'ways' of communication in a different sense and included:

- telephone
- letters
- fax
- memos
- minutes
- meetings

- briefings
- appraisals
- interviews
- electronic data interchange
- computer print-outs.

These are ways in which communication is manifested or expressed; in other words, they are the means by which we communicate. They are not in themselves communication; computer print-outs, graphs and even language are only tools to enable the process of communication to take place.

For example, we might regard the passage of speech from one person to another as an example of communication. John, Shopquick's office accountant shouts across the room to Jim, the transport manager: 'It's important that we use an accurate rate of depreciation on the new articulated lorries. Do you think it would be more accurate to use a straight-line or a decreasing balance method?'. In fact, communication may or may not have taken place in this case. Has the intended recipient of the information heard the words spoken? Jim may be listening to someone else. Have these words been interpreted and meaning given to them? Jim might not have the same background and technical knowledge about accounting terms.

How can we define what communication really is? We now consider a few definitions. The first one is the most succinct: 'the exchange of information and the transmission of meaning' (Katz & Kahn, 1966).

Other definitions consider the 'exchange of information' and flesh this out as a process during which symbols are formed and passed between people. For example, communication can be defined as 'sorting, selecting, forming, and transmitting symbols between people to create meaning' (Rasberry & Lemoine, 1986).

The idea of symbols reminds us, as Activity 1 does, that words, for instance, are only symbolic and that meaning does not reside in the words themselves but in the meaning which we, as the recipients, can give them. Activity 1 shows us that symbols are many and diverse.

This is true of all aspects of our lives including the environment of organisations. An organisation is complex and to meet its goals, its activities need to be managed. Within its environment there are many goals, directives and symbols aimed at achieving these ends. It also consists of people and systems, which are constantly changing and which impinge on the communication that takes place. The ways in which an organisation communicates to other organisations and the ways in which members communicate to each other is not a 'bolt-on' facet. We can argue that communication is at the heart of what the organisation is, in other words, its culture. These factors lead us towards a definition of communication within the organisation as follows: 'Organizational communication is an evolutionary, culturally dependent process of sharing information and creating relationships in environments designed for manageable, goal orientated behaviour.' (Fisher, 1993)

1.2 Purposes of organisational communication

Having discussed various definitions of communication and organisational communication, we can now appreciate the purposes of communication in organisations.

ACTIVITY 2

We can consider organisational communication as having three main aims or purposes. Bearing the *Shopquick* case study in mind, suggest what these might be using brief labels for the categories.

Compare your answers with Figure 1. Even if the labels you choose differ from those in Figure 1, you will probably have identified the same three purposes for organisational communication and recognised their inter-relationship:

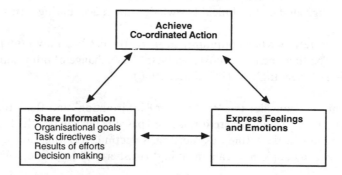

Figure 1: Three purposes of organizational communication
Source: Moorhead & Griffin, 1995

- The first, **achieving co-ordination,** is often considered to be the primary objective; this accords with our previous discussions on administration and control in Unit 1. Reginald is keen to achieve this objective.

- Clearly, the second, **sharing of information** is closely linked to this need for co-ordination and is linked to strategy and feedback on plans and directives. This information flow is probably largely one way, to Reginald only.

- The third objective is not directly linked to either of the other two. If, for example, we feel that something is important, then we need to **communicate that feeling**. If that feeling is concerned with a particular directive or linked to co-ordination then it will, of course, reinforce the message. Other examples might include management wanting to convey its excitement upon the launch of a new product or, conversely, its disappointment at losing a major contract. Reginald probably does not value this as an objective.

1.3 Time spent by managers in communicating

We can see how important communication is, if we consider that some theorists have carried out research to suggest that managers spend as much as 80% of their time in communication of one sort or another. Henry Mintzberg, in one detailed study of five chief executives, found that they spent 78% of their time communicating orally and that this accounted for 67% of their activities (Figure 2).

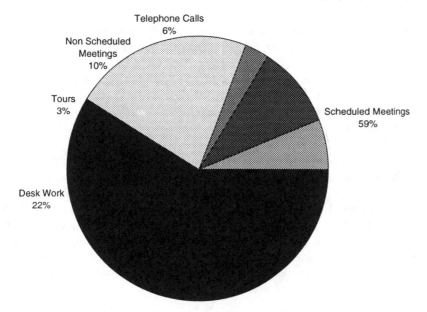

Figure 2: Managers and communicating.
Source: Mintzberg, 1980.

Thus, we may conclude that if wars, governments and companies devote so much time and attention to the practice of communication, that it is more than likely that it is extremely important to organisations, whatever their form.

1.4 Communication and leadership

If we accept that managers have a leading role to play in the organisation and co-ordination, leading, controlling and planning of work, then one way to look at the importance of communication would be to analyse its application within the management situation.

Consider leadership, for a moment. John Adair, one of the present British leadership 'gurus' talks about leadership in terms of achieving the common task, building the team and meeting the needs of individuals. As he says: 'To lead at all requires communication; to lead well requires that a leader communicates effectively' (Adair, 1989).

Look at the quote from the *Art of War* (war, it would seem brings the requirement for good leadership to the fore!) written by the Chinese, Hsun Tzu: 'If the words of command are not clear and distinct, if orders are not thoroughly understood, the general is to blame'. Good communication is put squarely in the court of the leader. We suggest here that time has not dulled this message in the theatre of war, nor in the war-like theatre of modern businesses.

ACTIVITY 3

At Shopquick, Reginald has been sent by senior management on a week's executive training course in the USA, leaving Sheila to run the supermarket in his absence. No sooner has Reginald's plane taken off when a message from an outside sales representative reaches Sheila that their arch supermarket rival 'Savings-U-Like' has negotiated the lease of a factory unit adjacent to Shopquick and is set to immediately develop it, already announcing that it will open within the month.

Sheila phones head office with the information and faxes the details through, as far as she knows them. Head office thanks her and somewhat vaguely instructs her to 'take appropriate action'. Sheila decides that she needs to act on two fronts. Firstly, to reassure staff that Shopquick staff are not under immediate threat of redundancy as head office will support the store and that plans for handling the situation will be given by Reginald upon his return. Secondly, in the meantime, she wants all of the views of the staff in their various departments about how they can improve the service and image of the store.

What do you think might be the main problems facing Sheila in carrying out her two strategies? How might Sheila communicate with her staff to help overcome these problems?

Clearly, Shopquick staff may feel anxious and despondent. They fear that Shopquick may be forced to cut down on staff to remain competitive or even, that head office may be forced to close the store. Staff may not believe that head office will support the store if it becomes unprofitable. Staff may not believe that Sheila carries any authority and not respond to her wish to pool ideas.

As a leader, Sheila will need to address all of the above points. The ways in which she communicates with her staff will be vital if she is to achieve her stated aims and she will need to devote a large part of her time to it. She has, to date, had a certain amount of success with her participative style of leadership and she may wish to capitalise on this.

A good sequence of communication might be to talk firstly to the supervisors to gain their support, and later to all staff. With both audiences, she needs to prove the credibility of herself and the organisation.

Her message needs to be:

- clear
- strong
- conveyed with energy.

She must lead by example and convey this by communicating a general demeanour of appearing:

- confident
- determined
- in control.

We should remember the definition of a leader. A leader is someone whom others follow. Also, we may hear but we don't listen. And, although effective communication means that we understand the meaning (we don't have to agree with the message), if we don't listen, how can we follow?

1.5 Verbal and non-verbal communication

In Activity 1, we noted that we can convey meaning not only by words, **verbal** methods, but in other ways which we classify as **non-verbal**.

Some writers also classify the written and oral use of words as separate categories. Figure 3 gives this kind of framework.

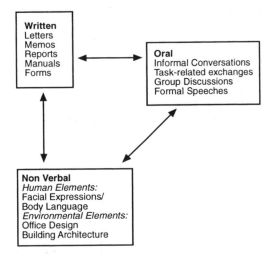

Figure 3: Verbal and non-verbal communication.
Source: Moorhead & Griffin, 1995, p. 353

We have already mentioned many of these terms. An example of the environmental elements in Figure 3, might be a managing director's office featuring a large, imposing desk and leather chair to signify the power of the occupant. All the categories of communication identified in Figure 3 offer a rich field of study and writers have devoted entire works to areas such as 'body language'. See, for example, Michael Argyle, 1988 for further information. As the name suggests, body language is essentially the ways in which we communicate through our bodies, other than by language.

ACTIVITY 4

How can we communicate through body language, including facial expressions?

Perhaps you are surprised at how many different ways we can communicate in just by using our bodies to different effect. Manning and Curtis (1988) provide the following guidelines:

- **Facial expressions**
  Perhaps the most informative area of our bodies. We might exchange meaning by: smiling, frowning, grinning, blushing, looking worried, anxious, smug, puzzled, satisfied, sly, angry, friendly, tired, energetic, etc

- **Eye contact**
  Steady, shifty, interested, dull

- **Head movement**
  Nods of the head to signify acceptance or willing the other person to continue
  Shakes of the head to signify non-acceptance

- **Hand and arm gestures**
  Pointing, beckoning, stopping
  Folded arms – defensive
  Arms uplifted outward – puzzlement, disbelief
  Hand to mouth whilst talking – can indicate lying!

- **Body posture**
  Fidgeting – nervousness, boredom
  Hands-on-hips – arrogance, confrontation
  Slouching – indifference, apathy, depression
  Shrugging shoulders – uncertainty, disbelief

- **Dress**
  Business suits – formal, serious, denotes profession
  Casual – informality of the event, for example. a weekend residential course, also denotes the prevailing culture within the organisation, for example, film studio

Non-verbal communication has clearly many dimensions. Even in verbal communication there is often a non-verbal element. As John Townsend reminds us,

'It's not what you say, it's the way that you say it'. The manner in which we say something will affect the message – a phenomenon studied under the category of paralinguistics.

ACTIVITY 5

List the ways in which you can alter the message by the way in which you speak.

Townsend (1988) lists the following seven categories:

- timing, length of utterances
- emotional tone, inflection
- speech errors, such as umm and err
- national or regional accents
- choice of words, sentence structure
- verbal 'tics', for example, repeated use of 'you know'
- stressed words.

USE OF SILENCE

Often combined with body language and other actions, such as staring, walking out of the room, silence can be an incredibly powerful means of communicating: perhaps pausing for effect in a speech; perhaps to show anger; to stop dead in mid-sentence to gain attention from an audience whose attention has wandered; to punish by 'sending someone to Coventry' [not speaking to them].

1.6 Five models of communication

We have introduced the concept of communication, discussed its importance within organisations and briefly considered how it might be manifested in verbal and non-verbal ways. However, in order to make a deeper and more meaningful analysis of communication in the work situation, it is extremely useful to use models. These models give a simplified view of a complex situation; they enable us to make sense of what is going on; they act as the basis for further analysis, providing common terminology and concepts.

Fisher (1993) provides an overview of five well-known models:

- **one-way model**
- **interaction model**
- **two-person relationship model**
- **communication-in-context model**
- strategic model: **organisation-environment transaction model.**

ONE-WAY MODEL

In the one-way model of communication, someone sends a message to a passive receiver, as depicted in Figure 4. It is the simplest of the models.

Figure 4: One-way model of communication

Many types of oral communication – speeches, lectures, courtroom arguments, presentations, TV commercials – are often one-way.

REQUIREMENTS FOR EFFECTIVENESS

True one-way communication does not allow for any feedback from the receiver and so the single most important factor for effectiveness will be the sender's knowledge of the audience or 'receiver'. In particular, you would need to know:

● audience's existing technical knowledge

● likely appeal of the presentation and its approach to their interests

● relevance of your topic in their view.

You would need, in other words, to 'put yourself in their shoes'. This is because you are attempting to persuade or educate your audience. You need to 'get it right first time' because there is no means by which the audience can obtain clarification.

The next most important factors to communicate successfully would be:

● structure and language of the talk

● your delivery of it.

The talk needs to be set up to keep the audience with you. This will mean that you need to:

● tell people where the talk will go

● provide 'signposts' on the way so that they know which stage you have reached at any one time

● summarise from time to time to indicate the completion of sections and remind the audience of key points covered so far.

You will, of course, need to keep their interest, or else they will simply not listen! Try applying this same exercise to an after-dinner speech where the objective is one of entertainment and this need then becomes paramount.

WRITTEN ONE-WAY

Messages do not have to be delivered orally. Written directives, for instance, and material given in books, journals, magazines, etc is one-way. Again, all of the points given above, structure etc, would apply with regard to the receiver or reader, although there would be a difference in technique. Oral presentations would be short and biased towards impact and key facts; books can be very much longer and go into a lot more depth.

ADVANTAGES OF ONE-WAY COMMUNICATION

As we have mentioned, one-way communication is widely used and carries with it the following advantages:

- fast and efficient delivery of the message in question

- easily recorded, this may be done in advance of delivery.

Senders often think that one-way communication is

- more logical, although, in fact the sender's logic may differ from the receiver's

- it is 'messy' – it doesn't allow for 'distractions' such as people wandering off the theme.

Senders may also favour it if they are short of time, and if there are any controversial issues they do not wish to discuss!

DISADVANTAGES OF ONE-WAY COMMUNICATION

The major disadvantage with strictly one-way communication is the lack of feedback. This means that mis-judging the knowledge, interest, expectations or motivation of the audience, or not bothering to find them out, can be catastrophic as the sender has no way of knowing whether or not the message is arriving at its destination.

Poor structure and delivery also mean failure. It is easy to lose the interest of an audience through monotonous delivery, or to antagonise a reader by a pompous, patronising or peremptory tone in a written communication. A report or lecture which is confusingly ordered and not clearly signposted will equally fail to communicate.

There are many books which can help presentations and report writing skills, for example, Stanton, 1990.

ACTIVITY 6

Imagine that you work in the Department of Transport. How would you use the principles of one-way communication if you were asked to prepare a presentation or speech on road safety to be delivered to primary school children of:

1   5 years of age

2   10 years of age.

We suggest the following guidelines:

1   5 year olds

- **knowledge:** limited knowledge of cars and road safety – keep the talk direct and highlight key areas only, keeping the message as simple as possible

● **interest:** use a mixture of methods to keep attention as young children have very short attention spans, consider the use of cartoons or puppets, for example, Tufty the squirrel

● **relevance:** a need to stress that road sense is a skill to be learnt like any other at school, reward correct answers, give badges to reinforce this relevance, involve the class teacher who is the central authority position for a young child.

2   10 year olds

● **knowledge:** a growing awareness of the potential ability of cars to maim and kill, remember this but don't be un-necessarily gruesome, foster the notion that we care for each other and we need those around us to use road sense as well, by this age children will be developing a strong sense of ethics

● **interest and relevance:** develop a sense of responsibility and awareness not only for ourselves as pedestrians but also about how it feels to be a driver as this is only seven years away, show the driver's perspectives, for example, how difficult it is to stop quickly or see people.

INTERACTION MODEL

This model assumes that two-way communication is taking place. It is a good model for us to look at because it introduces some useful ideas and terminology. Even in many so-called 'one-way' situations, the speaker will be looking for tell-tale responses from the audience; do they look bored, excited, puzzled, for example? The skilful presenter will alter the talk as he proceeds. Two-way communication of a sort is happening as the receiver is responding by body language. The speaker might even stop the talk and invite questions if he sees a lot of puzzled frowns; he has then entered into two-way communication much more fully. Look now at the model in Figure 5.

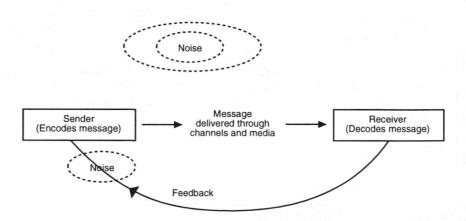

Figure 5: The interaction model

Recall that communication concerns 'the exchange of information and the transmission of meaning'. As it is not possible for someone else to know what it is we are thinking, we need to use some form of symbols, such as language, to form a message. The process by which the sender achieves this is called **encoding**.

CHANNELS AND MEDIA

The message is sent via one or more **channels** or cues. In face-to-face conversation, for instance, we might typically use the five senses of:

● sight

● sound

● touch

● smell

● taste.

These are sensory channels (Berko et al, 1995).

Fisher (1993) defines channels in the broad sense as 'the means by which senders convey messages: oral; written; and non-verbal'. Often a message carries more force if it is repeated or delivered through more than one channel. Thus a face-to-face conversation is likely to be more effective than a telephone conversation because in addition to using sound, the channels of sight, for instance, facial expressions and touch may be used.

We could use various **media** to assist us. Fisher defines media as 'the various tools or vehicles of communication'. A talk could make use of a microphone or a television programme. A written message might be given on a letter, a fax or electronic mail. Note also that the medium itself can have an impact upon the effectiveness of the message; for instance, a fax carries more urgency than a letter. Figure 6 suggests the most effective media and channels for various types of communication.

MEDIA	Characteristics		Best for Communications that are:
	Feedback	Cues and CHANNELS	
Face-to-face	Immediate	Audio and Visual	Ambiguous, emotional divergent in background
Telephone	Rapid	Audio	
Addressed documents	Slow	Limited Visual	Clear, rational, similar in background
Unaddressed documents	Slowest	Limited Visual	

Figure 6: Effective use of media and channels
Source: Adapted from Steers, 1991

We might a so speak of sending messages via certain channels in the organisation, by this we r ean via certain departments or individuals. In this sense, a channel is the conduit ; ong which the message travels. Note, channels and media are closely linked. Some writers use the terms interchangeably. Although we have differentiated these terms you may see them in the literature in either context.

Feedback is the process by which the receiver responds to the message. As we mentioned earlier, this can be oral, verbal or non-verbal. Feedback is an extremely important feature of communication.

Noise is anything which diminishes the impact of the message. It can be physical, for example, loud traffic, or it can be defined in other ways, for example, boredom, pre-occupation with something else, or anger. We consider other types of noise when we look at 'barriers to communication'.

ACTIVITY 7

What channel and media would you use to:

1 Inform someone that they had been successful in a job interview held last week? Why would you use this method(s)?

2 Inform someone that you were very sorry but that you were going to have to make them redundant because of work shortage? Why would you use this method(s)?

---

1   You would inform someone by written letter, because of its:
- formality
- record purposes
- details of start date, salary, etc can be attached

2   You would inform someone by one-to-one conversation, privately, and follow later with an official letter, because:
- it shows that you think it is important
- it offers a forum for feedback from the receiver, no matter how unpleasant the message is
- it gives you the opportunity to offer further advice or consolation
- the letter is brief and is there for your records after you have discussed the matter.

TWO-PERSON RELATIONSHIP MODEL

This model states that the way in which we view ourselves and the other party and the way in which we behave, for example, communicate, are affected by the way in which the other party views itself and us and the way in which it behaves. This may sound complicated but an example will illustrate.

People tend to act in ways which reinforce their own self-perceptions. A manager may thus act differently towards subordinates than towards colleagues because of his perceptions that they expect different kinds of behaviour from him. His behaviour, and communication, with subordinates is affected by his perception that they expect an authoritative approach from him. He, therefore, adopts the role of leader that he feels is expected. Equally, the subordinates see him as leader and take on their expected role of subordinates to him. With colleagues, who expect a more friendly style of communication and behaviour, he adopts an approach that reflects their perceived equality of status.

This communication model, with each person adapting the perceived roles and status relationship of the situation, can be carried into any inter-personal relationship.

COMMUNICATION-IN-CONTEXT MODEL

This model incorporates elements of all of the previous models and then considers the organisational back-cloth or 'context' in which communication takes place (Figure 7). It sees communication as shaped by other important factors as well as the individuals directly involved. These include:

- **task characteristics,** is the task complex or straightforward, design, for example, is a complex task, following a recipe, is a straightforward task?

- **group characteristics,** for example, how big is the group, what sort of people are in it, what are their relationships to each other?

- **organisation structure and culture,** for example. how is work allocated, tasks carried out, what are the values of the organisation?

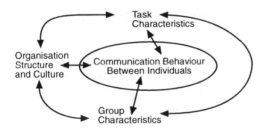

Figure 7: Communication-in-context model
Source: Fisher, 1993, p. 14

Consider the following two scenarios; both have a set task to achieve and require good teamwork for their success. Both situations actually occurred in Himalayan mountaineering.

The first situation concerned an attempt by an international team in 1971 to climb Everest by the (as then) unclimbed south west face. The group was characterised by its inability to act cohesively; it was rather a collection of individuals with personal (nationalistic) ambitions (values) at heart. Organisation structure was weak. There was more than one leader and there were too many people for a single route. The task itself was highly complex in terms of the logistics of supplying camps high up on the mountain, open to much uncertainty (where would such a route go?) and would involve very difficult climbing.

In such a situation, communication was immensely difficult due to the tensions outlined above. Even if the expedition had been blessed by having people with superb communication skills, the effectiveness of their messages would probably be severely impaired by such problems. In the event, there was a great deal of conflict and the expedition failed.

In comparison, Chris Bonington's 1975 expedition on the south west face had to contend with the same task but the group size was small and there was no nationalistic agenda. Ultimately (allowing for input from the group) there was one leader and communication flow was clearly defined up and down the structure. The group of climbers had already evolved their own culture and values having climbed together previously on other expeditions.

Again, communication was essential but given the factors outlined above it was much more effective as evidenced by the high level of teamwork shown on the expedition and its success in forcing the route to the summit. (Bonington, 1994)

ORGANISATION-ENVIRONMENT TRANSACTION MODEL

This model is even wider based than the communication-in-context model. It is a strategic model which takes into account the wider context in which organisations operate and the environment they communicate in. Thus many organisations are now keen to promote a 'green' image to their customers and also to other competitors, pressure groups and local government.

1.7 Perspectives of communication

So far we have analysed communication in terms of models, going from the simple one-way model to the more complex strategic model. Which model is the 'right one' to use? It is, in fact, quite possible to use one, several or indeed all of the models to analyse a particular situation.

Which of the models we use and the bias we place upon them is governed by our perspective, in other words, the way in which we view the situation. To give an example, take the case in which a manager asks a worker to work some overtime that weekend and the worker refuses.

- From one perspective, we could question the way in which the manager asked (was it verbal or written?) – the emphasis is clearly on the medium and channel of communication.

- From another perspective, we could look at the communication processes in terms of what perceived importance the manager gave to the message (it could be very important) and his perception of the worker (he wanted the work), and the perceptions of the worker (it was not so important, he didn't want the work).

- From another perspective, we could look at the message in terms of the culture of the organisation ('people never work Saturdays here – its just not done!').

REVIEW ACTIVITY 1

Suggested time: 45 minutes.

Read the case study, *Helenne,* and answer the questions that follow.

Helenne

Gordon McGreal is the marketing manager for Godiva Beauty Products Ltd. In the past, Godiva has concentrated its product range on moisturising lotions and creams under the 'Dermiplex' label designed to 'rejuvenate sagging and tired skin' as the sales blurb says. The company has enjoyed a degree of success with these but has recently been the subject of scrutiny from animal rights activists after a local newspaper revealed that the Dermiplex range had been initially tested on animals.

Now Gordon has decided that the future for Godiva Beauty Products lies in products which are made from natural ingredients, not tested on animals. He has thought of a name for the new product range – *Helenne* (after Helen of Troy, famed for her beauty) – which will feature a soap, facial scrub, and shampoo.

Of course, he is aware that this is no longer a totally unexploited 'niche' market (Body Shop, in particular, is already well known) and is aware that he will have a tough fight on his hands to convince his own company to agree to his plans. However, he is adamant that this is the direction for the company to take; he is tired of those in the company's management who are afraid to 'move with the times' and feels passionately that the time to get into the 'natural market' is 'now or never'. In fact, he feels so strongly that he is prepared to resign if the board turns him down and he has another job lined up as a back-up.

Deep down he feels that his role as marketing manager means that he must be the catalyst for new products; this is a view shared by the majority of senior managers and directors. He tries to communicate an appropriate self-image by always appearing energetic and wearing 'sharp' suits complete with loudly contrasting ties and braces.

Gordon had gained approval from Mr Dermot, the managing director, to give a presentation of his ideas at the next monthly board meeting. Approval had not been easy to obtain, for Mr Dermot was a busy man. Gordon had made an appointment to speak to him but, as usual, Mr Dermot had been behind schedule and was busy putting various papers into his briefcase prior to leaving for the airport when Gordon was summoned in by the secretary. Gordon had tried to quickly explain the whole business of *Helenne.* Mr Dermot, now searching for something in his desk, had scarcely looked up, only acknowledging Gordon's idea with the occasional grunt. Wanting to complete his packing, Mr Dermot had muttered 'Yes, McGreal, put it on the agenda. See Norma on the way out. See you at the meeting'.

Gordon had indeed seen Norma (Mr Dermot's secretary) and had also persuaded her to include a paper headed 'Natural products: the way forward?' to accompany his presentation which was listed as item number 2 on the meeting agenda. This paper firstly, showed how profits appeared to have stagnated at a moderate level and secondly, introduced the field of natural beauty products for future product portfolio consideration. All board members had now received this information and with the monthly meeting only a week away, Gordon was already receiving nods of approval and equally threats of opposition. The production director, Alec Smallfield, in particular pointed out to Gordon over the telephone that neither his staff nor his factory were set up to manufacture the proposed range.

If his strategy receives company backing, Gordon will have to sell the idea to major stores and pharmacies as the company does not have its own sales outlets. However, final approval will only come from the customer!

It will be important to launch the *Helenne* range at the most auspicious time. Gordon has decided that an ideal launch date would be immediately after a nationally publicised day of action ('Animals have feelings too!') by animal rights activists. It will, therefore, be essential to have the first of the product range available and in the stores by this date and to have all of the publicity sorted out well in advance.

1   How are the three purposes of organisational communication illustrated in the case study?

2   Describe the following communication models and comment on features in the above scenario which relate to each:

● one-way

● interaction

● two-person relationship

● communication-in-context

● organisation-environment transaction.

3   Identify different types of non-verbal communication in the case study.

4   What media and channels:

(a) has Gordon McGreal used to communicate with senior management?

(b) would you use if you were Alec Smallfield, production director, assuming the following situation: Gordon's proposals have been accepted and you have to tell your staff that there will be big changes ahead for everyone but that their co-operation will be vital for the organisation's success? Why would you use these particular media and channels?

Summary

In this section, you have been introduced to communication as a means of exchange of information and transmission of meaning, and have discussed its specific meaning within an organisational context. You have examined its purpose and importance in organisations, particularly in relation to management and leadership. You have analysed different types of verbal and non-verbal communication and identified examples of each, emphasising the fact that messages are constantly being conveyed non-verbally and informally.

You have also examined in outline five models of communication and you have identified, in practical examples, basic features of some of these models.

SECTION 2

Barriers to Communication

Introduction

In this section, we look at barriers to communication in the organisation. Barriers, as we see, come in many shapes and forms and they are potentially present in all communication and in all of the models we have so far considered. Barriers range from the obvious, for example, language differences, to the more subtle, for example, difference in perceptions.

Understanding how barriers to communication can arise is essential, if we are to suggest ways in which communication might be improved. This section is, therefore, devoted solely to the many types of barriers and we cover the more common instances. However, it is impossible to include every example due to their diverse nature.

2.1 Barriers to communication

All of the models of communication are concerned to a greater or lesser extent with barriers to communication. These can take many forms.

ACTIVITY 8

List all of the barriers to communication that you can think of.

Barriers
Message ambiguity
Physical noise, for example, the background noise of road-works
Distance, for example, sometimes it is better to meet in person
Language
Jargon
Lack of interest by receiver
Mismatch of knowledge, for example, receiver might not have the relevant technical background
Distortion of the message
Lack of time
Length of the communication chain, for example, through many levels of hierarchy
Information 'gatekeepers'

Psychological
Difference in perceptions
Emotions – happiness, anger, sadness
Fear, anxiety
Mistrust

Cultural
Differences in values of sender and receiver
Status
Deliberate by-passing
Assumptions, jumping to conclusions
Expectations
First impressions
Stereotyping
Polarisation
Tendency to evaluate too early and not really listen

Many of these barriers you will have identified either as we have given here or in equivalent terms. Others may be unfamiliar, but these will become clear as we explain the most significant barriers.

2.2 Message ambiguity

Consider the following statement in a pharmacy window:

We dispense with accuracy

At first glance, this is a perfectly sound statement. We assume that the pharmacy is accurate in its dispensing of drugs and medicines. We could, however, interpret the statement as meaning that the pharmacy does not use or dispenses with accuracy!

The following statement was drafted as part of a university regulation:

> 'The student will fail and must repeat the subject if he/she fails to produce any work with regard to the three assessments'.

This statement caused much confusion at an examinations board. Did the statement mean that the student:

- failed and had to repeat the subject if there was non-submission of any one assessment? (that is, failure to submit one or more), or

- failed and had to repeat the subject if there was no evidence whatsoever of submission? (that is, failure to submit all three assessments).

2.3 Language

We could argue that the cause of the ambiguity was the language used, specifically the word 'any'. Here, the word has been used too loosely. As we mentioned earlier, meaning does not lie in the words themselves but in the meaning that we give them. Of course, it takes time to learn all of the symbols in a language and some of us might have a larger vocabulary than others. Language may be a barrier between people of different nationalities in a multi-national company, for instance, and even between different cultures.

Consider this example: Little Johnny (from the north east of England) explaining to his (Scottish) teacher what he had done over the previous weekend:

'Please, Miss, I didn't do anything. I was bad.'
'Oh, Johnny, what did you do?' asks the concerned teacher.

Unless you are acquainted with the north east you may not be aware that 'bad' means 'ill', and not 'badly behaved' and you may make the same mistake as the teacher.

In organisations, the use of jargon – words which only have meaning within the organisation or profession– can cause barriers. Sometimes, this might be done deliberately to either exclude others or to foster a sense of mystery and difficulty.

2.4 Distortion

A message does not have to be ambiguous to cause problems. Quite often the problem is that the person sending the message intends that it can only be interpreted in one way; the problem is that the encoding process hasn't been very good and what the sender communicates isn't quite what was intended. For instance, details of an office plan are sent via a fax machine; the sender has tried to send a full size plan by cutting the original into A4 size sheets and faxing these across. Unfortunately, the equipment distorts the images at the edges and when the receiver pieces together the faxed sheets certain words and dimensions are erased or disfigured.

ACTIVITY 9

Consider the following examples of ambiguity, language problems and distortion and comment upon them and identify the type of barrier:

1 Nothing is better than this product.

2 This ice-cream is really wicked!

3 I found it very educational.

4 This job requires a part-time man.

5 That's not very pc.

---

1   ambiguous – does it mean that the product is the best or that anything is preferable to it?

2   a language problem – a child telling the merits of a new ice-cream, but it could be ambiguous if taken out of context.

3   it could be used in a sarcastic, intentionally ambiguous way – 'It taught me a lesson! I'll know next time not to do that!

4   distortion – what the sender meant was for a man to take up the position on a part-time basis, not for the person to be a man part-time.

5   language – use of jargon, pc meaning politically correct.

2.5 Physical noise and distance

Clearly physical noise can be a barrier. Distance can compound the problem. People have recognised this. For instance, construction sites can be noisy places. To make themselves understood, engineers often use a series of hand signals to the person working with them when surveying with a theodolite. Crane operators and banksmen (person on the ground directing and informing the crane operator) and taxiing aircraft and ground personnel may also use hand signals or more increasingly mobile phone or radio communication.

What is important is that the symbols have been previously agreed and are unambiguous and they will still make sense even if subject to a fair amount of distortion. Take the case of two rock climbers tied together. One climbs out of sight of the other and the wind is so strong that it carries all sound away. How does the second climber know that the first one is safe and that it is time to climb? If the pre-arranged signal is that one tug on the rope means 'Climb!' and two tugs means 'Don't climb, I'm not ready!' then disaster awaits if the two tug message is sent and only one tug is received. One practice is for three sharp tugs to mean 'Climb!' and no signal for anything else. Thus, even if the distorted message of one or two tugs is received, the climber will know that it is time to climb.

Distance can also be a problem, especially if people have never met before. We gain so much useful information from body language. We are also much more likely to feel a sense of commitment if we meet someone in person. It's hard to tell someone face-to-face that the order is going to be late! It is important to build a relationship with those with whom we communicate. What are their values? How do they view the situation? How important is the issue to them? If distance prevents or reduces meetings to such an extent that these relationships suffer, then we can create barriers.

2.6 Emotions – fear, anxiety, mistrust, anger

ACTIVITY 10

Imagine that you work for a small, family run business, D R Giles Ltd, which employs a workforce of semi-skilled craftsmen. It is taken over by a national company, Reckitt UK, with factories all over the country and with its headquarters over 200 miles away. As yet, you have not even seen the new managing director. How are you likely to view the new parent company? How might these views affect communication between your small organisation and the national company?

It is possible that you will fear for your job security or status, be anxious about new working practices and be mistrustful in general about Reckitt's intentions.

If so, these would be common feelings. It is usual for people to have such feelings about the unknown, and most changes mean an element of the unknown. People tend to fear the worst. In this kind of atmosphere, it is only too easy for such an unhealthy climate to develop.

The effects upon communication can be dramatic. Fear and mistrust will block out organisational goals of effectiveness and efficiency from Reckitt's headquarters to the small organisation. Personal survival will take precedence. Perceptions may form of a 'them and us' type and these may be self-perpetuating as each side acts out its role.

Of course, people in D R Giles may be quite right to be fearful. However, if there is no real justification for such fears, it would be wise to break down the barriers regarding these misperceptions before they become any worse. The business needs to know that it is welcomed and needed by the larger parent company. A visit by the managing director and (truthful) reassurances would be welcomed; a statement outlining the direction the parent company is moving in and where the smaller company fits into the plan would be welcomed.

ACTIVITY 11

Imagine that you are a worker in D R Giles Ltd and you have just heard a rumour that your pay is to be reduced. You are very angry. At this point, your manager requests that all workers attend a briefing on the new terms and conditions. The message she is about to deliver is that the pay package will be restructured; whereas previously you were paid on an hourly basis (including overtime) you will now be paid a basic salary plus performance-related bonuses. Your manager wants to explain that, although at present, this would mean a cut in take-home pay because the factory is quite old and inefficient, as soon as the new methods and machinery are installed in line with Reckitt UK's systems, you will actually end up with an increase in your weekly take-home pay.

How do you think your anger will affect the communication process at the briefing?

It is probable that your anger will act as a barrier, initially, at least. It may influence your perception of the deal offered by Reckitt UK to the extent that you do not believe that this is (probably) a better deal. You might be particularly vocal at the meeting and arouse the anger of the managers, remember the two-person model, so that you finish by having a fruitless argument.

Perhaps, you are so angry that 'words fail you' and you resort to insulting personal remarks. If this happens, your argument will probably fail. Your ability to express yourself has been diminished because of excessive emotion, in this case, anger. What is more, communication failure will apply in the opposite direction. You will simply not 'listen to reason' in the other person's mind and any attempt to communicate with you is a waste of time.

We have seen in our discussion that emotions may be a barrier either to the reception of a message or to the ability of the sender to communicate the message effectively. Manning and Curtis have a simple diagram which highlights our ability to express ourselves as a function of our emotions (Figure 8).

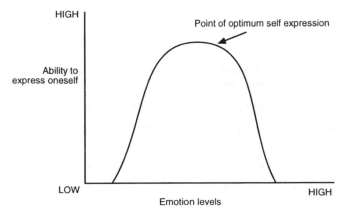

Figure 8: The relationship between emotion levels and the ability to express oneself
Source: Manning-Curtis, 1983

It is interesting to note that there is an optimum level – that a certain amount of emotion is good. For one thing, it shows that we are interested! For another, a certain amount of adrenaline usually brings out the best in us as communicators. Actors recognise this fine balance.

Anger is just one emotion; other emotions can equally assist or hinder the process of communication. Take 'happy' versus 'sad', for instance. Again you can probably think of instances when we either don't want to communicate or the situation is so overwhelming that we are quite unable to communicate.

2.7 Perceptions

Perception must always be a paramount consideration. It is applicable to so many situations, as we have just seen . To illustrate this further, take the concept of 'danger'. Danger may be minimal, but if we perceive that some activity involves an element of danger, then our fear will be very real.

ACTIVITY 12

In the earlier example, what do you think may be the perceptions of both the managers and the workers of D R Giles Ltd to the role of work in their lives? How might these perceptions raise barriers to communication?

Managers may:

- view work as a career
- not intend to stay with the company but use it as a 'stepping stone' to a better position somewhere else
- take the view that the company buys their professional expertise
- regard additional work hours (including work at home) as part of being a 'professional'
- assume that they do the thinking and the workers do the 'doing'
- see themselves as 'fitting in' (or not!) with the new management.

Perhaps the most relevant of these perceptions to this scenario is the last one. If a managers sees him or herself as the sort of person whom the new company encourages then he or she will want to stay and will seek out as much information as possible on the goals and objectives of the company. Conversely, it may be that the manager does not or cannot work in the style of the new owners. Such a manager will not listen to head office directives or will at best simply pay 'lip service' to them.

Workers may:

- view work as a job – the means to earn a livelihood
- intend to stay with the company and gradually work their way up the ladder, at least to a better paid position
- believe that they will never work again if made redundant
- have the view that the company buys their time, 9 till 5, with overtime being paid for any work after this
- as a 'time'-based commodity they are easily replaced
- view that it is their job only to follow management's instructions.

If workers regarded their work as a means to a livelihood and thought that they would never get another job again then they will tend to be anxious and suspicious of anything that management says. The whole situation is much more likely to erupt into one of conflict.

Some of the other perceptions could act as barriers to communication. For instance, the Reckitt UK Ltd's approach to the work situation might expect workers to contribute their own ideas and to accomplish the task – even if this occasionally meant unpaid overtime. If this were the case, workers' minds would not be open to any such initiatives.

2.8 First impressions and frozen evaluations

The saying is that 'first impressions count'. We tend to make snap judgements upon first encountering someone or some situation for the first time. It is claimed that the first few minutes in a job selection interview are crucial to the potential candidate's success. Often our first impressions are somewhat superficial and subjective as we have little 'hard' information to work on; it is easy to gain a false impression under these circumstances. The fact that this occurs is bad enough, however, the fact that it is often compounded by our unwillingness to change our evaluation when presented later with conflicting evidence to our initial 'judgement' is even worse. This unwillingness to change our opinion is sometimes referred to as a **frozen evaluation** and has been recognised for some time now as one of the barriers we erect to communication (see Haney, 1974).

Again, recall the danger of making assumptions. Assumptions are inferences we make – sometimes without realising! We observe one thing and then infer something from that. We assume people will be interested because they have turned up for our speech – they might have been coerced. We assume that they don't need further information because they don't ask questions, whereas, in fact, they might be so confused that they don't know what to ask!

2.9 Stereotyping

There is often a strong tendency for us to want to put people into certain categories or **stereotypes**. For instance, this may be according to profession, race, sex. In our own mind, we have built up a 'mental picture' of the characteristics of this group – how its members look and behave, and what their attitudes are.

The use of the stereotype model simplifies the process of 'getting to know' an individual; once the individual has been 'pigeon-holed' into a certain category it is then easy to infer that person's characteristics.

Of course, what stereotypes do not do is discriminate. In reality, people are not identical. Just because a person belongs to a certain profession does not mean that such a person must conform to our stereotype. Take the case of the professional stereotype of an accountant.

ACTIVITY 13

What personality characteristics come to mind when you think of an accountant?

Your list might include the following:

- dull
- grey
- methodical
- painstaking.

Or you might have adopted a more modern approach. You actually think accountants lead exciting, thrusting lives surrounded by computers and advising major corporations and might have listed characteristics such as:

- dynamic
- astute
- ruthless
- business-like.

This is a very different stereotype! If you use both then you have been more discriminating and used two 'pigeon-holes'. However, if you rigidly apply these patterns to all accountants then you are still using stereotypes.

The danger of using any stereotype is that the person might only have some of the characteristics and not others. Indeed, the person might possess none of the characteristics at all! As our perceptions about the receiver of our communication will strongly affect what and how we communicate, using stereotypes can seriously impair our effectiveness in the communication process.

2.10 Polarisation

If we think of the poles of a battery we think of 'positive' and 'negative'; if we think of the north and south poles we are looking at opposite ends of the earth's surface. In communication, we talk of people thinking in 'black and white'. This tendency to think of something as either one thing or the other, all or nothing, is known as **polarisation**. It can be a significant barrier to communication.

Consider the statement: 'Chocolate makes you overweight because its loaded with fats and calories'. But is this is a valid statement? Chocolate does contain a high percentage of fats and calories; this part of the statement is true. However, the next part of the statement is highly polarised; chocolate will not necessarily make you overweight. For instance, what if you only eat a little? What if you use a lot of calories because you are an active person?

In organisations there are very few things which are completely 'black and white', most are shades of grey. For example, a polarised management statement might be that 'unions are counter-productive to profits and efficiency in the work place'. It is true that union activity can be counter-productive. After all, the union's members probably view the company in a different light to management. However, it is also true that an exploited work force will tend to work grudgingly and will have long-term problems such as absenteeism, high labour turnover and even sabotage which may have been avoided if there was dialogue between the two power bases of union and management. Also unions play a positive leading role in the provision of training for members.

2.11 Evaluate too early and not listen

Carl Rogers (1991) argues that one of the main barriers to communication is the tendency to evaluate, that is to approve or disapprove of what the other person is saying too early, that is, before the person has finished communicating.

ACTIVITY 14

What do you think are the dangers of doing this?

The problem is that once you have made an evaluation you will then simply twist the rest of the communication to fit this evaluation, whether it is approval or disapproval. You may thus stop listening to the real arguments put forward by the sender.

ACTIVITY 15

How do you think you could reduce this tendency to evaluate?

Rogers suggests that what we should try to do is to put ourselves 'in the shoes' of the person sending the message. What is their background; their hopes, aspirations, and values. How will the outcome of the situation affect them? We should try to express empathy with the feelings of the other party.

Managers need to encourage people to talk frankly with them so that they can offer their support; sometimes by acting as a 'sounding board' and getting their employees to answer their own questions. 'So, Tim, you say you've had problems with the machine. Have you any ideas on how to solve them?' Managers can assist by a process of 'active listening'.

We need to make a conscious effort to suspend evaluation until all angles have been covered. The danger of this, as Rogers concedes, is that our own view of the situation might be unduly influenced and we end up agreeing when we don't really want to!

REVIEW ACTIVITY 2

Suggested time: 40 minutes.

Re-read the *Shopquick* case study given at the beginning of the unit. Then answer the following questions.

1   Look at the section in the case study entitled *Perceptions and attitudes*.

Briefly describe the essential differences in perceptions between the staff, Sandra and Barbara, and Reginald Homeworthy towards the work situation, that is, their values and attitudes towards work.

2   Reginald receives a fax from head office which reads: 'Stock Records: Discrepancies on confectionery items type 56. Please explain these losses'.

Reginald immediately orders the secretary to place a poster in the works canteen which reads: 'It has come to my attention that a certain amount of pilfering has been going on in the store. May I remind you that this is a sackable offence and any one discovered partaking in such action will be instantly dismissed? Signed Mr R Homeworthy (Store Manager).

Comment on

(a) Reginald's interpretation of the message from head office

(b) The way in which he transmits the message to his staff

(c) What sort of barriers to future communication are likely to arise from this action?

3   Upon reading the notice, Fred who works in the bakery and never misses an opportunity for a good argument, announces to the rest of the staff in the canteen 'Well, it doesn't surprise me at all. This always happens. I told you so before but now, perhaps you'll listen. The only way to treat management is with contempt. I vote that we all go on strike to show our solidarity against this blatant slur on our characters. Its either that or we become their lapdogs!'

'But we promised Sheila that we'd work late tonight' says Sandra. Fred retorts 'Sheila! She's management as well, and don't you forget it!'

Comment on Fred's statements.

4   In the meantime, Sheila has pointed out to Reginald that confectionery item 56 was, in fact, a large batch of last year's Easter eggs which he himself had ordered to be thrown out at the beginning of the month because they were long past their sell-by-date.

(a) Comment further on Head Office's message and Reginald's interpretation of it.

(b) Reginald now has an irate staff to deal with. Have you any suggestions about how he might communicate that a genuine error has been made?

5   Imagine that Reginald is told by Sheila that he ought to improve his human relations style. What sort of barriers do you think Sheila might have to contend with in order to get her message accepted?

6   Suppose that Reginald understands and accepts the message from Sheila about his management style. What barriers, apart from the recent confectionery fiasco, do you think he might face as he attempts to communicate to the workforce his intentions to adopt a more co-operative and friendly approach.

7   How do you think Reginald might attempt to overcome these barriers?

Summary

In this section, we have looked at barriers to communication. Barriers are present in many situations and have a wide range of sources. For instance, we have looked at examples where the message itself has become distorted; barriers which we erect ourselves due to our unswerving opinions of other people; and barriers which arise out of our emotions. You have analysed these barriers by looking at some examples and doing the activities.

SECTION 3

Formal and Informal Communication

Introduction

In this section, we look at how communication occurs within formal organisation structures. We consider the role of communication in decision-making and then look at the need for communication to occur informally, as well as through formal channels. We also cover formal information sources inside and outside the organisation.

3.1 Formal and informal communication

Firstly, you need to note that the use of the words **formal** and **informal** can be confusing as writers occasionally use these terminologies in different ways. For our purposes here we define **formal communication** firstly as: 'concerned with the flow of information through the authorised channels in the organisation'. This definition covers **downward** and **upward** communication and also some of the **network patterns** we cover.

Secondly, we often talk of **formal** and **informal sources of information**. For example, we might say that a supervisor gave an 'informal' verbal warning (off-the-record) to an employee rather than a formal, written warning (as laid down in the rules and regulations of the organisation). This leads us to another consideration of the terminology. A **formal information source** uses the organisation's own approved media which is usually capable of retrieval, for example, a letter to job applicant informing him or her of success at interview. By inference, any other source is informal. For example, a request for stationery within a company might have to be made formally on the correct requisition form rather than informally over the telephone.

We can define informal communication along similar lines: **informal communication** is concerned with the flow of information outside of the authorised channels in the organisation.

This does not mean outside of the organisation. We cover this aspect when we look at **horizontal communication** and again in some types of the **network patterns** we discuss. This definition also covers the so-called **grapevine**.

3.2 Vertical communication

Communication in an organisation can be either vertical or horizontal. **Vertical communication** can occur either **downward** or **upward** communication and is usually formal. Although it may be considered informal if a subordinate communicates with his superior's boss as we see later.

Vertical communication concerns the passing of commands down the way and the flow of control information up the way, in the sort of organisational structure proposed by writers such as Fayol.

DOWNWARD COMMUNICATION

Katz and Kahn (1966) splits communication 'down the line' into five categories:

- **job instructions**
- **job rationale** – explains why a task is being performed
- **information about procedures and practices**
- **feedback** to subordinates
- **indoctrination of goals** – mission

Consider a typical organisation chart as in Figure 9. This chart is useful in that it lays out diagrammatically the authority and reporting relationships between people in the organisation. It is often the first thing that is given to a newcomer upon arrival. Vertical communication is typically through this hierarchy.

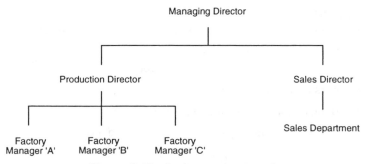

Figure 9: Typical organisation chart

ACTIVITY 16

Can you think of any drawbacks to downward communication through this hierarchy?

The first thing to note is that the majority of downward communication is one-way in nature. Katz included feedback as one of his categories but, in reality much downward communication does not invite the discussion of subordinates as most managers like to think that they are right! It assumes that all operations can be carried out by following a systematic series of rules and directives sent down through the hierarchy. In fact, as we see, when we discuss informal communication, it is almost impossible to allow for all likely happenings in the course of the working day. We only have to look at the chaos caused by people 'working to rule' to understand this.

The second thing to note is that there is often information loss, especially if there are many levels within the organisation, see Figure 10.

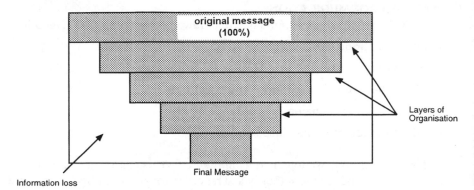

Figure 10: Downwards information loss
Source: Adapted from Fisher, 1993, p. 38

UPWARD COMMUNICATION

Katz and Kahn summarise upward communication from subordinate to superior as one of the forms:

- about him or herself, performance and problems
- about others and their problems
- about organisational practices and policies
- about what needs to be done and how it is to be done.

> ## ACTIVITY 17
>
> Imagine that you are one of several sales representatives working for D R Giles Ltd, which you will recall has just been taken-over from Reckitt UK. Your immediate superior is your old boss, the sales director Mr Brown, now merely a sales manager reporting to Reckitt UK's sales director, Mr Plunkitt. You are sorry that Mr Brown has been, in effect demoted, because you always seemed to 'get on' with him. The new situation looks far from certain, though, and you think that 'old Brownie' has been lucky to keep his job so far.
>
> 1 Can you see any barriers to your communications upward with Mr Brown?
>
> 2 What do you think about communications between Brown and Plunkitt?

1   You are sympathetic towards Mr Brown and will probably confide in him to a certain extent. You might try to help by making useful suggestions about how to improve operations.

2   Mr Brown is likely to be extremely wary of communicating with Mr Plunkitt; he will be acutely aware that the majority of information will be of the 'performance' type and used as control information. If such control information shows that either he or his section is performing badly it could threaten the security of his job.

Additionally, Mr Brown is unlikely to think that he should be offering information other than this to Mr Plunkitt. He has, he thinks, been demoted; so why should he help? He is likely to be protective of his sales reps and will certainly be wary of discussing any of their weaknesses with Plunkitt. In any case, Mr Plunkitt is trying to establish his authority and that probably means he will adopt a telling approach rather than a listening one.

This scenario indicates that upward communication is difficult for both superior and subordinate!

3.3 Network patterns

Information networks describe the pattern in which communication is carried out. Research carried out by Harold J Leavitt in the early 1950s provides five well-known models, for example, see Greenberg & Barron, 1993. In each of these models, communication, for our purposes, is two-way between each of the circles which represent people (see Figure 11).

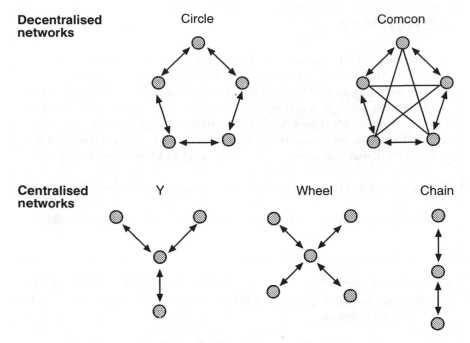

Figure 11: Centralised and de-centralised networks

The chain, Y and wheel represent centralised networks, that is, control information flows to a central point where decisions are made. These decisions are then disseminated out from this central point to the other members who are, in effect controlled from the centre. Communication is usually formal.

The circle and comcon networks are de-centralised. Communication flows between group members for the purposes of sharing information, achieving co-ordination and expressing feelings. Control is not held by any one member; members are free to make their own decisions. Communication is often informal.

CENTRALISATION VERSUS DE-CENTRALISATION

The decision to centralise or de-centralise has to be made with regard to the following factors. However, what you should realise is that the question is not simply 'Do we decentralise or not?' but 'What decisions should we centralise and de-centralise?'

Advantages of centralised networks are:

- good for simple tasks
- fast
- strong leadership can be demonstrated.

Advantages of de-centralised networks are:

- better for complex tasks requiring multiple inputs from members
- involves people in decisions and gives them ownership.

For example, a division within a large company might have its budget decided centrally at corporate head office and management development might also be a centralised function but the division might be able to make decisions itself on how to spend its budget and upon hiring and firing of its work force.

Often, in the early stages of growth within an organisation it is relatively easy for certain managers or directors to act as 'nerve centres'. Control is 'tight'. Often, in an internally competitive environment, managers will want to retain information themselves both as protection from company rivals and as a means of controlling their work situation.

However, as the organisation grows there is a tendency for the sheer volume of decision-making to increase. There will come a point at which the manager can no longer deal with his or her work in the way in which he or she did previously. At this stage, an overload situation has been reached. Various strategies can be adopted by the manager to cope:

- spending less time on decisions
- managing by exception, that is, only looking at those decisions which are noted as requiring special attention and pushing the rest through a routine system
- dealing with complaints – fire-fighting – and hoping that the other decisions will resolve themselves!

Often one or more of these strategies will have been tried before the manager reluctantly admits that the situation is still not effective and likely to get worse as the company grows. Decisions aren't being made or else they are being poorly taken.

One way to deal with this overload is to decentralise. This has both structural and communication implications for the organisation. This empowerment of others should then free the manager for the more important of her tasks albeit at the loss of direct control in exchange for a co-ordinating role.

ACTIVITY 18

Now that DR Giles belongs to Reckitt UK it can no longer function as it used to. In particular the flows of information and the focus of decision-making are likely to change. Several issues need to be tackled by senior management of Reckitt UK with regard to the takeover, namely:

1 collation of detailed end of month management accounts, this shows for instance, profit on individual product lines

2 summary of management accounts, this gives overall profit/loss and key financial information only

3 collation of debtors and creditors accounts, this shows detailed information of customers owing money and suppliers that D R Giles owes money to

4 sales 'intelligence gathering' on competitors

5 equal opportunities statistics compiled by D R Giles, for example, number of workers with disabilities, number of women managers

6 company newsletters

Which of the above areas do you think Reckitt UK will centralise and which do you think it should de-centralise to D R Giles Ltd? Give brief reasons for your choices.

Some of the above areas fall squarely in one or other of the two approaches. Others are open to debate, depending upon the advantages sought. Your answers may have included:

Centralised decisions and information flow

Item 1: detailed management accounts. Unless Reckitt feels confident it might ask for this information to be sent to headquarters as well.

Item 2: summary of key financial information. Reckitt must have access to this information for overall control of all of its units and factories and to know at any time the overall financial health of the entire organisation.

Item 5: equal opportunities statistics. For the sake of comparison amongst factories and units and to demonstrate an organisational commitment, this information would be best dealt with centrally.

De-centralised decisions

Item 3: Probably best to deal with this information at individual units, that is, at D R Giles, as it would only overload a centralised system and is best left to the individual units to manage directly.

Centralised or de-centralised?

Item 4: Intelligence gathering. This could be de-centralised, for example, using a comcon network pattern, so that each unit feeds information to other units, allowing for rapid information flow. However, if Reckitt (UK) feels that it wishes to retain a tight control as the 'nerve centre' then it may prefer a wheel type of centralised information flow.

Item 6: Essentially is there to be one newsletter for the whole organisation or will D R Giles have its own? The advantages of an organisation-wide newsletter include learning about other factories in the group and a sense of 'belonging' to it. Information would flow to an editor at head office. The advantages of a D R Giles newsletter concern retaining identity and information would be focused within D R Giles Ltd.

3.4 Horizontal (lateral) communication

Earlier in Unit 1, we covered Fayol's principle of chain of command through which communication flows and authority were exercised. Fayol recognised that the formality of the chain could prove to be extremely cumbersome in some cases and he advocated the use of a gang-plank in which people communicated directly with each other across the chain of command, rather than following the formal route through it (Figure 12). This communication route involved people on the same hierarchical level – their 'peers'.

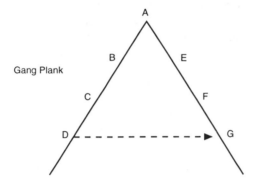

Figure 12: Fayol's gang-plank

Horizontal communication is extremely important in an organisation. It has been estimated that two-thirds of communication flow occurs informally in this way.

ACTIVITY 19

Can you identify the important functions in an organisation served by horizontal communication?

The purpose of horizontal communication is primarily to co-ordinate work, formal activities, goals and objectives of a particular sub-unit or department. Departments are established with this in mind. Many writers thus describe horizontal communication as having a formal role, for example, Rasberry & Lemoine, 1986, 97.

There are other purposes for horizontal communication. Katz and Kahn (1966, p. 244) refer to the socio-emotional support for people in both unorganised and organised work groups. In other words, people 'in the same boat' have a natural need to talk to and help each other.

Mintzberg discusses horizontal communication in a different light. If something cannot be achieved by way of formal directions from above and requires an informal approach of co-ordination to achieve, then it is part of the informal communication network. He talks of 'communicating outside the chain of formal authority'. You will recall that this is consistent with the definition we are using. Mintzberg gives the example of a management information systems manager engaging in such informal activity by gathering the 'real information and intelligence' from informal contacts. 'Soft' information – 'intangible and speculative' gathered from talking to these contacts – was no less useful just because it had not come through official channels and could not be quantified. He gives the types of informal communication depicted in Figure 13.

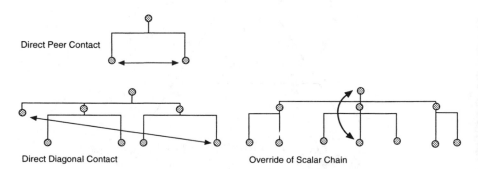

Figure 13: Informal communication
Source: Mintzberg, 1979, p. 51

ACTIVITY 20

Suppose that you are a design engineer working on a new project. You report to the project manager. However, it soon becomes apparent that you need to talk to your counterpart, Samantha, within another division of the company to solve a technical question that you have. During your telephone conversation, Samantha tells you that she's heard a rumour that your boss is about to leave the organisation. You tend to believe her, especially as recently the operations director, the project manager's boss, has been sending instructions directly to you.

What sort of communication is occurring here, according to Mintzberg's model?

Communication with Samantha is peer-based and is informal and outside the chain of command. Communication with the operations director is an over-ride of scalar chain and is again informal. The rumour mentioned by Samantha is worth noting in that the message itself is informal. We consider rumours shortly when we look at the grapevine.

TRIST AND BAMFORTH

Trist and Bamforth's coal mine studies in the early 1950s are one of the best known studies on formal and informal communication. This study looked at the effects of mechanisation in the coal mines. Before mechanisation, the miners used to work in small groups, each able to do all of the tasks required, and each group co-ordinated by informal communication within itself. Mechanisation brought about a system in which tasks were specialised and the old groups were broken up; a coal face might be blasted by one shift of workers and dug out by another, the groups of workers never meeting each other. It very soon became apparent that productivity was suffering because of this new system and that one of the factors responsible for this was the inability of the new system to replace, by the use of managers and standardisation of work practices, the co-ordination which had been achieved by the old system of informal communication.

This need was recognised and a new socio-technical system devised in which groups were again established. These could communicate effectively by informal methods. The result was that productivity was restored.

As Mintzberg (1979) states: 'Most work simply cannot be done without some form of informal communication'. He goes on to explain that the reason for this is that, even in what we might regard as the simplest and stablest of work, there are so many variables that mere rules and regulations are unlikely to work on their own. What is required are people to make the system work (sometimes in spite of itself!) and this requires informal communication. Strauss (1962-3, p. 52), talks of: '. . . oiling the wheels of bureaucracy through the use of lateral relationships which rely upon friendship, favours and their own political power'.

Figure 14 shows the breakdown:

- 20-35% in documents of the formal system
- 65-80 % in verbal communication
- 45% of this outside of chain of command

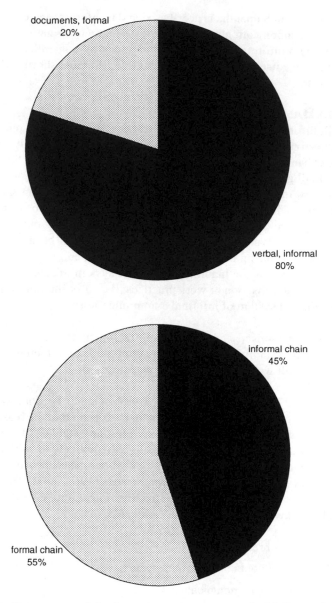

Figure 14: Documents of the formal system versus verbal information of the informal system

COMPARISON OF INFORMATION SOURCES – FORMAL WRITTEN VERSUS INFORMAL VERBAL

Below we highlight the essential differences between formal and informal information sources. The thing to note is that it is not a question of 'formal' being somehow 'better' than 'informal', rather that the two are complementary. Indeed, often the best way to get a message to 'stick' is to repeat it in both formal and informal ways.

Formal

- public – large potential audience
- information permanently stored and retrievable
- information relatively old
- orientation of information chosen by originator
- moderate redundancy in information
- no direct feedback to originator

Informal

- private – restricted audience
- information typically neither permanently stored nor retrievable
- information more likely to be up to date
- information primarily user-selected
- sometimes much redundancy of information, that is, it is not required
- often considerable feedback to the originator

ACTIVITY 21

Mr Brown has just received an internal memorandum from Mr Plunkitt. Plunkitt has been reviewing the last six months sales figures and has expressed surprise that there is a dramatic dip half way through this period in the northern area. As this is your area, Mr Brown has urgently tried to contact you (you are visiting customers), by fax and car telephone and also leaving messages at the places you are likely to visit. As you quite often spend a long time on the car telephone talking to the other sales reps, it is not until late afternoon that the message reaches you.

You explain that one of your major customers, Quickchange, tightened the tolerances (that is, it has reduced the acceptable variation in size of your product) on its product specification and word of this didn't reach you or your firm's production department. This resulted in an enormous number of rejected goods which meant issuing credit notes. You have only found this out yourself through talking in the pub the previous night with Fred, one of Quickchange's foremen who you know personally. Fred was most surprised that you were not aware of the change of specification. It was common knowledge as far as he was concerned, details of the new specification had been given to everyone from their section leader and had been backed up by large reminders on the notice board. As it happens, a letter was sent to your company but it had been addressed to 'The Quality Department', which your company does not have, and was lying gathering dust on some shelf in the midst of the disturbances of the take-over by Reckitt UK.

You reluctantly explain to Mr Brown that the sales figures projections for the next six months for the north are wildly inaccurate too, as they are far too high! What they do not show is one of your major customers, Maxisell, has altered its product range just this month and is not renewing its contract. Your monthly report to Mr Brown, which is now being typed, shows this. Mr Brown sighs and wonders how he might 'massage' the figures.

1   What are the major shortfalls of the formal communication system?

2   What are the benefits of the formal system?

1   The major shortfalls of the formal communication system are three-fold

● Old information: because of the time it takes in the formal routes
Quickchange letter lying gathering dust
Maxisell loss of contract not included in sales projections
Your report to Mr Brown has information which can be up to a month old.

● Lack of feedback to the originator
In the above case, back to Quickchange for the specification change.

● Accuracy
Old information has a tendency to be inaccurate. Also, Mr Brown's thoughts on 'massaging' the figures indicate that the presentation can mask the true situation.

2   The benefits of the formal system include:

Permanent records, in this case, of past sales
Written plans, in this case, profit projections which can be shared with a wide audience – the sales team, senior management, accounts
Concise
Easily understood – acceptable format
Potential use as control data, for example, 'Shall we sack old Brown?'

3.5 The grapevine

The term **grapevine** is often used to describe the way in which 'interesting' bits of information travel informally around an organisation, for example, what the next pay rise is going to be, who is getting promoted or sacked, whose wife is expecting a baby, if that important contract has been secured, etc.

The grapevine is an extremely fast communication channel. It does not respect hierarchies or departments with the result that within a very short space of time, many people in the organisation are aware of the message. Suppressing the grapevine only makes people more determined to promulgate it. It has often been accused of supplying erroneous information – rumours, for example. However, studies have shown that the grapevine is often highly accurate, not least because those who are part of its transmission wish to value their reputation as providers of accurate, up-to-date information.

Keith Davis's work on grapevines showed four ways in which the grapevine could operate (Figure 15).

- **Single strand** represents the 'Chinese whispers' type of chain in which information is passed one-to-one down a line, the message is liable to distortion at each stage. Single strand was singled out as being the most inaccurate because of this distortion, whilst the cluster group was much more accurate and the most dominant form in organisations.

- In the **gossip chain**, one person is actively on the look out for messages and then tells everyone.

- The **probability** chain starts with someone who has a message but only delivers it on an ad hoc basis, depending more or less upon whom he or she happens to be in contact with.

- The **cluster** chain is more selective; an individual will only pass on messages to a select group or 'cluster', one of whom might then become the message source for subsequent clusters. Sometimes different ways were used depending upon the perceived importance of the information.

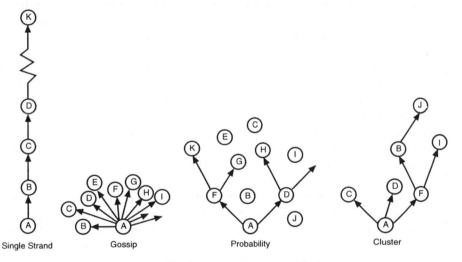

Figure 15: Types of grapevine chains
Source: Davis, K, 1953

ACTIVITY 22

Briefly list the advantages and disadvantages of informal communication networks.

Advantages
Fast
Informs a large number of people
Often highly accurate

Disadvantages
Single strand prone to distortion
Can supply rumours and incorrect information

REVIEW ACTIVITY 3

Suggested time: 60-75 minutes.

Re-read the case study, *The Roving Area Representative,* and answer the questions which follow.

The Roving Area Representative

Jane Cassidy is the recently appointed sales director in a national company which packages and distributes various grades of motor oil to haulage contractors, travel operators and agricultural users. She had a university education in which she studied marketing and commerce and has worked her way up the ranks in sales since getting her first job eight years ago. Jane's 'inherited' sales team consists of area representatives whose job it is to visit both existing and prospective clients. The majority of these managers have risen to their current positions by 'being in the right place at the right time', for example, taking over someone else's job after that person has left the company. They tend to have varying amounts of experience and have attended the occasional short sales course although few have any professional or academic qualifications. Even now it appears that there are some managers who are undoubtedly good at their job but, by the same token, there are some who Jane would rather get rid of.

Sales contracts are normally negotiated for a yearly period. The market is highly competitive and so area representatives have traditionally been given certain discretion, within boundaries prescribed by the sales director, to set contracts with their clients according to the variables of volume, price and delivery. They can receive up to 25% bonus depending upon the volume of business they generate and how this relates to agreed individual targets. Up until now, the area representatives have operated on a written call card basis, that is, cards which are kept for each client and which record details such as company name and address, key contact person(s), last date visited, type of contract, expiry date of contract, price, delivery terms, and other comments. Information from these cards is summarised and has, in the past, been sent to the sales director so that he could co-ordinate on a national basis.

Area representatives like to feel that they lead exciting working lives, though, in reality, their job can be rather lonely so they constantly chat to one another over the car telephone during the long hours of motorway driving. Cliques exist which share local sales information and gossip. These have previously excluded the sales director.

Jane feels that the reporting mechanism is far too slow for her purposes as oil prices fluctuate dramatically. Additionally, she feels that she is not always receiving the 'full picture' and that some of the area representatives are somewhat cavalier in their deals, to say the least. For example, it may emerge that they are offering unrealistic delivery times, and giving 'freebies' such as oil storage tanks etc. In a bid to obtain up-to-date, accurate and full information, Jane is thinking of giving area representatives portable laptop computers and developing a whole new system of working. The idea is that the area representatives would take the laptops on their travels and enter the information into them each night, either at home or in their hotel room. They would have to 'report in' at least once a week at pre-set times by downloading their laptop information via a modem to the central head office computer. Jane is also thinking of using the system in reverse and sending messages to each area representative via her office computer to their home computer terminal which they will be told to access upon their return. In the past, communication has proved problematic due to the roving nature of the area representatives, also she is slightly suspicious that managers sometimes choose not to receive messages!

Jane also has doubts about whether or not all of her representatives can be relied upon to use this new technology. She intends to provide training specifically for this but has started to think that perhaps she should introduce a programme of careful recruitment of younger, more 'professional' staff, both from outside the organisation and through careful management development of promising 'high flyers' within the organisation.

Jane is also thinking of holding monthly meetings in her office at which all of the area representatives must be present. Each manager will be asked to give a report on progress within his or her area. The format of these reports will be standardised and will include details such as the number of clients visited, the number, type and value of successful contracts serviced and those obtained, as well as any contracts lost. Previously managers were more or less left to their own devices and there was little monitoring of their progress. She intends to initially use the reports as the basis for determining good performance, as given by these indicators. Given that the good performers are likely to be the sort of manager she is seeking to develop she intends to involve one or two of them in future development of specific sales methods and procedures. She will ask these good performers to assist in training and selection, using their existing knowledge of the industry.

She also would wish to go further than this by then applying her own ideas with regard to efficiencies to be gained through computer routing of calls, so as to minimise 'dead' time on the road between calls, and of drawing up schedules to visit existing clients, rather than waiting until their contract is almost expired. She has promised them that any useful suggestions will be looked at seriously. She also thinks that this would be a good time for area representatives to socialise with more than their immediate 'neighbour' and Jane intends meetings to be completed by 1pm so that a relaxed business lunch may be arranged. Jane is well aware of the coolness of relations between the area representatives and previous sales director and intends to adopt a more constructive approach. She intends also to arrange a company-paid annual weekend break for managers and their partners at a 4-star hotel. Key customers will also be invited. An internal company magazine is a further idea which will be pursued and notable events covered.

And, of course, there is the issue of bonuses. This has long been a thorny problem. It is true that large bonuses have been awarded in the past but the gripe has always been from those who were not awarded them that they did not reflect issues such as the number of contracts involved or the degree of competition. For example, one area representative received a large bonus whenever one particular very lucrative contract was renewed allegedly because he was 'well in' with his opposite number. The other issue is the size of the market – the potential number of clients and how geographically spread they were. Some managers complained that in some areas a 'monkey could do the work and get a bonus' whereas in other areas it was 'well nigh on impossible' to hit the targets. Jane is aware of this unfairness and feels that it undermines the motivation of managers in poor areas and over-rewards managers in 'good' areas.

Of course, if the managers follow the proposed new systems Jane is confident that they will soon be hitting targets they never thought possible, and she has plans to make this a key note in her initial meetings with them. However, she proposes to devise a points system which would weight the bonus according to the degree of difficulty of achieving targets. In theory, the bonus maximum would remain at 25% but privately she is wondering if this is the right level. Certainly, she intends to monitor the degree of difficulty allowed by her points system against the actual securing of individual contracts within her best managers' portfolios. She suspects that difficult targets which do not allow sufficient 'difficulty weighting' will restrict success because the payoff for additional work is seen not to be worthwhile. By systematically analysing targets, their difficulty weighting and actual performance achieved over the next 6 months, Jane will set the next targets.

1   How do you think Jane Cassidy might successfully use Katz and Kahn's five categories of communication 'down the line' with her proposed system?

2   (a) What sort of communication network(s) do you think existed amongst the area representatives before Jane took control? Why?

(b) What sort of network do you think Jane would like? Why?

3   What sort of issues do you think the area representatives might communicate about with Jane Cassidy using the proposed system, use Katz and Kahn's four categories as a framework?

4   Jane is thinking of using standardised reports. She hasn't said so yet but her initial thoughts were that the area managers would circulate the written report in advance of the meeting and then each manager would back this up with a quick verbal summary at the monthly meeting. What are the advantages of doing this?

5   Apart from the 'official' presentation of reports, are there any other advantages in communication terms, for having a monthly meeting?

6   How do you think the informal networks of the area representatives might change as a result of the new proposals?

Summary

In this section, we have considered the role of formal and informal communication and the roles of both vertical and lateral communication within the organisation. The conclusion we have reached is that both types of communication are vital to effective and efficient operations. We introduced communication network patterns, such as the wheel and comcon, and used them to illustrate the flow of information and directives in centralised and de-centralised decision-making. We considered informal information according to messages which lie outside the chain of formal command. The advantages and disadvantages of formal written versus informal verbal communication were briefly covered. Finally, we discussed the notorious grapevine and found that it is usually quite accurate! The activities and Review Activity 3 have allowed you to demonstrate your understanding of formal and informal communication channels and networks, with the advantages and disadvantages of each, and to identify how communication is an important factor in issues such as centralised and de-centralised decision-making.

Section 4

Communicating Culture

Introduction

You will recall from Unit 4, the topic of organisational culture. We first remind you about its definition and some of the theory, before we address the purpose of this section – the ways in which culture may be communicated in the organisation :

Culture is a 'pattern of basic assumptions invented, discovered or developed by a given group as it learns to cope with its problems or external adaptation and internal integration – that has worked well enough in the past to be considered valid and, therefore, to be taught to new members as the correct way to perceive, think, and feel in relation to those problems' (Schein, 1990).

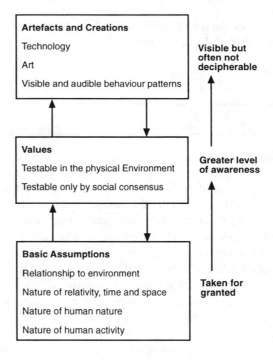

Figure 16: A framework for culture
Source: Schein, 1985

Schein (1985) provides us with a framework for culture at three levels of awareness (Figure 16). We can describe the first level of **artifacts** as symbolic evidence of 'the way we do things around here'. They include stories, metaphors, myths, heroes, logos, slogans, rituals, ceremonies, etc.

The second level of **shared values** is not so visible but employees in a strong culture will be aware of them; for example, integrity and loyalty might be highly prized values.

The deepest level of culture occurs as **basic assumptions** – these are 'taken-for-granted' truths. For example, a university might at one time have implicitly assumed that its primary purpose was to further academic research and excellence. It is only when challenged that these assumptions surface, and many universities have now had to re-assess their most basic assumption as they realise that the business of education in providing degree qualifications on a much wider basis than previously, might now be their main purpose.

ACTIVITY 23

Why do you think present-day managers are so interested in organisational culture?

The reasons that managers are so interested in culture stem from the four areas which Martin and Siehl (1990) identify:

1   Culture provides a **history** which can be used by members as a guide for their own behaviour at work.

2   Culture can help establish **commitment to management values.**

3   Cultural norms and values can be used as **control** mechanisms by management.

4   Culture might possibly be related to **productivity and profitability.**

Some organisations might already have a strong culture which they wish to retain; others might have cultures which are still embryonic. In both cases, there is a need to at least maintain if not develop these cultures. Some writers would argue that culture is extremely difficult to alter. Morgan in *Images of Organization* (1986) states: 'Managers can influence the evolution of culture by being aware of the symbolic consequences of their actions and by attempting to foster desired values, but they can never control culture in the sense that many management writers advocate'. We need, therefore, to approach the influence which management can exert over culture in a realistic and careful fashion.

4.1 Communication of culture

As we stated earlier, our intention within this unit is to show ways in which organisational culture can be communicated within the organisation. One way of achieving this, is to view this process as one of socialisation. Socialisation is defined by Schein (1968) as: 'the process by which a new member learns the value system, the norms, and the required behaviour patterns of the society, organization, or group which he is entering'. Mintzberg uses the term 'indoctrination' to describe the process by which the organization formally socialises its 'members for its own benefit'. Pascale set out the elements of the process in his 'steps of organisation socialisation' (Figure 17).

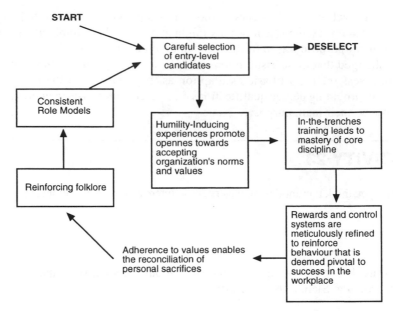

Figure 17: Steps of organisation socialisation
Source: Pascale, 1992

4.2 Selection of candidates

An organisation is its people; if we accept this fundamental premise, then the obvious way in which culture with its shared values and meanings can be maintained, is to try to ensure that the people who are involved in this sharing process are the 'right' sort of people in the first place. Are they likely to have attitudes and beliefs which are in line with the organisation? This is becoming as important now in companies with strong cultures as the possession of relevant qualifications and skills. Nissan, for instance, appears to have a strong work ethic in its production areas – the commitment to tasks which are physically demanding and which require endurance is very important. It is extremely useful for such a company to be able to choose people who are 'not afraid of hard work'. With the plentiful supply of well trained workers in an area which has high unemployment due to the demise of heavy industries such as ship-building and coal, there is no lack of suitable candidates and the company can afford to be selective.

4.3 Reputation

Even before a candidate walks into an interview situation at Nissan, he or she will be already aware of certain cultural aspects of the company. The potential recruit might well have asked friends 'What it's like to work there?'.

ACTIVITY 24

Think of some issues that might be behind this question.

You might have included:

● how 'hard' the working life is

● how 'Japanese' it is – is there exercise at the beginning of the day, for instance?

● are people rewarded for being good at their job or for long-term loyalty, or both?

Local newspapers might have mentioned the plans of the company; or the importance which it places on its values, quality, for example, might have become apparent. Indeed, the company's products can be seen to 'speak for themselves'. The Nissan Micra and Bluebird have both been highly recommended in car magazines in recent years for their quality and reliability. Quality products do not just happen – they require a dedicated approach to quality within all areas of the organisation.

A reputation carries with it and helps to transmit both explicit and implied cultural values. Within the car industry, a good reputation is paramount to successful sales. It also says much about the company to the prospective worker. Consider the company, Skoda, which now belongs to the Volkswagen group. It has attempted to transpose its once poor reputation for quality to that of its new owners by encouraging potential buyers with the words: 'Before we changed the car, we changed the company' (advert for Skoda Felicia in *Daily Mail Magazine,* Saturday 20 May 1995). The advert ends with three brief 'soundbites'. 'We heard the criticisms. We changed our company. Now, are you open enough to change your mind?'.

4.4 Job adverts

When a company places adverts for its jobs, these also provide some information to the candidate about the type of culture and values espoused by the organisation.

ACTIVITY 25

Consider the following three mythical job advertisements and identify any key words and phrases which indicate the organisations' values.

Advert 1

Purchasing Professionals
c £22,500-£25,250 + benefits

To support Dojan's further European development we are looking for individuals with initiative, commitment and flexibility to enhance our professional Purchasing team in the following areas:

Production Component/Materials Purchasing: Working closely with our European Technology Centre, key plant interfaces and suppliers you will develop Sourcing Strategies on a European-wide basis. You will be responsible for selecting and developing suppliers to enhance delivery, development and management performance against quality, cost and business improvement targets.

Facilities and General Purchasing: You will source and develop suppliers of capital equipment, services and other indirect materials in order to support a diverse and dynamic production environment.

Advert 2

Maintenance Officer
Salary £12,915 to £15,624 (under review)

Edge of the Tyne is a leading regional housing association and consultancy. Following expansion we now require a qualified and experienced full-time Maintenance Officer to provide a high standard, comprehensive maintenance supervision and administration service to approximately 800 properties and a range of clients throughout the north east.

You must have an HNC level qualification in building studies or equivalent and at least 3 years' experience in the construction industry. You must be able and prepared to travel throughout the north east and to work sympathetically and sensitively with a wide range of elderly and other clients.

Edge of the Tyne supports equal opportunities and we particularly welcome applications from members of ethnic minority communities.

Advert 3

Cash Collector
£7,074 to £7,643 + Car + Benefits +PRP

Technic Ltd is the premier electronic leisure supply company in the UK and part of a major PLC with ambitious plans for further development. Opportunities now exist in the north east area.

Duties include the collection, conciliation and documentation of cash from a wide range of electronic equipment located in our customers' premises.

Applicants must be numerate and physically fit. A current driving licence is essential. Experience is preferred but full training will be given.

Benefits include a competitive salary, an excellent pension and life assurance scheme, participation in the Company share ownership scheme, sick pay, four weeks' annual holiday, service bonus, profit-related pay scheme, and various other group discounts and allowances.

If you feel you meet the requirements of this challenging opportunity, then please apply in writing to.

We are an equal opportunities employer.

Advert 1

The car industry is highly competitive and innovation and the ability to respond quickly to change is essential. Dojan's culture reflects this in its advert through the use of words such as:

- initiative
- flexibility
- delivery
- quality
- cost
- business improvement targets
- dynamic.

Loyalty is expressed through the words:

● commitment

● professional.

The company is portraying a **task culture** in which influence is based more on expertise than position or personal power.

Advert 2

We are continually told that we are in the 'Caring '90's'. Organisations have followed the recent surge of public opinion and attempted to adopt these caring values. Edge of the Tyne Ltd talks of the need to:

● 'work sympathetically and sensitively'

and it goes further than the simple 'we are an equal opportunities employer' of Technic by its positive action in particularly welcoming:

● 'members of ethnic minority communities'.

Advert 3

The cash collector advert demonstrates a focus on the individual, as opposed to the team, in what would appear to be a tough environment.

Values are demonstrated by the words:

● ambitious

● development

● physically fit

● challenging opportunity

● performance-related pay.

4.5 Brochures, job descriptions, person specifications

No longer is it the case with large companies that the job advertisement is immediately followed by a single one-to-one interview leading to either acceptance or rejection of the candidate.

It is quite usual for the company to send the candidate written material in advance of any meeting. This would often include information about the company, a job description and, more revealingly from our point of view, a person specification. Rodger's seven-point plan lists 'special aptitudes', 'interests' and 'disposition' amongst its criteria (see Torrington & Hall, 1992). Through these means, the potential candidate will glean further details on the organisation's culture, the type of person and commitment the company is looking for and whether he or she will 'fit in' – perhaps even to the point of 'de-selecting' themselves.

4.6 Interviews and the selection process

We have already considered these in depth but it is worth noting that there are opportunities, in this case, face-to-face, for transmitting cultural values. Some of the values might be apparent in the selection process itself. How tough is it? How many stages of interview are there?

The prospective candidate will observe the surrounding settings and gain an impression of the organisation through symbols such as:

- photographs – the product, aerial view of large site, team and chairman
- company magazines
- trophies – quality, charity
- decor – spartan, opulent
- building size and importance
- building layout – open plan, closed offices
- number of personal computers and other high-tech equipment
- dress – formal, informal
- activity – busy, quiet.

It is quite common, even before selection has taken place, for candidates to be taken around the place of work and shown the various departments and rest and social facilities. In addition to the interviewing panel, candidates may be allowed to talk to staff to ask questions of them like 'What is it like working for the company?'.

The surroundings and ambiance experienced during the selection process convey very strong messages about the culture to a newcomer whether these are consciously absorbed or not. The buildings themselves are quite literally concrete symbols. And their messages affect long-serving employees just as strongly as newcomers – a phenomenon that is particularly highlighted when changes are proposed or occur, as the following example illustrates.

CULTURAL IMPACT OF A BUILDING

Take the case of the business school at the University of Sunderland in the UK. Previous accommodation had been a rambling Victorian house with a warren of small offices, basic facilities with an old-fashioned pigeon-hole mail system. Lecturers could hide away in their own cosy rooms with old-fashioned gas fires and second-hand armchairs and assorted memorabilia, shut off from the outside world. The new accommodation was the prestigious St Peter's Campus on the River Wear; the accent was now upon an efficient and modern business-like operation.

The old individual offices were replaced by open plan 'pods'. Note the use of the new terminology. These had three to seven people in an office, allowing for personal interaction with the emphasis upon team work, collaboration and exchange of ideas. And, of course, everything was new – carpets, toilets, even the kitchen sink, with each pod having its own rest area.

Under the old regime only those wanting to use a personal computer had one, those who preferred not to use, or could not use, computers made do with hand-written slides and asked the administrative staff to type letters, notes and other documents. In the new system, every member of staff was given a personal computer at their work-station and expected to use it. Self-sufficiency through technology was the new order of the day. For example, no more lecturers' notes were to be typed by the administrative staff.

The electronic mail system superseded the pigeon-hole system to a large extent; the pigeon-holes were now reserved for bulky documents and non-urgent information. The emphasis was on fast and accountable flows of information.

Additionally, the architects had deliberately given the campus a marine-like quality, making use of its commanding position on the River Wear, traditionally the artery of local commerce. The head of school's office was approached via a concrete 'gangway'. There was light-hearted banter amongst staff about this being the 'bridge' with the head of school being the captain of the 'ship' and the 'engine room', where they worked, being where the real work was done.

A member of the administrative staff describes the change in culture in one of her poems, *The Assignment* (Dewart, 1995). Note also the reference to dress.

From Thornhill Park we moved in days
In boxes in crates, in bags the whole phase
Packing and unpacking, the moving was slow
Old habits, old furniture they had to go
New occupants already had viewed
The notion to stay considered quite rude

The kitchens all fitted with all mod-cons
Tea, coffee, hot beverages for all old dons
Politically correct, non-sexist, person not man
Smoking who do, an all building ban
IT, technology, key boards, PCs abound
News flashes, gossip, fast E-Mail around

Pods not offices, levels not floors
Dirty windows and squeaky doors
Bright classrooms, new carpets, toilets galore
It's got to be better who could want more?
. . .
Admin. staff what gems, what stars
All dressed in navy, like jolly jack tars
The naval style, runs like the brine
Right on the bank of the Wear not the Tyne

4.7 Induction training

As part of the formal induction, a new recruit will often go on an induction programme. This might include a brief history of the organisation, its founding members and their successes and failures, leading up, through various critical incidents to where the company is today.

It is at this stage that newcomers are often made aware of the symbols and embodiments of the organisation's culture:

- stories
- myths
- sagas
- heroes
- written artifacts – slogans, logos, manuals

STORIES

You have probably heard the story about Henry Ford who when asked what colour he could provide for his famous Model T car said, 'Any colour, as long as it's black!'. This emphasised the sheer dominance of the Ford Motor Company. It was in the business of producing mass produced cars and the customer simply had no choice if affordable motoring was the reason for buying the car. The dominance of the company extended to the company's influence over its personnel who endured noisy, difficult and repetitive tasks because the company had them in its power by paying high wages. This sort of culture is a **power culture**.

MYTHS

Myths are expressed, unproven beliefs. In the early 1960s, Triumph was one of the major British motor bike manufacturers. The belief generally held was that the Japanese who had entered the market with the small moped would never challenge the British dominance. The myth was that the Japanese couldn't build 'big bikes'. British manufacturers clung on to this belief even when large, modern, Japanese bikes came onto the market. These 'sewing machines' with their button start engines, as opposed to the traditional kick start, were somehow not the 'real bikes' that the British made. This myth was such a strong part of the old, traditional, bike manufacturing culture amongst British firms that it prevented the development of new, modern designs and was a major factor in effectively killing off the majority of British bike manufacturers.

SAGAS AND HEROES

Sagas are often associated with founding stories. Typically, the story concerns the early, difficult days of the business with corporate 'heroes' fighting and overcoming adversity against all odds. These stories might become exaggerated in the course of time to the point where reality is left behind and the story then becomes a myth. Consider the example of Severnside, now a major recycler of waste paper, based in South Wales and a division of a large paper company. In its early days, it had to be bold and determined if its expansion plans were to succeed in an extremely competitive market. During this early expansion, it moved its headquarters out of its previous portacabins and into a large but rather ramshackle Victorian house. The story goes that on the first big storm over a weekend, a section of the slate roof was lost. Upon hearing this, the managing director summoned the assistance of his fellow directors and spent the rest of the weekend climbing between rafters fixing polythene sheeting as a makeshift roof.

The managing director, an entrepreneur, never tired of relating this saga to newcomers. The symbolism was evident, even directors had to get their hands dirty if necessary and they had to be prepared to lead by example. What is more, they needed to use their initiative and make the most of whatever resource was available. The postscript to this story is that the building itself became a symbol. The managing director personalised it by painting it pink, it was known as the Pink Palace – especially by the other, more established divisions in the group – and it became symbolic of the individualism and entrepreneurial flair of its founding members.

ACTIVITY 26

Richard Branson of music group Virgin and airline Virgin Atlantic hit the news headlines in his attempt to cross the Pacific in a hot air balloon. Clearly, this episode says something about the company but under which of the previous headings – stories, myths, etc – would you classify it? What do you think it suggests about the company's culture and values?

The most appropriate category would appear to be that of 'saga' with Branson the 'hero' battling against the odds, in this case, the forces of nature. It says much about the company and the way it is managed. It suggests an organisation, where people:

- 'lead from the front'
- are not afraid to take risks
- like the 'big gesture'

and that the products and services are

- adventurous
- innovative.

Also, it suggests, because we always associate 'heroes' with 'decent values', that the organisation is run with:

- integrity
- open-ness.

WRITTEN ARTIFACTS: SLOGANS, MISSION STATEMENTS, LOGOS, MANUALS

Company slogans attempt to encapsulate some basic value in a neat soundbite. A good slogan is relevant, interesting and memorable. Consider, for example, 'I think, therefore IBM'.

Mission statements go further than this. They reflect the very reason for the existence of the organisation and its primary purpose(s). 'Ford Motor Company is a world-wide leader in automotive and automotive-related products and services as well as in new industries such as aerospace, communications, and financial services. Our mission is to improve continually our products and services to meet our customers' needs allowing us to prosper as a business and to provide a reasonable return for our stockholders, the owners of our business' (Brown, 1995).

LOGOS

Some organisations go a long way in order to get the 'right' logo as they believe that it can be a strong symbol of its values. Colour, shape and size are all important. Consider ICI; it went to very great expense to change its old black and white logo of waves on a round background, to one of gentler waves in a blue and white logo; this was considered much more in line with its increasing commitment to environmental issues.

MANUALS

Manuals can convey a great deal of detailed information on an organisation's values. Even the thickness of the manual and its complexity can give an indication of this. Many rules and regulations would be consistent with a role or bureaucratic culture, for instance. How are the manuals laid out? Are they concise or verbose? Up-to-date?

4.8 Humility-inducing experiences and in-the-trenches training

---

At this stage, after the initial induction, the candidate really begins his or her **initiation**. This can range from quite pleasant experiences to the not so pleasant! These might include rites and rituals, for example, many Japanese companies insist on everyone singing the company song first thing in the morning, and further elements of induction training.

ACTIVITY 27

Identify some examples of rites, rituals and induction training.

Military examples are obvious, although you may have listed others:

- regulation haircut
- getting 'kitted out' for the first time
- 'square bashing' – marching in formation
- assault course
- being 'eyeballed' by a corporal or sergeant
- inspection parades.

These are formalised methods of communicating to the individual that obeying orders without question is one of the core values. Informal ways of communicating core values are sometimes carried out by members of organisations who feel that an individual needs to be 'brought in line' with their way of thinking. These can be much harsher than the formal system, as the newcomer is likely to discover.

In-the-trenches training can be particularly effective at showing new managers, for instance, the ways in which their would-be subordinates think – their values and norms are often wildly different to those of management. The insight of sub-cultures within an organisation is extremely useful to the manager who will have to manage, lead and communicate with his or her staff.

In-the-trenches training is recognised as a formal means of allowing the individual access to the values of an organisation. However, such values may be transmitted both formally, for instance, the organisation's approach to the way in which customers are treated, and informally, for instance, the attitude of staff to working overtime, during the trainee's 'tour of duty'.

Having such training included in a programme also shows the new manager that senior management values those who can relate to their subordinates. Again, some of the training might be **humility-inducing,** for instance, cleaning out a machine. Such companies probably believe in their staff 'knowing the ropes' and 'leading from the front' and do not want 'smart alecs' in their organisation.

Often training is deliberately difficult. It may involve spending time in different parts of the organisation and different parts of the country; it may involve early morning starts and late-night finishes or travelling over weekends. It may also include experiential learning, that is, learning by 'doing', and group and leadership courses which may be activity-based.

ACTIVITY 28

Can you think of any reasons why an organisation might do this type of training?

You might include the following reasons:

- as an initiation rite – 'We all had to do it so why shouldn't they?'

- to reinforce the values of hard work and/or teamwork as being necessary for success

- as a core value of a task culture, where nothing is allowed to get in the way of the task

- as a core value of a power culture, which maintains absolute control over its subordinates.

4.9 Rewards and control systems

A very critical way in which shared norms and values are communicated within the organisation is reward and control. At its simplest, this is close to the 'carrot and stick' principle. Appraisals are very often held each year between manager and subordinate; feedback will be given to the subordinate on achievement of targets. This is a formal procedure during which the subordinate is likely to have cultural norms and values reinforced. 'Well, normally, Jack, we expect sales people such as yourself to be a little more dynamic . . . you should have been able to secure the Z36 contract. Mind you we liked your emphasis on quality with the Y24 product – that's the message we want to get across to our customers – and its starts with us.'

ACTIVITY 29

In what sorts of ways, do you think that compliance with cultural values could be symbolically rewarded within the organisation? In what ways might non-compliance with cultural values be symbolically handled?

Symbolic rewards could include:

- salary increase
- promotion
- keeping your job
- status symbols – nice office, car, etc
- interesting and prestigious work.

Non-compliance could be flagged on the spot or at appraisal time. Symbolically this could be reinforced by punishments such as:

- no salary increase
- demotion
- sacking
- side-ways moves
- being given little or demeaning work
- being given too much work.

4.10 Reinforcing folklore and consistent role models

People who survive and fit in by adopting and internalising the organisation's norms and values are then in a position to act in such ways that they begin to be the actors in the stories, rather than the audience. They become the role models against which newcomers to the organisation must aspire if, they too, are to be successful.

As consistent role models, they communicate the culture of the organisation by their behaviour and attitudes. It is usual in some companies for such role models to be used as **mentors** – people whom the newcomer can confide in and ask for assistance and advice during their formative time in the new work situation.

REVIEW ACTIVITY 4

Suggested time: 50-60 minutes.

Read the case study, *Soapworks,* and answer the questions that follow it.

Soapworks
Just east of Glasgow, on the main road to Edinburgh, lies a great sprawl of grey council blocks, thrown up on bare fields. This is Easterhouse and it houses 55,000 people. Supported by a handful of churches, boarded-up pubs, barricaded shops and a surfeit of schools, the dreary blocks of flats were built after the Second World War when the councils cleared the Glaswegian slums and had to house 75,000 people. Twenty years ago, gang warfare brought a notoriety that today is maintained by a drugs culture where solvent abuse-related deaths are common.

Unemployment is high here; 56% of the men are out of work. There's an industrial estate at Queenslie in the middle of Greater Easterhouse, but it's pretty quiet. The Glasgow factories, steel works and shipyards that used to employ residents have disappeared. Companies like Olivetti which once employed thousands locally have long gone. Who can blame them?

Indeed, it's all too easy to write off a place like Easterhouse, lacking as it does any superficial allure. Parts like these have been recognised by the European Community as the nearest thing to Third World conditions in the developed West. But, fortunately, not everyone here has given up. There are jewels to be found – the Calvi project, for example, shows what can be made of these drab blocks to change them into desirable homes. The council, meanwhile, wages an endless war on the all-pervasive damp that afflicts so much of the housing in the area. And there are phalanxes of council and community workers fighting for improvements.

It was one of these interested parties, Chris Elphick of Community of Learning Initiatives, who stood up at a meeting in London late in 1987 and accosted Anita Roddick, founder of Body Shop International. She was giving a talk to the Business Network, a group of people which looks at running business in a holistic way.

Roddick is one of Britain's most publicly unorthodox managers. When her husband decided to spend a year horse-trekking across South America in 1976, she started a small shop in Brighton to support her family. She sold a handful of naturally based toiletries, adapted from materials she had seen being used in less developed countries. Packaged in urine sample bottles with hand-written labels and offered in five sizes the products were an immediate hit. Today, she and her husband Gordon, who is chairman of the company, run a £220 million empire with 350 shops in 34 countries. The company owns 13 of these shops; the rest are franchises, the factor that enabled Body Shop's stupendous expansion.

The company is imbued with the Roddicks' principles of honest trading, value for money, a high level of support for the environment and the community and a total belief in the people who work for the company. As Anita, who is fond of epigrams, says, 'I employed workers, but people came instead.' So Roddick is uniquely equipped to give a talk about holistic business, for she practises what she preaches. At the Business Network meeting, Elphick suggested that she might care to go and practise some of it in Easterhouse. She immediately arranged to visit Scotland in January. 'What struck me was that there was so much skill here,' says Roddick, recalling her visit. '1 just decided instantly – it's wonderful, you can do that when you're at the top.' On her return to headquarters in Littlehampton, Sussex, she told her husband that he should go and see it for himself. He came back and said, 'Right, let's put in a soap factory and we'll put 25% of the profits back into the community,' and that was it. Done.

'Going into Easterhouse we were dealing with hard traditional socialists with no real belief in change,' says Roddick. 'You go in and you're suspect because you're business. So we got in all the councillors from the area and talked. I think passion persuades – if they were doubting before, they certainly weren't afterwards. We said, you're getting a factory and employment and you're not dealing with a traditional company. We bombarded them with the Body Shop. They came in like lambs. They asked about unions, I told them you only need unions if management are bastards. We like to talk to people one-to-one if there's a problem.'

Having convinced the community of their good intentions, the Roddicks then had to figure out who in the company would run the factory. Gordon Roddick and director, Stuart Rose were heavily committed to the operation currently being set up in the US, while Anita Roddick spends much of her time looking for new products, which includes travelling for at least two months each year. Eric Helier, the manufacturing director recently appointed to the board, was a natural choice as one director, and Michael Ross, a franchisee who owns two shops with his wife in Aberdeen and Dundee, had expressed a wish to work on a wider front within the company. Ross, who helped find the 36,000 sq.ft Scottish Development Agency site at Queenslie Industrial Estate, was appointed managing director of the factory, which was christened Soapworks.

Next, Ronnie Morgan was hired as factory manager. Morgan had spent 20 years as an engineer and latterly in senior management in the construction industry. Made redundant after a take-over of the business he was running, he suffered a traumatic time looking for another job. After a brief stint in Australia, he came back looking for the right job in Scotland. He remembers going for the interview in Littlehampton with Gordon Roddick: 'I was the only guy dressed in a suit and tie – I lost the tie very quickly.' Morgan came moulded as a traditional manager, but says, 'I found I fitted in very easily with the ethos, the feel for Body Shop. We hold views in common.' He reflects, 'I was sufficiently cynical to wonder if the whole environment thing they support was a gimmick, but I honestly don't believe it is. Body Shop is a tremendously honest company; people genuinely believe in what they are doing.'

Morgan wasn't alone in his initial suspicion of the company. Recruiting was a harrowing time for those involved. 'We were looking for personality really that would gel into a team. We can add the training,' says Ross. 'We went for a balance of sexes and ages. I was almost dreading that moment, starting recruitment. You don't come away from an experience like that unmoved.' They interviewed 100 people, all unemployed, for 16 jobs. 'The employees are the ambassadors for this – they're crucial,' Ross adds.

Yvonne Anderson, 30, from Easterhouse and Linda McGovaney, 21, from nearby Garthamloch, part of Greater Easterhouse, came to the Body Shop from a training scheme run by Poldrait, a publicly funded employment training group. 'Employment training is a bit of a con,' says Anderson 'You're given to understand you'll get what you want, but they put you into what they have for you. We were treated as ignorant people, patronised. So there was a certain amount of suspicion to begin with – these English people coming up.' McGovaney nods in agreement.

Both women say they'll feel more secure when the first year in the job is up. They are naturally further unsettled by the new factory's teething problems but are happy working for Body Shop. The job has strings – no smoking (nearly everyone is a smoker), and rather healthier food with more salads than they would personally choose. 'I like something a bit more substantial myself,' says McGovaney. But the factory is spotlessly clean and the facilities pleasant. 'It's a really good, caring company,' says Anderson. They are interested in making sure that people know what's going on.' McGovaney adds, 'Anita is really down-to-earth and Gordon is really nice. It's good to work for people like that.'

The five most skilled staff, including Morgan himself, his office administrator, a graduate chemist, the production supervisor and the maintenance engineer, came from just outside the Greater Easterhouse boundary. The rest live in the area. They started work in October. It had taken just eight months from Roddick's visit, to get the factory up and running.

That first week in October was, in fact, spent at the Body Shop Training School in London. 'It was brilliant,' says Linda Bruff, Soapworks' bubbly receptionist. She was delighted to get the job – even though her brother is a manager with Safeways and her sister is a dealer on the Glasgow stock exchange, she felt that she had been discriminated against by potential employers just because of where she lives. 'The training was more practical; learning things about yourself, mind games to see how you coped. It wasn't them and us. We were made to feel welcome, made to feel part of Body Shop, to feel at home.'

This was followed by a week in the factory at Littlehampton, shadowing workers there to see how the company operated. The aim was to mould a disparate group of people – single parents, long-term unemployed, an ex-soldier, a 16-year-old school leaver – into a team. The result: 'We all started here knowing each other,' says Bruff. 'All we had to do was learn our jobs properly.'

It is inspiring to listen to these people talk about their work. Even though Soapworks is designed to employ 100 people eventually, and the current 25 rattle round in it, there is a busy, happy atmosphere. They want to do their jobs well and get to grips with new machinery that doesn't always do what it's supposed to do. There are constant references to 'the family', which is how they view their group. 'I thought we might have big problems here,' says Ross, who was originally given dire warnings about Easterhouse. 'I thought we'd have to spend 90% of our management time on it, but we haven't. They're good people to work with and it's been very rewarding.'

But it really isn't all that surprising. The people who work at Soapworks are treated well and with respect by their employer. They are made to feel their role is important, and they are told what is going on and why, both informally and in a more formal monthly meeting with Morgan. As a relative newcomer to the company he walks a delicate balance between the superficially laid-back Body Shop style and the more paternal role of the traditional factory manager. He won't stand for any nonsense, but some of his workforce might be surprised at how much he knows about their lives outside the factory, and how much he cares about them.

Perhaps it has sometimes been hard for Morgan, and it has certainly proved difficult for other business traditionalists in the city, industry and the press, to understand what makes the Body Shop work. It demands that the observer step outside a 'normal' mental framework and look at the company in a different way. After all, how many companies build environmental and community issues along with community work into their mainstream business? And how many companies would choose to set up a new factory in one of the blackest spots in the country and commit themselves to ploughing a quarter of that factory's profits back into the community? Sadly, all too few.

That 25% figure was pulled out of the air at random, as Roddick, Ross and Morgan all confirm. Ross is committed to ensuring that it is 'a significant amount – not just peanuts'. He reckons the factory should be in profit in 18 months, maybe two years. Until then, his concern is to get Soapworks running at full stretch; on current equipment producing 3 million bars of soap this year. 'I asked for a budget,' says Morgan of his original interview, 'but they didn't seem to have one. It seems like the company has so much money that it doesn't have to look after it. That's not true, they look after it very carefully. They don't present me with money in the way I'd like them to, but I suppose there are certain things it's not necessary for me to know. I reconcile myself to it. I want the information but I don't need to know it. I have to trust Michael [Ross]; he knows what he wants me to do.'

Ross explains, 'We've got budgets and business plans, but they've been revised about six times. We've got to be flexible, not guided by bits of paper. We know how much we'll commit this year, and next year, but we want to leave room to add things.' As it happens, Morgan has never been refused whatever he has considered necessary, and by not knowing what's available he probably takes even more personal responsibility than usual for keeping what he spends to a minimum.

The speed with which Body Shop has set up Soapworks is extraordinary – eight months compared to an industry standard of about 18 months – especially considering that it has never made soap before. While 98% of Body Shop products are made in the UK, only about a third are made by the company itself, at the facility in Littlehampton. 'As we get bigger we need to secure lines supply and ensure that we know about the products we are selling,' says Ross. 'With soap we see sales increasing 50-60% a year, and even given full production here we'll only meet a fifth of our demand in a year. So we'll continue to subcontract, and we are concerned that our suppliers are confident in us, too.' For Soapworks' future, a dry powder plant is being considered, for making talcum powders and related products, along with a bath salt filling line and certainly a second soap line.

But even before the plant makes a profit, Body Shop already have contributed to the community. Every year the company holds an international conference for all franchisees. Last year the franchisees were told about Easterhouse. Roddick spoke of her dismay at the terrible lack of facilities in the community, not even a playground for the children. The response was immediate: £23,000 from their own pockets which was put into an account towards having a playground built.

Heather Forster, who like her husband Rob is an environment and community projects co-ordinator for Body Shop, is responsible for getting the playground built and managed. 'The idea was not for anyone from BSI [Body Shop International] to co-ordinate it,' she says. 'The idea was for someone like CLI [Community Learning Initiatives] to do it. Someone from the community has to carry the can for and run it'. Forster has involved local schools in designing equipment for the playground, and commissioned community architects in Glasgow to design it. A site has been found in the middle of Easterhouse and a steering committee staffed by members of the community has been set up. Since Roddick's initial contact with Easterhouse was via CLI, it is fitting that one of its team, Pat Boase, is responsible for co-ordinating the project locally. He has already delivered one playground in the Glasgow area and is currently trying to convince the regional and district councils along with the SDA, to fund this project's completion.

All the Body Shops are involved in community work of some kind, whether it's working with old people, handicapped kids or prisoners, or whatever staff choose. Both the central company and franchisees give staff time off in working hours to do it. Forster helps advise and inform employees on what they can do. Of course, it costs the company money, but the rewards are considerable. As Forster says, 'We have to make money to do something, but there's no reason for earning money if we don't do it.' This is Roddick's utter conviction and one she has instilled throughout her company. Steve Maguire, Soapworks' storeman. puts it most succinctly: 'They've got t'get before they can gie.'

To cynics, Roddick points out, 'Altruism in business is disarming. But the bottom line is you keep your staff – and good staff are hard to get and keep, especially in retailing.' Body Shop has a commendably low turnover of staff. 'We had an audience of young females in the company and community work opened up a well of caring . They're looking to do more than just earn their daily bread.' It's not, though, a female preserve. While the new staff at Soapworks won't be starting community work until the factory is running smoothly, Maguire comments that one of his colleagues, Paul, had already set up a football match with Soapworks staff and unemployed friends. The Soapworks team rented a pitch and provided the strips and probably bought the drinks afterwards.

It's a curious phenomenon that Body Shop seems almost too good to be true. Once tagged 'the share that defies gravity', the company has been able to circumnavigate the pervasive insipidity of most 'health products'. While its wares are based on natural and often ancient treatments for 'cleansing, -polishing and protecting the body', they are presented in a compelling way which informs the consumer about relevant and topical, moral and environmental issues. Of course, the company is riding the current 'green wave', but it was there long before the general public had expressed such an interest in green issues. In the five years since its flotation, the company has increased both its turnover and profits by a factor of nine to £46. 2 million and £9. 3 million respectively.

The reason for Body Shop's success is not a closely guarded secret. It can be attributed to two major factors. First of all, the company operates on principles and values that most individuals feel entirely comfortable with. Most of us don't earn money for the sake of earning money; we work so that we can afford to live and do the things we want to do. But most companies earn for the sake of earning; profits are bottom line, an end in themselves. Yet why should companies, which after all simply employ individuals, be any different from people? Why not earn so that you can spend the money on things that matter – informing and educating people, supporting your local community, paying decent prices for Third World goods, as well as providing decent dividends for shareholders? That is precisely what the Body Shop does, and extremely successfully at that.

The second major factor is that while the company and its founders appear to be flouting the traditional ways of doing business, they actually operate with extremely sound and well-recognised methods. Body Shop asks customers what they want and delivers. Since its earliest days the company has never diluted its image – it keeps it concentrated and clear by communicating it through training, videos, newsletters and meetings with staff from top to bottom of the company. It even bought its own video production company, Jacaranda, last year to step up its communications abilities as the company expands. Its staff are highly trained and motivated, and they are given the chance to excel. Yvonne Anderson says she would like to be an 'ideas person' in the factory, while Wee Willie, at 16 the youngest member of the Soapworks family, is nursing a clear ambition to run the factory one day. Both will get their chance.

But Body Shop never forgets that it is money that enables it to do what it wants. Behind the apparently casual image, every movement of every penny is carefully tracked. And while Roddick proudly points out that Body Shop has never advertised or marketed its products, she is nevertheless an instinctive marketer.

Suspicious observers analyse Body Shop on their terms, sure that the company must be hiding something. Yet even a cursory glance reveals excellent business principles embedded in all its operations. What the critics have not grasped is that unlike many traditional businesses which struggle to integrate these principles, Body Shop, almost by accident, was built on them right from days of the first shop. The Roddicks' astuteness rests not on an ability to fool outsiders, but in spotting a good idea and exploiting it for all its worth. If you don't look at the business and its good deeds in this light, you just won't see it. In the traditions of the Quakers, Body Shop wants to trade as fairly as possible and benefit the world around it.

Roddick believes in an ethical code of behaviour for the global citizen – and that means multi-national companies. She believes in empowerment of people through jobs, work, honest earnings. 'Our idea of success,' she says, 'is the number of people we've employed, how we have educated them, and raised their human consciousness, and whether we've infused them with a breathless enthusiasm. Products in industry are no more than a by-product. I mean how can you take a moisturiser seriously – it's not the body and blood of Christ, it's water and oil. All we're doing is trading, but, like the Quakers, trading in an honest way, and that brings a morale and a sense of purpose. I don't know how we'd have succeeded without it.' As for Easterhouse – 'Its like love – the more you put in the more get out.'

(Anne Ferguson, *Management Today,* May 1989, pp. 94-100.)

Using Pascale's steps of organisation socialisation (Figure 17) as your framework and the headings in this section, analyse the case study and list ways in which the culture of Soapworks has been communicated to its staff.

Summary

In this section, we have considered culture in the organisation and the many ways in which the assumptions, values and artifacts which it embodies may be communicated to those within and external to the company. Using Pascale's model of socialisation, we have investigated processes which a person would typically go through from the time of joining the organisation to the point at which he or she feels 'part of' the organisational fabric. You have analysed these processes, for example, using the job adverts activity to highlight possible cultural values, and seen how reputation and even building design can communicate a great deal in terms of the priorities and ways of operating within organisations. We also discussed stories, myths and other artifacts of culture.

Finally, you have looked at the potent use of rewards and punishments to symbolise approval and disapproval of a person's adherence to the cultural values of the organisation and how the rewarded eventually become role models that future trainees are urged to imitate.

Unit Summary

In this unit, we have covered basic elements of communication in organisations. You have been shown various models of communication to help and develop your understanding. In particular, you should now be able to analyse barriers to communication in the work place and be able to suggest ways in which communication might be improved.

You have also considered through reading and the use of examples the benefits and pitfalls of formal and informal communication so you should now have a more informed basis to help you decide which of these, or what sort of mix of the two, you would use in certain work situations. The issues of centralisation and decentralisation have been analysed in relation to the flows of information and directives required for decision making. Finally, you have reviewed the concepts of organisational culture and then observed and discussed ways though which organisations attempt to promote their cultures using a range of socialisation processes.

References

Adair, J (1989) *Great Leaders,* Talbot Adair Press

Argyle, M (1988) *Bodily Communication,* London: Routledge.

Berko, R M Wolvin, A D and Wolvin, D R (1995): *Communicating,* Boston, MA: Houghton Mifflin.

Bonington, C (1994) 'The Heights of Teamwork,' *Personnel Management,* Oct, pp 44-47

Brown, A D (1995) *Organisational Culture,* London: Pitman.

Davis, K (1953) 'Management Communication and the Grapevine', *Harvard Business Review,* Sept-Oct, 31 (5), pp. 43-49

Fisher, D (1993) *Communication in Organizations,* St Paul, MN: West Publishing Company.

Greenberg, J and Barron, R A (1993) *Behaviour in Organizations,* Allyn and Bacon

Haney, W V (1974) *Communication and Organizational Behaviour: Text and Cases,* Homewood, IL: Irwin.

Katz, D & Kahn, R L (1966) *The Social Psychology of Organizations,* New York: John Wiley & Sons.

Manning, G and Curtis, K (1988) *Communication, the Miracle of Dialogue,* Cincinnati, OH: South Western Publishing.

Martin, J and Siehl, C (1990) 'Organizational Culture and Counterculture: An Uneasy Symbiosis', in Sypher, Beverley Davenport, *Case Studies in Organizational Communication,* The Guilford Press.

Mintzberg, H (1979) *The Structuring of Organizations,* Englewood Cliffs, New Jersey: Prentice Hall.

Mintzberg, H (1980) *The Nature of Managerial Work,* New York: Harper & Row.

Moorhead, G and Griffin, R W (1995) *Organizational Behaviour,* fourth edition, Boston, MA: Houghton Mifflin Company.

Morgan, G (1986) *Images of Organization,* CA: Sage Publications

Pascale, R (1992) 'The Paradox of Corporate Culture: Reconciling Ourselves to Socialization', *California Management Review,* 27, 2 Winter 1985 p. 38, as used in Luthans, Fred (1992) *Organizational Behaviour,* New York: McGraw Hill

Rasberry, R W and Lemoine, L F (1986) *Effective Managerial Communication,* MA: Kent Publishing Company.

Rogers, C R (1991) 'Barriers and Gateways to Communication', *Harvard Business Review,* 69, 6, 105-111.

Schein, E H (1968) 'Organizational Socialization and the Profession of Management', *Industrial Management Review,* winter, p.1-16, as given in Mintzberg, H (1979) *The Structuring of Organizations,* Englewood Cliffs, New Jersey: Prentice Hall Inc.

Schein, E H (1985) *'Organizational Culture and Leadership: A Dynamic View',* Jossey-Bass, as used in Mullins, L J (1996) Management and Organisational Behaviour, (4th edn), London: Pitman Publishing.

Schein, E H (1990) *'Organizational Culture', American Psychologist,* 45, p.109-119, as used in McKenna, E F, *Business Psychology and Organisational Behaviour,* Hove: Lawrence Erlbaum Associates Ltd Publishers.

Schermerhorn, J R Hunt, J G Osborn, R N (1991) *Managing Organizational Behaviour,* New York: John Wiley & Sons, Inc.

Stanton, N (1990) *Communication,* London: Macmillan.

Steers, R M (1991) *Introduction to Organizational Behaviour,* 4th edition, New York: Harper Collins Publishers Inc.

Strauss, G (1962-3) 'Tactics of lateral relationships: The Purchasing Agent', *Administrative Science Quarterly,* P. 161-186.

Torrington, D & Hall, L (1991) *Personnel Management: A New Approach,* Englewood Cliffs, NJ: Prentice Hall.

Townsend, J (1988) 'Paralinguistics: It's not what you say it's the way that you say it' *Management Decision,* 26, volume 26, number 3, Bradford: MCB University Press Ltd.

Recommended Reading

SECTION 1
Mintzberg, H (1980) *The Nature of Managerial Work,* New York: Harper & Row.

Verbal and non-verbal communication:
Greenberg, J and Barron, R A (1993) *Behaviour in Organizations,* Allyn and Bacon, Chapter 13

Argyle, M (1993) *Bodily Communication,* London: Routledge, Chapter 1.

Communication models:
Fisher, D (1993) *Communication in Organizations,* St Paul, MN: West Publishing.

SECTION 2
Rogers, C R and Roethlisberger, F J (1991) 'Barriers and Gateways to Communication', *Harvard Business Review,* 69, 6, 105-111.

Haney, W V (1974) *Communication and Organizational Behaviour: Text and Cases,* Homewood, IL: Irwin.

Bolton, R (1986) *People Skills,* New York: Simon & Schuster.

SECTION 3

Communication networks and upward, downward and horizontal communication
Greenberg, J and Barron, R A (1993) *Behaviour in Organizations,* Allyn and Bacon.

Mintzberg, H (1979) *The Structuring of Organizations,* Englewood Cliffs, NJ: Prentice Hall.

Upward and downward communication
Francis, D (1987) *Unblocking Organizational Communication,* London: Gower Publishing.

Section 4

Levels of culture:
Schein, E H (1991) *Organizational Cultures and Leadership,* Jossey-Bass, Chapter 1.

Handy, C (1993) *Understanding Organizations,* fourth edition, Harmondsworth: Penguin, Chapter 7.

Pascale's model of the socialisation process, around which the section is based is discussed in:
Luthans, Fred (1992) *Organizational Behaviour,* New York: McGraw Hill.

Answers to Review Activities

Review Activity 1

1   The three purposes of organisational communication are to:
   - achieve co-ordinated action
   - share information
   - express feelings and emotions.

These are illustrated by the case study in the following ways:

Achieve co-ordinated action
The first people to 'get on board' are the members of the board. The purpose of the monthly meeting will be to approve or to reject Gordon's approval. If approval is granted the company will then be able to co-ordinate its planning. Even Alec Smallfield will be included in this.

Other activities to be co-ordinated will be concerned with the product launch: liaison with major stores, who will stock the product; and publicity agents. These activities will probably involve further meetings, letters, telephone conversations etc.

Share information

The first person Gordon shared his idea with was the managing director in his hurried meeting. The agenda and the paper 'Natural products: the way forward?' was the next instance of this sharing. Gordon did not have to share his ideas at this stage; however, the fact that he did so shows that people like to know about new developments. The information he is sharing relates directly to organisational goals and results of efforts (the Dermiplex range).

Express feelings and emotions

The animal rights activists' day 'Animals have feelings to!' is an obvious expression of strongly felt beliefs and emotions. Alec Smallfield's telephone conversation to Gordon was also partially to express his feelings over someone else trying to alter his entire production set-up! Gordon might also use the monthly meeting to show how he feels about the conservative policies that the company has been following for so long.

2   See section 1.5 for communication models.

One-way

Gordon's paper was written as a 'one-way' message, its intention was to raise doubts in the minds of the board members and suggest that perhaps there was a new way forward. He would have to be most careful in his choice of phrases and very carefully consider all of his intended readers and their interest and knowledge in natural products.

Interaction

The most obvious illustration of the interaction model is the planned monthly meeting. Conversation will definitely be two-way on such an important issue. The board members will probably ask for clarification on some points and question the validity of others.

Two-person relationship model

This model considers the ways in which others expect us to behave and the ways in which we think we should behave towards them. Gordon clearly thinks it is his role to be creative and dynamic. His new proposals clearly communicate this. Likewise, other managers see his role in the same light; they expect him to act and communicate in this way.

Communication-in-context model

This model takes into account the context in which communication takes place. If we consider the monthly meeting, or even communication now going on in the company subsequent to Gordon's paper, we can see that the following will impact upon the effectiveness of communication:

- The task: this is not straightforward which would mean a major upheaval in production as a minimum.
- Organisation structure and culture: Alec Smallfield informs us that 'neither staff or his factory' is set up to deal with the proposed changes.
- The change in strategic focus from synthetic to natural products would cause a change in the values of the company.
- Group characteristics: Gordon's task at convincing the Board would be much easier if they were not such a bunch of old-fashioned conservative thinkers! Additionally, he has Alec Smallfield to contend with.

All of these factors shape the communication process.

Organisation-environment transaction

This is a strategic model which demonstrates the ways in which the organisation communicates with the outside world and the ways in which elements of the outside world communicate with the organisation.

By adopting and promoting *Helenne* as a natural product, the organisation would be telling existing and potential customers and interested bodies, for example, animal rights activists, that its new values were friendly to the animal environment. 'Natural must be best', as in kindest to the skin, is also implicit in this message.

It is equally clear that the values of people outside organisation have permeated their way into the core of the company's strategy.

3   Typical forms of non-verbal communication include:

- Gordon's sharp suits, tie and braces
- his appearance of 'buzzing with energy', he is conveying the message: 'I'm your ideas person'
- Mr Dermot busy packing papers and not looking up during his meeting with Gordon, his message is: 'I'm too busy right now'
- nods of approval to Gordon's paper

4

(a) Gordon has used the following media and channels:
media: written his paper; channel: limited visual
media: telephone to Alec Smallfield; channel: audio
media: face-to-face initial meeting with managing director; channel: audio and visual.

(b) Alec Smallfield has a difficult message to communicate. His staff may feel that their jobs are threatened. They will certainly not like the major changes in their daily routines.

Alec should choose media and channels which can best deal with the strong feelings his workers are likely to experience. Face-to-face communication could be via one-to-one meetings and also group discussions and should be audio and visual to allow for feedback and also for the sake of clarity.

He might want to reinforce these meetings with a personally addressed letter explaining the company's new proposals. This has the advantage of laying out the issues in a clear, rational format. It is easy for someone to miss a vital point in a meeting, or indeed for someone such as Alec to either forget or not attach sufficient bias to the point. The personally addressed letter at least shows that the company thinks that the issue is important to its employees.

Review Activity 2

1   There are obvious differences in perceptions to the work situation.

Sandra and Barbara regard work as:

- not their main priority – home life takes precedence
- a means to an end – their pay packets
- a place to have a chat with friends and to share problems.

Reginald views work as:

- his main priority
- an end in itself
- a place where he can put into effect his ideas regarding efficiency.

2

(a) Reginald' s interpretation of the message is incorrect. He jumps to conclusions, perhaps he has pre-conceived stereotypes of his staff as people whom he cannot trust.

(b) Reginald has fallen down very badly in this area! He has made a number of basic errors:

- using one-way communication for a very sensitive issue, allowing no further explanation or feedback
- a group setting arouses emotions amongst the staff
- tone of the message is very autocratic and condescending
- no checking on the validity of the message.

(c) Likely barriers are:
    fear
    mistrust
    anxiety.

He is likely to distance himself from the staff even more than he is at present.

3   Fred's statement of 'Either that or we become their lapdogs!' is one of polarisation. It only offers a black and white choice with no in-between-ground. His statement about Sheila being 'Management as well' is one of stereotyping; it doesn't matter that Sheila is, in fact, very different to Reginald. She has been put into the same category as Reginald and the other managers.

4

(a) The message has misled Reginald, probably on two counts:

●   Item 56 clearly has not registered in Reginald's mind; 'Easter eggs' might have done

●   'account for these losses'

Reginald has read this as 'losses' through theft. In fact, the discrepancy is the way in which the stock was 'written off'. Of course, it might not have been due to losses at all but an error in data fed into the computer. The word 'losses' is emotive.

(b) Reginald really is in a difficult position now. Quite apart from the new barriers of mistrust, anxiety and fear that his management style is in danger of producing, he now has the added barrier of anger. His staff are even less likely to hear what he has to say than before.

He could put up another poster to apologise but this would appear crass and distant. He needs to time his communication; perhaps allowing a cooling off period, passing word through the grapevine via Sheila that he intends to hold a meeting, in work time and at the end of their shift, to say that he has noted their comments and he can understand their anxiety. He will attempt to use this event as a 'springboard' to launch a new commitment between management and worker with more meetings etc. Well, its worth a try!

The other option is for him to quietly take the poster down and hope that it will 'all blow over'.

5   Sheila might have difficulty in getting Reginald to accept that his managerial style is in drastic need of an overhaul.

Barriers which Reginald might put up could include:

●   Pride (yet another emotion!): He has to admit that his style of management has its weaknesses. He might also resent this suggestion coming from Sheila if he has a stereotype about her as a woman and his subordinate.

● Perceptions: Reginald might simply not perceive the problem as his! He has, in his eyes, merely pointed out (albeit a little heavy handed) what employees already know. Pilfering will lead to dismissal.
Although, he mistook the discrepancy to be due to pilfering that does not detract from his message which is still valid and it shows staff that he intends to run a tight and efficient store.

6   Obviously there are barriers due to the differences in perceptions and possible mismatch of knowledge, skills and interest. However, one of the major barriers will be that of credibility. Quite simply, will the staff believe that he is about to reform his ways? He might try to explain to his staff how things will be in future but they might have a tendency to evaluate him too early and not really listen to what he has to say. They might even have a frozen evaluation of him for months if not years to come and never accept the 'new' Reginald, even if he does begin to behave differently

7   A difficult one this! Reginald needs to convince people of his genuine desire to change. Actions, as they say, speak louder than words and so many of his staff might suspend judgement until his actions become consistent with his words.

Reginald needs to repeat his message in different ways – hold meetings, briefings, manage more by 'wandering around', adopt an 'open door' policy, be seen to react to staffs' comments and to give feedback. He needs to reward staff appropriately and to recruit the sort of people who will fit in with his style of management. Most of all, he needs time and patience and a genuine desire to improve communication.

Review Activity 3

1   Katz and Kahn(1966) split communication 'down the line' into five categories:

1   Job instructions

2   Job rationale (explains why a task is being performed)

3   Information about procedures and practices

4   Feedback to subordinates

5   Indoctrination of goals (mission).

● Jane is going to use computers to download information and monthly meetings to issue job instructions 'on the spot'. Memos and telephone conversations are not mentioned, although Jane may use them on an ad hoc basis.

- One aspect of her communication to the area representatives will be to explain why she is introducing the new system and what it is she hopes it will achieve. Hopefully, there are benefits for both the company and the reps. She will need to explain why she is preferring the use of computers. Probably the rationale she will use is one of standardisation and efficiency, coupled with up-to-date information.

- As important – or more important to the sales reps! – will be her rationale for the new bonus system; why she thinks the old system is unfair and why her new points-weighted system will be better.

- She will certainly have to give information about procedures and practice. For instance, the procedures relating to the downloading of computers and the ways in which the standard report forms must be completed; procedures to be adopted at meetings.

- Feedback to subordinates is one area which has been sadly lacking in the past! Feedback will now be formally given in two ways: through the forum of the meetings; and via a modem to the area representatives' laptops.

- Indoctrination of goals. Sheila will be trying to indoctrinate her new goals and values to the sales team. She might have difficulty as inevitably there will be some resistance to change. She will try to win over the high performers in the organisation. Additionally, she could use training events, for example, the 'high flyers' programme as a means of communicating these new values. And the new 'professional' staff she will be taking in to the organisation will be put through an induction programme in which they will be immersed in these new values.

2

(a) The communication networks which existed before Jane took control were probably of the circle or comcon type amongst the cliques. This represents decentralised control, information sharing and decision-making are carried out among the group members.

There is probably an element of grapevine communication, probably of the cluster type with the sharing of unofficial information – gossip, rumours, etc – amongst selected members of the clique.

This system probably came about for two reasons:
- It was the natural and preferred style of the area representatives; they would have sales areas which would border, or possibly overlap, with their neighbours and they would need information regarding what contracts they were dealing with. They might even be dealing with the same client. They required information in order to up-date their knowledge and as a means of co-ordinating their efforts. It was a lonely life; they needed others in a similar situation to talk with and share their everyday problems.

- There appears to have been little control or co-ordination from the previous sales director, thus leaving little choice for any other form of communication!

(b) It is evident that Jane wants a centralised information system, a wheel, in which control information is sent to her and she sends directives out to the sales representatives. She wants this for control purposes. She wants to have the overall picture of a very-fast moving market. She also wants accountability of staff to herself.

3

Upward communication

Katz and Kahn summarise such communication from subordinate to superior as one of the forms:

1   About him or her self, performance and problems

2   About others and their problems

3   About organisational practices and policies

4   About what needs to be done and how it is to be done.

This list gives a list of areas which could be covered. In the event, it is unlikely that all of them will actually be used. At first the area representatives will be wary of giving any information voluntarily concerning themselves or others. The information which they will have to provide concerns performance with their various contracts. In other words, they are providing control information. Of course, control information is likely to be used by Jane to determine bonuses, etc. It is highly likely that under-performing individuals will only want to present the minimum of information. There is, after all, the element of 'big brother' watching in Jane's new system.

There is likely to be concern over the new policies, procedures and what is to be done. Thus, some of the area representatives are likely to seek advice from Jane on these issues, certainly as a preliminary measure and possibly also in an ongoing manner.

4   There are advantages in using the standardised report and also in using the verbal summary. There are also advantages in using the two in tandem. To take each in turn:

The report provides:

- a permanent record which reaches all of the relevant people, Jane and the sales reps and allows them to read the information in their own time and convenience

- a consistent format, hopefully, Jane will have chosen an appropriate format

- only relevant information and, if succinct, should be relatively quick to read.

Verbal summary
The first advantage of this method is that it allows Jane, or the others, to ask questions and to seek clarification on data presented to them. It also allows more probing questions along the lines of 'that's interesting, tell us more'. This two-way process involves those present, and this involvement is a great stimulator of ideas and a motivator of initiatives.

Reports can be dull depending upon your perception and what the sales people really want is some personal interaction. Think about the amount of time they spend on the car phone. Remember as well, that a verbally delivered summary also makes use of body language, and paralinguistics. If delivered with gusto and clarity, it can be so much more interesting than the report.

In tandem
Putting the two together reinforces the message; these monthly meetings are evidently important; the new reporting system is important. Some people will want to carefully analyse the reports; others would prefer to 'hear it from the horse's mouth'. Some people will have a knack at writing good reports; others will write turgid ones, although the standard format will hopefully overcome some of these problems. Some people will deliver their message better in presentation form.

Putting the two together is likely to have a synergistic effect. The combined effect is likely to be greater than the simple benefits which could be derived from having one or other forms of communication on their own.

5   Some of the benefits of having a meeting other than for official reporting include:

- area representatives get to know more than their immediate neighbours

- area reps get to know Jane Cassidy.

These two factors in themselves are of vast importance to communication. Although, it is quite possible to develop some sort of understanding of another person over the telephone, it is never quite the same as meeting that person face-to-face. Again the body language says much about a person. Feedback is also possible.

In this respect, the apparently informal nature of the rest of the afternoon – the lunch, for instance – is useful for icebreaking. This is also a time when more favourable impressions of people may be formed. Perhaps so-and-so isn't so bad after all – he or she seems to have the same sort of homelife as myself. This might help us to avoid the stereotype scenario or the frozen evaluation we mentioned earlier. The more comfortable we feel with someone, the more likely we are to communicate at a deeper level with them. We might discover how they see things – their perceptions – again this is extremely useful.

From a network point of view, it should increase the size, number and/or strength of the networks.

6   It is unlikely that the informal networks of the area representatives which have built up over the years will suddenly vanish. Nor is this necessarily desirable. Hopefully, the networks will carry more meaningful information and have more sense of purpose than previously. The cluster chains of the grapevine will probably still persist.

The networks grew out of a need for self-support amongst the area representatives. This need for information and group identity will persist but because it is now only one of the ways in which communication takes place, its importance as the sole provider of information is likely to decrease with the introduction of the meetings, written reports and the computer.

Review Activity 4

Careful selection of entry level candidates
Soapworks chose people who were likely to be receptive to the socialising process:

- We were looking for personality really that would gel into a team.
- They interviewed 100 people, all unemployed, for 16 jobs.
- The employees are the ambassadors for this – they're crucial.

There is, in effect, a person specification.

Reputation
It is likely that all of the recruits had an idea of the caring and 'green' image of Body Shop, the parent company, probably through buying the products for themselves or for their families.

Interviews and the selection process
Dress is featured at managerial level, for example, Ronnie Morgan's interview, 'I was the only guy dressed in a suit and a tie – I lost the tie very quickly'.

There are clearly 'no-nonsense', 'let's call a spade a spade' values with managers prepared to 'roll up their shirt sleeves' rather than standing on ceremony.

Induction training
Staff are sent on an induction training course. 'The first week in October was, in fact, spent at the Body Shop Training School in London.'

Here the norms and values of Body Shop would be an integral part of the socialisation process. These are stated as:

- caring – internal and community
- honest
- natural – green
- enthusiasm – 'breathless'
- family
- work
- empowerment through jobs
- education
- unconventional.

This is an in depth process, designed to first of all unfreeze any previous values and norms by allowing the individual to look at him- or her-self – 'learning things about yourself, mind games to see how you coped'.

It is interesting to note that people weren't subject to other techniques such as humiliation as this is not consistent with the 'caring attitude'. It is likely that all of the employees learnt about the history, and hence stories, heroes, slogans etc, at this school.

This was followed by a week in a factory in Littlehampton, shadowing workers who would be the consistent role models for in-the-trenches training.

The workplace itself: rules and regulations

The green, caring and paternal values are evident in the workplace:

- no smoking
- healthy eating – salads, etc

Stories

There is plenty of evidence of stories:

- Founding story – Anita Roddick and the small shop in Brighton whilst her husband is away in South America on horseback! In fact, this is probably more accurately described as a saga in which the heroine is Anita Roddick. This says a lot for the sheer energy and zeal of Roddick and the somewhat unconventional style of business.

- Then there is the founding story of Soapworks, of how Roddick was 'accosted' by Chris Elphick. This story shows the conscience of the company being pricked and responding to the needs of the local communities.

- Another story in the making is the playground project for Easterhouse Estate.

Mission statements, logos, slogans, etc
The case study suggests what the mission statement could be but it does not actually give one. However, it is likely that the company has one.

Slogans appear to be a speciality, for example, Roddick's: 'I employed workers, but people came instead'.

It continues communicating its 'image' through training, videos, newsletters and meetings with staff from top to bottom of the company. It even bought its own video company.

The products themselves
These communicate values very strongly themselves. The packaging of the products suggests a no-nonsense approach; people buy the contents and not the packaging. Simplicity is consistent with the naturalness of the product itself which speaks for the overall caring attitude of the company.

Unconventional
The values placed on money and managing the business are not those of the accountant. 'I asked for a budget', says Morgan, 'but they didn't seem to have one.'

Rewards and control systems
Rewards – the ethos of education is communicated; this is a reward in itself. Hard work and ability – that Soapworks communicates the chance to become 'someone' is apparent. Young Willie, at 16 the youngest member of the Soapworks factory, has a clear ambition to run the factory one day.

Caring attitude
'All the Body Shops are involved in community work of some kind'. Staff are given time off to do these activities. Such activities are clearly looked upon with favour by senior management.

RESOURCES

▷ RESOURCE 6.1

G H Rice Jr and D P
Lindecamp
Source: Journal of
Occupational
Psychology, 1989,
vol 62 pp. 177-182

Personality Types and Business Success of Small Retailers

'The business incomes of 102 owner-managers of small retail stores were correlated with their Jungian personality types, measured on the abridged version of the Myers-Briggs Type Indicator. It was found that thinking extroverts did best as small retailers.'

There has recently been some interest in using the Myers-Briggs Type Indicator (Myers & Briggs, 1962) to identify managerial decision styles on the basis of Jungian personality typologies (Henderson & Nutt, 1980; Hoy & Hellriegel, 1982; Lyles & Mitroff, 1980).

'. . . the dominant problem solving style of managers may influence: (1) the types of information perceived in the environment, which, in turn [may] impact on how unstructured problems are defined and what issues become conceptualised as problems; and (2) the process and criteria for generating, judging and selecting both the means and goals.'

The study described here was designed to examine the relationship between Jungian personality type and the financial success of small businessmen.

Very few field studies have examined the relationship between managerial performance and Jungian personality types. Much of the published work has been speculative (eg. Mitroff & Kilmann, 1975), and most of it has concentrated on the way managers approach decision-making problems (Hellriegel & Slocum, 1980; Hoy & Hellriegel, 1982; Mason & Mitroff, 1973; McKenney & Keen, 1974; Slocum, 1978), although some of these authors have argued that certain personality profiles contributed to successful management. Myers (1962) herself argued that 'thinking-judging' people comprise 'executive types', and should do well as managers.

By studying simulated investment decisions, Henderson & Nutt (1980) showed that decision style as identified by the Myers-Briggs Type Indicator (Myers & Briggs, 1962) was related to the likelihood of adoption of innovative projects, and to assessments reported by executives of the projects' riskiness. 'Sensing-Feeling' executives were more venturesome than others.

In contrast, Crooks (1972), after correlating the performance of graduate students who took a written 'in-basket test' with the Jungian types identified by the Myers-Briggs instrument, reached no overall conclusion regarding managerial performance, and produced several findings that disagreed with Myers' predictions.

Given the limited amount of relevant research and the apparently contradictory results of simulation exercises, an exploratory field study was undertaken to correlate Jungian personality types with business success. Based on the literature, the following hypotheses were proposed:

Hypothesis 1: Extroverts would be more successful businessmen than introverts

Hypothesis 2: Thinking-Judging type managers would be the most successful businessmen

Hypothesis 3: Thinking-Sensing type managers would be the most successful businessmen.

Method
Subjects
The sample consisted of a stratified random selection of 121 of the 242 white male owner-managers of retail stores in the Natchez, Mississippi-Vadalia, Louisiana trading area. The selection excluded branch stores of larger companies, stores owned or operated by women, and stores owned or

operated by persons from minority groups. Restricting the sample in this way avoided many of the identified intervening variables and made the sample relatively homogeneous. The use of owner-managers of small businesses was considered to be most appropriate for this study. These men are the dominant, and often the only, decision makers in their respective organisations. Success or failure of their organisations rests almost completely on their guidance of activities (Friedlander & Pickle, 1968; Hoy & Hellriegel, 1982).

The 121 men owned and operated 127 establishments. Eighty-three of these were various kinds of store; most of the remainder were petrol stations, car dealerships or eating and drinking places. From these 121, 109 participated in data collection sessions. Usable data were obtained from 102 of them.

Measurements
Two measurements were made. The first was a measure of personality type, using the abridged version of the Myers-Briggs Type Indicator (Hellriegel & Slocum, 1975). The second measurement was of business success, using self-reports.

The Myers-Briggs Type Indicator (Myers & Briggs, 1962) and the abridged version of the Myers-Briggs Type Indicator (Hellriegel & Slocum, 1975) are based on the psychological model of Carl Gustav Jung (1875-1961), and result in a scale of measurement of personality along each of four dimensions described by Jung (1923) [1].

According to Jung, although each personality is unique, everyone has made four fundamental choices:

1. whether to be an extrovert (symbolised here by an E) or an introvert (I), in terms coined by Jung

2. whether to emphasise sensing (S) or intuition (N) in perception

3. whether to emphasise thinking (T) or feeling (F) in making evaluations

4. whether to emphasise perceiving (P) or judging (J) in dealing with the world outside oneself.

A person's standing on the four basic choices yield 16 possible personality types: ESTJ, ESTP, ISTJ, ISTP, ESFJ, ESFP, ISFJ, ISFP, ENTJ, ENTP, INTJ, INTP, ENFJ, ENFP, INFJ and INFP.

Evaluations of the dependent variable, the economic performance of the small business owner-managers, were derived from their reported annual personal incomes. In view of the recognised possibility of overstatement or understatement by the businessmen, these incomes were examined carefully by the researcher. For those cases which seemed out of line with industry standards (or were very much different from earnings by others in the same line of business in the town studied), incomes were verified by a more intensive and exhaustive investigation.

Procedure
Appointments were made with owner-managers of the small businesses chosen for the study, and the researcher visited each at his place of business during working hours. After explaining the object and nature of the research, each businessman was asked a set of questions to obtain a demographic and financial profile, then was asked to complete the abridged version of the Myers-Briggs Type Indicator (Hellriegel & Slocum, 1975).

Analysis
There are several ways that the quality of management could be assessed, ranging from gross personal income of the managers to return on assets, return on sales, age and reputation (both financial and performance) of their companies, projected future success, comparative performance with other similar companies, or the managers' own personal social reputations within the community.

From all of these measures of performance, it was decided to use two to evaluate managerial performance of the small businessmen: (1) income from the business and (2) income from the business compared with expected income from a business of this size.

The first measure is a gross measure,

readily recognised and acknowledged by the small owner-managers themselves. The second is a much more accurate measure of the efficiency with which managers utilise their assets, and can be seen as a surrogate for the more commonly proposed measures of return on assets or return on investment. Number of employees was used as the measure of size of the business, rather than the sales, in order to avoid the 'high volume-low mark-up vs. low volume-high mark-up' controversy. A simple linear regression was used to obtain expected values of income rather than the usual Cobb-Douglas function (Cobb & Douglas, 1928), since the range of values was so small.

Results

For the total sample of small business retailers, there was a significantly greater (at the 0.01 level) number of extroverts than introverts, a significantly greater (at the 0.01 level) number of sensing than intuitive types, and a significantly greater (at the 0.5 level) number of judging than perceiving types. There was no significant difference noted in the numbers of thinking vs. feeling businessmen. Table 1 summarises the performance of businessmen by personality types.

Hypothesis 1: Extroverts would be more successful businessmen than introverts

Criterion 1 (income from the business). The average income of all 67 extroverts in the sample was $32,000 and the average income of all 35 introverts was only $21,500. The difference is significant at the 0.01 level. Does this mean that all extroverts managed larger businesses, and therefore made more money? Extrovert businessmen averaged 9.8 employees, and introvert businessmen averaged 6.6 employees. This difference is not significant, so it cannot be said that extroverts owned and managed larger businesses.

Criterion 2 (income compared with expected income from a business of this size).

In only four of the eight sets (ESTJ, ESTP, ENTJ, ENTP) did extroverts' incomes exceed that which might be expected from a business of the size they were managing.

Hypothesis 1 was, therefore, not fully supported. Although extroverts made more money, they did not seem to be more efficient in their use of capital (ie. employees) than introverts.

Hypothesis 2: Thinking-Judging type managers are the most successful businessmen

Criterion 1: There were more Judging

Table 1. *Annual income from the business by personality type*

Personality type	Income ($'000)	Employees (average)	Expected income ($'000)
ENTP	75.0	27.7	66.9
ESTJ	39.5	8.5	27.0
ENTJ	32.8	3.0	15.6
ENFP	30.6	10.8	31.8
ESFP	28.7	13.1	36.6
ISFJ	25.6	4.4	18.5
ISTJ	25.6	10.6	31.4
ESFJ	25.0	10.1	30.3
ESTP	23.8	5.9	21.6
ISTP	23.3	4.7	19.1
INFJ	17.5	2.0	13.5
ISFP	15.1	9.3	28.7
INTP	10.5	5.0	19.7
INFP	10.5	2.0	13.5
INTJ	10.5	0.0	9.3
ENFJ	7.8	4.3	18.3

types ($n = 52$) than Perceiving types ($n = 30$) in the sample, but there was no significant difference between the number of Thinking ($n = 50$) and Feeling ($n = 52$) type businessmen in the sample.

Thinking type managers made an average of $33,900 and Feeling type managers made an average of $23,700. The difference is significant at the 0.01 level. For six of the eight sets, Thinking types had higher incomes from the business than did their corresponding Feeling types. This is a significant difference (at the 0.05 level by the sign or binomial test).

Mean income for all Judging types was $1,600 higher than for all Perceiving types. Using a t test to compare means, or a U test to compare the Judging and Perceiving income distributions, this difference is not significant. Also, the tau relating individual Perceiving-Judging scores to income from the business was a near zero 0.0012 (which would be significant at the 0.988 level).

Of the four Thinking-Judging groups, three were in the top half of the 16 type groups in income. Average income of the Thinking-Judging groups was $27,100 compared with $24,500 average for all other groups. the difference is not significant at the 0.05 level (by t test).

Criterion 2. Six of the eight Thinking groups had average incomes which exceeded incomes expected from businesses of this size. This difference is significant at the 0.05 level by sign test. However, only five of the eight Judging groups exceeded their expected incomes, and this is not a significant difference. Three of the four Thinking-Judging groups exceeded their expected incomes from businesses of this size but, from such a small set, this is not significant.

Therefore, there is insufficient evidence to claim that Thinking-Judging types did significantly better than other types in the sample.

Hypothesis 3: Thinking-Sensing type managers are the most successful businessmen

In order to test this hypothesis, data were grouped according to those mental functions which define distinctive decision-making styles (Mason & Mitroff, 1973).

Criterion 1. Although Thinking types make more money than Feeling types, there is no significant difference between the incomes of Sensing types and Intuitive types. Average income of the four Thinking-Sensing type groups was $31,300 as compared with the average of all other groups of $26,400. However, this difference was not significant.

Criterion 2. In three of the four Sensing-Thinking groups, men earned greater incomes than might be expected from the size businesses they were managing. However, with such a small sample, it is not possible to say that this is a significant percentage.

Therefore, Sensing-Thinking type businessmen did not perform significantly better than others in the sample. In retrospect, it can be seen that the data support an alternative hypothesis.

Alternative hypothesis: Thinking-Extrovert type managers are the most successful businessmen

Criterion 1. Average annual income of the 33 Thinking-Extrovert type managers was $38,600, while the average for all other managers was only $23,500. This difference was significant at the 0.001 level, by t test.

Criterion 2. All four of the Thinking-Extrovert groups exceeded their expected incomes. With only four groups, it is not possible to get a probability of success that reaches the level of significance used in this study. However, it is interesting to note that the probability of seeing this degree of success (four out of four) is 0.0625, which does approach significance.

Discussion and Conclusion

This study of 102 small business retailers constituted about a 50 per cent sample of white males in a specific geographical trading centre. It appears to be representative of that population. Whether or not the population is representative of all retailers in the United States is debatable.

The study found no convincing support for any link between Jungian personality types and performance of small businessmen, and this includes failure to support the expectations of Myers.

An important caveat should be noted. All Jungian criteria constitute continua.

Therefore, it is possible for a person to fall near the centre or at the extreme of a characteristic and still be classified as having that characteristic. For example, a person might be classified as an extrovert, yet be very nearly an introvert. He might be classified as a Thinking type, yet be almost a Sensing type, etc. In any such case, the person might be expected to behave 'almost like' or 'very often like' a person having the opposite trait. In fact, Jung (1923) argued that maturity consists of a conscious choice among behavioural alternatives, or deliberately moving towards the middle position on all four of the traits involved. The study reported here did not attempt to measure the degree to which each subject exhibited a characteristic. It is interesting to speculate whether or not managers exhibiting extreme positions on the continua would be more successful than managers who exhibited more central positions. Perhaps this could be the focus of some future study.

Notes

1 There are no published validity studies of the abridged version of the Myers-Briggs Type Indicator. The authors conducted a study of 117 white male college students, comparing scores on the full and abridged versions. Spearman rhos ranged between 0.80 and 0.91 with a median between 0.88 and 0.89, indicating that the abridged version would be a valid and administratively convenient instrument for field use. Full details of the abridged version and the validity data can be obtained from the first author.

References

Cobb, C.W. & Douglas, P.H. (1928) 'A Theory of Production', *The American Economic Review,* March, 139-165.

Crooks, L.A. (1972) The in-basket study: A pilot study of MBA candidate performance on a test of administrative skills as related to selection and achievement in graduate business school. Brief no. 4, Research and Development Committee, Education Testing Services.

Friedlander, F. & Pickle, H. (1968) 'Components of effectiveness in small organisations', *Administrative Sciences Quarterly,* 22, 289-304.

Hellriegel, D. & Slocum, J.W. (1975) 'Managerial problem solving styles', *Business Horizons,* 18, 29-37.

Hellriegel, D. & Slocum, J.W. (1980) 'Preferred organisational designs and problem solving styles: interesting companions', *Human Systems Management,* 1, 151-158.

Henderson, J.C. & Nutt, P.C. (1980) 'The influence of decision style on decision making behavior', *Management Science,* 26, 371-386.

Hoy, F.S. & Hellriegel, D. (1982) 'The Kilmann and Herden model of organisational effectiveness criteria for small business managers', *Academy of Management Journal,* 25, 308-322.

Jung, C.G. (1923) *Psychological Types,* London: Routledge & Kegan Paul.

Lyles, M.A. & Mitroff, I.I. (1980) 'Organisation problem formulation: an empirical study', *Administrative Science Quarterly,* 25, 102-119.

Mason, R.W. & Mitroff, I.I. (1973) 'A program for research on management information systems', *Management Science,* 19, 475-487.

McKenney, J.L. & Keen, P. (1974) 'How managers' minds work', *Harvard Business Review,* 51, 75-90.

Mitroff, I.I. & Kilmann, R. (1975) 'Stories managers tell: a new tool for organisational problem solving', *Management Review,* 64, 18-28.

Myers, I.B. (1962) *Manual for Myers-Briggs Type Indicator.* Palo Alto, CA: Consulting Psychologists Press.

Myers, I.B. & Briggs, C.K. (1962) *Myers-Briggs Type Indicator.* Princeton, N.J: Educational Testing Service.

Slocum, J.W. (1978) 'Does cognitive style affect diagnosis and intervention strategies of change efforts?', *Group and Organisational Studies,* 3, 199-210.

Counterfeits, Conceits and Corpses: The Failure of the Mask in Corporate Performance

Hopfl

The Implications for Organisational Behaviour

The training of organisational staff to perfect dramaturgical roles to be played out in specific performance areas and for a defined audience leads to a level of exchange where actors who are devoid of personalities play to audiences who are deprived of theirs. This travesty is the fundamental inauthenticity of the contemporary preoccupation with the debased notion of 'people values'. The theatricalities of organisational life have produced corporate actors who are humiliated, debased and undervalued. Only fellow actors understand the sense of misappropriation which they share. This appears to be particularly true of customer/client contact staff where the most intensive dramaturgical approaches have been tried. The customer cannot appreciate the personal costs of performance and yet has expectations of continuity, regularity and, indeed, improvement. The customer comes to be regarded by the organisational actor with disdain thinly masked by the persona of professional competence. The fundamental hypocrisy of this behaviour produces a contemptuous attitude to the customer and gives emphasis to a cognoscenti inwardness among professional players. One former Lufthansa flight attendant confided that the main reason she had left the airline was that, "The more you were trained to be nice to the passengers, the more you began to despise them".

Likewise, the audience qua customer, being now separated from the performance, which has become self-serving, finds its dignity in a scornful abhorrence of the actor's craft. The customer is led to expect delight, arousal, and even magic from the encounter with the organisation through its actors but now approaches the performance arena as a sceptic with some revulsion for the counterfeit experience at the heart of the performance: alienated actors playing to alienated audiences. The apparent coherence and consensus regarding the definition of the event depends on masking. The dramatic mask conceals ambivalence about the role. about performance and about the play itself but it is not infallible. When the mask fails the performance is thrown into question: becomes ludicrous. For the actor, the extent of his/her degradation is revealed. For the audience, the encounter is shown up for what it is, mere illusion. The implications are all too clear. Without making the parallels between theatre and organisational life too clearly and recognizing that comparisons are a two-way street (a theatre is an organisation too, afterall), it is possible to entertain alternative ways of using theatrical analogies which give more specific attention to the nature of theatrical work and the specific issues which attach to the work of the actor. There are a range of issues which, though fascinating, go beyond the scope of this paper: the annihilation of the audience and the significance of the dramaturgical theory adopted being just two. However, the most important implication for organisational behaviour of the argument presented above rests on the commitment to the regulation of behaviour via manipulation of the role. Ultimately, the regulation of the actor appears to produce contempt. The practical implications of this assertion need further consideration. In the meantime, those who proclaim the virtues of "human process re-engineering" may have something to discover in eighteenth century theories of acting.

Notes

(1) Staff of a theatre, players and non-players, are referred to as "the company" and note the etymology of the word company: the Latin con- with panis- bread.

(2) The literal and metaphorical annihilation of the audience fits well with Diderot's conception of "the fourth wall" of the auditorium between actors and audience. The actors are unselfconsciously absorbed in their actions to the extent that the audience becomes irrelevant.

RESOURCE 6.3

by Crawley, B, Pinder, R & Herriot, P
Source: *Journal of Occupational Psychology*, 1990, vol 63, pp. 211-216.

Assessment centre dimensions, personality and aptitudes

Assessees at two assessment centres (N = 117 and N = 157) completed personality inventories and aptitude tests. Correlations between personality attributes and assessment dimensions were generally low, and suggested that some attributes permitted competencies to be expressed in behaviour. Correlations between intellectual aptitude and dimensions were higher, with aptitude being related to the more cognitive dimensions. Implications for assessment centre practice are explored.

Following the work of Boyatzis (1982), much emphasis has recently been placed upon managerial competencies. Indeed, they form a basic plank in the programme of the Management Charter Group (Jacobs, 1989). However, the exact status of this construct is not clear. One interpretation suggests that competencies are the expression of underlying personal attributes in various types of work situation. Boyatzis' list of competencies resembles a typical list of dimensions assessed in a managerial assessment centre. It comprises the following: accurate self-assessment; conceptualisation; concern with impact; developing others; diagnostic use of concepts; efficiency orientation; logical thought; managing group processes; perceptual objectivity; positive regard; proactivi v; self-confidence; self-control; specialised knowledge; spontaneity; stamina and adaptability; use of oral presentations; use of socialised power; use of unilateral power. It is, therefore, not surprising that those who perceive managerial performance as a function of a universal set of competencies favour assessment centres as a method of ascertaining training needs, evaluating training effectiveness, assessing potential and selecting for promotion.

Unfortunately, it seems unlikely that assessment centre dimensions can carry the load of responsibility thus thrust upon them. They possess very weak construct validity, as demonstrated by Sackett & Dreher (1982) and Robertson, Gratton & Sharpley (1987). These authors found that, using the multitrait-multimethod technique, the ratings of different dimensions within each exercise correlated more highly than did the ratings of the 'same' dimension across different exercises.

Another method of assessing construct validity is to relate dimensions to more underlying attributes of the person. Let us assume that assessment centre dimensions are representative of competencies as defined by Boyatzis (1982). If Boyatzis is correct in assuming that specific competencies are the expression in managerial behaviour of specific personality attributes, we would then expect to find significant correlations between individual dimensions and individual attributes. If, however, certain personality attributes simply make the expression of behaviour in the assessment centre situation more likely, we would then expect correlations between certain specific social attributes and a wide range of assessment centre dimensions. In the latter case, personality would be generally facilitating the expression of behaviour rather than underlying specific types of behaviour.

Method

Two assessment centres (A and B) were investigated. Centre A assessed 117 accountants in order to select them for promotion to partner level. The 13 dimensions, assessed by five exercises,

were: problem analysis; judgement; decisiveness; initiative; interpersonal sensitivity; persuasiveness; stress tolerance; planning and organising; delegation; management control; subordinate development; business awareness; and environmental awareness. Assessees also completed Saville & Holdsworth's Occupational Personality Questionnaire (OPQ) and the Myers-Briggs Type Inventory. The OPQ was analysed in terms of 10 domains: assertive; gregarious; caring (relationships with people); practical and data rational; artistic and behavioural; abstract; structure (thinking styles); anxieties; controls; and energies (feelings and emotions). There are 10 rather than the recommended nine domains since the practical and data rational, and the artistic and behavioural, scales were negatively related to each other. Furthermore, three of the 30 scales were negatively related to the other scales in their domain and were therefore omitted. The Myers-Briggs Type

Table 1. *Correlations of OPQ and Myers-Briggs with dimension ratings for Centre A (N = 117)*

Dimension	PA	J	D	I	IPS	P	ST	P/O	DG	MC	SD	BA	EA
OPQ													
Assertive	15	16*	20*	13	20*	19*	15*	10	09	07	23**	26**	10
Gregarious	01	05	09	-01	13	04	14	06	11	07	25**	36***	11
Empathy	-13	-17*	-09	-17*	-03	12	18*	-06	09	10	-03	09	18*
Practical and data fields	10	10	10	06	18*	12	13	02	05	13	22*	05	03
Artistic and behavioural fields	16	18*	14	-01	19*	19*	19*	15	16*	07	09	14	10
Abstract	17*	18*	17*	08	15	18*	02	-02	05	04	17*	21**	05
Structure	14	03	05	04	-07	-02	-01	12	08	07	10	-05	-14
Anxieties	00	02	-16*	-11	-09	-15	-20*	-01	-05	-07	-05	-30**	-16*
Controls	00	01	00	07	02	-01	08	19*	06	15	14	-11	—
Energies	05	08	11	13	12	01	01	03	06	11	28**	39***	06
Myers-Briggs													
Extraversion-introversion	-02	03	06	-08	22**	16*	10	11	19*	18*	16	28**	33**
Sensing-intuition	-02	06	09	00	05	03	-09	-02	-02	02	00	11	08
Thinking-feeling	16*	16*	-01	-08	04	11	11	-08	-02	-19*	-18*	-16*	-02
Judging-perceiving	01	07	01	01	06	04	10	-17*	01	-10	-09	-09	-01

* p < .05; ** p < .01; *** p < .001

Note. Decimal points omitted.

Key. PA, Problem analysis; J, Judgement; D, Decisiveness; I, Initiative; IPS, Interpersonal Sensitivity; P, Persuasiveness; ST, Stress Tolerance; P/O, Planning and Organising; DG, Delegation; MC, Management Control; SD, Subordinate Development; BA, Business Awareness; EA, Environmental Awareness.

Inventory measures personal orientation and styles of information processing on four dimensions: extroversion-introversion (E-I); sensing-intuition (S-N); thinking-feeling (T-F); and judging-perceiving (J-P).

Centre B assessed 157 supervisors in a large service organisation. Its purpose was to identify those who would be promoted to a new level of supervision involving more human resource management and planning demands than was required of them in their present grade.

The nine dimensions, which were assessed by six exercises, were: problem investigation; problem solving; planning and organising; interpersonal sensitivity; influencing skills; assertiveness; oral communication; written communication; and flexibility. In addition, assessees completed the following six personality and aptitude tests:

1. FIRO-B. This assesses characteristic behaviour towards others on six scales: expressed inclusion; expressed control; expressed affection; wanted inclusion; wanted control; and wanted affection. Assessees who score highly on the three 'expressed' scales wish to include, control and be affectionate towards others. Those scoring highly on the 'wanted' scales wish to be included, controlled, etc.

2. Leadership Opinion Questionnaire (LOQ). This assesses two aspects of leadership behaviour: consideration and structure

3. Ravens Standard Progressive Matrices. A non-verbal test of general intelligence

4. Saville & Holdsworth's VP1. A test of verbal intelligence

5. Saville & Holdsworth's NP2. A test of numerical reasoning

6. ACER. A test of clerical accuracy against speed.

In Centre A, assessors were not informed of test results until after they had made their dimension ratings. In Centre B, an interpretation only of test results could be requested from a psychologist in those rare cases where the assessors could not arrive at a consensus rating. In neither assessment centre, therefore, were the actual test results known to assessors when they rated dimensions. Both assessment centres were designed by occupational psychologists after a job analysis exercise, and required the assessors to be trained (albeit briefly).

Results and Discussion

Table 1 presents correlations of OPQ domains and Myers-Briggs types with the 13 dimensions assessed in Centre A. Table 2 presents correlations of FIRO-B and Leadership Opinion Questionnaire scales with the nine dimensions assessed in Centre B.

Considering the OPQ (Table 1), it is clear that certain domains tend to be associated with several dimensions: assertive with seven dimensions, abstract with six, and artistic and behavioural with five, while empathy is negatively related to four. Two dimensions, subordinate development and business awareness, are more highly correlated with OPQ domains than are other dimensions. While the assertive, abstract and anxieties domains are also significantly related to several other dimensions, this is not the case with gregarious and energies. These latter two domains are relatively highly related to subordinate developments and to business awareness, but not to any dimensions other than these.

A similar pattern emerges for the Myers-Briggs. Extroverts tend to be rated significantly more highly on six dimensions. On the other hand, there is also some evidence for specificity, in that thinkers are likely to be rated higher on problem analysis and judgement, but feelers on management control, subordinate development and business awareness.

The results for FIRO-B (Table 2) demonstrate even fewer significant relationships. The wanted inclusion scale predicts four of the nine dimensions and expressed control three. Furthermore, the dimensions predicted are not the more social ones which one would expect to be related to FIRO-B scales, but rather the more intellectual ones. In the case of the LOQ (Table 2) the only significant relationships are between consideration and two dimensions. Given that only 10 out of 72 correlations were significant for FIRO-B and LOQ, these results must be treated very cautiously.

Thus, the results of the personality tests are certainly not clear cut. The overall level of correlations obtained between personality attributes and dimensions is low, and the pattern of relationships obtained allows both interpretations to be made, ie. that some personality attributes permit dimensions in general to be expressed in behaviour, and that certain attributes are specifically related to certain dimensions.

When we consider the results of the aptitude tests for Centre B, however, different results were obtained. There were only moderate intercorrelations between tests, ranging from .40 to .59, suggesting that to some extent they may be measuring different aptitudes. Table 3 indicates much higher relationships between aptitudes and dimensions than those obtained between personality attributes and dimensions. Indeed, it is only the less cognitively based dimensions (interpersonal sensitivity, assertiveness and flexibility) that tests of aptitude sometimes fail to predict significantly. The three more specific aptitude tests are overall better predictors than Ravens Matrices, but there is no indication that specific aptitudes are related to specific dimensions. This finding supports that obtained by Dulewicz & Fletcher (1982), who found a strong relationship between intellectual aptitude and overall assessment rating.

In conclusion, this evidence must be

Table 2. Correlations of FIRO-B and LOQ with dimension ratings for Centre B (N = 157)

Diemension	Problem investigation	Problem solving	Planning and organising	Interpersonal sensitivity	Influencing skills	Assertiveness	Flexibility	Oral communication	Written communication
FIRO-B									
Expressed inclusion	14	16*	09	00	09	13	13	13	08
Expressed control	15	10	06	10	18*	15	17*	17*	06
Expressed affection	02	-05	-09	-09	02	05	03	01	-02
Wanted inclusion	17*	17*	11	09	09	06	28***	15	21**
Wanted control	-12	-04	-04	-08	-08	00	04	-08	-12
Wanted affection	00	05	-02	-05	-07	-09	-02	-02	14
LOQ									
Consideration	12	03	05	15	15	07	20**	14	16*
Structure	11	02	04	02	08	08	02	07	08

* p < .05; ** p < 0.1; *** p < .001
Note. Decimal point omitted

Table 3. *Correlations for four aptitude tests with nine dimensions for Centre B (N = 157)*

Diemension Test	Problem investigation	Problem solving	Planning and organising	Interpersonal sensitivity	Influencing skills	Assertiveness	Oral communication	Written communication	Flexibility
Ravens	25**	30***	27***	14	20*	08	18*	22*	11
VPI	28***	35***	36***	13	20*	18*	25**	40***	19*
NP2	12***	44***	42***	18*	25**	26**	33***	42***	23**
ACER	36***	42***	43***	10	20*	25**	33***	31***	18*

* p < .05; ** p < .01; *** p < .001
Note. Decimal points omitted

treated with caution. Correlations obtained are low, particularly those for the personality tests. However, we cannot be sure that their lower predictive power is not due to their lower reliability and validity in comparison with the tests of aptitude. Moreover, the ipsative nature of certain of the personality tests renders correlations with dimensions a dubious procedure. There is a little support for the idea that personal attributes permit competencies in general to be expressed in performance, and the overall construct validity of dimensions is not enhanced by these results. On the contrary, the only reasonably firm conclusion is that the more intellectually oriented dimensions are related to general intellectual ability.

The general implication for assessment centre design is to cast further doubt on the use of the 'sign' as opposed to the 'sample' rationale (Wernimont & Campbell, 1968). In other words, the inferential sequence should not be from job analysis to task areas to dimensions to exercises designed to assess those dimensions. Rather, it should be from job analysis to job sample exercises with content validity. More specifically, the research also suggests ways in which the psychometric tests which are often administered during assessment centres might more profitably be used. If assessees are low on those personality attributes (eg. assertiveness, extroversion) which permit expression of desirable assessment centre behaviours, more attention should be paid to the results of tests of intellectual aptitude, and less to their assessment centre ratings. Then the danger of misinterpreting poor situation-specific performance as a general lack of competence might be avoided.

Future research could profitably investigate whether certain personality attributes moderate the validity of assessment centre dimensions.

As a footnote, multitrait-multimethod analyses were conducted for both centres. For Centre A the overall mean correlation for different dimensions within the same exercise was .43, while that for the same dimension across exercises was .14. For Centre B, the correlations were .56 and .40 respectively.

References

Boyatzis, R.E. (1982) *The Competent Manager: A Model for Effective Performance,* New York: Wiley.

Dulewicz, S.V. & Fletcher, C. (1982) 'The relationship between previous experience, intelligence and background characteristics of participants and their performance in an Assessment Centre', *Journal of Occupational Psychology,* 55, 197-208.

Jacobs, R. (1989) 'Getting the measure of management competence', *Personnel Management,* June.

Robertson, I.T., Gratton, L. & Sharpley, D. (1987) 'The psychometric properties and design of managerial assessment centres: dimensions into exercises won't go', *Journal of Occupational Psychology,* 60, 187-195.

Sackett, P.R. & Dreher, G.F. (1982) 'Constructs and assessment centre dimensions: some troubling empirical findings', *Journal of Applied Psychology,* 67, 401-410.

Wernimont, P.F. & Campbell, J.P. (1968) 'Signs, samples and criteria', *Journal of Applied Psychology,* 46, 417-419.

Steering the Middle Road to Car Production

RESOURCE 7.1 ◁
Source: Personnel
Management, June
1993, pp. 34-38.

Peter Wickens, Director of Personnel and Information Systems at Nissan Motor Manufacturing

The job-enrichment-driven motor vehicle production techniques pioneered by Volvo and Saab in Sweden in the 1970s have been out of favour for some time now. But many of the Japanese concepts involved in the new 'lean production' ethos are facing heavy criticism. Peter Wickens offers a middle way – a new 'synthesis' of teamworking, flexibility, continuous improvement and 'ownership of change' leading to high efficiency and high quality of work and jobs.

In 1991, when visiting Volvo's new assembly plant at Uddevalla, 80km north of Goteborg, I was told: 'If we can't build cars this way in Sweden, we can't build cars in Sweden.'

However, that same year Saab closed its Malmo factory, which had been hailed as the 'auto factory of the future' and regarded as one of the most 'worker-friendly' in the industry.

And then, at the end of 1992, Volvo announced its intention to close both Uddevalla and Kalmar, the 1970s Mecca for those who believed there was a better way of building motor cars. Both factories would close by the summer of 1993. What went wrong?

In a declining market Volvo and Saab simply do not need the capacity of these small plants, which undertake only final assembly operations and not fully integrated manufacturing.

Volvo's early objectives were clear: Kalmar opened in 1974, driven by the difficulties of getting Swedes to work in line-paced assembly plants and inspired by Pehr Gyllenhammer's vision of a better way.

It is commonly assumed that Volvo still employs groups of people to undertake the final assembly of the whole car – the 'dock assembly' process. In fact, that system lasted only a few years, as the increasing number of model variants made material supply difficult, and failure to complete the tasks on time caused problems with the production flow.

The official report on the dock assembly system at Kalmar suggested that the employees did not enjoy the procedure. 'It was sometimes experienced as stressful, and there was always some uncertainty as to exactly where the workers were in the work cycle at any particular moment and how much time remained for the allotted tasks,' said the report.[1]

A return to traditional line-paced assembly work, but with tasks organised on a team basis, was therefore welcomed.

The strength of Kalmar came not from the physical process but from the genuine building of teams – 'the little factory within the factory' – perhaps a two-person team working together along the line on a variety of tasks, with each foreman's group having its own 'precisely limited production tasks, its own leisure areas and its own financial framework.'

While teamwork proved popular, however, absenteeism remained high. Volvo had aimed to get absenteeism down to 10 per cent in Uddevalla, and in Saab the worker-friendly plant did not result in significantly lower absenteeism. But the then Saab president, David Herman, did not blame Sweden's welfare system. 'Absenteeism is more a question of management than of the macro-economic system,' he argued.[2]

Learning from Kalmar, Uddevalla sought to return to a form of dock assembly, believing that it had resolved the material supply problem. 'I hope that one day somebody will be able to stand here and say 'Henry Ford invented the assembly line but Volvo did away with it',' said car division president Roger Holtbach.[3]

Uddevalla has teams of eight to 10 'car builders' undertaking the complete final assembly of four cars a shift on static platforms in individual work cells. The material supply breakthrough came from having a separate materials centre where components are stored, sub-assemblies built and placed on automated guided vehicles, which are routed to the cells at programmed intervals. There is a low degree of automation and a job cycle of up to two hours.

In developing the project, the management and union 'working commitment group' aimed to achieve quality and productivity in 'a pleasant working environment where people are happy to work and can continue to develop throughout their working lives'.

The teams are responsible for much of their own training, maintenance, planning, selection and tooling. Each team has a spokesperson, a role which is rotated between members at intervals determined by them, and the selected person assigns work, guides the team, plans and reports, leads discussions and resolves individual and practical problems.

What then, are the difficulties? First, eight people building four cars a day means a final assembly time of 16 hours. The best European plant is achieving body construction, paint application and assembly in 10 hours. Similarly, Saab found that Malmo took twice the European average time to build a car.

Secondly, the extensive training needed to teach a two-hour job cycle means that, with continuing high labour turnover and absenteeism, each operator is at a different stage of the learning curve, and with high inter-dependence this can lead to frustration.

Thirdly, it is extremely important to recognise that long-term high quality demands not only motivation of the workforce but also control of the process. But the long job cycle and freedom to determine the build sequence that are inherent in dock assembly results in a loss of control. As a result, 'right first time' suffers and high 'post-build rectification' is needed.

Lean Production
In their book *The Machine that changed the world,* which introduced the term 'lean

production', Womack, Jones and Roos (WJR) say of Uddevalla: 'We are very sceptical that this form of organisation can ever be as fulfilling as lean production. Simply bolting and screwing together a large number of parts in a long cycle rather than a small number of parts in a short cycle is a very limited system of job enrichment.'[4]

This comment is somewhat unfair to the totality of the Volvo experience, but it is true that the actual manufacturing process is not the most important element. It is the organisation of the total process, not just the technology, which brings about success.

A better way, according to WJR, is lean production, which is seen as the successor to mass production. It is a collective term for many aspects of the so-called Japanese production system (just-in-time, zero buffer stocks, quality built-in, delegation, small lot production, problem-solving, teamworking, quick set-up times etc.). Lean production uses half of everything – effort, space, investment time and inventory. It results in fewer defects and greater productivity. And the results are remarkable.

Taking the standard measure of direct labour hours used for body construction, paint and final assembly, WJR show the best and worst productivity levels measured by hours per car in 1989:

	Best	Worst
Japan	13.2	25.9
North America	18.6	30.7
Europe	22.8	55.7

Quality performance follows the same pattern. And it is not just automation that causes the difference. The least automated Japanese plant is the most efficient, and the most automated plant in the world requires 70 per cent more hours per car than the most efficient. According to WJR: 'Lean organisation must come before high-tech process automation if a company is to gain the full benefit.' And, I would add, whoever heard of a machine improving anything? It is only people who make improvements.

The Critics
However, everything in the lean garden is

not rosy. There are critics. In February 1992 the Japan Auto Workers Union (JAWU) highlighted what it called the triple sufferings of the Japanese automobile industry: 'The employees are exhausted, the companies make only little profit and the automobile industry is always bashed from overseas.'[5]

JAWU argues that excessive competition in Japan's domestic market demands constant innovation and 2,200 working hours a year. It queries what will happen if it manages to reduce the working year to 1,800 hours. It does not, however, criticise the detailed practices of the Japanese production system.

Heavy criticism comes from the Canadian Auto Workers Union (CAWU), which sees the objectives of lean production as being to intensify the work effort, increase managerial control and undermine the independence of trade unions. To the CAWU the critical issue is 'who controls the shopfloor?'[6]

The union sees just-in-time and the elimination of waste and buffer stocks as being against the workers' interests, requiring jobs to be standardised and imbalances eliminated.

But, it argues, it is these imbalances that provide workers with flexibility and the opportunity to create personal time (doubling up, banking etc.). No manufacturer can eliminate the need for buffers – there will always be problems. But lean production shifts the buffer from being stock in production to the workers' personal time. 'Our willingness to make up after hours the production lost during the shift . . . makes us the buffers,' it says.

The union sees the process of *kaizen,* continuous improvement, as 'appropriating workers' knowledge', aimed at replacing 'worker solidarity with total identification with the goals of the company'. Clearly the CAWU's starting point is that a capitalist enterprise can only succeed by exploiting the workforce. But it does serve to highlight the potential dangers of management abusing its position.

The elimination of buffer stocks does mean that 'catch back' (catching up) may be achieved by overtime working. If properly managed, this is no problem but, if abused, it is justifiably criticised.

The 'appropriation of workers' knowledge' accusation defies logic. If you believe that workers' interests are inherently opposed to those of the management, you can take this view; if you believe that by sharing knowledge then success and security will accrue to all, it is the right thing to do.

A criticism from the German union, IG Metall, is that the attempt by management to introduce such concepts tends to concentrate solely on reducing production time and labour costs.[7]

In arguing that firms should seek to combine benefits to the company with benefits to the workforce, the union is correct. If there are no reciprocal obligations, there are no reciprocal benefits. It is also right when it says: 'It is an illusion to think that employees will readily work for improvements to which they fall victim.'

In any organisation, true commitment demands security of employment so that change can take place naturally in a manner which is non-threatening.

So we have Volvo and Saab and their problems; lean production and its critics. What is the way forward?

The key to the future lies in a phrase coined by Werner Sengenberger of the International Labour Office. What we should be seeking is 'a new synthesis between higher efficiency and higher quality of work and jobs.'[8]

How can this be achieved? Some unions and some companies are seeking this middle way – beginning with teamworking.

One of the great problems is a total misunderstanding of teamworking. David Herman said of Saab that, in a nation regarded as egalitarian, 'there was a benign neglect by the middle manager who failed to relate to the workforce and did not create a team spirit within the company.'

Herman perceived that teamworking is not about organisation structures or changing from sequential to cellular manufacturing. It is not about interlocking circles, nor is a team built by assembling an 'ideal' amalgam of various personality types who undertake teambuilding exercises.

A team begins with individuals whose contributions are recognised and valued and who are motivated to work together to achieve clear, understood and stretching goals for which they are accountable. The best team results come with positive leadership and tough goals. Flexibility, another loosely applied term, is not simply about more skills of the same type; it is about expanding the roles of the individual to the greatest extent possible.

Two elements
All work is divided into two elements: 'prescribed' and 'discretionary'. Prescribed elements are those which have to be done in a specific place, way and time. Discretionary elements are those which are not time-specific or task-specific and over which the organisation and individual can have some flexibility such as maintenance, continuous improvement activity, housekeeping and training.

For a senior executive, perhaps 95 per cent of the job is discretionary and 5 per cent prescribed. For the line-paced shopfloor operator the proportions are reversed. What is essential is to make that 5 per cent as meaningful as possible for those who have only 5 per cent.

The shift from the Tayloristic 'control' model to the human relations 'commitment' model is often suggested as a reason for enhanced performance. However, in their rejection of the control model the proponents throw the baby out with the bath water. If we are to achieve long-term high quality we need to combine commitment of the workforce and control of the process. These two seemingly opposed objectives are the paradox of production. One is a top-down imposition; the other comes from the bottom up.

If all we have is a committed workforce, then, while this may achieve short-term high quality, it may lead to people doing what they, individually, believe to be best. The consequence could be anarchy. Alternatively, if all we have is control of the process, this takes away the feeling of ownership, with a subsequent lack of motivation. The objective is to resolve the paradox.

Every car manufacturer has a standard operation for most tasks – F.W. Taylor's 'one best method' for doing a job in a safe manner at the required quality level in the right time. This standard operation is normally the property of the engineers. They prepare it and pass it to production, who have little influence on it. But the person doing a job knows more than anyone else how to do it better. In most companies that knowledge is at best withheld and at worst is used against the company.

Ownership of change
The key to opening the door is to give responsibility for that standard operation to the production people. They work to it, they prepare it, and it is their responsibility to improve productivity, quality, safety and ease of working.

In order to resolve this paradox we must give ownership of change to the people doing the job: in other words, the process of *kaizen,* which if properly implemented can be satisfying and constructive, but if abused can be seen as management adding to an already difficult task.

This concept of continuous improvement is critical, but the Germans are right when they argue that it should not simply be about efficiency, quality and short-term results. The process is as important as the results. It must begin with the workforce and allow expressions of creativity and also be concerned with safety and the working environment.

Under no circumstances can any *kaizen* activity threaten employment, but equally it is foolish to think that efficiency improvements are not going to result.

It is ironic, however, that, as efficiency levels move towards what the critics denigrate as '60 seconds of added value work a minute', the opportunities for spending time on *kaizen* activities get less.

We have to recognise that eliminating waste – whether wasted time or wasted actions – does stretch the system and, if undertaken in isolation and taken to the extreme, can create significant pressures. It then becomes important to build in an appropriate staffing level and/or schedule paid overtime for these activities.

As organisations progress down this road, control by the process changes to control of the process. Job satisfaction arises from performing the prescribed task well, achieving high levels of productivity and quality, and, at the same time being involved in changes to the process and the range of discretionary tasks.

This results in a much higher degree of integration between the worker and the process, with the workers being involved in decisions which affect the company. The distinction between white-collar and blue-collar workers becomes blurred, and the relationship between management and workers changes.

However, the process of building motor cars is demanding, both physically and mentally. One objective of continuous improvement must be to make the tasks easier. Involving people in the discretionary activities contributes to this, but the area of great neglect in the design and manufacturing engineering disciplines has been the failure to apply ergonomic principles to the build process. The education of undergraduate engineers barely recognises the need, and manufacturers have done little more than pay lip-service to the concept.

Within Nissan we have established a policy that 'the ergonomics of building a car will be a fundamental factor in the original design, engineering and specification of the product, facility, tooling and processes. Such factors will also be included in all changes, improvements and *kaizen* activities.'

As a result the input into new model programmes specifically requires the study of difficult jobs on the current model to eliminate them at source on future products. The capital budget approval process has an 'operator care' section as one of the justifications for capital expenditure. Ease of working requirements are included in facility specifications and standards.

The only long-term solution is to design for manufacture, but in the short term the most exciting development over the last few years has been the total commitment of production management to the principle and practice of people care via process improvement.

'Ownership' is everything. Supervisors have developed their own systematic method of assessing the difficulty of jobs in a quick and accurate way. It is not a professional ergonomist's analysis. But it is easy to use and allows, not just one specialist, but 200 people to study jobs and initiate remedial action, whether it be facility change, process change, training or revised job rotation. The method is being refined – it is not yet precisely right, but it is the commitment that brings results. Without that, systems achieve very little.

The mistake is to believe that the production system itself gives the results. What counts is the relationship of people with the process. A controlled Taylorist process need not alienate if the workers are able to contribute, and long-cycle dock assembly will not satisfy if that is all there is (nor will it last if it cannot compete). What we must aim for is lean, people-centred volume production.

The big challenge is the integration of new technology, new management practices and the people in the new flat organisations. No company has yet got it right. But if we are to have lean production, it must be managed by people who care about people. A synthesis between higher efficiency and higher quality of work and jobs is possible.

For personnel managers this must be *the* issue for the second half of this decade.

References

1 *Volvo, Kalmar revisited: 10 years of experience,* Development Council of Sweden, 1984.

2 'Saab's new big wheel', *Scanorama* (Swedish Airlines inflight magazine), October 1991.

3 *Financial Times,* 9 November 1989.

4 Womack, James, Jones, Dan and Roos, Daniel, *The machine that changed the world,* Rawson Associates, 1990.

5 *Japanese automobile industry in the future,* Japan Auto Workers Union, 1992.

6   Robertson, David. 'New management technology: the development of a trade union counter strategy', *Vauxhall Motors' Shop Steward Committee Conference*, January 1992.

7   Roth, S. (1992) *Japanisation or going our way*, IG Metall.

8   Sengenberger, Werner, *Lean production: the way of working and production in the future*, ILO, 1992.

▷ RESOURCE 8.1

by S R Clegg
Source: Human
Resource Strategies,
eds. Salaman, G,
Cameron, S,
Hamblin, H, Iles, P,
Mabey, C &
Thompson, K,
London: Sage
Publications in
association with the
Open University.

Modernist and Postmodernist Organisation

Japanese work organisation is premised on self-managing teams rather than workers striving against each other under an individualistic and competitive payment and production system. In Japanese enterprises the functional alignment of activities is achieved by extensive use of the market principle through subcontracting and a (quasi-) democratic principle through self-managed teamwork. (As it takes place within an overall structure of hierarchy and private ownership it is clear why the principle can only be described as quasi-democratic. Within the self-managing teams work roles overlap and the task structure is continuous, rather than discontinuous, in which the workers themselves allocate the tasks internationally (see Schonberger, 1982). Production is not accelerated by redesigning work downwards in its skill content, by simplifying it further and separating the workers more one from the other, as in the classical modernist organisation under Fordism. This is clear from studies of Japanese organisations in other countries, such as the research by Lincoln et al. (1978) into 54 Japanese-controlled Californian organisations, which found an inverse relationship between functional specialisation and Japanese control. Within Japanese organisation practices, work in the internal labour market seems to be designed with a eye to the collective worker rather than in opposition to the collective worker. It appears to be designed to facilitate such collective work.

'With work teams, the pace of production can be changed by adding or removing workers, and management and team members can experiment with different configurations for completing specified tasks. In cor rast to US mass production where work arrives on a conveyor belt, Japanese workers often move with the production line . . .

'Work groups perform routine quality control. This allows Japanese quality control departments to focus on nonroutine aspects of quality control, such as advanced statistical measurement or even work redesign. There is substantial evidence that work groups detect and remedy mistakes much more quickly than designated 'inspectors', saving considerable rework and scrappage. Japanese work organisation has led to the integration of quality control and shopfloor problem solving.' (Kenney and Florida, 1988: 132)*

Quality circles have been seen as a major achievement of the Japanese system, and not only because they serve as a substitute for quality surveillance as a separate management function. They include both operatives and staff specialists such as engineers in the same circle, oriented towards not only reducing the wastage rate but also making technological and process improvements. Once more this is related to the 'deepening' of technological development. Quality control is not 'externalised', nor is maintenance, to anything like the same degree as in more traditional modernist organisations. Much of the routine preventive maintenance is done by the operators who use the machines. Kenney and Florida (1988: 132) note that 'downtime' is considerably less on machines in Japan than in the United States (the figures cited are 15 per cent compared to 50 per cent downtime). This confirms Hayes' (1981) view that the Japanese succeed because of meticulous attention to every stage of the production process.

The greater flexibility of workers extends to the technological design of work itself. Production lines in Japanese enterprises are organised to be more flexible than the simple linear track of a Fordist factory. They can be easily reconfigured between different product lines (Cohen and Zysman, 1987: ch. 9) and do not necessarily conform to the linear layout. Kenney and Florida (1988: 132-3) note that in some industries the lines may be 'U'-shaped or modular, so that operatives can 'perform a number of tasks on different machines simultaneously while individual machines 'mind' themselves'. As they note, for such a strategy to succeed, multi-skilling is essential.

Mechanisms of Co-ordination and Control
Mechanisms of co-ordination and control of the different functions and alignments of the organisation depend, in part, on the strategies of power pursued. There are two aspects to this: power in the organisation and power around the organisation.

Japanese organisations are not based on familism. Nor are authority relations of · co-ordination and control. In Japan superiors are expected to make their subordinates accept the practice of groupism so that the trust is constituted which transcends particularlisms, binding each person to the universal love of the enterprise. According to Rohlen (1973),

drawing on fieldwork in a Japanese bank, about a third of Japanese organisations give their employees 'spiritual training', akin to techniques of religious conversion, therapy and initiation rites, which emphasise social co-operation, responsibility, reality acceptance and perseverance in one's tasks. Tanaka (1980) also describes similar phenomena of socialisation to and indoctrination in company goals. Organisational commitment would not appear to be left to chance in many cases. In the case of Japan, organisational commitment is of most moment for those workers who are secured by the golden chains of the internal labour market. These core employees are securely incorporated as members with benefits. Such benefits are not typically approached where there is a much greater reliance on the external labour market as a source of recruitment. (In some instances, as in the case of skilled labour in New Zealand and Australia for much of the post-war era, this reliance on the external labour market has led to a positive neglect of questions of skill formation.) Where skill formation has not been marginalised, as in the Japanese case of the core internal labour market, then it is important to remember that the benefits are not spread throughout the industrial system. Those workers who are subject to domestic outwork, seasonal working or extended subcontracting will secure none of the benefits of the much vaunted core workers (Dore, 1973; McMillan, 1984), yet it is upon their 'flexibility' that the system rests. It is a system which works well in securing loyal commitment, by virtue of low turnover and dissent, even if it does not produce markedly more satisfied workers than elsewhere.

Empowerment on the shop floor appears to be more widespread in Japanese enterprises than it does in the bureaucratically conceived Fordist structures of Western modernity. This is achieved through mechanisms like extensive firm-specific basic training and learning. In part, this is accomplished through being involved in the work teams with more experienced workers. Job rotation also facilitates this learning. Such rotation takes place not only within the work teams but also more widely in the enterprise.

'*Workers sequentially master the complexities of different tasks and grasp the interconnectedness among them. By breaking down the communication barriers among work groups, rotation enhances the flow of information between workers and across functional units. Rotation generates a storehouse of knowledge applicable to a variety of work situations and enhances problem-solving capabilities at the enterprise level.*' (*Kenney and Florida, 1988: 133*)

The empowerment strategies of Japanese enterprises have been identified in a generalised commitment to 'learning by doing' (Kenney and Florida 1988: 133-5). The Kanban system, which is used to co-ordinate work between different work teams, has been seen as a part of this empowerment. Instead of top-down co-ordination of the work-flow in the form of superordinate commands and surveillance, the kanban system allows for communication flows which co-ordinate horizontally rather than vertically. Work units use work cards (kanbans) to order supplies, to deliver processed materials and to synchronise production activities. Communication is through the cards, laterally rather than vertically, reducing planning and supervision, creating empowerment as workers 'do' for themselves.

▷ RESOURCE 8.2

Tim Dickson
Source: *Financial Times*, 17 March 1995

Look, Listen, Learn and then Alter

Behaviour analysis has transformed an old city firm.

How do you turn an old-fashioned City of London partnership into a dynamic and properly managed insurance organisation?

Thomas Howell Group, part of the world's second-biggest reinsurance company Swiss Re, has recently sought to achieve this transformation in a rather unusual way. Led by chairman and chief executive John Stitch it called in a firm of 'professional voyeurs'.

Voyeurism is how Tony Hipgrave of Huthwaite Research describes some of the work his company has been doing over the past three and a half years for THG, which is the UK's biggest loss adjuster with a turnover of more than £100m.

Through techniques such as behaviour analysis – in which records are made of what happens and fed back to groups and individuals – Huthwaite set out to make the group's board meetings more effective, and to encourage directors to think ahead strategically rather than just to react.

Loss adjusters, who investigate and settle claims on behalf of other companies, enjoyed buoyant demand throughout the 1970s and 1980s as they followed their big domestic clients into international markets. But about the time THG was acquired by Swiss Re in 1988 the UK domestic market started to plateau and competition from the insurance companies intensified.

Under pressure from its new parent it became clear that the classic partnership structure with all its fiefs and often meaningless titles was no longer appropriate, not least given the need to continue expanding globally. Incorporation on its own and a thinning out of the management hierarchy, moreover, were not enough.

Michael Reeves, THG's marketing director and European chief executive designate says the departure of a couple of 'difficult' individuals and the injection of younger blood in 1992 made a perceptible difference. But he also accepts that the behavioural approach of Hipgrave and his Huthwaite colleagues has improved the board's performance.

'Board and team skills don't normally form part of a loss adjuster's armoury,' he admits.

Hipgrave says Huthwaite's contribution was in part to help the directors 'unlearn' old habits. 'The early meetings were over-long, poorly structured and air-time was shared very unequally. There were tricks and 'games' going on. In fact, the meetings were scarcely worthwhile.'

The 'airtime' problem was dealt with by behavioural analysis – literally timing the length of each contribution and examining whether individual styles of persuasion were of the 'push' (advancing arguments) or 'pull' (asking questions) variety. This helped shorten and better structure the meetings.

The 'games' were tackled through a series of intimate interviews with each board member using a variety of psychological tools, followed by detailed and at times painful individual feedback and a board meeting where participants were forced to face up squarely to who needed to change and how.

'This has resulted in a more honest recognition of how decisions are really made and contributed to the new structure which the group will have in place in April,' says Paul Clayton, CEO designate.

Hipgrave says it is one thing for a consultant to be called into an organisation to sort out its internal structure and processes, and to re-think its strategy. It is 'very rare' to be also asked to observe meetings at board level in the way it has happened at THG.

'Boards are rarely honest enough to say we are not behaving properly with each other. That is something that they are usually only happy to see going on further down the organisation,' he says.